CW01367207

MORGAN
Sports Cars

The Heritage Years
1954 -1960

Forewords by
Charles Morgan & Lew Spencer

*J.D. Alderson & Chris Chapman
with Craig Atkins*

© J.D. Alderson, Chris Chapman & Craig Atkins

Published by Plus Four Books
539 Manchester Road
Huddersfield HD7 5QX
United Kingdom

Printed in Slovenia

British Library Cataloguing-in-Publication Data
A catalogue for this book this available from the British Library

ISBN 1 872955 30 4

Contents

Forewords	*iv*
Introduction	*7*
Chapter One - 1954	*9*
Chapter Two - 1955	*71*
Chapter Three - 1956	*120*
Chapter Four - 1957	*175*
Chapter Five - 1958	*218*
Chapter Six - 1959	*277*
Chapter Seven - 1960	*337*
Acknowledgements	*411*
Index	*413*

Forewords

Authors' note

The story we have to tell is truly international, the two most important countries being Great Britain and the USA. For this reason we have commissioned two Forewords. The first is from Charles Morgan, who was growing up at the time within the Morgan family in Malvern, and the other is from Lew Spencer who was racing and selling Morgans in California.

Charles Morgan

The period 1954-60 covers a period of Morgan history that coincides with my boyhood when I was perhaps most receptive to everything around me. I can still vividly remember my father breaking the family holiday in Cornwall in 1959 to race in the 6 Hour Relay Race at Silverstone. He arrived back on the Sunday with a laurel garland and a car still smelling of the racetrack. I spent the following two days sitting in the stationary car pretending to race it myself.

The family home, Braeside, in Malvern saw some interesting prototypes in the driveway and there was a particular route around the Malvern Hills that my father would use to demonstrate the superior handling of a Morgan to me. His example led me to try and emulate him, first of all with a lovely lightweight wooden pedal car that reputedly belonged to Stirling Moss and later with one of the first garden tractors, a Trojan, hotted up and fitted with a foot throttle by the factory.

More seriously it was a period where my father was wrestling with some of the most important Morgan development issues of its history. The company was 50 years old but my grandfather, the company's founder, had just died unexpectedly in 1959, months before the anniversary. Apart from the obvious succession issues, there was my father's desire to remain competitive on the racetrack with more streamlined cars. In this period my father thought long and hard about doing a more modern Morgan. I remember a wooden scale model he made and kept at home which bore a striking resemblance to an AC Bristol.

Charles Morgan with his mother Jane, father Peter and sister Jill at Prescott.
(Morgan Motor Co collection)

Counter balancing this desire to do a 'modern looking' Morgan was the success that the traditionally styled Morgan was having on the race track, due to its inherent balance and high power-to-weight ratio. In the USA news of 'Baby Doll' winning SCCA events on a regular basis prompted a trip by my parents to the USA in 1961. The success of 'Baby Doll' and the enthusiasm of a number of dealers led to the USA taking 70% of the factory's output. This export success story made the front page of the *Daily Express* in 1960 with a picture of all 120 of Morgan's workforce taken in the chassis shop. Of course at home Christopher Lawrence was simply obliterating the opposition in BARC sports car events where he was often seconds quicker than everyone else on the same lap.

All of this forms the bedrock for the following success of the Morgan Motor Company and it is the initiatives launched in these years that helped the company survive the next turbulent years in the British motor industry. It seems incredible today that of the 50 or so British motor manufacturers of the early 1950s the Morgan Motor Company is almost the only one left. It is time to reappraise the achievements of the enthusiastic contributors to the Morgan legend between the years 1954 and 1960. Perhaps this book will go some way to explain why Morgan survived where others failed.

Malvern
2007

Lew Spencer

What a wonderful time period for sports cars and Morgans in particular. The 1950s saw the blossoming of sports cars for the average person who wanted the freedom to drive and have fun with a car that handled and performed in a manner that gave the driver real enjoyment. To me, that just spells out Morgan and the 50s.

Living through that period in California was exciting. Seems like there was always something new happening, another track opening up, an airport allowing races to be held, an experiment to see if a new site would work out just by trying it the first time, new cars hitting the market.

Some of us just stumbled on to sports cars. Servicemen returning from England and Europe brought some back, along with the desire to drive 'fun' cars like they had never seen before, everyone had their own story.

General Curtis LeMay, who headed the Strategic Air Command (SAC), was an enthusiast and he arranged for SAC fields across the U.S. to become road race courses for the weekend. At March Air Force base I saw Masten Gregory crash his beautiful C-Type Jaguar into the hay bales. At Golden Gate Park in San Francisco, there was no crowd control and we stood right on the edge of the pavement watching Bill Pollack make Tom Carsten's bowlegged 'Cad Allard' (Cadillac-Allard J2) fly by only feet away. Now this was exciting! The sport was growing, getting better organized and being recognized. The Sports Car Club of America was gaining new members with activities all across the country. The California Sports Car

Lew Spencer prepares to race Baby Doll No 3. (Lew Spencer collection)

Club was bursting with new members, activities and races. Rallying was becoming popular and on weekends parking lots were filled with spectators watching slaloms.

Cars had always just been transportation to me until I happened to see a Morgan parked in a lot in Hollywood. Someone told me what it was and where they were sold. Went to the dealership and was hooked immediately. A salesman at the dealership wanted to go racing and wanted me to go too, but I was concerned because it was my only car and it was needed for work. Turns out he was a great salesman!

So, February 7th 1954 found us at the Singer Owners' Club Willow Springs hill climb. He had to show me how to downshift. Still won second in the stock Morgan class and was hooked. Then to Palm Springs, California for an SCCA race on the airport. Smashed the radiator of my Morgan. On to Bakersfield Airport and a piston problem. Now it was time to drop out and help the sport by working at the races.

Sports cars continued to grow in number; clubs constantly putting on races, rallies, slaloms. Rene Pellandini became Morgan distributor for the western United States. He and others like him brought in sports cars and sold them in increasing numbers to the fans. By now, there were huge numbers of 'street' sports cars in the spectator areas of the races. (The United States of America became the single most important market for the Morgan Motor Company, taking around 30% of Plus Four production in 1954 but rising steadily to a staggering 90% by 1959). The public really began to notice sports cars.

Rene wanted to publicize the Morgan. I bought a 1956 Plus Four, ran it at the first Pomona Fairgrounds Cal Club races and won overall. Now Rene was hooked. He decided to field a Morgan and I would drive it. This started what became a well known, popular and very successful series of five 'Baby Doll' Morgans, of which the first three are covered in detail in this book. They were the terror of Cobb Mountain hill climb in Northern California. They raced over the entire western U.S.A., California to Kansas, Arizona to Salt Lake, Utah and on up the coast to Kent, Washington. Wherever we raced, more and more people learned about Morgans and Rene established more dealers. One of the most crowd pleasing races was always Lew Spencer in 'Baby Doll' versus Ronnie Bucknum in his Porsche. There was never a dull moment.

Later, when the Super Sports version came out, they were switched up a class or two, away from the Triumphs, but still fighting Porsches. In fact, on the shorter, tighter courses, like Del Mar in California, they held their own against the Corvettes. It didn't hurt at all that 'Kas' Kastner, the Triumph wizard, started building our engines. He didn't like the Porsches either. If a Triumph wasn't racing against them, at least a Triumph engine would be.

Wherever Morgans raced they did well. They were competitive, they were easy to drive and they gave pleasure to everyone that owned or raced one. They were truly a sports car for the average guy, price was reasonable, pleasure was unlimited. I don't think there will ever be another sports car to match the Morgan.

Texas
2007

Introduction

By the mid 1950s the various economies of the world had started to recover from the austere period following the Second World War. Motor sport was a popular hobby for those young men and women with enough disposable income to allow the purchase of a sports car. It was a time when it was possible to buy a sports car from a high street showroom, use it for ordinary duties during the working week and then compete with it in motor sport events at the weekend with reasonable chance of success.

Events open to the sports car enthusiast included race meetings, rallies and trials. The races were often held at abandoned Second World War airfields in Britain and overseas. Rallies in those days were usually held on public roads, with navigation and driving tests as major components, and trials used un-metalled steep hills. Trials were more popular in Britain than elsewhere. Many car clubs also had sprints at various venues, and hill climbs (up-hill sprints on metalled roads) were popular too. It was a golden period for anyone running a sports car.

Looking at the involvement of the Morgan sports car in motor sport, as we have done with this book, it is clear that the Morgan at this time was eminently suitable for all branches of the sport. Many sales of Morgans went to owners new to the marque who quickly found that they could actively compete in them as well as using them as everyday cars. It was an era of the sports car being true to its name.

Many of those who started their motor sport in Morgans went on to a greater motor sport career. In the UK several of the top 'works' team rally drivers of the 50s and 60s became noticed by their successes with a Morgan. These include Jimmy Ray, Doc Spare, Brian Harper with Ron Crellin, and Pauline Mayman with Val Domleo. In America it was racing that made the driver famous, such notables as Lew Spencer, Gaston Andre, Bob Bondurant and Peter Revson beginning their racing careers with Morgans. There were others who became not only first rate drivers but also top quality engineers. Outstanding examples are Chris Lawrence in England and David Van Dal in Australia. The Morgan factory team of Peter Morgan and Jim Goodall was also pretty impressive in many fields of motor sport.

By the early 1960s specialist cars were beginning to be produced suitable for just one aspect of motor sport. The true sports car was now at a disadvantage, and to do well it was necessary to modify the car considerably.

The Morgan Motor Company was privately owned by the founder HFS Morgan and his family. HFS Morgan was a keen designer and experimenter all his life. He was to die in 1959, just before his Company celebrated 50 years of Morgan car production. His son Peter continued the tradition admirably and made the Company successful.

In this book we describe the developments at the Morgan factory from 1954 to 1960, having had considerable support from Peter Morgan and access to the Morgan Motor Company minute book and archives for this period. We have also sought out and interviewed many of the drivers, agents and others involved with the Morgan car both in the UK and overseas. During the late 1950s the main market for the Morgan models was the USA and we have concentrated heavily in researching this area thoroughly. Without this market it is likely the Morgan Company would have ceased trading. We have not mentioned any changes in the layout of the various shops at the Morgan factory, as any changes were quite minor during the years covered by this book.

The Morgan Plus Four was proudly advertised as the fastest sports car at its price by the Morgan factory. When the Triumph TR series was introduced in direct competition using the same engine there was a reduction in the number of engines made available to Morgan. As a result HFS Morgan looked elsewhere and introduced the Ford powered 4/4. We describe the reasons behind its development and introduction. It was to become successful in later years too, and the association with the Ford Motor Company has been a very good one for the Morgan Motor Company, still continuing today, an association of over seventy years.

We hope you will enjoy our story. The research has taken well over ten years, but has been most enjoyable for us.

Jake Alderson and Chris Chapman
2007

This mid 1950s California photograph shows one of the Plus Fours fitted with 'interim' bodywork, designed by HFS Morgan and introduced at the 1953 Motor Show. It was only in production for a few months before being replaced by a new version designed by Peter Morgan, which had higher headlamp pods and a curved radiator grille. (The front bumper on the car shown is non-standard.) (Curt Warshawsky)

Chapter 1
1954

The Morgan Motor Company had been building the Plus Four model with the 2,088cc Standard Vanguard engine at its small 46,000 square feet factory in Pickersleigh Road, Malvern Link in Worcestershire since late 1950. As 1954 dawned the Morgan Motor Company had just switched production from the original chromed radiator-shell Plus Four, to a newly bodied version of the same model, redesigned by HFS Morgan, the founder of the Company. The new bodywork featured a cowl around the radiator, and new front wings. As these front wings now covered more of the front suspension than before they gave the car a much cleaner and more modern overall outline. The front headlamps were faired into these wings, enabling the Lucas seven-inch headlamp inserts to be used, Lucas concentrating future production on these units instead of the previously used free-standing type. This new 'interim' bodywork also allowed the increase in under-bonnet room that was required for the twin SU H4 carburettors on the new Triumph TR2 engines that the Morgan Motor Company wanted to fit to the Plus Four. These engines were currently awaited from the Standard Motor Company.

Some forty of these newly bodied cars had been built during the latter three months of 1953, but few had reached the home agents, for they preferred to wait for delivery until 1954 to sell them as 1954 models. Furthermore the non-delivery of the promised TR2 engines by the Standard Motor Company meant that all were being built with the more sedate Standard Vanguard unit. They were to prove difficult to sell with this engine as enthusiasts waited for the more powerful TR2 version to become available.

Only one TR2 engine had so far been received by the Morgan factory, this being engine number TS 1ME. It had been built into the prototype two-seater fitted with the new bodywork, chassis number T3000, in the autumn of 1953. Peter Morgan needed a TR2 engine for his own 'works' two-seater Plus Four KUY 387 (chassis number P2316) so he arranged for it to exchange engines with T3000, thus acquiring TS 1ME early in January.

Peter himself was somewhat disappointed with the styling of the new cowled radiator and front wings that his father HFS Morgan had designed, so in late 1953 he had asked Charlie Cummings, the foreman of the sheet metal shop, to make up a more rounded radiator grille than the flat one designed by his father. He had also commissioned Felix Day of Mudguard Supplies Limited to adapt the front of the mudguards to take a curved lamp-holder instead of the straight 'bean can' design of his father. This made the headlights higher so that they now complied with the British headlight height requirement. Both the new grille and the new wings were to be fitted to KUY 387 at this time. Charlie Cummings, incidentally, had also been very helpful to Peter during the original development of the Plus Four. It was he who produced the all metal bulkhead and tool box, replacing the wooden items of the 4/4 design.

The engine removed from KUY 387 in the exchange with T3000 had actually been a very special experimental Vanguard engine, number X540E. Originally built by the Standard Motor Company's experimental department, probably for the stillborn Triumph TRX in 1950, it was fitted with twin SU type H4 carburettors, and had been tuned at Standard to produce 72 bhp at 4,250 rpm, an increase over the standard Vanguard engine of 4 bhp.

Morgan production was approximately five or six Plus Fours per week, all using the 2,088cc

Standard Vanguard engine, with the three body styles of sports two-seater, four-seater, and two-seater coupé. Experimental four-seater coupés had also been produced, but this was yet to become a production model.

The development of the new TR2 engine from the earlier Vanguard unit had been undertaken by the Standard Motor Company for its own TR2 sports car which was introduced in July 1953, but the Morgan Motor Company had earlier commissioned the Standard Motor Company to try to extract more power from the Vanguard engine in order to make the Plus Four into a genuine 100 mph sports car. A few Morgans had actually been built with twin carburettor Vanguard engines, and Standard Motor Company engineering drawings show that hollow pushrod tubes using Reynolds 531 tubing were drawn for the Morgan engine in September 1952, to replace the original heavy and solid versions. These lighter pushrods had been one of the suggestions made to HFS Morgan by his friend Harry Hatch, the ex-Blackburne engine designer, whom HFS had asked to look at the Vanguard engine for possible ways of achieving the magical 100 mph back in 1952.

Another change being introduced to the Plus Four at this time was to the steering system. Criticism of the original Burman-Douglas box for having far too much play and not being adjustable had been received by Peter Morgan, particularly from rally drivers who needed precision steering whilst performing driving tests. Eventually HFS had agreed with Peter that something should be done, and the whole system was changed. Thompson track rod ends (as fitted to Rootes Group cars) appeared on new Morgans in late 1953, replacing the original Harrisflex system, and a new steering box appeared in early 1954. HFS and Peter Morgan both agreed that the Marles type of box was too heavy for a Morgan, so the replacement chosen was a Bishop-type cam and lever adjustable steering box. It was produced by the long established company Cam Gears Ltd, based in Luton, Bedfordshire, but with manufacturing facilities at the associated company of George Kent Ltd in Resolven, South Wales. Cam Gears was supplying a good proportion of the British motor industry with steering systems at this time, either the Bishop cam and lever type box, as chosen by Morgan, or a rack and pinion system. Cam Gears Ltd was collaborating with the American Ross Gear and Tool Company; eventually in 1965 it would become a subsidiary of this American firm's successor, later named TRW Inc. Peter Morgan told us that the relationship with Cam Gears was purely business, whereas the Burman family were Morgan family friends, and the choice of Oundle for Peter's own schooling had been influenced by the fact that the Burman boys went there too.

The little Malvern factory where the Morgan cars were made had not made any real profit since the war. HFS had realised very early on in his career how precarious the motor business could be, so he had invested wisely and it was his investments that kept the company afloat by buffering difficult times.

Since the war the British Government had insisted on a major proportion of manufactured cars being exported, as Britain tried to recover from virtual bankruptcy caused by the war. As a result HFS's Managing Director, George Goodall, who was in charge of sales, had managed to set up several overseas agencies, including two particularly important distributorships in the USA.

The founder of the Morgan Motor Company, HFS Morgan, was of course the Company's Governing Director and Chairman of the Board, whilst his son, Peter, was the Deputy Governing Director and Deputy Chairman. The other directors were Harry Jones, who had joined HFS in 1912 and who was in charge of servicing and repairs, Major William Kendall, the Company's accountant, who had been with HFS since the death of his father, and finally HFS's wife Ruth, but she took little part in the running of the Company.

The failure of the Standard Motor Company to deliver the promised new TR2 engines to the Morgan factory was causing despair to the Morgan directors. Initially the problem was Sir John Black, the Standard Motor Company's managing director, who according to Harry Webster, the company's chief chassis engineer, was reluctant to supply the TR2 engine to the Morgan Motor Company. He only relented when the TR2 began to attract large sales but by then the demand was overwhelming the ability of the Standard Motor Company's engine plant to keep pace with orders, with the supply of engines to Morgan suffering as a consequence. The new TR2 sports car had also still to reach its own planned target of 100 per week at Standard's Coventry factory. Obviously a precarious engine supply was no good for Morgan and HFS wondered whether an alternative engine supplier could be used. HFS Morgan had built his Company's name on supplying inexpensive but fast small capacity cars and three-wheelers. Way back in 1949 when Peter Morgan and Repair Shop Foreman, Jim Roberts, had begun constructing the prototype Plus Four chassis, HFS had noticed that the enlarged chassis would allow a complete Ford 'C' type 1,172cc side valve engine plus its gearbox to fit within the engine compartment. At that time consideration had been given to fitting this engine to the 4/4 as a new model to replace the Standard Special engined 4/4, but as the engine was already fitted to the excellent Morgan Model 'F' three-wheeler it was not pursued. Now of course three-wheeler production had ceased, so this argument was no longer valid. In November 1953 HFS told the board that he was going to look further at this, as he believed there would be considerable interest in the home market in producing a Morgan car at a 'popular price'.

The Morgan Company had always had very good relations with the Ford Motor Company, from whom engines had been reliably and uneventfully purchased for nearly twenty years for the F-Type three-wheeler. Conditions in Britain were very difficult still, following the Second World War, and new cars were subjected to 50% Purchase Tax, making most very expensive to buy, and out of reach of the average householder. Indeed food rationing, introduced during the war, was still in force for some items, and would only finally be stopped in June when meat products became freely available once more. Life was quite austere, so the idea of a cheap Morgan made a lot of sense.

No doubt HFS Morgan had also had a good look at the newly introduced Ford Anglia and Prefect models at the October 1953 Motor Show at Earls Court. They were powered by a new version of the old 1,172cc side valve engine, which was externally the same size as the earlier version, but this engine shared little with its predecessor apart from its bore and stroke (63.5 x 92.5mm) and cylinder spacing, thereby enabling some of the previous tooling to be utilised. Its development had been led by George Halford at Dagenham. The new engine, given the nomenclature of the vehicle model 100E by Ford (the '100' being the model number and the 'E' referring to it being an English production model), had a much improved cooling system, including a water pump, larger inlet ports, adjustable tappets and an improved crankshaft with larger diameter bearing surfaces and improved counterbalancing. There was a by-pass oil filter. The compression ratio was 7 to 1, producing 36 bhp at 4,400 rpm, some twenty percent greater than the earlier Prefect engine. The maximum torque was 54 lb ft at 2,150 rpm, with excellent low speed pulling capacity. A hydraulic clutch led to a three-speed gearbox, with synchromesh on just the two upper gears, the production gearbox ratios being 3.403, 1.863 and 1 to 1 for first, second and top gear respectively. These were very wide ratios, hardly ideal for a sports car, and worse than the previous E93A model which the 100E had replaced. The ratios were to get even wider during the production of the 100E Fords.

The use of the Ford engine in another Morgan model would have the great advantage for the Morgan Company of it not having to rely on one company (the Standard Motor Company) as a sole engine manufacturer, a company which had attempted to take over Morgan not too long ago, but had been rebuffed. In addition there was now new 'unproven' management at Standard, for Sir

John Black had just been ousted by the rest of the Standard board, and had been replaced by the young Alick Dick. The Ford Motor Company, on the other hand, had a proven record of reliability in supplying engines to Morgan in the past and was keen to restore this relationship.

At the Morgan directors' meeting held early in 1954, on Wednesday January 20th, it was reported that only four TR2 engines had so far been received at the works, although a further sixteen were expected shortly. Not surprisingly, HFS Morgan reported his continued enthusiasm for a Ford engined 'Popular Model' Morgan using the 1,172cc side valve Ford engine and gearbox. His initial costing suggested a saving of approximately £70 could be made building a coupé version against the equivalent Plus Four coupé. By the directors' meeting held on Wednesday February 24th HFS Morgan was able to present detailed costing of the proposed model. The engine would cost £66 from Ford, compared with £119 required for the TR2 item. Having just one spare wheel, a non-folding windscreen and less complicated bodywork construction would save another £16. He believed the Company should be able to sell the 'Popular Model' at approximately £100 less than the Plus Four. The Ford Motor Company had agreed to supply an engine on loan for trial purposes.

It was not until the meeting on Wednesday April 21st that it was reported that a promise had been received from the Standard Motor Company to deliver four TR2 engines per week. Peter Morgan advised that there were approximately ninety Standard Vanguard engines in stock, or in cars being produced, so the board resolved that for the time being the TR2 engine should only be used for the two-seater Plus Four. In later years Peter expressed relief that he had ordered so many Vanguard engines, as it kept the Plus Four at a reasonable level of production at a difficult period. (There had been problems with wear in big-end bearings in Triumph TR2 engines, so a revised engine with a cross-drilled crankshaft was introduced by Standards in March at engine number TS 881E.)

The Plus Fours built with Vanguard engines were being allocated chassis numbers having the prefix 'P' for Plus Four at the Morgan factory, but there was a change of prefix introduced with the new TR2 engines, a 'T' being used to indicate the Triumph version. However, Charlie Curtis in his Morgan factory tester's report book still prefixed Triumph engined chassis with 'P', and eventually the Morgan Motor Company ceased to bother with the prefix altogether.

Something else for motorcar manufacturers to think about was the new 'Motor Vehicles (Construction and Use)' regulations which had come into force on January 1st 1954. Included was the legalisation of flashing direction indicators, although these remained an optional fitment. The new regulations also stated that cars parked on a highway at night must be parked on the nearside of the road.

The competition year had started at the beginning of January with the running of one of the classic trials. The Morgan factory had always supported the Motor Cycling Club (MCC) long distance trials since the very early days of three-wheeler production, led admirably by HFS Morgan himself. Before the Second World War many sports car manufacturers entered trials as a form of motor sport, but since the war it was only really Morgan and one or two smaller companies that continued to support trials. Originally the idea of trials was to drive at a set speed between major cities, proving the reliability of the motor cars, but as cars and roads became better the organisers sought out ancient unmade roads up the sides of steep hills, and included these as special sections. In MCC trials a First Class Award or Gold was awarded for climbing all the special sections without stopping, and for keeping to time. A Second Class Award or Silver was awarded to those failing just one hill, and a Third Class Award or Bronze to those failing two. The MCC ran two long distance trials each year, the 'Exeter' at the beginning of January, and the 'Land's End' at Easter. The club had also run the Edinburgh Trial at Whitsun in pre-war days, but many of the old hills had been tarmacked, and this annual event had been replaced by a rally.

The MCC Exeter Trial was held over the Friday night and Saturday, January 1st and 2nd, and attracted no fewer than twelve Morgan entries. From the Morgan factory came W A 'Jim' Goodall, George Goodall's son and manager of the machine shop, with the prototype Plus Four two-seater HUY 982 (chassis number P2100), and Sonny McCann who also worked in the machine shop, entered in the short chassis 4/4 trials car BWP 47 (chassis number 380) dating back to 1937 and now running with a Standard Special engine. Peter Morgan had not entered this year, but had loaned his Plus Four coupé JNP 239 (chassis number P2038) to Peter Garnier, the sports editor of *The Autocar* magazine and a great Morgan enthusiast. In the absence of Peter it was the Worcestershire farmer John Moore who completed the Morgan team of three cars in his black Plus Four coupé KNP 5 (chassis number P2216). 'Joe' Huxham, the Bournemouth Morgan agent since the early 1930s and a keen motor sportsman, was in a 4/4 Le Mans Replica with 1,086cc Coventry Climax engine, probably FOH 812, no doubt prepared as usual by his business partner Tom Bryant. Alan Hobbs was in his white Plus Four OHW 273 which had slightly unusual bodywork. John Ahern was driving his Plus Four NXH 394, Ernest James his Plus Four NYU 993 (chassis number P2638), P Norgard his Plus Four NYF 452 (chassis number P2548), C Neale was in Plus Four GJN 5, and I Elkington was also in a Plus Four, but we have no registration number for that one. Les Griffiths non-started in his Plus Four. John Ahern's four-seater had been owned by him from new and he had designed a boot conversion for the rear, with the spare wheel fitted on the outside. This was made for him by the London coachbuilder J Jarvis of Walmer Road. Peter Garnier's entry was listed as having a TR2 engine, but the borrowed Peter Morgan coupé JNP 239 was still running with a Vanguard engine at this time. Perhaps it was originally envisaged that he would drive Peter Morgan's two-seater KUY 387.

One hundred and thirty-four cars had entered for the trial, starting on the Friday night from the

Sonny McCann passengered by Terry Hall in the Morgan factory short chassis trials car BWP 47 in the MCC Exeter Trial.
(LAT Photographic)

three alternative starting places: Kenilworth, Virginia Water and Launceston. The Morgan team started from Kenilworth and was met by dense fog with icy roads all the way to Bristol, falling behind time until they reached Somerset where the fog cleared and the ice melted. John Moore navigated through the fog with both of the coupé's doors open, enabling him and his passenger to search for the kerbstones lining the sides of the road. Of the hills, Simms was a real stopper, and none of the Morgans managed to climb it, Jim Goodall being the best, but coming to a halt just ten yards from the top with wheels spinning. Second Class Awards were won by Jim, Alan Hobbs, John Moore, John Ahern and C Neale, whilst Ernest James and Peter Garnier received Thirds. Joe Huxham retired and the others finished out of the awards.

Within a few days of the trial John Moore drove his black coupé KNP 5 to Twickenham for the international rugby match, suffering the misfortune of running the big-end bearings just as he arrived. He paid to have new ones fitted whilst he watched the match and then returned to Worcestershire, unfortunately running the replacement big-ends as well. He wasn't too concerned however, for on Wednesday January 6th the coupé was taken to the Morgan factory to have one of the few available TR2 engines fitted. The front end of the car was updated at the same time to the factory approved Peter Morgan redesign, which had superseded the 'interim' design of HFS Morgan. Jim Goodall was to follow suit with HUY 982, receiving TR2 engine number TS 423ME, and probably a 3.73 to 1 rear axle at the same time.

The Vintage Sports-Car Club obviously catered for motor sportsmen with vintage cars, but it did allow a class for 'visitors' cars' in the Measham Rally over the weekend of January 9th and 10th. Keen Morgan rally driver Les Yarranton, whose family ran a motor coach business in Eardiston in Worcestershire, entered his Plus Four KWP 926 (chassis number P2372), which had been bodied at his family's own premises. The rally traversed a 250 mile night route through Wales before arriving at the Measham Motor Sales Organisation's car auction ground for two final driving tests. Here Les Yarranton made fastest time in the first test, and made the best performance overall in any class, getting a nice silver trophy.

Rallies were a very popular form of motor sport in Britain at this time, with many including long night navigation sections against the clock, and with driving tests to separate those with similar times. There was a host of motor clubs spread around the country keen to run rallies, such that the enthusiast had a choice of several on most weekends. One such was the Thames Estuary Automobile Club's 'Cats' Eyes' Night Navigation and Map Reading Rally held over the weekend of February 6th and 7th. Over two hundred started, the Mayor of Southend-on-Sea flagging off the first few starters at one minute intervals with the crews receiving the route card just ten minutes before departure. There were 320 miles to be covered during the night, split into four sections, before the cars returned in the morning to Southend-on-Sea for the final driving test. The most amazing performance was that of Bernard Clarke with his Plus Four PKK 769 (chassis number P2222) navigated by Ian McKenzie, for they lost no marks at all, winning the rally outright. Second in class was the Plus Four of Hugh Denton (JNV 654, chassis number P2712) with two hundred marks lost.

The 'Cats' Eyes' Rally had been a 'Closed Invitation' event, indicating it was open only to the organising club's members, and those of invited clubs. The British Trials Drivers Association was to award their Silver Star Rally Award to the driver doing best in his pre-selected eight of fifteen possible contributing events. The Gold Star Award was to be awarded for best performance in nine major 'Open' rallies in 1954, being open to all comers. A Silver Garter Award would be given to the best lady driver in the latter competition.

Also run that weekend was the Kings College Motor Club's Allendale Rally, attracting twenty-eight starters to wild Northumberland. After jointly leading the overnight section Raymond

Bernard Clarke holds the torch whilst his navigator plots the route for the 'Cats' Eyes' Rally. (Charles Dunn)

Patton had to settle for second place in his Plus Four after losing six minutes on the Sunday.

The Yorkshire Sports Car Club had a reputation for toughness with its winter Yorkshire Rally and the one held over the weekend of February 12th and 13th was no exception, only thirty-five of the ninety-five starters returning to the Town Hall at Harrogate after the overnight section! Fog and drifting snow were the culprits. Peter Reece, a director of the Liverpool Ford dealership 'Blakes', but a keen Morgan driver, retired when he hit a stone wall head-on with his coupé. Bill Whiteley at least made it back to Harrogate, but his Plus Four PKK 256 (chassis number P2402) was seriously damaged and no Morgans made the award sheet. Bill was an enthusiastic member of the Ilkley and District Motor Club, and regularly entered local events. His family business was a paper processing mill at Pool-in-Wharfedale, near Otley.

During 1952 and early 1953 Peter Reece had been driving one of the three special lightweight Morgans produced for the RAC and Alpine rallies. This car was registered KUY 475 but it had now been passed to Marion Parry (always known as 'Pip'). Her father ran the Blakes business in Manchester (Vauxhall dealers). The Morgan had also been driven by 'Jock' Sinclair, who had competed with it in 1953. Peter Reece was now driving a blue coupé, OFM 200 (chassis number P2254). Peter and his cousin Jack were the main force within the Liverpool Motor Club, and many top drivers were to start from humble beginnings in that club.

Over the weekend of February 27th and 28th the Falkirk and District Motor Club ran the first Closed Invitation event of the Scottish season. Several Morgans were entered. The famous rallying sisters Andie and Chrissie Neil, who worked in the family pig farming business at Tollcross near Glasgow, were entered in their Plus Four KYS 41 (chassis number P2508) which was nicknamed 'Toots'. Stanley Kay was entered in the special, unique closed-body Plus Four of Roy Clarkson (chassis number P2483), the body having been copied from the Touring body of Roy's previous car, a 2.3 litre Ferrari. The Morgan was registered VNO 600. Howard Sturrock completed the Morgan entrants with his Plus Four, and was the only Morgan driver to feature in the main awards, winning the class for open cars over 1,500cc.

Another of the events for the Silver Star Rally Award was the Bolton-Le-Moors Car Club Rally held on Sunday March 7th at Blackpool, attracting an entry of 161. This was really a day of driving tests, and Peter Reece excelled in his coupé, winning the Standard Car Award.

The Lanarkshire MC and CC's Clydesdale Rally, held on March 10th again saw Howard Sturrock on the award sheet, for he was victorious in the open cars unlimited class with his Plus Four.

The greatest event for the British rally enthusiast was undoubtedly the RAC's annual event, the British International Rally. This year it was to start on Tuesday March 9th and finish some 1,900 miles later on Saturday March 13th, with the traditional 'Rally Ball' that final evening. This year, to try and avoid too much congestion on the English roads, there were two starting places, namely the seaside towns of Blackpool and Hastings. Odd numbered competitors started from Blackpool and the even numbered from Hastings. Amongst the 240 accepted entrants were eleven Morgans, of which six formed two teams of three, competing for the team prize.

Morgans usually did well on the RAC, for the special tests suited the nimble Plus Four, and of course many of the top rally drivers of the day drove Morgans for this very reason. One of the best was Doctor John Spare, a General Practitioner from Taunton in Somerset, who rallied another of the special lightweight Plus Fours used in the Alpine Rally in 1952. This was KUY 476 (chassis number P2321). In January he had contacted another top driver, Jimmy Ray from Prescot, who worked in the family confectionary business and owned the third of the special lightweights, KUY 474 (chassis number P2315), to see if they might form a team. Jimmy replied that he was actually getting married (in Bath) on Saturday March 6th, and was then competing in the RAC Rally as part of his honeymoon. His future bride, Kath, had yet to get a driving licence, and had never been in a rally in her life, so Jimmy suggested he was not likely to be competitive and that John might try elsewhere! John, who was to be navigated by a Bridgewater GP, Dr Peter Legat, did just that, forming a team with fellow Morgan enthusiasts Barrie Phipps and Hugh Denton. Barrie, in the fruit canning business in Worcestershire, ran a special Dellow-bodied four-seater Plus Four KUY 714, and was to be navigated by Robin Butterell. Hugh Denton and his navigator Richard Colton were both from Northamptonshire and in the leather business. Hugh was in shoe manufacturing and Richard in the shoe wholesale and retail trade; they had been friends from school and were in Hugh's Plus Four JNV 654. This team was using the Hastings start.

The second Morgan team was that from the Morgan factory. This year the Company wanted to run and demonstrate the new Plus Fours with TR2 engines and Peter Morgan's revised cowl and wings. Consequently the team consisted of Peter Morgan navigated by an enthusiastic Morgan factory apprentice named John Bodin in KUY 387, Jim Goodall navigated by his regular rally co-driver Terry Hall in HUY 982, and John Moore in KNP 5 navigated by Les Yarranton. Terry Hall loved being with Jim in the works team, but being a pharmacist in Bromsgrove meant he always had difficulties in getting a locum to keep his shop open whilst away on rallies. Also starting from Hastings was Les Griffiths, a regular RAC Rally competitor and garage proprietor from Bridgwater in Somerset who was navigated by T Pascoe. This was his first RAC in a Plus Four, but his fourth overall.

Starting from Blackpool were Jimmy Ray and his new wife Kathleen, the Neil sisters Andie and Chrissie in KYS 41, Alec Newsham and Doc Steel. Alec Newsham, who was from Blackburn and in the 'fish and chips' restaurant business, was navigated by Preston solicitor Tony Beaumont in his Plus Four OKC 208 (chassis number P2554). Doctor William Steel owned the prototype four-seater Plus Four JWP 537 (chassis number P2121). 'Doc' Steel had previously been a regular member of the Morgan factory team, but not this year because his Morgan didn't have the new bodywork or a TR2 engine. His Plus Four still had the Vanguard engine and was regularly serviced at the Morgan factory, where the black car with hood erect was christened 'The Hearse' by the employees for obvious reasons. As he lived close by in Worcester, Doc Steel had bought a paratroopers' bike for factory service visits, carrying it dismantled in the back when delivering the car, assembling it once there and riding it the few miles back home. His navigator was John Dodd, the competition secretary of the Worcestershire Motor Club. Apart from the factory team all the Morgans had Vanguard engines and the older chrome radiator and free-standing headlights.

The RAC Rally was subtitled 'The Rally of The Tests', for whilst the road section was long, the required average speed of 30 mph was hardly in the same league as the great Continental rallies, which were virtually road races along tricky roads. To compensate, tests were set at various venues on the route, including the motor sport venues of Silverstone, Goodwood, Oulton Park, Prescott, and Charterhall, and the traditional 'scissors' test faced the competitors at the starts. On the Friday, after the stop at Blackpool, the two sets of competitors joined up for the less busy final day's northern route returning back to Blackpool for the finish.

The weather could always play a part in the 'RAC' and so it proved this year. The first stage for the Blackpool contingent was held at night in Wales and dense fog caused major problems. The Neil sisters damaged the front of their Plus Four beyond repair and had to retire. Doc Steel had been concerned about low oil pressure in the Plus Four, but gamely followed the grass verge as quickly as he could in the foggy conditions. Suddenly he saw a gate in front and the car rolled right over, luckily finishing upright and back on its wheels. It turned out he had put one wheel up the steeply sloping entrance to a cottage on a right hand bend. His passenger was knocked unconscious and Doc spent the rest of the night seeing that he was OK (he made a full recovery), vowing in the process he would give up rallying forthwith.

Another driver having problems was John Spare, who was nursing a sick engine, eventually limping into the Blackpool overnight halt with big-end trouble. The car was placed in 'parc ferme' overnight and couldn't be touched until after the following day's start, so John arranged with a nearby garage for them to drop the sump and replace the big-ends immediately following the Friday restart. This was done in the amazing time of 23 minutes, but there was now a rush to be on time for the first control, allowing no time for running in, and sadly the bearings began to fail once more. He limped round the course and then slowly made his way home. Les Griffiths' rally

Alec Newsham's Morgan is scrutineered at the Blackpool start. (Charles Dunn)

Doc Steel's four-seater after its mishap in the RAC Rally. (George Goodall)

finished in the Welsh section when he retired. Meanwhile the surviving Morgans were doing well in the various tests, often putting up the best times, but they were being let down with delays on the road sections. It is rumoured the Morgan team even misread the night control of Newcastleton in Scotland as Newcastle (on Tyne) in England, going several miles off course before the mistake was realised! Newly wed Jimmy Ray had discovered his new wife was not up to rally driving, so she drove no more than twenty miles in the whole rally whilst he drove the rest, an amazing endurance feat. Many rally drivers took 'Benzedrine' tablets (an amphetamine) to stay awake on the long sections, this being socially and legally acceptable then, but not today.

When the results were calculated the winning car was the new Triumph TR2 of Johnnie Wallwork, losing no marks at all on the road sections and, with another TR2 coming second, this was excellent publicity for the Standard Motor Company. The best Morgan performance was that of Jimmy and Kath Ray in seventh place, with Alec Newsham just behind in eighth. No others finished in the first twenty-five finishers, and neither of the Morgan teams was complete at the finish, with Barrie Phipps retiring in the Lake District section as did John Moore.

No doubt all still found time for enjoyment at the evening ball on the Saturday, many pranks and high jinks being undertaken as the crews relaxed. Favourite 'games' included going as fast as possible in hotel revolving doors (one of Peter Morgan's favourites) and racing spare wheels down the promenade!

A new windscreen, radiator and sundry other items were soon dispatched to Scottish agents Murray and Neilson to repair the Neil's car. Doc Steel's was returned to the factory, rebuilt and sold on to a surgeon. Doc Steel had indeed retired!

Whilst the works cars KUY 387 and HUY 982 had been updated with cowled radiators fitted with the new curved grille, and also the redesigned wings with the curved headlamp holders, the production Plus Fours were not yet being built to this specification. They were still leaving the Morgan factory fitted with the HFS-designed 'interim' flat-grille cowls and his original 'bean can' wings, which had lower headlamps. Presumably stocks of these components were being used up and recent research by Gerry Willburn, assisted by Hermen Pol and one of the authors (JA) suggests around forty-six Plus Fours were produced to this specification, being dispatched from late 1953 to March 1954. It seems apparent that whilst the stock of flat-type radiator grilles of the interim design was then exhausted, there were still some of the lower-headlamp-type wings in stock, such that several cars (around nineteen) were then built with a specification combining the later rounded grilles and these early wings. By the end of May, however, the full 'Peter Morgan redesigned front end' was being fitted to dispatched cars and continued from then on. The surviving works records make it nearly impossible to be completely certain.

In Scotland the Lanarkshire MC & CC ran its Clydesdale Rally on Wednesday March 10th. It was a difficult rally, with many entrants having problems in finding a way to the quoted map reference points, such that the final test was eventually abandoned. Howard Sturrock did well with his Plus Four, winning the unlimited class for open cars.

On Saturday March 13th the Omagh MC in Northern Ireland ran a trial as a 'dress rehearsal' for the forthcoming Ulster AC's Circuit of Ireland Rally in April. John Howe did well in the pylon-circling tests, making fastest time in this section, and finishing second overall in the class for open cars, behind a Dellow, with his Plus Four.

At Kirkistown Airport, County Down in Northern Ireland, the 500 Motor Racing Club of Ireland staged its Championship of Ireland meeting for 500cc cars on Saturday, March 20th using a 1.6 mile circuit, the championship being won by the great Don Parker. Also on the race card was an open handicap for all comers, comprising two ten lap heats and a ten lap final. Qualifying for the final by finishing fifth in heat one was the Plus Four of Arthur Clapham, but he was out of the places in the final, coming home eleventh.

The Scottish Sporting Car Club ran its 'Winter Half Day' on Sunday March 21st starting at Giffnock and finishing at Troon, with a mixture of trials and rally sections for the competitors to enjoy. Howard Sturrock won a Second Class Award with his Plus Four. Charlie Robertson made a valiant attempt on Sparnelbank trials hill, but just failed to crest the top. No doubt he was driving his Plus Four JSG 320.

That same day Mike Warner made fastest time of the day in the Eastern Counties MC's autocross meeting. He was running his Vanguard engined Plus Four APV 607 with no headlights and with cycle-type front wings.

The fifteenth British Automobile Racing Club (BARC) Members' Meeting was held at Goodwood on Saturday March 27th in perfect sunny weather. Two Morgan Plus Fours took part

Basil de Mattos sets off for victory in the BARC Handicap race at Goodwood. (Basil de Mattos collection)

in Race 8, a five lap handicap event. These were the TR2 engined coupé KNP 5 of John Moore, and Peter Morgan's TR2 engined two-seater KUY 387 borrowed by Morgan enthusiast Basil de Mattos for this meeting. Basil was Sales Director of Laystall Engineering and a well known and experienced racing driver. An Alvis led for four of the five laps before being swamped by the later-starting and faster cars. After overtaking John's coupé Basil just managed to hold off Major Bailey's thundering vintage 4.5 litre Bentley to win the race at 71.58 mph. This win was excellent publicity for the new TR2 engined Plus Four, for it was well covered in the motoring magazines.

There were sixty-two starters for the Herefordshire MC's four hundred miles Welsh Rally that same weekend, but it was a tough event with almost one third retiring. Equal first on points, and receiving the award for best club member, was Les Yarranton, passengered as usual by D 'Tommy' Thompson, who had been a rear gunner in bombers during the Second World War.

The following weekend there was yet another rally in Wales (!) when the Midland Centre of the MGCC held its Welsh Rally. At the end of the first day Hugh Denton was the joint leader, with a penalty-free score, but he lost fifteen marks on the Sunday's regularity test, having to settle for a First Class Award.

The Eastern Counties MC ran a closed-to-club race meeting at Snetterton circuit on Saturday April 3rd, not getting a particularly large entry. Once again Mike Warner was victorious, his handicap over the two following Jaguars being too lenient, giving him an easy victory. In the programme the engine of his chrome radiator Plus Four was noted as 2,488cc, perhaps just a misprint for 2,088cc.

The Bristol MC and LCC ran a race meeting at Castle Combe that same day. Although racing in his 4/4 Le Mans Replica JUO 177, Jeff Sparrowe didn't finish in the awards.

On Saturday April 10th the London Motor Club ran its 'Little Rally', with entries for London Motor Club members only, it being a closed-to-club event. There were still 335 entries for this popular event, with eighteen teams, each of three cars, contesting the team award. One of these was the Morgan 4/4 Club team, but all had to be London Motor Club members too of course. The team consisted of the Plus Four JNV 654 of Hugh Denton navigated by friend Hugh Ladds, an Allard belonging to Peter Homes, and the new geranium pink TR2 of Bill Parkes navigated by Barrie Phipps. At this time the Morgan 4/4 Club was primarily a motor sport orientated club, just like most other motor clubs, and ownership of a Morgan was not essential for membership.

Despite the lack of Morgans in the Morgan team, there were several others competing. D L Franks was navigated by Miss L MacRae in their early Plus Four OHW 611, and P Norgard by his wife in their Vanguard engined Plus Four NYF 452.

Jeff Sparrowe at Castle Combe with JUO 177. (Charles Dunn)

Ernest James slides his Plus Four on the slippery Hustyn surface during the MCC Land's End Trial. (The Autocar)

L Jenner was in his Plus Four, Les Griffiths and Alex Blair both in theirs, whilst A W Taylor was navigated by R A French in a Standard Special engined 4/4.

The Morgan team did well to come second in the team competition, whilst Hugh Denton came second in the class for open cars over 1,500cc. Alex 'Sandy' Blair, a Harpenden farmer, had bought his 1953 two-seater chrome radiator Plus Four NXY 859 from a London agency, possibly Basil Roy. For fairly obvious reasons this green Morgan was christened 'Nixie'.

The MCC's Land's End Trial was held as usual over the night of Good Friday, finishing on Easter Saturday (April 16th and 17th). There were three starting points: Launceston, Kenilworth and Virginia Water. The competitors converged at Taunton in the early hours of Saturday morning and followed a common route through the north of Devon and finally into Cornwall. The Morgan team consisted of Jim Goodall in the TR2 engined HUY 982, Peter Morgan in his Vanguard engined coupé JNP 239 and Terry Hall with the short chassis 4/4 with Standard Special engine, BWP 47; they started from Kenilworth. Joe Huxham was this time driving a Vanguard engined Plus Four. Other similar Plus Fours were entered by I Elkington, John Ahern, Ernest James and P Norgard, presumably the same cars they used in the Exeter Trial.

Whilst good weather made most of the hills easy, a stream on Hustyn caused many to fail, including Peter Morgan, Elkington and James. There was much spectator interest in the TR2 engined Morgan of Jim Goodall, which of course had the new shape front end, and was one of the first seen on the trials hills with this new configuration. It proved to be very powerful on the hills, and Jim took a First Class Award along with Joe Huxham. Peter won a Second Class Award and the others Thirds except for Terry Hall, who had to retire.

The Pembrokeshire MC held regular hill climbs at Lydstep, these being popular events, attracting over seventy entrants and 1,500 spectators to the one held on Easter Saturday, April 17th. John Moore was outstanding in the TR2 engined coupé KNP 5 breaking records in three classes. He finally lowered the 3 litre sports car record from 36.4 seconds to 35.5seconds, and he was victorious too with his runs in the unlimited class, with another class record of 35.1 seconds. In the popular 1,500cc to 2,000cc sports car class he eventually had to settle for second place with a time of 35.4 seconds, just 0.2 seconds behind Trelfall's Turner-Lea Francis. John also won the saloon car handicap (!) with a time of 35.1 seconds, finishing off an excellent day's driving, and collecting a bag full of trophies!

On Easter Sunday the Northampton and District Car Club ran its first autocross, at the Wakefield Lawns Estate near Towcester. The course was exactly half a mile, with plenty of corners laid out in a large field. Hugh Denton had entered his Plus Four JNV 654 and Richard Colton was also driving Hugh's car. Hugh was unbeatable, with a time of 57.8 seconds for fastest time of the day, whilst Richard came second, just 0.4 seconds slower.

Also over the busy Easter weekend the Scottish Sporting Car Club ran its Highland Three Days' Rally, starting on Easter Saturday and finishing on Easter Monday. Several Morgans took part. Roy Clarkson was passengered by Stanley Kay in his special-bodied saloon Morgan. More conventional chrome radiator Plus Fours were entered by the Neil sisters, Charlie Robertson and Howard Sturrock. The Morgans all performed well, with Howard Sturrock and Andie Neil both winning awards in the class for open cars of unlimited capacity. Roy Clarkson won an award in the class for saloon cars, unlimited capacity, and the Neil sisters took the Ladies' Award.

The Ulster AC's 1,000 mile Circuit of Ireland Trial started on Good Friday, with starts in Dublin and Belfast, and finished on Easter Tuesday. Two Vanguard engined Plus Four Morgans took part, both from Belfast, driven by Albert Acheson and John Howe. Friday night was the all night run, and after that there were night stops at Killarney on the Saturday and Sunday. There were eight driving tests along the route. At the end of the first day Albert Acheson, probably driving his 1952 green Plus Four KUY 625, was in sixth place in the class for sports cars. Despite good performances in some of the driving tests he finished out of the top six places, a Dellow winning overall.

On Saturday April 24th the Pathfinders and Derby Motor Club ran its Midlands Rally, held over two circuits of 100 miles in Derbyshire. The event attracted thirty-three starters, despite cold and overcast conditions. There was a shortage of marshals on the grassy, rocky hill tracks used, but despite that Ernie Sneath from Sheffield finished second to a TR2 in his Morgan. Ernest Sneath was a keen member of the Sheffield and Hallamshire Motor Club, and had previously run a Morgan three-wheeler. He was a greetings card publisher and printer in Sheffield. His usual navigator was his son Rodney, a doctor.

That same evening the Wirrall 100 MC ran the Wallasey Corporation Rally, cars starting from 10 pm onwards and covering 300 miles in Wales. The following morning the cars returned to the

Richard Colton in Hugh Denton's Plus Four at the Northampton & DCC autocross. (Richmond Pike)

Ian Hall with the coupé after the Wallasey Rally. (Ian Hall collection)

car park at The Baths, New Brighton for the final tests. Once again a TR2 was victorious, driven by the Triumph dealer Denis Done, but Ken James in a Plus Four navigated by Ian Hall finished eighth of the forty-nine starters. Ken James worked for Peter Reece at Blakes in Liverpool. Peter had lent him his coupé OFM 200 for this event.

The Morgan 4/4 Club held its AGM at the Warwick Arms Hotel at Warwick on this Saturday. Peter Morgan was elected President, with Dick Pritchard Chairman and Barrie Phipps Club Secretary. HFS Morgan was still the Club's Patron.

Les Yarranton again demonstrated his mastery of rallying when he took first place in the Coventry and Warwickshire MC's T G John Cup Rallyette on Sunday April 25th, beating forty-five other competitors with his Plus Four KWP 926.

There were several small club sprints in existence at which enthusiasts could have fun. One such event was that held at Bushmead, near St

Richard Colton at the Bushmead Sprint. (Richmond Pike)

Neots, organised by the Bedford Automobile Enthusiasts Club this same Sunday. Hugh Denton was competing in JNV 654, and Richard Colton was also competing, this time in his own Morgan, a 1953 two-seater, RYC 777, which he purchased with low mileage from a Somerset driver, meeting him in Wiltshire to do an exchange for his own MG TD. The Plus Four was red with red upholstery. It was chassis number P2684, and had been originally dispatched to the Taunton agency, Silver Street Motors, on Friday August 13th. Neither Morgan featured in the awards.

Several rally drivers were now having their Plus Fours converted to the new Cam Gears steering box, for better steering control in driving tests. In April both Hugh Denton and Andie Neil had this box fitted to their cars.

John Spare had a busy weekend over May 1st and 2nd, for on the Saturday he won his class in the Torbay MC's third Torbay Rally, whilst on the Sunday he finished second in the class for open cars in the Welsh Counties CC Rally.

That same Sunday the Singer OC ran its team driving tests at Bovingdon Aerodrome. The Morgan 4/4 Club had entered Hugh Denton, Les Yarranton, Barrie Phipps and John McDonagh, and they came away with the main prize, the Singer Challenge Trophy. The best individual performance

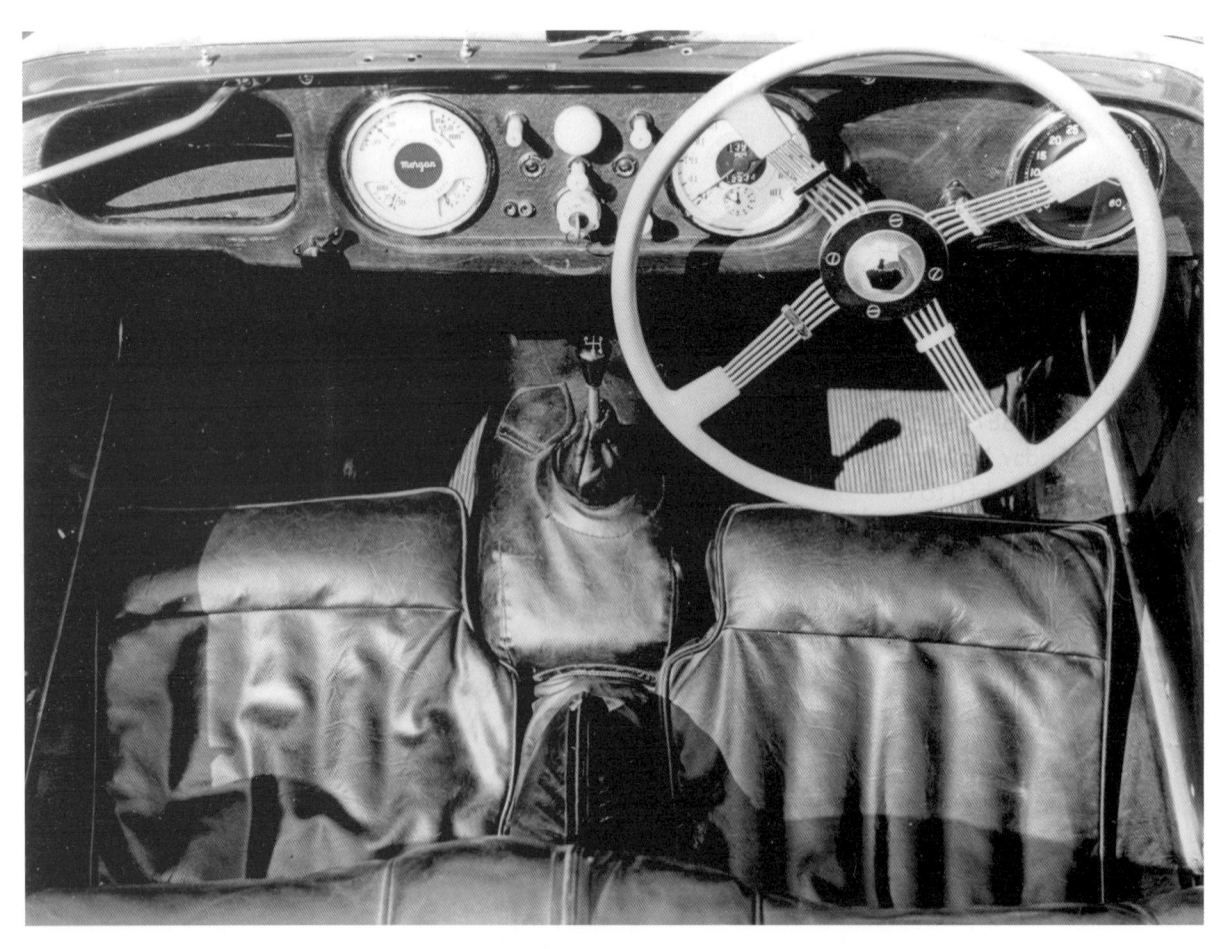

The interior of Peter Morgan's KUY 387. Non-standard features include the padded central arm attached to the backrest of the seat, built in at Peter's request for better driver location whilst racing. The rev counter is pre-production, the production models having matching cream dials. A hand throttle for preventing stalling during driving tests is also fitted, but is not visible here. (The Autocar)

Peter Morgan in the Prescott paddock in KUY 387, John Moore's coupé alongside. (Morgan Motor Co collection)

went to Warwick garage owner John McDonagh, whilst the best lady driver was Aileen Jervis in her 4/4 Le Mans Replica JTT 703. Also that Sunday Charlie Robertson was second in the class for open cars over 1,200cc in his Plus Four in the Lothian CC's rally.

The Autocar magazine borrowed Peter Morgan's two-seater KUY 387 for a road test published in the issue of Friday May 7th. The TR2 engine gave acceleration figures of 0 to 60 mph in 13.3 seconds, covering the standing quarter mile in 18.5 seconds, and reaching 102 mph top speed. The new Cam Gears steering was found to be light, sensitive and accurate, and the only real criticism was of the brakes which had a rather dead feel to the pedal, and required a lot of pressure to work fully. 'It does not pander to the creature comforts and, in exchange for a slightly Spartan outlook on behalf of the driver, it will give him real pleasure,' the tester commented. The Morgan Plus Four with TR2 engine was priced at £585, which with Purchase Tax at 50% gave a total cost of £829 17s 6d. (£829.88). The four-seater cost £600, the coupé £640, before tax, but with the Vanguard engine fitted instead of the TR2 £20 could be deducted from these prices. A heater was available for an extra £8 12s 0d. (£8.60), but few were fitted at this time.

The West Hants and Dorset Car Club once more managed to borrow the old Ibsley airfield from Lord Normanton for a race meeting on Saturday May 8th. Crop cultivation prevented the previous circuit being used, but a 1.9 mile lap of the perimeter substituted admirably. Court Corner (old Paddock Bend) was particularly tricky, catching out the experienced Jeff Sparrowe in his fast Le Mans Replica JUO 177, for he spun on the second lap and failed to finish in the places.

The Bugatti Owners' Club ran a National hill climb at its Prescott venue on Sunday May 9th. Peter Morgan took along KUY 387, and John Moore KNP 5, both being entered in the class for sports cars of 1,501 to 3,000cc. The class was dominated by the Bristol engined Kiefts, but Peter had the satisfaction of beating the three TR2s by over a second with a time of 51.69 seconds, finishing fourth, whilst John was seventh in 52.8 seconds.

There were sixty entrants for the North Devon MC's fourth Ilfracombe Rally that same weekend. There were four starting points for the rally competitors, being Ilfracombe, Bristol,

John Spare positions his Morgan correctly in the Ilfracombe Rally driving tests. (John Spare collection)

Salisbury and Plymouth, finishing at Ilfracombe some three hundred miles later, after an overnight run, for driving tests held near Ilfracombe Pier. The winner was Hugh Denton in JNV 654, whilst John Spare was second in KUY 476. This showed just how successful these two drivers had become in club rallies with their Plus Fours. For driving tests John used to borrow his passenger's seat cushion and put it on top of his own for extra visibility, and he always used minimal strength throttle return springs to make sure he had immediate maximum engine response. The Team Award too went to the Morgans, for Hugh and John had teemed up with Barrie Phipps as the Morgan 4/4 Club entry.

On Saturday May 15th the Daily Express International Trophy meeting was held at Silverstone, organised by the British Racing Drivers' Club (BRDC). On the programme was the International Trophy race itself, attracting Formula 1 cars such as Ferraris, Maseratis, Connaughts etc. Peter Morgan had entered the International sports car race with KUY 387. A record crowd of 120,000 came to watch, despite the heavy rain. Peter's opposition in the two litre class consisted of a bevy of Cooper Bristols, Horace Gould's Kieft Bristol and Leslie Brook's TR2. Unfortunately Peter's Morgan failed to last the distance.

The Scottish Centre of the MGCC staged its annual weekend rally and gymkhana over the weekend of May 15th and 16th. Charlie Robertson did well with his Plus Four, finishing second in the class for open cars, behind an MG but ahead of a TR2.

1954 marked the fiftieth anniversary of the MCC's very first Edinburgh Trial and the club decided to commemorate it with a run from London to Edinburgh, as in the original 1904 trial, with participants limited to those with long standing Edinburgh Trial history, or those driving ancient but appropriate vehicles. HFS Morgan had first entered the Edinburgh Trial in 1911 in his three-wheeler (the programme stated 1912) and decided to enter in a coupé, co-driven by his son Peter. Also entered in a Morgan was Basil Roy, the prestigious London agent. He had first entered this event in 1928. Roy Clarkson had never competed in the Edinburgh Trial, but managed to get his entry accepted because he was to drive his 1902 Panhard et Lavassor. Amongst other notable entries was George Brough, the famous pre-war motorcycle manufacturer and competitor.

A total of forty-eight starters, comprising thirty-four cars and fourteen motorcycles, was dispatched by Sir Algernon Guinness at one minute intervals on a cold and wet evening on Friday May 21st from the London GPO building. Twenty-four hours and 397 miles later they all checked in at Edinburgh, with just three absentees, one of whom was Roy Clarkson who had retired at Hitchin. This was to be HFS Morgan's last ever 'competitive' event.

The Lancashire Automobile Club's eighth Morecambe National Rally also began that Friday, attracting 221 competitors to the eight starting points of Morecambe, Shenstone, Bristol, Leeds, Luton, Manchester, Preston and Glasgow. They faced a route of 200 miles on the Friday, the routes converging at Samlesbury, and thence arriving in Morecambe for a night's rest, before a 140 mile run on the Saturday.

Several Morgans took part. From Morecambe there was the Southport agent Gerry Hoyle in a new TR2 engined Plus Four KFY 1, which we think was probably chassis number T3092, and J Waddell in a Vanguard engined 1952 car. Mr J Waddell was the Deputy Town Clerk of Lancaster. Andie Neil started from Glasgow in KYS 41. There were several Luton starters, being Les Yarranton in KWP 926, John Moore in his TR2 engined coupé KNP 5, Sandy Blair with his Vanguard engined car NXY 959 and Hugh Denton with JNV 654. From Bristol came John Spare with KUY 476 and Les Griffiths with his 1953 Plus Four. Miss M Parry was starting from Preston in a 1952 Plus Four (perhaps this was Pip with KUY 475). The Morgan 4/4 Club

Gerry Hoyle in the Morecambe Rally, ahead of Kinns' HRG. (Charles Dunn)

team consisted of Hugh Denton, John Moore and Les Yarranton.

Up in the leaders early on was Hugh Denton, but he then seems to have had problems. Andie Neil certainly did on the Saturday, bending back the Morgan front suspension to cause a retirement. John Moore had broken the throttle pedal in his coupé, making the driving tests difficult. Les Yarranton took the award for Class A3, for production sports cars, 1,300 to 2,600cc, whilst Les Griffiths took the 'Bristol Starting Control Prize'. The Team Prize went to 'The Hundreds', a team of Austin Healey 100s.

The Eastern Counties' MC ran the Felixtowe Rally over the weekend of May 29th and 30th. Hugh Denton, Barrie Phipps and Sandy Blair, presumably in their usual Plus Fours, entered as the Morgan 4/4 Club team, and came away with the Team Award, whilst Hugh Denton also won his class.

Saturday May 29th was the date of the popular 'Eight Clubs' meeting at Silverstone. Two forty minute high speed trials began the proceedings, D I C Brunt covering 21 laps for a Third Class Award in his modified early 4/4 in the first, whilst John Moore covered 24 laps in the second in his coupé. In Event 13, a five lap handicap, John Moore was on scratch and only just failed to take third place from Goodearl's HRG. In Event 15, a five lap scratch race, John took an early lead, holding on to it despite spinning at Woodcote on the first lap, but eventually finishing second to Simpson's Austin Healey.

On Sunday May 30th John Spare won the Exmoor Rally by a large margin from a Dellow. Peter Reece took part in the Mid-Cheshire MC's autocross held the same day at Pott Shrigley near Macclesfield. He destroyed the opposition, winning not just his event but also the final. We suspect he was now driving a chrome radiator, red two-seater NAD 409, which had received 'The Reece Treatment', being fitted with a tuned engine and low back axle ratio, giving impressive acceleration. It also had a Morgan factory option of a front bumper. Also on that Sunday Ernie Sneath from Sheffield did well in the Sheffield and Hallamshire MC's sprint at Bircoates, coming second to Yates' Frazer Nash-BMW in the class for 1,501 to 2,600cc with his Plus Four.

The MCC's Edinburgh Trial traditionally took place over Whitsun, but had now been replaced by a rally since several of the roads previously used by the trial in North Yorkshire and the Lake District had been tarmacked since the war. Much of the same route was used, the event starting on the evening of Friday June 4th from the three starting points of London, Edinburgh and Tewkesbury, and running over night to Harrogate. From there began a 270 mile rally which finished back at Harrogate. Several Morgans took part in this, the fourth MCC Whitsun Rally, the best performance being by Jim Goodall who won his class, no doubt driving HUY 982. P W S White and P Norgard gained First Class Awards with their TR2 and Vanguard engined Plus Fours, whilst Basil Roy and Ernest James took Seconds, again TR2 and Vanguard powered. Bernard Clarke retired from the event and Jimmy Ray failed to start.

The twelfth Scottish Rally, an International event, was to start from Glasgow on Monday June 7th, finishing four days later. Jimmy Ray had ordered a new TR2 engined Morgan for rallying this year, and he managed to take delivery the Thursday before the start. Jimmy was keen to save weight for better performances in driving tests, so this Morgan two-seater, chassis number T3118 fitted with TR2 engine TS884, had some aluminium body panels. It was registered NAB 217, and was painted the same colour as his old car, namely white with red leather upholstery. It had the 3.73 rear axle. Ken James, then working at Blakes in Liverpool, bought Jimmy's old Morgan KUY 474.

Three other Morgans were entered for the Scottish Rally: the TR2 engined car of Gerry Hoyle from Southport (presumably KFY 1), Albert Acheson from Belfast in his Vanguard engined car (probably KUY 625), and Bill Whiteley from Pool-in-Wharfedale in PKK 256. The Morgan drivers were also members of mixed teams. Jimmy Ray was in 'The Stargazers' with a Standard and Austin

Healey, Bill Whiteley was in the 'Ilkley and District MC' team with a Hillman and an Austin, and Gerry Hoyle was in the 'Nil Desperandum' team with two Jaguars. Albert Acheson joined two Northern Ireland Citroën-entered colleagues in the 'Ulster Automobile Club' team. The Neil sisters were running, but not in the Morgan, which was being rebuilt at the Morgan factory after its Morecambe Rally damage; they were entered in an MG.

Jimmy Ray was outstanding. He was being navigated by his new wife Kath, and Jimmy excelled in the driving tests, drawing much praise from spectators. The *Autosport* reporter commented, 'Jimmy Ray was a delight to watch in all of the eight driving tests and his crisp handling of his familiar white Morgan wasted no movements in manoeuvrings and was always allied to speed.' Jimmy had the best score of all, winning the class for sports cars, 1,601 to 2,600cc. Second in this class was Gerry Hoyle. This was the last time Kath passengered for her husband Jimmy Ray. She decided rallying was not for her.

The 500 Motor Racing Club of Ireland had good weather for its race meeting at Kirkistown airfield on Saturday June 12th. Competing in his Plus Four was Arthur Clapham, coming home second in Heat 2 of the Open Handicap behind a Ford special. He was out of the prizes in the final. On Sunday June 13th John Moore competed at the Prescott hill climb, presumably with his coupé KNP 5. He was second to an Aston Martin DB2 in Class 2, for sports cars 1,501 to 3,000cc.

There were sixty entrants for the Maidstone and Mid-Kent MC's rally and concours, starting on Friday June 18th from Bearsted, and finishing on Saturday June 19th after two loops including driving tests at Brands Hatch. The rally included tests held on the local constabulary's skid pan in Maidstone, and on the Saturday finished with more tests on the esplanade. Winner of the over 1,500cc open class was P W S White, from Camberley in Surrey, with his green TR2 engined Morgan. This two-seater Plus Four had been dispatched to Basil Roy Ltd on Saturday May 15th, with chassis number T3096 and engine number TS845. Whilst the Vanguard engines used by Morgan had used a consecutively numbered series unique to them (beginning at V1ME), the Triumph engines, although starting at TS1ME, did not run consecutively, and used an engine number series shared with Triumph TR2s.

Bill Whiteley, passengered by Leslie Winder, undertakes a test in the grounds of Castle Grant at Grantown on Spey during the Scottish Rally. (Aberdeen Journals Ltd)

The Midland Automobile Club (MAC) ran a National hill climb at Shelsley Walsh on Sunday June 20th. As well as the top racing cars competing, there were also classes for sports cars and even a 'team challenge' for them. Peter Morgan entered a team comprising himself, presumably in KUY 387, Jim Goodall, presumably in HUY 982, and John Moore, presumably in his coupé KNP 5. Peter was fastest with 44.50 seconds; Jim recorded 45.58 and John 46.93 seconds. Glorious sunshine was the order of the day. The times for the team gave them second place behind three Bugattis.

The Plymouth Motor Club's '1946 Presidential Trophy Rally' was a popular annual rally, this year covering 360 miles of lanes in Cornwall and Devon over the weekend of June 25th and 26th, with seven tests en route. There were three starting points: Bristol, Salisbury and Plymouth. Several of the top Morgan drivers had entered, including John Spare with KUY 476, Les Yarranton with KWP 926 and Jimmy Ray with NAB 217. Jimmy had just retrieved his Morgan from the Morgan factory where an annoying steering wobble had been subdued by supplying two new tyres. The final tests were held on Plymouth Hoe, and Les Yarranton was best of all in these, being given the Final Tests Award. In the Morgan class John Spare was victorious, with Les second. John also participated in the winning team, with two TR2s.

The Royal Scottish Automobile Club staged its sixth International speed hill climb at the Rest-and-be-Thankful on Saturday July 3rd. The weather was awful with relentless heavy rain. The best Morgan performance was that of Andie Neil back in her Morgan, winning the Frew Cup for the best time of the day by a lady, with a time of 83.35 seconds, two seconds better than the second placed TR2.

At Silverstone the same Saturday the MCC ran its Club meeting containing the traditional one hour high speed trials, with passengers as pre-war at Brooklands. In these a given number of laps was the target for a First Class Award in each class. F Elkington achieved his, but P Norgard was only able to claim a Second Class Award. Presumably both were driving their usual Vanguard engined chrome radiator Plus Fours.

On the Sunday July 4th Peter Reece was at the Lancashire Automobile Club's hill climb at

Hugh Denton at the Prescott inter-club meeting. (Hugh Denton collection)

The new rear end of KUY 387 as photographed at Prescott. (Morgan Motor Co collection)

Clerk Hill near Walley. Although this 250 yard hill was not tarmacked, every effort had been made to smooth the surface. Peter was outstanding in NAD 409, the Plus Four with low back axle ratio and tuned engine which took him to an easy class win in the over 1,500cc class for open cars. Indeed he made third fastest time of the day. The top six fastest cars took part in a handicap at the end of the event. Peter Reece had already left for home, but Gerry Hoyle upheld the Morgan name with victory in his Plus Four.

That same day Hugh Denton was autocrossing his Plus Four at the Chiltern CC's meeting at Wakefield Lawn near Towcester. He came second in class behind an MG. At Horley Barrie Clarke made the best performance in the London Motor Club's driving tests with his Plus Four.

The Brighton and Hove MC held its Brighton Rally on Saturday July 10th. It was won by John Spare in his Vanguard engined Plus Four KUY 476, beating five TR2s and the TR2 engined Plus Four of P W S White, although the latter made best time in the bay test.

An inter-club hill climb competition was run at Prescott by the Bugatti Owners' Club on Sunday July 11th. There were twenty-four teams entered. The usual Morgan factory team was representing the Worcestershire MC, comprising Peter Morgan in KUY 387, Jim Goodall in HUY 982 and John Moore in KNP 5. Other Morgans were entered, by Barrie Phipps for the Worcester MC (KUY 714), and by Richard Colton and Hugh Denton for the Northants and District MC (JNV 654 and RYC 777 respectively). The two litre class looked likely to be a battle between the various TR2s, but Peter Morgan and Jim Goodall beat the lot of them. The Bugatti type 51A of Jack Smith eventually took the class. Club handicapping left the Morgans out of the places in the team competition.

Peter Morgan's car KUY 387 appeared at Prescott with a new rear-end treatment. Since the road test of KUY 387 reported in the Friday May 7th edition of *The Autocar* the rear had been modified to take just one spare wheel. This was done by altering the shape of the cutaway in the rear panel from the previous 'hourglass' to what was virtually a square with rounded corners. A strip-steel mount was fastened to the wooden fuel tank support platform to hold the single spare wheel at an angle sloping forwards within this, whilst the original spare wheel supports were

Ross Lomax in the David Brown Challenge Cup Relay Race. (Charles Dunn).

either removed from the trunnion tubular chassis cross member, or this member was replaced.

That same Sunday Jack Reece borrowed a Morgan from his cousin Peter for the Lancs and Cheshire CC's autocross held at Eaton near Tarporley. He made the best time by a series-production car with the Plus Four.

Seven thousand spectators lined the course at Bouley Bay in Jersey on Thursday July 22nd for the annual hill climb organised by the Jersey MC and LCC. L R Olver beat all the TR2s with his 1952 Vanguard engined Plus Four, and was second overall in the sports car class, 1,501 to 2,500cc, behind a Kieft Bristol. The *Autosport* reporter commented, 'One shudders to think of the slaughter if ever Olver invests in a TR2 engine for his car.'

At Silverstone on Saturday July 24th the Aston Martin Owners' Club ran its St John Horsfall Trophy meeting. Several Morgans took part. Roy Clarkson had entered with his special bodied Plus Four VNO 600. Also entered were Richard Colton in KYC 777, Hugh Denton in JNV 654, Barrie Phipps with KUY 714, and the two 4/4s of Ross Lomax (JK 7381) and Ray Meredith (EAX 377). Barrie collected a Second Class Plaque for covering nineteen laps in the half-hour regularity trial. The AMOC had devised a handicap relay race for teams of three cars, competing for the David Brown Challenge Cup. Each car had to complete five laps, and the team cars were identified by carrying coloured panels, one on each side of the bonnet and one on the right hand front wing. The colours required were red for the first car, then white and blue for the two others. The Morgan 4/4 Club had entered two teams. Team 1 consisted of Richard Colton (red), Barrie Phipps (white) and Hugh Denton (blue). Team 2 consisted of Ross Lomax, Ray Meredith and Roy Clarkson. The event was won by a team of Aston Martins, but much fun was had by all.

The same Saturday as the Silverstone meeting the Midland AC held a hill climb and gymkhana at Shelsley Walsh, John Moore taking his class with a time of 48.2 seconds in his coupé.

Roy Clarkson made best time of the day by a saloon at the Maidstone and Mid-Kent MC's sprint meeting, held at Brands Hatch on Sunday July 25th, with his special bodied Plus Four VNO 600. This car was running with a TR2 engine, TS 911ME, which had been supplied by the Morgan factory in March and no doubt had been fitted shortly afterwards to replace the original Vanguard unit.

On Saturday July 31st the very first autocross to be held in Ulster was run by the Newry and District MC at Tullyhappy near Newry. The course was only wide enough for one car so they were sent off every twenty seconds along the half mile grass course. Robert Moore covered the distance in 2 minutes 11 seconds in his Morgan Plus Four to finish second to a Dellow in the class for open cars up to 2,600cc.

The Birmingham newspaper *The Birmingham Post* had recently run a feature on the cheapest available 100 mph car, but without mentioning the Morgan Plus Four. The Morgan Motor Company wrote to the newspaper to correct this and offered a Plus Four for testing, the write-up appearing in the issue of Wednesday August 4th. After apologising for not having previously mentioned the Morgan as being the actual cheapest 100 mph car, the road test suggested that the hood was not normally required, commenting, 'The Morgan should be driven with the hood down to extract the maximum enjoyment. Even in the rain driver and passenger do not get wet with the hood down, the rain blowing over the windscreen - except of course at halts. The hood however is easily and quickly erected by driver alone.' The only dislikes were the non-adjustable backrest and the fact that, 'the fly-off handbrake lever on the model tested was more inclined to fly-off than to brake'.

The motor sport magazine *Autosport* published a road test of the two-seater Morgan Plus Four in the Friday August 6th copy. The tester was none other than motor-racer-cum-journalist John Bolster, and for part of his test he used Silverstone. The car carried registration HUY 982, but the car was actually a left hand drive Plus Four bound for America, the number plate doubtless being 'borrowed' from Jim Goodall's usual car for the test. Quite early on in his report John summed up the current status of the Morgan thus: 'The Morgan has always been a formidable contestant in rallies by virtue of its exceptional acceleration and controllability. Now the adoption of the Triumph TR2 engine has added 100 mph motoring to those assets, and at £585 this is the cheapest car which can encompass "the full ton".' He recorded a 0 to 60 mph time of 10.8 seconds with a standing quarter mile of 17.9 seconds, and a maximum speed of 100 mph, the latter achieved after a long run on the test route, but genuine in both directions. There was much he liked, although he found the steering wheel too close to the dashboard for his taste. He finished, 'Above all the car has been greatly improved without losing its essential character, and I am sure it will make many new friends for this old-established name.' Comparing this report with the earlier one in *The Autocar*, the much better acceleration figures recorded by John must have greatly pleased the Morgan directors.

Lambert Motors, of Leeds Road, Bradford were appointed Area Distributors in August, taking out a large advertisement in the *Yorkshire Observer* of Thursday August 19th. All three current Plus Four models were stocked and the company even offered to obtain pre-war Morgan spares at short notice.

On Sunday August 22nd the Falkirk and District MC ran its Bairns Trophy Rally, Howard Sturrock finishing third equal with his Plus Four and winning the team award with R J Traill in an Austin A40.

The Sheffield and Hallamshire MC ran its Rally of the Dams under a National permit this year over the weekend of August 28th and 29th. There were three starting points, Manchester, Leicester and Sheffield, attracting 69 entries for the 500 mile rally. Best of the production sports cars was Jimmy Ray in NAB 217, with Ernie Sneath winning the award for the best performance by an S & H Club member. Ernie now had a new Plus Four: chassis number T 3133, which had been supplied to Silver Street Motors, Taunton on Wednesday July 14th. It was green and had a 3.73 to 1 rear axle ratio.

The annual 750 MC's National Six Hour Relay Race, known as the 'Six Hours', was held at Silverstone on Saturday August 28th. This was always a popular event with the various motor clubs, and this year there were thirty-nine teams entered. Two were entered by the Morgan 4/4

Club, one team of Plus Fours, and the other comprising, somewhat surprisingly, Austin Healeys! The 'A' car in the Plus Four team was Sandy Blair's NXY 859, the 'B' car was Richard Colton's RYC 777, and the 'C' car was Hugh Denton's JNV 654. Twenty-five credit laps were given to this team. This was to be Sandy Blair's first track race in his Morgan. The Austin Healeys were driven by Geoff White, Gordon Stratton, David Scott, John Pither, J Dolton and Gerry Corbett, this team receiving nineteen credit laps. The race was won by the Singer team, which, with the addition of the thirty-nine credit laps, covered 190 laps in the six hours. The Morgan 4/4 Club's Austin Healey team came second with 185, whilst the Plus Four team was thirteenth with 180.

On August 29th the Morgan hill climbers returned to Shelsley Walsh with four TR2 engined Morgan Plus Fours. Fastest of the Morgan drivers was Peter Morgan driving KUY 387 with 44.60 seconds, whilst Jim Goodall was close behind recording 44.84 seconds driving HUY 982. John Moore climbed in 46.69 seconds, no doubt driving his coupé KNP 5. Also entered was a Mrs Ward who recorded 49.44 seconds.

The London Motor Club's fourth annual London Rally took place over the weekend of September 3rd and 4th. There was the usual massive number of entries, no fewer than 378 this year, including Jimmy Ray, the winner of this rally in both 1952 and 1953, in NAB 217. He was navigated by the brilliant Jeff Dixon. Also in Plus Fours were John de Blaby navigated by A W Brucher, Sandy Blair navigated by I Sinclair, and Dr John Spare. The great British lady rally driver Nancy Mitchell was to fulfil an ambition by driving Peter Reece's Morgan NAD 409 with Peter's wife Doreen as navigator. Les Yarranton was navigated by Tommy Thompson, and Barrie Phipps by his secretary and girl friend Angela Palfrey. Hugh Denton was navigated by his friend Richard Colton. Apart from Jimmy Ray all the above were in Vanguard engined cars. Other TR2 engined Plus Fours were entered by Ken Lee from Leeds navigated by A R Bould, Jim Goodall navigated by Terry Hall, and John Moore navigated by none other than Peter Morgan. There were two Morgan teams, being the factory team of Jim Goodall, Jimmy Ray and John Moore all in TR2 engined Plus Fours, and the 4/4 Club team of Les Yarranton, Barrie Phipps and Hugh Denton with Vanguard engined cars.

Peter Morgan at Shelsley in KUY 387. Note the strained front tyre and the hump on the bonnet side to clear the front carburettor. (LAT photographic)

Nancy Mitchell and Doreen Reece in the London Rally. (Doreen Bennetts collection)

The night navigation section caught out several entrants, including Jimmy Ray and Nancy Mitchell, but Jim Goodall managed the best times in a couple of the driving tests with HUY 982. After the seven hundred miles were completed the only Morgan to finish in the awards was that of Nancy Mitchell and Doreen Reece, winning the Coupe des Dames Challenge Trophy. Nancy had enjoyed this, her only competitive drive in a Morgan, but it was otherwise not a good event for Morgans. Peter Morgan remembered urging John Moore to go ever faster, but still there had been no success.

An autocross using a half mile course, covered twice, was run at Shelsley Walsh on Sunday September 12th. Fastest time of the day was made by Les Yarranton in KWP 926, and he therefore took home the Humphreys Cup. Barrie Phipps came second in the open cars class behind an Allard, but he won the closed-cars class in the Austin A40 Sports he shared with his secretary Angela Palfrey. She finished second.

The Birmingham Post newspaper sponsored an annual rally, which was organised by the Midland Automobile Club (MAC). It began in the evening of Friday September 17th with departure from the Birmingham Civic Centre's car park, heading then through the mountain tracks of Wales to arrive in Llandudno in the early hours of Saturday morning for a two hour rest. The competitors then returned through the mountains to Shelsley Walsh before finishing at the Lido car park Droitwich after 400 miles of driving.

Several Morgans were entered. Peter Morgan, who had won the event in 1953, was accompanied by Jane Morgan. Jim Goodall and Terry Hall were presumably in HUY 982. Les Yarranton was accompanied by Tommy Thompson in KWP 926. These three made up one of the Worcestershire Motor Club's teams. John Moore was in his coupé, Peter Reece was passengered by Barry Davies, and John de Blaby was in his Plus Four navigated by D Oakley, whilst Barrie Phipps was in KUY 714 navigated by Angela Palfrey. Dr John Spare had travelled up from Taunton in KUY 476 with local lawyer Mervyn Meredith navigating for him. Jim Bishop was in his Standard engined 4/4 FWD 376 navigated by Tony Perks. The 1953 ladies winner had been Aileen Jervis in her 4/4 Le Mans Replica JTT 703 and she was back this year in a new car, a Plus Four coupé OWD 750 navigated by Mary Freeman as usual. Aileen's white coupé was chassis number P2750, originally finished in October 1953, but Aileen had actually bought it new in May 1954 through her friend John McDonaugh, who owned The Bridge Garage in Warwick. We believe it was converted to the modern cowl radiator front-end before she bought it.

This year the Daimler Conquest Century of Ken Rawlings was the rather unlikely winner of the rally, but the over 1,300cc sports car class was won by Les Yarranton, whilst second was John Spare, and third was Jim Goodall. Aileen Jervis came second in the ladies' event this year. As the Morgans failed to be listed in the leading team results, we presume Peter Morgan had a bad rally.

There is a story from Peter Morgan relating to Peter Reece which we will fit in here, although the actual date is not now known. Morgan Plus Fours were notorious for breaking the saw-steel steering dampers and many Morgan rally drivers took spares for long rallies. On one event Peter Reece broke one, mentioning this to Peter Morgan. Peter Morgan replied that he had a spare and that he would fit it, which he did. Peter Reece couldn't get over the boss of a motor company doing such a thing, commenting that William Morris (Lord Nuffield) would hardly be seen working on his customers' cars in rally conditions!

The long established Sutton Coldfield and North Birmingham Automobile Club (SUNBAC) held a race meeting at Silverstone on Saturday September 18th, attracting the Plus Fours of Hugh Denton and Richard Colton. They both took part in the first of the thirty minute high speed trials for cars, completing nineteen laps each. Also held that Saturday was an autocross at Pewsey by the 750 Motor Club. A half mile circuit was laid out in a large field, with a number of interesting bends and a good straight. Competitors were set off in pairs. In the class for open cars over 1,800cc P Norgard in his familiar Vanguard engined Plus Four finished second to a Triumph TR2.

The fifth annual Clacton Rally took place over the weekend of September 25th and 26th, organised by the East Anglian MC. Hugh Denton did well in the tests and eventually finished third in the class for sports cars over 1000cc in JNV 654.

That same weekend the sixth annual Lakeland Rally took place in North Wales, organised by the Lancs and Cheshire CC. Amongst the 108 entries were the three top Morgan rally drivers Peter Reece, Jimmy Ray, and the previous year's winner Ken Lee. They all battled with each other for fastest

Ken Lee at Llandudno performing in one of the driving tests in the Lakeland Rally. (The Autocar)

driving test times, with Jimmy Ray finishing second in NAB 217 and Ken Lee third in TUB 400 in the over 1,500cc open cars class. Peter Reece was driving one of the 'interim cowl' Plus Fours in this event, possibly OXL 875. Peter was in charge of second-hand sports car sales for the Liverpool Ford agent 'Blakes' and toured the country seeking suitable vehicles. A regular source of suitable Morgans was Mercury Motors at Sudbury near Wembley in London.

The Scottish Sporting Car Club's three day 'Heather Rally' was also held on the last weekend in September, based at Braemar. Frank Dundas, a great motoring enthusiast from Dumfries, made excellent times in many of the tests in his TR2 engined Plus Four PSM 508, but he threw it all away when he hit the kerb in the parking test at the finish. Andie Neil took the Ladies' Award with her Plus Four KYS 41.

A new regulation for cars used on British roads was introduced on Friday October 1st, namely the compulsory fitting of two rear red reflectors, of size 1.5 inches diameter or the equivalent surface area. This was an attempt to prevent stationary vehicles being hit from behind in poor visibility. The Morgan Motor Company complied by fitting angled Remax reflectors to the rear wings. It was still legal to have just one rear red light, this rule finally being changed to make two compulsory in October 1956. Also included in these new lighting regulations was a requirement for all cars manufactured after July 1954 and fitted with reversing lights operated by a switch, to have a tell tale light indicating to the driver when they were in operation. Many a rally driver forgot to switch off his reversing light after a nocturnal driving test, causing confusion to other road users.

The Northern Centres of the MG Car Club ran the club's Northern Rally on October 1st and 2nd, with three starting points of Leeds, Manchester and Edinburgh. Second overall was Ken Lee, whilst Ernie Sneath won Class 3 in his Plus Four, with Harry Jacoby third in the ex-Jimmy Ray Morgan MLV 58. On the Sunday the Morgan 4/4 Club held a day of driving tests, attracting twenty competitors. The outright winner was Hugh Denton with JNV 654, whilst Ray Meredith won the open class in his ex-Bill Allarton 4/4 EAX 377 with Robin Butterell second. Barrie Phipps won the closed class, but we don't know what he was driving. Also competing in the closed section was Aileen Jervis. Her coupé had been modified via Peter Morgan to have a rear window with zip fastening, as in Peter's own coupé JNP 239, allowing better rearwards visibility for such occasions by unzipping the rear window.

The MG Car Club's Weston Rally was held on Friday October 8th and Saturday 9th attracting ninety starters. Barrie Phipps came home with a First Class Award, after a difficult rally that only 52 finished. Both John Spare and Hugh Denton were forced to retire. Dr John Spare's usual passenger was unavailable so he had persuaded a friend to do the driving whilst he navigated. Unfortunately John was easily car sick whilst trying to map read in a moving car and the end result was the Morgan went straight on at a T-junction, forcing retirement. John suffered a black eye and the Morgan initially didn't seem too bad, but it was soon apparent the chassis was twisted and the Morgan was returned to the Morgan factory for a new one. John decided it was a good opportunity to upgrade the Plus Four to the latest specification with a TR2 engine and cowled radiator.

The South of Scotland CC ran its Ayrshire Rally that weekend on the Saturday and Sunday, Frank Dundas doing very well in his Plus Four PSM 508 making the best performance by a club member and winning the class for open cars over 1,500cc.

Morgans also did well in autocrosses that Sunday with Charlie Robertson taking the class for open cars over 1300cc at the MG Car Club's Scottish Centre event at Biggar, whilst Edgar Cubley took the 1,601 to 2,600cc class for open cars at the Liverpool MC's 'Swan' event at Frodsham. Edgar had bought Peter Reece's Plus Four NAD 409.

John Moore always did well at the Pembrokeshire MC's hill climbs at Lydstep. At the event held on Saturday October 16th he recorded 39 seconds to finish third behind a Dellow and an AC Ace in the class for sports cars up to 2,000cc.

In his runs for up to 3,000cc sports cars he improved on his time by 0.15 seconds to finish second, behind the same AC, but in the unlimited capacity runs he recorded 38.55 seconds to take the class. Also competing was Hugh Denton in his Vanguard engined Plus Four JNV 654. Unfortunately he tried just a bit too hard, rolling the Morgan, luckily without serous injury. His Morgan too was to return to the Morgan factory for attention the following week. The replacement of the rear gearbox end-cover required a separate visit on Thursday October 28th, but Hugh had now decided he would have his car upgraded to the latest TR2 specification with cowled radiator and 3.73 axle, and this was undertaken early in November, engine TS 3820 being fitted.

The North Midland Motor Club ran the Hopkinson Trial on Sunday 17th October. Ernie Sneath in his Plus Four finished second in the class for open cars behind an MG TD.

The Motor Show was held at Earls Court from Wednesday October 20th to Saturday October 30th. BBC television broadcast a preview of the manufacturers' new cars by outside broadcast from Kenwood House in North London, and Morgan was represented by rally driver Jimmy Ray. The Morgan Motor Company was this year introducing one new model, the Plus Four drophead coupé four-seater. HFS Morgan's own car MAB 696, a works prototype, had been updated to the cowled front end and was specially prepared as the press demonstrator. HFS Morgan was always looking for new markets for the Morgan and had developed this car for the family enthusiast with two young children. Jimmy drove this Morgan around the drive of Kenwood House before being interviewed by Raymond Baxter. The new four-seater coupé was priced at £620, with Purchase Tax of £259 9s 2d to be added, and *The Motor* in their review of the new Morgan commented that, 'the occasional four-seater drophead model will make the sporting Morgan a practical car for many family motorists.' The single spare wheel was located within a locker at the rear, the lid of which hinged down to act as a luggage carrier. HFS Morgan also liked this feature, for it was ideal for carrying a crate of pullets from Malvern to his home in Bray as his wife Ruth kept chickens there. The two- and four-seater coupés and the four-seater tourer Plus Fours were advertised as being fitted with the Standard Vanguard engine, whilst the two-seater

Jimmy Ray with HFS Morgan's four-seater drophead coupé is interviewed by BBC reporter Raymond Baxter at Kenwood House. (Jimmy Ray collection)

Jimmy Ray in the Blackpool driving tests. Note the single spare wheel. (Jimmy Ray collection)

tourer had the TR2 engine. The Motor Show stand featured the full range of Morgan models, which had chassis numbers 3176 to 3179. These comprised a green four-seater (3176), an ivory two-seater (3177), a red two-seater coupé (3178) and an ivory four-seater coupé (3179), all powered by Vanguard engines except the TR2 engined two-seater. The latter had a basic price of £595, some £30 less than its competitor, the Triumph TR2. Morgan had a very satisfactory show, with George Goodall reporting considerable improvement in demand for the Morgan car at the following directors' meeting in November.

A driving test 'challenge match' was held between the North and the Midlands at Blackpool on the Middle Walk Promenade on Saturday 30th October. It was followed on the Sunday by another driving test competition open to seven club teams. The two teams on the Saturday each had fifteen drivers, with both Peter Reece and Jimmy Ray competing in their Morgans as members of the Northern team. Despite their efforts the Midlands team was victorious. On the Sunday Peter Reece took the class for the best sports car, and along with Jimmy Ray and the Triumph TR2 of Johnny Wallwork he took the team prize as well, as a member of the 'Red Rose' team.

Jimmy Ray's Morgan NAB 217 now had a different rear end treatment. As he was only interested in rallies, the two spare wheels of the normal Plus Four two-seater, which were fitted really for trials use were not required, a single spare sufficing. Jimmy had an uncle in the sheet metal business who had modified the rear end to Jimmy's instructions. Later a spare wheel cover was also fitted giving a streamlined effect.

That same weekend the University Motor Clubs ran the Inter-Varsity Rally. This attracted seventy starters from all the university motor clubs to the four starting points of Bedford, Kidderminster, Huddersfield and Durham, the routes converging near Buxton on Saturday evening. Best performance in the special tests was made by Harry Harrop in his two-seater Plus Four, and his team, Manchester University, came third behind Cambridge and Oxford.

The Lanarkshire MC and CC also ran a rally that weekend, calling it the 'Tumshies Turnoot' as it was Halloween, tumshies being turnips to those south of the border. Howard Sturrock was outstanding in his Plus Four, taking the Premier

Award, and also the Team Award with D Jack in a Riley. Frank Dundas was also impressive in the driving tests with PSM 508.

On the Sunday the Scottish section of the MG Car Club staged the Moorfoot Rally, with Charlie Robertson taking the award for best open car with his Plus Four.

One week later the Scottish Sporting Car Club held its annual Anniversary Run, commemorating the first event the club organised some twenty-two years earlier. The Neil sisters Andie and Chrissie took the Chairman's Cup for the best all-ladies crew in their Plus Four KYS 41. Morgans were certainly doing well in Scottish events!

The most important British rally in the autumn was the MCC's National Rally, this year sponsored by the petrol additives firm REDeX, and taking place from Wednesday November 10th until Friday November 12th. It was one of the Open events contributing to the BTDA's Gold Star Award. Several Morgans featured amongst the high-class rally field. Competitors could choose to start from Manchester, Glasgow, Norwich, Cardiff, Plymouth, Kenilworth or London. Starting from Manchester were several Plus Four drivers. These were Sandy Blair (NXY 959), Barrie Phipps (KUY 714), J Holmes, Ken Lee, and Harry Jacoby (MLV 58). Three Morgans non-started, being those of Jimmy Ray (NAB 217), W Wilson, and Roy Clarkson (VNO 600), the latter car having received Thompson track rod ends at the Morgan factory in September.

Starting from Glasgow were the two regular Scottish Morgan rally drivers, Frank Dundas (PSM 508), and Andie Neil (KYS 41). There was just one Morgan starting from Norwich, the TR2 engined Plus Four of Ted Cleghorn (RVF 142). Ted had no right arm, the result of an injury from a lorry accident some twenty years previously, but his performances in driving tests, either with his Dellow or his new Morgan, showed having only one hand was no handicap to Ted. His Morgan, a blue two-seater with red interior, chassis number 3184, had been dispatched on Friday October 22nd to Harvey Lane Garage in Norwich. It was fitted with TR2 engine TS2961. It is interesting that just about every new Morgan fitted with a TR2 engine was being used for motor sport at this time.

No Morgan drivers chose the Cardiff start, and there was just one from Plymouth, the Plus Four four-seater of E M 'Monty' Rogers from Southampton. Monty had bought the Morgan specifically for 'motor sport in the vintage

One-armed Ted Cleghorn on the MCC REDeX Rally. (Mrs Delf collection)

On the Wednesday run to Harrogate, Terry Hall, navigating for Jim Goodall, makes an entry in his logbook at the North London control in Neasden. (The Autocar)

tradition', it being chassis number 3153, dispatched on Friday August 27th to the London dealer Basil Roy Ltd. It was registered PLB 111, fitted with Triumph TR2 engine TS3153, was ivory in colour, had red upholstery and a khaki hood.

There were three Morgan starters from Kenilworth, namely the Morgan factory team of Peter Morgan in the coupé JNP 239, Jim Goodall in HUY 982, and Les Yarranton in KWP 926. Their navigators were respectively Patrick Mallam (often John Moore's navigator), Terry Hall and Tommy Thompson. Peter Morgan's coupé had now been upgraded to the cowl front. The final start point of London had two Morgan starters, these being Plus Fours driven by P W S White and C E Neale.

Competitors left the seven starting points on the Wednesday with separate routes of over 360 miles to meet up at Harrogate, where the routes converged into one for the rest of the rally (some 1,200 miles), finally finishing on Friday morning at Hastings with a series of driving tests.

Severe storms were the order for the rally, making driving very unpleasant for the open cars, but one particular fifty mile stretch in Wales caused havoc to the entry. The Glasgow Morgan starters both suffered here, Andie Neil being over the allowed time, forcing her retirement, and Frank Dundas getting a pile of penalty points for lateness. Another collector of mass penalty points was the Norwich starter Ted Cleghorn. Monty Rogers, who started from Plymouth, had earlier experienced the flexible windscreen wiper drive breaking but had managed to buy a replacement and fit it. However, he was also over the allowed time in Wales and had to retire. The Morgan factory team was brilliant however and when the final results were to hand Les Yarranton had fewer points than any other competitor, just 10.27. This did not give him the rally championship, for the MCC awarded this to the competitor having achieved the greatest improvement over the average for each class, and this gave the overall victory to Parson's Jaguar Mark VII. Les was second, Peter Morgan was fifth and also the winner of Class G2, for closed cars over 1,300cc, and up to 2,600cc. Jim Goodall finished sixth overall, and he took Class G1 for open cars over 1,300cc and up to 2,600cc. P W S White was second in this class, and twelfth equal overall. The Morgan team won the team competition. Les took the MCC Members' Award,

Graeme Anton tackling the CUAC driving tests in his Dellow bodied Plus Four. (Raymond Pike)

and also the Kenilworth Starters' Award, whilst P W S White took the London starters' equivalent. It had been a very successful rally for Morgans, and the Company lost no time in advertising its successes. REDeX too were pleased as the first three place winners used their products.

The best rally team of small saloons had been three Ford Anglias, one of which was driven by Peter Anton, and he had even managed to beat the brilliant Morgan times in the final driving tests. Peter was from Bridgnorth, not too far from Malvern, and was also a member of the Morgan 4/4 Club. He had got to know Peter Morgan during Club events and following the final tests in the REDeX Rally Peter Morgan approached him commenting that he was obviously very keen and could he could have a word in private. He told him that a new prototype Morgan was weeks away from completion at the Morgan factory, fitted with the same Ford engine and gearbox as Peter's saloon, and wondered if he would like to borrow it and assess it for him. Peter Anton was happy to do this and awaited a call that the car was now available.

The Cambridge University AC ran driving tests at a nearby aerodrome on November 14th, attracting a good entry. Graeme Anton, a cousin of Peter Anton, driving his special Dellow-bodied Plus Four LAB 276 finished third.

Dr John Spare visited the Morgan factory during the week of the MCC Rally to discuss the rebuild of his Plus Four. The following week he received a letter from Harry Jones advising that the Morgan factory had now received authorisation from his insurance company to proceed. A TR2 engine and current front end styling were to be included in the rebuild, and the rear axle was changed for the 3.73 ratio type, together with a speedometer to suit. Total cost was to be £166, which included a £10 excess on the insurance.

On the evening of Saturday November 27th just over twenty competitors braved gales, sleet and rain for the North Midland MC's Moonlight Rally. Despite getting lost on the Derbyshire Moors Ernie Sneath, navigated as usual by his son Rodney, finished second in the green Plus Four. That same evening severe flooding did not deter just over forty competitors from starting the Herefordshire MC's Hereford Rally. Les

Yarranton finished third in the class for open cars and, together with a Riley and a Jaguar, he won the team prize. The Morgan 4/4 Club ran its fourth annual Night Rally over the same Saturday night, organised by Dick Pritchard. Just twelve started on a night of torrential rain, with floods and open man-holes to contend with, the covers having washed away. Peter Morgan was one of the unfortunate marshals in these dreadful conditions. The winner was Peter Anton in his Ford Anglia, with Richard Colton winning the Morgan Cup for best 4/4 Club member in his Plus Four. Jim Bishop won the open class in his 4/4.

One week later, on Sunday December 5th in perfect weather, Ted Cleghorn was best of the forty competitors in the Signpost Rally, organised by The Sporting Car Club of Norfolk. Each competitor had to pinpoint the seven controls using photographs of signposts handed out by each control. Ted also won the up to 2,000cc open class with his Plus Four RVF 142.

Monty Rogers had discovered two 'factory faults' with his new Morgan. The first was vagueness in steering. This was eventually discovered to be due to the tab washer holding the steering drop arm securing nut onto the Cam Gears steering box having not been properly fitted, allowing the arm to become loose on the splines. This was soon sorted. The second fault occurred whilst changing gear on one occasion. The gear lever knob and part of the lever came away in his left hand! This was replaced on a visit to the Morgan factory on Tuesday December 7th, when the front suspension was also overhauled.

The new Morgan agent for Somerset and Gloucestershire was Horace Gould, the famous British motor racing driver, known as the 'British González' on account of his exuberant style of driving and his similar build (González was affectionately nicknamed 'The Pampas Bull'). George Goodall took HFS Morgan's four-seater coupé MAB 696 down to the new agency in mid-December as part of a promotion, and various tradesmen and newspaper journalists were invited to Horace's garage in Newfoundland Street, Bristol. Introduced to the press as Horace's first Morgan customer was Ian 'Tiny' Lewis, (so named because he was somewhat large), who demonstrated his Morgan driving skills to them and said he would compete with his own four-seater coupé in many events in 1955. Tiny ran a small garage in Bristol, and was a notable competition driver. George Goodall commented that the time from order to delivery of the new four-seater coupé would be six weeks, until production was stepped up, but that all other models were for immediate delivery.

On the evening of Saturday December 18th, following the final competition for the trial competitors competing for the British Trial Drivers Association trophies, the organisation held its annual dinner and awards presentations in Maidstone, Kent. In the rally section Jimmy Ray had won the Gold Star competition, for best performance of 62 entrants in the major Open rallies with 103 points from five scoring rallies, way ahead of second placed Johnny Wallwork, but with Les Yarranton in third place. In the Silver Star competition John Spare too had a runaway victory with 131 points from six scoring rallies, despite 28 other entrants. To cap the Morgan successes Jimmy Ray's passenger Jeff Dixon received the *Autosport* Rally Navigator's Trophy.

The rebuild of Dr Spare's Plus Four was complete by the middle of December. It was virtually a new car, with little of KUY 476 remaining. He decided to re-register it, getting the registration TYA 1, and the Morgan factory also gave it a new chassis number, 3206. It was painted a light blue.

At the Morgan directors' meeting held on Wednesday December 22nd George Goodall reported that the London agent, Basil Roy, had returned to the factory four old style chrome radiator Plus Four models that had remained unsold. The Morgan factory later managed to

Dr John Spare with his 'new' Morgan TYA 1 and the BTDA Silver Star. (John Spare collection)

sell these by offering a discount of £18. Peter Morgan also reported that construction of the Ford engined Morgan prototype would begin early in the New Year.

Tiny Lewis took a Morgan to the annual Cecil Kimber Trial, run by the South West Centre of the MGCC on Monday December 27th. It was not the promised four-seater coupé, but an early Vanguard engined Plus Four with chrome radiator, to be registered THY 60 early in 1955. This was chassis number P2738, coloured blue with red upholstery and had actually been built in 1953, but had been sold to Tiny by Horace Gould on Thursday December 9th. It had originally been supplied to Basil Roy Ltd, and was probably one of those returned to the factory and sold at a discount. He was accompanied in the trial by Dave Warren and H J C Lidden with their Morgans, and Tiny and Dave Warren took home First Class Awards, whilst Mr Lidden took home a Second. No doubt the organisers were pleased that an MG, the MG TF driven by Geoff Dear, was first overall as the Morgan of John Spare had won the event the previous year.

Dave Warren had recently purchased a white Vanguard engined Plus Four two-seater, MYP 802, as he had been impressed by the performances of Doc Spare and Les Griffiths in their examples, and decided it was the obvious way to go. He wasn't disappointed!

1954 had been a good year for Morgans. Despite the threat of the newly introduced Triumph TR2, the Morgan did well in British rallies, the BTDA 'Stars' showing the other makes that the Morgan was still the major player. The Morgan factory was still making the cheapest car available to the British public capable of achieving 100 mph. However the problems in getting the TR2 engines from the Standard Motor Company had no doubt contributed to poor production figures of no more than five cars per week being manufactured. This had lead to a loss of £3,140 being recorded at the factory for the trading year. Development of the new Ford engined model was well underway, and it was hoped that the introduction of this model would allow production to be increased during 1955.

France

Since the introduction of the four-wheeler Morgan in 1936 the Paris Agent, Stuart Sandford, had been the sole agent for the Morgan car in France. He was very popular with HFS Morgan and the Morgan directors. He was now in his mid 60s, and still dealing in Morgan cars and British motorbikes. His business had been destroyed during the war and he had become a prisoner of the occupying Germans, but since then he had doggedly rebuilt his business back into profit.

Whilst we have no information on French competitors with Morgans at this time, cross channel events were popular with some British competitors. Several made the trip to the famous track at Montlhéry for the 'Coupes de Paris' series of races held on Sunday April 25th. They had banded together as 'Ecurie Bull Frog', one member being Roy Clarkson who had doubtless been involved with the organisation of the trip, with the special bodied Plus Four VNO 600. Unfortunately the high speed possible on the banked track did no good to his new TR2 engine, which broke two pistons, and he failed to finish his race.

One of the great European rallies of the early 1950s was the annual Alpine Rally, organised by L'Automobile Club de Marseilles et Provence. Held in July it was basically a race over the various Alpine passes, starting in Marseilles and finishing in Cannes. Bridlington dentist Derek Howard and his girl friend Kath (entered as Miss Jumbo) had taken part in the previous two Alpines in Derek's black Plus Four, but for the 1954 event Peter Morgan had agreed to lend him a new TR2 engined Plus Four. This was chassis number T3125, fitted with engine number TS 1549, a white two-seater with black upholstery, and having a Cam Gears steering box. Engine cooling could be a common problem in July in the South of France, so the two additional driving lights were spaced well clear of the radiator. The Plus Four was registered NAB 463 on Monday June 14th.

The Alpine Rally started on Thursday afternoon July 8th with a run overnight and through the following day to St Moritz in Switzerland. Unfortunately unseasonable cold and wet weather caused havoc with the route, some roads being snowbound (in July!) and others flooded. Of the eighty starters only thirty-two arrived at St Moritz without penalty. Only sixty-two were still in the rally to start the following day, Saturday. Again the bad weather played havoc, for the famous Stelvio pass was closed due to snow, forcing a diversion to get to the Autobahn test at Munich, which was held in torrential rain. The poor Morgan could only achieve 84.5 mph on the flying kilometre, whereas the Triumph TR2 of Ken Richardson did a more respectable 95.9 mph. The event continued with more detours until eventually the overnight stop at Cortina in Italy was reached.

The Sunday saw the competitors racing around the 188 mile long circuit of the Dolomites, along closed roads. At the end of the day there were just twenty competitors un-penalised with clean sheets. The Monday morning heralded the final and most gruelling stage of all, 884 miles long, finishing at Cannes on the Tuesday afternoon. The rain gradually eased and the passes were now open to traffic, but snow on the roads was still a hazard. Cannes was finally reached in brilliant sunshine for a final driving test on the tree lined Allée de la Liberté by the harbour.

Derek Howard and Kath had experienced major problems. The engine seemed gutless compared with the Vanguard in Derek's own Plus Four. Then two of the engine mountings had broken, forcing Derek and Kath to remove some of the car's floorboards to wedge the engine in place. As a result they finished with a massive 1,137 penalty points, but still seventh in the 1,600 to 2,000cc class. There was one triumph however. Derek had nothing to lose in

Morgan *Sports Cars* 1954

Derek and Kath prepare to start on the first day of the Alpine Rally at Marseilles. (Photo-Junior)

the final Cannes driving test, so he really went for it, beating everyone with a time of 28.8 seconds and winning the Coupe de Cannes. Some of the spectators were not too sure that it was correct practice to change down into bottom gear at maximum revs as an aid to stopping quickly, but it worked for Derek!

Just eleven Coupes des Alpes were awarded for un-penalised runs. The greatest achievement was that of Stirling Moss in a Sunbeam Talbot, who was one of those finishing with a clean sheet and claiming a Coupe des Alpes. However this was also his third Coupe in a row, so he now won the prestigious Coupe des Alpes en Or, the Gold Cup awarded for three consecutive un-penalised runs in Alpine Rallies, an amazing achievement for a great driver.

Another Morgan driver competing was Jimmy Ray. After winning the Scottish Rally in June he had been approached by Standard Triumph to passenger Lyndon Mills in one of the Triumph TR2s taking part. They were forced to retire when a rear hub bearing failed on the final section, but the TR2 team did take the Team Award.

When Derek returned the car to the Morgan factory he reported to Peter Morgan how disappointed he was with the poor engine performance. Peter apologised that it had been so bad. The battered Morgan was repaired and finally left the Morgan factory on Tuesday October 19th bound for the long established Edinburgh agents Rossleigh Ltd and a new owner.

46

1954   The Heritage Years

Derek and Kath complete the driving test at Cannes in the fastest time. (The Autocar)

Roy Clarkson was back at Montlhéry for the Coupe du Salon races held on Sunday October 10th with his special Plus Four. In the event for Touring cars up to 2,000cc, over seventeen laps, he came in first at 76.4 mph, beating Chavy's Peugeot and the Porsche of Mme. Perray.

Roy Clarkson at Montlhéry for the Coupe du Salon. (Vachon)

Luxembourg 1953

The story of the Luxembourg Morgan came to light after our first book was printed. We felt it should be included in this volume despite being one year out of sequence.

Paul Conrardy from Luxembourg was the son of a coachbuilder, whose trade was making bodies mainly for commercial vehicles and buses. Paul had fun after the Second World War with two MG TCs, but fancied a modern style body on an MG chassis. After the 1949 Paris Salon Paul contacted the great French stylist Philippe Charbonneaux, and arranged for him to produce plans for a two-seater closed coupé body for the MG chassis. Paul unfortunately found difficulty in obtaining the MG chassis, so when he realised that in the Morgan Plus Four chassis the centre of gravity was actually lower than in the MG, he decided to switch his plans to a Morgan chassis. There was no Luxembourg Morgan agency so the chassis P2506, with Vanguard engine V452ME, was obtained via the Belgium agent Lucien Riga of Brussels, being dispatched from the Morgan factory on Friday November 21st 1952.

Construction of the body began immediately, Paul working in the evenings and into the night at the family coach building premises at 9-13 Rue Henri VII. A light tubular steel framework was used to support an aluminium alloy skin, (Aluman, supplied by Allusuise, and rare at this time). The new enclosed radiator was made locally in Luxembourg. The front windscreen was specially made by the same company in Belgium that made safety glass for the buses that were bodied by the firm. The large rear window was made from Perspex, shaped in a water bath at 80 degrees

The Conrardy Morgan Grand Sport under construction. (Paul Conrardy collection)

On the streets of Luxembourg. (Dries Jetten)

Centigrade. Two-tone cellulose paint, in ivory and navy blue, made the finished car look very attractive and beige leather was used to trim the interior. The whole car weighed about 850kg. Paul called it the 'Morgan Grand Sport' and described himself as 'Agent et Constructeur'.

Unfortunately the hard work involved in building the Morgan took its toll on Paul for he became very ill with pleurisy, and he was forced to rest and abandon the Morgan and other projects. The Morgan was disposed of, and it went to Leige probably in late 1953.

Scandinavia

In Norway at this time there were no permanent motor racing circuits. In the summer it was sometimes possible to race on horse racing tracks, but in the winter the easiest way to get a track was to plough away the snow from a frozen lake to produce a course. Most courses had a straight and several curves, and a lap distance of one to two miles. Banks of snow formed the outer limits of the track, and protected the spectators against sliding and spinning cars.

Standard car classes allowed the use of snow chains on normal road tyres, but the faster sports cars used rubbed down tyres, run at high pressure and fitted with steel spikes through the casing. The spike lengths were regulated for the different classes.

The Morgan agency was held by Andres Berge and Co in Oslo. Erik Hellum, who ran the family business A S Frankering in Oslo, had asked this company to import a Morgan for him. Erik had previously been quite successful ice-racing an Austin, but realised that the Morgan could be much more suitable, being a particularly well balanced sports car. Erik was also keen to obtain this Morgan agency for himself, but does not appear to have ever done so. The Morgan he received was a red two-seater, with beige upholstery, and left hand drive. It had chassis number P2736 with Vanguard engine number V629ME, and had been dispatched from the Morgan factory on Wednesday November 25th 1953. One of his first events was a Sunday meeting at Årungen in Akershus. The event was organised by the Follo branch of the Norsk Motor Klubb (usually known as the NMK and translated as the 'Norwegian Motor Club'). A newspaper report of Erik's driving translates as,

Morgan *Sports Cars*   1954

Erik Hellum in his Morgan at Østensjø. Spiked tyres are fitted, and the front wheels are apparently non-standard. (Harald Hellum collection)

BASSE HVEEM: „*Har aldri kjørt på bedre olje!*"

**VIKINGOLJEN VANT
I VINTERENS ISRACE**

VIKING OLJERAFFINERI A/S — OSLO — RØYKEN

ERIK HELLUM: „*Vikingoljen er fantastisk!*"

Viking Oil of Oslo used the local Østensjo race results to advertise the company's oil in the local newspaper, the caption translating as the oil having 'won in the winter ice race', whilst Ford V8 driver Basse Hveem 'has never driven on better oil', and Erik Hellum said, 'Viking oil is fantastic.' (Harald Hellum collection)

50

'His red Morgan goes at full steam through the corners, just as surely as if it was on rails.' Each class ran twice, with the times added together. Erik achieved the fastest time of the day.

The NMK's Oslo branch ran ice races upon the frozen lake at Østensjø, a southeastern borough of Oslo, probably on Sunday February 21st. The snowploughed course was 1.7 kilometres per lap and most races were of five laps duration. Despite a temperature of minus 15 degrees C there were 5,000 spectators there to see Erik Hellum win his class in the Plus Four, and give him a great ovation. The two fastest finishers in each class then took part in a final race, and once again Erik gave the crowd a demonstration of how to race by easily finishing first.

When the new TR2 engined Morgan Plus Four became available Erik realised the more powerful engine could be even better for racing, so he ordered a new Plus Four via Andres Berge. It was also red, but with black upholstery and according to the Morgan factory records was chassis number T3101, fitted with TR2 engine TS657, and dispatched on Friday May 28th to Norway. Norwegian sales records however suggest it was chassis number T3103, fitted with the same numbered engine, so a clerical error is apparent somewhere!

Erik tried the new Morgan, but preferred the characteristics of the older one, so the TR2 engine was transferred to P2736, and the papers for T3103 were transferred to the older car too, thoroughly confusing which car was which! The newer Morgan was later sold on, fitted with the Vanguard engine.

The Fluberg branch of the NMK ran the first post-war hill climb held in Norway on Sunday August 22nd. The Fluberg course of 1.5 kilometres was very demanding, with difficult corners as well as being steep. The weather was good and an excellent crowd of 1,500 came to watch the action. Once again Erik was in a class of his own, easily setting fastest time of the day with a climb in 1 minute 41.2 seconds, his nearest competitor being Kåre Madsen's Triumph, nearly 4 seconds slower.

Macau

In June 1953 Gordon 'Dinger' Bell had collected his Vanguard engined four-seater Plus Four, chassis number P2677, from the Morgan factory. It was registered NOM 260, but had been ordered through Far East Motors in Hong Kong because Gordon was taking the Morgan there when he returned from leave in England later in the year. He was the scientific officer at the Royal Observatory in Kowloon, and was also the commanding officer of Hong Kong's Royal Auxiliary Air Force. In November Dinger had returned the Morgan to the factory for new front shock absorbers, damper blades, rebound springs and rear springs. Presumably he returned to Hong Kong shortly afterwards, where he was a popular member of the Hong Kong Motor Sports Club.

The tiny Portuguese colony of Macau on the Chinese coast was not known for motor sport, but a group of three residents thought it might be fun to run a treasure hunt around the city streets. Having no experience of such an event they approached the Hong Kong Motor Sports Club, whose member Paul Dutoit rapidly developed the idea into a proper street race using a 3.9 mile circuit, called the Guia circuit after a bordering hill of that name. Part of the circuit was paved, but the back stretch was just dirt.

The event was scheduled for the weekend of October 30th and 31st, the first day being for a 'Speed Regularity Trial for Production Cars' over five laps, whilst the 'Grand Prix' was to be over four hours' duration with a Le Mans start.

A motley selection of vehicles made up the fifteen starters for the Grand Prix, there being three TR2s, an Austin Healey, three Fiat 1100s, a Hillman, a Citroen, a Mercedes Benz 220, a Riley 2.5, an MG special, two Fords and Dinger's Morgan. To make his Morgan more competitive Dinger had up-rated the engine to TR2 specification, fitting a new aluminium bonnet to

Dinger Bell gives the 'thumbs up' sign to the pit crew before the disastrous fifth lap. (Dick Warrall collection)

accommodate it. A home made racing screen was also fitted.

Some 20,000 spectators came to watch the Grand Prix on an overcast Sunday, and as the Governor dropped the Portuguese flag the drivers sprinted across the track for the Le Mans start just after 12 noon. The Morgan was in second place in the line up to the Austin Healey, but Dinger was first away, despite the floor mat slipping to cover the foot pedals as he leapt in.

After the first lap Dinger was half a mile ahead of a TR2, and by the fourth lap he was a quarter of a lap ahead of the field, lapping one of the Fiats, and setting the fastest lap of the race at 4 minutes 12 seconds. Unfortunately just after he gave the 'thumbs up' signal to his pits the nearside front hub broke in two at the notorious Reservoir Bend, the liberated wheel flying through the air and into the sea, whilst the Morgan came to a precarious halt on the inclined sea wall a few feet from the edge. The three TR2s now had things all their own way to finish in the first three places. The Morgan suffered considerable damage, but Dinger rebuilt it, keeping it for several years.

Australia

1954 was the first full year that a new body, the Confederation of Australian Motor Sport (CAMS), took over the responsibility of overseeing competition Australia-wide. In 1952 the Australian Automobile Association (AAA) had decided to relinquish national control of the sport and, even though CAMS had actually opened its doors in Melbourne for business in February 1953, the first meeting of the national body was not until November that year. The CAMS Deed of Agreement was drafted and executed by the RAC of Great Britain in July 1954.

There were two Morgan agencies in Australia in 1954. The oldest was that of Bry-Law Motors Pty Ltd, importing Morgans from 1936 onwards. The company was originally based in Melbourne, Victoria, but now also had a branch in Sydney, New South Wales. Although this agency had supported motor sport with Morgans pre-war, particularly the company's own racer driven by Jim Boughton, they had also become agents for Lea Francis and Jaguar, and were now concentrating on the latter commercially more successful dealership. The other was the Perth, Western Australia, agency of Bill Richards, who had been importing Morgans since 1949, running Bill Richards' Motors Pty Ltd in Fitzgerald Street in North Perth. He had been involved earlier with Mortlock Bros Ltd, the Triumph agents.

The roads in Australia, whilst generally acceptable for using Morgans in the urban conurbations, could be little more than dirt tracks away from such areas. Morgans were not really suited to such conditions, and previous agencies in Adelaide were not successful partly for this reason. Bill Richards' customers did not appreciate the absence of an air cleaner on the Plus Four, so he fitted Citroën air filters to the single Solex carburettor of the Vanguard engine. With the introduction of the TR2 engine Bill had the Morgan factory supply cars to him already fitted with an air filter, which was attached to the twin SU carburettor intakes by a specially fabricated assembly. Bill Richards had always supported motor sport, competing himself on several occasions, but mainly assisting his local Morgan enthusiasts. One in particular was achieving superb results with his tuned Plus Fours, namely David Van Dal.

David had studied at the University of Western Australia, majoring in mechanical and high voltage engineering, after which he worked as an engineer for the Stanford X-Ray & Radium Co Pty Ltd in Melbourne. Here he met John Cummins (known as 'Cummo'), who had been an apprentice at the Rolloy Piston Co Pty Ltd under Bob Chamberlain. They became the 'Dreadful Duo', playing 'motor cars, booze, music, and girls, but not necessarily in that order'. Included amongst their friends was Phil Irving, the ex-Vincent and HRD motorcycle designer and author of the tuners' bible 'Tuning for Speed'. Charlie Dean, noted for preparing the Maybach racer and becoming Chief Development Engineer at Repco engineering, was also in the group along with Bob Chamberlain, so they all had many informative and exciting evenings and weekends together.

David realised that the development of racing motorcycle engines seemed far ahead of those in the motor car. He was particularly impressed by the BSA DBD34 Gold Star 500cc single, which he regarded as the best performing pushrod engine ever made, and held its designer, Peter Pugh, in great admiration. He decided therefore to redesign the Vanguard engine along the lines of four joined BSA scrambler pushrod engines. A similar concept was to be followed by the Vanwall Grand Prix team, but based on overhead camshaft Norton engines. Early Vanguard engine development had been undertaken by David in his Plus Fours of 1952 and 1953, but he really wanted to build a Formula 2 (under two litres) racer, based on the Morgan, from scratch.

In 1952 David had visited the Morgan factory on behalf of Bill Richards to discuss his ideas for the racing Morgan. David remembers he also suggested improvements to the current production model, by triangulating the chassis to reduce the propensity to oversteer, and introducing minor rear spring leaves of progressively greater radii together with telescopic rear shock absorbers to give progressive rate springing and greater tyre adhesion. He finally suggested using new German self-lubricating nylon instead of the bronze bushes in the front sliders. David also visited the Standard Motor Company in Coventry where he shared his ideas on tuning the Vanguard engine with their Technical Engineer, Lew Dawtrey, and possibly the TR2 Development Engineer, Ken Richardson.

In August 1953 while working at Newton Victor in Taunton, Devon, in England, he again visited the Morgan factory and outlined plans that he and Bill Richards had for the racer. David didn't want to use the traditional Morgan suspension, and had designed one based on an improved version of the front end of the Fiat Topolino, similar to the Cooper, but further improved. He also planned using a frame-mounted differential, using the modified Ford Model 'A' system, as used in the 'Speedcar' speedway racer. He recalls talking to the board (including Peter Morgan and George Goodall) but they were not at all interested in the project unless the standard Morgan front suspension and full drive-train currently used in the Plus Four were incorporated, along with a radiator and cowl which was obviously 'Morgan'. These conditions were reluctantly accepted and David believes that the factory contributed significantly

The Bill Richards demonstrator. Note the signwriting on the car! (David Van Dal collection)

(£834) to the cost of building and developing the car. Sadly we have been unable so far to find any surviving record of this having happened or of the extent to which there was cooperation between Bill Richards' dealership in Perth and Pickersleigh Road.

Whilst David began the design of the racer he made an arrangement 'over a Chinese prayer mat' to take over the blue Plus Four demonstrator used by the Bill Richards dealership, to use for sports car racing. This was in spite of his opinion that this type of production car racing was much more dangerous than racing full blown racing cars, due to the inexperience of some of the drivers. This chrome radiator Vanguard engined Plus Four had already been mildly tuned by David, with twin 1.5 inch SU carburettors on a fabricated manifold, and a copper-plated head, to reduce pre-detonation.

In Perth the Standard Triumph distributor for Western Australia was Mortlock Bros Ltd, located in Hay Street. The same company was also the BSA agent, with premises further along the same street, so David got to know the Managing Director, Bernie Mortlock, quite well. Most of the Vanguard engine parts David wanted were recovered from the 'Guarantee Claims Bin', at 'no charge'. At this time (1953 and 1954) David was very busy commissioning X-Ray units, travelling extensively both in Australia and overseas and also setting up electro-medical manufacturing facilities in Western Australia.

On Monday March 1st the annual Car Racing Carnival was held at Narrogin, Western Australia using the same 'round the houses' course that had been used for the Australian Grand Prix in 1951. The previous afternoon some speed trials were held on Boundain airstrip and Ted Barker, a motor mechanic, was third in the standing quarter mile, recording 19.75 seconds in his Vanguard engined Plus

Four, some way behind the winner, Syd Anderson with his amazing twin V8 engined special with 16 seconds. Ted 'Limpy' Barker had previously modified the Vanguard engine in his chrome radiator Morgan, under the influence of David Van Dal, fitting twin Solex carburettors and a Lucas Vertex magneto as well as copying the short stub exhausts that David Van Dal had fitted to his more highly modified engine in 1953. However the stub exhausts reduced its performance and so he reverted to a much less noisy manifold arrangement during 1954. He was also reported to have made a lightweight fibreglass body for the Morgan but there is no record of it having been used in racing.

On the Monday two Plus Fours were entered, those of Ted Barker and Arthur Littlejohns. We believe that Arthur Littlejohns was an Englishman who worked in the country town of Toodjay as a bulldozer driver. He entered his chrome radiator Plus Four in many events during 1953-54 but was never competitive with David Van Dal or Ted Barker who had Morgans that were more modified.

A crowd estimated at five thousand was present for the Narrogin races. Ted Barker and Arthur Littlejohns between them entered all the races on the card but did not meet with much success. In the feature event, The Great Southern 50 (actually 51 miles), Ted Barker initially went very well, running third for eight of the twenty-four laps, but then ran off the track on lap eleven and was unable to finish. The fast MG driver Noel Aldous had more excitement than he bargained for when he hit and killed a stray dog, the resultant skid sending him sideways towards a crowded footpath. Luckily the kerb stopped his progress. The race was won by the 'flying dentist', Sid Taylor, in his Dodge engined TS Special.

Competing in the State of Victoria during 1952 and 1953 with some success in his second-hand Plus Four was Richard Reynolds. After strengthening the chassis for the poor roads of the period Richard had then improved the performance by shaving the head to raise the compression, and by fitting twin Stromberg carburettors, as fitted to the Australian Holden car. He entered the races held at Fisherman's Bend, a two mile 'T' shaped track, constructed from redundant runways built adjacent to a Government Aircraft Factory during the Second World War. It was in an industrial area of Melbourne, just two and a half miles from the city centre. The races were

Richard Reynolds at Fisherman's Bend gets a good start. (Richard Reynolds collection)

Morgan Sports Cars — 1954

The Uffindel treatment to the engine of Gavin Sandford-Morgan's Plus Four. (Gavin Sandford-Morgan collection)

held on Tuesday March 23rd. There was a Le Mans start and Richard got away well. Sadly, at half distance the carburettor linkage (from a Riley) broke and he had to retire. He located someone in the pits to weld the linkage together, and was able to drive the Morgan home. This was his last event with his Morgan.

South Australia was also seeing some Morgan racing. During 1953 that great motoring enthusiast with the very appropriate name, Gavin Sandford-Morgan, had been developing his Plus Four for racing. The car had been getting more competitive, and the Vanguard engine was now fitted with properly located valves, after correspondence with the Standard Motor Company in Coventry. The car also had twin carburettors and Riley rack and pinion steering. Gavin had now consulted the local and legendary tuning wizard Ron Uffindell, to improve top end performance. Ron developed a much improved inlet manifold arrangement, with stabilising struts for the carburettor float bowls, and he fabricated an extractor type exhaust system. As is the way of racing, these modifications were only just completed at midnight before the Easter Speed Meeting at Port Wakefield on Saturday April 17th. The final operation necessitated waking up a friend who possessed a gas stove in order to solder a leaking petrol union! There were eighteen entries for the thirty lap Morton Motors scratch race for sports cars, including several Austin Healeys, an Allard and a Jaguar XK 120. The Morgan went very well, despite problems with new brake linings, of 'Don' manufacture, which were excellent until hot, when they became unpredictable and finally disintegrated. For twenty-six laps Gavin battled for the lead with the Austin Healey of his friend Greg McEwin (an ex-Morgan racer), until another Austin Healey baulked Greg allowing Gavin to the front, where he remained to the finish for a most satisfying, if somewhat brakeless, victory.

Competing at the same meeting with a Vanguard engined Triumph Roadster was Tony Innocenzi. He noted the speedy Morgan with interest.

On Easter Monday the Australian Hill Climb Championships were held at Collingrove, Angaston, in South Australia. Gavin was there with his Plus Four, and so was M J Thomson with his own rapid Plus Four. Gavin had never managed to beat him during 1953, but this time his 44.6 seconds was 0.9 seconds quicker. Greg McEwin got his revenge, with a time of 43.8 seconds, to beat Gavin into second place, with M J Thomson third. This was the last time Gavin

Gavin Sandford-Morgan wins at Port Wakefield. (Gavin Sandford-Morgan collection)

raced his Morgan, for he decided to sell it to raise some finance towards a new house and workshop. The new owner was to be the aforementioned Tony Innocenzi.

The next of the 'round the houses' races was the 'Flying 50' event organised by the West Australian Sporting Car Club (WASCC) on the streets of Northam on Easter Monday, April 19th. The only Morgan representative was Ted Barker and he enjoyed no success. He was sixth after four laps and fifth after eight but then had to withdraw with mechanical problems. He returned later and gamely reeled off lap after lap in an impossible chase, and indeed had to be called off the course for safety reasons after the race had been won by Syd Negus in his reliable Plymouth special for the second year in succession.

A hill climb was held by the Victoria Sports Car Club at Foley's Hill on Sunday May 16th, at which the Morgan 4/4 of H Colley finished sixth in 25.69 seconds with J Hearne's similar (possibly the same) Morgan just 0.26 seconds behind.

On Monday June 7th the Goomalling Speed Classic, another 'round the houses' event, was organised by the WASCC and the Ariel Motor Cycle Club of Western Australia. Arthur Littlejohns entered two of the five lap events in his Plus Four and although he finished the unrestricted handicap he was not in the places. He only completed four of the five laps in the handicap event for sports cars and did not start in the longer Speed Classic over fifteen laps.

Also in June the Northam Car Club ran its initial event at the club's new hill climb, situated seven miles from Northam on Mr Justin Walsh's grazing property, 'Egoline'. A report of the day indicates that there was considerable interest in the event and even the Western Australia State Premier, The Hon Mr A G Hawke (uncle of Bob Hawke, Labour Prime Minister during the 1980s), who was patron of the NCC, came to open the hill. After being driven over the hill by the club's president he then drove his own car over the climb before leaving for other engagements.

As well as the local members of the Northam CC many drivers from Perth came to try out for the first time what became known as the Justin Walsh hill climb. They included Keith Lindsay who entered in his Plus Four, achieving fastest time of the day (50.8 seconds) despite or possibly because of a wet road during his runs. Keith's Vanguard engined chrome radiator Plus Four was prepared by his friend, well known Perth motor racing identity, Don Hall. Don's garage in Subiaco and later his 'speed shop' in the same area was well known to those wanting to get their production sports cars going that bit faster. As Don was sponsored for racing by the petrol company 'BP', he developed a close relationship with their staff in Perth, maintaining their executive vehicles at his garage. He was always immaculately turned out in white overalls at his equally immaculate garage, such that David Van Dal referred to him as, 'Dirty Don and his Aegean Stable-like Service Station!'

On the outskirts of Sydney, racing was held on the two year old circuit in the Park at Parramatta on Monday June 14th. D Wright scored a second place in an open handicap event for sports cars.

In September 1954 the WASCC ran a hill climb at Byford. Two Morgans were entered, both Vanguard engined chrome radiator Plus Fours. They were Arthur Littlejohns' car, and the Bill Richards demonstrator, to be shared by David Van Dal and John 'Cummo' Cummins. Arthur Littlejohns was not competitive (43 seconds) but John Cummins dead heated for the fastest time (39.1 seconds) in the sports cars over 2,000cc category with Syd Anderson's supercharged 100 Austin Healey. Although David Van Dal recorded a 39.4 second run his other two runs were much slower.

On Monday October 11th the Sporting Car Club of South Australia ran the Labour Day Speed Meeting at Port Wakefield, and attracted the ex-Gavin Sandford-Morgan Plus Four, in the hands of its new owner Tony Innocenzi. Tony entered two races, the ten lap 'Hambley Clarke B Grade Scratch Race', and the twelve lap 'Hannon Bros Saloon and Touring Car Handicap', but there was no success for him at this meeting.

Five days later at the Caversham airstrip at Middle Swan in Western Australia, David Van Dal turned the tables on Syd Anderson during the WASCC meeting, winning the three lap unrestricted handicap from the Healey, with Geoff Way driving his MG TD third. Syd retrieved his dominant position later by winning a four lap event and a 'special' three lapper, both just ahead of David. After his success in the Justin Walsh hill climb Keith Lindsay had entered his Plus Four in what would have been his first circuit race, but apparently failed to start as there are no lap times in the results sheet.

The Sunday November 21st WASCC meeting at Caversham saw the Morgan entries return in force. This meeting was in aid of the Spastic Welfare Association of Western Australia and the main event was a fifteen lap handicap named for the Association. The then Governor of Western Australia, His Excellency Sir Charles Gardiner, came to the track and after driving his own MK VII Jaguar around in a rather sedate 2 minutes and 30 seconds (the chauffeur relegated to the back seat), rode for two laps at racing speed with Syd Anderson in his Austin Healey. Keith Lindsay had entered his Plus Four for his first circuit races, but Arthur Littlejohns did not start. David Van Dal and John 'Cummo' Cummins again shared events with the blue Bill Richards demonstrator. The day was fine and clear and, as it turned out, the racing was both exciting and eventful.

David and Cummo had been disappointed with the performance of the demonstrator at the last Caversham meeting, and decided to make it more reliable in the oil pressure department. The engine was stripped to the block. The oil pump pickup was reworked to fit two inches lower into the extended and baffled sump. New bearings and valve springs were fitted and the compression raised to 9.1 to 1 from 8.5 to 1. A 3.73 differential replaced the 4.1. As is usual with such rebuilds it wasn't finished until 1.15am. on the day of the Caversham races. After practice the first race was a three lap scratch race for cars over 1,500cc and David had the edge on the TR2 driven by speedway driver Laurie Stephens and was well ahead of Syd Anderson's Austin Healey. The 'flying dentist', Sid Taylor, won in the TS Special.

Oversize tyres were now fitted for the five lap 'All Powers Handicap' for racing cars, but Cummo found the gearing now too high and finished out of the places.

On the card was a four lap sealed handicap event, for sports cars, that featured a Le Mans-type start. Cummo was to drive the Bill Richards demonstrator, but David Van Dal had felt Cummo stood a better chance if he could practice the Le

Mans start. David and Cummo had therefore arrived early at the track, and armed with white handkerchief and stopwatch at the end of the main straight, set about refining Cummo's Le Mans start technique. They had practiced until his time fell from an initial fifteen to around ten seconds.

At the start of the race Sir Charles dropped the national flag and Cummo sprinted across to the Morgan. He leaped over the door but as he slid down he realised one foot had actually entered through the steering wheel and was jammed into the dash. He removed the foot and again slid into the seat, but came to an abrupt halt as the gear lever entered the leg of his white overalls. A third attempt at last had him seated and turning the starter, only to hurtle backwards as the gear lever had moved from first to reverse in the confusion! After scattering the pit crew and officials, who by this time were becoming quite vocal in their assertions about 'wise men from the east' (Cummo was from Melbourne) the Morgan joined the fray, a little in arrears, but at least going in the right direction. He battled with the TR2 to the finish, being second over the line.

Surprisingly when the envelopes for the sealed handicaps were opened Cummo had actually won! Keith Lindsay was second in a dead heat with the Citroën special entered by E Davies and driven by Johnny Metcalf.

David Van Dal took over for the four lap unrestricted handicap race for 'stock' and sports cars to again engage the supercharged Austin Healey but came to grief on the third lap. A grey-brown Austin A70 Utility with a fairly inexperienced driver had swung very wide and close to the wire going into the right hand hairpin at the end of the main straight. The blue Plus Four, in very close company with Syd Anderson and Laurie Stevens' TR2 and doing more than 70 mph, suddenly had to take evasive action. The A70 must have seen the trio bearing down in his rear view mirror and in panic pulled across the track towards the inside of the corner. Whilst taking avoiding action a rear wheel of the Morgan went off the track and dug into the sand. The poor Plus Four rolled three times with David's weight actually pulling the safety harness from its anchorage. The last roll put it back on its feet but

The sorry state of the Bill Richards demonstrator after the inversion by David Van Dal at Caversham. John 'Cummo' Cummins is in white racing overalls, with hand in the car. Sydney Van Dal, David's father, is wearing the pith helmet, to the far right of the photograph. (David Van Dal collection)

the car was a mess. There was good deal of blood as a windscreen pillar had passed through David's arm and there was considerable concern for his health. David was taken to hospital with concussion, broken ribs and shoulder, and arm and hand injuries.

Thankfully he was later released from hospital just in time for the event break-up party. He made a grand entrance, seated on a commode into which some lager and cooked sausages had been placed for effect, pleading, 'Wheel me to the keg.' Interestingly the WASCC newsletter, *The Visor*, reported that Laurie Stevens had stopped at the start-finish line to inform the stewards of David's accident, costing him a place at least for his concern.

The win by Cummo earned Bill Richards the princely reward of £8 which was not a great deal towards the rebuild of one very bent Morgan! However, it was quite a successful race day for Keith Lindsay; he came in fourth in an unrestricted production car handicap over four laps after his equal third with Johnny Metcalf's Citroën special in the Le Mans handicap event. When the handicaps were applied Keith had actually dead-heated for second place with R A Davies' MG TF, each of then receiving cheques for £5.

New Zealand

New Zealand took a major step forward towards becoming an important motor racing country in 1954 with the first International New Zealand Grand Prix, which was held at Ardmore Aerodrome on Saturday January 9th. The top Australian driver Stan Jones won the event in his Maybach, from the British driver Ken Wharton in the V16 BRM. An international series of races was now being developed in New Zealand to attract those racing during the summer months in the European Grands Prix to come over to New Zealand during the European racing's winter closed season. These events were to include Wigram, Ohakea and Dunedin. Often a sports car race was to be on the programme too, and Morgans were sometimes to take part in these races.

Despite being a sparsely populated country there was an overall speed limit in New Zealand of 50 mph. This did not dampen the spirit of the motor sport enthusiast however, for it was usually quite easy for car clubs to arrange the closure of public roads for motoring events.

Jack Shelly ran Independent Motor Sales Ltd at 125 Wakefield Street in Wellington, on the North Island of New Zealand and was the importer for Morgan cars at this time, although he himself had been singularly unimpressed by the Morgan factory methods when he had visited England. His main business was as a Jaguar dealer. During the early part of 1954 Jack had in stock a new green, Vanguard engined, chrome radiator Plus Four two-seater. This had been in the showroom for some considerable time and which he had failed to sell. We think it was either P2499 or P2501, both of which had been dispatched from the Morgan factory on Saturday November 8th 1952. Jack's son Tony had noticed it during 1953 whilst still a schoolboy at Scots College and had asked his father whether he could have the Morgan if it was still unsold on his next birthday. His father agreed, so on Tuesday February 2nd 1954, on his son's seventeenth birthday, Jack gave Tony the unsold Morgan.

That great Dunedin Morgan enthusiast Ted Reid took his 1952 green Plus Four, chassis number P2412, to Wigram Airfield near Christchurch on Saturday February 6th. This operational Royal New Zealand Air Force Station had been originally used for training pilots during the First World War, and in 1931 it was extended following a gift of further land by Sir Henry Wigram. Motor racing began annually in 1949 and a circuit of 2.073 miles was produced from perimeter roads for 1954 by The Motor Racing Club of Christchurch. This year the main 100 mile race was held under an international permit, attracting several overseas drivers, including Ken Wharton with the V16 BRM. Ted Reid finished in fifth place in the first event, the twelve lap Redex Sports Car Handicap, the winner being J Kerr in his Singer. Ted had set off on the 225 mile journey to Wigram in the early hours of the Saturday with his wife and two children in the two-seater Morgan, competed, and then made the return journey the same night.

The Hutt Valley Motoring Club organised a race meeting on a section of East Hutt Road on Saturday February 20th, with proceeds from the paying spectators to go to the local carnival. It was just a short 0.9 mile circuit in an industrial area. Tony Shelly had entered his new Plus Four, unbeknown to his father, and actually won the eight mile race for sprint cars and sports cars over 1,500cc. Sadly inadequate control of the spectators reduced the number of races possible, and as a result the police decided not to allow any more races at this venue in the future. Upon his return home Tony was forced to confess to his father of his day's activities, for fear his father would otherwise first learn all about it when he read the results in the local paper!

On Tuesday February 23rd Ted Reid entered his Morgan in the Otago Sports Car Club's, Night Trial; it was his local club and he came home in first place.

The Wellington Car Club staged the New Zealand National Hill Climb Championship on Saturday February 27th and attracted two Plus Fours, Dr Graham Cowie in his usual black coupé and Tony Shelly in his green two-seater. Also present was ex-Morgan racer Allen Freeman. At the Houghton Bay hill climb late in 1953 Allen Freeman had put up for sale his own red Plus Four, chassis number P2290, as he had now purchased from England the Cooper Mark IV raced by Grand Prix driver Peter Collins. With the Cooper powered by a 1,098cc V-twin JAP, Allen recorded a very fast 47.20 seconds to gain him second place overall in the championship. The two Plus Fours returned 53.50 seconds for Tony Shelly and slightly quicker, 53.05 seconds for Graham Cowie.

Ohakea airfield was once again used for racing by the Manawatu Car Club on Saturday March 6th. The local handicappers didn't seem to appreciate that the Morgan was quite a bit faster than MG T types and gave the Plus Fours very generous handicaps. As a result Maurice Orr from Palmerston North came home easily in first place in his Vanguard engined Plus Four, with Tony Shelly second and Graham Cowie third, also in their Plus Fours, in the sixteen mile sports and racing car handicap. In the main race, the 5th Ohakea Trophy race held over fifty miles, 'Morrie' Orr came home second on handicap and fifth overall in 47 min 15 seconds, the winner being the Cooper JAP of Bob

Graham Cowie in his lightened coupé, possibly at Ohakea. (Graham Cowie collection)

Ted Reid goes around the outside of Godfrey Paape's TR2, and is followed by Dave Edmiston's Singer, at Waitati. (Ted Reid collection)

Gibbons. Morrie was actually the hero of the race, for he had reeled off laps 2 to 23 of the 25 lap race with no more than seven seconds variation. In the final few laps he had really put his foot down, recording two laps in 1 minute 49 seconds. Then, in the twenty miles sports car handicap Tony Shelly was the victor, with Morrie in third place. It had been a good day's racing for the Morgans due mainly to the very kind handicapper!

To make his 1952 black coupé, chassis number P2303, more suitable for racing Graham Cowie had considerably lightened it. An aluminium bonnet replaced the steel original, the heavy doors were replaced by canvas ones, and the windscreen and hood were removed and an aero screen used instead. Graham didn't think the top speed was increased by these means, but acceleration must have been better. It was otherwise un-tuned as indeed was Tony Shelly's Plus Four. In our previous book 'Morgan Sports Cars – The Early Years' we inadvertently recorded Graham Cowie as George Cowie. Author's brain fade (JA) is the only excuse!

Ted Reid continued to campaign his green Plus Four in a whole variety of events. He entered the Mosgiel grass track races near Dunedin on Saturday April 3rd, but we have no results for this meeting. On Saturday May 15th the Otago Sports Car Club ran a 'Mud Trial' and Ted Reid once again showed his Morgan could tackle anything. He proved victorious and won the event, collecting the South British Challenge Trophy.

On Saturday August 7th the Otago Sports Car Club held its Hill Climb Championship on Patmos Avenue in Dunedin. Once again Ted Reid was entered, and he finished first in Class C for cars of 1,240 to 3,000cc, and won the James Challenge Cup, which was awarded to the club member with the fastest time in the championship.

Ted Reid also made fastest time of the day at the Waitati grass track meeting near Dunedin held later in the year, and he finished a most successful year by being awarded the Otago Sports Car Club's Elms Trophy for having accumulated the most points in speed competitions during the year. For the second year in succession he also won the General Accessory Co Challenge Trophy which was awarded to the winner of the grass hill climb.

USA

The Morgan Motor Company exported cars to the USA via two importers, who distributed the cars to different areas. Cavalier Motor Cars Ltd in Los Angeles covered territory to the west of the Mississippi and Fergus Motors Inc, based in New York, covered the east, and this system worked well for Morgan. Fergus Motors was founded much earlier by Joseph B Ferguson, originally from Northern Ireland, who was now into his seventies. He kept a tight rein on the finances of the company, leaving much of the car sales to his enthusiastic son Joe Junior. Joe

Senior (known as JB) was intensely religious, such that he disapproved strongly of racing on Sundays.

Enthusiasm for sports cars was growing in the USA, with many drivers wanting to race them on proper European style road circuits. However the USA had few of these, American racing traditionally being on oval tracks, so redundant airfields became the popular alternative. Due to the enthusiasm of General Curtis Le May many of these airfields belonged to the USAF Strategic Air Command, with charities benefiting from his 'hiring out' of these venues. Several proper road circuits were planned for the future and one, Willow Springs in California, had just been completed.

Most sports car racing in the USA was organised by the Sports Car Club of America (SCCA), and to ensure close racing it had introduced a classification system for sports cars which used the engine displacement, adopting the European cubic centimetre engine capacity rather than the American cubic inches. The classes were divided as follows:

Class A – above 8,000cc, B – 5,000 to 8,000cc, C – 3,000 to 5,000cc, D – 2,000 to 3,000cc, E – 1,500 to 2,000cc, F – 1,100 to 1,500cc, G – 750 to 1,100cc, and H – 500 to 750cc.

These classes were further subdivided into 'Production', representing unmodified production cars, and 'Modified' including purpose built sports racers, specials and modified production cars. The classes were keenly policed by the SCCA.

The SCCA covered America with a series of 'Regions', each of which could organise its own races. Certain races were to be given status as 'National' events, with points scored going to an annual SCCA National Championship.

Regular competitors in Regional events could be allocated the same race number throughout the season, which was displayed on the side of the car, along with letters indicating the class in which the car was running. Thus a Vanguard engined Plus Four would carry 'DP' indicating Class D Production.

As yet the new TR2 engined Plus Four Morgans had not arrived in sufficient numbers in the USA for the model to be given a Production classification, so it was temporarily allocated to the Modified class, where it was at considerable disadvantage, competing against purpose built racers.

In addition to the SCCA there were many other smaller clubs that organised events for sports cars, of which the most popular was undoubtedly the California Sports Car Club (CSCC), commonly known as the Cal Club. Most of these clubs used their own car classifications for racing, but they were usually based on that of the SCCA.

Making his first foray into motor racing in January was a Californian commercial kitchen designer by the name of Lew Spencer. It has been extremely difficult to date the three events in which Lew began his racing career, and we originally thought the first, a hill climb, took place in 1953. Lew had been persuaded by Ralph 'Pete' Peterson, a salesman at Cavalier Motor Cars, to take part in a hill climb held at Willow Springs by the Singer Owners' Club, using his daily transport, a Morgan Plus Four.

Having watched several cars do their runs he asked Pete for some advice. When he mentioned 'downshift' Lew asked him what that meant. Pete demonstrated the art to Lew and Lew responded by then coming second in the Morgan class! Lew has a trophy dated February 7th, but contemporary reports date this event one week earlier, on January 31st! Having enjoyed this, Lew was persuaded by Pete to enter the Cal Clubs race meeting at Palm Springs, over the airport course. The programme dates this event as the weekend of January 23rd and 24th, but it was actually held over the weekend of February 6th and 7th! Two other Morgan Plus Fours were also entered, one driven by Pete, and the other by Robert Avedon, although the latter was actually driving the Morgan owned by Ed Mann from Los Angeles (probably his 1953 red coupé).

None of the Morgan drivers tasted success but Lew 'had a ball' in the Saturday races and

Lew Spencer has a 'moment' at Willow Springs. (Curt Warshawsky collection)

eagerly awaited the more important events on the Sunday. During these, in a mixed 'Modified' and 'Production' classes race, 'The Eliminator', an American flathead V8 powered hotrod, built and driven by Frank 'Duffy' Livingstone, overtook Lew on a straight. He promptly spun at the following 180 degree corner and Lew had a disaster when he tried to turn inside (rather than the more natural outside) to avoid the sideways car but found he couldn't and damaged his Morgan. The chrome plated radiator was destroyed, a very expensive part on a Morgan, but Lew did manage to get the Morgan returned to his home town of Culver City with the front end lifted onto the truck of Lou Falcon, the very same person who had aligned the tracking on the Morgan for him before the race.

Whilst Lew repaired the Morgan he was forced to borrow another car for daily transportation, but he hadn't been put off racing and duly entered the races to be held at Minter Field, an ex-Second World War B24 bomber base, near Bakersfield on Sunday March 21st. He was joined at the races by Pete Peterson once more, and this time both drivers did well, with Pete taking the 'D Stock'

class, with Lew finishing second. Unfortunately for Lew the strain had damaged the Vanguard engine, cracking a piston and Lew reluctantly decided he couldn't afford any more racing that year.

Unusually there was no Morgan entered for the third annual Sebring 12 Hour Race held on Sunday March 7th, no doubt to the annoyance of Fergus Motors for whom this event provided desirable publicity for the Morgan sports car. This prestigious endurance race had acquired full international status from 1953 onwards when it became one of the contributing events to the FIA World Sports Car Championship. It was really beneficial to Morgan sales in the USA to have a Morgan do well in this race. The Morgan entrant in 1953, Mike Rothschild, was entered this year, but in a Healey Silverstone, which only managed seventeen laps before retiring. This year the American Oil Company (AMOCO) was beginning a six year exclusive deal to supply fuel, and all competitors received this free high octane petrol in five gallon containers.

Over the weekend of May 1st and 2nd 60,000 spectators braved the hot sun at the National Capital Sports Car Races, held at the Andrews Air

Bob McKinsey on the vast expanse of runway at the Andrews AFB meeting. (Jake Alderson collection)

Force Base near Washington DC. This was one of the USAF Strategic Air Command (SAC) meetings run by the SCCA. Bob McKinsey didn't do well. In fact he finished last in his Plus Four in the George Washington Trophy Race for production cars under 3,000cc. He was running the Plus Four complete with its windscreen, bumpers and even the hub caps still fitted, so perhaps he was just enjoying the ride. The Shell Oil Company supported this meeting by supplying a fuel tanker and setting up impressive lubrication facilities in one of the hangars. The trophy for the main event, the President's Cup, was actually presented by the U S President, Dwight D Eisenhower, the following Monday at the White House, the first time any form of U S auto-racing had been so honoured. The same weekend Charles Yost from Overland Missouri finished a fine third in class in his Plus Four at the novices' races at the Iowa City meeting.

The American professional racing organization NASCAR (National Association for Stock Car Auto Racing) decided to allow non-American cars to race in selected races this year, calling these races 'International Races'. One such was held at Linden Airport in New Jersey on Sunday June 13th comprising fifty laps of a two mile circuit. Linden Airport had been built across the street from a General Motors factory during the Second World War when that factory began producing military aircraft. It was now privately owned by a motor racing enthusiast and the course was produced from runways and taxiways. The race was the eighteenth of thirty-seven races contributing to the Grand National Championship in 1954 (equivalent to the Nextel Cup series today).

Entered in a Morgan Plus Four was a 'Jack Farnell'. According to Jaguar driver Bill Claren, 'Jack Farnell' was really Joe Ferguson Junior, who, wary of the likelihood of losing his SCCA licence by entering a professional NASCAR event, had decided to use this alias. His wife Henrietta's maiden name was Farnell. The Morgan lasted just ten laps, and was credited with 41st place of 43 starters, but the classification system in use meant that 'Jack' did get $25 of prize money! The race was won by the Jaguar XK120 coupé of Al Keller at an average speed of 77.569 mph, and Al collected $1,000.

According to Bill Claren Joe had previously raced his Morgan on the half mile dirt oval at Morristown, New Jersey, finishing in fifth place. Bill finished in second place in his Jaguar behind an Allard. Joe and Bill were two of the founder members this year of the Sports Car Owners and Drivers Association (SCODA) which ran races for sports cars on oval tracks. By 1955 these races were under NASCAR sanctions.

There was little opportunity for circuit racing in Pennsylvania at this time, but the State had plenty of hills suitable for hill climbs, and as a result this became a popular sport. At Sewickley on Sunday June 13th Ralph Zeigler from Pittsburgh came second in the 'Stock' class.

One week later another hill climb took place, this time in Vermont. It was the famous Mount Equinox event. This was hardly a hill climb in the traditional manner, for the hill was 5.2 miles long, with thirty-six sharp bends and ten 'S' curves, winding to the summit at 3,848 feet at a rate of 500 feet per mile. The road was actually privately owned by Dr J G Davidson, and was normally a toll road. Morgan driver Daniel Hastings III did well claiming second place in his class.

The second annual 'Seafair' sports car races run as part of the Seattle powerboat festival were moved from the Payne Air Force Base at Everett to a new airfield at Bremerton in Washington this year. This move was partly in response to complaints from the Highway Patrol who were forced to deal with major traffic jams following the 1953 races. A 3.9 mile circuit was laid out at the Kitsap County Airport, with long straights and two hairpin turns. The races took place on Sunday August 8th and attracted just one Morgan, the chrome radiator Plus Four of Dick Carruthers from Salem in Oregon. He was entered in the one hour and fifteen minutes Seafair Trophy race, running as a Modified car in Class D, this race being for over 1,500cc Modified cars. The race was won by the Ferrari 340 of Sterling Edwards from California but we have no result for Dick.

Race promoter Red Crise ran an ambitious race at Linden Airport in New Jersey using the two mile course over the weekend of August 21st and 22nd. It was his own version of the Sebring 12 Hour Race and was run professionally under a NASCAR sanction. The race was due to be held on the Saturday, but was postponed for a day to Sunday because of rain, the twelve hour race starting at midday and finishing at midnight. A good crowd, estimated at ten thousand, came to watch the action. One Morgan took part amongst the forty starters, being a cowled radiator TR2 engined two-seater, shared by two drivers named as Jock Parnell and Eric Peterson. The Morgan was classified into the 1,500cc to 3,000cc class. It seemed to go well, for it finished sixteenth overall and fourth in class behind the class winning 1952 British Ford Zephyr Six and two Austin Healeys. As this was a professional race no doubt the SCCA deeply disapproved and had prohibited its members from competing, the SCCA being very strict on such things. Bill Claren has confirmed that 'Jock Parnell' was actually another alias of Joe Ferguson Junior and believes that 'Eric Peterson' was really Ray Errickson,

Dick Carruthers races his Morgan at Bremerton during the Seafair races. (Chuck Brown)

a good friend of Joe Ferguson. When we questioned Ray he remembered racing a Jaguar XK140 at Linden, but not a Morgan. Ray had studied mechanical engineering at the prestigious Stevens College of Technology at Hoboken in New Jersey, frequently visiting Fergus Motors where he got to know Joe well and the two became life long friends. Ray worked for a while as a salesman at Fergus Motors before running Fergus Motors' repair and engineering shop. He became invaluable as a race car engineer.

Back in California the Cal Club ran its second race meeting at Santa Barbara Airport at Goleta over the weekend of September 4th and 5th. Jane Marie McBratney entered the fun in her four-seater Plus Four, but could only finish fifteenth in the 'Girls' Race'. Jane was a doctor's wife living in Glendale who, having bought her Morgan, had been told by the salesman that Leo Caton also owned one in Hollywood. She visited him and discovered he had been racing his car, so she had decided to follow suit!

Following the death of a young spectator and the injuries to twelve others during the 1952 races, the original racing circuit through the town of Watkins Glen in the Finger Lakes region of New York was abandoned. However, the townspeople had been keen to preserve the financial bonanza of the earlier races, so for 1953 they hastily produced a transitional 4.6 mile circuit on township roads. It wasn't satisfactory to the SCCA for 1953, although the races did go ahead, but the SCCA did approve the circuit for 1954. The meeting was held on Saturday September 18th, but the long drive from his home in McClean, Virginia was to no purpose for Bob McKinsey. He finished next to last in the eleven laps unrestricted event, which included Formula 3 cars, for the Seneca Cup, but at least he was fourth in Class D Production.

On Sunday October 10th Edwin Hebb Junior from Detroit was possibly the first SCCA member to race the new TR2 engined Plus Four. The event was the SCCA Northeast Ohio Region's meeting held at Akron Municipal Airport. In the Forest City Trophy race, a thirty minute race for sports cars over 1,500cc, he finished eleventh overall behind a number of Jaguar XK120s, an Austin Healey and a Triumph TR2. He did beat all the other TR2s entered, indicating that the Morgan should provide great fun in the future racing against these identically engined cars.

That same day Mike Rothschild and his English wife Hanni (always known as Honey) had taken their Plus Four from their home in New Jersey to Thompson in Connecticut. Mike again tasted success with a third in Class D Production whilst Honey took part in the 'Girls' Race', finishing an excellent fifth.

One week later Jane McBratney was racing her four-seater Plus Four at Palm Springs, having an excellent day, finishing ahead of the Austin Healeys, and being only beaten by a Jaguar. Jane was racing again over the weekend of November 6th and 7th at the very last SAC race which was held at March Field Air Force Base at Riverside. It was a SCCA National meeting and attracted 25,000 spectators. Jane finished fourth in the ladies' race, beating the TR2s and Austin Healeys. Racing possibly the same Morgan, (same race number), was Leo Caton. Leo finished thirtieth of the thirty-nine starters in the seven lap race for 'Junior Drivers', but this should be put into context by many of the entries being higher powered Jaguars and Austin Healeys.

Leo Caton's usual Morgan was a red two-seater, chassis number P2138, and one of the very first Morgans imported to California. It now had a modified road-wheel securing system following the loss of a wheel which cracked and pulled over the locating nuts whilst racing at Pebble Beach in 1952. As a result of this Leo had converted the wheel fitting to one popular in American racing. New hubs were made having unthreaded wheel studs to just locate the normal wheels in place, but a specially cast magnesium spacer was then placed over the studs and tightened onto one central locking stud, effectively sandwiching the wheel centre between the brake drum and the spacer. This system prevented further breakage, and Leo believes he also made a similar system for the rear wheels of Jane's car.

Another modification Leo made to his car was to fit two Holley single throat carburettors, as used on Ford cars, using a special manifold cast in aluminium to a pattern that he had made. Leo remembered races of this time as being very amateur, with little in the way of prizes to be won. Many races were held as a way of raising money for charity, the SAC races being a good example of this. This meeting marked the end of the SAC races, held over the previous twenty-six months on Strategic Air Command Bases, and the end of an era for sports car racing in the USA. These races had been invaluable in providing safe courses for sports car racing on airfield circuits whilst this racing got established. Now several purpose built courses were being constructed or planned in different areas of the country. The sports car movement was indeed deeply indebted to General Curtis LeMay for allowing racing on these military facilities.

With the increasing interest by Americans in sports cars it was not long before the domestic motor industry decided to join in. The first of the American big league to break in to this market was General Motors with the cautious introduction of the Chevrolet Corvette in 1953, whilst Ford was not far behind with the more powerful V8 Ford Thunderbird in 1955.

The initial version of the fibreglass bodied Chevrolet Corvette was hardly a pacesetter, for the 150 bhp six cylinder 'Blue Flame' engine of 3,840cc (235cid) was unfortunately attached to General Motors 'Powerglide' two-speed automatic transmission and could only manage eleven seconds for 0 to 60 mph.

For 1955 the Chevrolet small block V8 of 4,346cc (265cid) was introduced, along with other performance enhancers, and in 1956 a three-speed gearbox at last gave the sportsman something to use. The Ford Thunderbird was initially much better equipped with 200 bhp on tap from its 4,786cc (292cid) V8, which was coupled to an optional manual gearbox, and it was to easily out sell the Corvette. Later on, Ford changed the concept of the Thunderbird into a four-seater convertible and it lost its sporting credentials.

Leo Caton's method of keeping the wheels in place on his Plus Four consisted of a modified hub onto which the hub spinner screwed in place, holding the cast spacer which fitted over the wheel centre, the wheel being located by modified studs. Below the mounted wheel is shown the spacer and wheel spinner from another hub. (Chris Towner)

For 1955 onwards a new and enthusiastic agent was to take over the distributorship of Morgans to the western States of the USA from Cavalier Motor Cars Limited. This was a company originally called Worldwide Westwood, and later Worldwide Imports; it was situated on Santa Monica Boulevard in Los Angeles. Originally this business had been founded by Al Landau in 1951 as a small repair shop when he was unable to get his own Triumph properly serviced elsewhere. In 1954 he sold the

> *We are pleased to announce that we are now Official Distributors for the*
>
> **1955 MORGAN**
> (WITH THE TR-2 ENGINE)
>
> *You Are Cordially Invited to Visit Our Showroom and See the New Sports Car*
>
> "Hand-Built for the Enthusiast and Costing No More"
>
> **WORLDWIDE WESTWOOD**
> 10860 SANTA MONICA BOULEVARD, LOS ANGELES 25
>
> ARIZONA 9-0227   BRADSHAW 2-7605

business to a Swiss sports car enthusiast named Rene Pellandini, and it was Rene who had taken over the Morgan agency. He immediately began advertising the Morgan marque in the local motoring press. The first Morgan cars taken by Worldwide Westwood were chassis numbers 3134 and 3135, which were dispatched from the Morgan factory in England on October 4th 1954.

In December the American *Motor Sport* magazine published a road test by Joe Wherry of a couple of the new TR2 engined Plus Fours, loaned by Fergus Motors. The new cowl styling was thought much improved over the unhappy interim style of 1953 and the magazine summarised the car as, 'darned good', reminding readers that the kerb weight was almost 200lbs less than the TR2. A 0 to 60 mph time of 11.4 seconds was achieved and it was suggested that Laycock de Normanville overdrive might be available at a later date (it never happened). The two-seater Roadster was priced at $2,450, the four-seater at $2,500 and the coupé at $2,650 f.o.b. at any port.

Canada

Just across the Canadian border from Detroit, the home of the American car industry, is the city of Windsor where Windsor Motorcycles held the Canadian Morgan agency. The proprietor was Douglas Ellis, always known as 'Curly'. Although British by birth, Curly had been brought up in New Zealand but whilst convalescing from a motorcycle injury he had set out on a 'world tour' with his mother. After visiting an uncle in the Windsor area he decided to stay, feeling comfortable in the area and, after the Second World War, he set up a business buying up war-surplus Harley Davidson motorcycles and converting them for civilian use. He had a partner in this enterprise called Victor Finch. Their premises were situated at 2504 Howard Avenue, on the corner with Ypres. Curly began importing some British and German motorcycles, including NSU, and in 1952 he also imported a Morgan Plus Four on the request of a local Englishman named Al Weed, which Al had raced during 1953. We think this was chassis number P2464, a green two-seater, dispatched from Malvern on Wednesday September 10th. As a result Curly became a Morgan agent!

The Ford Motor Company ran an important Trade School in Windsor where apprentices undertook a four year course in mould making, tool and die work etc. Obviously most of these young apprentices lived in boarding houses in the area and they tended to be interested in anything special in the car world. The close proximity of Detroit itself and the surrounding USA towns meant that several sports car enthusiasts from the USA willingly crossed the border to visit Curly's establishment. Thus Curly had ready made markets for Morgans on his doorstep.

One of the Ford Trade School pupils at this time was Frank Boulton, who had bought an MG TD. The sight of this made another School pupil, Les Burkholder, buy a new black MG TF. Yet another pupil, named David Elcomb, was running Ford Model T coupés. Frank was a founder member of the Essex County Sports Car Club with Al Weed and others.

Morgan Sports Cars 1954

Al Weed's first Morgan, at Windsor Motorcycles by the railroad track. (Curly Ellis)

During a Michigan all night car rally Al Weed experienced clutch trouble in the Plus Four and had stopped at an intersection at the bottom of a hill. Les came over the hill at high speed in his new MG TF and because of the clutch problem Al wasn't able to get into gear to get out of the way. The MG struck a glancing blow on the rear of the Morgan, damaging the woodwork, but leaving the MG unscathed.

Chapter 2
1955

As usual the MCC's Exeter Trial heralded the new motor sport year. It began on the night of Friday January 7th, from three starting points at Virginia Water, Kenilworth and Launceston, finishing at Bournemouth on the Saturday. Just four days earlier the West Country had been subjected to severe snow blizzards, blocking some country roads, but the event itself was held in fine weather, with only a few reminders by the side of the roads of the previous inclement weather. With the Edinburgh Trial not happening in 1954 this Exeter Trial also counted towards the MCC's Triple Award for 1954, for those select drivers who managed to complete the Exeter and Land's End trials with First Class Awards.

As usual there were several Morgan entries amongst the starters, thirteen in fact. One, the Vanguard engined Plus Four of L Jenner, NLU 620, was preceding the motorcycles at the front of the trial competitors, Mr Jenner being a travelling marshal. There were two teams of three Morgans entered. The Morgan factory team consisted of Jim Goodall in HUY 982, John Moore in KNP 5, and Terry Hall in Peter Morgan's coupé JNP 239 passengered by Horace Roberts. The other team was that of Horace Gould in a Vanguard engined Plus Four, Tiny Lewis in his Vanguard powered Plus Four, now registered THY 60, and John Spare in TYA 1.

Also competing was Joe Huxham in a 1,086cc 4/4 (probably FOH 812), the two TR2 engined Plus Fours of Monty Rogers (PLB 111) and G Day, and the three Vanguard engined Plus Fours of John Ahern (NXH 394), P Norgard (NYF 452), and Ernest James, but the latter, who usually drove his chrome radiator Plus Four NYU 993, non-started. Simms proved a stopper for the coupés of Terry Hall and John Moore, and they had to settle for Second Class Awards. There were no such problems for Jim Goodall or the members of the Horace Gould team, for all were awarded Firsts. Jenner, Ahern and Day took Seconds, Huxham, Rogers and Norgard claiming Thirds. Gould's team won the team competition.

Having obtained a First, Jim Goodall was awarded one of only two MCC Triple Awards given for 1954, showing he was one of the very best trials drivers in his Plus Four.

Monty Rogers in the Exeter Trial. (Monty Rogers collection)

That same weekend, over the Saturday and Sunday the VSCC ran its sixth annual Measham Rally. There was snow and ice to contend with on the hills of Wales before the final driving tests on the Sunday morning back at Measham. The snow and ice suited the vintage cars better, but Andy Polack in a Morgan Plus Four was best in the driving tests. Andy was studying engineering at Loughborough College. His Morgan was a 1952 registered Vanguard engined coupe, red with beige upholstery, registration ECF 495.

On the Sunday the North Midland MC ran a standard car trial, and the best performance was that of Ernie Sneath with his Plus Four, who also finished in the winning team.

The January issue of *Motor Sport* carried an advertisement from Ray Meredith wishing to sell his 4/4. This ex-Bill Allarton car, EAX 377, was advertised as follows: '1940 Le Mans Morgan, 1,098cc, red, latest front suspension just rebushed, practically new tyres. D D (downdraught) SU 32mm carburettor, Scintilla Vertex magneto, 7.5 compression ratio, new valves, rings, brake linings this September, £250'. Ray wanted to continue his Morgan motor sport with a Plus Four, so he had sought out Terry Hall at a local Morgan 4/4 Club meeting to seek his advice (they both lived in Bromsgrove). Terry had, of course, driven all types of Morgan, being Jim Goodall's regular co-driver. He wasn't as yet impressed with the TR2 engine, preferring the low down torque of the Vanguard. Good deals were currently obtainable on old chrome radiator Vanguard engined Plus Fours, and Ray managed to find a nearly new green two-seater. It was chassis number P2732, dispatched from the factory to the Birmingham agent Henry Garner at the late date of November 30th 1954, and registered POP 560. We think it was also one of the unsold cars originally taken by Basil Roy Ltd, having been tested at the Morgan factory during the week of September 14th 1953.

There were twenty-five starters for the Liverpool MC's New Year Rally for the Stott Trophy on January 16th. Snow fell heavily all day creating havoc with time schedules and causing the cancellation of the special tests. Only six crews reported at the final control, and of those only one was on time, namely Ken James navigated by Peter Dingley in their Plus Four. The other two Morgans, of Harry Jacoby (MLV 58) and Marion 'Pip' Parry who was navigated by Peter Reece, failed to finish.

Ken James was driving the ivory Plus Four KUY 474 he had bought from Jimmy Ray the previous year. The engine had shown it needed work when he acquired the car so Ken had taken this to Laystall Engineering in Liverpool for rebuilding. It was fitted with Ferguson tractor pistons and liners giving a capacity of 2.2 litres, a TR2 camshaft, and also a Barwell gas-flowed cylinder head. The crankshaft assembly and flywheel were all balanced. Jimmy Ray had run this Morgan with twin SU carburettors, which tended to dribble fuel through the louvres, staining the side of the bonnet red. After the Stott Trophy event Ken therefore decided to solve this problem by having the Morgan repainted in Rolls-Royce Regal Red metallic paint!

Jimmy Ray himself had again been asked by the Standard Motor Company to drive a works rally car for them (this time a modified Standard 10 in 'GT' trim) in the Monte Carlo Rally held from January 17th until 24th, and he finished an excellent third in class. Jimmy now realised that his rallying future was likely to be with Standard, a company which would be able to offer him more than Morgan was ever likely to, so he put his lightweight Plus Four NAB 217 up for sale. John Moore decided to buy it, reasoning it must be faster than his coupé KNP 5 and Peter Reece in turn bought the latter from John.

The Cambridge University AC ran its annual Lent Term Rally over the weekend of Saturday and Sunday January 29th and 30th, with eighty-six starters from the two starting points of St Neots and Harrogate. Five hundred miles later the tired competitors finished at York, with E G Jackson finishing fourth overall in his TR2 engined Plus Four, and second in class. That same Sunday John Spare took his Plus Four TYA 1 to second place in the sports car class of the Taunton Motor Club's driving tests, and finished in the winning Weston team.

The Thames Estuary AC's 'Cats' Eyes' night navigation rally was held over the night of Friday February 5th, starting from Lamb's Garage in Woodford Essex and finishing the following day some 450 miles later on the front at Westcliff. It was a National event for the first time. Several Morgans competed, but the best was that of Bernard Clarke who finished second in class to a Triumph TR2, presumably in his Vanguard engined Plus Four PKK 769. J P Russell was in a TR2 powered Plus Four PLL 234.

Construction of the Ford 100E engined Morgan prototype went on quite quickly, with design led by HFS Morgan and assembly in the capable hands of Jim Roberts, the repair shop foreman. Once the basic design had been agreed all the factory foremen were called together and asked to suggest ways in which costs could be saved in production. All pulled their weight according to Peter Morgan, one such saving being the absence of louvres on the bonnet top. Peter Morgan played a major role in the body design of this car and he was pleased to find that the engine sat much lower in the chassis than in the Plus Four, for this allowed him to lower the bonnet line. Also, by moving the fuel tank from the Plus Four's wooden platform to a new lower position on the chassis it was possible to lay a single spare wheel on a sloping rear panel. Peter had always liked the way the spare wheel was recessed into the rear panel on post war 4/4 Le Mans Replicas, and he was pleased he could use a similar design on the new car.

One particular problem for the new car was the gear lever, for the Ford gearbox was of course directly behind the engine as in the Ford car. This meant that on the Morgan the gearbox resided in the engine compartment. HFS Morgan asked Peter to devise a gear shift system, and he produced a linkage from the cut down Ford gear lever with a rod passing through a 'flexible bearing' (rubber mounted tube) attached to the Morgan bulkhead and hence into the passenger compartment. This was simple and proved effective, pleasing HFS who 'quite liked it'. The clutch of course was much easier to sort, having hydraulic operation.

Cheaper instrumentation, a non-folding windscreen, a cheaper Salisbury back axle (type 6HA of 4.4 to 1 ratio), and smaller tyres (5.00 x 16) all helped in saving money. The trunnion rear mounting for the rear springs was also replaced by a much simpler rubber bushed shackle system. The engine, number 3601, had originally been supplied by Ford in early 1954 and the new car was given chassis number 3242 in the Plus Four series and was coloured blue.

It was tested by Charlie Curtis during the week of February 7th, but was not registered for the road at this time. At the Morgan directors' meeting held on Thursday March 3rd Peter Morgan reported that the new car had completed 150 miles very satisfactorily, presumably being driven on trade plates.

The Bristol MC and L CC ran its very first rally, starting at Bristol Cathedral after lunch on Saturday February 19th, and finishing the following day at a Bristol restaurant after approximately 450 miles in Devon and Somerset. The event was sponsored by 'Maggi Soups' so the rally was named the 'Maggi Carlo Rally'. Two tests were put in by the sponsors for fun, and not counting in the results. The first was to row a boat around a pylon in a lake and then drink a carton of Maggi soup, and the second to drive from one line to another without spilling a can of soup on the car's bonnet! Best of the 53 starters in the main event was Dr John Spare in TYA 1.

John Spare also did well in the Plymouth MC's '200 Trophy' Reliability Trial held in snowy weather on Sunday February 27th. Despite heavy snow causing the cancellation of two of the hills John won the Trophy, even beating the Dellows.

The Bolton-Le-Moors Rally Driving Tests always sorted out the most skilful of the rally drivers. Peter Reece had won the last two, and was leading this one, held on March 6th, until the very last test when he over ran the stop line, thereby finishing second of the 162 starters to

Morgan Sports Cars   1955

Ken James during the Bolton-Le-Moors driving tests in his Rolls-Royce Regal Red Plus Four. (Charles Dunn)

Ken Fleuriot in a Triumph TR2. Peter was driving his ex-John Moore coupé KNP 5 which had earlier received some new Thompson steering joints. Also in Morgans were Hugh Denton in JNV 654 and Ken James in KUY 474. Hugh and Ken both won special awards, Ken also joining Peter Reece and John Waddington in the winning team.

Several rally drivers had booked their Morgans in to the factory for work prior to the forthcoming RAC Rally. John Moore had NAB 217 generally checked over on Monday February 28th, and Tiny Lewis had Cam Gears steering and Thompson track rod ends fitted to THY 60 on Wednesday February 23rd and a 3.7 back axle on Thursday March 3rd. The RAC Rally itself was to start on Tuesday March 8th and finish on the following Saturday March 12th. Again the two starting points of Hastings and Blackpool were used, with the finish at Hastings some 2,000 miles later, after just one twelve hour rest period. Despite this, the event was fully subscribed with 240 entrants and ten reserves.

Starting from Hastings were several Morgans, including two teams. The non-team Morgans were the TR2 engined Plus Four of G E Day from Forest Hill in London, navigated by F E T Reeves, and Tiny Lewis in THY 60. The first team consisted of P W S White navigated by G W D Vaughan in his usual TR2 engined Plus Four, Barrie Phipps, navigated by his girl friend Angela Palfrey in KUY 714, and John Moore with Les Yarranton in NAB 217. John and Les were to share the driving tests. The other team was John Spare in TYA 1 navigated by Mervyn Meredith, Jim Goodall navigated by Terry Hall in HUY 982, and Peter Morgan navigated by Ralph Stokes in KUY 387. Ralph Stokes lived just the other side of Malvern Link from the Morgan factory, and was a well known top rally navigator who had passengered for Lionel Creed pre-war, in Morgan three-wheelers. Starting from Blackpool was the Plus Four of Harry Jacoby (MLV 58) navigated by W K Webster, and the Plus Four of Yvonne Jackson from Leeds navigated by Miss J Crossley, both cars with TR2 engines.

Three ex-Morgan drivers were in works cars, namely Jimmy Ray in a modified (GT) Standard 10, Ken Lee in an MG TF, and Peter Reece co-driving for his cousin Jack in a works Ford Zephyr. It also appears that Frank Dundas managed to get an entry with his Plus Four PSM 508, despite not appearing amongst the list of competitors or reserves.

1955 — The Heritage Years

The RAC Rally's start at Hastings. John Spare makes an adjustment to TYA1, Peter Morgan at the rear of the car. Behind are the works cars HUY 982 and KUY 387. Note the cleared snow on the side. (John Spare collection)

The severe winter weather was atrocious, with much snow and ice, and many competitors took two spare wheels shod with winter tyres and Parsons chains, and also carried shovels for snow drifts. The Welsh sections were particularly bad, with many cars getting stuck and those following unable to get past. Peter Morgan found himself behind time, but his attempt to speed up only led to KUY 387 sliding into a bank. Although the Morgan was only travelling at about 20 mph the impact was sufficient to bend back the front crosshead and Peter was out of the rally. An Austin Healey driver made the same mistake, but just backed out of the bank and was on his way. Whilst

John Moore with the ex-Jimmy Ray car at Goodwood during the RAC Rally. Note the shovel attached to the spare wheel. (Les Yarranton collection)

the fragility of the Morgan front end was good for protecting the passengers, it did mean that front impacts usually meant retirement, whereas stronger cars just kept going. Another who did the same was Tiny Lewis in his Plus Four. He too retired.

It was not a good rally for Morgans, none appearing in the final prizes, although Jim Goodall and Frank Dundas survived to the finish, making good times in the final test. The winner was the amazing twin carburettor Standard 10 'GT' of Jimmy Ray, navigated by Brian Horrocks, with another Standard 10 'GT' driven by Ken Richardson third, sandwiching a TR2 in second. The Team Award went naturally to the Standards.

After the rally Tiny Lewis decided it was opportune, whilst repairing the front end damage, to convert his chrome radiator Plus Four Morgan to the latest cowled radiator style, and also to fit a Triumph TR2 engine.

Frank Dundas's many achievements with his Plus Four had impressed another rally driver from the Dumfries area. He was Jim Hughan, and he had decided that he too would try rallying a Morgan. As his father-in-law ran a garage in Kirkcudbright he suggested to him that the best way to get a Morgan was for him to become a Morgan agent! This he duly did and Jim went down himself to Malvern to collect his TR2 engined Plus Four two-seater on Thursday March 3rd. It was coloured ivory with black wings, carried chassis number 3245, and was registered ASW 222. Unfortunately the factory forgot to tell Jim that the inflatable seat cushions needed some air, and as he was unaware of the system, he had a most uncomfortable journey back home! This was the sole Morgan taken by the J J Aitken agency.

On Sunday March 13th the Chiltern Car Club ran an autocross at the One Hundred Acres Estate at Amersham. A 'B' shaped course was used and only one car at a time was allowed on the track. The master proved to be Hugh Denton in JNV 654 setting the best time of the day.

The British Automobile Racing Club (BARC) ran its first Members' race meeting of the year, its eighteenth, on a wet and windy day at Goodwood on Saturday March 26th. In the second novices' handicap, over five laps, the two TR2 engined Morgan Plus Fours of Brian Odoni and Monty Rogers (PLB111) just failed to catch the better handicapped Morris Minors and had to settle for fourth and fifth respectively, with Brian setting the fastest lap. Brian Odoni's Plus Four was a green two-seater, chassis number 3189, which had been dispatched from the factory to agent Basil Roy Ltd on November 6th 1954. It was registered PUV 42, Brian living in London.

Event 6 was a five lap Members' handicap and two Morgans took part, Basil de Mattos in a 'borrowed', probably works, Plus Four and John Hayles in his own Plus Four. Basil had a start on scratch of 15 seconds and finished seventh overall making the fastest lap in the process at 1 minute 59.2 seconds, whilst John Hayles was two places and eleven seconds behind having started 15 seconds earlier. Basil was out again in the Plus Four for the final five lap Members' handicap and this time finished sixth.

On Sunday April 3rd the Westmorland MC ran its Spring Regularity Trial, with victory going to the Morgan of Cecil Hall, who also took the team prize together with the Morgan of W Rigg, and a Sunbeam-Talbot. Cecil's Morgan was a 4/4, registered LKP 766, chassis number 1891, originally dispatched on July 11th 1949 to the Ashford, Kent agency of Hayward. Also held this Sunday was a hill climb at Brunton by the BARC, in which Richard Colton came second to an Austin Healey with his Plus Four.

As always the Easter Holiday brought a plethora of motor sport. The traditional MCC Land's End Trial set off on the evening of Good Friday April 8th from the three starting points of Kenilworth, Virginia Water and Launceston. One hundred and fifty seven cars were entered, several being Morgans. From the Morgan factory came Peter Morgan in KUY 387 and Jim Goodall in HUY 982. Completing the factory team was Terry Hall in the coupé JNP 239. Tiny Lewis was in THY 60, B Thorne in a chrome radiator four-seater MLX 521, and Jim Banbury in a two-seater

JJY 221. All the above were listed as having TR2 engines, but we do wonder whether in fact JNP 239 still had a Vanguard unit. Vanguard engined Plus Fours were driven by Joe Huxham and P Norgard (NYF 452). R Dowle was in a Standard engined 4/4.

The weather was glorious, but previous rain left the hills very challenging. First Class Awards were won by just Jim Goodall and Tiny Lewis of the Morgan drivers. Peter Morgan failed one hill for a Second Class Award as did Norgard, whilst Terry Hall and Thorne claimed Thirds. The other three retired. For this event Jim Goodall had fitted an 'auxiliary fuel tank' to an extension on the rear of the chassis for more rear end weight. Despite being called a fuel tank, it was actually full of water! It seems to have worked well for him.

Jim Banbury hailed from mid-Devon. He had been hill climbing a home-made special comprising the usual mixture of Austin 7 and Ford 10 bits, but then came into some money, allowing him to buy his green Plus Four, chassis number T3131. He had collected the Plus Four directly from the Morgan factory on Wednesday July 14th 1954.

On Easter Saturday the Bristol MC and LCC ran races at Castle Combe. Monty Rogers entered his four-seater Plus Four PLB 111 for the thirty lap sports car race, running the Morgan with an aero screen fitted. Bill Boddy in his report for *Motor Sport* recorded that, 'Considerable tail slides characterised E M Rogers' second place in the 2,000cc class in his Morgan Plus Four.'

Whenever the Pembrokeshire Motor Club ran hill climb events at Lydstep and John Moore entered a Morgan the results were never in doubt. So it proved once more at the Easter Saturday meeting, for John driving NAB 217 won all three classes he entered and broke two class records, clipping 0.2 seconds from the sports cars up to 2 litres time, and 0.33 seconds off his own record in the class for cars up to 3 litres! He won the 2 litre class with a time of 35.0 seconds, the 3 litre class with a time of 35.2 seconds and the unlimited class with a time of 35.4 seconds.

On Easter Sunday the West Cornwall Motor Club ran a hill climb at Trengwainton, attracting several competitors staying over from the Land's End Trial. Best of the Morgans was the TR2 engined Plus Four JJY 221 of Jim Banbury, who finished second in class behind an AC Ace. He was to become one of the best drivers of this tricky course.

The 1,000 mile Circuit of Ireland Trial (really a rally) started from Dublin and Belfast on Good Friday, finishing at Bangor on Easter Tuesday. John Howe had entered in his Vanguard engined Plus Four and Marshall entered in a TR2 example. Frank Dundas had taken his Plus Four PSM 508 from Dumfries and did well initially, but then seems to have faded from the results. We have no record of the fates of the other two.

The London Motor Club's 'Little Rally' was anything but, for despite being a Closed event for club members only, it attracted 466 entrants, the largest ever received for a motor sports event in the UK. The reason for the 'Little Rally' title was that it was intended largely as a social affair, with a fairly easy 200 mile route through Surrey and Sussex on Saturday April 16th. As a result the eight driving tests determined the winners, and John Spare battled all the way against the TR2 of Dick James for overall victory. He just failed, but was second to Dick in the class for open cars over 1,499cc.

One week later the North Devon MC ran the fifth Ilfracombe Rally, starting from Ilfracombe, Bristol, Plymouth or Salisbury on Friday evening April 22nd. It finished at Ilfracombe the following day some 400 miles later, with the final test being by the pier. Morgan Plus Fours were entered by R D Boney (Plymouth start), Barrie Phipps and John Spare (Bristol start) and P W S White and Monty Rogers (Salisbury start). Once again John Spare was the best of the Morgan drivers, finishing second in the open car class to the rally winner Geoff Dear's MG TD. John also won the Bristol Start Award, and was the winner of the award for the best Morgan, donated by the manufacturer.

Over the same two days the MAC ran its third Birmingham Post Rally, starting from the Civic Centre in Birmingham, and finishing at Droitwich.

The route was kept secret, being handed to the navigator just as the starting signal was given. There were 154 starters, including eight Morgans. The Morgan factory team consisted of Peter Morgan, navigated by Ralph Stokes in KUY 387, Jim Goodall navigated by Graham Stallard in HUY 982 and Les Yarranton navigated by Tommy Thompson in a Vanguard engined car. It was possibly his old one, KWP 926, although we believe he was about to, or indeed had already, sold this car. Peter Reece was navigated by Barrie Davies, presumably driving his coupé KNP 5. Andy Polack was navigated by H Hughes in his coupé ECF 495 and Mr and Mrs Cleghorn were in Ted's Plus Four RVF 142. Yvonne Jackson was navigated by Leonie Kinns and John de Blaby by R Dillow. Les Yarranton finished third in the over 1601cc sports car class, but the other members of the Morgan factory team had big problems with Test C, the driving test held on the grass at Shelsley Walsh, and finished well out of the team competition. Peter Reece finished in fourth place behind Les Yarranton. Andy Polack was excluded for exceeding the permitted maximum 40 mph during the night section following secret checks, whilst the Cleghorns lost many points during the night. Yvonne Jackson had problems with the final test at Droitwich, but John de Blaby drove consistently well to finish well up in the results.

The last of the motor races held at Ibsley by the West Hants and Dorset MC and LCC was held on Saturday April 30th, attracting many top drivers. Competing in his four-seater Plus Four was Monty Rogers, entering the novice race. The day before, the race competitors were allowed to practise, but it was raining hard and a moment's inattention had Monty aquaplaning off, straight for a parked ambulance. He managed to avoid that but in the process the Morgan leapt up into the air, throwing Monty out whilst it rolled, and finally stopped upright on all four wheels. Monty was uninjured and his cousin then took command of the situation, transporting the Morgan to his workshop close by (he was a builder). Using his expertise as a joiner and carpenter the damaged bodywork was soon repaired.

On that Saturday, the Torbay MC ran its fourth Torbay Rally, attracting several Morgan entries. There were starts from Plymouth, Ilfracombe, Taunton and Torquay. The TR2 engined Plus Four of Jim Banbury (JJY221) and the Vanguard Plus Four of Leon Fredman started from Plymouth. Starting from Taunton were the TR2 engined Plus Fours of Dr John Spare and P W S White and also Dave Warren with his Vanguard engined Plus Four MYP 802. Starting from Torquay was the Standard engined 4/4 of P T Shipman. John Spare had problems on the road section with TYA 1, gaining penalties which put him out of the running, as did P T Shipman. It was Jim Banbury who won the event, also winning the Plymouth starting control award and his class. It was a great day for Jim as he savoured his success. Leon Fredman was runner up and also won the over 2000cc open cars class, and Dave Warren was in the winning team of the Burnham-on-Sea Motor Club. It proved quite a successful event for the Morgans. Leon Fredman was a family member of Plymouth furniture shop owners.

The Lancashire Automobile Club's Morecambe National Rally was always a popular event, attracting over 160 starters from the starts at Morecambe, Manchester, Leeds, Shenstone, Glasgow, Luton, Bristol and Preston. Several Morgans were entered. Starting at Morecambe was Morgan agent Gerry Hoyle in a TR2 engined Plus Four. Starting from Leeds was Yvonne Jackson, and from Glasgow Andie Neil in KYS 41 and Frank Dundas in PSM 508. Starting from Luton was Sandy Blair in 'Nixie' and Romek Michalkiewicz in his Morgan. Romek was from Rainham, and had purchased his green two-seater Plus Four, chassis number 3205, from R Rootes Ltd, the Morgan agent in Maidstone in Kent. It had been registered TKT 100 on November 30th 1954, and had been dispatched from the Morgan factory the following day. Starting from Bristol was John Spare in TYA 1, and from Preston Les Yarranton and J Carefoot, a Blackpool driver.

The event started on Friday May 13th with the competitors converging at Morecambe for a braking test before setting off again for the night navigation test in the Lake District, then returning to Morecambe for the driving tests on the promenade on the Saturday. Les Yarranton won the class for the larger sports cars, whilst Frank Dundas took the Glasgow Starters' Award and Sandy Blair the same from Luton. Frank and Sandy also shared the fastest time in the final test at Morecambe, known as the 'Monte-Morecambe run'.

The BARC ran its first Members' Meeting at the Aintree circuit, the famous horse racing venue near Liverpool, on Saturday May 21st, using a new 1.64 miles club circuit for the racing. John Moore took along NAB 217 and faced a field of no less than ten Triumph TR2s in the scratch race for sports cars between 1,500 and 2,000cc. John refused to be overwhelmed by the opposition and drove in his usual forceful style to an impressive victory by 0.8 seconds.

The MCC ran its fifth Whitsun Rally on Friday and Saturday May 27th and 28th, with starts at London, Kendal and Taunton. Four Morgan Plus Fours were entered. Ernest James was in his usual Plus Four NYU 993. Tom Threlfall, then undergoing his compulsory stint of National Service in the RAF, was entered in the ex-Jimmy Ray Morgan KUY 474 which he had recently purchased from Ken James. Monty Rogers was in PLB 111 and Jim Banbury was in JJY 221. None collected awards.

Les Yarranton borrowed a Morgan for the Hereford MC's May driving tests held on May 29th, winning the open cars class from Barrie Phipps in KUY 714.

Plus Fours began leaving the Morgan factory towards the end of May with enlarged front brakes, still nine inches in diameter but now 1.75 inches wide, replacing the 1.25 inch version. These Girling brakes, type HLSS, indicating 'Hydraulic Leading Shoe, Sliding', were as fitted to the current Austin A40 and A50 Cambridge models. Obviously new front hubs with integral brake drums were required and this gave the Morgan factory the opportunity to strengthen this item, eliminating breakages of this part in the future. The first production car to be so fitted appears to be chassis 3297, tested in the week of May 23rd, but the Girling catalogue gives 3333.

The 13th Scottish Rally was held during Whitsun week, starting on Monday May 30th and finishing four days later on Thursday June 2nd. Several Morgans were amongst the 110 plus entrants. Roy Clarkson was in VNO 600, Frank Dundas and Eric Dymock were in PSM 508, Romek Michalkiewicz and John Ross were in TKT 100, Andie and Chrissie Neil were in Toots, KYS 41, and finally John Howe

Roy Clarkson in VNO during the Scottish Rally. (James Brymer)

had made the trip from Northern Ireland, presumably in his Vanguard engined car. The first test on the Monday was a brake test at Gleneagles, where competitors had to drive between 30 and 35 mph and brake hard when shown a red light. There were several speed tests, these being a flat out 'blind' on Connel airstrip, and speed hill climbs of Rest-and-be-Thankful and Monument Hill near Dalmally. Several manoeuvring driving tests were also laid out in a car park at Ganavan, just a few miles from the rally headquarters at Oban. When the results were announced Roy Clarkson had won Class 6, for Touring cars between 1,301 and 2,000cc, in VNO 600 whilst Andie Neil won the Scottish SCC's award for the best performance by a lady who was a club member, as well as finishing in 26th place in Class 9, for sports cars over 1,600cc. In fourth place in that class was Frank Dundas, an excellent performance by him. Romek Michalkiewicz was in twentieth place, with John Howe in 25th. In thirteenth place was the Austin Healey of Billy Potts, navigated by Jim Clark who was competing in his first International rally.

On Saturday June 4th the Eight Clubs ran their annual Silverstone race meeting. The meeting began with two 40 minute high speed trials, during which a compulsory pit stop was required to either change a wheel or spark plugs. Twenty-two laps was the number needed to be completed for an award and David Hiam in NWP 776, Hugh Denton in JNV 654 and John Moore in NAB 217 all managed twenty-four.

Race 11 was a five lap handicap which saw David Hiam drive furiously through the field from the five second mark, taking second place on the very last corner. The next race was another five lap handicap and John Moore stormed through from the 25 second mark to win. Unfortunately he didn't see the chequered flag and continued racing, but as he raced around Woodcote the nearside rear wheel came off and he spun to a halt. Thinking the racing was still going on he decided it was probably safer to stay in the Morgan rather than risk sprinting for the side of the track. Eventually he heard the race commentator announce, 'Put the driver out of his misery. Tell him he's already won.' Two races later John had fitted a replacement wheel and took part in the five lap scratch race, finishing second to Standbridge's AC Ace.

David Hiam's father worked for the Dunlop Rubber Company and he had ordered David's Morgan directly from the Morgan factory, possible because Dunlops were original equipment suppliers to the Morgan Motor Company. His ivory two-seater Plus Four with black upholstery, chassis number 3199, was fitted with Triumph TR2 engine number TS 2994 and had been collected from the Morgan factory on January 1st 1955 by David and his father. It was registered NWP 776.

The Snetterton racing circuit in East Anglia had been an airfield base for B17 Flying Fortress bombers of the 96th Bomb Group of the US 8th Army Air Force during the Second World War. The redundant airfield had been purchased after the war by a local farmer, Fred Riches. A local motor sport and Aston Martin enthusiast named Oliver Sear persuaded the farmer that he could get an income by using the runways for motor racing, and the two men formed a company to promote motor racing there named Riches and Sear Ltd. During October 1954 a 24 hours endurance record for the circuit had been set by a Morris Oxford at 54 mph. Ted Cleghorn had decided that this record should be easily within the grasp of a Morgan Plus Four and Ted had approached Peter Morgan earlier in the year for support. Peter had agreed that the factory would support the project by supplying a Morgan and helping to run the attempt. The group of drivers consisted of Ted Cleghorn and all the drivers involved with the previous Morris Oxford record, namely racing driver Jack Sears, Oliver Sear the managing director of the Snetterton Circuit, and Dennis Allen, the motoring correspondent of the *Eastern Evening News* newspaper who wrote as 'Conrod'. They all tested Ted Cleghorn's Morgan Plus Four RVF 142 at the circuit on Tuesday May 3rd, easily exceeding the 60 mph lap speed they required for the record. The attempt on the record was booked for Saturday and Sunday June 4th and 5th, and Jim Goodall had agreed to be pit manager and bring a works car for the event.

The record attempt was due to start at 3 pm on the Saturday, but was delayed by 90 minutes whilst the local fire brigade pumped recent rainfall flooding away from 'The Esses'. It was sponsored by the *Eastern Evening News* newspaper, the Morgan Motor Company, National Benzole Ltd (petrol) and the Dunlop Rubber Company (tyres). Jack Sears began the attempt, soon lapping the blue works Morgan (thought to have been HUY 982) at 70 mph, until flagged down to lap at the planned 65 mph. Jack's very first sports car in 1948 had been a Morgan so he was immediately at home. After two hours Oliver Sear took over for his 48 lap (two hours) stint and then Ted Cleghorn for his. By now it was dark. Conrod (Dennis Allen) then took over for his stint after Ted had done his 48 laps, but disaster struck on the 161st lap when he lost his steering and there was a shower of sparks from under the front of the car. Luckily Dennis was able to stop without mishap. Jim Goodall quickly assessed the damage, finding a steering arm had fractured, allowing the track rod to hit the ground and hence make the sparks. Despite the drivers wanting to replace the stub axle with one taken from one of the other Morgans present the attempt was abandoned, for Jim Goodall pointed out that this was likely to take some three hours. Until this mishap the Morgan had covered 390.24 miles at 65.2 mph, using fuel at 23.7 mpg. Following this the group inquired of Peter Morgan if another attempt could be arranged and Peter Morgan agreed, deciding he would be the pit manager this time. The track was then booked for Saturday and Sunday July 23rd and 24th.

That same weekend, June 4th and 5th, the BARC Yorkshire Centre ran a full weekend at Scarborough with the Scarborough Rally on the Saturday and the Wilson Trophy Trial on the Sunday. The rally had only short road sections, the main feature being the driving tests. Despite, or because of, the heavy rain the winner was Alan Walker in his Plus Four, whilst Ernie Sneath won Class 8 and was a member of the winning 'Normids' team (presumably indicating it was from the North Midlands MC). Peter Reece hit a pylon on Test 6, ruining his chances.

On Sunday June 5th D J H Donovan won the Haslemere MC 'Mini-Rally' with his Morgan.

The Bedford Auto Enthusiasts' Club also ran its first autocross that day, at Wendy near Cambridge, with victory going to the TR2 engined Plus Four of Alf Thomas, with Richard Colton second in KYS 777. Another autocross was run the same day at Dunstable by the Sporting Owner Drivers' Club, the unlimited sports car class being won on his last run by Sandy Blair in Nixie, with P Norgard third in NYP 452, behind an Allard.

The Le Mans 24 Hour Race was run from 4 pm on Saturday June 11th to 4 pm Sunday June 12th. It was always a popular event for motoring enthusiasts, but this year it hit the headlines for a far more tragic reason. After just two and a half hours of racing Pierre Levegh driving a Mercedes Benz 300SLR hit the rear of Lance Macklin's Austin Healey 100S. The Mercedes became airborne, hit an earth bank, landed amongst the spectators and exploded. Eighty-two spectators and Pierre himself were killed, with even more being injured. The whole world was horrified and many countries took urgent steps to make sure a repeat of the accident couldn't happen there. Several immediately banned motor racing, including France, Spain, Mexico and Switzerland, the latter's ban still being in operation today. The forthcoming French Grand Prix was one of several cancelled and Mercedes Benz announced they were pulling out of motor racing. In England the governing body of motor sport, the RAC, announced the imposition of new safety measures to prevent wayward cars hitting spectators, and all racing venues had to comply. Some of the smaller ones, such as Castle Combe, found these too expensive to implement, and motor racing ceased there for several years (motorcycle racing was unaffected).

Derek Howard had been intending to compete in the Alpine Rally in July, but as this was cancelled too he married Kath instead.

The Morgan factory began to phase out the trunnion mounting for the rear springs in late June, when the four-seater Plus Four coupé, chassis number 3307, was fitted with rubber bushed spring shackles instead. Armstrong shock absorbers also began to replace the Girlings as from chassis number 3313, with the rears being of the lever arm type.

On Saturday June 19th, several Morgans were at Shelsley Walsh for the MAC's hill climb. From the Morgan factory came the entries of Peter Morgan and Jim Goodall, presumably in KUY 387 and HUY 982 respectively. John Moore was entered in NAB 217, which had been back to the Morgan factory on Monday June 13th for a lower ratio back axle to be fitted (given as 4.7 in the car's factory service card, but more likely to have been 4.56 to 1, as 4.7 was not a production item for the 3HA axle). It had also received new tyres, and had the radiator repaired. Also competing in TR2 engined Plus Fours were Mrs Ward and John McKechnie. John McKechnie's family were involved with George Hopkins' garage at Ledbury. His two-seater was chassis number 3270, dispatched to Hopkins' garage on April 7th. It was green, with leather upholstery, fitted with TR2 engine TS3608 and registered MVJ 101. Fastest of the Morgans by a long way was Peter Morgan, recording 48.57 seconds, the closest of the others being John Moore with 50.49, but this was two seconds faster than the other Morgans, suggesting the new rear axle was of some value.

The Plymouth MC's tenth annual National Rally was held over the weekend of June 25th and 26th. There were six starting points: Plymouth, Bristol, Ilfracombe, Salisbury, Virginia Water and Birmingham, the routes becoming identical from Bridgwater. Several of the top Morgan drivers were competing, including Dr John Spare in TYA 1, Tiny Lewis in THY 60, and Les Yarranton. The event was won by the remarkable 750cc Renault 4CVs, with Tiny Lewis being best of the Morgans and the winner of the Bristol Start Award. Jim Banbury made best time in the final tests in JJY 221. Monty Rogers had an eventful rally in PLB 111. He was going 'great guns' on a clear stretch of road approaching Dorchester when a tractor with a trailer laden with straw bales pulled out of a field and then into his path as it attempted a turn into another field. Monty desperately tried cadence braking, but hit the trailer, luckily at quite low speed. Unfortunately the Morgan was not built for frontal impacts, and a garage in Dorchester was required for temporary repairs to render the Morgan driveable again. It was returned to the Morgan factory for a new chassis and further repairs. The farmer admitted his liability for the accident.

The Westmorland MC ran a Summer Regularity Trial for cars and motorcycles on Sunday July 3rd. C Hall proved the victor with his Plus Four. That same day a National hill climb was held at Catterick barracks, with Yvonne Jackson from Thorner near Leeds proving to be the fastest lady driver in her TR2 engined Plus Four. Her Morgan was chassis number 3167, painted red with red upholstery, and she had purchased it new from her local agent H R Martindale in Leeds on September 23rd 1954. It had been twice returned to the Morgan factory this year (February and March) for accident repairs.

The 750 MC's Six Hour Relay Race was very popular with car clubs, and for the event held on Saturday July 9th the Morgan 4/4 Club entered no less than three teams! Once again there was a team of Austin Healeys, driven by club members Gerry Corbett, David Scott, Gordon Stratton, R Tucker and Geoff White, the team manager being Dick Pritchard. This team had ten credit laps over the scratch team of Jaguars. There was a team of Morgan Plus Fours with 1991cc Triumph TR2 engines, the 'A' car being the red 1954 two-seater of W D (Douglas) Bertram from Scotland (MFS 374, chassis number 3180), the 'B' that of Jim Goodall (HUY 982), the 'C' that of John McKechnie (MVJ 101), the 'D' that of Peter Morgan (KUY 387). The 'E' was driven by Barry Thomas, and the final car, running as the 'F' car, was JNV 654 driven by Hugh Denton. This team had twelve credit laps, and was managed by Bill Parkes. The final Morgan team comprised Plus Fours with 2088cc Vanguard engines. The 'A' car was KUY 714, the driving of which was shared by Barrie Phipps and his girlfriend Angela Palfrey, the 'B' car was POP 560, driven by Ray Meredith, and the 'C' car was OWP 38, driven by John Looker. This team had twenty credit laps and was managed by John Pither.

John McKechnie's Morgan had been returned to the Morgan factory on Monday July 4th to have a set of wheels especially fitted with Dunlop racing tyres for this event. Ray Meredith had Cam Gears steering fitted to his on Tuesday July 5th. John Looker's Morgan was a four-seater, chassis number 3295, coloured blue and fitted with Vanguard engine number V697. It had been dispatched to the agency of H A Saunders Ltd in Worcester on Friday May 27th, and was unusual in having no louvres on the top of the bonnet. John lived in Pershore and ran a laundry.

As usual the race got underway at 1pm with a Le Mans start. It was a glorious cloudless sky. One of the first away was Hugh Denton for the '1991' Morgan team, who put in a very consistent first spell of one hour. He was called in, giving the team's sash to Douglas Bertram, who again put in a consistent hour before handing the sash to Jim Goodall. Jim developed problems with the front brakes, leading to several excursions amongst the circuit marker oil drums, luckily without contact, but he still managed to complete his allotted hour in good time. He was relieved by John McKechnie who ran off his hour without incident, handing over to Peter Morgan. Peter then gave the others a demonstration of how to do it, regularly lapping three seconds faster than the others had managed to do. He did do one slow lap, drawing an imaginary circle in the air as he passed the Morgan pits to show the reason! At this time the team was running fourth, just behind the Triumph TR2s and just ahead of the Morgan team of Austin Healeys. Barry Thomas was sent out for the final hour, but his lap times were slow and Bill Parkes finally called him in after eight laps when a TR2 hit the Morgan in the rear. As a consequence Peter Morgan was sent out again for the final time to the finish at 7 pm, having one more spin in an otherwise typically fast run.

The '2088' team had drama right at the end when Barrie Phipps lost a wheel on the very last lap when a front wheel bearing broke up and John Looker had to go out to retrieve the sash so that the team could be classed as finishers.

The winning team comprised various saloons (Fords, Volkswagen and Fiat), was named 'Tinlids' and had started with 41 credit laps. The Morgan

Ray Meredith driving POP 560 during the 750 MC's Relay Race at Silverstone. (Charles Dunn)

4/4 Club's '1991' team finished sixth, but beat one of the teams of TR2s which had had two more credit laps. That team finished eighth, just ahead of the Morgan 4/4 Club's Austin Healey team. Another of the TR2 teams finished third, one lap ahead, but had had three more credit laps than the Morgans. Overall the Morgan performance was very good.

No doubt the wider front brakes fitted to the factory cars were the talk of the club racers, for both John McKechnie and Ray Meredith decided they needed these on their own cars for racing, John returning his car to the factory for conversion on Tuesday July 19th and Ray on Monday August 8th.

The day after the Relay Race, Sunday July 10th, Hugh Denton took his Plus Four JNV 654 to Snetterton for the East Anglian MC's sprint meeting. He won the unlimited class for production sports and 'grand touring' cars.

On Sunday July 17th the Coventry and Warwickshire MC ran its 'Attelboro' Trophy Driving Tests and P B Bradshaw finished second to a TR2 in the open car class.

There was a heat-wave for the Aston Martin Owners' Club Silverstone meeting held on Saturday July 23rd. Once again the David Brown Challenge Cup was being awarded for a team handicap race, and several Morgans had entered. The meeting commenced with a half hour regularity trial, John Looker, Ray Meredith and Barrie Phipps all claiming First Class Plaques for covering twenty laps in their Vanguard engined Plus Fours, OWP 38, POP 560 and KUY 714 respectively. H E White completed eighteen laps in his Vanguard Plus Four for a Second Class Plaque.

The Morgan 4/4 Club had entered three teams for the David Brown Challenge, named 'Red', 'Amber' and 'Green'. The 'Red' team consisted of the three Austin Healey 100s of Gerry Corbett, Geoff White and Gordon Stratton and was given 3 minutes 50 seconds start over scratch. The 'Amber' team comprised Ross Lomax with his 4/4 JK 7381 as the 'A' car, H E White in his Vanguard engined Plus Four as the 'B' car and John McKechnie in his TR2 engined Plus Four MVJ 101 as the 'C' car. This team was on 7 minutes 10 seconds start over scratch. The 'Green' team comprised Ray Meredith in POP 560 as 'A', John Looker in OWP 38 as 'B', and Barrie Phipps in KUY 714 as 'C'. This team was on 6 minutes 50 seconds start. Each car from each three car team had to complete seven laps. This year the 1954 system

A hot day at Silverstone waiting for the David Brown Challenge relay race. Ross Lomax is on the far left, wearing a shirt and tie and crash helmet, by his 4/4. Alongside is White's 1952 Plus Four, with John McKechnie's car adjacent to that. (Charles Dunn)

of coloured panels on the cars had been replaced by the more conventional 'A', 'B' and 'C' suffixes to the team numbers. We do not have detailed results, but a Frazer Nash team won and the Morgan teams did not finish in the first three.

On Saturday July 23rd the new attempt at the 24 hours record at Snetterton was flagged off by Dr Ian Pearce, the chairman of the Sporting Car Club of Norfolk with 'Conrod' at the wheel of the blue works Plus Four. He soon settled in to a 65 mph lap and handed over after his two hours to Oliver Sear, after covering 130 miles. 132 miles later Oliver handed over to Ted Cleghorn. The heat of the mid-afternoon sun made the track temperature so high it began to melt and become slippery causing a couple of spins, but the engine's oil temperature remained low. Presumably an oil temperature gauge was fitted, but we can see no signs of an oil cooler. An aero screen was used on this attempt, whereas the normal windscreen had sufficed on the earlier one. We believe it was Jim Goodall's car HUY 982 that was being used once more.

The fourth two hour spell was undertaken by Oliver Sear as Jack Sears had not yet arrived, being busy on his Norfolk farm with harvesting, and by the end of Oliver's stint the Morgan was averaging 66.6 mph. As dusk fell Conrod again took the wheel for the next session, which was uneventful, apart from a brief stop to sort out the lighting dip-switch which had become stuck on dipped beam. Jack Sears had by now arrived so he took the first of the night sessions, easily maintaining the 66 mph average. Unfortunately when Ted Cleghorn took over from Jack the mist that had been drifting over the old aerodrome circuit began to thicken, and his lap times fell as fog enveloped the circuit. As a result Peter Morgan signalled Ted in, and Jack Sears took over once more for he knew the circuit well and could lap faster in these difficult conditions. Luckily the mist began to fade as dawn approached.

Conrod now took over but had the front near side brake lock up, sending the Morgan skidding through the marker tins. This entailed a twelve minute stop to file down the front of the linings of the grabbing brake shoes. The average speed at the end of his spell was 65.1 mph, but Oliver Sear and Ted Cleghorn in their next two hour spells

The victorious record attempt at Snetterton. The Morgan receives champagne from 'Conrod'. Jack Sears (behind the bottle) is talking to a hidden Peter Morgan. Ted Cleghorn holds a glass behind the car. (I C B Pearce)

brought it up to 65.6 mph. The final two hour stint was in the hands of Jack Sears. By now the silencer was holed, and oil stained the bodywork due to oil surge under cornering. Jack set out to improve the average speed, turning in one lap at an incredible 75 mph, which was very impressive considering twenty-two hours had already been completed at racing speeds. Eventually he crossed the line after the full twenty-four hours had been completed, covering 586 laps or 1,588 miles at an average speed of 66.25 mph. (Fuel consumption was 25.2 mpg. The front tyres were Dunlop racing, and had been changed after 12 hours. The rears were Dunlop Fort). Peter Morgan opened a bottle of champagne for the drivers, whilst the Morgan, after receiving its share of the bottle too, was given a change of engine oil!

That Sunday the fourth annual Bugatti Owners' Club inter-club hill climb meeting was held at Prescott, and several Morgans participated. The Morgan 4/4 Club had entered a team of Plus Fours with Vanguard engines, this comprising John Looker with OWP 38, Ray Meredith with POP 560, and Barrie Phipps with KUY 714. Hugh Denton with JNV 654 and Richard Colton with RYC 777 were in a Northampton and District CC team, and Tiny Lewis with THY 60 was in a Bristol MC and LCC team. Obviously the Morgan factory drivers were absent because of the Snetterton event. Hugh Denton was by far the fastest of these Morgans with 50.57 seconds, giving him fifth place in the individual class for cars between 1501 and 2000cc, behind an ERA, a Cooper Bristol, an AC and a Lister Bristol, and beating all the TR2s.

In the class for 2001 to 3000cc Richard Colton was fourth with a time of 53.94 seconds. Most spectacular was the second run of Tiny Lewis, for as he approached the 'Semi-Circle' the front offside wheel, complete with brake drum, left the car and decided to return to the paddock on its own, eventually colliding with the door to the ladies toilet, which luckily was not occupied at the time! Presumably a hub casting or stub axle failure was the cause. The handicap club event was won by the VSCC.

Another hill climb was held at Trengwainton on August 1st (Bank Holiday Monday). Jim Banbury took second place to a Lotus in the class for sports

Barrie Phipps corners hard at Prescott in July. (Charles Dunn)

cars up to 2,000cc with a time of 26.60 seconds. In the later unlimited class runs Jim improved his time to 26.34 seconds, and finished fourth behind the winning Lotus, Ashley Cleave's potent Morris special and a Dellow.

The West Hants and Dorset CC ran an autocross at Sway in Hampshire on Sunday, August 14th, using an interesting and bumpy course set in a field of stubble. Best time of the day was set by Tom Bryant, Joe Huxham's partner at the Bournemouth Morgan agency, using a Vanguard engined Plus Four.

On Sunday August 21st John Spare took TYA 1 to the Plymouth Motor Club's Allen Trophy Tests at Hemerdon Mine in South Devon. The seventh and last of the driving tests was a small speed hill climb, and John made the mistake of getting the inner wheels on an incline as he cornered. The Morgan rolled, trapping John underneath (no roll cage in those days) with petrol pouring over him. Fortunately there were plenty of onlookers to lift the Morgan off, 'before my next breath was overdue,' he told us. After the Morgan was back on its wheels John had to try and disguise the mishap from his mother whom the family had arranged to meet for a picnic. The Morgan was then gingerly driven back home as usual with two of his children behind the seats and one on mum's lap in the front, but with a flattened windscreen and a twisted chassis. John was luckily uninjured, although he was always to remember the severe pain caused by the petrol that had found its way into his ear and which took a long time to finally disappear.

Just before this weekend Peter Anton was pleased to learn from Peter Morgan that he could now borrow the prototype Ford engined Morgan for a few days and see what he made of it. He took it down to Goodwood on the Saturday for the Nine Hours Race, and the new Morgan attracted much attention in the car park. Peter then drove it back home to Bridgnorth via London, finding the Morgan a delight to drive and making the fastest time back from London he had ever done. He found the cornering and road holding to be superb. The following week he returned it to the Morgan factory where Peter Morgan asked him for his opinion. He told him it was an excellent car, apart from one thing, the gearchange, which he didn't like. Peter Morgan said it couldn't be changed now, and asked whether Peter Anton might be interested in a production 4/4 when announced at the forthcoming Motor Show. 'Yes please' was the reply, so Peter Morgan put his name down for one.

At the Morgan directors' meeting held on Thursday September 1st HFS Morgan confirmed that the new Ford engined Morgan would be shown at the forthcoming Motor Show. It was to be known as the Morgan 4/4 Series II. George Goodall submitted detailed costings of producing this model, and it was eventually decided to price the car at £450, which with Purchase Tax would bring the cost to £638.15.0. For the Morgan agents the wholesale value would be £371, some £87 less than the Plus Four with Vanguard engine. It was thought this £87 could be saved in the overall cost of manufacture of the new 4/4 compared with a Plus Four.

At the same meeting it was decided to discontinue production of the Plus Four four-seater coupé, which had not sold well (just 49 were to be produced in total, excluding two works cars). Peter Morgan always felt that the agents were wrongly trying to sell this model as a full four-seater, which it wasn't, rather than as just a coupé for two adults and two small children. The directors also decided to cease the practice of supplying agents with cars on a sale or return basis.

Whilst the Triumph TR2 engine was an excellent and economical design, many felt that by getting it to breathe more easily extra performance at higher revs would be obtained. The tuning company V W Derrington was long established and the proprietor well known to the Morgan Company, for Vic had been involved with taking records at Brooklands with a Morgan three-wheeler back in 1927. He manufactured a new inlet manifold for the TR2 allowing the standard twin SU H4 carburettors to be replaced by two

H6s, giving an improvement in the bore from 1.5 to 1.75 inches. He also added a balance pipe to the inlet manifold casting. A much improved exhaust system replaced the original and poorly designed factory exhaust manifold of the TR2. This new system had tuned pipes, those from cylinders one and four being paired together as were two and three before they united just before the silencer. John Bolster borrowed Vic's TR2 as fitted with these modifications, finding useful improvements in performance which he described in *Autosport*. Of course the Standard Motor Company was not unaware of how to develop the TR series of engines and had a new version nearly ready for production anyway.

The London Rally always attracted a huge entry, and for this year's event, held on Friday and Saturday September 16th and 17th, there were 454 entries in total. Several Morgan Plus Fours were entered of course. Starting from Leeds in the 'Experts' section were Mrs Yvonne Jackson, navigated by Mrs Leonie Kinns, Peter Reece, presumably in KNP 5 navigated by Barrie Davies, and Frank Dundas in PSM 508, navigator unknown. Starting from Yeovil were Tiny Lewis navigated by J Flook in THY 60, and Dr John Spare navigated by Mervyn Meredith in TYA 1. Starting from Norwich were Ted Cleghorn and his wife Mibs in RVF 142, and Mr Williams navigated by K Tomblin. Starting from London were many Morgan entries, these being P W S White navigated by D Donovan, A W Taylor navigated by A G Harris, L Jenner in NLU 620, navigator unknown, Romek Michalkiewicz navigated by E Clarke in TKT 100, David Hiam navigated by his father in NWP 776, and P Norgard (navigator unknown) in NYP 452. Starting from Birmingham were Barrie Phipps navigated by Angela Palfrey in KUY 714, Les Yarranton navigated by Tommy Thompson, Jim Goodall navigated by Peter Morgan, and Andy Polack navigated by John Baker-Courtenay in ECF 495. Peter Morgan had loaned his Morgan KUY 387 to Les Yarranton, whilst he passengered for Jim in HUY 982. All the Morgans were powered by TR2 engines except for those of L Jenner, P Norgard, Barrie Phipps and Andy Polack, theirs having Vanguard engines. John Spare, Les Yarranton and Jim Goodall comprised the Morgan factory team, whilst Barrie Phipps, P W S White and A W Taylor comprised the Morgan 4/4 Club team.

The event was tough, with 650 miles being covered in 26 hours, and the retirement rate was

Andy Polack's coupé at scrutineering at the start of the London Rally. (Charles Dunn)

Les Yarranton driving Peter Morgan's car nears the top of the 'Devil's Staircase' in Wales during the London Rally. (Les Yarranton collection)

high, no less than 196 being non-finishers. Jimmy Ray had won this event in two of the last three years, and he did it again this year, navigated by Jeff Dixon in a works Triumph TR2. Best of the Morgan drivers was Les Yarranton who won the Harradine Trophy for the best time in the driving tests. The Morgan team was second to the TR2s in the team competition, whilst Yvonne Jackson won the Coupe des Dames for best lady competitor. David Hiam recalled being amazed his father could tolerate being the navigator for his 18 year old son. He believes this was made somewhat more acceptable by a supply of pre-mixed gin and dry ginger that his father had brought with him and from which he regularly imbibed. The week after the London Rally David's Morgan was returned to the Morgan factory for a new frame front and front suspension springs. This was required, so David told us, because of his reluctance to slow down for the bumps on the rally route!

The Aston Martin Owners' Club ran the third United States Air Force Trophy race meeting on Saturday September 17th at the delightful Cheshire circuit of Oulton Park. It had been opened as a circuit in 1953, but had been extended for International races for 1954. It was a real drivers' circuit with dips and difficult corners throughout its picturesque 2.76 miles lap. The weather was fine but chilly for the event. Three Plus Fours took part in the second part of the first event, a half hour's regularity trial for sports and 'touring' cars, being those of Ray Meredith, (POP 560) John McKechnie (MVJ 101) and John Looker (OWP 38). There was a Le Mans start, which added to the fun, and the TR2 engined car of John McKechnie finished with a First Class Plaque for covering thirteen laps, whilst Ray managed one less for a Second. John also took part in a five lap scratch race, but the competition (a Lister Bristol and various Coopers and Lotuses) proved too strong.

One of the highlights for the British motor racing enthusiast was the Mid-Cheshire MC's International Gold Cup meeting held at Oulton Park on Saturday September 24th, sponsored by the *Daily Dispatch* newspaper. On the programme was the 150 mile International Gold Cup race for Formula 1 cars, which was being covered by both BBC radio on the Light Programme and also by BBC television. An excellent entry had been received with works entries from Ferrari, Vanwall,

Connaught, BRM and Maserati. Stirling Moss was to win, driving a factory Maserati, with Mike Hawthorn second in a Ferrari-entered Lancia. Stirling had won the previous year's Gold Cup too, but this time raised the lap record to 87.81 mph.

Also on the programme was a thirty lap race (84 miles) for standard production sports cars, attracting entries from four Morgan drivers, namely Peter Reece, Roy Clarkson, John Looker and A S Bubman. Only Peter Reece and John Looker actually started and Peter Reece had borrowed Peter Morgan's car, KUY 387, fitted with Dunlop racing tyres. The opposition included thirteen TR2s, with drivers including Johnny Wallwork, Jimmy Ray and Syd Hurrell. There were also six AC Aces, one of the works cars being driven by Basil de Mattos, six Austin Healey 100s, two being driven by Morgan 4/4 Club members Gordon Stratton and Gerry Corbett and a lone Sunbeam Alpine. During practice Peter Reece had some problems with grabbing brakes, but managed to correct these before the race took place.

The sports car race was held just after the Formula 1 cars had completed theirs and they had left a lot of rubber on the circuit, making it very slippery. At the start Peter took an immediate lead, but relinquished the place to the two Austin Healeys of Gerry Corbett and D Scott. These two ran away and battled against each other, whilst Peter played a waiting game. On lap 8 Gerry lost control at Old Hall Corner, taking off Scott, and both overturned, luckily without injury. This left Peter Reece back in the lead, fending off the AC Aces. At half distance Peter was 39 seconds ahead. He went on to victory in a time of 1 hour, 10 minutes and 47 seconds at an average speed of 70.21 mph. Second and third were the AC Aces of Bob Standbridge and Basil de Mattos, the latter being nearly one minute behind. Basil, who was a great Morgan fan too, later told us that he always thought that Peter Reece's Morgan would beat the ACs because the Morgan lapped two seconds faster in practice. At such a major and well publicised meeting this win was excellent publicity for the Morgan Motor Company.

John Looker had not gone so well, finally retiring his by now somewhat battered four-seater OWP 38 at his pits. His Morgan was returned to the Morgan factory on September 26th for a new front wing, a radiator tie bar and repairs to the hood.

The seventh Lakeland Rally organised by the Lancashire and Cheshire CC took place that same weekend, but the attraction of the Oulton Park meeting meant entries were down 20% on 1954. To appease the local population the Sunday run was omitted, leaving just the driving tests at Llandudno that morning. Ernest Sneath drove well in his Plus Four, finishing second overall to a TR2 and winning the Tom Leigh Trophy. Ernie's Morgan was now running with new front brakes and drums to the improved wider pattern, following an upgrade at the Morgan factory in August.

By the end of September two-seater Plus Fours were now being fitted with just a single spare wheel, the rear bodywork being redesigned by Arthur Cridland, the body shop foreman, to accommodate this. Obviously it was cheaper to have just one spare, but the need to have two spare wheels fitted with knobbly tyres for off road trials had largely disappeared anyway. Chassis 3361, dispatched on Monday September 26th, was probably the first with the new rear end treatment.

The Worcestershire MC ran an autocross at Shelsley Walsh on Sunday September 25th, in conjunction with the Herefordshire MC and the Morgan 4/4 Club. Fastest time of the day was set by Angela Palfrey in Barrie Phipps' Morgan, whilst John Looker took the prize for the fastest sports car with OWP 38. Barrie Phipps of course owned the Vanguard engined Plus Four KUY 714, but he had either just bought, or was about to buy, Hugh Denton's potent TR2 engined Plus Four JNV 654, Hugh now retiring from Morgan motor sport.

Another famous car changing hands was NAB 217, the ex-Jimmy Ray lightweight Plus Four, owned by John Moore. John had decided to buy a Jaguar and Ray Meredith heard that this special car was for sale, visiting John at Shelsley Beauchamp to clinch the deal. John had maintained NAB regardless of expense, and it was now green, with the original Morgan factory twin spare wheels rear-end reinstalled following accident repairs. Ray wanted to race and had realised that Terry Hall had originally given him bad advice when he suggested he bought the Vanguard engined Plus Four, despite getting a very good deal on POP 560. He now advertised this car for £600.

Ted Cleghorn did well in the East Anglian MC's Clacton Rally held on Friday September 30th and Saturday October 1st, finishing second in class with his Plus Four RVF 142.

The MCC organised a trial in Derbyshire for Friday October 7th and 8th. This was named the Derbyshire Trial, and replaced the previously run Testing Trial. Four starting points were used on the Friday evening, competitors starting at one minute intervals from Penrith, Norwich, Alveston or London. Rain on the Friday and preceding days made some of the hills treacherous, particularly Bamford Clough. Four Morgans had entered: B J Thorne in MLX 521, Ernest James in NYU 993, Jim Goodall in HUY 982 and P Norgard in NYS 452 but he non-started. None of the Morgans managed to climb Bamford Clough, but Jim gained a Second Class Award, whilst the other two gained Thirds.

That same weekend, on the Saturday and Sunday the MG Car Club ran the Weston Rally, with Tiny Lewis winning the Bristol Start Award in THY 60.

The Motor Show held at Earls Court from Wednesday October 19th to Saturday October 29th had several important changes to the Morgan range on show. The most important was the introduction of the new Series II 4/4 two-seater, the Show model being chassis number A200. It was beautifully prepared in ivory with black interior and special wheel embellishments. It was a most attractive car, and Peter Morgan rated this as a most pleasing body shape for a Morgan. This car, fitted with Ford 100E engine number 110046, had been tested at the factory during the week of October 10th, along with chassis A199, A201, A202 and A203. A199 was actually the refurbished original prototype now given a new chassis number to bring it into numerical order with the new 4/4s which were being given chassis numbers beginning with A200. It had previously been using the Plus Four chassis number 3242. The Morgan publicity for the new model gave the dry weight as 12.75 cwt, and described an eight gallon petrol tank and gear ratios of 15.07, 8.5, and 4.4 to 1. However, the instruction book for the 4/4 gives a back axle

The beautifully prepared new 4/4 Series II on the Morgan show stand. Jim Goodall is standing behind, to the left. The Plus Fours are to the right. (The Autocar)

ratio of 4.44 to 1 rather than 4.4, and gear ratios of 17.29, 8.91 and 4.44. The petrol tank is given as holding 8.5 gallons and the dry weight as 12.5 cwt! The back axle actually used a crownwheel of 40 teeth and a pinion of 9 teeth giving a ratio of 4.44 recurring. The road wheels were as on the Plus Four, but fitted with 5.00 x 16 inch tyres, one size smaller. A top speed of 77 mph was claimed for the little car, but Peter Morgan did not feel the car had sufficient performance to justify being called a sports car. As a result it was advertised as a two-seater tourer.

Also on show were several Plus Four models. Two were two-seaters, being chassis numbers 3361, which was ivory with green interior, and 3365, which was coloured Ming Blue with beige upholstery. A four-seater and coupé completed the exhibits, being chassis numbers 3362 (red with black interior) and 3364 (blue) respectively. All had TR2 engines except the coupé, which was Vanguard powered. The new single spare wheel rear-end treatment was shown on the two-seater models, and Morgan also announced the improved Girling brakes, Armstrong shock absorbers and replacement of the rear spring trunnion mounting with rubber bushed shackles. Whilst the two-seater Plus Four was available with just the TR2 engine at a total price of £844.0.10d, the four-seater and coupé could be bought with TR2 or Vanguard engines, the prices with TR2 power being £865.5.10d and £907.15.10d respectively. Fitting the Vanguard engine took £30 from the basic price of each model.

A new model was exhibited on the Triumph stand too. It was the TR3 sports car, derived from the TR2 and having increased power from the same TR2 engine, achieved just by fitting two larger (1.75 inch) SU H6 carburettors. It was priced at £921.19.2d, in basic form £25 more than the TR2 which continued alongside it. Obviously the increased power of the TR3 engine (95 bhp at 4,800 rpm, compared with the TR2's 90 bhp) was of interest to the Morgan Motor Company, although it was realised that this power increase was achieved at the expense of higher petrol consumption.

Also new to the British motorist was the latest MG model. The new MGA, powered by a 1.5 litre 68 bhp engine, was identical in price to the TR2 engined Plus Four at £844.0.10d. Morgan still made the cheapest 100 mph car available on the UK market, and with the introduction of the new 4/4 the Company also made the cheapest sports car too.

During the last week of the Motor Show the Chancellor of the Exchequer announced a change in Purchase Tax applied to new car sales, this rising from 50% to 60%, whilst that on commercial vehicles rose from 25% to 30%. This rise followed a tightening up of 'Hire Purchase' terms, and was part of Her Majesty's Government's plan to control consumer spending, and encourage exports. Morgan's strategy of producing the cheapest sports cars available on the British market was obviously a sound one.

On Sunday October 30th the Falcon Motor Club ran the Guy Fawkes' 200 Trial, using eleven sections in the Cotswolds. Four Morgans participated, of which the best was Ted Cleghorn's RVF 142.

Les Yarranton took delivery of a new Plus Four on Monday October 31st. It was chassis number 3369, and registered PUY 306. It was a red two-seater, with black upholstery, fitted with TR2 engine TS 7161. Before he took delivery he had the Morgan factory fit a heater. Perhaps he was getting soft!

The *Autosport* magazine in the issue of Friday November 4th printed details of a new championship it was sponsoring for 1956. A series of races of not less than thirty miles distance were planned for production sports cars, specifically excluding the sports-racing cars built just for racing which had been pushing the cheaper production ones out of the awards in motor sport. Four classes were planned, Class I for cars up to 1,200cc, Class II for cars from 1,201 to 1,500cc, Class III for cars from 1,501 to 2,500cc, and Class IV for those over this engine size.

The new Morgan 4/4 was placed in Class I and the Plus Four in Class III.

A certain amount of tuning was to be permitted, thus engines could have modified or proprietary heads, providing the compression ratio increase did not exceed 10% of the original manufacturer's figure. Valve springs were unrestricted, but valves could only be replaced by others listed by the manufacturers. Only standard camshafts could be fitted, and twin carburettors were allowed for side valve engines under 1,200cc (this including the Ford engined 4/4) but otherwise no change in the number was permitted. Choke sizes were unrestricted but twin-choke carburettors counted as two carburettors. The gearbox had to contain standard ratios, but the back axle could have alternative manufacturers' listed ratios, but not limited slip or locked differentials. Road springs had to be standard, but any shock absorber was acceptable. The aim was to keep the cost of competing in the series reasonable for the ordinary clubman. It would have better suited the TR2 engined Plus Four drivers if the Class III limit had been 2,000cc, but apart from that it was an attractive series and John McKechnie was certainly interested.

The Blackpool and Fylde Club ran its annual 'Rally Driving Tests' at Blackpool on Saturday November 5th, devising seven different tests for the best rally drivers to attempt, and the event continued on the Sunday with the inter-area team challenge match. It was bitterly cold on the Saturday and this year none of the Morgan drivers was victorious, Peter Reece having his transmission fail during the 'scissors test' in KNP 5. The only Morgan driver to feature in the awards was Les Yarranton, who was a member of the victorious Hagley and District LCC team (along with a Ford and a Dellow) in the team competition. On the Sunday the Midlands area won the challenge match.

That same Sunday Barrie Phipps put up the best performance in the Evesham AC's driving tests.

At the Morgan Motor Company directors' meeting held on November 9th HFS Morgan reported back on the Motor Show. He reported that the new 4/4 Series II had created great interest and been well received, with 66 written orders received since the beginning of the show. There was however no great interest from export buyers, the Plus Four still being the favoured model overseas. There appears to have been a problem with supplies of side-screens, hood frames, windscreens etc for the new 4/4, but HFS stated his eventual aim was that the Company should produce no less than four 4/4s per week.

However, it was some time before any more 4/4s were made and indeed after the sale of A200 to Basil Roy Ltd after the show, no more were to be dispatched until May 1956!

George Goodall also mentioned production problems from the sheet metal shop at the directors' meeting, and suggested production would be much improved if the front cowls were subcontracted elsewhere.

The fifth annual MCC National Rally began on Thursday November 10th. This year it was un-sponsored and received fewer entries than usual, just 221 cars starting. As usual several starting points were available, these being London, Kenilworth, Taunton, Cardiff, Norwich, Glasgow and Manchester. There were lots of Morgans entered. Starting from Kenilworth was the Morgan team which consisted of Peter Morgan, navigated by Ralph Stokes in KUY 387, Jim Goodall navigated by Graham Stallard in HUY 982 and Les Yarranton navigated by Tommy Thompson in PUY 306. Also starting from Kenilworth was the Morgan 4/4 team, which was made up of three crews of Morgan 4/4 Club members. These were Sandy Blair navigated by C Weir in Nixie, an all ladies crew of Angela Palfrey and Aileen Jervis, probably in KUY 714, and Barrie Phipps navigated by Robin Butterell in JNV 654. Completing the Kenilworth Morgans was Stan Keen navigated by L Lord in the former's Vanguard engined Plus Four HDY 603. Stan's Morgan was an ivory two-seater with green upholstery, chassis number 3198.

Starting from Taunton was Doc Spare navigated by Mervyn Meredith in TYA 1. The Neil sisters were entered from Glasgow but non-started in KYS 41, as did J and V Holmes who were entered to start from Manchester in

Morgan Sports Cars — 1955

Peter Morgan and Ralph Stokes at Hastings during the MCC Rally. Behind, Tommy Thompson is seen adjacent to Les Yarranton's new Morgan. (Morgan Motor Co collection)

their TR engined Plus Four. There was one family crew in a TR engined Plus Four starting from Manchester, this being Mr and Mrs J Carefoot, but they retired early on.

The routes from the various starts converged at Harrogate and then covered the North of England followed by Wales before making for the finish at Hastings some 48 hours and 1,200 miles later. As was usual with MCC rallies the road section was thoroughly route-carded, making life easy for the crews with no complex navigation to unravel, and as a result some 86 arrived un-penalised at the finish.

There were nine driving tests to determine the winners, five held en route and four at Hastings. Sadly for the Morgan team Jim Goodall broke a half shaft during Test 5, a flat out forward and reverse test at Eppynt. Sandy Blair retired shortly afterwards too, whilst Barrie Phipps was over the time limit at the Cirencester control. The overall winner was decided by the car exceeding by the greatest margin the average penalties (ie time in minutes to do the tests) of the best 50% in that class. It was to be Freeman's pre-war MG TA that was declared the winner, with John Spare, the best of the Morgans, in equal 24th place.

Many felt the moral victor was the one with least penalty points overall, irrespective of the class average, and here the Morgans really scored, for first was John Spare, with Les Yarranton second and Peter Morgan third. Indeed the MCC recognised this interpretation and awarded the cup for the competitor losing the least number of penalty points to John. He obviously won the class for open cars from 1,300cc to 2,600cc too, with Les second and Peter third. John was not finished with awards yet, for he also won the Starting Control Award for Taunton and the MCC Members' Award. Poor John, who had already packed his Morgan ready to return home, now found himself embarrassed and overwhelmed by the amount of silverware he somehow had to find stowage space for in the Morgan!

Les Yarranton took the Starting Control Award for Kenilworth, whilst Angela Palfrey took the Kenilworth Ladies' Starting Control Award. She also won the rally's overall Ladies' Award. It had been an excellent rally for Morgans.

On Sunday November 13th Dick Pritchard took home a First Class Award from the Nottingham Sports Car Club's Autumn Trial, driving his Le Mans Replica 4/4 KPH 486.

There was great sadness in the British motoring world when the deaths in a road accident of Peter Reece and his navigator Barry Davies were reported over the weekend of November 19th and 20th. Peter had been a most popular and brilliant driver. He had made a major contribution to the success of Morgans, and was to be badly missed. His ex-John Moore coupé KNP 5 was to pass to Edgar Cubley. The same weekend in Scotland the Kilmarnock CC ran the Dunlop Rally, with Tony Cochrane from East Kilbride setting the fastest time in the open class driving his TR2 engined Plus Four.

The Herefordshire MC ran a night navigation rally over the night of Saturday November 26th. The outright winner proved to be Les Yarranton with his Plus Four. The following Wednesday, November 30th, Les Yarranton returned PUY 306 to the Morgan factory to have the gearbox replaced and for a general check over. He was only charged half of the labour cost!

Hugh Denton and Richard Colton organised the Morgan 4/4 Club's fifth annual Night Rally on Saturday 3rd December. Luton and Evesham were the alternative starting places for the 44 entrants, the routes converging in Northamptonshire where they were scrutineered and sent on their way again at minute intervals from 12.50 am onwards. After 250 miles the competitors returned to Weston Fowell with just three still un-penalised, these being Harold Rumsey in a TR2, Barrie Phipps in the ex-Denton Plus Four JNV 654 and J Shove in a Renault. The deciding driving test gave victory to Harold Rumsey from Barrie by 0.4 seconds, thereby winning the Morgan Cup, whilst Barrie collected the Committee's Cup. These two were now not eligible for the class awards, so Ted Cleghorn was upgraded to finish second behind another TR2 in the open cars class, 1,501cc to 2,000cc, whilst Tiny Lewis finished second to a Jaguar XK 120 in the similar class for cars over 2,000cc.

The British Trial Drivers' Association announced the winners of its rally competitions at its annual dinner and awards presentation at the St Nicholas Hotel at Scarborough on December 17th. There had been 40 entrants for the Gold Star competition, with the best five out of seven nominated events counting. The winner was John Waddington, who rallied a TR2, with 66 points, but four points behind in second place was Les Yarranton. John Spare was fourth with 38 and Peter Morgan fifth with 23. In the Silver Star competition, with the best six of eight nominated

Les Yarranton at the Morgan 4/4 Club's Night Rally. Barrie Phipps' cup winning Morgan is partly visible behind. (Les Yarranton collection)

Morgan Sports Cars — 1955

events to count, Ernie Sneath was the best of the 38 entrants with 120 points, just beating John Waddington by three points. Fifth was PWS White with 75.

At the Morgan directors' meeting held on Wednesday December 21st Peter Morgan reported that it was hoped to start production of the 4/4 Series II in the New Year. George Goodall reported that there had been problems for Morgan in obtaining supplies of the new TR3 engine for the Plus Four. To sort this out he had visited the Standard Motor Company in Coventry, and was pleased to report they had now agreed to supply four engines per week throughout the year. He commented that he thought the reluctance to supply this engine was due to the successes of the current Plus Four in motor sport.

The directors noted that there could be clearance problems under the bonnet with the wider carburettors on the TR3 engine, but HFS Morgan felt sure these could be overcome without upsetting the general appearance of the car. HFS Morgan also reported that he had had further discussions with the Ford Motor Company about a possibility of using a Ford engine to replace the TR3. HFS was aware that the Ford Motor Company was about to introduce a new enlarged Ford Consul (Mark II or 204E), which was powered by a bigger version of the current Consul's ohv four cylinder engine. In its

Dave Warren winning the Kimber Trial. (Dave Warren collection)

new capacity of 1,703cc (82.5 x 79.5mm bore and stroke), the engine put out a respectable 59 bhp at 4,400 rpm, with maximum torque of 91 lb.ft. at 2,300 rpm. This car was to be introduced in February 1956.

George Goodall informed the directors that the Bradford agency, Lamberts, was in liquidation. He had visited to find out the situation regarding the three Morgans held by the firm.

The first TR3 engine fitted by Standards to its sports car had been TS 8997E, and from TS 9095E onwards replaceable camshaft bearings were introduced as standard.

Twenty-seven competitors took part in the MG Car Club's Kimber Trophy Trial held on Boxing Day. The trial began with four tests in Coles Quarry at Backwell in Somerset, where the unsuitability of the new MGA and the TR2 for trials was soon obvious. Then the competitors moved to Naish Hill, where rain and mud contrived to prevent many from even reaching the last two observed sections. Once again it was a Morgan that won this annual event, this time being the Plus Four of Dave Warren, MYP 802.

The second British Racing and Sports Car Club Boxing Day meeting went ahead in appalling weather, with heavy rain and strong winds. The last race was the Martini Trophy, for sports cars un-supercharged of 1900cc and above. There was a very strong field, but no Morgan appeared in the main results.

France

There were 52 starters in the Bol D'Or 24 Hours Race at Montlhéry, held on Saturday and Sunday May 14th and 15th by the Automobile Club de l'Ile de France. The race was for cars of under 2,000cc and used a circuit of 8 kilometres. Just one Morgan was entered, the TR2 engined Plus Four of Hayles and Mainwaring. The race began with a Le Mans type start at 4 pm on the Saturday, and first away was the Hayles Morgan, leaving rubber tyre marks as it got under way. The circuit was terribly bumpy, but the little Morgan was running in eighth place in the two litre class after the first hour. Unfortunately the fast pace told and a big-end shell went, forcing early retirement.

The Automobile Club de l'Ouest organised the VI Rallye de Dieppe from May 21st to 22nd, and Roy Clarkson entered in VNO 600, but didn't finish in the top twenty-five.

Roy Clarkson in VNO 600 on the Dieppe Rally. The radiator grille is missing for this event. (J Appert)

The disaster at Le Mans on Saturday June 11th not surprisingly caused much reaction in France. The French Grand Prix was immediately cancelled, and the French Government banned all motor racing in France for some time. The Government went on to ban open sports cars from future rallies run over French territory. This caused much consternation amongst many British rally enthusiasts, and clarification was sought as to just what was permissible. After all, the Monte Carlo Rally was a major international event in the winter rallying calendar. Many felt this latter ban was an over-reaction, and of course it meant the popular trips across the Channel by British Morgan owners to compete in smaller French events were now unacceptable.

Scandinavia

The Oslo branch of the NMK ran another successful ice race meeting on Østensjø lake on Sunday February 27th, having postponed it once due to mild weather and unsatisfactory ice. The event attracted around 15,000 spectators on a fine winter's day. The snowploughed course was 1.65 kilometres per lap this year. Erik Hellum competed in a Fiat 1100 TV as well as in the Plus Four, coming second with the former in the 1001cc to 1300cc standard car class behind a VW.

In the 8 lap race for racing cars up to 2,000cc Erik won easily in the Plus Four, making the best time of the day in the process. The Plus Four was

Erik Hellum shows the others how to race on ice at Østensjø. (Harald Hellum collection)

running with spiked tyres fitted onto normal Morgan wheels.

The frozen lake at Jaren in Oppland County was the venue for the last ice race held in Norway in 1955. The race was organised by the newly established Hadeland branch of the NMK, in conjunction with the Fluberg branch. The racing car class was dominated by Erik Hellum in his Morgan and Arne Hindsvaerk in his Ford special, with the latter setting the fastest time of the day, whilst Erik scored several heat victories and was regarded as the day's best driver.

Australia

On the last day of January, Sunday 31st, (Australia Day) the inaugural Busselton Derby was run by the WASCC in the coastal town of Busselton some 120 miles south of Perth. A 'T' shaped circuit was marked out by hay bales on the runways of Busselton Airport. Arthur Littlejohns and Keith Lindsay both participated in a number of events but with little success.

John 'Cummo' Cummins, writing in the *West Australian Newsletter*'s 'The Filter' column in Feb 1955, reported on David Van Dal's inversion the previous November at Caversham. The article went on to mention that, 'now under way, one Morgan Special space frame F.I.D. body, 11 inch Alfin drums, Rudge wheels, four type 29 Amals with four exhaust pipes and a Waggott cam'. This is the initial and not quite accurate report of the David Van Dal designed racer for Bill Richards, which was to have been based around the wrecked demonstrator Plus Four. However the mess did not provide enough bits, most coming from another wrecked Plus Four purchased from Geoff Hawes through Ken McConville (long time President of the Australian Motor Sporting Club) in North Melbourne, late in 1954.

As we have previously mentioned, David Van Dal was a design and development engineer specialising in high voltage electrical and mechanical fabrication, particularly in the X-ray field. His father's medical supply business in the inner Perth suburb of Subiaco provided the environment in which he was able to transform his ideas into a range of unique diagnostic devices. However, an abiding interest in motorcars and how they could be made to go faster was a passion that remained throughout his life. With the backing of Bill Richards, David began work on a Formula 2 two-litre racer based on the Plus Four in December 1954. The special Morgan emerged after just six months.

The rear suspension of David Van Dal's racer. (David Van Dal collection)

The Plus Four's rather heavy and flexible chassis had been replaced with a highly rigid tubular space frame incorporating the original Morgan front end insisted upon by the Morgan factory, but widened by two inches and using Austin A40 stub axles welded to the Morgan sliders. Gilbert (Gil) Ford at Avon Industries (a tubing products manufacturer) in Bayswater (Perth) had fabricated three space frames for the racer, one being kept as a spare and one reportedly shipped to the Morgan factory in England. The fate of the latter is not known. Interestingly, a visitor to the factory from Perth has recounted seeing a space frame there, 'in a loft', in the late 1960s, but this has never been confirmed.

A Peugeot 203 rack and pinion steering was fitted, together with a fabricated steering column having a fifteen-inch sliding collapsible centre section. Locally made 11.5 inch by 1.75 inch finned, alloy brake drums based on those of a Fiat 1300, together with Fiat backplates, replaced the originals. The wire wheels were Dunlop 15 inch by 4.5J, with 5.50 section front tyres and 6.40 rears. Although the original Morgan rear axle was used, it was located by a parallelogram linkage and Panhard rod. The rear suspension was comprised of telescopic Armstrong dampers within coil springs of 50lb/inch neutral load.

As we have previously mentioned, David's idea for the Vanguard engine was to develop it as if it was four connected BSA Scrambler engines, each with a separate Amal carburettor (he chose 32mm) and a tuned exhaust pipe.

The extent of the engine development previously undertaken by David Van Dal on the original Vanguard engine had made him worry about the life of the big-end and main bearings, which he considered the weak point of the Standard design. Whereas the newly introduced TR2 engine achieved 1,991cc by reducing the bore (the cheapest option) David wanted to reduce the crankshaft and conrod load, so he reduced the stroke by 2mm, giving 1997cc. New unmachined crankshafts had to be purchased direct from the Standard Motor Company factory, and machined locally. The hard chromed crankshaft was cross-drilled for increased oil flow to the big-end bearings, balanced and polished and the big-end bearings enlarged (in width) to take silver-plated bronze-steel shells. Despite these improvements the crankshaft was still to be the Achilles heel, lasting only 18 hours of flat-out racing before needing to be replaced (at 20 hours it simply shattered at the rear web and the engine literally exploded!).

Early development of the Vanguard engine had been undertaken in David's 'Letterbox' Plus Four which had also suffered crankshaft-bearing failure on a regular basis and despite trying a range of bearing materials David was unable to overcome the problem. However, Bob Chamberlain had pointed out that the Hobourn Eaton double eccentric rotor oil pump on the Vanguard engine could fill with air and stay filled with air and not oil when the engine suffered oil surge. With this realisation a Holden sump was modified and the oil pump fitted into an inverted top hat that prevented air intake.

For the Letterbox Plus Four, which had only developed 108 bhp, this proved adequate, but David did realise a better system would be needed for the new racer, so the engine in the Letterbox had been further developed. Initially he used a gear pump from a Bedford truck, and fitted an oil cooler, made from a refrigerator condenser, to keep the oil temperature below 200 degrees Centigrade. On the Letterbox this was fitted below the radiator, behind a wire grille. However, for the new special a better arrangement was needed. David decided the best way to go was to dry-sump the engine. He purchased for £5 an external oil pump as fitted to a radial aero-engine, possibly the Bristol Pegasus, found brand new in its oilskin wrapper at Andy's salvage store in Perth. It was driven from the camshaft nose by chain at 1.5 to 1 reduction, and mounted on a special cast aluminium cam drive cover. The oil supply was held in a one gallon tank mounted on the bulkhead, feeding through a filter to the pump and then to a large oil-cooling radiator that was again a modified refrigerator condenser, before entering the crankcase oil gallery.

The cylinder head on the racer was modified to give a 9.6:1 compression ratio, and was copper-plated to help dissipate heat. David had used copper-plated heads on his earlier Plus Fours and felt they were a useful modification. High compression solid skirt pistons and a highly unorthodox camshaft were fitted; the latter designed by Peter Pugh, the camshaft wizard at BSA. They were ground by Bill Kirkham of Kayes Engineers, an engine reconditioning shop in Perth. Enlarged Norton valves or possibly BSA Gold Star 350cc 'Scrambles' valves, stronger BSA-type Federal valve springs, alloy caps with proper colletts as opposed to the double drilled cap system used by Vanguard, and tubular alloy pushrods completed the valve gear specification. The camshaft had the profile 38-76/76-38, with Gold Star 500 Scrambles acceleration ramps. This gave close to a 152 degrees overlap in valve timing and as a result the engine ran very roughly below 1,550 rpm. The camshaft was drilled from the nose to a depth of 5.5 inches to remove distortion occurring due to natural periodicity at circa 5,600 rpm, raising this point to 6,500 rpm. This same problem was solved by the Standard Motor Company for the TR2 engine by increasing the diameter of the front half of the camshaft. The ignition was from a Lucas Vertex magneto, 10 degrees BTDC Static and 38 degrees at 2,200 rpm. David didn't like the way the Standard Motor Company had loaded the vulnerable skew gear to drive the distributor, oil pump and rev counter on the Vanguard and later the TR2, so he took the rev counter drive directly from the camshaft via a motorcycle knuckle, mounted on the new cast aluminium cam drive cover for the oil pump. Dynamometer tests on the new engine gave an incredible 138 bhp at 6,100 rpm, held for 90 seconds, with maximum torque of 128ft/lb at 4,900 rpm.

When the gearchange on the Moss box proved to be difficult it was made more positive by the simple expedient of fitting a large solid brass knob. There were numerous other unusual features on this car, such as a lightweight aluminium flywheel and a hydraulic clutch from a Holden FX, which reflected David's skill and attention to engineering detail. Cliff Byfield in Perth fabricated the smooth, quasi two-seater body from aluminium. The all up weight with a full tank was 1486 lb.

As the '+4' badge could be easily changed to read 'R4', the 'R' being for 'Racing', the new special was so named. It was usually entered by Bill Richards however, as the 'BRM Morgan', standing for Bill Richards Motors. Involved in the project from the beginning had been John 'Cummo' Cummins, who now worked as a 'trouble shooter' for Perkins Diesels of Melbourne. That company's Western Australian agent was Comet Motors, of Jolimont, and much work was done there. Assisting was David Beattie, another excellent engineer, who raced a very rapid self-tuned Ariel Square 4, and Don Anderson, a qualified fitter and turner at a local firm of engine reconditioners. Many aspects of design and fabrication were considered frequently by these gentlemen with their sponsor Bill Richards, in the public bar of the Rosemount Hotel, situated conveniently opposite Bill's showroom at 416 Fitzgerald Street, North Perth.

The 3.125 mile circuit of asphalt roads around the lake in Melbourne's Albert Park had been used for the Australian Grand Prix in 1953, and was used again for the Moomba festival over the weekend of Saturday and Sunday March 26th and 27th. The South Australian driver Tony Innocenzi is recorded as competing there.

Tony Innocenzi returned to South Australia for the Port Wakefield Races on Easter Saturday April 9th, driving his ex-Gavin Sandford-Morgan Plus Four. The circuit facilities had been improved with a three hundred seater grandstand and permanent pit facilities. Tony entered the 'C' Grade scratch race held over eleven laps, but on the first lap whilst tackling the hairpin he ran into the back of Graham Hoinville's MG TC, forcing its retirement. The Morgan front end didn't fair too well either. He entered a later handicap event for fifteen laps for Grade 'B' cars, but was unplaced there too.

The local enthusiasts had nicknamed him 'Tony In-a-frenzy', because of his Latin temperament!

Morgan Sports Cars — 1955

The Victorian Sporting Car Club (VSCC) had built a 2.3 mile bitumen circuit around Cherry Lake, in wetland in the Melbourne industrial suburb of Altona in 1953. S J Thompson competed with a Plus Four in three of the races on the VSCC card on Sunday May 29th, gaining a second place in the Packard Cup, a third in the VSCC Invitation Trophy and a fourth in the Superior Cars Trophy Handicap for sports cars. It was at this meeting that Raymond Bridson rolled his Morgan-Vincent Special (a four-wheeler, built using Morgan three-wheeler parts), ending upside down in a lake, having lost control in a right-hand corner after negotiating the esses! Tony Innocenzi was at the Rob Roy hill climb on Monday June 13th, his Plus Four achieving 37.47 seconds on the hill but not being placed, whilst S J Thomson, in his Plus Four, recorded a time of 69.13 seconds at the Templestowe hill climb in the following month on Sunday July 3rd. The Templestowe course had been constructed by members of the Victorian Sporting Car Club in 1951, and was a challenging course, particularly at 'The Wall', which had a gradient of one in two and a half!

The annual Northam 'round the houses' races were held on Sunday August 14th. The premier event, as in the past, was the Flying Fifty race comprising twenty-four laps around a mixture of sealed and dirt roads in the town centre. There was a crowd of close to eight thousand and the organisers in their report to the Northam Car Club observed that, had everyone paid, quite fat cheques might have gone to the Local Police Boys Club and the Infant Health Centre. As it was they only received £100 each.

There were two Morgan Plus Fours entered, these being the TR2 engined cowled radiator cars of Bill Staker (1954 model) and Geoff Way (1955). Geoff, from Northam, had raced an MG TD for several years, tuned but still useable on the road as daily transport. Wanting more 'grunt' he had purchased a cream (probably ivory) two-seater Morgan, with red leather upholstery, from Bill Richards. This was possibly chassis number 3210 (ivory with red upholstery) dispatched from the Morgan factory on December 20th 1954. Geoff was friendly with Fred De Bonde, who owned a motor repair shop in Northam, and also raced an

Geoff Way at Northam.
(Geoff Way collection)

Austin Healey. He helped Geoff prepare the car. However, on the day, Geoff was forced to withdraw with brake failure and Bill did not feature in the results either. The victor was Syd Anderson in his Le Mans Austin Healey. Also entered for the Northam meeting had been David Van Dal with the R4. We believe, however, that the entry was premature, for the racer was still undergoing development.

The following month on Sunday September 11th, Geoff met with more success at Caversham, placing second in each of two events, one of which was the first heat of the WASCC State Sports Car Championship (over 1,500cc), on handicap. He also won both the quarter mile sprint and a Southport-style race organised by the Beverley Car Club later in September. Geoff recalls that the Plus Four had good power to deal with the competition he faced but that the Morgan's brakes were its downfall on the tight street circuits like Northam. In the longer races brake fade left him with little option but to slow significantly into the right-angled bends of the town's streets. At Caversham on the airstrip, with faster and more open corners, this disadvantage was minimised.

Also competing at that Caversham meeting was David Van Dal with his new racer, the R4, in its first really serious outing. He shared the driving with the experienced racer Noel Aldous. Despite Noel only travelling two laps of the Caversham circuit in the first heat of the 'State Championship for Racing Cars', the time for the second lap (1 minute 54 seconds) was close to those of the first three drivers (Maurie Maurice in his Chrysler Special, 1.49; Mick Geneve, 1.51 and Syd Anderson, 1.50). However, the next three meetings at Caversham saw the R4 develop into the fastest and most successful racing car that year.

Early on in the development a set of nineteen-inch, five degree, Lilley megaphones, suggested by engine guru Phil Irving, were fitted to straight exhaust pipes, giving a total length of 68.5 inches. As a consequence the engine produced just 20 bhp at 3,150 rpm but a shattering 80 bhp at 3,160 rpm, making the car completely undriveable, especially between the gears whilst cornering! The megaphones were not used for long!

After much testing the carburettor float chambers were found to be prone to produce fuel frothing, giving flooding at 4,500 rpm, so the system was to be modified with fuel level weirs, with a return pump to the fuel tank. The megaphones were replaced by straight pipes, each 87.5 inches long, with no attempt at silencing, peaking at 6,000 rpm, and the Amal inlet tracts were later to be increased from 9.5 inches to 16 inches, by fitting 6.5 inch parallel trumpets, peaking at 2,500 rpm. The whole set-up was very satisfactory, giving a highly driveable car, and only losing around 8 bhp at 6,100 rpm. The R4 was now really very quick, going from 0 to 60 mph in six seconds with a recorded top speed of 128.3 mph and a standing quarter mile of 13.6 seconds.

Certainly details of how 138 bhp had been coaxed out of the Vanguard engine would have been of some interest to the Standard Motor Company in the subsequent developments of the TR engine. Again, there is no documented evidence that these details were made available, or were used, but David remained sure that the Research and Development Department at Standards was kept fully informed.

At the WASCC Benefit Cup event on Sunday October 23rd Noel Aldous and David Van Dal shared the driving. Noel Aldous was renowned for his speed and skill in an MG TC and he placed the R4 third in a scratch race for racing cars over 1,500cc. David Van Dal then went one better, placing second in the handicap race for the Benefit Cup and managed third in the scratch section of the same race.

The Spastic Welfare Cup meeting the following month on Sunday November 20th saw Noel and David again sharing the R4; now painted in opalescent blue and with some of the bits chromed. Noel Aldous won the six lap racing car handicap and David Van Dal placed second in a three lap scratch race for racing cars. In the feature

Morgan Sports Cars — 1955

The engine of the R4, but with the Amals not yet fitted with inlet trumpets. (David Van Dal collection)

race of the day, the Spastic Welfare Cup over 20 laps, David had the R4 in front within the first lap when the condenser failed in the distributor and he ground to a halt. Despite these continuing teething problems the R4 equalled the lap record for the Caversham circuit (1 min 46 sec), signalling to others in the racing fraternity that they would need to improve the performance of their cars to meet the Morgan's challenge. Geoff Way also campaigned his now familiar Plus Four at this meeting but had some mechanical problems and did not feature in the places.

David Van Dal drove the R4 to first place in a three lap scratch race at Caversham on Sunday December 18th and then in the Christmas Cup, an open race for all comers, established a new lap record for the track and won the race. David's

The R4 in the paddock during the November Caversham meeting. (David Van Dal collection)

The victorious R4 after winning the Christmas Cup. The Amal inlet trumpets are now in place. Around the car, from right front wheel behind the car to the left front wheel are: David Beattie, David Van Dal, Sydney Van Dal (behind David), Don Anderson, George Wakeland, Bill Richards and Colin Uphill. (David Van Dal collection)

old rival Syd Anderson was second with his blown Le Mans Austin Healey but his lap times were four to five seconds slower than the R4. In winning the Christmas Cup the R4 lowered the fastest lap time by no less than an incredible six seconds and was clocked at 128.3 mph at the end of the main straight. This lap record was to remain intact until the Australian Grand Prix came to the west in 1957, when the Lex Davison 625/750 Ferrari lowered it from 1 minute 40 seconds to 1 minute 34.8. Jack Brabham's Cooper only managed to equal the R4's record in the Australian Grand Prix that year!

Whilst 1955 ended on a very successful note for Morgans, it was in fact the last year of the decade that there were exports from Morgan in England to Australian agencies. Bry-Laws were now concentrating on Jaguar sales, and Bill Richards had taken the last of some fifteen TR2 engined Plus Fours he received during 1954 and 1955. He was still continuing to promote the marque however.

New Zealand

The very first international New Zealand Grand Prix had been run on an old Second World War airfield at Ardmore, some distance from the nearest town of Papakura, on January 9th 1954 by the Auckland International Grand Prix Association Inc. It had been a very successful event so the same organization, now renamed as the New Zealand International Grand Prix (Auck) Inc, set about organizing another Grand Prix at the same

Morgan Sports Cars — 1955

John Moorhead in his blue four-seater at Ohakea. (John Moorhead collection)

venue in 1955 on Saturday January 8th. As previously, sports cars were allowed to enter the preliminary heats of twelve laps, the results of which determined the grid positions for the 100 lap Grand Prix itself. Six sports cars qualified for the race, these being three Austin Healeys, two Triumph TR2s and a Morgan Plus Four. Fastest of the Austin Healeys was the modified ex-Ross Jensen car driven by Auckland clubman Les McLaren, father of the soon to become famous Bruce McLaren. Ross Jensen himself was driving a much-modified TR2. The Plus Four was due to be driven by seventeen year old Tony Shelly from Wellington, but Tony had elected not to start. He reasoned that the eventual race winner, B Bira, would be working his 250F Maserati up to around 160 mph on the back straight and the speed differential to his standard Plus Four was potentially just too dangerous to contemplate.

During 1954 John Moorhead from the farming community of Bulls on the west coast of the North Island, not far from Ohakea, had purchased a blue four-seater Plus Four from Independent Motor Sales in Wellington. It was chassis number T3105, fitted with engine number TS 457. It had been dispatched from the Morgan factory in England on Friday July 9th. John had the radiator cowl chrome plated, finding it made the car look more attractive. This was something HFS Morgan was to do back in England on his four-seater coupé MAB 696 too. John took the Morgan to Ohakea on Saturday March 5th for the sports car race. We do not have the results but John advised us that he finished simply somewhere in the field!

The Otago Sports Car Club ran its hill climb at Patmos Avenue on Saturday November 19th. As in 1954 Ted Reid won the class for cars between 1,240 and 3,000 cc in his Plus Four.

USA

One of the most interesting, and certainly one of the coldest events on the calendar for the northeastern enthusiast was the annual snow race at Franconia in New Hampshire. This year, on Sunday January 30th, a one mile twisty course of packed snow at Lovett's Field was being used for the first time. Mike Rothschild made the journey north with his Morgan, and came back with a second place, following home an Austin Healey.

Good news came on Saturday January 15th when the Plus Four with the 1991cc TR2 engine was given Production status by the contest board of the SCCA, allowing the new car to compete in Class E for Production sports cars between 1,500 and 2,000cc.

This year Fergus Motors Inc was determined to have the Morgan marque entered once again for the international Sebring 12 Hour Race, for sports cars, on Sunday March 13th, having missed out in 1954.

The company decided to support two entries. One was that of previous Sebring entrant Mike Rothschild, who was entered with Dr Hal Kunz as his co-driver in a new TR2 engined Plus Four that he had purchased. The second entry was that of New York fashion designer John Weitz, who had previously been racing Allards, and already had the necessary FIA licence (Sebring was held under FIA rules). Joe Ferguson promised him a car and some assistance if he would organise the teams, so he contacted a friend, a Jaguar XK120 racer named Gordon MacKenzie. Gordon worked for IBM in Poughkeepsie New York and was well known for his Scottish ancestral eccentricity. He agreed to be one of the Morgan drivers, the third relief driver being Joe Ferguson.

To publicise their Morgan entries Joe Ferguson arranged for some photographs to be taken one Sunday morning in February outside the Fergus Motors showroom on Broadway. In addition the Morgan team captain John Weitz designed a shield-type cloth patch for the crews' racing overalls, containing the Morgan wings logo and the words 'Team Sebring 1955'.

The bright red Plus Four for John Weitz (probably chassis number 3244, with a 3.73 back axle ratio) arrived about 10 days before the event. The competition numbers were soon appended at Fergus Motors and a straight through exhaust system was fitted. John and Gordon, after sitting in the car, were concerned that the steering wheel was far too close to the dashboard for racing so the wheel was removed and put into an arbor press to dish the centre two inches. This allowed much better clearance for fingers.

Before setting off for Sebring, Gordon drove down to stay overnight with John and his wife in New York City for a planned early start the following day, at 4:30 am. The Morgan meanwhile was parked overnight opposite John's Manhattan apartment block on East 35th Street. Setting off the following morning the noise of the unsilenced exhaust reverberating around the tall buildings was such that Gordon was sure that they would be arrested, and this seemed all the more likely when they then entered the close confines of the Lincoln Tunnel connecting Manhattan with New Jersey. Gordon is positive that the police must have had them under observation but thankfully they left them alone, and let them continue on their noisy way south, on the 1,300 mile journey to Sebring.

The Morgan needed running in, so speeds were slow to start with, but following the changing of the engine, gearbox and back axle oils in North Carolina they began to speed up. They then negotiated forest fires, an unexpected hazard in Georgia, clouding the road in dense smoke and slowing progress. Eventually they reached Sebring where at last they could check-in to their somewhat rickety hotel and relax.

The following day a young mechanic and his bride contacted them, and checked the car over (he was from Fergus Motors), and scrutineering was then successfully completed. The Morgan was rather surprisingly running on ordinary white-wall tyres, a somewhat suspect commodity for 12 hours of racing, but it was hoped they would last the distance. Both spares were to be carried, and they had no other tyres available if they had problems.

Practice was uneventful, and so John and Gordon walked off to study a particularly tricky part of the circuit, just after the chicane. To their surprise they saw their own car coming through! They raced back to the pits to find Joe Ferguson allowing the Morgan to be driven by a prospective Morgan customer he had located!

Meanwhile Mike Rothschild was at the centre of much ribbing because his car was carrying race number 55. On American television at that time was a series about a police car, number 55, in which the catch phrase was, 'Car 55 where are you?' Wherever Mike went he was followed by that greeting!

Both cars received liberal application of masking tape to the front lights and wings to try and reduce the likelihood of stone damage. As always John Weitz made sure his car was immaculately presented, as befitted a top fashion designer!

John Weitz, being tall, decided he should do the Le Mans start of the race, with his other team drivers taking subsequent two hour shifts. With Sebring being an endurance race John was instructed by his colleagues to take the start gently to avoid mishaps. An aero screen was fitted to the car for the race with the normal windscreen folded flat. A seat belt had also been fitted for the driver. The race this year was to be run in glorious weather, further increasing concern for tyre wear, particularly the trendy white-wall variety!

The two Morgans both got away well, and settled down to the regularity of endurance racing. One of the excitements for the drivers was being overtaken by the top seeded drivers in the works Ferraris and Jaguars now being attracted to this annual event. Gordon remembers approaching a bend, being already committed to the line he would take, when he saw Mike Hawthorn's D-type Jaguar filling his mirror. Mike roared by, but then failed to take the next corner. Gordon drove on but then Hawthorn passed again, turning round to wave and gesture as if to say, 'Come on - see if you can catch me now.' Top drivers were always so gentlemanly especially when tackling the slower cars and this made the event such fun.

Gordon did have one 'moment' when he messed-up the chicane and hit the far kerb, throwing the Morgan into the air, but it landed straight so he was able to carry on immediately.

During the afternoon, as Joe Ferguson brought the Morgan in to hand over to John Weitz, the gear knob snapped off, leaving just a sharp spike.

Mike Hawthorn passes the Weitz Morgan, as they both approach the hairpin. (John Weitz collection)

John was to quite badly cut his hand during his shift, before he came in to hand over to Gordon MacKenzie for the final stint. Luckily Gordon was wearing double thickness leather United States racing gloves, and these helped protect his hand.

Leading Class E was the team of Arnolt Bristols which ran one, two, and three for much of the race. In the last few hours the Arnolt of Rene Dreyfus and Bob Grier slowed after developing lighting and brake troubles, and this allowed Mike Rothschild to move up to third in class. Behind this Arnolt, in fifth place, was the Weitz car. As the end of the race beckoned Gordon feared he would run out of fuel so he pitted for a further gallon. This meant that as he left the pits the fourth placed Arnolt, that of the great French driver Rene Dreyfus, was bearing down on the Morgan. Gordon managed to stay ahead to finish just a car's length in front, but it transpired the latter was three laps ahead anyway.

Mike Rothschild had managed to complete 149 laps to finish third in class, and John Weitz's Morgan covered 145 to finish fifth. They were 27th and 30th overall respectively, the winner being the Mike Hawthorn/ Phil Walter Jaguar D-type with 182 laps. The white wall tyres had also survived!

A slightly faded photograph showing Gordon MacKenzie with the Sebring Morgan. Note the white wall tyres. (Gordon MacKenzie collection)

The Mike Rothschild and Hal Kunz Morgan is prepared in the Sebring pits. (Ozzie Lyons)

John calculated the cost of the Sebring adventure at just $300, and even Scot Gordon MacKenzie was happy to contribute his share! Both Morgans had gone well, and both crews had uneventful return drives home.

The following month the annual Pebble Beach races were held once more in California, on Sunday April 17th. The Cypress Point Handicap for Production cars of over 1,500cc included two Morgans. In Class D was the Vanguard engined Plus Four of Dr. Charles Thompson, who was up against three Austin Healeys, one of which was to be driven by a rising star named Richie Ginther. In Class E was the TR2 engined Plus Four of Reg Parsons, a Texan living in Woodland Hills, California. He was competing against seven Triumph TR2s and a Swallow Doretti. Neither Morgan finished in the places.

There was a new name driving a Morgan at Thompson, Connecticut on Sunday April 24th, this being Gaston André, who was a dealer in foreign cars in Newton, Massachusetts. Born in Switzerland, he had settled in the USA in 1952 aged 25. During the winter of 1954-5 his business partner had told him of a brand new TR2 engined Morgan which had been involved in an accident and could be bought cheaply. It was suggested that Gaston rebuild and race it, and he agreed. The car was stripped and straightened and new parts purchased from Fergus Motors. By April it was ready and taken to the Thompson track. In practice it handled well, and Gaston immediately felt at home in it, finding he could keep up with much bigger cars. It only had one vice: the brakes, which faded badly. It was painted pale blue, and we think it was chassis number 3099, which was a Ming Blue car with red upholstery, originally dispatched from the Morgan factory on September 7th 1954 and fitted with TR2 engine TS 442. Come the races, and Gaston Andre managed an excellent second in class in what was described as an informal event.

Further racing by Gaston showed up a weakness of the new cowled-front Morgan namely the method of locating the bonnet, for it came loose as the cowl flexed and then disappeared over his head! Gaston thought this to be very dangerous, so he used a couple of trouser belts to make a temporary bonnet strap passing from both wings over the top of the bonnet. Returning home he went to see Adolf, the local belts supplier, and got him to make a good leather belt, with felt glued to the underside to protect the bonnet paint. This was then fitted as a bonnet strap, attached to hinges on each wing.

On Sunday May 1st Pete Peterson and Jane McBratney were in the places at Bakersfield, in California. Pete came third in the race for Class D, and Jane also had a third place, in the women's race when she was only beaten by a Ferrari Mondial and a Frazer Nash Targa Florio.

The same day three Morgan Plus Fours were entered for the ten lap Class D and E Production car race at the SCCA New York Region's meeting at Thompson. Mike Rothschild was in his navy blue car, John Weitz in his red ex-Sebring Morgan, still carrying race number 52, and the other Morgan was driven by Harold Ellis. Most of the entries were Austin Healeys in Class D and there was just one Triumph TR2 contesting Class E with the three TR2 engined Morgans.

Despite the lack of Class E opposition it was a great race, for the Morgans of Rothschild and Weitz were really moving, and Mike beat all the Austin Healeys (fifteen of them) to finish second overall behind an Aston Martin DB2. Unfortunately John Weitz got crowded out on one of the corners by an Austin Healey whilst running fifth, took evasive action and shot over an embankment, becoming airborne for a good six feet before returning to tarmac. The bonnet came loose and landed on John's chest. John then grabbed hold of the flapping bonnet and held it in place whilst he drove to the pits for a quick check for damage before rejoining the race once more. He now had to hold the bonnet in position with one hand whilst steering and gear changing with the other, but he still finished third in class behind Harold Ellis, completing a truly epic Morgan performance. John later discovered that he had broken three ribs during the flying bonnet incident. John wore a body belt while racing, following a suggestion from Stirling Moss in 1954, and believes this prevented further injury and allowed him to continue racing. John had actually already advertised the Morgan for sale in the newsletter of the New England Region of the SCCA, asking for $1,900.

Mike Rothschild was racing again two weeks later at the Cumberland circuit in Maryland for another SCCA meeting. The circuit was 'tight', of 1.6 miles length, with two right angle bends, two hairpins and four curves, one of which gradually tightened and overhung a frightening 200 ft drop into the Potomac River! Four Triumph engined Plus Fours took part, these being Mike's navy blue car, the pale blue one of Gaston Andre, complete with his new bonnet strap, the yellow car of Gunnard Rubini from Toledo Ohio, and completing the quartet was the Plus Four of Edwin Hebb from Detroit, Michigan.

They were entered in race seven which was of thirty minutes duration for Classes E and F, and from the start it was Mike Rothschild who led the way. By the end of the first lap, however, he had been passed by Andre, Hebb, Rubini and TR2 driver Jim Robinson. Mike managed to re-pass Robinson whilst Gunnard Rubini took the lead from Gaston Andre around mid-distance. Rubini and Andre then had a fine tussle for the lead, which was finally resolved in Gaston Andre's favour, with a speed of 58.2 mph. Robinson was third, Mike Rothschild came in fourth and Ed Hebb finished sixth.

On Sunday May 22nd, another new road racing circuit was used for sports car racing. It was at Marlboro in Maryland, just 15 miles southeast of the nation's capital, Washington DC. The group of 63 local enthusiasts, led by local dentist Richard Thompson, had contributed 50 dollars each to fund an extension of the southern end of an existing third of a mile oval, then in use for stock car racing. They called themselves 'The Lavender Hill Mob Racing Association', after an Alec Guinness film about a London criminal gang, and their financial contributions allowed the construction of a seven tenths of a mile circuit. The new course was successful from the beginning, and, despite a rather wet day, Chas Shinn managed to finish second in the novices' race in his Plus Four.

On Sunday May 29th the northeastern racers returned to Thompson. Besides Gaston Andre and Mike Rothschild, Benjamin Dane had also entered a TR2 engined Plus Four. The three Morgans took the prizes in the E Production race, Mike finishing first, with Gaston second and Ben third. This particular race was run in conjunction with the E Modified race, so the Morgans had found themselves racing alongside Maseratis, Arnolt Bristols and other sports racing cars.

The programme for the Cal Club's meeting at Santa Barbara on Sunday May 29th contained an advertisement for the new Morgan four-seater drophead coupé, and also introduced an additional Los Angeles agent named Ed Savin whose premises were situated on the eastern side of the city. Rene Pellandini was still the West Coast distributor of course, and he also continued to look after the western side of the Los Angeles metropolis as a dealer. His business had been renamed Worldwide

Gaston Andre chases Gunnard Rubini at Cumberland. (Sports Cars Illustrated)

Imports Inc, and had relocated to 1968 South Sepulveda Boulevard where he had a small showroom, an office and one closed work area. In the same premises, but separately operated, was the repair business of Norm Hitchin. He had previously worked for the former Morgan distributor Cavalier Motor Cars Ltd, relocating when they had closed. Norm consequently picked up some work from Rene.

Included in the programme were two Morgans, the Vanguard engined Plus Four of Dr Charles Thompson (who failed to start) and the red TR2 engined Plus Four coupé of Reg Parsons. The latter had loaned his car to Maxine Elmer, the wife of Briggs Cunningham. He was famous for his support of sports car racing in America and had built his own Cunningham cars specifically to tackle Le Mans. Maxine recalls that she had an interesting battle with Mary Davis who was driving the MG TF belonging to Hal Butler, during the ladies' race, in what was generally thought to be a rather disorganised race meeting.

One of the most fascinating events on the SCCA calendar was the annual race meeting held by the Cleveland Sports Car Club on the picturesque island of South Bass in Lake Erie. This was a genuine 'round the houses' race meeting held over a roughly rectangular 3.2 mile circuit around the town of Put-in-Bay. 1955 was the third year of this annual race which took place on Saturday June 11th. To get to the island the cars had to be sent by ferry, but the drivers and spectators had the option of flying in Island Airlines' vintage 1928 Ford Trimotor airplane to the island's small airport.

Because of the width of the streets, competing sports cars were restricted to two litres and below, and this allowed in two TR2 engined Morgans this year, one belonging to Edwin Hebb from Detroit, and the other belonging to Ben Hall. No doubt both drivers were pleased they could race without worrying about exceeding the 50 mph maximum speed limit in force on roads in the State of Ohio at this time.

Ben, who ran a refrigerated trucking business in Cleveland, had previously visited Fergus Motors in New York to try to exchange his tired MG TD for a new Plus Four roadster. Unfortunately Joe Ferguson didn't have a roadster available, but could offer Ben a red Plus Four coupé with tan trim. It was this car Ben had entered at Put-in-Bay.

The races had rolling starts, with the cars lined up in two long lines behind a pace car. Ed Hebb made a great start and was out in front for the first two laps, but then began dropping back. He failed to finish, and the race was won by Joe Bojalad's AC Ace. Brake fade proved to be a major problem for Ben Hall, and forced his retirement too.

On Saturday and Sunday June 18th and 19th the Cal Club arranged a one-off race meeting at Hansen Dam, using a 1.3 mile, narrow and tight course in the dam park within the City of Los Angeles. Dr Charles Thompson entered with his

Advertisement for the four-seater drophead coupé in the Santa Barbara programme.

Plus Four but the event was won by a TR2 engined Swallow Doretti. Taking third in his class with a modified Triumph TR2 was a tool and die maker from Whittier named Bob Oker. Los Angeles agent Ed Savin was now preparing a Morgan for entry into sports car racing, and he engaged Bob Oker to drive it. Bob had been racing for quite a few years, initially with motorcycles, even at one time professionally, but he had switched to cars in 1952 after his wife Ila complained of yet more of his injuries. He was tough.

The airport runways of the quiet little southern Illinois town of Lawrenceville made a 3.3 miles long circuit for the SCCA Regional races held on the weekend of June 17th to 19th. Sixteen thousand spectators watched Gunard Rubini finish third in class behind a Ferrari Mondial and a Triumph TR2 in a 12 lap race, and improve on this to second in class in the later 30 lap race. The Ferrari Mondial of Bob Magenheimer again took the class win.

On Sunday June 19th the pine covered slopes of Mount Equinox in Vermont were the venue for the annual 5.2 mile hill climb up the privately owned toll road of Dr Davidson. Gaston Andrey (his name now commonly 'Americanised' with a 'y' added) proved to be the master of Class E as well as beating all the larger engined Class D competitors. He was a brilliant hill climb driver.

Another new circuit was in use on Monday July 4th for an Independence Day race meeting, namely Beverly in Massachusetts. A 2.6 mile course had been laid out on the airport's runways and a taxiway, and some 30,000 people donated to the local hospital building fund in order to watch the racing.

The second race was over 18 laps for Production Classes C, D and E, and no less than 19 of the 34 starters were Jaguars. Gaston Andrey and Mike Rothschild were to continue their supremacy battle here with an epic race, eventually finishing in tenth and eleventh places overall respectively and first and second in their class. Many Jaguars were completely out classed by the flying Morgans.

Race 5 was a 30 lapper (78 miles) for D and E Production and also included F, G and H Modified cars, there being 37 starters. Once again there was a tremendous battle between Gaston Andrey and Mike Rothschild, Gaston finally passing Mike on lap 28. They finished fourth and fifth overall, behind three sports racers, but ahead of all the Austin Healeys of Class D. They were also class winners once more.

Mike Rothschild at Beverly.
(Alix Lafontant)

Mike Rothschild next headed south to the new circuit at Marlboro for the races on Sunday July 10th, and took a class win, finishing second overall to a Lester MG.

Over in California the Ed Savin Morgan Plus Four was driven by Bob Oker at Torrey Pines on the same day. (The Torrey Pines circuit was a marvellous one of 2.5 miles, using the roads around the coastal army training facilities of Camp Callan and being situated just to the north of San Diego.)

Immaculately prepared in a turquoise blue-green colour, and carrying race number 59, this Morgan was the Class E victor in the Production race, with Ralph Peterson sixth in Class D in the same event. In the main sports car race over 40 laps Bob again finished first in Class E, but was also classified third in Class D behind a Ferrari 750 Monza and an Austin Healey. Ralph Peterson completed just three of the 40 laps before he had to retire.

On Friday July 22nd Gaston Andrey was hill climbing once more - this time in Pennsylvania at the Giants Despair hill climb near Wilkes-Barre. It was a 5,700 ft course, with average of a one-in-eight gradient but with one section at one-in-five. Fastest overall was Duncan Black's Ferrari 375MM Spyder, and Andrey came fourth in Class D, just beaten this time by Edwin Hebb who was third with his Plus Four behind two 'gull-wing' Mercedes 300 SLs (Class E was combined with Class D for this event).

The weekend of August 13th and 14th marked the SCCA's annual Mount Washington hill climb. Newcomer to the scene was John, the younger brother of Gordon MacKenzie, who had recently purchased John Weitz's ex-Sebring Plus Four for $1500. He had fitted a straight-through silencer complete with a butterfly valve to control the exhaust.

Mount Washington was a formidable hill, with the temperature at the base in the seventies Fahrenheit, whilst the summit was often at freezing point. During the Saturday practice fog also blanketed part of the course, and John entered this just as he reached 'The Meadow', a long right-hand sweeping turn. He made for a gap in the fog and found himself on a small overhang with a thousand foot drop beneath! He reversed and completed the rest of his run uneventfully.

The night of Saturday August 13th was notable for the havoc wreaked by Hurricane Connie as it journeyed through the northeastern USA. Mount Washington did not escape, and part of the course was washed away making the hill climb impossible. The stewards therefore decided to move the event to an airstrip at nearby Berlin, New Hampshire (a flat hill climb!), where Gaston Andrey finished second in Class D behind the Mercedes 300 SL of Paul O'Shea. Theodore (Ted) Leonard finished 5th in his Plus Four, behind a couple of Austin Healeys.

On Sunday September 4th the northeastern enthusiasts moved to Thompson for an SCCA National meeting. The weather was perfect and a large crowd was present. Five Morgans were entered for Race 4, a 10 lap race for Class E Production and E Modified. These were the cars of Gaston Andrey, Mike Rothschild, Ben Dane, Captain Mike Ashley of the US Marines, and John MacKenzie. They were to battle amongst themselves for class positions together with an AC Ace and a Triumph TR2.

John MacKenzie was having a good race, running in the places, until just before the finish when he braked hard from 80 mph and turned into the 90 degree right-hander to find no response from the steering! The car just went straight on, onto an embankment and then shot into the air, losing the bonnet in the process, which luckily missed John by inches. The Morgan eventually landed safely on all four wheels and came to a very abrupt stop, for both front wheels were pointing outwards. A broken right hand steering arm was the culprit.

Meanwhile Gaston Andrey had finished the race victorious once more, and with a record speed of 64.56 mph, ahead of Captain Mike Ashley who was second, with Ben Dane third and Mike Rothschild seventh.

A rather shaken John MacKenzie had decided that his Morgan racing days were over, but he was still faced with the immediate problems of what to do with his damaged Plus Four and how to get home. The first problem was solved by a friend present with a trailer, who delivered the damaged Morgan to a garage for repairs. The second was solved by the generosity of Briggs Cunningham's son who kindly lent John his T type MG in which to drive home to Millbrook in New York State. It proved to be somewhat of a nightmare of a drive, for the MG's lights were temperamental, and the damage from the recent Hurricane Connie caused many delays with several floods and fallen trees along the way.

John claimed the cost of the Morgan repairs on his ordinary car insurance which failed to include a disclaimer for racing. The bill was paid but subsequently all his motor insurance policies were to contain an appropriate exclusion clause for racing! The Morgan was repainted Cadillac Eldorado grey and later sold. Gordon MacKenzie, thinking about the steering failure, remembered back to his own mishap with the car at Sebring, and wondered if the steering arm had been cracked at the time he hit the kerb with the right front wheel.

The California Sports Car Club also ran an event on September 4th, at Santa Barbara airfield. Ed Savin had entered Bob Oker once more, and Reg Parsons also made an appearance. The third race was for cars under 2,500cc, and Bob managed to finish fourth, the winner being the famous ex-Velocette motorcycle racer John McLaughlin in an Arnolt Bristol. In the ninth race, for all Production sports cars, Bob finished eighth just behind Willet's Arnolt Bristol. The Ed Savin Morgan was, as usual, prepared by Ed's mechanic Bill Binney and Bob himself. It is believed that the Ed Savin Morgan was chassis number 3128, originally a blue two-seater, dispatched from the Morgan Factory to Worldwide Imports on Tuesday January 11th.

On Sunday September 11th the SCCA ran a race on the newly reconstructed Wisconsin track, 'Road America'. Beautifully designed by Clif Tufte it ran amongst the rolling wooded countryside near the Village of Elkart Lake to the north of Chicago, close to the Canadian border. The four miles long circuit was one of the longest purpose-built tracks in the USA, and replaced an earlier 'round the houses' one.

Entered in a Morgan was Tom Payne, who ran a car dealership in Ypsilanti, Michigan, specialising in selling VWs and sports cars. He was purchasing Morgans from the Canadian agency of Windsor Motorcycles and driving them back the 40 miles over the border to Ypsilanti, where he sold them. As we mentioned before, the city of Windsor in Ontario was just across the river from Detroit and 'Curly' Ellis, the Morgan agent, was able to sell to enthusiasts based in the Detroit area as well as to Canadians. Whether Fergus Motors were aware he was taking their business is not known!

The second race was to last 45 minutes and Tom finished third in class, the winner driving a Mercedes 300 SL. The race of the day, and some said of all time, was between Phil Hill in a three litre Ferrari 750 Monza and Sherwood Johnston in Briggs Cunningham's D-type Jaguar, with future world champion Phil Hill eventually proving the victor after an epic battle of 148 miles of close and exciting racing.

For the Saturday September 17th SCCA meeting at Watkins Glen the interim track used in 1954 was still in use, and the event attracted seven Morgan entries, although one, John MacKenzie, had since withdrawn following his dramatic retirement from racing at Thompson. The usual northeastern racers were present: Gaston Andrey, Gunnard Rubini, Mike Rothschild, Edwin Hebb and Captain Mike Ashley. Also present was Ben Hall with his Plus Four coupé, travelling to the event from Ohio. The track seemed very slippery and there were spills a plenty in the early races; Gordon MacKenzie was lucky just to break his nose when he rolled his Jaguar. There was also quite a lot of oil on the course before the start of the Glen Trophy race of 50.6 miles for production cars of Classes E and above, so the race marshals liberally sprinkled cement powder on the corners to try and improve grip. Despite this the Jaguars and a Corvette had great difficulty in staying on the course, whilst the Morgans seemed far more stable.

Ben Hall remembers this event well, for the leading cars threw up the cement dust into an impenetrable cloud screen, the following cars therefore facing absolutely blind bends. Luckily the dust settled as the race progressed and visibility improved.

The race was won by Paul O'Shea from Rye in New York State, driving his 'gull-wing' Mercedes 300 SL, whilst Gunnard Rubini took Class E, in front of John Dowd's AC Ace. Gaston Andrey was third in class, Ben Hall fifth, and Mike Ashley and Mike Rothschild finished seventh and eighth. Ed Hebb failed to finish.

Gaston Andrey's impressive drives in the Morgan were achieved despite the major problem of brake fade, necessitating screaming down through the gears when approaching corners to scrub off speed. 'I thrashed my car mercilessly', he told us. After every practice session new brake linings would be fitted but still brake fade would handicap the Morgan towards the end of the races.

Another problem Gaston had found with racing was a worrying drop in oil pressure from surge or whilst braking. He and his pit crew were wise to this now and changed the big-end bearings after every meeting. They also drilled extra holes in the crankshaft to try and get constant oil pressures, but even this did not completely solve the problem. Being in a Production class meant little could really be done to the car except for careful preparation for there was always the fear of being reclassified into Modified.

Gaston's excellent drives of the Morgan were beginning to attract considerable interest, with several private owners considering asking him to drive their cars for them. His successes were also being noticed by the business community, which lost no time in using him and to advertise its products.

On Sunday October 9th Gaston was back at Thompson accompanied by several other Morgan drivers. Once again he was victorious, followed home in Class E by Ted Leonard and Ben Dane, giving a Morgan one, two, three.

By Sunday October 16th Gunnard Rubini, Mike Rothschild and Gaston Andrey were down in Maryland for a National SCCA race over a 2.4 mile course at the Fairchild Aircraft facility at Hagerstown. They were joined by the Morgans of Ed Hancock and George Parks in Race 3, a 15 lapper for Production Classes D and E, in which the opposition included Austin Healeys, TR2s, Swallow Dorettis, an AC Ace, a Kaiser Darrin and a Lancia Aurelia. In less than a lap Andrey, Rothschild and Rubini were in front of everything else and going away. Gaston then dropped to third, whilst Gunnard and Mike regularly swapped the lead as they disappeared into the distance, never more than a few car lengths apart. Around lap 15 the pair lapped Jim Robinson's TR 2 right in front of the start-finish line, and Jim's gestures to the officials left no doubt that he would be filing a

GASTON ANDREY WINS WITH

OILZUM

1st Class E, 2d Class D, Thompson, 4/24
1st Overall, E & F, Cumberland, 5/15
1st Class D & E, Mt. Equinox, 6/19
1st Class E, Race 2 } Beverly, 7/4
1st D & E, Race 5

As a top contender in Class D & E, "Gus" Andrey uses OILZUM *only* in his Morgan Plus 4. As President of Gaston Andrey, Inc., Newton, Mass., sports-car garage, he sells and recommends OILZUM *exclusively!*

For Name of Nearest OILZUM Dealer . . . and FREE racing poster for your garage . . . write:

THE WHITE & BAGLEY CO.
100 FOSTER STREET, WORCESTER, MASS.

Choice of Champions Since 1905
BEST FOR YOUR CAR, TOO!

protest! This he duly did, and later the white Plus Four of Rubini was found to infringe the strict Production class regulations and disqualified from first place. Mike's black Morgan however was found to be standard, so he was promoted to first, with Andrey now second, Ed Hancock fourth and George Parks seventh. This protest also altered the class positions of Race 6, in which Mike had beaten Gunnard into second place, with Gaston Andrey third. No doubt these impressive top-finishing Morgans were all fitted with the larger brake drums phased in at the Morgan factory on production cars from May, but still brake fade was a problem, when racing.

The California Sports Car Club once again used the excellent Torrey Pines course around Camp Callan army training camp for a race meeting held over the weekend of October 22nd and 23rd. A six hour race with Le Mans start was held on the Saturday. Two Morgans were amongst the fifty-five starters, Bob Oker with the Ed Savin Morgan, and Reg Parsons's TR2 engined Plus Four shared with journalist Jim Mourning. The latter Morgan finished in twenty-ninth position overall and was third in Class E Production, but was over forty-three laps (over 116 miles) behind the winning C-type Jaguar of Pearce Woods. Jim Mourning in his column in the Californian racing paper *MotoRacing* wrote that the Morgan finished with, 'highly wrinkled bearings!' Bob Oker was doing well in the race but failed to finish after bending back the front crosshead on a hay bale. As a result of this mishap Bob raced in a Jaguar XK140 in the following day's thirteen lap race for Production cars over 1,500cc. As the Parsons/Mourning Plus Four also failed to appear the only Morgan entered was to be the Plus Four of Rudy Cleye, who was sixth overall and second in Class E.

Mike Rothschild at Hagerstown, the Morgan awaiting eligibility inspection. (Mike Rothschild collection)

By Sunday November 13th the Savin Morgan was healthy once more, for Bob took it to a fine first in class in the fifteen lap over 1,500cc Production race held on the Glendale Grand Central Airport circuit. This was originally the main Los Angeles airport in pre-war days, but was now being turned into an industrial estate. This was the only time this circuit was used, surrounded as it was by the suburbia of Los Angeles, from which many complaints were received about noise.

On Sunday December 4th, at the Cal Club's Palm Springs meeting, two Morgans took part, the Bob Oker Plus Four and the Plus Four of John Watkins. In the Saturday six lap race for Production Classes E and above Bob finished sixteenth overall and took a third in class, being beaten by an Arnolt Bristol and a TR2. John Watkins failed to finish in his Morgan, having lost oil pressure. On the Sunday in the main race for all cars above 1,500cc over thirty-eight laps Bob was again sixteenth, but this time the victor of Class E Production.

Throughout the year the drivers winning National SCCA races had been collecting points towards the various class championships. A win in a National race gave the driver 1000 points, with 750 being awarded for second place, 500 for third, 300 for fourth, 200 for fifth, and finally 100 for six. Just National graded races counted, the top drivers therefore touring the country to race in these. The lesser Regional graded races were more useful for the ambitious local drivers who wished to learn more of the craft of motor racing before attempting the National races. With there being more National SCCA races held in the northeast it followed that most class champions were to come from that area, and so it proved with Class E where Gaston Andrey's 5000 points gave him a clear victory. Second was Mike Rothschild (2750), then Al Newton with his TR2 (2000). Fourth equal were Captain Mike Ashley, who was from Quantico, Virginia, and Gunnard Rubini.

Morgans had certainly done very well with no fewer than nine of their drivers gaining points in the SCCA Championship. 1955 had been an excellent year in the USA for Morgans.

Canada

A Ford Trade School pupil at Windsor was Don Broadbent, who regularly borrowed a friend's blue chrome radiator Plus Four for commuting. He gave Frank Boulton a ride, and Frank was hooked and decided he had to have a Morgan.

A batch of three Morgans was dispatched from the Morgan factory on Wednesday April 6th, bound for Windsor Motorcycles. They were all two-seater TR2 engined Plus Fours, chassis number 3257 being green with black upholstery, 3258 being black with red upholstery and chassis number 3260 being ivory with red upholstery. They were purchased respectively by Frank Boulton, Al Weed and Don Broadbent. When the Morgans arrived at the dockside in Toronto Curly Ellis drove the three new owners along to collect them. Frank remembers that there was a wooden cover fitted over the cockpit of each car which had to be removed, and then the hood and side curtains could be attached. The owners then drove the cars back to Curly's where a little servicing was done on the cars. Frank was only twenty years old and not really able to withdraw the purchase money from his bank on his own but he recalls Curly co-signed for him and all was satisfactorily completed. Frank regarded Curly as being a true friend as a result. Al Weed showed the others how to polish the combustion chambers, Curly generously letting his premises be used. Don was to experiment with a partial copper exhaust pipe and special manifold, which made a hell of a racket. His father worked as a mechanic at Windsor Motorcycles.

Don Broadbent tended to be quite an aggressive driver on the road, such that the other Ford Trade School pupils gave him the nickname of 'Broadslide'. He had the misfortune once to be stopped for speeding in a 50 mph zone. When the police officer approached the Morgan Don quickly countered, 'but officer it will only go up to 50', pointing at the tachometer. He got off with a warning!

During the Second World War Canada had played a major role in the training of allied airmen by setting up major training centres within what was called the British Commonwealth Air Training Plan (BCATP). This had been set up in December 1939 specifically for the war. Many thousands of airmen were trained in Canada at seventy-four training schools with two hundred and thirty-one sites, including a large number of airfields. After the War these airfields were no longer required, and as in Great Britain they became popular for motor racing.

One such was at Edenvale, near Stayner, west of Barrie. Al, Frank and Don all decided to enter the races to be held there on Saturday August 13th. It was a wet day. Frank had problems at scrutineering because of his young age and lack of parental consent. Al was able to sort this out for him, but Frank did miss practice as a result. From the start Al, who knew the 1.73 mile track well, was near the front of the field with the other two Morgans further back. Then a TR2 spun in front of Frank and Don as they were coming onto the start and finish straight. Frank went to the right, whilst Don took to the left, passing between a telegraph pole and its guy wire, and receiving marks on both sides of the Morgan as a consequence! Frank and Don then started to improve positions until Frank attempted to pass Don at a right hander, spinning and losing his position. Al finished best of the Morgans, possibly second or third overall from Frank's memory of the event. Frank's TR2 engine had developed a noisy big-end bearing, which he replaced at Curly's once he got home. A result of over revving he assumed. Not long after this race Al Weed had his car resprayed white.

Two of the Morgans at Edenvale. Al Weed's car is number 26, and Frank Boulton's is 24. (Bob Harrington)

Chapter 3
1956

Les Yarranton's Morgan PUY 306 was back at the Morgan factory early in January for pre-season attention which included strengthening of the rear axle U-bolt plates. He was preparing his Morgan for the VSCC's Measham Rally, to be run the following weekend, starting on Friday January 6th. This, the seventh Measham Rally, took the competitors overnight into Wales through rain, sleet, snow and ice before finishing at the Measham Motor Sales Organisation's premises for final driving tests and a welcome breakfast. There were 78 entrants, 33 of whom were driving vintage cars and 36 driving modern cars. One of the final tests was a jacking competition, with Andy Polack the fastest in his Plus Four coupé, ECF 495. Whilst others messed around with the primitive jacks supplied with their cars from new, Andy had bought a small telescopic hydraulic jack which was adjusted to be ready to slide under the front crosshead. Just one pump with the handle and the wheel was airborne and could be spun to comply with the test. It was completed in under a minute. Les Yarranton used a garage jack for PUY 306. When the results were announced Les Yarranton was the overall winner, gaining the Silver Cup whilst the vintage section was won by Pat MacNaughton's 1926 Sunbeam, these being the same two victors as in 1955! Andy Polack won the class for visitors' cars.

As Andy was training in engineering he was well able to improve his coupé. The lights were much enhanced, including adding a spotlight which was adjustable from inside to read signposts, and there were navigator's lights too. The Vanguard engine was now virtually giving TR2 performance, and was fitted with twin SU H4 carburettors on a modified TR2 inlet manifold. Plenty of tools and spares for most eventualities were carried behind the seats and between the twin spare wheels, but the rough treatment in rallies caused several rear spring breakages. In the end he fitted a set of locally made springs with an extra leaf. Extra-wide Town and Country tyres were used on the rear, and Andy remembers the Morgan was virtually unstoppable in snow or muddy conditions, and much better than most of the opposition, the weight of the tools and spares in the back also helping considerably. A Ford heater, sold as an after sales accessory, had been modified and fitted. Andy had dramatically reduced the wear in the front suspension bushes by fitting rubber gaiters over the rebound springs, these being cut from those used to cover motorcycle telescopic front forks. He mentioned this simple modification to Peter Morgan, but Peter replied that the Morgan factory saw little need for this. Andy had also experienced a fracture of a front hub, causing a wheel to come off the car complete with the brake drum, but thankfully at low speed. Damage to the front wing required the purchase of a second-hand replacement from the Morgan factory. Andy was surprised that the Morgan factory had little interest in this failure, but Andy's father was the manager of an ICI plant and he soon had his metallurgist investigating the casting, finding the malleable iron was too brittle, possibly from poor quality control.

As usual several Morgans had also entered the MCC's Exeter Trial, held over the same two days. The Morgan factory team comprised Jim Goodall in HUY 982, Terry Hall in the coupé JNP 239, which still had the Vanguard engine, and Dr John Spare in TYA 1. Tiny Lewis and Monty Rogers were in their usual TR2 engined Plus Fours, THY 60 and PLB 111. Tom Threlfall was in the ex-Jimmy Ray and ex-Ken James car, KUY 474, with the modified

Vanguard engine. Vanguard engined Plus Fours were also entered by the Hobbs brothers, Alan and Ken, and by B Thorne (NYX 521), L Jenner (NLU 620) and P Norgard, but the latter non-started in NYF 452, despite his Morgan having recently been overhauled at the Morgan factory. Alan and Ken Hobbs had both bought blue Plus Four four-seater coupés, registered LAK 767 and UHY 277 respectively. Alan's coupé was chassis number 3238, originally dispatched to Lambert Motors in Bradford in February 1955. Ken's was 3214, originally ivory, and had been dispatched in December 1954.

The south of Britain had been shrouded in a blanket of fog and smog for most of the previous week, but this luckily moved away north just a few hours before the start on Friday evening January 6th, allowing competitors a clear run overnight towards the West Country. As usual the three starting points of Kenilworth, London and Launceston were used and there was a new hill this year at Tillerton. It was reported that Jim Goodall's attack on Simms hill seemed to be jet propelled as he simply shot up, the Plus Four leaping from ledge to ledge as Jim went on his way to a First Class Award. Equally successful were Terry Hall, B Thorne and Ken Hobbs, whilst Tom Threlfall and Alan Hobbs took Seconds. John Spare, Tiny Lewis and L Jenner had to make do with Thirds, whilst Monty Rogers missed out on an award. Earlier in the trial his Morgan had developed handbrake trouble.

The Liverpool Motor Club held its annual New Year Rally in conditions of ice and snow in the hillier parts of Lancashire and the West Riding of Yorkshire over the weekend of Saturday 14th and Sunday 15th of January. Snow caused much disruption but at the night halt Edgar Cubley, driving Peter Reece's old coupé KNP 5 was in the lead from the TR2 of Ken James. Snow then delayed these two and by the finish a Standard Vanguard was the victor. As Edgar had entered the coupé in the closed car class, the open class victory went to Ken James, but Edgar was in the winning team.

There was a directors' meeting held at the Morgan factory on Wednesday January 16th. Peter Morgan was able to tell the board that a number of chassis frames had been delivered for production of the new 4/4, and that axles were expected over the next week or so. Some 88 firm orders had now been received for this new model. HFS Morgan informed his fellow directors that he was still exploring the possibility of using the new 1,703cc Ford Consul engine, type 204E. Nothing more seems to have been heard of this, and when we asked Peter Morgan about this

'Tiny' Lewis in the MCC Exeter Trial on Stretes Hill. (Norman Miller)

proposal he replied that his father was always looking at ways of saving money on the Morgan range, but they didn't necessarily lead anywhere.

By the end of January new Plus Fours began to be delivered fitted with stronger stub-axle steering arms, after experiencing several failures, and from early in February they were fitted with tubeless tyres. A new version of the Triumph TR engine had been introduced by the Standard Motor Company for the TR3, superseding the previous TR2 type as from engine number TS 9350. The cylinder head was still based on the TR2 design (low port) but now had enlarged inlet ports to match the SU type H6 carburettors. These cylinder heads were known as 'Le Mans heads' because they were based on those used on the Triumph TR2s raced at Le Mans in 1955. One of the first fitted by Morgan was TS 9654, which was fitted to the car (chassis number 3421) dispatched to the USA on Tuesday February 7th, for racing at Sebring. It wasn't until near the end of the year that these cylinder heads completely replaced the earlier version on Morgan engines.

The fourth Thames Estuary AC's 'Cats' Eyes' Rally took place over Saturday night February 4th and finished the following day. There were 250 entrants starting either from Southend-on-Sea or Dunstable. They met up at the north end of London Bridge before heading south to Maidstone in Kent. There were then four more rally sections before the final driving tests on Sunday morning near Lingfield. There was always a good selection of Morgans entered for this popular rally, which was a tough navigation event, giving the rally navigator a busy time. Romek Michalkiewicz was best of the Morgan drivers, finishing third in the under two litres open car class with TKT 100, behind a TR2 and an AC Ace, the latter driven by ex-Morgan driver Bernard Clarke. The following Thursday Ted Cleghorn, one of the other Morgan drivers that had entered this rally, had the Morgan factory fit the latest type 1.75 inch front brakes to RVF 142.

The Yorkshire Rally had a notorious reputation for being a really tough event weather wise, giving the competitors a hard time, but the weather didn't seem too bad this year at the start. A total of 140 started from the Crescent Hotel at Ilkley on the 580 miles day and night journey, setting off from 10 pm onwards on Friday February 10th. All went well

Ted Cleghorn reversing hard during a driving test on the 'Cats' Eyes' Rally. (National Motor Museum)

until the competitors tried to approach the sixth control on the moors at Little Blakey. The control was situated at the top of a steep hill and here snow caused havoc, with cars strewn all over the hill side as they made their attempts to get there. One who did get through without losing too many penalties was Bill Whiteley navigated by Les Hopps. He went on to achieve the best performance of the rally in his faithful Vanguard engined Plus Four PKK 256, whilst Yvonne Jackson took the Ladies' Award in her TR2 engined Plus Four. First Class Awards were also won by W A R Crowther and Dr E Townsend in their Plus Fours. Many top class rally drivers found themselves humbled by this event.

The Scottish Sporting Car Club's Starlight Rally attracted sixty-one starters to Glasgow during February for the start of this all night rally. The weather conditions were atrocious, with ice and snow being major hazards. Many of the smaller roads were blocked completely, and black ice made fast driving dangerous. The route from Kinlochleven to Fort William was particularly icy, but Jim Hughan in ASW 222 amazingly averaged 60 mph for this section to have the only clean time sheet at this point. On the snowbound secondary road through the Cairngorms Jim had a magical experience as a herd of red deer leapt over the top of the Morgan whilst he was travelling along a road through a shallow defile. At the finish at Stirling Jim Hughan was pleased to find that he had actually won the rally overall, collecting the Smith Quaich Award, whilst Ken Sturrock and J T Gray both won First Class Awards in the open cars class with their Morgans.

The Scottish Sporting Car Club also held a short evening rally entitled the 'Moonbeam' during February, attracting 67 starters and again Ken Sturrock won a First Class Award.

A Spring Rally was held by the Cirencester CC on Saturday February 25th and Sunday February 26th. Barrie Phipps won the open cars class, presumably in JNV 654, whilst Aileen Jervis took the Ladies' Trophy with her coupé OWD 750. The Morgan 4/4 Club's team took the team prize.

The RAC International Rally was held this year from Tuesday March 6th to Saturday March 10th, finishing at Blackpool. As usual there were several Morgans entered amongst the 200 starters, all TR2 engined Plus Fours, except for the Neil sisters who were competing in their usual Vanguard engined Plus Four, 'Toots'. Starting from Blackpool were Les Yarranton navigated by Tommy Thompson in PUY 306, Jim Goodall navigated by J Thomas in HUY 982, John Spare navigated by Mervyn Meredith in TYA 1, and Andie Neil navigated by her sister Chrissie in KYS 41. Peter Morgan was entered in KUY 387, to be navigated by Ralph Stokes, but he was forced to pull out following the illness and death of his mother Ruth in February, and he handed the car and entry to Ralph. Starting from Hastings were Tiny Lewis in THA 60, and Barrie Phipps navigated by John Pither in JNV 654. The rally itself had the usual mixture of difficult navigation and seventeen special tests, many at motor racing venues. The road section exceeded 2,000 miles, and from the welcome break at Hastings on Wednesday there was no break worth speaking about until the finish at Blackpool in the early hours of Saturday morning. Dr John Spare used Benzedrine (an amphetamine) to try and stay awake on these occasions (quite legal then), but always remembered how difficult it was towards the final stages of the rally to perform quite simple calculations for average speed required to the next control. Poor Jim Goodall and his navigator were so tired they missed the turn off towards the finish at Blackpool, going several miles out of their way before realising the mistake. John Spare finally resorted to smelling salts (880 Ammonia) to keep him awake for the last few miles into Blackpool. After a rest the competitors then undertook the final three big tests on the sea-front, culminating in the traditional 'Monte-Blackpool' test. When the results were announced Dr John Spare had finished third overall, winning £100 and a Souvenir, a magnificent achievement. The winner in an Aston Martin DB2/4 was Lyndon Sims. John obviously won the class for production sports cars over 1,000cc, with Les Griffiths second in an Austin Healey and Les Yarranton third in his Plus Four. Pat Moss, Stirling's

Dr John Spare corners hard at Goodwood on his way to a magnificent third place in the RAC Rally. (Charles Dunn)

sister, had been comfortably leading the Ladies' Award until the final tests when she went the wrong way round a pylon in her MGA, giving victory to Angela Palfrey, navigated by Aileen Jervis, in her Austin A40 Sports.

Several companies advertised the success of John Spare, including Ferodo brake linings. A perhaps unexpected advert was that for Mory radiator blinds. John told us he really had fitted one of these to his Morgan!

Ralph Stokes had had an eventful rally in Peter Morgan's car KUY 387. He had collected the car from the Morgan factory just a couple of days before the rally started, and an engine had been fitted which still needed running in. As a result he didn't drive flat out until the RAC Rally Goodwood test, where he found the performance lacking, blaming retarded ignition. He wondered whether Mr Goodall (whom Ralph didn't care for much) had had something to do with this. Earlier, at Prescott, the Morgan initially hadn't operated the timing beam, so Ralph had to repeat the climb, but he slid at the top left hand bend, spoiling this run. Ralph also had problems with his passenger, whom he had chosen at short notice and now found was not experienced, getting them lost in Devon. He had said to Ralph, 'Oh I know this country, my uncle lives here', but he still got them going too fast into a T junction, sliding into a hedge and damaging the front suspension!

The sad death of HFS's wife, Ruth Morgan, in Chelsea Women's Hospital at the age of 71 years robbed the Morgan world of a wonderful person. From the moment she had married HFS in 1912 she had supported her husband in every way she could, and in between pregnancies she was his regular passenger in his Morgan three-wheeler in the many trials that he entered in the early days of the Company. Many were amazed that she would tolerate the frequently appalling weather and conditions of trials on a regular basis, the early Morgan having minimal weather protection, but she did and no doubt her presence alongside her husband helped to sell these cars. Following her cremation in London her ashes were interred in the Morgan family grave at Stoke Lacy.

A crowd of 8,000 attended Goodwood on Saturday March 17th for the BARC's 21st Members' Meeting, held in brilliant spring sunshine. In the second five lap novices' handicap Tony Cochrane set fastest lap with his Plus Four four-seater, but could only finish fourth. The winner was driving a Morris Minor fitted with a Jowett Jupiter engine, a Standard 14 gearbox and Wolseley 4/44 back axle!

The Morgan 4/4 Club ran a driving test meeting on Sunday March 18th. The best individual performance was achieved by B Randall in an MG TF, and he was a member too of the MGCC team which took the Team Challenge Trophy. Runner up was Barrie Phipps, presumably in JNV 654, whilst the Morgan 4/4 Club Team of Barrie, Les Yarranton in PUY 306, and Sandy Blair in Nixie was second in the team competition.

Barrie Phipps and Les Yarranton formed a team the following weekend for the Herefordshire MC's sixth Welsh Marshes Rally, starting on Saturday March 24th and finishing the following day. They took the team prize and Les, navigated by Tommy Thompson, also finished first in Class 3, presumably driving PUY 306. Barrie was navigated by his girl friend Angela Palfrey, presumably in JNV 654, and they won the prize for the best mixed crew, whilst Aileen Jervis, navigated by Mary Freeman, in her coupé OWD 750 won the prize for the best ladies' crew.

There was beautiful Easter weather for the MCC's 36th Land's End Trial, starting on Good Friday March 30th from London, Kenilworth or Launceston, with an overnight drive and ten testing hills before the finish the following day, 225 miles later at Land's End. Amongst the 135 car starters were five TR2 engined Morgans. The Morgan factory was represented by Peter Morgan in KUY 387, Jim Goodall in HUY 982 and Terry Hall in JNP 239, although we do wonder whether the latter coupé didn't really still have a Vanguard engine. Also entered were Tiny Lewis in THY 60 and B Herbert in NRY 979. Jim, Terry and Mr Herbert collected First Class Awards, Peter a Second after failing Beggars Roost, but Tiny had troubles and got no award at all.

Starting on Easter Saturday and finishing on Easter Monday was the Scottish Sporting Car Club's Highland Rally. Despite not doing well on the road sections Bob Grant made best times in the driving tests for sports cars of 1,601cc and above. Bob was an enthusiastic member of the Lancashire and Cheshire Car Club, and had bought in 1955 a new 'cream' (ivory) Plus Four, with red upholstery and wheels, this two-seater having twin spare wheels and being registered TKC 389. He

B Herbert on Hustyn in the MCC Land's End Trial. (Norman Miller)

bought it from a car showroom in Manchester, although it had originally been dispatched to Carrs Motors in Liverpool and he had traded in his rallied Renault 4CV for it. It was chassis number 3276, originally dispatched on Tuesday April 26th 1955, and Bob believes that the original purchase had fallen through. Bob was in the timber trade in Manchester. His navigator was, as always, Lorimer Darwent.

The big motor racing event held on Easter Monday April 2nd was the BARC's International meeting at Goodwood, with 60,000 spectators present on a sunny day to watch the action. On the programme at this prestigious meeting was the inaugural race for the *Autosport* magazine's new Series-Production Sports Car Championship with a thirteen lap scratch race for twenty starters. We are not sure if John McKechnie ran his Plus Four at this event, and certainly no Morgans featured in the main results, the race being won by Ken Rudd in an AC Bristol. John had suffered a bad winter with his Plus Four MVJ 101, for it had twice been back to the Morgan factory for major repairs after accidents.

A hill climb event was held at Trengwainton the same day. The course had been repaired since the previous meeting and times were faster in consequence. Jim Banbury managed to finish third in the class for sports cars up to 2,000cc in JJY 221, despite wheel spin on the bends, recording a time of 26.20 seconds. Ahead of him was Skinner's winning MG powered Dellow and the second placed MG engined Lotus of Willmott.

Also held on Easter Monday was the North Devon MC's autocross, and Dave Warren proved victorious in the class for sports cars over 1,500cc, with his Plus Four MYP 802, beating an HRG and a Frazer Nash. In the handicap event the places were reversed however, Dave finishing third, with the HRG victorious and the Frazer Nash in second place.

By early April the traditional fold down windscreen of the production two-seater Plus Four had been discontinued and replaced by a fixed screen. By the mid 1950s trials had become relatively less important in the world of motor sport so the need for folding the screen flat to allow the driver to see through muddy trials sections became less important. It was of course cheaper anyway to manufacture a fixed screen and Peter Morgan had also been concerned for some time about the dangers of these screens. Once he had had one fly upright whilst travelling at high speed, breaking the glass, luckily without any injury, and he felt a clip was really needed in the middle of the bonnet to hold the screen down. Of course this was not readily possible with a side opening bonnet as on the Morgan.

The 22nd Members' Meeting of the BARC was held at Goodwood on Saturday April 14th, with dry weather but a bitterly cold wind. R S Benson competed with his Plus Four in the last of the five lap handicap races, finishing third behind the winning Brooklands Riley and a Triumph TR2. The Herts County A & AC and the North London Enthusiasts' CC jointly ran driving tests the following day at Heston, and Sandy Blair was best in the unlimited open car class, beating two TR2s with Nixie. In the Morecambe CC Driving Test Rally Cecil Hall was the overall winner with his Standard Special engined 4/4 LKP 766. He also won his class, and the prizes for the best performance by a member of the Morecambe CC, and also the Westmorland MC.

In the West Country on the same day Dr John Spare won the Premier Award of the Taunton MC's Allen Memorial Trial, whilst Leon Fredman was a member of the winning team in the Plymouth MC Manor Trophy Rally.

The London Motor Club's famous Little Rally began from the Queens Hotel Farnborough on the morning of Saturday April 21st, finishing at the same place that afternoon after eight tests. As usual a huge entry was received, several starting in Morgans. There were two TR2 engined Plus Fours, being those of Les Yarranton navigated by Tommy Thompson in PUY 306, and Barrie Phipps navigated by his girl friend Angela Palfrey in JNV 654. There were three Vanguard engined Plus Fours, being those of Sandy Blair navigated by J Sinclair in Nixie, the Norgards in NYF 452, and P W E

Constantine navigated by F J Foster. Barrie Phipps, Sandy Blair and Bill Parkes formed the Morgan 4/4 Club team, Bill driving his Triumph TR2, navigated by Aileen Jervis. None of the Morgans took home trophies this year, but the Morgan 4/4 Club team did finish third out of 63 entries in the team event.

Having finished the Little Rally on Saturday afternoon Barrie Phipps went on to take part in the sixth Ilfracombe Rally, which began that evening and finished the following day. Dr John Spare was best of the Morgan drivers in this rally, winning the Class B Award and the Morgan 'One-Make' Award with TYA 1, whilst Leon Fredman took the Starting Point Award for Plymouth with his Plus Four.

Unfortunately Barrie Phipps hit the headlines for the wrong reason when he hit a Renault head-on in the narrow Mill Lane, near Twitchen, whilst both drivers were looking for a control post, and the navigator of the Renault (no seat belts in these days) was killed when he hit the windscreen, despite the fairly low speed of the impact. Later, at the formal inquest, a verdict of 'misadventure' was recorded, but the jury was critical of the speeds being driven by rally drivers on narrow roads and also of the actual organisation of a rally in allowing such collisions to be possible. Barrie's Morgan, JNV 654, went back to the Morgan factory for a check-over of the stub axles and steering on Monday April 30th.

Sandy Blair travelled to The Thames Estuary AC's 'Day of Dicing' on the day after the Little Rally, Sunday April 22nd, and he showed the rest how to drive by convincingly winning the event in Nixie, even beating the Dellows. That same Sunday April 22nd Stan Keen won a Second Class Award with his Plus Four, presumably HDY 603, in the Coventry & Warwicks MC National Benzole Trophy Rally, and formed part of the winning team along with another Plus Four driven by Peter Brayshaw. Peter's Morgan was a blue two-seater with black upholstery, registered PKV 131. It was chassis number 3213, and had been dispatched from Malvern on Wednesday July 20th 1955.

This year's Birmingham Post Rally organised by the MAC was once again awarded National status, and was one of the qualifying events for the British Trial Drivers' Association Gold Star Rally Competition. There were several Morgans amongst the 150 entries. Romek Michalkiewicz was navigated by E Clarke in his Plus Four TKT 100. Yvonne Jackson was navigated by Mrs Leonie Kinns in her usual Plus Four, whilst Stan Keen from Coventry was navigated by L K Lord in his Vanguard engined Plus Four HDY 603, and no doubt hoping to do as well as he had the previous weekend. Peter Morgan was navigated by John Moore in KUY 387, Jim Goodall by J Thomas in HUY 982, and Les Yarranton by Tommy Thompson in PUY 306. These three made up the Morgan team. Dr John Spare navigated by Mervyn Meredith was in TYA 1, Barrie Phipps was in JNV 654, and J F 'Robin' Brown from Blackwell, near Bromsgrove in Worcestershire, was navigated by Don Shead in the ex-David Hiam Plus Four two-seater NWP 776. Robin had bought David Hiam's Morgan from a second-hand car dealer in Cotteridge, Birmingham. David had sold the Morgan after being posted to Germany for part of his National Service.

Robin's previous car, a Dellow, had been registered LAD 1 and because of this registration Robin had got a better price than expected for this car when he sold it, thereby allowing him to buy the Plus Four. Robin worked in his father's coal, corn and seed merchant business, and along with Barrie Phipps he was to become a stalwart of the Morgan 4/4 Club. Robin was a member of one of the club's two teams for this event, teaming up with Stan Keen and John de Blaby, the latter driving an 1,172cc Ford. Barrie Phipps was entered in the Morgan 4/4 Club's other team, along with Dr John Spare and Angela Palfrey, Angela driving her Austin A40 Sports, navigated by Aileen Jervis.

The competitors started from the Civic Centre car park in Birmingham at one minute intervals from 10pm onwards on Friday April 27th, first away being Romek Michalkiewicz. Not until the start did they see the route card, which had a series of map references for the first half of the forthcoming 400 mile route, and they could not stop to plot the route until clear of city traffic. The route took them into Wales, finally finishing at Droitwich Spa on Saturday afternoon.

The event was won by John Waddington in his Triumph TR2, with the best Morgan placing being that of Dr Spare in fourth place in the open car class for over 1,600cc. The Morgan factory team just won the team competition from a Morgan 4/4 Club team, whilst Angela Palfrey won the ladies' competition as well as being an excellent third overall.

This was probably the last event for Dr John Spare in TYA 1, for the Standard Motor Company had been most impressed by his performance in the earlier RAC Rally, and was now to put a Triumph TR3 at his disposal.

The Sporting Owners Drivers' Club ran an autocross at Dunstable on Sunday May 6th. Morgans once again took the prizes, for Sandy Blair won the production sports cars competition in Nixie, John Looker won the open cars class up to 2,000cc in OWP 38, and Mrs Pauline Mayman achieved the 'Best Ladies' Performance'.

Pauline and her husband Lionel Mayman were the proprietors of Kay Garages, a smallish service station with workshops, situated in Shadwell Street in the centre of Birmingham and serving the gunsmith area of the city. In the course of their business a few customers had asked them to prepare cars for them to rally. The Maymans knew nothing of this sport so they decided to find out what it was all about, initially entering with an Austin 16, then progressing via a Morris Minor to a Triumph TR2. Both became hooked on motor sport, but sharing a car did not make for good matrimonial harmony, so Lionel had bought Pauline a second hand black TR2 engined Plus Four, registered TTD 318. This was chassis number T3138, fitted with engine number TS 2011 and had been originally dispatched to the County Garage Morecambe on July 16th 1954. Pauline loved this Morgan, and found the twin spare wheels ideal for autocrosses as she could carry two wheels fitted with knobbly tyres for use on the rough courses of these events.

The fact that John Looker won the under 2,000cc class suggests the original Vanguard engine of 2,088cc was no longer fitted and had been replaced by the Coventry Climax engine that John was definitely using by June. Coventry Climax Engines Ltd had produced a lightweight four cylinder overhead camshaft engine of 1,020cc for

Pauline Mayman wins the Ladies' Class at the Dunstable autocross. (Pauline Mayman collection)

a post war Government fire-pump contract. Designed by Harry Mundy, with Walter Hassan, this engine produced 37 bhp at 3,500 rpm. During the third year of production, in 1954, Harry had produced a sports car version, designated 'FWA', the 'FW' being an abbreviation for 'Feather Weight' and the 'A' for 'Automotive'. This engine was over-square, with a bore of 72.4mm and a stroke of 66.6mm, giving a capacity of 1,097cc. Production engines in 1955 used a compression ratio of 9.8 to 1, and initially produced 75 bhp at 6,250 rpm. The dry weight of the engine with twin 1.5 inch SU carburettors, distributor and engine mounting plates was just 215lb.

Bill Boddy, the editor of *Motor Sport* magazine, had visited the Coventry Climax factory during 1955 and it is interesting that in his following report in *Motor Sport* he described an old Morgan 4/4 being used as a mobile test bed. It is possible that this car was the blue 4/4 two-seater, chassis number 530, which had been dispatched from the Morgan factory pre-war on Wednesday March 2nd 1938 to Coventry Climax Engines Ltd. Recent research by the Coventry Climax expert Des Hammill however proposes it might have been a modern Morgan re-engined. Leonard Lee, the wealthy managing director of the company had several cars re-engined with his company's products for promotional visits. He himself had a choice of Rolls-Royces for his usual transport, complete with chauffeur.

John Looker had bought his FWA engine from the noted 1950s racer Alan Brown, and Morgans had supplied him with a 4/4 bell-housing and other parts in October 1955. In December the factory had fitted a bulge into the nearside bonnet (presumably to make room for the carburettors, which were on the nearside of this engine). John had also bought three wheels in March at a special price of £1.5.0 each (£1.25p) from the factory, presumably making a set with the normal spare, probably for racing. John was an early exponent of Michelin X radial-ply tyres for racing, but others found the sudden loss of adhesion off-putting and preferred the gradually worsening slide of conventional cross-ply types as being more predictable of when the limit of grip was reached.

The Marconi AC ran its May Rally on Sunday May 6th, with a class win for Ted Cleghorn, navigated by his wife Mibs, in RVF 142. He was also a member of the victorious team from the Thames Estuary AC.

The Bugatti Owners' Club ran an International hill climb on May 6th at Prescott. Four Morgans participated, all TR2 engined Plus Fours. Barrie Phipps was fastest of the four with a time of 51.45 seconds in JNV 654, giving him sixth place in class, the winner being the Cooper Aston Martin of Tony Everard, with a time of 49.18 seconds. Ray Meredith was just 0.43 seconds slower than Barrie in NAB 217, but the times were all very close and he was only in eleventh place in class, whilst John McKechnie in MVJ 101 was twelfth, 0.4 seconds slower than Ray. Bob Grant in TKC 389 recorded 52.77 seconds to finish sixteenth. The winning Cooper Aston Martin was hardly a true sports car, for it had started life as Mike Hawthorn's Formula 2 Cooper Bristol, before being fitted with a sports car body by Alan Brown, and then converted to take the 2,580cc Aston Martin engine for Tony to drive.

The Bristol MC & LCC ran a speed hill climb up the drive of Naish House on Saturday May 12th. Peter Hubner did well with his Plus Four, taking the class for sports cars from 1,300cc to 2,000cc in a time of 48.6 seconds, and the unlimited class in 49.0 seconds. Naish House was the home of the great motoring enthusiast and special builder Dick Caesar. Peter, from Bishop's Sutton near Bristol, was driving VHT 198, an ivory two-seater Plus Four originally supplied to the Bristol agent Horace Gould on December 3rd 1954. It carried chassis number 3202, but wasn't actually registered for the road until July 12th 1955. Peter was the second owner, the first having sold it after hitting the side of a lorry, the Morgan receiving a rebuilt front end at the Morgan factory in August 1955.

That same weekend the Lancashire AC ran the 10th Morecambe National Rally, with sponsorship from the *Daily Mirror* newspaper. There were 272 starters, setting off on Friday evening May 11th from Glasgow, Luton, Morecambe, Buxton and Pontefract, all converging at Skipton for the rally proper which began in the Yorkshire Dales. The rally then routed via Penrith into the Lake District before returning to Morecambe for the usual Saturday's driving tests, culminating in the famous 'Monte-Morecambe'.

The Morgan entries starting from Buxton were Barrie Phipps in JNV 654, Angela Palfrey, possibly driving KUY 714, Les Yarranton in PUY 306, Bob Grant in TKC 389 and Ted Cleghorn in RVF 142. Only one Morgan started from Morecambe, that of Yvonne Jackson. Starting from Glasgow was Andie Neil in KYS 41, and also Jim Hughan in ASW 222, whilst starting from Luton was R D McNair. There was a Morgan 4/4 Club team which consisted of Barrie Phipps, Les Yarranton and Dr John Spare, but the latter was now in his TR3. The outright winner was the Burnley driver John Waddington, who had flown back from competing in the Tulip Rally just before the start to take part in his TR2. First Class Awards were won by Barrie Phipps, Angela Palfrey, Les Yarranton, Bob Grant and Ted Cleghorn of the Morgan drivers, whilst the Morgan 4/4 Club team won the Team Award. The Sunday following the rally the same five driving tests used at the finish in Morecambe were used again for the Turner Trophy competition. Barrie Phipps did well to win the over 1,600cc sports car class, whilst Les Yarranton won the trophy for best performance in all the Rally and Turner Trophy tests.

Production of the Ford engined 4/4 was now well underway at the Morgan factory, and the first cars were dispatched during May. Unfortunately increased costs of labour, both at the factory and with suppliers, had led the Morgan board to add another £25 to the sale price, the car now costing a basic £475.0.0, which came to £713.17.0 when Purchase Tax was added. The original prototype had now covered several thousand developmental miles to everyone's satisfaction, and it was registered RNP 504 in mid-April. Publicity for the new model was now required, so the prototype was made available to newspapers and magazines for road testing, and Peter Morgan was to begin using the car in motor sport.

A modified version of the Moss gearbox was fitted to Morgan Plus Four models from May onwards, this close ratio box (or 'high ratio' as Moss Gears

Bob Grant undertakes the final driving tests of the Morecambe Rally on the promenade. (Charles Dunn)

termed it) had altered constant mesh gearing. The input primary gearing changed from 26 and 39 teeth to 28 and 37 teeth, all other gears remaining the same as before. The change was instituted on gearbox 1217 onwards and gave new ratios for first gear of 11.05 to 1 (from 12.5), for second gear 6.5 (from 7.3), and for third 4.5 (from 5.1) with the 3.73 back axle. Top being direct was unchanged at 3.73 to 1.

The Royal Scottish Automobile Club started its fourteenth Scottish Rally on Monday May 21st, and it finished five days and 1,220 miles later. There were three Morgans amongst the 101 competitors. Andie Neil made the journey from Glasgow in KYS 41, whilst James Bertram from Barton, and Jim Hughan from Auchencairn in ASW 222, completed the Morgan entries. James Bertram was driving a green two-seater, possibly chassis number 3238, one of two Morgans apparently built with the same chassis number! Apart from Andie Neil, who was still Vanguard powered, the others all used Triumph TR engines.

James Bertram was a member of the 'TK+4' team, with the other team members driving a Triumph TR2 and Jaguar XK140, from whence came the name of the team. Andie Neil and Jim Hughan were in the same team as a Ford Anglia, this team being called the 'What a Sandwich' team, presumably relating to the Ford sandwiched by the two Morgans! James Bertram's brother David was piloting the TR2 in the 'TK+4' team, and he had previously driven down with his other brother Douglas to Silverstone in 1955 to watch him compete in his Plus Four in that year's 750 MC Relay Race for the Morgan 4/4 Club team. It is interesting that both James and Douglas had bought their Morgans over the winter of 1954 to 1955 from Rossleigh Ltd, the Edinburgh agents, and that they were identical except for the back axle ratio, with James's having been supplied with the 3.73 ratio, and Douglas's the 4.1 to 1. Douglas later had his uprated to the 3.73 ratio during October 1955. The Bertrams were in engineering.

Most competitors did well on the road sections, so the final places were determined by their times in the fourteen tests. Once again the Triumph TRs beat the Morgans, Dr John Spare winning the 'Firth of Scotland' award in his TR3, but Andie Neil did take the Ladies' Sports Car Award. John Spare told us that the Triumph was much less tiring to drive than the Morgan, the softer suspension playing a great part here. There was however much comment that the easy road sections of the Scottish Rally were really not up to international rally standards, and that the whole event needed toughening up. One who possibly did not agree was Jim Hughan. Jim had been battling hard when he came to a downhill bend through a forest, touched the brakes to slow but his efforts had no effect as water had got to the linings. Sliding off sideways into the trees did not appeal so he chose to drive straight on through the trees and was saved from a fate too awful to contemplate by a huge pile of sawdust conveniently placed by the foresters who had been sawing up recently fallen trees!

On Friday May 25th Peter Anton acquired his new blue 4/4 Series II, chassis number A202 and one of the first batch to be built. It was registered RUY 255. At the end of the following week he returned his new car to the Morgan factory for a service and a general check over, with special attention being required to the steering. A new exhaust pipe was fitted too. He was to rally it in the Hagley and District Light Car Club Welsh Twelve Hour Rally run over Saturday night and Sunday morning that weekend, but had the misfortune in Wales to slide the car on a gravel track, damaging the front suspension. He returned the Morgan to the factory the following Monday where Peter Morgan asked him if he thought the car was to blame. Peter Anton dismissed this suggestion admitting the accident could only be blamed on him, and that the car had behaved beautifully.

On Saturday June 2nd the Lancashire and Cheshire Motor Club held a race meeting at Oulton Park. The first two events were half hour high speed trials, and Bob Grant and R Benson took part in the first, Bob Grant driving TKC 389. Also competing at this meeting was Barrie Phipps in JNV 654, but the Morgan developed big-end trouble, but not until he had qualified for an award in the second of the high speed trials, along with John Looker. The final event of the meeting was a complicated fifteen lap handicap race for sports cars, John Looker finishing second in OWP 38.

On Tuesday June 5th Barrie Phipps took JNV 654 to the Morgan factory for a general overhaul to the engine, including the fitting of a new crankshaft. Andy Polack collected his new Morgan the same day. Peter Morgan had previously asked Andy if he would like one of the new 4/4 Series II cars about to come on to the market. We think he had demonstrated the prototype RNP 504 to him as well as showing him around the factory, where he was astonished to find hand operated drills happily still in use. Andy had liked the modern stylish lines of the new Morgan and the much lighter steering, but wasn't impressed by the gear lever!

Peter used to practice for driving tests in the factory yard. A hand throttle was fitted to his car and set to prevent stalling in driving tests and Peter found the push-pull gear change ideal for tests requiring quick changes of direction. He could brake to lock the rear wheels whilst still sliding forward, push the gearlever sharply forward and let out the clutch now in reverse gear, all before the car had stopped. Andy had been impressed by this manoeuvrability and decided to order a 4/4 for himself. He was allocated another one of the first batch made, a blue car, chassis number A203 and registered TOK 144.

It is clear that Peter Morgan was keen that early examples of the new 4/4 should go to sporting motorists, with the cars for Andy and Peter Anton being prime examples.

Racing returned to Oulton Park the following Saturday, June 9th, for the North Staffordshire Motor Club's National meeting, this including the second round of the Autosport Championship. It was a cold, dull day, and this ten lap scratch race didn't start until 6.30pm. There were thirteen starters, John McKechnie making the front row of the grid in MVJ 101. On the first lap another Morgan, that of F Newby, retired. After two laps John McKechnie was lying fourth, and kept the Jaguar XK120 of P Salmon behind him for four laps. Once again Ken Rudd was the Class 3 winner (1,501 – 2,500cc), with John in fourth position behind Robinson's AC and Syd Hurrell's TR2.

The following day the Sporting Owner Drivers' Club ran another autocross on Dunstable Downs at the London Gliding Club's field. Sandy Blair was fastest in the open cars class for over 2,000cc in Nixie.

John McKechnie had taken his Morgan to Prescott for the hill climb this Sunday, finishing third in class with a time of 50.67 seconds, Tony Everard's winning Cooper Aston Martin recording 48.66 seconds. Also competing in Morgans at this event were Pauline Mayman in TTD 318, recording 54.45 seconds and T Dixon Smith with a Series 1 4/4 with the Standard Special engine, recording 62.39 seconds. This was no ordinary Series 1, for two years earlier Dixon had been looking to buy a sports car, and noticed a Morgan advertised for sale in the next Worcester village for £220.0.0. by Graham Stallard. This was CAB 652, the ex-Morgan factory racer of the 1930s and 1940s. Dixon bought it and was to keep it until 1961.

Also held this weekend was the BARC Yorkshire Centre's Scarborough Rally. D A Walker made the best overall performance in his Plus Four, leading his class on both the Saturday and the Sunday, whilst Yvonne Jackson was third in the same class on the Saturday in hers.

The third round of the Autosport Championship was actually a hill climb held at Shelsley Walsh on Saturday June 16th. John McKechnie's second run was in an impressive time of 50.16 seconds. Also competing were Robin Brown in NWP 776, recording a best time of 53.28 seconds, and Pauline Mayman who only competed one run in TTD 318, recording 59.45 seconds.

John McKechnie was now third equal in the championship with six points. The run-away leader with 23 points was Ken Rudd with the AC Bristol, whilst Syd Hurrell was second in his TR2 with eight points. Syd Hurrell was soon to be famous

Robin Brown at Shelsley Walsh during the June hill climb. (Robin Brown collection)

as the founder of the SAH Accessories range of sports modifications for TR sports cars.

The Northampton and District Car Club held a sprint meeting at Silverstone on that same Saturday June 16th, and Ray Meredith won the class for open cars between 1,501 to 2,000cc with a time of 1 minute 39.4 seconds driving NAB 217, whilst John Looker finished third in the class for open cars, 1,001 to 1,500cc.

On the following Sunday Yvonne Jackson came second in the open cars class driving her Plus Four in the driving tests held jointly by the MGCC and the Riley Car Club.

The Field magazine of Thursday June 21st carried a road test of the Morgan Plus Four by none other than Sammy Davis, the famous racing motorist of pre-war days, and a previous Sports Editor of *The Autocar*. It was Jim Goodall's car that he had borrowed, HUY 982, now fully updated with the single spare wheel rear end treatment, and running with a TR3 engine. The Plus Four brought back fond memories of the Morgan three-wheeler he had co-driven with Gwenda Stewart at Montlhéry in 1930 for record breaking. He summed up his drive by writing, 'Now this is the kind of car that the normal person may neither appreciate nor understand. It is a "he-man" car, needing an experienced enthusiast as driver; but to that enthusiast it will appeal in no small measure, and although it is said that old age should bring a reflective calm, for me the thrill of driving the Plus Four is augmented by the memories it evokes.'

The Plymouth Motor Club's 11th annual Plymouth Rally was organised by Leon Fredman. As usual there was a choice of starting place on Friday June 22nd, the competitors converging on Exeter Airport for the first test then continuing overnight through Devonshire lanes before finishing at Plymouth for the final tests. Once again John Waddington was outstanding, not losing a single mark to win the rally with his TR2. The only Morgan to feature in the prizes was in the team entry of Dr John Spare, Les Yarranton and Neville Jarrett which won the Team Award. Whilst Les was in PUY 306, John and Neville were both in Triumph TRs.

On Sunday June 24th the South Western Centre of the BARC held an experimental interclub team hill climb at Brunton between teams of three cars. The times were scored according to the improvements or otherwise over existing class records. There were two Morgans competing, Monty Rogers' Plus Four for the West Hants and Dorset CC 'B' team, and John Looker in his Coventry Climax FWA engined Plus Four for the BARC 'B' team. John's team finished third. Of interest are the comparative times of Monty with a normal TR2 engined four-seater Plus Four, and John's similar vehicle with the 1,098cc Coventry-Climax engine. John's best time was 29.15 seconds, whilst Monty's best time was 30.23 seconds.

Once again the Morgan 4/4 Club supported the Lancia Motor Club's Inter-'One-Make' Club Driving Tests held at Heston Aerodrome in Middlesex the same Sunday, June 24th, but this year apathy led to just one team being entered and with no reserve! The handicap section was won by the Lagonda 'A' team, whilst the scratch section was won by the MG Car Club's 'B' team, with the Morgan 4/4 Club team finishing in second place. The Morgan team consisted of Ray Meredith in NAB 217, Sandy Blair in Nixie and John McKechnie in MVJ 101. Also held that Sunday were the Sheffield and Hallamshire MC Team Driving Tests, with victory going to the North Midland MC's team, which included Ernie Sneath in his Plus Four.

The *Autosport* magazine of Friday June 29th carried an advertisement for the unique Morgan van, XEV 795, chassis number P2479, now offered for sale at offers around £275 by the original owner Sandy Lumsdaine. Since being built in 1953 this unusual car had covered 34,000 miles, and the Vanguard engine now had twin 1.75 inch SU carburettors and a 7.3 to 1 compression ratio. A neat multi-branch exhaust manifold system was fitted which exited by the normal route through the hole in the offside of the chassis. In March 1954 the back axle had been changed at the Morgan factory from 4.1 to 3.73, and in September 1955 a Cam Gears steering box and Thompson track rod ends were also fitted at Morgans. This interesting Morgan, which also had a heater and screen washer, was now purchased by Dave Thomas, a development engineer at the Ford Motor Company Experimental Works at Rainham in Essex.

Peter Morgan does well at the MCC Silverstone meeting in the new 4/4. (James Brymer)

The MCC ran its annual Silverstone race meeting on Saturday June 30th. As usual the traditional one hour high speed trials began the day's events, and First Class Awards were won by Jim Goodall in HUY 982 who covered 41 laps, Pauline Mayman in TTD 318 who covered 39 and Peter Morgan in the new 4/4 prototype RNP 504, who covered 37. Peter covered the same number of laps as two MGAs, an excellent performance for the new car.

At the Morgan factory the nine inch rear brakes on the Plus Four model were being increased in width from 1.25 inches to 1.75 inches by the adoption of the Girling type HL3 system, as used on the Austin Cambridge and others. The 'HL' indicated 'Hydraulic, Lever handbrake', this replacing the 'HW' or 'Hydraulic, Wedge handbrake' system used previously. Production Plus Fours left the factory in July with this new braking system (chassis number 3529, although the Girling catalogue lists 3550 as the first). The new 4/4 model still retained the 9 inch by 1.25 inch system used on Plus Fours prior to 1955, at both front and rear (HLSS at the front and HW at the rear).

On Saturday July 21st the Aston Martin Owners' Club celebrated its 21st birthday party at Silverstone during the seventh St. John Horsfall Trophy meeting This included a procession of 100 Aston Martin cars through the ages. Several Morgans joined in the fun. Robin Brown was driving NWP 776, John Looker his 1,098cc Coventry Climax engined Plus Four OWP 38, John McKechnie MVJ 101, Ray Meredith NAB 217, Barrie Phipps JNV 654, and Alan Smith was in KUY 714. Alan, a monumental mason from near Evesham, had bought this Vanguard engined Plus Four from Barrie Phipps. As usual the meeting began with two 30 minutes 'regularity trials', and Robin Brown, Ray Meredith and Barrie Phipps entered the second one. There was a Le Mans start to add to the excitement and all the Morgans covered the required nineteen laps for First Class Plaques, Ray Meredith actually covering twenty-one.

The big event of the meeting for the Morgans was the team relay race for the David Brown Challenge Cup, where 24 teams of three cars took part, each car covering seven laps before handing over a sash to the next runner. A time handicap

Barrie Phipps, Ray Meredith and John McKechnie wearing victory laurel garlands proudly display the AMOC's David Brown Challenge Cup on NAB 217. (Charles Dunn)

was given to each team. The Morgan 4/4 Club had entered two teams. The first had John McKechnie as the 'A', Ray Meredith as 'B' and Barrie Phipps as 'C', with a start over the scratch team of Aston Martin DB3Ss of five minutes ten seconds. The second Morgan team had John Looker as 'A', Alan Smith as 'B' and Robin Brown as 'C', with a start of five minutes, fifty seconds. All the team cars were lined up in echelon along the pit area, and the first cars were set off according to handicap. After seven laps they returned to hand over the sash to the 'B' cars, and this change over of cars caused pandemonium and appeared incredibly dangerous, as did the subsequent change after the next seven laps to the 'C' cars. However, the first Morgan team came first, beating a team of Austin Seven specials into second spot and a team of Austin Healey 100s into third.

That same Saturday the Herts County Automobile & Aero Club ran its fourth hill climb at Westbrook Hay, near Kings Langley, this year achieving National status for the 650 yard climb. Lionel Mayman entered in his TR2 and his wife Pauline in her Morgan, TTD 318. Neither featured in the awards, but Pauline was now a regular competitor on the hill climb circuit.

Also that weekend the Thames Estuary Automobile Club ran its Southend 'Three Hundred' Rally, attracting three Morgan teams to this Restricted event. Romek Michalkiewicz, passengered as usual by E Clarke in TKT 100, just beat Ted Cleghorn with passenger Mibs in their Plus Four RVF 142 to take their class. The other Plus Four, crewed by Mr and Mrs Randall, retired.

One of the first Series II 4/4s to be modified for motor sport belonged to Andy Polack. It was soon clear to him that the standard Ford 100E engine was gutless for any form of motor sport, but he had been impressed with the possibilities of the new Elva cylinder head specially designed for converting the Ford 100E engine to overhead inlet valves and marketed by Frank Nichol of the Elva Engineering Company of Bexhill-On-Sea. The name 'Elva' was Frank's anglicised version of the French phrase 'elle va' meaning 'she goes'. This special head cost £58.10.0. and a power output of 54 bhp at 4,500 rpm and 65 bhp at 5,600 rpm was claimed when the engine was also fitted with a modified camshaft and 8.9 to 1 compression ratio. This head had been gas flowed and tested in association with Harry Weslake, the engine guru, and is believed to have been originally designed

Pauline Mayman passes watching farm workers at Westbrook Hay. (Pauline Mayman collection)

by a Mr Macwhitts. Andy was interested and took his 4/4 down to the Elva factory for the conversion to be fitted.

The Bugatti Owners' Club ran its fifth annual inter-club hill climb at Prescott on Sunday July 29th. In the individual competition Ray Meredith did well in NAB 217 to split two ERAs in the 1,501 to 2,000cc class and finish second with a time of 53.71 seconds. Barrie Phipps recorded 56.36 seconds in JNV 654, John McKechnie recorded 57.82 seconds in MVJ 101, and Peter Hubner recorded 59.55 seconds in VHT 198, whilst Pauline Mayman recorded 60.14 seconds in TTD 318. John Looker was in the class for sports cars under 1,300cc in OWP 38 with its Coventry Climax engine and recorded 61.41 seconds.

In the team competition the Midlands Motoring Enthusiasts' Club was victorious, one of the three team members being the irrepressible Pauline Mayman with her Morgan, who recorded times of 59.70 and 57.62 seconds on her two runs. The Morgan team of Barrie Phipps in JNV 654, Ray Meredith in NAB 217 and John McKechnie in MVJ 101 couldn't overcome its handicap. Peter Hubner competed in the Bristol Motor Cycle and Light Car Club team.

A new racing circuit at Mallory Park had been opened on Wednesday April 25th. This little circuit was shaped rather like the head of a golf club, with just 1.35 miles to the lap. In July a National meeting had been held there, featuring a round of the Autosport Championship, but John McKechnie did not participate, nor had he at the earlier Aintree meeting. The Nottingham Sports Car Club was to run several meetings there, and at the club's meeting on Bank Holiday Monday August 6th John McKechnie did take part in MVJ 101, unfortunately spinning off on the third lap of the ten lap race for Sports Cars, 1,501 to 2,700cc. He did manage to rejoin after outside help.

The August issue of *Motor Rally* magazine published another road test of HUY 982, undertaken by Ian Walker. Much was praised, particularly the steering and road holding abilities. A 0 to 60 mph time of just 10 seconds was recorded and a maximum speed of 105 mph. Ian summed up the car by writing, 'The Morgan's successes in all forms of motor sport are evidence of its worth, and in the right hands is virtually unbeatable in driving tests. In exchange for some concessions to luxury and comfort, the car will give a great thrill and considerable pleasure to drive.'

Meanwhile *The Motor* published a road test on the 4/4 Series II prototype RNP 504 in the issue of Wednesday August 8th. Acceleration was nowhere nearly as impressive as the Plus Four, the car taking a sluggish 26.9 seconds to reach 60 mph, and achieving a top speed of just 75.0 mph. It was of course the cheapest open two-seater on the market, selling some £200 less than other sports cars, a considerable amount of money in the difficult and austere times of a Britain still recovering from the effects of the Second World War. The car was enjoyed by the tester, and summed up by the final sentence, 'Smart in appearance, inexpensive to buy and run, steering and holding the road in sporting fashion, and with 75 mph performance which can be further improved by engine tuning if required, the Morgan 4/4 will undoubtedly appeal not only to young people acquiring their first new car, but also to many others whose tastes are not easily met within their financial resources.'

The 750 Motor Club ran its ever popular annual Relay Race at Silverstone on Saturday August 18th. As usual the Morgan 4/4 Club entered a team, comprising John McKechnie in MVJ 101 as the 'A' car, Ray Meredith in NAB 217 was the 'B' entry, Barrie Phipps in JNV 654 was the 'C' entry, with Angela Palfrey sharing this car as the 'D'. The final driver was Alec Newsham in his new green Plus Four HBV 883 as the 'E' car. Since selling his previous Vanguard engined Plus Four, OKC 208, Alec had been very successful in rallies and driving tests with a Ford Anglia 100E. His new Plus Four was collected directly from the Morgan factory on Tuesday July 10th, but became stuck in first gear on reaching the first road junction! Stiff Moss gearboxes were not infrequent in new Morgans, and several gearboxes ended up being returned to their manufacturers for attention.

There were twenty-four teams entered, and all drivers were required to be experienced racers as this was a National event. The Silverstone circuit being used was a 2.5 mile extended Club circuit, including a long downhill straight along the runway from Maggotts corner towards Club, then a hairpin turn back along the runway to a long left hander (Tower) to rejoin the usual Club circuit straight down to Woodcote. After the usual Le Mans start at 1pm the racing began, but John McKechnie was soon back in to hand over to Barrie Phipps after damaging a rear wheel during a spin.

At the finish the Morgan team had covered 178 laps, of which thirteen were handicap credit ones, finishing in eighth position. A team of MG Magnettes proved victorious with 183 laps of which 33 were credit, whilst a team of TRs came second with 182 of which fourteen were credit. Alec Newsham now returned his Morgan to the factory where the stiff gearbox was replaced, and play in the steering ball joints taken up.

Pauline Mayman was looking forward to driving her Morgan at the MAC's Shelsley Walsh International hill climb on Saturday August 25th, but disaster struck the week before the event when a bulk milk transporter drove into TTD 318 whilst it was neatly parked in the centre of Birmingham. The Morgan was badly damaged and Pauline was devastated. Her father realised just how upset she was and he helped her buy a brand new British Racing Green Plus Four two-seater which was standing in a Birmingham showroom. This was chassis number 3527, which had been dispatched to Henry Garner Ltd, the Birmingham Morgan agent, on Tuesday July 17th, and it was registered TON 919. Pauline was now faced with running in the new car and having new competition brake linings fitted over the four days before Shelsley. The Morgan went back to the Morgan factory as well, for a replacement gearbox and its first service. She made the meeting and recorded a best time of 55.19 second. John McKechnie was fastest of the Plus Fours with 52.11 seconds, with Robin Brown recording 54.80 seconds.

Pauline's damaged Morgan, TTD 318, was returned to the Morgan factory for repairs, including a new Cam Gears steering box and Thompson track rod assembly, and was later sold. Pauline liked her new Morgan very much, but missed the extra spare wheel of her earlier car

Alec Newsham receives the sash to set off in the 750 MC's Relay Race at Silverstone. (A Hollister)

Jeff Parker-Eaton in TOK 258 leading Pauline Mayman in her Morgan and her husband Lionel in his TR2 into Woodcote corner at the SUNBAC Silverstone meeting. (Autosport)

which carried two spare wheels fitted with knobbly treads for autocross meetings.

The SUNBAC ran a race meeting at Silverstone on Saturday September 1st. It was a dull overcast, cold, windy day with scattered showers. The car events began with two half hour high speed trials, and Pauline Mayman particularly impressed David Pritchard, *Autosport's* reporter, with her 'excellent driving' of TON 919. In the second of the six lap handicap events for sports cars Ray Meredith in NAB 217 stormed through the field from virtual scratch to victory. Second was Millard's 750 Formula Austin, whilst in third place was the red Plus Four of Jeff Parker-Eaton. His Morgan was a two-seater Plus Four, registration TOK 258, a car to become much more famous under the later ownership of Chris Lawrence. It had chassis number 3464, engine TS 8829, and had been dispatched to the Birmingham agent Henry Garner Ltd on Thursday April 5th. Jeff was studying at an agricultural college near Warwick and had bought the Morgan new from a small Birmingham showroom. It was the only Morgan they had on show, he remembers, and the garage may not have been Henry Garner's. He was a member of the Midlands Motoring Enthusiasts' Club, which had been invited to the SUNBAC meeting, and he had driven the Morgan down to Silverstone, with no fewer than five enthusiastic passengers somehow wedged in it!

Following the damage to Bob Grant's Morgan TKC 389 in France in July, it had been returned to the Morgan factory for repair. George Goodall invited Bob down to the factory once the car was dismantled to show him what was required, so he took his co-driver Lorimer Darwent with him. George showed him two piles of Morgan parts from his car; one of useable items and one of scrap, and proceeded to give Bob a lecture on how anyone could do such damage. Bob quickly corrected him, pointing to his co-driver, and insisting that he should take all the blame as he was driving. The Morgan was rebuilt on to a new chassis, and the front brakes were upgraded at the same time to the new 1.75 inch type. Bob had complained how bad the original brakes were for competition, and was told he could have upgraded to the larger size earlier if he had told them he was racing the car. The newly repaired Morgan was back in Bob's hands early in September.

The Bugatti Owners' Club ran an International meeting at Prescott on Saturday September 8th. The weather was fine and the event was contributing to the Autosport Series-Production Sports Car Championship. John McKechnie had the misfortune to hit the bank on one run, bending back the front suspension and damaging a wheel, but he managed to complete one run in 55.32 seconds. He was now lying in fifth place in the championship's Class 3 (1,501 – 2,500cc). The final race in the championship was

Morgan Sports Cars — 1956

Robin Brown and an admirer in the Prescott paddock with NWP 776 after making the fastest Morgan time. (Robin Brown collection)

to be the three hour race at Oulton Park on Saturday September 22nd. Robin Brown was also at Prescott, competing in Class 1C, for sports car between 1,601 and 3,000cc, recording a best time of 54.16 seconds in NWP 776. Ray Meredith did a very slow first run in NAB 217, but improved to 54.71 seconds in his second.

The weather was foul, with torrential rain throughout, for the Romford Enthusiasts' Car Club's hill climb held on perimeter roads at nearby Stapleford Aerodrome the following day. Dave Thomas was entered in the over 1,501cc closed car class with his Morgan Plus Four van XEV 795. Preparation consisted of removing the spare wheel which lay loose on the van floor. There was much good natured mickey-taking about Dave's Plus Four van in the paddock before the event, it being christened 'The Flying Hearse' by another Ford employee! Despite using Blue Peter retread tyres, which were hardly the most desirable for racing, Dave still showed the others how it was done, and came first in class with a time of 44.78 seconds, beating the second placed Ford Zephyr by over one and a half seconds! Dave was amazed and delighted by how far sideways he could throw the Morgan on the bends, and still recover the situation with certainty.

The Autocar magazine carried a road test of RNP 504, the 4/4 Series II prototype, in the issue of Friday September 14th. The 4/4 was summed up as a 'creature of compromise'. The article continued, 'Main items on the debit side are performance which is not exciting in standard form, difficulty in getting in and out, the laborious hood mechanism, and the lack of accommodation for luggage. On the credit side are low price, fuel economy, handling of a high order, the ease with which engine power could be increased and the accessibility of those parts subject to routine attention.'

On Saturday September 15th the Aston Martin Owners' Club ran the 'Martini Speed Match' at Brands Hatch circuit in Kent. It was basically a sprint meeting, with various 'Matches' for different classes. Just one Morgan was entered, the 4/4 Series II of Andy Polack, which was running with the Elva head. In practice all seemed well with the Morgan. Opposition in 'Match F' comprised two Lotus Mk VIs and the Austin special of Major Arthur Mallock, but poor Andy had the misfortune to strip the teeth off the gearbox primary shaft without even completing a lap.

Andy had discovered that the Achilles heal of the new 4/4 was the wide ratio three speed gearbox, which just wasn't strong enough, stripping the gears on the primary shaft with some regularity, even after changing to proprietary items made from better steel. Apart from the input and output shaft bearings in the gearbox casing all the internal bearings were sintered bronze bushes, and they just were not up to racing. Andy soon became adept at changing the gearbox primary shaft, performing this by the roadside on occasions.

Andy had also had problems with the Elva head conversion, finding the engine just did not rev as it should. Elva seemed unable to help him so Andy used the facilities at Loughborough College to investigate further. Using the strobe light on the valve springs he soon found that the new inlet valve springs were not adequate, developing valve spring surge at high revs. This was caused by secondary vibrations occurring within the spring. Working with his friend John Baker-Courtenay, Andy softened the springs, took out one coil, stretched the spring to the original length and re-tempered them. Two of the six springs they made snapped, but the other four were fine and immediately allowed the engine to rev to 7,000 rpm. A sample was taken to Terrys, the valve spring manufacturers, for a batch to be professionally produced, but the company declined to make any, believing the specification to be too extreme for long spring life.

On Sunday September 16th the Worcestershire Motor Club held an autocross in conjunction with the Morgan 4/4 Club and the Herefordshire Motor Club, with practice in the morning and the event in the afternoon. Some thirty-nine competitors were present, but fastest time of the day went to Jim Goodall in his Plus Four (presumably HUY 982) with a time of 64.8 seconds. Barrie Phipps took the open car class for 1,601 to 2,600cc with a time of 66.3 seconds in JNV 654, whilst John Looker took the open class for up to 1,100cc in his Coventry Climax engined Plus Four OWP 38 with a time of 69.1 seconds. Jim Goodall and John Looker were joined possibly by Peter Morgan in the 4/4 RNP 504, to win the team competition.

That same dull day the Midlands Motoring Enthusiasts' Club ran a sprint meeting at the Second World War aerodrome at Honeybourne, using a standing quarter mile runway course with two corners, one quite acute, and then a quarter mile straight sprint, the times being added together to give the results. Lionel Mayman took the open car class for 1,601 to 2,500cc in his TR2 with 64.1 seconds. Also competing was Jeff Parker-Eaton in TOK 258, now with a dent in the right side front wing following an altercation with an approaching vehicle, on a narrow bridge, whilst travelling to the venue. Pauline Mayman's old Plus Four TTD 318, newly rebuilt by the Morgan Motor Company, was being driven there, but we don't know by whom, for Pauline herself was at the South Wales

Jeff Parker-Eaton prepares to start in the MMEC Honeybourne sprint. Pauline Mayman's old Morgan is behind. (Jeff Parker-Eaton collection)

AC's Castel hill climb near Bridgend where she took TON 919 to third place in Class 3 (1,501-2,500cc) behind two TR2s.

The climax of the Autosport Series-Production Sports Car Championship was the three hour race held during the Mid-Cheshire Motor Club's Daily Herald Gold Cup meeting, at Oulton Park, on Saturday September 22nd. It was the first event on the programme, starting at 11am on a warm and dry morning. There were twenty-one starters for the Le Mans start, just John McKechnie in MVJ 101 representing the Morgan marque. It was a handicap event, John receiving six credit laps along with Syd Hurrell in the TR2. After fifty laps John pitted for fuel and oil, and had an uneventful drive to the finish, completing 79 laps (including the six credit ones) to finish second in Class 3 to Ken Rudd who covered 81 laps (scratch), with Syd Hurrell third after suffering misfiring, with 77. Overall John was fifth, but Ken Rudd, who had led the series all through the year, was beaten into second place by the MGA of R Fitzwilliam and Robin Carnegie. Thus the MGA drivers won the prestigious Autosport Trophy, together with a replica trophy and £100. Class awards however were allocated according to cumulative results in all the events of the championship, and Ken Rudd had a run away score in the 1,501 to 2,500cc class with 76 points, with Syd Hurrell second in his TR2 with 41. John McKechnie came third with 30 points. The fact that the Championship Cup was awarded to the MGA drivers and not Ken Rudd caused much controversy for he was way ahead of everyone in points scored throughout the championship events. *Autosport* promised to look at the championship rules for 1957.

The London Rally attracted over 300 entrants to the starts at Farnborough, Shenstone, Norwich, Yeovil and Leeds on Friday September 21st. After running to Hagley and Kidderminster the serious part began that evening with the competitors tackling a route in Wales in southern Cardigan and northern Camarthen. The roads were described as, 'diabolical, yet drivable' by *Autosport*, and as, 'the best standard car trials course I have come across' by Sydney Allard. The route was so tricky that the driving tests held on a disused airfield for tie-breaking purposes were not needed. Only 171 crews completed the course of 750 miles within the 3 hours 30 minutes of permitted lateness. Best of the Morgan crews was Les Yarranton and Tommy Thompson, who achieved 'Best performance by a member of the London Motor Club not winning any of the Premier Awards' in PUY 306 and also the 'Best aggregate time in the driving tests'. The Ladies Crew Award was won by Yvonne Jackson and Leonie Kinns in Yvonne's Plus Four. Overall winner was John Waddington in his Triumph TR2, whilst previous winners Jimmy Ray and Jeff Dixon won the best saloon award in a Sunbeam Rapier.

Alec Newsham had the misfortune of the Plus Four's bonnet flying off whilst speeding along a rough road during the night section. By the time he had stopped the Morgan they had travelled some way from where it had happened, and it took a while to find it in the dark. Others later suggested he should have carried on without it as he had been doing quite well up to then. He returned his Morgan to the factory for the dents in the bonnet to be removed, a new oil gauge and flexible exhaust pipe to be fitted and for another replacement gearbox!

Another rally driver requiring repairs to his Morgan was Romek Michalkiewicz, for TKT 100 was also returned to the factory after the London Rally for extensive repairs following an accident, possibly in this rally. At the same visit a new TR3 engine replaced the previous TR2 version, and the hubs were changed for a heavier pattern. This Morgan had now covered just less than 12,000 miles.

The Lancashire and Cheshire Car Club's eighth Lakeland Rally attracted fifty-one starters from Manchester and Llandudno on Friday evening September 28th. The first part of the event was an overnight road rally section of 350 miles, with one driving test, this being followed by a series of driving tests held at West Shore, Llandudno the following day. One of the best at driving tests was

John Looker in his Coventry Climax FWA engined Plus Four winning his class at the Hagley & DLCC Staverton meeting. (Charles Dunn)

Alec Newsham, and he took first place in the tests for open cars over 1,600cc in his Plus Four OKC 208. He also took a First Class Award in the rally part of the event.

The Hagley and District Light Car Club had glorious sunny weather for its sprint meeting held at Staverton Aerodrome near Cheltenham on Sunday September 30th. John Looker was entered in his Coventry Climax engined Plus Four OWP 38, and came second in the class for sports cars under 1,500cc to Ashley Cleave's amazing Morris. As Ashley was also given the Award for the 'Best Sports Car under 1,172cc', John ended up as the class winner.

The West Hants and Dorset CC held an autocross meeting during September, which Monty Rogers won in his four-seater Plus Four PLB 111.

The MCC held its second annual Derbyshire Trial starting on Friday October 5th, and finishing the following day. Starting points were Penrith,

Monty Rogers wins the WH & DCC Autocross during September. (A Hollister)

Norwich, London and Bristol, from where the fifty-three cars converged on Cromford in Derbyshire for the 111 miles main event. Peter Morgan was exceptional in RNP 504, the 4/4, winning a First Class Award whilst Terry Hall in a Vanguard engined car (presumably the coupé JNP 239) and Jim Goodall in HUY 982 could only manage Seconds.

On the Saturday the Shenstone and District Car Club ran its Buxton Rally, with the best performance achieved by the unstoppable Alec Newsham in his Morgan. The following day the Hagley and District LCC and the Hereford CC jointly ran competitive driving tests, the Hagley club winning easily and Les Yarranton being best in the open cars class.

The Sheffield and Hallamshire Motor Club's National Rally of the Dams was held over the weekend of Saturday October 13th and Sunday 14th. There was some criticism of the organisers for using some of the rough trials roads that had been part of the Derbyshire Trial the previous weekend. Fog made timekeeping and navigation extremely difficult, but Les Yarranton managed second place in the class for sports cars 1,601 to 2,000cc.

On the Saturday, at Oulton Park, the Lancashire and Cheshire CC ran a race meeting attracting the Plus Fours of Bob Grant and John Looker (Coventry Climax engine), but neither featured in the awards.

The International Motor Show was held at Earls Court, London from Wednesday October 17th to Saturday 27th, and the Morgan Motor Company had a specially prepared 4/4 chassis on show, with several items chrome plated, There were also two complete examples of this model, these being a Ming Blue car with beige trim (chassis number A237), and another in Hillman Grey with black trim (A238). The three Plus Four models were represented by a four-seater, a two-seater, and a coupé, these being chassis numbers 3558, 3559 and 3560 respectively.

At the Show the Standard Motor Company announced the introduction of Girling type 'B' front disc brakes on the TR3, making this the first British car in volume production to use disc brakes.

An improved cylinder head was also announced, known as the 'high port' and it was gradually phased in to TR3 production from engine number TS 12606E until it was standard from TS 13052E. This head gave improved engine breathing enabling 100 bhp to be obtained at 5,000 rpm. Morgan soon received them for new Plus Fours.

Each year during the Motor Show period the Guild of Motoring Writers ran a test day at Goodwood. This year the Morgan Company had an improved 4/4 available, it being fitted with an Aquaplane head, and twin SU carburettors. We suspect it was the prototype RNP 504 which Peter Morgan had been using successfully in competition, and was no doubt developing. Cyril Posthumus from *Autosport* commented, 'It is an enchanting vehicle to drive at Goodwood for whatever silly things one might do the 'Moggy' obligingly gets one out of them. Initially I lamented the absence of a 2 litre Plus Four this year, but soon found the 4/4 was equal fun. The "poke" from the twin carburettor Ford engine is amazing, and on the handling of the whole car one could wax lyrical. In fact I note I already have!'

It is interesting that just the small engined 4/4 was being demonstrated to the Guild by Morgan, and not the larger engined Plus Four. One of the reasons may have been because things were beginning to turn nasty for the British motorist. The Egyptian President, Gamal Nasser, had nationalised the Anglo-French Suez Canal in July. The 'Suez Crisis' ensued with petrol becoming in short supply as supplies from the Middle East were reduced. The British Government was to reduce the availability of petrol by 10% in consequence and ask for a voluntary reduction in travel. Motorists feared rationing might be needed, and new car sales began to suffer in consequence, particularly of those cars with large capacity engines. Motorists looked for cheap-to-run cars and 'bubble cars' from Germany and Italy became popular.

It is also interesting that it was Peter Morgan's developed factory car being driven at Goodwood by the press, rather than a standard 4/4 as shown at the Motor Show. Perhaps press reaction to a developed version of the 4/4 was also being tested.

On Saturday October 27th the Falcon Motor Club began its Guy Fawkes Trial, with 59 cars starting from the four starting points of London, Birmingham, Taunton and Southampton. Twelve non-stop Observed Sections, stop and restart tests, and three timed climbs, all situated in the Stroud Winchcombe and Nailsworth area, were to be encountered before the finish the following afternoon in Cirencester. Ted Cleghorn came first in his class with his Plus Four RVF 142.

The following week Peter Anton returned his 4/4 RUY 255 to the Morgan factory for a replacement Ford gearbox to be fitted free of charge, the old unit being returned to Ford for examination. It appears Peter was having Ford gearbox problems just as Andy Polack was.

The MCC's annual National Rally, starting on the morning of Thursday November 8th and finishing two days and two nights later, was again unsponsored this year, and only attracted 172 entries, of which 151 actually started. The same seven starting points were used as in 1955, and the 1,200 miles road course was virtually identical to the previous year. The 1955 event had been criticised as being too easy for the experienced rally team so this year there was a special navigation section of 54 miles starting at Kirkham, soon after the Harrogate route convergence point. However, as the route card for this was handed out upon arrival at Harrogate the average crew had plenty of time to plan it in advance. Four tests were taken during the route with a final batch at the finish at Hastings. Barrie Phipps had particular difficulties with the second test, a stop and restart

The MCC Rally's Stockbridge control, as the competitors left Wales and headed east. At the control is Patricia Ozanne in a Ford Prefect and P Norgard in his Vanguard engined Plus Four. (The Autocar)

on the approaches to Hardknott Pass, for his starter had burnt out and he had to run backwards down the hill to get going again. Jim Goodall in HUY 982 and Les Yarranton in PUY 306 were joint second fastest here behind Doc Spare's Triumph TR3. As daylight made a welcome return on Friday morning Peter Morgan in the 4/4 RNP 504, Sandy Blair in Nixie and Harry Jacoby in a Triumph TR2 were equal second fastest at the next test at Keasden crossroads, again behind Doc Spare's Triumph.

The route now made for Wales where torrential rain caused many hold-ups on some of the poorly surfaced roads, particularly on the Hirnant Pass. The finish was in Hastings with four more tests, with Sandy Blair making the fastest time on the downhill 'wiggle-woggle', and also the 'forward and back' test. In the final 'scissor' test Les Yarranton was fastest, but poor P Norgard, in NYF 452, had major big-end troubles in the Vanguard engine of his Plus Four. When the results were announced Peter Morgan and his navigator Ray Meredith had won the class for production sports cars up to 1,300cc, whilst Barrie Phipps had obviously overcome the starter motor problem to finish second in the class for production sports cars from 1,301 to 2,000cc in JNP 654, finishing behind Harry Jacoby's TR3. The team award for sports cars went to the Morgan team of Peter and Ray in the 4/4 RNP 504, Jim Goodall and Terry Hall in the Plus Four HUY 982 and Les Yarranton and Tommy Thompson in PUY 306.

There was once again criticism of this event for being too easy, with the main results decided by the driving tests. 'Why drive 1,200 miles in order to compete in a driving test?' was the experienced teams' question. It was to be the last of these annual MCC rallies.

Whilst returning to Malvern Peter called in to see his father at Bray. Ray Meredith remembered being introduced to HFS, who apparently grunted in acknowledgement! HFS was intensely shy and preferred the company of his family to strangers or even Peter's friends.

Before this rally Jim Goodall had had a new high port cylinder head fitted to HUY 982, taken from the newly received engine TS 13033, whilst Peter Morgan's own Plus Four KUY 387 was to take the cylinder head from TS 13100. Both the donor engines were later built into new Plus Fours, chassis numbers 3570 and 3585 respectively, and presumably were fitted with the old heads taken from the two works cars.

The North Midland Motor Club ran its Autumn Sporting Trial, we think, during the weekend of November 10th and 11th. This year it was an invitation event, attracting many top drivers. There were separate routes for the out-and-out trials cars and production cars, but these ran alongside each other, the hills being easier for the production cars. Ernie Sneath came second in his Plus Four to a 1930s Austin Seven in the open car class.

With the petrol shortage due to the Suez situation increasing, the RAC announced on Tuesday November 20th that no more permits for motor sport events would be granted whilst the uncertainty of petrol supply continued. The British Government had been hoping that a voluntary restriction on petrol usage would be sufficient after its decision to restrict petrol supplies by 10%, but panic buying had occurred and many petrol stations were closing altogether at weekends. On Thursday November 22nd the British Government began to issue ration books as petrol rationing was to start from Monday December 17th and was expected to last for four months. The scheme was to be administered by the driving test examiners, so there would be no more driving tests either. Petrol stations were meanwhile asked to restrict sales for the period up to the introduction of rationing, but panic buying continued and the price of petrol rocketed to six shillings (30p) per gallon from a normal price of just over four shillings (20p). Car users were to be rationed to 200 miles a month, but businesses would get sufficient for 100 miles more. Farmers, priests and local authority essential users would be able to cover 600 miles per month, whilst doctors, nurses, vets and the disabled were to be unaffected.

Once details of rationing were introduced the RAC decided it could resume issuing permits for motor sport due to be held after December 17th. Few clubs believed they could attract many entries whilst rationing was in progress.

Petrol rationing was just a challenge to engineers, and so Andy Polack converted his 4/4 to run on liquid butane gas as supplied in Calor Gas containers by Calor (Distributing) Co Ltd to caravan owners and others. He ended up with two SU carburettors in series. The one nearest the engine was used to start the car with the rationed petrol in the normal way. The other had been modified by having a large diameter needle valve assembly replacing the usual SU jet housing. This received gas from one of two Calor Gas containers stored upside down in the luggage area behind the seats, and the accelerator pedal adjusted the gas flow through this carburettor. This was used once the engine was warm, the petrol supply then being turned off. The liquid gas received help to enable it to vaporise by wrapping the copper pipe, through which it flowed to the modified carburettor, around the Ford exhaust pipe! The only real problem was finding a reliable source of full Calor Gas containers en route to replenish supplies.

No doubt Rene Pellandini, the western USA distributor, was soon in touch with the Morgan factory in November when the California Sports Car Club banned Morgans from racing because several production road wheels had broken up during races. Obviously this was regarded as being very serious at the factory, with the USA being such a major market for the Morgan. Approaches were immediately made to the wheel manufacturers, the Dunlop Rim and Wheel Company, to see if stronger bolt-on wheels might be available. Peter Morgan recalled that they were not forthcoming with help, so it was decided wire wheels might be the only answer and Peter Morgan was to immediately investigate this. Wire wheels were not popular in the eyes of HFS Morgan, for he found they were so difficult to clean and keep looking presentable.

In its issue of Friday December 7th *Autosport* magazine announced details of the 1957 Series-Production Sports Car Championship it was again sponsoring. It was based on the successful formula used in 1956, but this time the championship would be awarded to whoever collected the most points throughout the year's events, rather than just in the final three hour race as in 1956. Both the Morgan Plus Four and the 4/4 were eligible.

The Midland Automobile Club announced the results of its Junior Hill Climb and Sprint Championship early in December. In eighth place was Robin Brown, whilst Pauline Mayman made eleventh.

With the rallying season having ended prematurely because of the petrol situation it took a while for the British Trial and Rally Drivers Association to decide how to deal with cancelled events, and the results for 1956 were only available at the end of February 1957. John Waddington easily won the Gold Star competition with 123 points gained in his TRs, whilst Doc Spare was third with 75 points after a mixed season, driving first his Morgan and later his TR3. Les Yarranton was fifth equal with 60 points in his Plus Four PUY 306.

In the Silver Star competition Alec Newsham scored 127 points to John Waddington's 118, securing the Championship. Again he had used two cars, a Ford 100E Anglia and latterly the Morgan Plus Four. In the Ladies' Silver Garter competition Angela Palfrey scored 38 points, mainly driving her Austin A40 Sports, beating Patricia Ozanne into second place on 24 points, whilst just one point behind in third was Yvonne Jackson with her Plus Four.

France

The French Government's ban on open cars remained in force for the January Monte Carlo Rally, which was won by the Jaguar Mark VII saloon of Ronnie Adams, Frank Bigger and Derek Johnston from Ireland, whilst ex-Morgan driver Jimmy Ray was a member of the winning team of Sunbeam Rapiers, the other two being driven by Peter Harper and Sheila Van Damm. Obviously open cars were not a popular choice for this winter endurance event, but clarification was still sought on the French Government's ruling for other French events.

By early February prominent French rally drivers had come up with their own set of proposals to hopefully satisfy the French authorities. These were to have three classes, one for normal series-production closed cars, one for special series-production closed cars, including Grande Tourisme, and the final one for series-production open cars. The aim was to ban thinly disguised racers from competing which was the idea behind the original governmental ban. It was suggested a minimum number of vehicles built by the manufacturer would be stipulated.

Later that month some clarification was given on the rallying of production sports cars, revealing that they were still banned, even if fitted with hard tops unless they had winding or sliding fitted windows, and at least 100 had been built before the end of January. This rule allowed in the coupé Morgans, but not the standard two or four-seater Morgan sports cars.

One of the first French rallies to be caught up in this controversy was the Rallye Lyon-Charbonnières, held from Friday March 16th to Sunday March 18th. The organising club, the AC du Rhône, scrapped its planned classes and decided to classify purely by engine displacement, expecting the Commission Sportif of the Automobile Club de France to only sanction the event for Grand Touring cars. Roy Clarkson's special bodied Morgan seemed likely to be approved, for it had fixed rather than removable side windows, and it was accepted as a variant of the Morgan Plus Four coupé, the special body having no weight advantage over the factory version, thereby complying with the 100 built rule. His passenger was to be Arthur Tatham.

There were starting points at London (Calais), Liège, Baden-Baden, Paris, Lausanne, Lyon, Milan, Nice, Bordeaux and Barcelona, with a run of 630 to 660 kilometres to Charbonnieres, where a common route was then followed, including the difficult Grenolhac-Privas section. This was plagued by black ice, and the Clarkson Morgan was three minutes late clocking in at St Agreve. Further on, rain froze as it hit the road, making driving even more hazardous, and Roy was now five minutes behind time on clocking in at Lancogne. Sadly he got little further, for he had to retire at Mende with loss of oil, presumably from a damaged sump on the TR2 engine.

Only 54 of the 113 starters finished and victory went to the 'Ecurie Noire' Porsche Carrera. Third was a Jaguar XK140, modified from the open version by having fixed side windows on the doors, but following a protest it was disqualified for being a modified open sports car! The rules of what was and wasn't allowed in France still seemed open to local interpretation and needed clarifying.

At the end of March the French Morgan agent Stuart Sandford sadly died after a lifetime of loyal support to the products of Malvern Link, as well as to British motorcycles. Stuart's death left Morgan without an agency in the important French market, but salvation was at hand because also situated in Paris was the garage of Jacques Savoye. Jacques ran a Rootes Group agency, having previously been a long time Singer agent. He had also been involved with the Le Mans 24 hour race since pre-war days. He had two sons, Claude and Guy, and when Claude heard that the Morgan agency would be available he asked his father to apply for it. Jacques wasn't interested in anything but Rootes Group products but his son's perseverance eventually won him over and a new loyal Morgan agency came into being, taking its first car in May 1956. This was a blue coupé, chassis number 3484, fitted with a Triumph TR3 engine. Jacques Savoye had been a noted competitor pre and post-war with various cars, but mainly Singers. His two sons were also keen motor sportsmen, and soon began using a Morgan Plus Four in competition.

Clarification from the CSI of the FIA allowed the Standard Motor Company to have the TR2

Lorimer Darwent and Bob Grant with the Albi Trophy during the London-Languedoc-Sète rally. (Studio Durand)

and TR3 models accepted as Grand Touring (GT) cars by simply fitting fixed door windows and exterior handles. This seemed such a simple solution it was surprising it had taken so long to make this decision.

Colonel Portham, who had spent the war years in France during the German occupation, had organised a rally from London to Languedoc and Sète in 1955 and he repeated the rally in 1956. It began in London on Monday July 2nd, attracting twenty-three starters, including the British Plus Fours of Bob Grant navigated as usual by Lorimer Darwent, and Ted Cleghorn navigated by his wife Mibs. Bob Grant had taken part the previous year too but in his Renault.

It was a semi-competitive event, with no time controls, the competitive element being restricted to regularity sections and driving tests. There was a considerable 'gastronomique' involvement!

On Wednesday July 4th the entourage took part in a regularity test near Albi, the correct time for the course being 30 minutes 7 seconds. Bob Grant was closest with 30 minutes 9 seconds, winning the test and collecting a beautiful glass bowl.

Following this most enjoyable rally Bob and Lorimer set off on the long haul back for the ferry. Lorimer was driving the Morgan when he unfortunately fell asleep and the poor Morgan mounted the doorstep of a French farmer's front door in the early hours. Luckily Bob, who was asleep in the passenger seat, was wearing a parachute harness that he had fitted to the seat, and this saved him from injury. The farmer gave the intrepid pair Cognac, for medicinal purposes. Although the Morgan body was not too badly damaged, the front end was a mess and Bob arranged for the Plus Four to be returned to the Morgan factory for repair.

The CSI of the FIA had by November updated the classification of sports cars with the publication of Appendix J of the International Sporting Code, in which open cars could be homologated into Category 2, providing at least 200 had been built during the preceding 12 months. This ruling would allow the Morgan Plus Four back into international rallies without modification, but had the desired effect of preventing highly specialised sports racers which were normally of strictly limited production.

Spain

A Morgan agency was appointed in Spain at the end of 1955. It was run by Francis Alcaraz, and his premises were situated at 88, Modesto Lafuente in Madrid. During the period from November 1955 to the end of January 1956 he took no less than fourteen Morgan Plus Fours. Seven were two-seaters, and six were coupés, of which two were four-seater coupés and all were fitted with leather upholstery. There was also one imported as a chassis.

On Sunday April 22nd a race meeting was held at the still operational Barajas airfield near Madrid,

Felipe Llopis de la Torre with his Morgan on the grid at Barajas, alongside the TR2. Note the aeroplane on the right (Spanish built CASA ES-1). (Morgan Motor Co collection)

The Spanish Morgan agent, Francis Alcaraz, lent support to the Morgan entry at Barajas. His Austin support vehicle is shown alongside a coupé that he was advertising, adjacent to the racer. (Morgan Motor Co collection)

the III Gran Premio Nacional Sport. A Plus Four two-seater was entered for the second race, held over 40 laps (112 kilometres) of the 2.8 kilometre circuit. It was to be driven by Felipe Llopis de la Torre, and the local Morgan agent was in attendance with a support vehicle and also a coupé to advertise his agency. Felipe started in tenth place, but by the eleventh lap was up to seventh position. He finally came home in sixth place after completing 37 laps in 56 minutes and 32 seconds, finishing just behind a Triumph TR2, but with the same finishing time. The race was won by the Porsche Spyder of Felipe Nogueira, who covered the forty laps in 55 minutes 29 seconds for an emphatic victory. Second was an Alfa Romeo Zagato, then two more Porsches. Felipe Llopis finished in second place to the TR2 in the class for 'Sport de serie de 1,601 a 2,000cc'. Besides the three races on the programme the large crowd was also entertained by an aerobatic display.

One or possibly two of the Morgans also took part in the 'Trofeo de Montan' hill climb where the Cortazar brothers were entered but we are unsure as to whether both brothers drove one car or whether they had two, and we have no results.

After taking its batch of fourteen cars the Alcaraz agency seems to have drifted away, taking just one two-seater, to our knowledge, in 1957.

Scandinavia

Early in 1956 the Kongelig Norsk Automobilklubb (KNA) arranged races on the horse racing track at Bjerke in Oslo. Some 4,000 spectators were attracted to the event, despite the alternative attraction of ski races nearby. Erik Hellum had entered with his Morgan, but was unable to use his spiked wheels on the track surface and had to fit chains. This proved disastrous, for he spun on the first corner, and struggled on until brought to a complete standstill by the chains. These had torn a great chunk out of the Morgan bodywork. It might have been a different story if only he had been allowed his usual spiked wheels.

Later this year Erik sold the Morgan, which had barely covered 5,000 kilometres, to a jet fighter pilot, Tore Paulsen, who wanted to develop the Morgan as a road car. Erik kept the special spiked wheels. He continued racing, notably in a Volvo PV544.

Australia

The tragic Le Mans disaster in 1955 had repercussions as far away as Western Australia, for the towns of Narrogin and Goomalling both decided they dare not allow future 'round the houses' races on safety grounds. Nonetheless Northam did decide the 1956 race could occur, but only because the circuit ran through a sparsely populated area north of the Avon river.

Bill Richards had other problems on his mind for his star driver and the developer of the R4, David Van Dal, had been hospitalised with poliomyelitis, thankfully in mild form. Bill and mechanics Don Anderson and David Beattie visited him regularly, seeking his advice on further development of the R4; visits which David believes hastened his recovery. Bill also asked David to recommend suitable drivers to deputise whilst he was out of action. One suggested was Merv Dudley, whom David rated very highly as a driver. He had spent three years racing on the Speedway circuits, before linking with Peter Bond to build their own open wheel special for road racing. This was named the 'Bondley Special', from their surnames, and was also Vanguard powered, indeed David Van Dal had helped them with this. The Bondley was considerably less powerful and slightly heavier than the R4. Bill approached Merv for the forthcoming race at Busselton airfield, and he agreed to drive the R4.

The second annual Busselton Derby was run on Monday January 30th by the WASCC, attracting a good number of entrants for all events, and a crowd of around five thousand spectators. Merv Dudley hired a 'Lend Lease' Chevrolet truck and towed the R4 to Busselton. A cartoon drawn by WASCC member Terry Trowell and later published on the front cover of the Club magazine *The Visor* in February, suggests there were problems en route!

This was Merv's first outing with the R4 and he placed fourth in a three lap Formula Libre scratch race for racing cars only. In the twenty-five lap Bussleton Derby itself Merv had a three minute pit stop, but resumed, really flying, establishing a new lap record for the circuit of 1 minute 59 seconds. Gremlins struck again, however, forcing his retirement on lap nineteen.

Geoff Way had also entered his Plus Four for this meeting and had a really mixed day, being disqualified in both the seven lap handicap for racing cars and a five lap handicap for production cars for exceeding the prescribed handicap limit established by him in a series of practice runs (he was by no means alone). However, he then won the seven lap handicap for sports cars that featured a Le Mans start because the two cars that finished before him were also disqualified! In the Busselton Derby he drove well to finish fourth overall.

During the heat of February in Western Australia the only WASCC event was a picnic club run with flying and standing quarter mile sprints. Merv Dudley made some good times in the R4 but missed a gear in a crucial run and so recorded a relatively slow time, well below the car's potential.

Geoff Way won all but one of the events (a standing quarter mile, a speedway and a track race), but not the time trial, at the annual Beverley Gymkhana, organised by the Northam Car Club on Sunday March 18th and comprising mostly country drivers. The lack of brakes in tight situations was not such a disadvantage when the competition was not so fierce!

On Easter Monday April 2nd at Caversham the WASCC got down to serious racing again and Merv Dudley scored two first places with the R4 in the preliminary events. However, in the twenty-five lap feature race of the meeting, the Westralian Cup, he lost a front wheel when the right front stub axle broke, whilst travelling at more than 70 mph on the first lap. The wheel and brake drum shot into the air, over the Morgan and over the two following cars too, without hitting anyone. It was a miracle the car did not turn over, but the left wheel was in the sand at the edge of the track whilst the right brake backplate being still on the bitumen just slid and the car pulled up safely. Sid

A cartoon drawn by Terry Trowell showing Merv Dudley on his way with the R4 to Busselton. (The Visor)

Taylor won the race in his TS Special, overtaking the misfiring Plymouth of Syd Negus, which had led from the start. In one of the preliminary races, a five lap race for sports cars, there was a Le Mans start. Geoff Way won the sprint and was first away, holding this position to the flag. When the handicaps were taken into account he was second.

A special six hour Le Mans production car race was to have been the feature of the Caversham meeting of May 13th, but the meeting was postponed one week because of rain to Sunday May 20th. The weather remained dull and overcast, but a good crowd came to see the racing, using a new triangle circuit, rather than the usual Caversham 'D'. Geoff Way had entered his Plus Four, with co-driver Fred De Bonde. Approaching the three hour point Geoff was in a comfortable second place overall, behind Syd Anderson's Le Mans Austin Healey, when disaster struck, for the water pump became loose on the front of the block, forcing retirement.

The afternoon was taken up with events for racing cars, and Merv Dudley and the R4 participated in a three lap scratch race managing fifth place, and the fifteen lap race for the 'Triangle Cup', being unplaced in this event.

After Caversham Geoff Way and Fred De Bonde decided to rebuild the engine of the Plus Four with racing in mind, fitting a slightly hotter camshaft, raising the compression, lightening the flywheel, porting the head and fitted special main and big-end bearings to the case hardened crankshaft. The radiator was increased in size to cure a tendency to overheating in the hot Western Australian summers.

Monday June 4th was the day of the Northam 'round the houses' races. Merv Dudley was driving the R4, and came in fourth in a four lap scratch race for racing cars. In the twenty-six lap 'Flying Fifty' Merv sadly failed to finish. Also competing once more was Arthur Littlejohns, now in a 1955 Morgan, but he was unable to finish in the first four places in the six lap handicap for production sports cars, or the five lap race for unrestricted stock cars.

The WASCC State Championship for Racing Cars was run at Caversham on Sunday September 16th with three heats. The R4 with Merv Dudley at the wheel placed first in two heats and third in another. As a result he and Sid Taylor 'the flying dentist' and his TS Special ended with the same point score. They decided to split the purse and compete over three laps for the title.

The TS just headed the R4 into the first corner and Merv Dudley tried all he knew to then try and pass Sid. In an all out effort Merv came through on the inside at the last corner and a hectic battle between the two experts ensued down the straight to the finish, Sid winning by just two feet. Rain had made the course slippery and dangerous giving the crowd more than its usual quota of thrills. In comparing these two locally built specials it is obvious that it was a real David and Goliath contest. The R4, in Formula 2 specification was less than two litres, whereas the TS Special was much larger with 3.56 litres. The TS (Taylor and Styles) Special had been built in 1949 by Rod and Cliff Styles whose garage was next door to Taylor's dental practice in Perth. The chassis was built up from 1.5 inch 16 gauge steel tube and carried a 3.56 litre side-valve 'stove-bolt' Dodge engine with a 3-speed Dodge gearbox driving a cut-and-shut Ford rear end. For the Australian Grand Prix held at Narrogin in 1951 the car had been rebuilt with independent front suspension based on telescopic shock absorbers and a live rear axle suspended by trailing quarter elliptic springs and rotary-type shock absorbers. With twin carburettors from a V8 Ford, the TS with its smooth monoposto body reached 97 mph at the end of a 17.3 sec standing quarter mile. Later, for the 1957 Australian Grand Prix at Caversham, Sid replaced the Dodge motor with a 4.43 litre GMC Chevrolet truck engine and gearbox. He drove the first Western Australia car to finish and was sixth overall. It is largely in this configuration that the TS Special competes today in historic racing events.

An absentee from recent racing was Geoff Way, who no longer worked for the family business, but was now the Western Australia Area Manager for the Caltex Oil Company, the travelling entailed preventing him from competing.

Although most Australian Morgan activity was in Western Australia, there was a Morgan competing in Queensland, namely the two-seater TR2 engined Plus Four of Mrs A Thompson who raced twice at local circuits in September. At the 1.4 mile 'up and down the runway' circuit at Strathpine, close to the northwest of Brisbane, she finished third in the twelve mile race. She also competed at Leyburn, on Sunday September 23rd. Leyburn was another Second World War airstrip, some 130 miles from Brisbane, previously home to B24 Liberators. It had hosted the Australian Grand Prix in 1949, and this circuit was a triangle of runways and service roads.

The Byford Car Club (Byford being a small town just south of Perth in Western Australia) ran a hill climb on Sunday October 14th, attracting just twenty-three entries, and only three sports cars to contest the over 1,500cc class. Syd Anderson took just a single run to take the class in his famous Austin Healey in 40.0 seconds, whilst R A Davies brought his Morgan Plus Four home second, one second slower but 0.7 seconds faster than the other Austin Healey. R A Davies had driven M T Chapman's MG TC at the State Championship Meeting at Caversham in September, but without success. Winning the over 1,500cc racing class race was Vin Smith driving David Van Dal's Bugatti type 57T. As we have mentioned David had been hospitalised earlier in the year recovering from polio and was there for eight weeks. After being discharged he still did not feel up to racing, but had bought the Bugatti in dismantled state from Phil Hines to see what he could do with it. It was the ex-Wimille Le Mans practice car brought to Australia for racing in 1938 by Duncan Ord. David came to regret the purchase of this difficult car.

There was excellent weather, but a sparse crowd, for the WASCC Speed Classic, at Caversham on Sunday October 28th. Merv Dudley and the R4 had yet more success winning the fifteen lap feature event, beating Syd Negus with the Plymouth Special after early leader Sid Taylor in the TS Special had retired. Merv was unable to finish an earlier five lap scratch race specifically for racing cars.

In Queensland Mrs A Thompson entered her car at Lowood for the Courier Mail TT Meeting held on Sunday November 4th, but with L Agnew named as driver. The Morgan came home third. Lowood was yet another ex-RAAF base, just 43 miles from Brisbane, and the Queensland Racing Drivers' Club

Ian McDonald starting at Templestowe, note the lightweight bonnet. (Terry McGrath collection)

had purchased it this year, although it had been previously raced on between 1948 and 1952.

In Victoria, also in November, the VSCC's hill climbs, firstly at Rob Roy and later (Sunday November 18th) at Templestowe, saw Ian McDonald compete with his Morgan. Ian had purchased his 1951 Plus Four second-hand from Heidelberg with just 11,000 miles on the clock. It had been converted to Peugeot rack and pinion steering, (just like the Plus Fours of two friends of Ian). Finance was tight, so Ian concentrated on sprints and hill climbs. To improve its chances the engine received a higher compression ratio, deeper sump, TR2 overhead valve gear, and a bigger carburettor, but Ian thinks the greatest improvement came from shedding weight, fitting a lightweight bonnet without sides, and later, light cycle-type front wings.

The Brookton Car Club attracted thirty-eight entries from all the Western Australian car clubs to its £100 Twelve Hour Trial, the cars starting at two minute intervals from 8pm onwards on Saturday December 1st, presumably from the small mixed agricultural town of Brookton itself, some ninety miles east of Perth. Just one Morgan was entered, a green Plus Four driven by L Bellairs, who drove well according to Geoff Way; he finished in twenty-fifth place.

The last Caversham meeting to be held on a Sunday was held on Sunday December 16th by the WASCC. The R4 did not generate the excitement of the previous Christmas Cup but the car, with Merv Dudley at the wheel, was again very competitive.

New Zealand

John Moorhead took his four-seater Plus Four to the International Grand Prix held at Ardmore on Saturday January 7th, where he competed in one of the support races. We have no results for this event.

The annual race meeting at Wigram airfield took place on Saturday January 21st, after a year's absence due to track resealing during 1955. First of the car races was an open car handicap which took place over twelve laps of the 2.1 mile circuit and was only open to cars not entered for the main Lady Wigram Trophy race. Tony Shelly proved victorious in his Plus Four, beating Vic Blackburn's Haigh–Citroën and the Vauxhall 14 engined RA Special of Ron Rutherford. Tony apparently did not compete again in the Morgan after Wigram. No doubt this was because he was soon to, as he

The start of Event 2, the sports car scratch race at Ohakea. John Moorhead's Plus Four can be seen partly hidden by number 18, Quirk's Austin Healey. (John Moorhead collection)

told us, 'stuff it into a Wellington tram, the tram surviving virtually unscathed, but the Morgan was a virtual write-off'. He thereby incurred a painful dent to his youthful ego.

Tony Shelly went on to become a very prominent driver in a range of Coventry Climax powered Cooper, Lotus and Lola open-wheelers and in later years campaigned for a short while in Europe as a privateer.

On Saturday March 3rd the Manawatu Car Club ran its Ohakea Trophy primarily as a fifteen lap (30 miles) scratch race but with a handicap event running concurrently. John Moorhead with his four-seater Plus Four was one of 48 entrants. He started on the second row along with Allen Freeman's 26C Talbot-Lago, Graham Wells' Brooklands Riley and a group of specials, but he did not feature in the results. He also took part in the earlier eight lap sports car scratch race.

Ted Reid took his Morgan Plus Four to the Otago Sports Car Club's Championship sprint meeting held over a standing quarter mile course on Fryatt Street on Saturday April 14th. On this occasion he finished third in the 1,240 to 3,000cc class. Ted Reid loved this Plus Four and it remained in his possession for the rest of his long life.

Dave Edmiston, a taxi driver in Dunedin and an enthusiastic motor sport competitor, ordered a new green Plus 4 two-seater from Independent Motor Sales Ltd in June and the car (chassis number 3569, engine number TS 13104) was dispatched from the Morgan factory on Monday November 5th. After arrival in Wellington it was then transported by air in a Bristol Freighter across the Cook Strait to Blenheim in the South Island of New Zealand from where Dave collected it. Ted Reid drove Dave up from Dunedin in his own Morgan to help him to collect the car.

This car was the last one ordered by Independent Motor Sales Ltd from Malvern. In 1957 a new company, McMillan Motors in Auckland, took over the agency, which they retained for several years. There were still some imports to the South Island, via T R Taylor of Invercargill, in addition.

USA

The terrible Le Mans disaster in 1955 had not gone unnoticed in the USA. The American public made it clear that sports car racing was 'on trial', and that safer racing must be achieved. As a result plans were prepared for several new purpose-built motor racing circuits, designed so that the spectators were properly segregated from the competing cars. Amongst those being planned was the new Watkins Glen circuit, a new circuit at Bridgehampton on Long Island, New York, one at Laguna Seca in California and one at Lime Rock in Connecticut. It was to be 1957 before most were available for racing.

The American Automobile Association (AAA) had also reacted to the Le Mans disaster, and had decided that, as from the end of 1955, it would no longer act as the American sporting representative of the Fédération Internationale de l'Automobile (FIA), which governed international motor sport through its Commission Sportive Internationale (CSI). The Sebring supremo, Alec Ulmann, was thus forced to make his own arrangements directly with the FIA to secure the immediate future of the Sebring 12 Hour Race in continuing as an international event, and it was to be Saturday October 19th 1957 before a new organisation (the Automobile Competition Committee for the United States), once again represented the USA on the FIA's sporting committee.

On Sunday January 15th the Cal Club returned to the roads of the army camp at Torrey Pines, for what was to be the last race held there before the site was redeveloped into a golf course. Once again a Le Mans start six hour race was the Saturday's event, attracting two Morgan Plus Fours, Bob Oker in the Savin car and Hayes Trukke in his own. This time the Morgans had a bad day, for Bob Oker broke the crankshaft of his Plus Four and crawled over the line in twenty-ninth position of the thirty finishers, some sixty-two laps behind the winning Jaguar D-type. This was good enough for fourth place in Class E Production. Hayes

Start of the first race at Walterboro. (Claude Haycraft)

Trukke failed to finish, sliding into hay bales just forty-three minutes into the event. The following day Hayes took his repaired Plus Four to the Production race for over 1,500cc, but once again had to retire after hitting the hay bales!

Mike Rothschild meanwhile was once more braving the cold at Franconia for the annual snow races held at Lovett's Field. As in 1955 he was able to travel back to New Jersey with a second in class.

The Ed Savin Plus Four was happily running well for the Cal Club's Palm Springs races over the weekend of February 25th and 26th. Bob Oker drove it superbly to take the class, and finished third overall, beaten only by a Porsche Speedster and a Carrera. He was ably supported by Hayes Trukke who finished third in class with his Plus Four. Mickey Trukke, presumably Hayes' wife, borrowed his Morgan for the ladies' race, finishing tenth of the eleven starters, and second in Class E Production.

The Porsche 356s were becoming most effective, if somewhat expensive, sports car racers in the USA. The Carrera version had been introduced in 1955, and featured a dry sump 1,498 cc flat four twin overhead camshaft engine complete with roller bearing crank and developing 100 bhp. It was basically a de-tuned Porsche 550 racing engine, making this model an excellent car to race, and a formidable competitor to the Morgan.

On the same day, in Florida, the SCCA had laid out a tight 2.3 mile circuit on the vast expanse of runways of the ex-Second World War bomber base of Punta Gorda. David Dukes was competing with his Plus Four and finished a fine third in class, the victor driving an AC Ace.

David then took his Morgan to Walterboro airfield in South Carolina on Saturday March 10th for another SCCA event. It was somewhat unusual for two circuits to be in use, one for smaller cars with just two miles per lap, and another for larger engined cars with 3.5 miles. This airfield had been the wartime testing base for General Jimmy Doolittle's B25 bombers, practicing short field take-offs prior to attacking Tokyo via aircraft carriers.

The first race for was over fifteen laps of the two-mile circuit for Class E Production and below, attracting 22 starters of which one was David Dukes, starting from the second row with his Plus Four. By the end of the first lap the Porsche Speedster of Lake Underwood was in the lead, and it stayed there to the finish, followed home by another Porsche and a Triumph TR2. David Dukes came in seventh overall and fifth in class.

The third race was for everyone from Race 1, plus Classes G and H Modified, and held over twenty laps of the two mile course. This time Frank Baptista's Lotus XI was victorious, with Dukes improving to finish sixth overall, and a third in Class E.

Over the weekend of March 17th and 18th the Cal Club ran a series of races at Santa Barbara

Airport. Amongst the Morgan drivers was a future star in the making, Bob Bondurant, who was entered for this his first race in his new Morgan Plus Four. Bob was not new to racing, having been competing with motorcycles for several years, learning particularly how to race in close proximity to other competitors without being nervous of colliding. A cousin had taken him to the previous year's Santa Barbara races, he had become hooked, had purchased the Morgan, and this year here he was entered. On arrival at the track he removed the windscreen and fitted a home made racing screen. The exhaust silencer was replaced with a straight pipe. In the fifteen lap Saturday preliminary for two litre cars Bob came third overall, behind Dick Heyward's SIATA V8 and Bob Oker's Plus Four. Dan Levitt finished thirteenth, eighth in class. Bob Bondurant was elated, believing he had nothing more to learn about motor racing.

Bob then lent his Plus Four to his girl friend Jackie Glorfeld, who finished fourth in the seven lap ladies' race, and second in Class E.

Just a few of the Class E racers joined the large number of Class F Production racers for a fifteen lap race on the Sunday, and Dan Levitt finished third of the thirty-six starters in his Plus Four, and first in Class E. There were thirty-one starters in the next race, over sixteen laps for Production cars over 1,500cc. After his successes on the Saturday Bob Bondurant had high expectations for this race. He was brought down to earth quickly because this race had much tougher opposition and he could only finish ninth overall and fourth in class. Best of the Morgan drivers by far was Bill Freedman who won the class, and also finished second overall to Rudy Cleye's Mercedes 300 SL.

Bob realised there must be more to motor racing than he had previously thought, and he resolved to learn how to become better. He began to study all the books he could find on driving techniques and entered as many races as he could find to get practice. He decided to become associated with the Ed Savin Racing Team, where Ed referred to him as, 'that punk kid!'

For this year's international Sebring 12 Hour Race held on Saturday March 24th there were two Morgans entered, one, a black twin spare wheel car for Mike Rothschild, to be co-driven by George Hunt from Fort Lauderdale, and the other a new single spare wheel car for John Weitz. Mike's black Morgan was to run with just one spare wheel in place, secured by a modified twin spare wheel clamp. The Weitz car was chassis no. 3421 and the first to be built at the Morgan factory with the new TR3 engine fitted with a Le Mans head (TS 9654). This engine had been prepared and balanced at an additional cost of $270, and could be run at up to 6,000 rpm. A side exhaust was used. Oversize Michelin X tyres, run at 30 psi front and 36 psi rear, helped reduce engine strain on the long Sebring straights. John had the Morgan delivered in the USA racing colours, white with a blue stripe, as he was financing the race himself and didn't see why he should display other than his national colours. No doubt both Mike's and John's Morgans were fitted with shortened gear levers, the new knobs being threaded on to a thicker section of the lever to prevent the breakage problem of 1955 recurring.

Gordon MacKenzie was originally to co-drive for John Weitz, as in 1955, but just before the event he was asked to co-drive a D-type Jaguar, an offer he felt he couldn't refuse. John therefore released him, and asked the Morgan factory if they could suggest a replacement with the appropriate FIA licence. Manuel Bos from Spain, who had raced a Pegaso Z102 Panamericana for Scuderia Madrid, duly appeared.

During practice John was faster than Manuel, but he found that the Morgan understeered badly. On the first night-training session Manuel asked for ten laps extra practice - and promptly rolled the Morgan, Manuel receiving minor injuries to his hands and arm. Ray Errickson had travelled down with the Fergus Motors contingent for the race and he recalled working all hours on the battered Morgan to get it race worthy. He just made it but John Weitz decided against competing with it. Ray believes John's decision was made

John Weitz and the Morgan during practice. (John Weitz collection)

purely because the Morgan was now not up to the usual immaculate standard of preparation associated with a John Weitz entry. John told us it just wasn't finished in time.

Mike Rothschild was able to start - he and George Hunt managed 87 laps before a front stub axle broke, and the car lost a wheel on the circuit. It was not the done thing at Sebring to give the true reason for retirement to the authorities, so Mike told them that the problem was 'transmission'.

After the race, whilst a disgruntled Mike was replacing the broken stub axle, a young racing enthusiast called Richard Vogel got talking to him. Richard, from Thiensville in Wisconsin, had been racing T-type MGs, and it quickly became apparent to him that Mike would be delighted to get rid of the troublesome Morgan, and would sell it to him at a very favourable price. The deal was struck for $2,000 for the Morgan and spares, and Richard found himself driving the rebuilt Morgan north to Wisconsin as the new owner. He particularly remembers the noisy straight through exhaust reverberating during the climb through the Appellation Mountains as he took Highway 41 through Tennessee on his way home.

Following the Sebring race the battered Weitz car was taken back to Fergus Motors where it was rebuilt and became the daily transport of Joe Ferguson. This Morgan was later to be road tested by *Sports Car Illustrated* for the November issue, where a 0 to 60 time of 11.2 seconds was recorded, despite the oversize rear tyres.

It is of interest that the Weitz car is listed in the Morgan factory records as actually having been prepared for a J Norwood. John Norwood, a journalist, was another regular Sebring competitor, well-known to the race organiser Alec Ulmann. Perhaps Joe Ferguson envisaged that he was going to take this entry originally.

Gordon MacKenzie too had a bad day at Sebring, for his co-driver destroyed the Jaguar very early on in the event. As a result Gordon made his way to John's pits to see whether he might be allowed to drive in the Morgan after all, only to learn of Manuel Bos's accident which had occurred

Bob Oker corners at Pebble Beach. Note the heavily wooded surroundings to the course. (Curt Warshawsky)

at exactly the same place (the chicane) that Gordon had had his 'moment' the previous year.

On Sunday April 22nd the very last race was held on the beautiful tree lined Pebble Beach course in California. Since the opening of the circuit in 1950 the speeds of the cars had increased tremendously, and this year the ex-Le Mans 4.4 litre Ferrari 121LM driven by Ernie McAfee crashed, killing its driver. The local residents had had enough. Racing his Morgan at Pebble Beach was Bob Oker and he finished tenth overall and first in class in the fifteen lap race for Production cars of 1,500cc and above.

The same day Gaston Andrey was at Thompson and he returned home with a second in class.

There was a tragedy at the races held on the airport of the small town of Willcox in Arizona on Sunday May 6th. A popular young architect from

Dick Vogel's Morgan in the St Louis paddock. (Dick Vogel collection)

The Wisconsin State Fair Park grid. (Dick Vogel collection)

Tucson, Bob Bender, rolled his red Morgan during the Willcox Civil Air Patrol Sports Car Races held by the Southern Arizona Sports Car Club. He was badly injured, breaking his spine and rendered paraplegic. He was not to be forgotten by the Californian Morgan owners however, for they were to run a concours named in his honour.

On Sunday May 13th Dick Vogel took his ex-Mike Rothschild Sebring Morgan to St Louis for the SCCA races at Smaart Field Airport. The Morgan went well, with Dick taking a class win during the forty minute race, finishing eleventh overall, the winner being Chuck Hassen in a three litre Ferrari.

One week later Dick took the Morgan to the Wisconsin State Fair Park in Milwaukee. This contained a traditional one mile oval, originally dirt but now tarmac, but for the sports cars a twisty infield section was added giving a two mile lap. Some 15,000 spectators saw Dick finish second in class behind Dan Fowler's TR2. The race was run within the main event, amongst the top racers, and overall Dick finished sixteenth, the winner being the Maserati 300S of Phil Stewart.

That same weekend the California Sports Car Club returned to the old bomber base at Bakersfield for races using a 2.3 mile circuit. Ten thousand fans endured blistering heat to enjoy the excitement. Bob Oker was supported by Bob Bondurant, Hayes Trukke and Dan Levitt, all in Plus Fours, but it was Bob Oker who excelled, being in a class of his own in the Savin Morgan. On the Saturday in the eight lap Modified race he finished sixth overall, behind the 300SL Mercedes of Tony Settember, a Corvette, a pair of Jaguar XK120s, and an Austin Healey. He was the class winner, and he repeated this feat on the Sunday in that day's ten lapper, with Hayes Trukke fifth in class. In the 'Strictly Stock' races the best of the Morgan drivers was Bob Bondurant with fifth in class, with Levitt seventh. Mrs Jackie Bondurant then borrowed her husband's Morgan to finish fifth overall and second in class in the six lap ladies' race.

The first race held on the Sunday was the consolation race, held over ten laps and Bob Bondurant finished fourth and took Class E Production, giving him a place in the main race for all-comers later that day. This race was for Modified cars over 1,500cc and covered 51 laps; Bob Oker finished ninth, and was beaten only by Jaguar C- and D-types, two Ferraris and a pair of Porsche 550s, a truly impressive performance against such top class racing machinery. He was second in Class E Modified to a Ferrari Milli Miglia. Bob Bondurant was forced to retire with a blown

Morgan Sports Cars

1956

Bob Bondurant at Bakersfield. (Bob Bondurant collection)

head gasket. All the Ed Savin crew wore black overalls with a Morgan patch, and each carried the wearer's name. These proved to be very hot in the summer sunshine, so Bob's wife Ila took pity on them and decided to make them some replacement shirts in turquoise to match the car.

On the same busy weekend, in the northeastern States, Gaston Andrey was taking a second in class at the Cumberland races, but poor LW Schroeder finished sixteenth and last in his Plus Four. Some 60,000 spectators had watched this National race meeting.

The annual Put-in-Bay races were held on Saturday June 9th. Two Morgans contested the fourth race held over twelve laps (37.2 miles) of the 'round the houses' course. This race was for

Ed Savin's Racing Team found that the heat required special headgear at Bakersfield. Left to right are Ed Savin, Bill Binney the chief mechanic, Bob Oker, mechanic Bill Rudd kneeling, and a Mexican assistant. (Ed Savin collection)

The starting grid at Put-in-Bay for Race 4. Robert J Shaver is in the Morgan, whilst ahead of him are Ben Hall in an AC Ace and Herbert Kouns in an MG TC. (Joe Brown)

supercharged cars up to 1,501cc, and non-supercharged cars up to 2,000cc. Edwin P Lawrence III from Detroit was in a TR2 engined Plus Four and Robert J Shaver from Grosse Point in Michigan was in a Vanguard engined chrome radiator Plus Four. Presumably he was allowed to start because the performance of his 2,088 cc engine, although over the two litre cut off for the race, was known to be slower than the TR engined entrants. He started at the rear of the field. Sadly we have no results for either Morgan.

The SCCA's annual races at Lawrenceville were held on Sunday June 10th. David Dukes did well to take second place in E Production with his Plus Four.

One week later the northeastern racers were in Vermont for the 5.2 miles climb to the top of Mount Equinox, along the toll road owned by Dr J G Davidson. With Gaston Andrey present with his Morgan the outcome of Class E was a foregone conclusion and he climbed in 5 minutes 48.2 seconds. Third in the class was Howard B Williamson, from Chambersburg Pennsylvania, who was usually known as 'Ike'.

On Sunday June 24th the SCCA ran what was to become an annual June race meeting at the Elkhart Lake course. Neither Ed Hebb nor Dick Vogel were very successful, coming in ninth and thirteenth in class respectively, but at least they finished, this race meeting being notable for the entire team of Briggs Cunningham's Jaguar D-types being race-damaged and sidelined.

Back in California Lew Spencer had returned to racing with an MG TC during 1955. For 1956 he decided to go back to a Morgan, consequently purchasing a red Plus Four from Rene Pellandini in the spring. His first event was to be the Cal Club's two day event at Pomona over the weekend of June 23rd and 24th. The two miles per lap Pomona circuit was laid out in the parking lot of the Los Angeles County Fairgrounds. Despite being flat it was a remarkably good course encompassing seven corners of varying severity, and was to be run clockwise for this and other early meetings, later meetings being held anti-clockwise.

Supporting Lew Spencer were Bob Bondurant, Bob Oker, Dan Levitt and Hayes Trukke with their Plus Fours, and they all entered the twelve lap Saturday race for Production cars from 1,500 to 2,000cc. Lew Spencer was best of the Morgans, with eleventh overall and seventh in Class E. Hayes

Trukke was fourteenth overall and ninth in class. None of the others finished. Bob Oker's Plus Four broke a tie rod, and Dan Levitt's suffered pushrod and rocker arm damage. Jackie Bondurant borrowed her husband's Plus Four for the eleven lap ladies' race, finishing tenth and third in Class E.

On the Sunday the twelve lap consolation race included the non-finishing Morgans from the previous day's race. Bob Bondurant did well to finish third overall and take Class E. Once again the others all failed to finish, giving lack of oil pressure as the reasons. The second event was an eighteen lap race for Production sports cars costing fewer than 3,000 dollars, this being an attempt by the Cal Club to counteract the domination of the expensive 'gull-wing' Mercedes 300 SLs and the Porsches, and give the cheaper cars a chance. Having done well in the consolation race Bob Bondurant was able to join Lew Spencer and Hayes Trukke on the grid. Lew drove superbly to win the race, while Bob Bondurant was fourth, and second in Class E. Hayes Trukke failed to finish, with a broken rocker arm assembly.

Bob Oker was also competing at Pomona with his modified Triumph TR2, running sixth against strong opposition in the main race, until a rod came through the side of the crankcase forcing instant retirement.

A victorious Lew Spencer celebrates his win with starter Cy Yedor at Pomona. (Lester Nehamkin)

On the other side of the country Gaston Andrey was co-driving 'Woody' Young's TR3 engined Plus Four at Thompson on Saturday June 30th in the New York Region's one hour race for Production cars of over 1,500cc After just fifteen minutes Gaston was in a secure second place, ahead of all the Jaguars, and he came into the pits at half distance to hand over to Woody for the final thirty minutes. Woody was unable to stay ahead of Evelyn Mull driving one of the first AC Aces raced in the USA fitted with the brilliant Bristol engine. These ACs were to become the cars to beat in E Production races. The following week Gaston returned to the 2.6 miles airport course at Beverly, Massachusetts, for the SCCA race being held once more for the benefit of Beverly hospital. He finished second in class, behind Bengt Soderstrom's Porsche 1600, whilst George Parks was eighth in his Plus Four.

One week later Gaston was at Mount Washington in New Hampshire for the 'Race to the Clouds' National hill climb. This formidable climb of 4,600 ft over eight miles was considered by many to be the most gruelling and spectacular event of its kind east of the Mississippi. There was no hurricane to prevent the event taking place this year, but the top of the mountain (6,288 ft above sea level) was capped by thick cloud, restricting visibility to 'pea soup' over the last two miles. Such conditions did not worry Gaston, for he knew the course well and would just drive where he thought the road to be, timing himself by counting 1-2-3-4-5, until he came through the fog. He also listened to the exhaust echo, and when the echo disappeared then he knew he had reached the end of the ravine just before a right-hand turn (he also recently told us that he would never drive like this now!). After each practice the Morgan would be put on stands and the chassis checked for cracks, welding up as necessary.

Gaston Andrey was outstanding, finishing fifth overall with a time of the 11 minutes 8 seconds. He was only beaten by the 1951 375 Grand Prix Ferrari (air freighted to America for Carroll Shelby to drive), a Cooper Mark IX, Dick Thompson's Corvette, and Paul O'Shea's Mercedes 300 SL 'gull-wing'. Carroll Shelby came to Gaston after his run and laughed saying, 'I just don't believe it', in disbelief at the Morgan's time. Gaston had shamed many famous drivers and many fast cars.

Meanwhile back in California William Snell had finished fifth in class with his Plus Four at Buchanan Field, an airfield east of San Francisco, during races held by the San Francisco Region of the SCCA on Sunday July 1st. He finished seventeenth and last in the main unlimited race over thirty-three laps. One week later Lew Spencer had taken his red Plus Four to Santa Maria, taking a third in class on the airfield races. The Los Angeles Region rather oddly also ran at this meeting a 'Shakedown Race', described as the 'Sports Car Equivalent of a Hooligan Race'! Lew finished last of the twenty finishers. Then, for the weekend of July 21st and 22nd, the Cal Club enticed several Morgan drivers to Montgomery Field airfield at San Diego for its rather grandly titled 'Fiesta del Pacifico'. These included Bob Oker, Lew Spencer, Bob Bondurant and Chas Winberg with their Plus Fours. In the Saturday race for Classes E Production and above Bob Oker confirmed his superiority with second in class, but Lew Spencer was only just behind him in third place, with Bob seventh and Chas tenth. This meant Chas missed the cut-off for the main event on the Sunday, racing instead in the twelve lap consolation race, finishing sixth overall and second in class. The main event, for Modified and Production Classes E and above was held over thirty-seven laps. Lew Spencer was the best Morgan placing, with sixteenth overall and fourth in class, with Bob Oker right behind. Bob Bondurant came in twenty-second overall, eighth in class, and Chas Winberg, given a run in this race because of his effort in the consolation race, was twenty-fifth and ninth in class.

In Pennsylvania Friday July 20th was the day of the 'Giants Despair' hill climb at Wilkes-Barre, whilst the following day Senator Woods allowed the SCCA to race around his nearby estate, named in Welsh 'Brynfan Tyddyn', meaning small hill cottage. The hilly, twisty and partly tree-lined

Brynfan Tyddyn course was restricted to cars of two litres and below. At least three Morgans took part, of which the best was the TR2 engined Plus Four of 'Ike' Williamson, who finished second in Class E, the race being won by Tom Payne in his Arnolt Bristol.

The same weekend, the Detroit Region of the SCCA held its annual hill climb on Haven Hill, situated forty miles northwest of Detroit in the Highland Recreation Area. The course was short, of just four-tenths of one mile, but full of bends as it climbed to a log lodge house. It was surrounded by trees, allowing no room for mistakes. Class C was for 1,601-2,700 cc Production and 1,301-2,000cc Modified cars, and the victor proved to be Ed Hebb, who just beat Cook's Arnolt Bristol by two hundredths of a second. Finishing eleventh was Dick Kennedy with his Morgan. Dick, a member of a family printing business in Detroit, had purchased his Morgan from Tom Payne's showroom in Ypsilanti. Tom in turn had previously bought the Morgan from the Canadian agent in nearby Windsor, Curly Ellis. This Plus Four was chassis number 3489, a red two-seater, with red leather upholstery and a TR3 engine, number TS8965. It had been dispatched from Malvern on Thursday May 31st.

Another hill climb, the Breakneck National, was held at Cumberland, Maryland on Sunday August 5th, attracting 64 entrants, of which seven were in Morgans. The overall victor was Carroll Shelby with the Grand Prix Ferrari once more, in 1 minute 12.41 seconds. Best of the Morgan drivers was Ike Williamson in 1 minute 29.87 seconds, 25th overall and fourth in class. Fifth and sixth in class were Frank Baptista and James Bullard, eighth and ninth were C Woods and L Schroeder, and twelfth and thirteenth were C Shinn and George Parks.

On Saturday and Sunday August 11th and 12th the Northwest Region of the SCCA held its Seafair sports car races at Kitsap County Airport at Bremerton, Washington, as a part of the Seattle Seafair celebrations. The top event of Seafair was the big powerboat race being held earlier at Seattle. As in previous years the Bremerton course was laid out using airport runways and taxiways giving a lap of 3.9 miles. In the fifteen lap (sixty miles) production car race Dave Troffer from Seattle with his Plus Four finished seventh overall behind Mercedes, Corvettes and Jaguars, but was first in class. This was an excellent performance, even beating Pete Lovely's Porsche. Dave had started his racing on ovals, later moving on to sports car racing with a VW before racing the Morgan. This green Plus Four two-seater was an early cowled radiator model with a TR2 engine. It had been brought into the USA by Dick MacAfee and Dick had asked Dave Troffer to race it for him. Earlier in the year an unfortunate chief turn marshall had been killed by the Morgan at Arlington airfield track in Washington. The marshal ran in front of it to attend to Pete Lovely's burning racer in the infield and gave Dave Troffer no chance to avoid him. The badly damaged Morgan had been subsequently rebuilt and sold to its new owner Gerry Barrett. This was Dave's last drive in the car before Gerry sold it. Dave moved on successfully to Corvettes before becoming a very notable racer with a Mercedes Benz 300SL

The California Sports Car Club had found another new course for its meeting over the weekend of August 18th and 19th. This was a challenging two mile course, set in the Santa Monica Mountains. The land, owned by Paramount Studios the movie company, was adjacent to a film lot used for Western movies. Ed Savin had entered Bob Oker in the Plus Four, running it in the Modified class this time, and also advertised the Morgan in the race programme.

Running in Race 3, for Production sports cars over 1,500cc and held over ten laps were Bob Bondurant, Lew Spencer and Jim Mourning with their Plus Fours, finishing third, fourth and ninth in class respectively. Race 6 was another ten lap race for Modified cars over 1,500cc, and Bob Oker managed eighth place overall despite some very fast machinery, being second in Class E Modified behind Bob Drake's Ferrari 166. On the Sunday Jim Mourning was in the consolation race over twelve laps in view of his low finishing position on

THIS MORGAN #59 IS CLASS WINNER IN 1956 AT SANTA BARBARA — PEBBLE BEACH — AND BAKERSFIELD.

Owned by Ed Savin   Driven by Bob Oker

♦

Ed Savin

AUTHORIZED SALES & SERVICE

A.C. ACE & ACECA	TRIUMPH TR-3
ALFA ROMEO	HILLMAN
MORGAN	RENAULT
RAPIER	

Two locations in Los Angeles

475 SO. ATLANTIC BLVD. • AN 8-3264
312 SO. SOTO STREET • AN 8-7151

---

the Saturday. He finished tenth, and fifth in Class E Production.

The main race was a one hour race for the fastest over 1,500cc cars. There was drama for Bob Oker when the left front wheel rim separated from the centre and he failed to finish. Lew Spencer managed twelfth overall, and second in class in this event, being beaten by the impressively fast Ruth Levy in her Porsche. Bob Bondurant lost his clutch.

Jim Mourning was a motoring journalist who had previously raced two Singers. The second of these had been sold after a crash at Palm Springs and replaced by the Morgan. He had been one of the founding members of the flourishing Los Angeles based Morgan Plus Four Club, which was formed in July 1955 following a meeting of interested Morgan enthusiasts at the home of Curt Warshawsky in Culver City.

The SCCA organised National races at Thompson for the Labor Day meeting over the weekend of Sunday and Monday September 2nd and 3rd, the Sunday races being short ten lap

Jim Mourning lines up on the grid at Paramount Ranch, in front of the Porsche of Harry Bonenberger, and the Jaguar of barman Harry Givens. (Lester Nehamkin)

Morgan Sports Cars — 1956

events popular with spectators, whilst Monday hosted one hour races, popular with drivers. Four Morgan racers were entered, these being Gaston Andrey, Woody Young, and two drivers from Rockville, Maryland, James Bullard and George Parks.

In the Class E ten lap race Gaston Andrey had a tremendous battle with Bengt Soderstrom in a 1,600cc Porsche, never more than a few yards separating them. Gaston just managed to win, and George Parks finished sixth, just ahead of James Bullard.

On the Monday the one hour race for Classes D and E was easily won by Paul O'Shea's Mercedes 300 SL, followed by Les Cizek's AC Ace-Bristol, which was second overall and first in Class E, ahead of Andrey and Soderstrom.

The same weekend the Cal Club ran races once more at Santa Barbara. For this meeting Ed Savin had entered Bob Oker in a different make of sports car that he had also begun to import - a turquoise coloured AC Ace, fitted with the excellent Bristol engine. It raced carrying their usual racing number 59E. The new car proved to have the edge on the Morgans, for Bob took it to first overall in the Saturday ten lap Class E race, with Bob Bondurant fourth, Chas Winberg sixth, Lew Spencer ninth and Jim Mourning fourteenth. Lew and Jim failed to make the cut for the Sunday main race, and took part in the twelve lap consolation race for Class E and above. Lew finished fifth overall and first in Class E whilst Jim was twenty-third and ninth in class. As a result of this performance Lew was allowed into the one

Gaston Andrey at the hill turn at Thompson, chasing a mixed Class D and E field. (Alix Lafontant)

The Savin Morgan and its many trophies in the Savin car showroom. (Jim Sitz collection)

hour over 1,500cc Production main event, joining Chas Winberg and Bob Bondurant. Once again Bob Oker and the AC Bristol ran away with Class E, finishing thirteenth overall. Chas Winberg was twenty-third. Lew would have been twenty-second but the Stewards decided he shouldn't have been running in this race after all and disqualified him. Bob retired with no clutch.

The Ed Savin Morgan had been a tremendous advert for the Morgan marque in the West Coast races; out of 23 starts it had taken twelve class wins in the hands of Bob Oker. Californian Morgan enthusiast Al Gebhard, a charter member of the Morgan Plus Four Club, remembers the turquoise Savin Morgan as having had the front inner wing valances extensively cut away, presumably to aid engine cooling. He was somewhat surprised that the car never collapsed!

The Road America course at Elkhart Lake staged the first of what were to become annual endurance races for the SCCA on the weekend of September 8th and 9th. This meeting started with a four hour race for the smaller engined cars on the Saturday, and finishing up with a six hour race for the larger cars on at the Sunday. Over fifty entries were received for the former, including the black Plus Four of David Vogel, and the red Plus Four of Dick Kennedy. The rules specified that there must be two drivers for each car, of which one should be the owner, and that the owner must drive as least one-and-a-half hours. As a result David Vogel asked Augie Pabst, noted TR driver but later to become a top flight sports car driver, to share his Morgan whilst Dick Kennedy asked Detroit MG driver Harry Constant to share his.

Taking the first stint in the Vogel Morgan was its owner and he soon found himself without brakes following serious brake fade, so he began to set up the car for corners sideways on, in a drift, finding the Morgan so easy to position, 'almost like a go-kart'. When he came in to hand over to Augie he told him, 'Oh, by the way, there are no brakes', but Augie found it handled beautifully and he scrubbed off speed with the gearbox before he too drifted around the corners. Pumping the brake pedal had no effect he found. The car went well and they finished third in class.

Meanwhile Dick Kennedy's car was not quite so quick. Harry Constant remembers it seemed to be falling apart around him with various items ceasing to function (no speedometer for example). They eventually finished seventh in class. The Detroit area drivers had developed their own 'club colours' for their sports cars, these being all red, with two yellow stripes across the bonnet. This was all in homage to their 'leader' Tom Payne, who was becoming well known as a semi-professional driver, and who used these colours on his own cars. The colours were said to be those of the 'Ypsilanti Yachting, Road Racing and Marching Society' and were in response to those of the 'Lavender Hill Mob Racing Association' and others!

On Saturday September 15th a race was held by the Glen Corporation at the newly built Watkins Glen course. The SCCA however felt the course to be unsafe and insisted its members should boycott it. This new 2.3 mile circuit, winding around a wooded hilltop, was designed by Bill Milliken with the assistance of computers at Cornell University. Two Morgans ignored the SCCA's advice and competed in the eleven lap (25.3 miles) Seneca Cup race for unrestricted sports cars, these being the Plus Fours of Ike Williamson and George Parks. Ike was sixth overall whilst George failed to finish. This new circuit was to be accepted by the SCCA in 1957 for racing, and was not altered again until 1971.

On Sunday October 7th Gaston Andrey was racing at Thompson and came home third in class.

In Missouri, on Sunday October 21st, Dick Vogel was back with the ex-Rothschild car at Smaart Airport, St Louis, where he finished third in class. David Dukes was also competing, finishing tenth.

The Cal Club returned to the Pomona fairgrounds for a two-day meeting that same weekend. On the Saturday Bob Bondurant was best of the Morgan drivers, finishing sixth in the ten lap race for E Production, with Chas Winberg seventh, and Jim Mourning thirteenth. Dan Levitt had his gearbox fail, hitting a hay bale on Turn 9 as a consequence. The following day the Morgans competed against the larger cars. In the twelve lap consolation race Jim Mourning retired when

Harry Constant leaves the pits in Dick Kennedy's Morgan during the endurance race, with the Morgan painted in the 'Ypsilanti Society' colours. (Harry Constant collection)

he hit an Austin Healey spinning ahead of him, and Chas Winberg lost a wheel at Turn 11, which rolled away to hit a policeman in the back, breaking his shoulder. It transpired that the wheel had pulled through the securing nuts. In the forty lap main event for cars over 1,500cc Bob Bondurant was the only Morgan entry and he failed to finish after he too lost a wheel. It was not a good day for Morgans.

The SCCA ran a race in California at Palm Springs on Sunday November 4th, but Dr Charles Thompson failed to finish.

Over the weekend of November 17th and 18th the California Sports Car Club returned to the tricky figure-of-eight circuit at Paramount Ranch, but this time the club announced that it was not allowing the Morgans, Renault 4CVs, and Citroen 2CVs to compete! This bombshell was no doubt forced upon the club by its racing insurers, who were worried about their liability at this tricky circuit. The Renaults were being banned because one had turned over at Pomona, the Citroens because of the worrying characteristics of the suspension, and the Morgans because of recent losses of road wheels. In addition, the California Club was to inspect Mercedes 300 SLs for anti-oil spill measures, and the tricky Paramount circuit was to be restricted to experienced drivers only, with a maximum number of 25 cars starting per race.

The Morgan bombshell caused a flurry of activity between the club and the car distributors, and no doubt also between Rene Pellandini and the Morgan factory itself. Whilst it was clear that Chas Winberg's Pomona incident happened when the wheel nuts pulled through the wheel centre, other wheel losses had happened for unrelated reasons. Bob Oker's Morgan had lost its left front wheel at the August Paramount meeting when the outer rim separated from the centre, for example. The Cal Club asked Rene if he would be prepared to accept liability if something happened whilst racing; obviously he couldn't do this, but something had to be done, for sales of new cars were beginning to suffer. It was reported that Ed Savin was about to complete the sale of a Morgan to a customer, until the prospective buyer's mother heard that Morgans were 'unsafe' and she quashed the deal. The Santa Barbara Morgan driver William Tuning was so incensed by the attitude of the Cal Club that he flew the Jolly Roger flag from his road going Morgan, emblazoned with the words 'CSCC Outlaw'.

Eventually an agreement was to be reached stipulating that only the latest approved wheels could be used, with safety plates fitted between the wheel centres and the wheel nuts to prevent the wheels from pulling through the nuts. It was clear though that the Morgan bolt-on wheels were not the most suitable for racing, and no doubt Rene Pellandini began pressurizing the Morgan factory for the fitment of the more acceptable wheel for racing, namely the wire wheel.

At the Chimney Rock hill climb in North Carolina over the weekend of November 30th and December 1st RC Buchanan drove his Plus Four up the challenging hill in 4 minutes 24.03 seconds. The course, near Asheville, was 2.75 miles long and had a 'Stop' box halfway up to reduce speed before a particularly dangerous corner! The climb was over two thousand feet and had eighteen corners. The surface was asphalt with a minimum width of eighteen feet.

With the year coming to an end, the SCCA was able to announce its National Class Champions, and this year Gaston Andrey finished second in E Production with 5,250 points, just 500 points behind Bengt Soderstrom's 1,600cc Porsche. Way behind in third place was 'Wacky' Arnolt's Arnolt Bristol, fourth was Les Cizek's AC Ace Bristol, and fifth was Tom Payne with his Arnolt Bristol. Yet again the Morgan had shamed many far more expensive sports cars.

1956 was also important to future American motorists, for it was the year in which authorisation was given for the construction of a national system of Interstate and Defense Highways. These new 'motorways' were to have a dramatic effect on long distance travel within the USA and were authorised by President Eisenhauer on Friday June 29th.

Canada

During July 1955 a sports car enthusiast from Niagara Falls named Ken Rigg put in his order for a Morgan Plus Four two-seater at Windsor Motorcycles. He believed it was the best car to buy at a reasonable price for road racing, being impressed by the way they were carving up the opposition in Class E Production in SCCA racing in the USA. His Morgan, chassis number 3401, engine number TS 7001, was dispatched from the Morgan factory on Tuesday January 3rd, and arrived in Toronto along with three others (chassis numbers 3402, 3406 and 3407) in two railroad boxcars in February. Ken had specified a non-standard colour, namely Jaguar Old English White for the body, with the usual red leather interior and black hood. He had also specified a black tonneau cover, a heater and rear overriders.

Ken's first competitive event was a hill climb run by the Toronto based British Empire Motor Club (BEMC) at Hockley Valley near Orangeville, on Saturday May 12th. As the authorities did not allow roads to be closed for motor sport the club was forced to find little-used tracks as hill climb venues, the Hockley Valley one being unmetalled with a surface of packed sand. The course was a steepish snaking 7/8ths of a mile. Ken improved on his practice time by over six seconds on his first run and by another two seconds on his second to record a best time of 1 minute 14.04 seconds. This remarkable performance gave him third fastest time overall out of forty-six competitors. He was only beaten by Fred Hayes' modified TR3 and Jerry Polinka's AC Bristol.

Ken entered another hill climb on Saturday June 2nd, run by the Sports Car Club. This was held at Rattlesnake Point, near Milton, Ontario, a winding unmetalled 1 in 4 gradient of 700 yards duration. Ken again did well, finishing eighth overall with a time of 52.47 seconds and finishing fourth in class E behind two AC Bristols and Fred Hayes' modified TR3 once more.

After the hill climbs Ken decided to race at the inaugural sports car meeting held at the old airfield at Harewood Acres near Jarvis, south of Hamilton in Ontario. The owners of Edenvale airfield had decided to move to staging just professional racing and were about to build a tri-oval there, so the British Empire Motor Club had now taken a lease on Harewood Acres. This airfield had originally been built as a safety airport by American Airlines for its route from Buffalo to Detroit before becoming a PCATP for Number 1 Bombing and Gunnery School during the War. Ken entered several races on the 3.5 mile circuit made up of runways and taxiways and featuring a hairpin. The meeting was held on Saturday June 16th, with practice and qualifying occurring the previous day. Ken had a dismal weekend. The brake-light switch was faulty and practice was virtually over before he had located and fitted a replacement. He eventually qualified in mid-field, helped greatly by the car's performance. It had rained, but the track was almost dry for the first race. There was another Morgan Plus Four entered, a green one, driven by Ed Russell. This was chassis number 3386, which had been dispatched to Windsor Motorcycles on Friday December 2nd. A Le Mans start was used for the race and Ken was surprised to find himself in the lead, followed by the green Morgan, but then the faster cars started to go by. On about the third lap a TR attempted to pass Ken, but slid in a wet area, taking out the Morgan, fortunately without too much damage. He was forced to retire from racing as a result but Ken kept the Morgan. He finally raced it again in 1987! The other Morgan at Harewood didn't finish either, for big-end trouble eventually forced its retirement.

On the comparatively well populated western side of Canada there was no Morgan agency, but there was sports car racing, the Canadians racing in British Columbia and in the northwestern States of the USA. Owning a garage since 1946 on East Sannich Road near

Sidney was George B Sterne, usually known by his initials 'GB'. He had been racing a black MG TD for two years at Abbotsford Airport, but was now looking for a similarly styled four-seater to accommodate his growing family. MG had introduced the MGA, the styling of which did not appeal, so he began to look elsewhere, and found details of the Morgan in an English sports car magazine. He decided to order one directly from the factory, but was rebuffed, and referred to Windsor Motorcycles. George was not one to give up easily and wrote back suggesting he should start a dealership for the west coast of Canada. Again he was rebuffed, but eventually, when he persisted with a patriotic plea that the Morgan Motor Company was ignoring a large number of Commonwealth subjects on the west coast, he was awarded a dealership, although he was told he was unlikely to get more than a handful of cars each year.

The first car a green two-seater Plus Four, chassis number 3504, was dispatched on Monday July 16th from Malvern, and used by George for publicity before being sold to Alex James of Victoria.

George was now awaiting delivery of his order for a four-seater Plus Four that he could use himself and race too.

Meanwhile in Hamilton itself a young sports car enthusiast named Lincoln Kinsman was working initially as a filing clerk and then as a 'gopher' for Canadian Westinghouse Co Ltd on the guided missile project for the infamous Canadian Avro Arrow fighter aircraft. He had traded in his 1952 MG TD for a Morgan Plus Four at Jim Ferguson Motors in Toronto in June. This ivory two-seater with beige leather upholstery was chassis number 3406 fitted with engine number TS8718. Jim Ferguson had obtained it from Windsor Motorcycles. Lincoln initially used it for his work, enjoying driving to pick up urgently needed parts, but then became interested in sports car racing. He became a founder member of the Hamilton Motor Sport Club and tried the Morgan at that club's driving test held at Harewood Acres in July, which he won!

On Saturday August 4th another race meeting was held at Harewood Acres. Four Plus Fours were entered to be driven by Lincoln Kinsman, Richard Kennedy from Detroit, Bruce McEachern and Ed Houlihan. Sadly we have no results available, but

Lincoln Kinsman after winning the driving test at Harewood Acres. (Lincoln Kinsman collection)

we do know that Lincoln was annoyed to find his Morgan was out accelerated on the straights. He reasoned that if others were bending the rules then he would need to do the same. As a result he and his best friend Michael Sopinka removed the engine and fully rebuilt it with 86mm liners and pistons to take the displacement to 2,138cc. The engine was balanced too and they played with the timing and used richer needles for the SU carburettors. A new set of front suspension rebound springs was also fitted. Lincoln took his Morgan to the Rattlesnake hill climb held in September and recorded the fastest time in his class. He also raced at Harewood Acres over the weekend of September 28th and 29th, along with Ed Russell and Ed Houlihan, but sadly we haven't found any results.

Another hill climb was held at Hockley Valley on Saturday October 13th, attracting five Morgans, namely the Plus Fours of Bob Crossan, Don Broadbent, J Thompson, Bruce McEachern and W Bradley. Bob Crossan was the most successful, recording a time of 1 minute 16.55 seconds to claim third place in Class E.

Starting a long Morgan career in 1956 was Alan Sands (he still has the car at the time of writing!). A friend named Luther Winchell had originally bought this green Plus Four, chassis number 3309, from Windsor Motorcycles in 1955, but disliked the 'brutal' ride, so Alan had traded his 1954 MG TF for it. Alan had been racing the MG fitted with a Judson supercharger.

The BEMC ran ice races during the winter months, although the prime function of these was as social events so no records were kept. A course of about a mile was ploughed clear of snow on a frozen lake, featuring straights, S-bends, fast bends and a hairpin. Alan found the Morgan handled extremely well, but thinks he also intimidated the field by replacing the Morgan's bumpers front and rear with two by eight inch wooden planks! The opposition moved out of the way when they saw these coming at them in the rear view mirror! On one occasion he broadsided an Austin Healey that had 'lost' it in front of him. He was doing about 60 mph and the Healey 2 mph less but sideways. He shoved the Austin Healey off into the snow with no damage to either car!

Lincoln Kinsman on his way to a class win at the September Rattlesnake hill climb. (Lincoln Kinsman collection)

Chapter 4
1957

The year began with petrol rationing still in force due to the Suez Crisis. All the traditional motoring events of the New Year were therefore cancelled, including the MCC's Exeter Trial. All motoring was severely restricted and there was little the motor sportsman could enter at this time.

On Sunday March 3rd the Shenstone and District Car Club managed to run a standard car trial, using a short fifteen mile course and this attracted an entry of over forty. According to *Autosport* magazine, 'M B Jarrett' was competing in the ex-Doc Spare car TYA 1, but we think this is more likely to be N B Jarrett. He did very well, collecting the Shenstone Trophy. Neville Jarrett had joined his grandfather's long established garage, Hunts (Birmingham) Ltd, after the war as Sales Director and had decided to deal in sports cars. During 1956 they had become one of the Birmingham Morgan agencies supplied with cars by Henry Garner Ltd, but in 1957 they were to become Morgan agents in their own right.

That same Sunday the Sheffield and Hallamshire MC and North Midland MC jointly ran a trial at Grasscroft, Dronsfield near Sheffield. Thirty-six competitors took part, and the trial was designed so that no more than one gallon of the precious petrol would be used by local drivers during the day. Two circuits of the eleven sections were undertaken by the production cars, and Ernie Sneath in his Plus Four finished in second place in the open car class, splitting two Austin Sevens.

On Sunday March 17th the Yorkshire Sports Car Club ran a combined trial and driving tests event at Hollings Mill at Sowerby Bridge, the whole event taking place within a circle of just a couple of hundred yards. It was the first motor sport event held in West Yorkshire since the previous November. Despite petrol rationing twenty-four cars entered the driving tests and twelve trials specials entered the trials event.

In the driving tests Ernie Sneath in his Plus Four came a close second to Hitchen's Dellow.

Meanwhile John Looker had decided to remove the Coventry Climax FWA engine from his Plus Four and fit a Triumph TR3 engine. He managed to buy a second-hand TR2 engine from the Morgan factory, and converted this to TR3 specification. The Morgan was returned to the Morgan factory at the beginning of April for a hole to be cut in the offside bonnet where it covered the foremost SU carburettor, and for a cowl to be fitted over this.

At the Morgan factory considerable developmental work was being undertaken, responding particularly to pressure from the important American agencies. Wire wheels were desperately required in California because of the ban by the California Sports Car Club on using the normal bolt-on road wheels for racing and Peter Morgan was busy with this, negotiating with the Dunlop Rim and Wheel Company Ltd. This conversion was undertaken quite quickly and the first cars were actually ready during early April for dispatch to the USA. The Morgan Motor Company's rear axle suppliers, Salisbury Transmission Ltd, had previously introduced in 1954 a wire wheel option for their 3HA axle, so there was no problem there. The wheels themselves were Dunlop type D 452, 60 spokes, with a 19mm inset, which Dunlop had designed to fit their type 42mm hubs. These hubs were used by other popular sports cars such as the Triumph TR series and were made by Dunlop under licence from the original designers Rudge-Whitworth. Whilst some British sports cars, including Triumphs, used a 48 spoke wheel, Peter Morgan didn't regard these as being strong enough for racing purposes on the Plus Four. The Morgan front hub drawings were undertaken by Peter, using drawings supplied by Dunlop which he then adapted. The wire wheels were fifteen inches in diameter, of 4.5 'J' section, and were to be fitted with 5.60 x 15 inch tyres at the Morgan factory. Early production Morgans with wire wheels were actually built fitted with conventional bolt-on wheels, and then converted in the repair shop before dispatch. The repair shop gave a job code number 20 to these conversions, presumably meaning that costs of the conversion were paid for by the car sales department.

The American agents in particular also wanted a more powerful engine fitted into the 4/4, and the Morgan factory's works car RNP 504 had been testing Aquaplane tuning equipment for several months now.

The Friday April 12th edition of *Autosport* carried a road test of RNP 504 by John Bolster. An Aquaplane 'Superhead' aluminium cylinder head raised the compression from 7.0 to 8.0 to 1, whilst twin SU carburettors were fitted onto a special Aquaplane manifold. We suspect that an Aquaplane exhaust manifold was also fitted as this was always recommended when the Aquaplane inlet manifold was being used. John recorded a maximum speed of 80.3 mph and a 0 to 60 mph time of 20.2 seconds, but he reported that the car still had one serious disadvantage and that was the low second gear of the Ford gearbox. He commented, 'With second gear raised to give an easy 60 instead of a doubtful 50 (mph) the car would be transformed.' As tested RNP had a map reading light fitted inside the glove compartment, for use by Peter's navigators in rallies. The report finished with the news that the car equipped as tested was now being catalogued as the 'Competition' model, and that this new model would be available for £531 basic price, including a rev counter, compared with the unmodified 4/4 at £475. The Morgan directors hoped this new model would be more successful in the USA than the standard 4/4 was proving to be. Again the conversion to Competition specification was undertaken in the repair shop on completed conventional production 4/4s, at least for the next year, and given the job code 20, as with the wire wheeled Plus Fours.

The Aquaplane Company had been founded at his home in Oulton Broad in Suffolk by hydroplane enthusiast Harmer Copeman. After the Second World War the Darby-One Design hydroplane had become a popular hydroplane to race and it was powered by a Ford 10 engine. Soon Harmer's tuning made his boat the one to beat, and hence the company was founded to sell his marine tuning equipment. He had now branched out into similar tuning equipment for Ford engined cars and specials, and his products were effective and good value for money.

Andy Polack had concluded that the Ford gearbox was neither strong enough nor suitable for competitive driving in the 4/4. He had tried fitting high tensile gears, and even tried an overdrive which gave six forward gears (although two were actually the same ratio). The overdrive was cunningly activated by raising or lowering the gearlever, making it easy to operate. Andy wanted a better gearbox. He purchased a large box containing two dismantled and slightly different ENV pre-selector gearboxes (one from a pre-war Rapier) for £45.0.0 and he decided to build up one good gearbox from the two and fit it to his 4/4. The gearboxes had no instructions for assembly with them and it was to take him over a year to complete the assembly, with several mistakes until he figured out the complex mechanism. He finally had the Morgan running with the ENV gearbox towards the end of 1958. The conversion proved to be excellent, using special hydraulic controls that he devised such that he could dispense with the normal clutch. The gearbox was fitted between the front of the seat and the driver's feet onto two new chassis cross-members and was quite wide, such that the occupants had the feeling of sitting within the machinery. In action it became very hot and was very noisy, requiring various forms of insulation, including rugs, placed over the gearbox to reduce the transmitted heat and dampen the sounds!

The London Motor Club ran an abbreviated 'Little Rally' on Saturday April 13th, occupying just three hours with mainly driving tests. Two Morgans were amongst the 180 entries, and Romek Michalkiewicz, navigated by E Clarke, only just missed the class award in his Plus Four TKT 100. Miss P Phillips and L Jackson in a Vanguard engined car also finished.

The MCC reluctantly decided it had no option

but to run a much abbreviated course for the Land's End Trial because of the ongoing petrol rationing and it used a 66 mile course within Devon and north Somerset on Easter Saturday April 20th. Several Morgans took part. The Morgan factory entered Peter Morgan in the 4/4 RNP 504, Jim Goodall was in a Plus Four (presumably HUY 982), and the third member of the team was Neville Jarrett, possibly driving TYA 1. Monty Rogers was in his Plus Four PLB 111, and there was another 4/4 Series II entered by D Samm. The weather was good this year and most hills were easy. Peter and Jim were both 'clean' gaining First Class Awards, whilst Neville and Monty failed just one hill for Seconds. Mr Samm didn't win an award.

Girling Ltd sent drawings of a Girling 10 inch by 1.75 inch HLS/S (hydraulic leading shoe, sliding) front brakes set up to the Morgan Motor Company for discussion at the end of April, presumably in response to criticism of the inadequacy of the current brakes during racing. This larger diameter drum brake system was doubtless a similar set up to that employed on the Singer Hunter 75. We believe the Morgan directors at this time really wanted Girling to produce a disc brake installation for the Morgan Plus Four and no doubt they encouraged the company to do so.

Despite petrol rationing the Wirrall 100 MC decided it could still run its annual 'Rally des Etages' event, starting at midnight Saturday April 27th. However, this year the road section mileage was reduced from 400 to 120. Seventy-four starters took part, and the event was won by the rally expert John Waddington who didn't lose a single mark in his TR2. Alec Newsham was in the winning team in his Plus Four HBV 883, together with two Triumph TR2s. Since February Alec's Morgan had been running fitted with yet another replacement Moss gearbox, installed at the Morgan factory, because of the car perpetually jumping out of second gear.

There was much excitement at the Bugatti Owners' Club's Prescott National hill climb held on Sunday May 5th with several records being broken, including the overall record which was lowered to 42.33 seconds by Tony Marsh driving his 1,100cc V-twin JAP engined Cooper. In Class 1C, for sports cars from 1,601 to 3,000cc, Barrie Phipps was fastest of the Morgan drivers in JNV 654, recording 51.82 seconds whilst Angela Palfrey in the same car recorded 52.78 seconds. She just beat Pauline Mayman who recorded 52.82 seconds in TON 919.

Competitors entered for the Autosport Series-Production Sports Car Championship were also eligible to score points here, and Ken Rudd was fastest of this group with a time of 47.95 seconds in his AC Bristol, gaining five points whilst Ray Meredith won two points with a time of 52.30 seconds in NAB 217.

The South Western Centre of the BARC held the first hill climb run at Brunton during 1957 on Sunday May 12th. Unfortunately torrential rain turned

Jim Banbury ascends Brunton hill climb course at the May meeting. (Morgan Motor Co collection)

the course into a river and the paddock into a liquid sea of clay, but it didn't stop John Looker claiming third place in the large sports car class with a time of 29.82 seconds. He was running with the TR engine in his Plus Four OWP 38, and finished behind a Frazer Nash and an AC Bristol. Jim Banbury in JJY 221 recorded 30.80 seconds, and Monty Rogers in PLB 111 made 32.40 seconds

Alec Newsham also did well in the MG Car Club North Eastern Centre's Night Navigation Rally in May, when he was one of two entrants to complete the sixty mile course centred on Leeds without losing a single mark. In the deciding 'cross-roads' driving test he proved faster in his Plus Four HBV 883 than Anne Hall in her Standard 10, thereby taking overall victory. In April his Morgan had the 3.73 to 1 rear axle changed at the Morgan factory for a 4.1 to 1, no doubt improving the acceleration in driving tests, and in early May yet another replacement gearbox had been fitted!

On Tuesday May 14th petrol rationing thankfully came to an end. It had previously been relaxed to a permitted 300 then 480 miles per month, but at last motoring could return to normal. In March the RAC International Rally should have taken place, but it had become one of the biggest casualties of the petrol shortage, and there was to be no such event in 1957.

Just caught out by the end of rationing was the Morecambe National Rally held over the weekend of May 18th and 19th, for the organisers had previously decided to abandon the usual road sections in case rationing continued and instead just ran the traditional driving tests on the promenade. One of the entries nearly didn't arrive at all, for Ted Cleghorn, on his way from Norwich, had broken a valve at Buxton, and he had telephoned home for a spare engine to be taken out to him! We doubt he was in his Morgan and think it more likely he was in his Dellow.

The Eight Clubs held their annual Silverstone race meeting in glorious sunny weather on Saturday June 1st. Before lunch there were two half-hour high speed trials, each having a Le Mans start and requiring a compulsory pit stop to change plugs or swap over the front wheels. Dr A G Turner in his Plus Four came through the event as a 'qualifier'.

The Bugatti Owners' Club ran a members' speed hill climb on Sunday June 9th at Prescott, attracting three Morgan Plus Fours with four drivers. Pauline and Lionel Mayman were sharing TON 919. Ray Meredith was in NAB 217 and Bob Grant in TKC 389. Lionel Mayman proved to be the fastest with a time of 51.04 seconds giving him fourth place in Class 1C, for sports cars from 1,501 to 3,001cc, behind three Bristol engined cars. Ray Meredith recorded 52.84 seconds, Bob Grant 53.46 seconds and Pauline Mayman 53.48 seconds.

The BARC held a National race meeting at Goodwood on Whit Monday, June 10th, attracting many top drivers to a top sports car event. Included in the programme was a seven lap Marque race, for drivers of production sports cars, but barring the more potent AC Bristols, Austin Healey 100S, and Lotus Fords, the BARC using a different classification to that used in the Autosport series. Paul Fletcher's AC Ace led from the start, closely followed by John Looker in his Plus Four, OWP 38. There were several spins and excursions off the course, but at the finish John was back in second place, behind Paul Fletcher, whilst John McKechnie came home in fourth place in MVJ 101.

After ten glorious sunny days the weather took a turn for the worse for the MCC's Silverstone meeting on Saturday June 22nd. As was traditional for the MCC the day began with a thirty minute high speed trial, with most entrants covering sufficient distance to claim First Class Awards. Peter Morgan was on scratch in his Plus Four KUY 387 for the second of the true races, a five lap handicap race, giving a minute start to a Jowett Jupiter. Try as he might it was too great a handicap for Peter to make up and he finished second. In a later five lap handicap Jim Goodall, driving HUY 982, came through the field to finish fourth. The next race was another handicap, but this time over ten laps and a wonderful scrap developed between Peter and Jim throughout the race, Jim eventually just beating Peter to the line for a well deserved win, averaging 70.13 mph. The final race was a five lap 'winners' handicap, producing the best handicapping of the day with practically the whole field crossing the finish line at once! The scratch Jaguar C-type of Johnny Bekaert tore through the field to victory, whilst Peter Morgan came home in third place.

That same day at Goodwood, under similar inclement weather, the BARC ran its 26th Members' Meeting. On the programme was a five lap Marque scratch race, using the BARC's classification and therefore open only to Triumph TRs, Austin Healey 100s, non-Bristol engined AC Aces, Morgan Plus Fours and MGAs. There were spins and incidents galore. On the fourth lap John McKechnie, driving his Plus Four MVJ 101, inherited the lead as those ahead of him spun off. On the final lap, on the run down to Woodcote the second placed MGA of Alan Foster closed up on braking (it was reported as having disc brakes, a non production item), and came alongside John's Morgan as they entered the chicane. Unfortunately there was only room for one and John's Plus Four erupted through the chicane wall and ground to a halt in a mass of planks and woodwork, being quite badly damaged. The Dick Jacobs prepared MGA went on to victory, whilst John Looker who had been driving steadily in his Plus Four came home in third place. The race meeting finished with another five lap handicap, which was noteworthy for fastest lap from a certain Chris Lawrence, driving the 'Rotacks-MG', a heavily modified N type MG running with six Amal carburettors, having originally been 'Porthos' one of the famous 'Three Musketeers' trials MG team cars.

The Plymouth Motor Club had 110 starters for its National rally, which started on Friday evening June 28th from Plymouth, Birmingham, Bristol, Southampton and London, with the routes converging about midnight at Exeter Airport where the real fun began in the West Country lanes. The event finished on Saturday afternoon with driving tests on Plymouth Hoe. Alec Newsham came second, but he had forsaken the Plus Four for a Ford Anglia. In eighth position was Pauline Mayman in TON 919, navigated by Val Domleo. Val Domleo and Pauline were at the beginning of a great partnership and would soon become a formidable ladies team in rallies. Val, a physicist, had graduated into motoring during 1954 after being a keen motorcyclist. She had rallied various vehicles during 1955 and 1956, but her true expertise was as a navigator.

It was really hot at Brands Hatch for a race meeting on Sunday June 30th organised jointly by Club Lotus, the 250 Motor Racing Club and the 750 Motor Club. Despite the unlikely looking clubs listed, 750 MC member J R Beasley entered a Ford engined Morgan 4/4. The bonnet was of unpainted aluminium. In the fourth race, a scratch race over seven laps for sports cars up to 1,250cc, all the field was made up by Lotus models, apart from Eric Broadley's Lola and Elkan's Austin 750. It was, as expected, the Lotus drivers who took the places. Later on in the programme was a five lap handicap for sports cars of any capacity, but excluding Lotus models. It was won by Wilks' Frazer Nash, but in second place came Beasley with the Morgan after a race long battle with Peter Arundell, a future Lotus F1 driver, in his rapid MG TC. Another future Lotus F1 driver, Innes Ireland, was fifth in a Cooper.

There had been correspondence in *Autosport* for some time as to whether Northern Ireland Ford specials were faster than those raced on the British mainland. To settle the matter the Irish challenged the British Ford drivers to the 'Ford Championship of Ireland' on Saturday July 6th at Kirkistown airfield. It turned out the British were the fastest, with Eric Broadley fastest of all in his 1,172cc Lola, just beating several Lotus cars. Besides the championship races there were some other races on the programme for which the Maymans had made the trip over from Birmingham to compete. Lionel won the Formula Libre race in his Cooper Climax, whilst Pauline took her Plus Four TON 919 to third place in the Triumph versus Austin Healey race. She was made an 'honorary Triumph driver' for this event, and finished behind a TR2 and a TR3.

Morgan Sports Cars 1957

The East Anglian Motor Club ran a sprint at Snetterton on Sunday July 7th and several Morgans took part. Alec Newsham was in his Plus Four, HBV 883, Ted Cleghorn in RVF 142, and Jim Banbury, who was now living in London, in JJY 221. These three were entered in the class for sports cars up to 2,000cc, whilst L M Walton had entered his Vanguard engined Plus Four in the over 2,000cc class. Best of the Morgan drivers was Jim with a time of 60.8 seconds, giving him third in class behind the first equal Peter Arundell in his amazing MG TC, and J Shand in a Triumph TR3. Alec Newsham was fifth equal with 61.6 seconds, whilst Ted Cleghorn was seventh, just 0.2 seconds slower. Mr Walton recorded 63.8 seconds.

No doubt it was HFS Morgan who had realised that the bumpers now being fitted to the Ford 100E cars would fit perfectly on the Morgan range and would be cheap to buy from Ford. Morgan had an excellent relationship with Bob Temple of Ford's Parts Division in Romford, and as well as using Ford engines and gearboxes Morgans were also using Ford handbrake levers (umbrella type) on the 4/4. With Ford having agreed to supply 100E bumpers the Morgan Motor Company asked the Pyrene Company to submit drawings for new brackets to mount them onto Morgan cars, which it did in July.

Severe rain showers that caused flooding of the track made racing particularly hazardous at the Aston Martin Owners' Club Silverstone meeting held on Saturday July 13th. As usual the day began with two half hour regularity trials for sports and 'touring' cars.

In the first, the four Morgan drivers entered all collected First Class Awards. These were J R Beasley in his 1957 4/4, and Robin Brown (UOL 490), John Looker (OWP 38) and Barrie Phipps (JNV 654) in their Plus Fours. As usual the AMOC was running its team relay race for the David Brown Challenge Cup and the Morgan 4/4 Club had entered two teams. Team 1 comprised John McKechnie in MVJ 101, Ray Meredith in NAB 217 and Barrie Phipps in JNV 654. Each car had to complete six laps, and the handicap of 2 minutes 50 seconds start was to be carried by the first car. The second Morgan team comprised John Looker in OWP 38, Pauline Mayman in TON 919, and Robin Brown in UOL 490 and the handicap was 4 minutes 15 seconds start. The bad weather meant the fastest teams were unable to use their speed to overcome the start credit handicaps of the slower teams, and a team of Morris Minors with twelve minutes start came home first, with a team of MGAs second and Morgan Team 2 third.

The South-Eastern Centre of the BARC held driving tests on Sunday July 21st on land near Rottingdean. Despite the slippery surface Horace Appleby won a First Class Award in his 4/4. This ivory Morgan, chassis number A207, registration KDY 183, had been dispatched on July 5th 1956 to Car Mart of Hastings for Mr Appleby of Hailsham in Sussex.

Several Morgans took part in the sixth annual inter-club event held at Prescott on Sunday July 28th. In the morning each car ran in the individual competition. Horace Appleby and D A Miller took part in Class 2, for cars between 1,101 and 1,500cc, Horace recording 58.10 seconds in his Series II, KDY 183, whilst Mr Miller recorded 62.86 seconds. This car was a post-war four-seater 4/4, registered DKG 853, and was with the Welsh Counties Car Club contingent.

There were three Plus Fours in Class 3, for cars between 1,501 and 2,000cc, being Les Yarranton with PUY 306, Bob Grant with TKC 389 and Lionel Mayman with TON 919. Bob Grant finished third in the 1,501 to 2,000cc class with a time of 52.62 seconds, beaten only by a Cooper Bristol and the Caesar Special. Lionel wasn't far behind in fourth place with 52.96 seconds, whilst Les recorded 55.64 seconds. In the afternoon the best three of each team competed for the Inter-Club Team Championship on handicap. The Brighton and Hove MC was the winner, and included in the three car team was Horace Appleby in KDY 183 recording an excellent 56.21 seconds. Lionel Mayman recorded 52.11 seconds as part of the Leicestershire Car Club team, whilst Bob Grant recorded 52.41 seconds as part of the Lancashire and Cheshire Car Club team.

Lionel Mayman cornering hard converts TON 919 into a three-wheeler during the inter-club Prescott hill climb. (Pauline Mayman collection)

A crowd estimated at 17,000 packed the spectator areas of the tight 1.39 mile Crystal Palace circuit in London on Bank Holiday Monday, August 5th for a BARC meeting. Racing had restarted after the war at this London park venue in 1953, but using a slightly different circuit to the pre-war one. Close proximity to suburban housing meant racing was restricted to just five events per year.

On the card were two seven lap Marque scratch races, open to Morgans, TRs, MGAs, Austin Healey 100s and non-Bristol engined ACs. In the first event Roy North's potent white TR2 led from the flag, closely followed by John Looker's Plus Four, but John went wide and through the straw bales at Ramp Bend on the first lap, damaging the front of his Morgan and retiring. John McKechnie failed to finish in the places. In the second Marque race Peter Hubner's Morgan, VHT 198, came home fourth behind three TRs.

Motor Sport magazine noted that Michelin X radial tyres were now proving popular for racing, for the first six finishers in this race were so equipped. John Looker had been an early convert to these tyres, but they didn't help him on this occasion!

The final race of the meeting was a five lap invitation handicap. First away was Allatt's TR3 and Peter Hubner in VHT 198, and these two led for four of the five laps before Ian Raby's Cooper Climax swept through the field from scratch to win, but Peter came home third behind Allatt after the spectacular Roy North had lost control of his TR2, spinning into the trees at the end of Glade.

At Trengwainton that same Bank Holiday, a large crowd packed the hillside at this Cornish venue to watch the West Cornwall MC's hill climb in glorious sunshine. In the class for sports cars up to 2,000cc Jim Banbury took his Plus Four JJY 221 to fourth place with a time of 26.60 seconds. Robin Brown finished just 0.04 seconds slower in UOL 490, whilst Ted Dennis recorded 27.16 seconds in his Plus Four, PUY 329. In the open class Robin Brown got his time down to 26.04 seconds to finish fourth.

Ted Dennis lived in Camelford in Cornwall and had successfully sprinted and trialled a 4/4 just after the Second World War. He had a succession of Morgans, and we think he was now driving a second-hand four-seater Plus Four, chassis number 3370, which had originally been dispatched from the Morgan factory on October 28th 1955. It had a Triumph TR2 engine.

The annual Six Hour Relay Race organised by the 750 MC took place at Silverstone on Saturday August 17th starting at 1pm. As in previous years the unique 2.5 mile circuit devised by Holland Birkett was used. Competitors turned right onto a runway at Maggotts, continued along this all the way to Club Corner where they came back on themselves, after a right hand hairpin, to join the Club Straight via a long left hand bend (Tower) using a crossing runway and hence to Woodcote Corner once more. This year the Morgan 4/4 Club had entered just one team, all the members driving 1,991cc Triumph engined Plus Fours. The 'A' car was Nixie, now fitted with a TR3 engine, and to be driven by Sandy Blair. The 'B' car was John McKechnie's racer, MVJ 101 and the 'C' was NAB 217, Ray Meredith's car, now also listed as having TR3 power. The 'D' car was JNV 654, to be driven by both Barrie Phipps and his girl friend Angela Palfrey. The 'E' car was TON 919, to be shared by Pauline and Lionel Mayman. The team manager was Bill Parkes, and the team was given fourteen credit laps. There was one other Morgan entered, the Ford engined 'Morgan Special' of K T Vernon running as part of the 'Individualists' team of mixed vehicles. From the records we have it looks as though the Morgan team disintegrated before it even got to the start, for neither Sandy Blair nor John McKechnie drove. Furthermore Ray Meredith was apparently driving the Maymans' car TON 919!

Ray Meredith did the start, we think driving the Maymans' car, and continued for a stint of just under forty laps covered in approximately one hour twenty minutes. Angela Palfrey then took over in Barrie Phipps' car for thirty minutes. She was followed by Lionel Mayman who lapped consistently quickly at around 2 minutes 6 seconds for about forty laps before he then handed over to Barrie Phipps for the next thirty. He was replaced by Pauline Mayman, who completed thirteen laps before bringing TON 919 back into the pits for refuelling, whereupon Lionel Mayman took over once more. He handed over to Ray Meredith towards the end of the six hours, and Ray crossed the finish line with the Morgan team having covered 165 laps. It was not a brilliant result for the team, for they finished in a lowly eighteenth place of the twenty-five starters. Bill Parkes calculated that the Mayman car TON 919 had covered 118 laps (275 racing miles) whilst the Phipps car JNV 654 had covered 46 laps (115 miles). The winning team was the 'Individualists', but we think the Morgan member of the team may have been missing too.

Whilst Sandy Blair's Nixie didn't manage to take part in the Relay Race, the story of how he acquired the TR3 engine is of interest. Sandy of course had got to know Peter Morgan well and he had asked him about the possibility of changing his original Vanguard engine for a TR3 unit. Peter had replied that there were no mechanical problems in the conversion, but that engines were in short supply at the Morgan factory and they were experiencing difficulties in keeping up with production. As Sandy was in a family farming business he then approached the local Ferguson tractor dealer, the Ferguson tractor engine being another derivative of the Vanguard engine. The dealer confirmed that they could get a TR3 engine for Sandy, but only on an exchange basis. As Sandy had already promised a friend the Morgan's Vanguard engine he exchanged an old Ferguson tractor engine for the TR3. Farmers are well known for being adaptable self taught engineers so Sandy then set about improving the performance of the TR3 engine before it was installed. Peter Morgan had told him how much he could safely take off the cylinder head to raise the compression and all the ports and manifolds were cleaned and polished. Once the engine was installed Sandy made a blister in the offside bonnet to accommodate the front carburettor, later making this into an air intake.

There was fine weather for the BARC's first Members' Meeting at Mallory Park, held that same Saturday August 17th. The third race was a seven lap Marque sports car race, to the BARC's definition, and John Looker was the sole Morgan representative. John had lost none of his verve after his previous escapade at Crystal Palace, for he drove away from the field to a comfortable two seconds win at 71.77mph, from the chasing TRs. Two weeks later on Saturday August 31st John

John Looker at the BARC Mallory Park meeting. (Charles Dunn)

Looker was at Goodwood for a BARC Members' Day. On the programme was a ten lap scratch race for Marque sports cars, to the BARC's formula. It was John Looker who led on lap 1, closely pursued by two MGAs, and eventually they both squeezed past, but one later retired on lap 5 with a leaking radiator. On lap eight John was back in front again, and he held this position to the finish. The BARC was very concerned about tidy driving and any excursions off the track were punished by exclusion from the results. Sadly John, and the third placed MGA of Alan Foster both found themselves subsequently disqualified, but this did push Peter Hubner up the order to fill third place.

That same Sunday the MAC held a hill climb at Shelsley Walsh, attracting four Morgan entries, but Robin Brown non-started. The fastest was Lionel Mayman in Pauline's Plus Four TON 919 with a time of 46.55 seconds, with Bob Grant in TKC 389 achieving 47.35 seconds and Pauline Mayman back in her own Morgan made 47.54 seconds. Fastest in the class for sports cars from 1,501 to 2,500cc by nearly a second was Ken Rudd in his AC Bristol with a time of 40.45 seconds.

With effect from Saturday August 31st the Morgan Motor Company announced substantial price increases across the Morgan range, consequent on wage increases and increased costs of materials and components. The two-seater Plus Four with Triumph TR3 engine rose to £968.17.0 including Purchase Tax, and the 4/4 to £748.7.0 in basic form and £826.7.0 for the Competition version.

The cramped cockpit of the Morgan range had been a source of criticism from the various agencies, particularly the American ones, so the Morgan body shop had been asked if more room could be obtained whilst retaining the same chassis. During September Plus Four two-seaters began being dispatched from the Morgan factory with wider bodies giving an extra four inches of inside space between the doors following a redesign of the wooden body framework. At the same time a shorter front grille was introduced to modernise the appearance.

This year's SUNBAC race meeting held at Silverstone on Saturday September 7th was blessed with sunshine, this being a considerable improvement on the previous year's miserable conditions. Several Morgan drivers entered, these being Ray Meredith in NAB 217, K T Vernon in a 4/4 Series II, and the Maymans. For this meeting Lionel was driving TON 919 whilst Pauline was entrusted with Lionel's 1,100cc Cooper Climax.

After the usual thirty minute high speed trials in which Ray Meredith and K T Vernon were entered, the first race was a six lap race for sports cars under 1,500cc. Pauline Mayman took an immediate lead, but she failed to finish in the first four with the Cooper. The main event for production sports cars was a fifty kilometre race, this being twenty laps of the Club circuit. John Venn soon had his Austin Healey at the front and went on to an easy victory. Behind it was very different, with a tremendous scrap between Lionel Mayman in TON 919, the TRs of Wagstaff and Gossage and the Jaguar XK120 of J R Axon. Wagstaff spun from second place, but rejoined and chased the Axon, Mayman, Gossage battle. Then Axon spun leaving Lionel Mayman in second place, but Wagstaff came past to take the position back, holding it until he ran out of fuel on the sixteenth lap. Axon then spun from third place, taking the unfortunate Gossage with him. This left Lionel to finish in an excellent second place, although he too nearly lost the Morgan on the final corner.

The Bugatti Owners' Club ran a hill climb at Prescott on Sunday September 8th, Class 1C, for sports cars from 1,601 to 3,000cc, being occupied by either Bristol or TR engined cars. Four Morgans took part, the fastest driver being John McKechnie in MVJ 101 with a time of 51.85 seconds. Lionel Mayman recorded 51.97 seconds in TON 919; Ray Meredith recorded 52.28 seconds in NAB 217, whilst John Looker recorded 52.95 seconds in OWP 38.

That same Sunday the Bentley Drivers' Club held a hill climb at Firle in Sussex using a twisty tortuous course with average incline of 1 in 7. Competing in the open class for cars up to 1,500cc was Horace Appleby who managed to finish second behind an MGA in his Morgan 4/4 KDY 193, with a time of 34.34 seconds.

On Saturday September 15th the South Western Centre of the BARC ran its sixteenth Brunton hill climb attracting Jim Banbury in JJY 221 and Robin Brown in UOL 490. Jim managed a climb in 28.19 seconds, gaining him the award for the fastest time of the day by a novice driver. In the under 2 litre sports car class Robin Brown came third with a time of 28.47 seconds to beat all the TRs with ease, but unable to get close to the times of the Frazer Nash of Rudd and the AC of A M Park. Also competing were Chris Lawrence and his uncle Tony Sanderson, both sharing the Rotacks-MG.

This year's London MC's London Rally began on Friday September 21st from starts at Farnborough or Shenstone, the routes converging near Birdlip and continuing to Hereford where the event proper started. The competitors were now faced with 200 miles of Welsh roads to navigate through overnight before a welcome breakfast at Llandrindod Wells and then the final journey to the finish at Farnborough. There were only 240 entries this year, perhaps a sign that the traditional format was beginning to lose its appeal. Fog and heavy rain made the Welsh section particularly difficult and 92 crews retired. Only twenty finishers lost less than fifty marks, but one of these was the Pauline Mayman and Val Domleo Plus Four TON 919 with 36 penalties, winning them the Coupe des Dames and finishing eighth overall. Val was enjoying her successful partnership with Pauline but was finding navigation in the cramped cockpit of the Morgan particularly difficult. 'If you couldn't find something in the car it had probably blown away', she told us. She used to buy Ordnance Survey maps in 'paper flat' option, and needed to fold them in a special way so as to stand any chance of reading them in the cramped cockpit of the Morgan.

The BARC held another race meeting at Goodwood on Saturday September 28th. As usual John Looker was entered for the Marque race, but in practice on the Friday a big-end bolt sheered on the TR engine, and a conrod came out through the crankcase after smashing the camshaft into three pieces. John wasn't one to give up easily so he telephoned his wife in Pershore to ask her to load up the Morgan's old Vanguard engine into the family car and bring it down to Goodwood. She arrived with the engine at lunch time on the Saturday and John just had time to fit it before his race. Sadly the performance was not good after the TR and he failed to make any impression.

That same weekend the Hagley and District Light Car Club ran its first ever sprint meeting at Chateau Impney, near Droitwich. The start was beside a lake, the twisty course finishing 550 yards later after a sharp right hand turn close to the imitation French Chateau. Practice for the fully subscribed event with 100 starters was on the Saturday, with each competitor having two timed runs on the Sunday. Several Morgans took part, with Ray Meredith being the fastest, finishing in third place in the class for standard sports cars up to 2,700cc behind two ACs which dead-heated for first. The Maymans were there of course, Pauline driving well in TON 919, whist Lionel was second in the class for sports racing cars up to 1,200cc in his Cooper Climax with a time of 25.95 seconds.

Alex Blair found the modified TR3 engine in 'Nixie' put him in the results of the East Anglian MC's Clacton Drivers' Rally that same Sunday, making the second best performance and thereby winning the Mann Egerton Trophy.

On Saturday October 5th the Pembrokeshire Motor Club ran another of its hill climbs at Lydstep. Jim Banbury took JJY 221 along and won the class for sports cars, 1,501 to 2,000cc, with a time of 36.95 seconds. The class records set by John Moore back at the Easter meeting in 1955 for the 2,001 to 3,000cc sports cars and also for sports cars over 3,000cc were still in place at the beginning of the day, but a 1,500cc Turner reduced the former by 0.53 seconds to 35 seconds dead, whilst a 5,420cc Allard J2X reduced the latter by 0.95 seconds to 34.15 seconds. The club's times for John Moore's records seem to differ from those reported by the motoring press at the time he took them!

That same Saturday the North Devon MC's Ilfracombe Rally started from Bristol, Salisbury or Newton Abbot, and finished the following day. The only Morgan to feature in the awards was C P Perriam's Plus Four, which won the Newton Abbot Start Award, and also the Agents' Challenge Trophy for Morgan cars.

The Border Motor Racing Club also held a 'Closed to Club' race meeting that same day on the northern racing circuit of Charterhall. This circuit had been built in 1952 using a runway and some perimeter roads of a wartime RAF base, and was situated in the Scottish border country, close to Greenlaw. The lap distance was two miles.

Robin Brown was racing a new green Plus Four this season and is shown starting at Chateau Impney. (Robin Brown collection)

Bob Grant hangs on to his Morgan on the delightful Oulton Park circuit whilst ahead of Alex McMillan's Lotus Climax. (Bob Grant collection)

The first race was a twenty minute handicap for production sports cars and after a shaky start the Morgan Plus Four of W R (Dick) Whitwell passed a Triumph TR and a Jaguar XK 120 to eventually finish in fourth place. Two Austin Healeys took the first two places, but finishing in third place was a local farmer by the name of Jim Clark driving Ian Scott Watson's ex-Billy Cotton Porsche 1600.

The final race of the day was another handicap, for the BMRC Trophy, the grid consisting of the first five finishers in each of the previous four races. Unfortunately rain spoiled things a bit, except to demonstrate just how good Jim Clark was, for he was the only driver to exceed his handicap on his way to taking first place in the Porsche. Dick Whitwell was fourth once more in the Morgan. Dick had purchased his red 1954 Morgan two-seater second hand but he didn't keep it long as he found it to be too unreliable. On this day it certainly seems to have behaved itself! Dick believes it was registered UTN 85.

In October the Ford 100E bumpers began to be introduced to the 4/4 and Plus Four ranges. Peter Morgan had commissioned a new works Plus Four two-seater with wire wheels, which was also fitted with some aluminium body panels, notably the bonnet. This green car had the newly introduced wider body and shorter grille, and had been given the chassis number 3779. It was fitted with the latest high port TR3 engine, number TS 18108. It was tested during the week of October 7th and was registered TUY 875 on Monday October 14th before being specially prepared by Charlie Curtis for the Guild of Motoring Writers' Goodwood Test Day.

On Saturday October 12th the Lancashire and Cheshire Car Club held races at Oulton Park in Cheshire. This attracted large numbers of competitors and spectators, and even ITV television, to this end of season meeting. It started with a half hour high speed trial, the thirty-four starters also having to perform a compulsory wheel change. Twelve drivers beat the club's set distances required to be covered to claim 'qualifiers awards' including Bob Grant in TKC 389 and John Looker in OWP 38. John had now fitted a replacement TR3 engine to his Morgan, obtained from the Standard Motor Company. The last two events of the day were fifteen lap handicaps for production and modified sports cars, but neither of the Morgans finished in the places. Bob Grant found that the Morgan brakes rapidly became useless at a long distance event at Oulton Park, consequently forcing him to brake earlier for the corners than the disc braked TRs, and relying more on engine braking to slow down, but the Morgan did handle better than the TRs.

At Snetterton the final race in the Autosport Series-Production Sports Car Championship was

Smith's Morgan Plus Four van wins at the Stapleford hill climb. (National Motor Museum)

held that same Saturday. It was a three hour event, starting at 5 pm to give drivers and spectators 'Day and Night Racing'. Although Ray Meredith was eligible to enter in view of his two points from Prescott, we have found no record that he did so.

The unique Morgan Plus Four van XEV 795 returned to Stapleford on Sunday October 13th in the hands of its new owner S Smith for the West Essex Car Club's National hill climb. He was competing in the saloon class and he recorded a time of 58.22 seconds to win the class.

John Looker's Morgan OWP 38 was returned from the Morgan factory on Wednesday October 16th after extensive repairs, suggesting the Oulton Park meeting had not been uneventful for him!

For this year's Motor Show, held at Earls Court from Wednesday October 16th to Saturday October 26th, the Morgan Motor Company was showing to the public several new features introduced on models during the previous year. The 4/4 rolling chassis shown at the 1956 Show was on display again, but this year it was upgraded to Competition model specification, the Ford engine being fitted with an Aquaplane head, 8 to 1 compression, stronger valve springs, new inlet and exhaust manifolds and twin SU carburettors. There was also a complete 4/4, coloured pearl grey and blue with grey upholstery (chassis number A344). There were two Plus Four two-seaters, both with the newly introduced wider bodies and one having wire wheels (3773 and 3774). There was also a coupé model on show, in left hand drive form and having the optional wire wheels as well as a radio (3775), and a four-seater in Ming Blue (3769) completed the Plus Four line up. All the Plus Fours had the new shorter grilles and TR3 engines, although Standard Vanguard engines were available as a cheaper alternative if required.

The Standard Motor Company was showing a revised TR3, the TR3A, which now had a full width radiator grille, slightly recessed headlamps, exterior door handles and lockable handles to the boot lid.

Peter Morgan was approached on the Morgan stand by Bob Grant and Ted Cleghorn who inquired whether Peter might make up a Morgan team of three with them to contest the Tulip Rally in 1958. They also asked whether the works might help prepare the cars. Peter replied that he was not able to compete in overseas events following a pledge he had given to his father some years previously, adding that the Company did not usually enter the Continental rallies. He asked what preparation to the cars would be required and Bob replied, 'brakes'! Bob continued, saying that good brakes were an essential requirement for the Tulip Rally, and asked when Morgans were to be fitted with disc brakes, as after all the Triumph TR3 was now fitted with them and had been since the 1956 Motor Show. Peter replied that he was concerned the front of the chassis might not be strong enough to stand the braking power of discs and might need strengthening.

On the middle Sunday of the Motor Show period (October 20th) the Guild of Motoring Writers were offered the chance to drive examples of the manufacturers' products at the Goodwood test day. This year Morgan made available Peter Morgan's new works car, TUY 875. This became the second car to be driven by the *Autosport* reporters on the day, and they noted the Plus Four had a small wooden handle from a file replacing the usual gear knob, this being a Peter Morgan 'customisation'. The reporters loved the car commenting, 'We cannot recall any other car of any type that was so much fun to drive.' They were lucky however, for the car spent most of the rest of the glorious sunny Sunday bogged down beyond Lavant Corner where it had come to rest after shedding one of its wire wheels!

On Saturday October 19th the Hastings, St Leonards and East Sussex CC ran a hill climb at Bodiam New House Farm using a course within this Guinness hop farm. In the class for open cars from 1,301cc to 2 litres A M Greig's pretty 1955 Plus Four climbed in 33.6 seconds on both runs for class victory, and his time was fast enough to be the sixth fastest of the day. Over that Saturday night the Yeovil CC ran a night navigation rally, finishing the following day. C Perrian won his class in his Plus Four, navigated by Miss Scott.

On Saturday October 26th the Falcon MC started the Guy Fawkes 200 Trial. This year two events were run concurrently, a tough one for trials specials and an easier one for standard cars. The starts were at London, Birmingham, Cambridge, Southampton, and Taunton, the field of over fifty cars converging at Andoversford near Cheltenham to visit twelve famous Cotswold trials hills. Peter Morgan was entered in the works 4/4 RNP 504 in the trials specials class, and did exceptionally well to collect a First Class Award. Ted Dennis drove his Plus Four to take the Sports Car Award, whilst F A Freeman took the Guido Vase, for the best standard car, with his Morgan. We think Mr Freeman was driving the ex-Odoni Plus Four PUV 42. Ted Dennis had his lights fail during the overnight run, but luckily David Hilliard had held back for Ted to follow close behind his Ford until dawn. Ted was also a member of the winning team, along with a Dellow and a Ford special.

The following day the Herefordshire MC ran a 'Sporting Half Day' event, challenging the Hagley and District LCC to tests. The class for open cars was won by Les Yarranton in his Plus Four PUY 306 whilst Frank Livingston was second in his Morgan. The Hagley Club won the Challenge.

The Oxford MC ran the Boanerges Rally on Saturday November 2nd. Pauline Mayman, no doubt navigated by Val Domleo, took the Ladies' Award. That same evening the BARC South Eastern Centre began a night navigational rally, and Horace Appleby managed to collect a Second Class Award in his 4/4 KDY 183.

Each year the Scottish Sporting Car Club ran an Anniversary Run to commemorate the club's formation and there were 74 starters for the run held on Saturday November 9th. As well as seven road sections the event had two driving tests held in the grounds of Trearne House, near Beith. Ken Sturrock came second in one of these in his Plus Four. This most sociable event ended with a fireworks display.

On Sunday November 10th the Harrow CC ran an autocross at Earls Colne, Essex in a field owned by the enthusiast Bert Westwood. Bert was sharing a Plus Four for the event, this being the ex-Alec Newsham car HBV 883 but we are not sure who now owned it. Tucker-Peake in his Tucker-MG won the class for the larger sports cars but F A Freeman's Plus Four was second, despite running with the hood erected, just ahead of the Morgan of H J Bone.

Whenever HFS Morgan introduced a new chassis he would always look at what body options might be built upon it to appeal to the public. The Ford engined 4/4 had duly received the HFS attention. During May a 4/4 chassis, number A296, appeared with four-seater bodywork to see whether or not this might be a model the Morgan Motor Company would add to its range. It was eventually decided not to proceed with this body for the 4/4 but this experimental four-seater was dispatched on Friday November 22nd to Royle and Sons in Romsey, Hampshire.

The Hagley and District Light Car Club held a combined sporting and production car trial on Sunday December 1st, victory in the open car class going to Frank Livingston in his Plus Four. That same day Bob Grant showed his versatility by winning the Chester Motor Club's standard car trial with TKC 389.

The BARC South Eastern Centre ran another night event on Saturday December 14th, this time the club's popular night driving tests. Horace Appleby was the open cars class winner in the 4/4 KDY 183. The following day the West Hants and Dorset Car Club ran the Christmas Cup Trial, which was won by future Morgan driver Harry Rose in a Morris Minor, but the best of the open car class was J Ashworth in his Morgan.

The British Trial and Rally Drivers' Association held its annual dinner and awards presentation on this Saturday, and the best performance of a Morgan driver in the Gold Star competition was this year by Alec Newsham in third place, although in several of his rallies he had not been driving his Plus Four. The winner was Ron Gouldbourn in his TR and second was Brian Harper.

As a post-Christmas treat the Nottingham Sports Car Club ran a race meeting at Mallory Park on Boxing Day. There were 29 sports cars amongst the entries, but a fine afternoon saw good racing. There were two twelve lap heats and a twenty lap final for the sports cars and John Looker went well in the second heat to finish in sixth place in OWP 38, behind various sports racing cars and two AC Bristols. In the final John was holding a remarkable fifth place amongst some exotic machinery when on lap six he had a front brake lock as he came into the hairpin, he went wide and the Morgan hit a very solid row of oil drums at the outside of the hairpin, which it mounted, coming to rest somewhat battered and unceremoniously on top of them!

France

Claude Savoye soon entered races on the banked track of Montlhéry with a Plus Four, discovering that the hard ride from the Morgan suspension was made much worse by the bumpy track, giving him a most unpleasant journey, with the car frequently airborne. He found it best to wear a body belt to reduce his discomfort.

The grid of the Grand Prix de Paris, run by the Association Générale Automobile des Coureurs Indépendants (AGACI) at Montlhéry. Claude Savoye is behind the front wheel, wearing his body belt. (Morgan France collection)

South Africa

Morgan Plus Fours had been imported into South Africa since 1952 mainly by Robb Motors in Cape Town, who were also distributors for BMC, Rover, Jaguar, Rolls Royce, and Studebaker as well as Norton motorcycles. Morgans were usually imported only to order and so in 1955 Peter Lawley, a member of a family printing and publishing firm, ordered a two-seater Plus Four to replace the Morris Minor he had been racing. Peter's father was actually a nephew of the Morgan Motor Company's very first works manager, Alfie Hales, and as such the name Morgan was revered in the family household. The ordered Plus Four, which was red with black upholstery and fitted with a TR3 engine, had arrived in late 1956, and Peter had been entering it in local club events, his first race being on his 27th birthday on November 3rd.

On Monday January 1st 1957 Peter took his Morgan to the South African Championship race meeting held at Gunners Circle, a road circuit made up from perimeter roads around a newly developing factory complex on the outskirts of Cape Town. During practice he was slip-streaming a Studebaker down the long main straight when a stone was thrown up and shattered his goggles. He went to hospital for glass to be removed from his eye and obviously took no further part in the proceedings. Also participating in a Morgan Plus Four was Eugene 'Gene' Bosman, a pharmacist from Kloofsig, Pretoria, who finished tenth overall in the False Bay 100, but second in the more important handicap division. He had bought his green Plus Four from the other Morgan importer, Haaks Garages in Johannesburg, during 1956, this being chassis number 3453 which had been dispatched from the Morgan factory on March 19th.

On Saturday January 26th a crowd estimated at 3,000 turned up at Krugersdorp, just west of Johannesburg for a hill climb organised by the Sports Car Club of South Africa. This was the second event to be held on a closed section of public road leading up from a sewage farm, and had two hairpins as well as a right-angled bend within its 960 yard length. The previous event had been won by a Morgan Plus Four with a time of 61 seconds, but this time some racing cars had entered so the time was expected to be beaten. Gene Bosman had entered his Plus Four in the 1,801 to 3,000cc sports car class, with eight TR2s to beat and a Le Mans Austin Healey 100. On the final run of the three undertaken Gene managed to beat all in his class, and had the distinction of being fifth fastest overall in 58.3 seconds.

Another South African Championship race meeting was held at the Eerste River aerodrome circuit just outside Cape Town on Saturday March 23rd. The main event was the 105 mile, sixty laps, International van Riebeeck Trophy race, which featured four overseas entrants driving two Cooper T41 Climaxes, a D-type Jaguar and a Connaught A-type. As was usual in South African racing at this time the local opposition ranged from locally owned single-seaters (Cooper Bristols etc) through home made specials to production sports cars. Peter Lawley drove extremely well in his Plus Four and managed to finish in seventh place overall. However the handicap division was always more important than the scratch and Peter was second in this to reigning South African Champion Bill Jennings in his home made Riley special. Peter's greatest thrill had been passing Lord Louth's D-type Jaguar on the outside of a long sweeping bend, but he later found out that the Lord was having tyre trouble. Peter received a large cup and a cheque for £75, a considerable amount of money.

Peter had modified the Morgan for racing by stripping it of unnecessary weight and replacing the driver's seat by one he made from some aluminium obtained from a scrapped Avro Anson aeroplane. Peter had found that if he uncoupled the flexible part of the exhaust system from the silencer and fastened it to the chassis just in front of the driver's door he got a considerable increase in performance. He also replaced the chrome grille in front of the radiator with wire mesh as he didn't want the original one damaged by stone chips.

Peter Lawley proudly displays his trophy at Eerste River. (Morgan Motor Co collection)

For some reason this also improved the engine cooling.

At the same meeting there was a twenty lap production and sports car handicap race. It was won by Mark Zoccola in an MGA, with Dave Colman second in a Plus Four. Dave was a motor mechanic, who tended to race whatever he had available.

A nine-race meeting was held at the 2.5 mile Halfway House circuit (Grand Central Aerodrome) near Johannesburg on van Riebeeck Day, Saturday April 6th, by the Sports Car Club of South Africa and the Transvaal Motorcycle and Car Club, five of the races being for cars. There was just one Plus Four in the third race, a five lap sports car handicap, but the Morgan didn't finish in the first three. The main race was the '1820 Settlers' Handicap', held over 65 miles and featured a massed start for the 27 competitors. At the start the Morgan driven by Gene Bosman was bumped onto the grass, narrowly missing a photographer, as the field roared under the bridge. It failed to finish in the places, coming home in ninth place overall and eighth on handicap.

Gene Bosman took his Morgan to the Roy Hesketh circuit at Pietermaritzburg on Easter Monday April 22nd for the 64 mile Coronation 100. He came home sixth on handicap. In the supporting 22 lap handicap race he did better, finishing third. On Sunday July 7th Gene took his Plus Four to East London where the 104 mile East London Winter Handicap was run on public roads, but he didn't feature in the main results.

Another hill climb was held at the sewage farm road course at Krugersdorp on Saturday September 28th, as part of the festivities to celebrate the town's founding seventy years earlier. In the class for sports cars up to 1,300cc there were six entries, one being a Morgan 4/4 Series II. An MG special took the class, the Morgan failing to beat 80 seconds for the run. No Plus Fours were entered in the larger sports car class. We think the 4/4 was one of two cars dispatched from Malvern to Robb Motors on September 3rd, chassis numbers A330 (red) and A331 (green).

Australia

The year started with the third of the annual Derbys on Busselton Airstrip on Monday January 28th and again Merv Dudley and the R4 participated, this time with no recorded problems in towing the racer from Perth.

1957 was to be a very significant year for motor sport in Western Australia. The second Australian Grand Prix ever to be held in the west was to be run on a very hot Monday March 4th at the Caversham Airstrip, on the 'D' circuit. In the annals of Australian motor sport this was probably the last of the 'local' post-war Grand Prix. It was in essence a mixture of the truly classic 1950s style racers and the highly prepared factory built entries that were to come and soon completely dominate. The Australian Grand Prix held at Narrogin in 1951, had featured seven MG TCs, a 4/4 (Colin Uphill) and a large number of specials, but by the time of the 1956 Australian Grand Prix at Albert Park in Victoria the entry was comprised almost entirely of factory built racers, Maseratis, Ferraris and Coopers. The 1957 event in the west combined both eras. More than half the starters were sports cars or specials, amongst which were two locally built Morgan Plus Four specials. The other half of the field had mostly come from the eastern Australian States and consisted of factory built racers.

The first of the Plus Four specials was the Bill Richards Motors R4 which was to be driven by Merv Dudley. The second of the specials was conceptually very different to the R4 and was to be driven by Barry Ranford. Barry was an extremely successful local Western Australian racing car builder and driver, who ran the Loftus Service Station in Leederville. When the Australian Grand Prix was announced for Caversham he came out of 'retirement' to build yet another special, and asked his son, also called Barry Ranford, if he would return from Singapore to share the driving. The basis was a Vanguard engined 1951-52 Plus Four that had suffered a 'write off' accident in someone else's hands. Starting from the original chassis the front suspension was very considerably softened and the geometry altered to enable the suspension and not the chassis to absorb the road shocks. As with the R4 a new rack and pinion steering was fitted (from a Morris 1000) which took care of the steering deflection caused by the original chassis flexing. The front suspension settings received considerable attention. General Motors (Holden) stub axles were married to the original sliders and the front suspension was lowered significantly. To the stub axles were added huge Ford Commercial front brake back plates modified to take two wheel cylinders and twin leading shoes. These were very effectively contained by beautifully finned Clyno brake drums. To balance the braking, larger rear wheel cylinders were fitted, resulting in a car that not even the disc-braked Cooper Climaxes could out stop. The brakes were so effective in fact that braking could be left until very close to corners, and when applied the tubular cross members of the front suspension could be seen to twist!

The rear axle and very reliable four speed Moss gearbox remained unaltered. The Vanguard engine was highly modified and received the attention to detail for which all Barry's specials were renowned. The crankshaft was ground, hard chromed and reground to size, and aluminium/tin bearings were used. Unlike the R4 the bore of the Vanguard engine in this Ranford Special was enlarged to the limit and special pistons (possibly Chrysler) and rings fitted. Everything was balanced. The head was ported and polished and fitted with maximum oversize valves with heavy-duty valve springs. The camshaft was reground to 'racing specs' but the final profiling of each lobe was painstakingly finished with emery paper over a flat file! The exhaust system had four equal length primary pipes, which were encased in an 'extraction chamber' and then reduced to a 3 inch diameter final pipe. Two SU carburettors had been fitted to the engine but were replaced with two Holden 'Stromberg' carburettors. These were far superior, each having an adjustable main jet fitted together with two accelerator pumps to supply extra fuel when needed. The cooling system had a thicker radiator core and an enlarged upper tank.

The car was enclosed in a rather simple but lightweight aluminium body fitted with detachable lights and mudguards enabling it to be used as either an open wheel racer or a sports car at the same meeting! The power to weight ratio was very favourable and, with the engine and gearbox moved further to the rear, the handling was exceptionally good. In the middle of a four wheel drift the car was easily steered by the throttle. Indeed Barry Ranford Jnr recalls that, 'by shifting one's bum in the seat the car could be steered with the power full on in a corner, a little like skiing!' It had neither oversteer, nor understeer and had superlative braking. Although the R4 had been racing consistently for more than two years, the Ranford Morgan Special only had its first real race in the heats two days before the Australian Grand Prix.

The Caversham Australian Grand Prix was a remarkable event not just because two very competitive Morgan specials were entrants. The two leading racing drivers were Stan Jones (father of future World Formula One Champion Alan Jones) in a 3 litre 250F Maserati and Lex Davison with his Ferrari 625/750. However, there was a string of Coopers including those of Jack Brabham, Len Lukey and Alec Mildren. The lap record at Caversham was still held by the R4 Morgan but in practice on the Saturday both Jones and Davison pulled it down from 1 minute 40 seconds to 1 minute 35 seconds (Brabham's Cooper equalled the R4 at 1 minute 40 seconds) and in the Australian Grand Prix race itself this was further reduced to 1 minute 34.8 seconds by the Ferrari. Merv Dudley fared very well in the twenty lap heats and the R4 managed to pass Alec Mildren's Cooper on lap 20 to take third place. Unfortunately, the marshals had flagged the finish of the heat on lap 19!

By Monday, the temperature had reached 104 degrees Fahrenheit in the shade when twenty-two cars faced the starter. The start was confused by one of the cars still being fuelled when the flag dropped and, although the R4 got away well with the first bunch, the Ranford Morgan, driven by Barry Ranford Senior, had been severely disadvantaged. By lap 10 the original field of twenty-six was reduced to twenty. There were frequent pit stops and a number of further retirements. Lex Davison came into the pits on lap 27 with heat exhaustion and handed over to Bill Patterson as relief driver. At the end of thirty laps, the order was Jones, Davison/Patterson, Mildren, Lukey, Brabham and then the R4. Lex Davison stepped back into the Ferrari on lap 45. Soon after, and no doubt by now suffering from severe heat stroke, Stan Jones hit the Ranford Morgan with his Maserati. Both continued but the Maserati had to be pushed to restart, and this, together with the rules regarding relief drivers, caused considerable controversy after the event. Stan Jones pitted to seek a relief driver but there was none available and he had to continue after a drink and just twenty seconds out of the car. The Maserati took the

A specially commissioned cartoon by Rod Waller of the finish of the Australian Grand Prix with Merv Dudley pushing the R4 over the line just before Barry Ranford finishes in the Ranford Morgan Special. (Rod Waller)

chequered flag, although there was some debate about on which lap the Ferrari and the Maserati had actually finished.

Both the Morgans had finished on lap 60 of the seventy. The R4 actually stopped just before the line, seriously overheated and with a burned piston; poor Merv Dudley had to push it across for eighth place. He was almost passed at the last moment by Barry Ranford, who finished ninth overall, but on handicap, the Ranford Morgan was in fact fifth. The R4 would have been the first Western Australia entrant to finish except for the incident on the last lap but was second to Sid Taylor in his TS Special. Sid had lost second gear in his special quite early in the race, so he did very well driving the car in just top gear. There were a number of drivers who required medical attention for the effects of the searing heat after the race, and following a number of protests quite a few positions were reversed, including those of the first two places. Stan Jones was flagged off as the winner on lap 70, with Lex Davison half a lap behind in second place. However a protest by Len Lukey against Alec Mildren meant the lap charts of Davison were used as evidence by Lukey, and it was found Lex was in fact ahead of Stan Jones by 0.43 seconds at the finish. Stan Jones protested at losing first place, but this was dismissed at a later meeting at Melbourne, leaving Lex Davison the winner of this twenty-second Australian Grand Prix, his second success in the events.

Making a welcome return to racing in the Australian Grand Prix had been David Van Dal, sharing his modified Bugatti 57T with his friend John 'Cummo' Cummins. He had fitted his own design of fuel injection using twin butterflies and suffered a bad misfire which eventually forced retirement. Later they found the cause was not the fuel injection system after all, but ignition.

Morgans took part in a number of hill climb meetings in Victoria. On Sunday May 5th L E Craddock with his TR2 engined Plus Four clocked 33.1 seconds at Rob Roy, and at Hepburn Springs a week later 38.8 seconds. At this latter meeting Craddock was just pipped by Ian McDonald (38.78 sec) with his lightened Vanguard engined Plus Four.

Following the Australian Grand Prix Merv Dudley rebuilt the R4's engine, which he detuned a little by replacing the head with one having a much lower compression ratio. Despite this the car remained competitive in Merv Dudley's hands, finishing fourth to Barry Ranford Junior's third in the ten lap Triangle race at Caversham on Monday June 3rd (but held on the 'D' circuit) and managing a 1 minute 44 seconds lap. The R4 was given a stiff handicap, starting ten seconds behind the TS Special, and there was some heated criticism of the stewards, for the TS had improved to the extent that Sid Taylor was lapping regularly at 1.40 or a bit above.

Back at Rob Roy in July Craddock was really flying, lowering his previous best by 0.89 seconds to 32.21 seconds and at Templestowe a week later he clocked a creditable 69.14 seconds to be second fastest on the day.

The two Morgan specials clashed again at the WASCC Caversham meeting on Saturday September 14th in the State Racing Car Championship. However, by now the competition was much more powerful. Sid Negus had acquired a Cooper Bristol and Syd Anderson a very well maintained Alta. Don Hall was driving a 57T Bugatti and Greg McEwin had come across from South Australia with his Mac-Healey. Barry Ranford managed third in one of the three heats but the R4 was now described as 'going badly'. It had been entered with both David Van Dal and Peter Bond as drivers, but in the event David and the current Western Australian Motorcycle Road-racing Champion Peter Nicol, were the drivers, and they fared poorly. After the first heat with David driving, the carburettor necks were found to have broken and Peter Nicol started the second heat with them simply 'taped together', only to pit after three laps. Syd Anderson became the Under 1,500cc Champion with his Alta and Greg McEwin the Over 1,500cc Champion in the Healey special. Sid Taylor had an eventful day, pulling the gear lever out of the TS. The Club magazine of the time, *The Visor*, suggested he had thought it was a tooth!

The WASCC Christmas Cup meeting was held earlier than usual in 1957, on Saturday November

Barrie Ranford Senior tackles Olympic Corner at Caversham with his special, probably during one of the last two events of 1957. (Barry Ranford collection)

23rd. The R4 (Peter Nicol) and the Ranford Special (Barry Ranford Senior) fared a little better in the five lap Champion's scratch race, placing fourth and fifth respectively, with Peter Nicol lapping in 1 minute 44 seconds, Barry Ranford in 1 minute 52 seconds. However, in the Christmas Cup itself, over ten laps, Barry Ranford's Special suffered a case of gremlins at the start and failed to move from the line for some time, but once going lapped in 1:50.

New Zealand

Dave Edmiston's first race with his new Plus Four was on Saturday January 26th at the Wigram airfield race meeting where he finished third in the twelve lap open car handicap for cars not entered in the Wigram Trophy race itself. The winner was B Kilkelly in a rapid MG from scratch. Bob Blackburn's Ford 1,172cc Mistral finished second off a handicap of two credit minutes, whist Dave had been given four minutes start. He recalls a most disgruntled Jaguar XK140C driver complaining about the cost differential and his inability to catch the Morgan that day.

One week later, on Saturday February 2nd, Dave entered the Morgan for the sports car event at Dunedin, where a street circuit was in use. This circuit of streets situated in the Victoria wharf area of Dunedin had first been used in June 1953 for the 75 mile New Zealand Championship Road Race, and the race meeting had been held annually since then. In 1953 Ted Reid had entered his Vanguard engined Plus Four for the supporting races, finishing in fifth place in the thirty mile Sports Car Handicap.

By 1956 the race meeting had developed to become part of the Dunedin Festival celebrations and had become a truly international event. Whilst the 43 lap Championship race was the main event on the programme and attracted an estimated 18,000 spectators to see Reg Parnell in a Ferrari beat Jack Brabham in a Cooper Climax, the Gregg Anderson Memorial Race for Sports Cars was also on the card. This attracted eighteen starters for the Le Mans start, one of which was Dave Edmiston. Dave had covered the front of the Morgan wings and cowl with masking tape to prevent damage from stones thrown up by other racers, and had removed the radiator stone guard to improve cooling. Two rear view mirrors were

Dave Edmiston spins his Morgan whilst racing at Dunedin. (Alex Stuart)

fitted to the windscreen support brackets on each side of the car, the windscreen being replaced by an aero screen. Bruce McLaren, the future World Champion from Auckland, was first away from the Le Mans start in his red Austin Healey, but was soon overtaken by Ross Jensen in a Ferrari Monza, and another future World Champion, Jack Brabham, in a Cooper Climax 1500 Sports bobtail, who went on to win. Dave Edmiston finished in equal sixth place overall, together with Avery's HWM Cadillac, but came second in Class II for cars under 2,000cc to Jack.

Two weeks later many of the Dunedin contingents had moved to the Ryall Bush circuit near Invercargill, this rectangular 3.65 mile circuit being the fastest in the country. The Southland Sports Car Club was to run the Southland Road Race on Saturday February 16th, and the weather was swelteringly hot, with hardly any wind to cool the 10,000 spectators. Dave Edmiston had entered the twelve lap sports car race, which was a handicap event, and he was to start 4 minutes and 30 seconds after the first competitor left the start. He took the lead and held it until he was just 300 yards from the chequered flag when Jack Brabham flashed by to win in his bobtail Cooper Climax. Jack had driven through the field after starting

4 minutes later than Dave. Ross Jensen was third in his Monza Ferrari.

Dave Edmiston continued to have success with the Morgan. He took first and second placings at the short grass track at Lovells Flat, and numerous placings in trials. He also won the James Challenge Trophy for the fastest stock car at the Otago Sports Car Club's Championship hill climb held at Patmos Avenue in Dunedin and recorded the fastest standing ¼ mile with time of 16.35 seconds at a sprint meeting held at the Fryatt street course.

On Saturday April 13th there were two Morgan entries in the Te Onepu hill climb event run by the Hawke's Bay (Sports) Car Club; Russell Buckthought in the over 1,500 cc class and Arthur Spargo in the under 1,500cc class. The hill climb enjoyed fine weather with entrants from Wellington, Masterton, Wananui and Manawatu. In the sports car class Arthur Spargo's Morgan 4/4 was sixth with 1minute 44.8 seconds, the fastest being Tom Fox (MG TF 1500) in 1minute 18.2 seconds. In the over 1,500cc class Russell Buckthought, driving the ex-Graham Cowie Plus Four coupé, was fifth with 1minute 15.5 seconds, the fastest being Hugo Hollis in a Jaguar XK120 in 1minute 9.0 seconds. Interestingly, Angus Hyslop was third in a Jaguar XK140 with 1 minute 9.2seconds. Russell Buckthought was also a

Dave Edmiston at Southbridge. (Dave Edmiston collection)

member of Allen Freeman's pit crew at race meetings.

Dave Edmiston took his Plus Four to Southbridge, just south of Christchurch, for races held on Monday June 3rd. The track was part tarseal and part gravel so Dave covered the front of the Morgan with masking tape to prevent stone damage. The event was a handicap race and, in Dave's own words, he was handicapped out of it.

Three Otago Sports Car Club drivers made the trip to Clellands Hill, near Timaru on Saturday June 22nd for the South Island Hill Climb Championships, organised by the South Canterbury Car Club. Each won a class, Dave Edmiston taking the up to 2,000cc class with his TR engined Plus Four, Ted Reid the up to 3,000cc class with his Vanguard engined Plus Four and W Ashton the up to 1,100cc class with his special.

Dave Edmiston again made fastest time of the day at the Dunedin Patmos Avenue hill climb, held over the October Labour weekend, October 26th and 27th, and actually broke the one minute barrier for the first time.

The enthusiastic Nelson Car Club was renowned for the annual New Year holiday two-day beach racing at Tahunanui Beach, but the club also organised other events. During October or November it ran a sprint meeting, attracting eighteen entrants, one of which was the Morgan 4/4 of the Club's Inaugural President, Halsey Logan. Halsey ran 'Logan Motors', a garage in Nelson. Tuned Ford Ten engined specials were popular for motor sport, but Halsey resorted to supercharging for his 4/4. It seemed to work, for he finished fourth in the standing quarter mile with a time of 20.4 seconds, and fifth in the flying quarter mile with a speed of 88.3 mph. This Morgan was chassis number A219, which was blue, and had been originally dispatched from Malvern on September 5th 1956. Halsey was the second owner, having purchased the car in August. On Saturday November 9th another hill climb was held at Te Onepu, on a fine sunny day. Finishing third in the class for sports cars of less than 1,500cc was P Langley in a Morgan 4/4, with a time of 1 minute 40 seconds, the winner being the MG TF of R Smith (1 minute 21 seconds). Arthur Spargo had entered an Austin Healey 100 Six this time.

On Saturday November 30th, the inaugural race meeting was held at the Teretonga circuit, at Sandy

Point near Invercargill. This permanent fully sealed purpose built 1.5 mile track had been built by the Southland Sports Car Club, and 5,000 spectators were attracted to view the action. Intermittent rain did its best to dampen the goings-on. There was a twenty lap 'Sports and Racing Car Race' on the programme, which was run as a handicap, and Dave Edmiston was set off five minutes after the limit car had been dispatched on its way. Dave was up to the challenge and finished first, Dr Ken McMillan's Austin Healey finishing in second place.

USA

In California the Cal Club's edict banning Morgans from its events at the end of 1956 had now been rescinded, providing safety plates were fitted to the wheels, and two Morgans were so equipped and entered for the Pomona meeting held over the weekend of January 19th and 20th. One was the well-known Plus Four of Charles Winberg, and the other was an entry from Rene Pellandini, the West Coast Morgan distributor. It was a Ford engined 4/4, and Rene had asked Lew Spencer to drive the Morgan for him, having been impressed by his racing in the previous year. Having an engine capacity of 1,172cc it was classified in Production Class F, which included sports cars from 1,100cc to 1,500cc. The car was prepared for racing by Rene's new mechanic, Claude Brun, who had left his homeland of France for the USA in June 1956 at the age of nineteen. In France Claude had been training as a chef at the restaurant of family friends, but also helping as a mechanic in his spare time at a back street racing garage. He had a natural ability as a racing mechanic, and the team of Rene, Lew and Claude were about to become the Morgan team to beat in the west of the USA.

The Ford engined 4/4 was not really to the taste of the American buyers, for its engine was just a toy in their eyes. Rene, just like other dealers, was finding this model hard to sell, and perhaps the racing programme was envisaged to help sales.

In the Saturday Pomona programme there was an under 1,300cc event (not really a separate class) and Lew Spencer took out the Pellandini 4/4, which was coloured red with two diverging white lines painted on the bonnet and was fitted with a white tonneau cover, but he could only manage tenth overall, the first six racers home being Alfa

Rene Pellandini at Pomona leans on the front of his 4/4 on January 19th. Note the safety plates on the wheels. In the car is Norm Hitchin, Rene's workshop manager, whilst Lew Spencer stands in front of Rene with hands in pockets and wearing a white hat. (Jerry Holscher)

Romeos. As a result Lew was not eligible for the main race on the Sunday, being relegated to the consolation race. In the E Production race on the Saturday Chas Winberg finished fifth overall, with Bob Oker the winner in Ed Savin's AC Ace. As a result Chas made the cut for the main race on the Sunday.

Unusually for sunny Southern California, Pomona was subjected to a day of heavy rain on the Sunday such that spins were common, with Caroll Shelby hitting a tree and even future World Champion Phil Hill retiring in the pits because he was, 'tired of making an ass of myself.' Lew braved the conditions for the twelve lap consolation Production race for cars under 1,500cc, finishing in ninth place, with a Denzel the victor. Chas Winberg also braved the conditions for the thirty-five lap main event, and managed to stay on the course, finishing twelfth overall and fourth in Class E.

That same weekend the Milwaukee Region of the SCCA borrowed a local farmer's frozen field and used it for an autocross, which was given the grand title of 'Cowpasture Traverse', using a one mile course. There was one Morgan entered, the ex-Richard Vogel, ex-Mike Rothschild black Plus Four, now owned by Ralph Rehberg. He finished third in the over 1,600cc event, behind a 'gull-wing' Mercedes 300 SL, and a Swallow Doretti.

One week later the even colder venue of Franconia in New Hampshire ran its annual snow races, using the usual one mile course. Of the two Morgans competing that of Benson came home second, whilst Laurence 'Woody' Young returned home to Lewisberg, Pennsylvania with a 'failed to finish' beside his name.

The tricky course at Paramount Ranch was once again used by the Cal Club for racing over the weekend of March 9th and 10th. As at Pomona, rain made the track exceptionally slippery for the Saturday's racing, with several spins, but no major injuries. Lew Spencer was seventh in the 4/4 behind five Alfa Romeos and an MG TF in the under 1,300cc ten lap race, whilst Chas Winberg was eighth in his Plus Four in the six lap Class E Production race.

The weather was brighter on the Sunday. Lew Spencer could manage no better than nineteenth in the ten lap Class F Production race with the 4/4. In the ten lap Production race for Classes C, D and E Chas Winberg did well to finish fourth overall and third in class with the Plus Four. Race

Lew Spencer in the 4/4 at Paramount Ranch. (Curt Warshawsky)

Chas Winberg at Paramount Ranch in his Plus Four. (Curt Warshawsky)

13 was an eight lap race for the ladies, and Ginny Simms borrowed the 4/4 to finish seventh out of eight.

It was now obvious to Rene that the 4/4 was not at all suitable for Production racing in the USA, its meagre power output and poor three speed gear ratios making it uncompetitive. He really wanted the 4/4 re-engined and fitted with a better gearbox, but he had more pressing problems for the Morgan factory to solve, namely the bolt-on wheel saga.

Fergus Motors too were having trouble getting anyone interested in the 4/4. When A272, an ivory 4/4, was dispatched for Fergus Motors in New York on Friday March 1st it was fitted with an Aquaplane head and two Solex carburettors, to try to improve the performance of the tiny (in American eyes) Ford engine. No doubt the two USA distributors were kept aware of the engine development being undertaken by Peter Morgan on the prototype 4/4 at the Morgan factory, and no doubt they were both asking for a performance 4/4 to be introduced. Eventually, in April, the Competition model was added to the Morgan range, but few reached the USA.

For this year's international Sebring 12 Hour Race, to be held on Saturday March 23rd, Joe Ferguson appears to have anticipated supporting the same two drivers who had represented the Morgan marque in 1956, for he ordered two cars to be prepared at the Morgan factory for Mike Rothschild and John Weitz. Both cars had been fitted with strengthened front ends, presumably achieved by means of additional chassis braces from the chassis to the top of the crossheads. The car prepared for Mike Rothschild was chassis number 3610, a blue two-seater with a central white stripe. The engine was specially prepared for racing, with matched and polished ports. An aluminium bonnet and leather bonnet strap was fitted and so too were 'Le Mans' lamps. It was dispatched on Wednesday January 16th.

The car for John Weitz was 3604, painted in the USA racing colours of white with a blue stripe (as in 1956). It had a tuned engine and racing tyres. Like 3610 it was fitted with black leather upholstery. On Monday January 28th it was driven to the docks for shipment to the USA, but suffered extensive damage in an accident on the way. It was returned to the Morgan factory for repairs, and was finally dispatched on Monday February 25th.

Unfortunately for Fergus Motors (now trading as Fergus Imported Cars Inc) both these drivers were otherwise occupied in the forthcoming Sebring race. Mike Rothschild was beginning an association with the Standard Motor Company as a works driver with a Triumph TR3, whilst John Weitz was to drive an Arnolt Bristol. John Weitz had accepted an invitation to join the 1957 Arnolt team immediately following his return to New York after the 1956 Sebring race. The invitation came from Rene Dreyfus, the great former Grand Prix driver and French Champion, who was the team captain for Arnolt. Rene also ran a French restaurant and bar in New York City called 'Le Chanteclair', situated at 18 East 49th Street, which had become a place to congregate for local motor sport enthusiasts (rather like the Steering Wheel Club in London).

In the event another regular at Rene's restaurant, called Bob Grier, who was also a regular Sebring driver, decided he would enter a Morgan, engaging as his co-driver Richard Kennedy from Detroit. Sadly we've been unable to trace anyone associated with this entry, but black and white photographs appear to show a dark coloured car with central white stripe and a bonnet strap, and we wonder therefore whether Bob Grier had taken over chassis 3610.

This year the class system for the entrants was changed to include a Grand Touring (GT) series of classes for production cars in addition to the usual sports racing classes - an attempt to encourage production cars and give them a chance of class awards. The Morgan was entered in the 1.6 to 2 litre GT class, along with the Triumph TR3s, AC Aces and Arnolt Bristols. The Morgan was prepared with a full width but cut down windscreen and on the right-hand side of this was a three lamp signalling system, presumably for communicating with the pits. The minimum number of laps between refuelling stops was set at twenty (104 miles).

This year the weather was tropically hot when the Stars and Stripes flag was lowered for the Le Mans start at 10:00am, unleashing 65 cars, with the eventual race winning 4.5 litre V8 Maserati of Juan Fangio and Jean Behra taking the lead after one hour and holding it to the end despite the heat. The Morgan completed 147 laps to finish in 29th position overall out of 38 finishers and fifth in the GT class behind two ACs and two TR3s, the two Triumphs having ex-Morgan drivers Bob Oker and Mike Rothschild in charge. Bob Oker had particular reason to remember this race - his works TR3 lost a clevis pin from the clutch and he drove the last eight hours clutchless. His engine was restarted at pit stops by engaging first gear and operating the starter until the car shuddered off on its way.

The Grier/ Kennedy Morgan is overtaken by a Maserati at Sebring. (Bill Foster)

Ralph Rehberg flies during the Milwaukee Trial. (Pierre Perrin)

John Weitz had a rather sad day, for the Arnolt Bristol team was withdrawn from the race after John had completed 51 laps, on the orders of factory owner 'Wacky' Arnolt. This followed the death of his driver Bob Goldich who was pinned beneath his works Arnolt when it somersaulted at the esses.

The ex-Rothschild 1956 Sebring Morgan, now owned by Ralph Rehberg, was entered by him in the SCCA's Milwaukee Region Trial held on Sunday March 31st. The event consisted of three timed trials sections and Ralph made off with the trophy for the best time for a car of over 1,600cc.

The problems with the Cal Club at the end of 1956 when it had banned Morgans fitted with production bolt-on road wheels from its races had led to much trans-Atlantic correspondence between Rene Pellandini and the Morgan Motor Company. At the factory the decision was made to contact the Dunlop Rim and Wheel Company Ltd to adapt the Plus Four to take wire wheels. This was undertaken quite quickly and the first cars were ready during April for dispatch to the USA. The first to arrive at Fergus Imported Cars, and possibly the first production Morgan fitted with wire wheels, was chassis number 3651, a two-seater painted Hunter Green, with black upholstery, which was dispatched on Monday April 1st. It was purchased by an enthusiast called Harry Reynolds, an industrial production engineering student at Lehigh University, Bethlehem in Pennsylvania.

Harry had been running an Austin Healey 100-4, which was proving unreliable and poorly built. Early in 1957 he ventured to New York just to look at the Morgans at Fergus Imported Cars. Unfortunately the Healey ground to a halt in the midst of the Lincoln Tunnel, requiring frantic work bashing the SU fuel pump to get it ticking again before the tunnel truck arrived to shove the car out. Feeling somewhat exasperated with the Healey he did an immediate deal to trade it in for a new Morgan at Fergus, and returned home by bus, expecting to receive his new black Plus Four within a month. As is the way of car dealers it was several months later before his car arrived. It was green, not black, and it had wire wheels. Initially he just used it for the street, but soon began entering mild motor sport, his first event being an autocross held near Philadelphia at Bakers Acre, a housing development with roads completed but not the houses. This was later in the summer.

Chas Winberg was entered for the April Palm Springs races in his Plus Four. On the Saturday April 6th he finished sixth in class and ninth overall in a five lap race and on the Sunday he took part in a ten lapper, finishing tenth overall and once again sixth in class.

On Sunday April 28th a new purpose-built motor racing circuit was introduced for sports car racing. This was at Lime Rock, built on his father's land in the northwest of Connecticut by Jim Viall, with help from John Fitch and Cornell Aeronautical Laboratories. This delightful circuit measured 1.53 miles and was to become a very popular racing venue. The first Morgan to feature amongst the awards was that of Bill Schade, following home the AC Bristols of Jordan King and Evelyn Mull to finish third in Race 4 of the inaugural event.

For its races in San Diego on the first weekend in May the Cal Club had set up a slow and tight 1.75 mile course around Hour Glass Field, the Naval Air Station at Miramar. Because the twisty (nine corners) course was so tight a two litre limit was imposed. The only Morgan entered was that of Dan Levitt, who lent his Plus Four to Rose Nelson for the first of the Sunday races, the eight lap ladies' race. She was disqualified however for racing without goggles. Dan entered Race 3, a seventeen lapper for Production Classes E and F, finishing ninth overall and sixth in class.

Two weeks later the Cal Club was at Santa Barbara, racing on the popular 2.2 mile combination of airfield and road circuit. Santa Barbara always attracted a large field, and so it was this time with a record entry of 240 drivers. On the Saturday (May 18th) the usually reliable California weather disappointed and rain was the order of the day for the races. This did not deter the brilliant Bob Oker driving the Ed Savin Plus Four and he finished second to Gordon Crowder's AC Bristol in the ten lap under two litre Production car race. Other Morgan finishers were James Evidon in eighth place and William Tuning, who lived in Santa Barbara, thirteenth. William Tuning had a January 1955 Plus Four two-seater, chassis number 3221, coloured black with red upholstery.

The following day the usual brilliant California sunshine had returned. Bob Oker was this time driving the Morgan in the over 1,500cc Modified class race, the main event of the weekend over one hour. Sadly the pace was too strong and a rod came through the side of the block of the Plus Four, ending a long and illustrious career for the Ed Savin Morgan with Bob Oker driving. The winner was Eric Hauser in the Balchowsky Special, ahead of the Ferrari 625TRC of John Von Neumann and the Ferrari 410S of Phil Hill.

In the ten lap race for Production Classes C, D and E the other two Plus Fours didn't fair too well, for out of the forty-five starters James Evidon was twenty-seventh, and seventh in Class E, with William Tuning fortieth, and fourteenth in class.

That same weekend in Maryland the SCCA ran its fifth annual 'Cumberland Classic' National races over the usual tricky 1.6 miles airport circuit. Several Morgans braved the rain to contest Race 6, over 45 minutes for Production Classes D and E, watched by some 45,000 spectators. The AC Bristols were invincible, claiming the first six places ahead of Archibald's TR3. First of the Morgan finishers was Erskine 'Rick' Kelly, finishing in eighth position, tenth was Ike Williamson, fourteenth Don Melvin, sixteenth Charlie Kolb and eighteenth Woody Young. The Morgans were not out-classed, for the rain caused chaos amongst the Class D Austin Healeys, of which the best finished in a lowly fifteenth place.

Charlie Kolb worked at a Triumph dealership named 'Auto City' in Silver Spring, Maryland (near Washington DC). He had initially raced one of their TRs, but found that he could make no impression on Gus Andrey and his Morgan. As a result he decided to try a Plus Four for himself, purchasing a green example from Fergus Imported Cars in New York. The car was again prepared at Auto City under the supervision of the English service manager Arthur Tweedel. Chas found the Morgan easier to race than the TR, although he recently described the ride to us as 'like riding a buckboard'.

Two weeks later, on the weekend of June 1st and 2nd, Charlie Kolb was riding his 'buckboard' at the airfield circuit of the small-town of Dunkirk,

203

in New York State, situated on at the bank of Lake Erie. The third race was the 'Lake Erie Invitation Race' for 20 laps of the circuit for Production Classes D and E. Bernard Miske, of Akron Ohio, took his AC Bristol to an easy class win, whilst Don Boyer was best of the Morgan drivers, with an excellent drive through the field, from eighth place at the start, to finish second. Charlie Kolb came home third in his Morgan, whilst Bill Jackson came in fourth in his.

The new circuit at Lime Rock hosted its first SCCA National race meeting over the weekend of June 8th and 9th. Whilst 24 starters took to the line for the fifteen lap race for Classes D and E, according to the British magazine *Autosport*, 'All eyes were on only two: Robert Kuhn's AC Bristol and Gaston Andrey's sky blue Morgan.' It proved to be a cracker of a race, with Robert Kuhn taking an early lead, until passed by Gus Andrey at Turn One. Robert Kuhn re-passed, only to be taken during Turn Two on the next lap, and so it continued with a seesaw changing of race leader. Finally Gus Andrey managed to pull off the victory, some two-and-a-half seconds ahead of Kuhn, at an average speed of 69.4 mph - beating in the process all of the Austin Healeys of Class D! Two other Morgans were competing, those of Jim Haynes (tenth) and David Michaels who finished twelfth. Once again Gaston Andrey had demonstrated his amazing ability to out corner stronger opposition with the little Morgan.

One week later Gaston Andrey was competing again at Mount Equinox, in the annual National hill climb. Oddly for Gaston he could only manage fifth place this time, with a time of 5 minutes 53.9 seconds, being beaten by the two AC Bristols of Jordan King and Mrs Eve Mull, an Arnolt Bristol, and the Morgan Plus Four of Ike Williamson (5 minutes 48.9 seconds).

The 3.2 mile 'round the houses' circuit at picturesque Put-In-Bay, was once again host to under two litre sports cars in June for the annual races held by the Cleveland Sports Car Club. Race 5, held over twelve laps for Classes F Modified and E Production, saw Tom Payne the victor in his Porsche Spyder, whilst Bill Johnson took third overall and first in E Production with his TR3 engined Plus Four. Listed as fifteenth overall out of the eighteen starters was the Morgan of Edward Houlihan from Detroit, but the results give positions for every starter whether they finished or not, and Ed didn't actually finish. He had made

Gaston Andrey on Mount Equinox. (Alix Lafontant)

The scene at the base of Mount Equinox, with 'Ike' Williamson's Plus Four. (Alix Lafontant)

an error at Cemetery Corner which led to him visiting the cemetery! Here he found a genteel couple having a quiet picnic, with fruit and cheese on silver plates accompanied by champagne. They invited the intruder to join them, but Ed politely declined. Ed was later to become famous as the chief starter at the Waterford Hills racing circuit, situated in Oakland County, Michigan. Also entered

Ed Houlihan's Plus Four is manhandled from its perch on a hay bale by the cemetery on Put-in-Bay. (Lake Erie Islands Historical Society collection)

in a Morgan Plus Four was Richard Kennedy, but he doesn't appear on the results sheet.

Rene Pellandini was still struggling to sell the Ford engined 4/4 on behalf of the Morgan factory. In May the factory had dispatched to Rene three cars modified with Aquaplane heads, chassis numbers A280, A284 and A285. We think these cars had twin SU carburettors, and improved exhaust manifolds, and had been modified to Competition model specification after completion as ordinary 4/4s in the Morgan factory repair shop. It may well be that Rene had previously had a standard 4/4 converted in the USA to Competition model specification. Rene had earlier lent an example of the standard 4/4, costing $2195, for road testing to motoring magazines, but the little side valve engine was too gutless for the American market. *Motor Trend* in March commented, 'This Morgan is far from powerful.' He now let *Road and Track*, test one of the modified cars, costing $2420, and the journal commented in the June edition, 'What is a British company thinking of to export to America a classic, fierce looking sports car…….. but with an 1,172cc engine?' The road test did record an 80 mph top speed for the modified car as against 75 mph for the standard one, whilst the 0 to 60 mph time was reduced from around 26 seconds to 20.5. Rene believed the car badly needed a new engine and gearbox for the USA market and he was keen for the Morgan factory to produce a very special 4/4 using the Coventry Climax FWB 1,460cc engine, which was an enlarged bore and stroke derivative of the famous FWA. He wanted this 100 bhp engine mated to the MGA close ratio gearbox, copying the use of this engine and gearbox combination in the successful Lotus Eleven 'Le Mans' sports racer. He promised he would immediately take fifty cars. News soon leaked out of the proposed super Morgan to the motoring world in California and this potentially extremely potent machine was awaited with considerable relish.

For the weekend of July 5th and 6th, Charlie Kolb took his green Morgan to Watkins Glen, for the 'Glen Classic' races. In the eleven lap race for Production Classes D and E, Charlie started thirteenth of the eighteen starters, but by lap ten he was in the lead. Just before the line he was re-passed by Robert Samm who managed to hold him off with his Austin Healey 100M, but Charlie did finish second, and first in class. As a result of their performances in this race both Robert Samm and Charlie Kolb were able to enter the 'Glen Feature', a 50.6 mile race of 22 laps for B and C Production cars (mainly Corvettes and Jaguars). These cars soon discovered that the Morgan was more than a match for them, for Charlie worked up to second place, before being passed once again by Robert Samm's Austin Healey. At the finish Charlie was fourth overall and first in class after a very impressive drive. Robert Samm was even more impressive for he finished second overall, beaten only by one Corvette.

One week later Charlie was at Marlboro in Maryland for a hot weekend of racing on the extended 1.6 mile circuit. The twenty lap race for E Production was won by Sarle with his AC Bristol, with Charlie fifth in the Plus Four, being literally pushed over the line by the AC Bristol of Bill Jordan, which had made contact from behind. The other Morgans of Don Boyer and Don Melvin finished tenth and eleventh, Bob Haas was fourteenth but Dave Spiegler and Rick Kelly both failed to finish. The local drivers had painted their cars lilac, showing their allegiance to the Lavender Hill Mob; even the starter Tex Hopkins wore a lilac suit for the occasion!

Jim Haynes, who had competed at Lime Rock in June, felt confident he could win at the meeting held on July 27th and 28th. He was entered in Race 4, a fifteen lapper for Production Classes D and E. After three laps Jim had displaced two ACs for the lead, but two laps later the extremely fast Harry Carter was right behind him with his AC Bristol, closely followed by Gaston Andrey in his rapid Morgan. Jim was trying all he knew, with the Morgan going sideways through the corners. Harry attempted to overtake Jim on the downhill section, the two cars unfortunately touched, and both finished up off the track on opposite sides. Gaston

Andrey took evasive action which entailed following Jim to the outside of the track. Gaston didn't do the front end of his Morgan any good when he finally hit the tow-bar on the rear of Jim's Morgan in the process (Jim's Morgan was also his towing car, for he also raced a Cooper JAP).

With these three fast cars out of the race, the two AC Bristols of Jordan King and Mrs Eve Mull finished first and second, with the Morgan of Tony Zuckert in third place (his speed was 67.62 mph).

Jim Haynes, who at this time was working for IBM in Poughkeepsie, New York State, was in the 1960s to become the Lime Rock track manager, a position he was to hold for over twenty years.

That same weekend the Cal Club was using the Pomona fairground circuit once more, running it anti-clockwise now and in the future. Just the Morgan of Keith Stratter took part, finishing sixteenth overall and ninth in Class E in the ten lap race for Production Classes D and E on the Saturday. On the Sunday in the nineteen lap 'Semi-Main Production Race' for Classes E, F and G he finished nineteenth overall and again ninth in class.

On the weekend of August 3rd and 4th a new track hosted its first race - Virginia International Raceway. It was a 3.2 mile circuit, roughly triangular in outline, with twelve corners and two 1.2 mile long straights. It was built on 1,200 acres on the Dan River valley, eleven miles southeast of Danville. Attracted to this first meeting were the Plus Fours of Gaston Andrey, Ike Williamson, George Elliott and Don Melvin. In Race 3, held over seven laps for Production Classes E and F (minus the MGs), the best Morgan placing was that of Gaston Andrey in twelfth position behind no less than eleven AC Bristols. George Elliott was sixteenth, whilst Williamson and Melvin failed to finish. In Race 9 for E Production over fourteen laps again the AC Bristols proved to be faster than the Morgans. Ten ACs and a well driven TR3 pushed the Morgans of Andrey, Elliott and Melvin into twelfth, thirteenth and fourteenth positions respectively, on this very hot inaugural day (104 degrees Fahrenheit).

So successful had been last year's inaugural races on Montgomery Airport that this year the SCCA gave National status to the event held on August 17th and 18th. Gaston Andrey was now being offered a regular drive in Mike Garber's Ferrari Mondial, so the Morgan was left at home. The marque was represented by Dr Norm McNamara, Michael Ben-Dror, Woody Young and Tony Zuckert, all entered for the twenty lap race for E Production. Despite fighting for third position with Jordan King's AC Bristol early in the race Tony Zuckert joined Woody Young as a non-finisher. Norm McNamara was tenth and Michael Ben-Dror thirteenth.

One weekend later the Wisconsin State Fair Park in Milwaukee was used by the SCCA. The course consisted partly of the usual oval and partly of a twisty infield section. W T Bosworth upheld the Morgan flag with a second overall and first in class.

The first weekend in September was a busy period on the racing calendar. For the races at Mansfield, Louisiana, Rick Kelly had driven down from Maryland to participate. He returned home with a fourth in class.

That same weekend several Morgans were competing at Thompson, using the new circuit completed over the 1956-7 winter period. This was built on land purchased by George Weaver adjacent to that rented for the original circuit. Just the former track's back straight and approach were retained, now coupled to a new one and a quarter mile long section featuring two hairpins, a chicane and a 3/4 of a mile gentle crescent, making a tricky two and a half mile circuit. On the Saturday in Race 2, for Classes D and E, the best performance of the Morgans was that of Tony Zuckert with sixth in class, whilst Joseph Daniels was ninth. The Morgan of Norm McNamara failed to finish. On the Sunday they all competed in the second one hour race, with Zuckert eighth overall, fifth in class, Daniels ninth in class once more, and McNamara once again failing to finish.

The Morgan of Norm McNamara, who lived in Boston, is particularly interesting in that it

Norm McNamara spins the Morgan in front of the Austin Healey of Mike Rothschild at the September Thompson meeting. (Mike Rothschild collection)

appeared to be painted in the USA racing colours (white with blue stripes), and also had the newly introduced wire wheels. We have been unable to locate this distinctive car in the Morgan factory records and wonder if it was possibly the Morgan prepared for Sebring since converted to the new wire wheels.

That same weekend witnessed the debut at Santa Barbara of Lew Spencer in Rene Pellandini's new racer prepared by Claude Brun at Worldwide Imports. This was a green Plus Four two-seater, fitted with wire wheels to get over the problems with the Cal Club over breaking standard Morgan bolt-on road wheels. Claude had fully balanced the TR3 engine, and the engine ports had been carefully polished and matched. It was to become a very famous car, later being named 'Baby Doll No 2'.

On the Saturday Lew finished fourth behind two AC Bristols and a Porsche in the ten lap race for Production Classes D and E. On the Sunday in the fifteen lap race for Production Classes E, F and G the results in Class E were the same, except that Lew was demoted one place to fifth overall by a Class F Production Porsche Carrera.

Also in the programme was William Tuning in his black Plus Four, Keith Stratter driving Dr Welles Forde's yellow one and Al Gebhard in his new blue car having bolt-on wheels. The only one to appear in the race results was local driver William Tuning, who finished fifteenth on the Saturday and twenty-sixth but thirteenth in Class E on the Sunday. The unfortunate Al Gebhard was trying out some brake linings that required heat before they worked and he spun out twice at the same Turn before being black flagged

During the summer Rene Pellandini had visited the Morgan factory. No doubt he had continued to push for the special Coventry Climax engined 4/4 that he knew he could sell. At the factory he was informed that the 4/4 model was designed to be very much a low cost entry model to the Morgan range, and to increase the specification would not only produce an expensive car but would detract from the current Plus Four. Rene still thought they should build his dream 4/4.

On Sunday September 8th W T Bosworth was at Elkhart Lake, but gave the major 500 mile race a miss, finishing fourteenth in the Production car race.

In Pennsylvania a couple of Morgans did well at the tricky Springtown hill climb, situated twelve miles from Easton. Although only 1.1 miles in length

Rene Pellandini at the Morgan factory in Malvern with the management. From left to right are Harry Jones, George Goodall, Jim Goodall, Peter Morgan and Rene Pellandini. (Morgan Motor Co collection)

there was little room for error, particularly approaching 'The Bump', two thirds of the way up, where the faster cars would leave the ground, hopefully landing in a suitable position to take the following lefthander. Winning Class E Production was Bill Worthington in his Morgan, with Frank Martin (of Martin Guitars) third in his Plus Four.

Ike Williamson and Tony Zuckert were both entered at the major meeting at Watkins Glen on Saturday September 21st. Only Ike started in the eleven lap (25.3 miles) Dix Cup race for D and E Production cars but he was well down the field in 26th position, and seventeenth in class.

A new California racing circuit held its inaugural races over that same weekend. It was Riverside International Motor Raceway, built at a cost of around $800,000, situated fifty miles east of Los Angeles in the hot desert below the San Bernardino Mountains. The circuit was of 3.275 miles per lap. Unfortunately Turn 6 was found to be very dangerous, being a blind uphill turn with banking on both sides leaving no room for driver error. Carroll Shelby stuffed his 4.5 litre Maserati into this bank in practice and was taken to hospital with facial injuries and later an MGA driver was killed when his car overturned on the bank. Rather surprisingly there were no Morgans entered.

On September 28th and 29th Lew Spencer with the new Worldwide Imports Plus Four was competing in Northern California, in wine growing country, at the Cobb Mountain hill climb event, organised by Sports Cars Unlimited. The original course was washed away by heavy rain on the night before the event, so a revised course of a one and a half miles of rough unpaved road, with a hundred yards section of foot deep mud, ended up being used - more suitable for trials than a hill climb!

Lew took Class E by storm, finishing nine seconds ahead of the field and recording a time of 2 minutes 38.2 seconds. He was followed home by the three other Morgan Plus Fours entered, being those of Al Gebhard, the black Vanguard engined car of Bill Hinshaw, and the TR engined 1953 Plus Four of Chuck Lowry. Following behind were the vanquished Triumph TR3s!

Al Gebhard, a merchant marine 'supercargo' (an agent responsible for a particular cargo at sea and in port) from San Pedro, near Los Angeles, gave the spectators something to think about when he left the course on one corner, crossing a four foot ditch, then proceeding through an apple orchard before finally regaining the course once more after crossing the ditch again! He blamed a lack of brakes, water having found its way onto the linings. Al had first seen a Morgan in 1951 in a dealership in Pasadena, and immediately fallen in love! His first Morgan, a 1953 two-seater, had been purchased and fully rebuilt by him in 1955. This car was previously owned by Dr Charles Thompson, but he had recently purchased a brand new two-seater for racing from Worldwide Imports. This was coloured blue with a red interior and had normal bolt-on wheels.

For this event Claude Brun had altered the back axle ratio of Lew's racer to a more suitable 4.56 to 1. Worldwide Imports had been aware for some time that the differentials from Studebaker cars could fit straight in to the Plus Four Salisbury casings. As these vehicles were abundant in the USA scrap yards, sets of differentials with different ratios were acquired for the racer. This allowed alternative back axle ratios of 3.73, 4.1 and 4.56 to 1 to be used, depending on the course or circuit.

It is possible that the local knowledge that Studebaker parts would fit the Salisbury came from the legendary special builder Max Balchowsky, who had been fitting General Motors V8 engines and Salisbury back axles to Swallow Dorettis for racing for a couple of years. The back axles manufactured by the English company Salisbury Transmission Limited, situated in Witton, Birmingham, were actually manufactured under licence from the Dana Corporation, based in Toledo Ohio in the USA. As Dana supplied Studebaker as one of its customers it was perhaps not surprising that these components fitted virtually straight into the Salisbury casing.

Lew's green Plus Four was now carrying the legend 'Baby Doll No 2' on the doors. Mechanic Claude Brun had recently seen the Warner Brothers movie, 'Baby Doll', starring Caroll Baker in the role of the sensuous nineteen year old in what was thought to be quite an erotic film for its day. Claude was much moved by this Elia Kazan directed film - he was later to even nickname his own wife 'Baby Doll'. Coming in to work one day he remarked, 'I wonder how our Baby Doll is today?' The name stuck and was adopted for the Worldwide Imports Morgan racers, with the previously raced 4/4 being credited as having been Baby Doll No 1 retrospectively. Claude had improved the engine of Baby Doll No 2, by having the camshaft accurately reground to factory specifications, and by replacing the valves and their springs by better 'Webco' types, as allowed by the racing regulations. Lew commented that this mod alone now allowed 6,500 rpm without valve bounce, although wisely 5,800 rpm was regarded as the optimum for the engine.

Baby Doll No 2 also carried two parallel white stripes close to the bonnet hinge, which continued onto the tail panel. These white stripes were edged with red to make them really stand out. On the left hand side of the bonnet was the legend 'Piloto Lew Spencer' whilst the right hand side carried 'Owner Rene Pellandini'.

Bill Hinshaw was a business studies student at the University of California at Berkeley. During his earlier education at the Ohio State University he had run an MG TC, but he had realized he needed more power for the drive across the USA to Berkeley in his birth State of California. Thus in June 1956 he had traded in his MG at Manhattan Auto in Washington DC for a red 1953 chrome radiator Plus Four that he was told had participated in the Nassau Speed Week in the Bahamas. Setting off in the Morgan for California with all his possessions in the back Bill was amused to find the air in the Moseley 'Float on Air' inflatable seat cushions expanded as he gained altitude crossing the mountain ranges, and contracted when he got into the valleys on the other side, necessitating changes in the volume of air to maintain his position! The red paint was tired, so the body was stripped by hand by Bill and he then had it repainted black. He had been a regular competitor in Northern Californian autocrosses and time trials during 1957, but the sight of Lew

Bill Hinshaw waiting to start at Cobb Mountain, the Buick behind was not competing! (Bill Hinshaw collection)

at Cobb Mountain left a lasting impression on Bill, for he had never heard a Triumph engine make so much racket before, or seen a Morgan so uncatchable. He immediately decided to trade in his Vanguard engined car for a new Plus Four and prepare it to go racing, visiting Frank Henry's Morgan dealership on Van Ness Avenue in San Francisco. He bought a late 1957 red Plus Four, with red leather upholstery and wire wheels.

The Northern California Morgan enthusiasts now announced in the motoring press that they had formed 'The Bay Area Morgan Plus Four Club' during the summer, with the first President being Wilson Cosby of Berkeley. It was more correctly titled the 'Northern Chapter of the Morgan Plus Four Club' which had been founded two years earlier in Los Angeles.

That same weekend Joseph Daniels was competing at another brand-new racing circuit. This was the new Bridgehampton circuit on Long Island, New York, replacing the previous street racing circuit used from 1949 to 1953, when it was closed following injuries to spectators. The new circuit of 2.855 miles length was a tough course to learn being very fast and tricky, with interesting gradients, a lot of sand and a breathtaking view of the Peconic Bay. Daniels unfortunately failed to finish in this inaugural meeting.

For the weekend of October 19th and 20th Lew, Rene and Claude were with Baby Doll No 2 in San Diego for races held at Hour Glass Field. On the Saturday Lew was running second in class when the clutch bearing unfortunately failed. As a result Claude, Lew and Rene, assisted by Al Gebhard and Stu Barnes spent most of the night in the workshop of British Motor Sales in San Diego replacing the clutch. On the Sunday morning Lew was driving well in the consolation race, running second in class and was certain to qualify for the main event of the weekend, when the clutch sadly went once more. He completed the last lap by jamming the gear lever into second with all his might and still collected his second place. Unfortunately it was a case of loading up the crippled Morgan now to return to Los Angeles. The horrendous sounds of protest from the gearbox had made Lew dread what would be found when Claude took the top off the box, but there wasn't even a mark. Lew commented, 'No abuse seems to make the slightest impression on it.'

Another new racing circuit held its inaugural meeting over at the weekend of November 9th and 10th. Replacing nearby Pebble Beach (where a concours event was still held on the Saturday) this exciting circuit of 1.9 miles with nine corners was built in record time. It was constructed in collaboration with the US Army from nearby Fort Ord and named Laguna Seca as it surrounded a usually dry lake. The circuit rose up a hill on to a ridge from where it descended into what became known as the 'corkscrew', a drop approaching five storeys in height between Turns 8 and 8A. Some 60,000 spectators attended this SCCA National event, and they witnessed a brilliant display from Lew Spencer in Baby Doll No 2, for in the over 1,600 cc all-comers race he was beaten only by two, these being the brilliant Bill Love driving an AC Bristol, and Cloyd Gray driving a Corvette. Bob Cole, the SCCA's reporter, called it an 'astonishing drive', for Lew had beaten many Corvettes and 300SL Mercedes, a total of 33 other cars. This twisting circuit really suited Lew and the Morgan, for he was able to out corner much more powerful opposition with ease.

One week later the Pellandini Equipe attended National races at Riverside, the circuit's second ever meeting. Riverside was to become a very important circuit, giving California, with Laguna Seca, two of the best circuits in the country. It was much faster than Laguna, with a back straight of over 1.25 miles. The difficult high-speed uphill esses contributed to it being a very demanding circuit of 3.275 miles, and no doubt Turn 6 had been made safer after the previous problems.

At this meeting Lew was again outstanding. On the Saturday, in the five lap race for Production Classes B to E he was sixth in class, but in the fifteen lap race on the Sunday for the same classes only Bill Love beat him in Class E, whilst he was sixth overall, out cornering many of the Austin

Lew Spencer in Baby Doll No 2 battles with the sliding AC Bristol of Bill Love at Laguna Seca. (Maurice Reichler)

Water for Baby Doll No 2 at Paramount Ranch. On the left is Rene Pellandini whilst Al Gebhard holds the watering can. (Bill Hinshaw)

Healeys and Jaguars and even holding them on the straights, where the Morgan was timed at 103-105 mph. We believe that it was at this meeting that the Pellandini team conducted experiments on car-to-pits contact using Citizens Band Radio (CB), the Morgan carrying a fancy aerial on the tail for this purpose. Unfortunately for the pioneers the local refreshment stall was using the same frequency!

The fourth Chimney Rock hill climb was held over the weekend on November 30th and December 1st. It was very cold in North Carolina at this time, particularly on the Saturday with the temperature barely rising above freezing, but this didn't stop Howard Kern from shattering the Morgan held Class E record by three seconds, recording 4 minutes 23.07 seconds. He was driving the chrome radiator Plus Four belonging to Ted Davison, this Morgan having been re-engined with a TR2 unit and it was running without an exhaust pipe. Ted himself was third in Class E, some thirty seconds slower than Howard! Howard's run was good enough for third place overall, behind Phil Styles' Davis Special and Bob McKaughn's Jaguar XK140MC.

The weekend of December 7th and 8th the Cal Club ran another Paramount Ranch meeting, and Lew Spencer was there with Baby Doll No 2. Sadly the racing was marred by three very serious accidents, and the tricky course was only to be used once more after this event.

Baby Doll No 2 suffered a holed radiator, forcing Lew to make several pit stops for water. His pit crew of Claude Brun, Al Gebhard and Chuck Lowry were kept busy running back and forth with the watering can and then dodging

Morgan Sports Cars — 1957

Lew Spencer driving Rene Pellandini's Plus 4 (TR3) Morgan No. 145 on the way to conquering 3rd Overall and 2nd in Class out of 36 contestants. The event was the beautiful Pebble Beach Laguna Seca Course.

IT DOES NOT TAKE $6000 TO BE SUCCESSFUL IN "E" CLASS
BE A "LEW SPENCER" TOO and
DRIVE A "MORGAN" TO VICTORY
(Special Consideration for Racing Drivers)

Four Different Models Available from $2195

★ 1st Class "E" at Cobb's Mountain Hill Climb
★ 2nd Class "E" & 6th overall out of 36 entries at Riverside
★ 2nd Class "E" & 3rd overall out of 36 entries at Fort Ord
★ 1st Class "E" Paramount Ranch

COMPETITION WIRE WHEELS AVAILABLE IN ALL MODELS

WORLDWIDE IMPORT, Inc.
Importer-Distributor for the 11 Western States
1968 So. Sepulveda Blvd., Los Angeles, Calif.
GRanite 7-6739

---

steam when the radiator cap was removed. In the ten lap Production race on the Saturday Lew finished fourth in class behind Bill Love's AC and two Porsches. On the Sunday in the eighteen lap race for Production cars of 2,000cc and below, and Modified cars under 1,100cc Lew was seventeenth overall and seventh in class, whilst later, in the 38 laps all-comers race he managed a magnificent sixth overall and second in class behind Alf Cadrobbi's Porsche Carrera.

That same weekend the Morgan Plus Four run by Wests Sports Car Center in Fresno (a Morgan dealership), ran at the Castel US Air Force Base (near Merced in California), making fastest time of the day, beating amongst others, two Jaguars, seven Austin Healeys and a Corvette. In Phoenix, Arizona, Roger Seargeant won his class with his Plus Four in the novices' race, finishing sixth overall.

When the SCCA announced its National Championship winners at the end of the year, Morgan had not done so well as previously, for the highest placing was that of Gaston Andrey in eighth position. However Gaston was now mainly driving the Ferrari of Mike Garber so his Morgan had latterly not been used very much.

1957 had been an important year. Many new racing circuits had been inaugurated and the future looked bright for sports car racing in the USA. In California the combination of Lew Spencer as the driver and Claude Brun as the preparer of the new wire wheeled Plus Four was rightly beginning to cause a stir amongst sports car enthusiasts. Rene Pellandini was delighted, and began a Morgan advertising campaign in the local motoring magazines. These achievements no doubt were rewarded by increasing interest and sales. Approximately 75% of all Plus Fours built in 1957 went to the USA, and just over 40% of the 4/4s.

Canada

Early in 1957 the various sports car clubs of Washington and Oregon in the USA and British Columbia in Canada got together to form the International Conference of Northwest Sports Car Clubs, commonly known as the 'Conference', the idea being to act as a focus point for sports car activities in the northwest. The Conference produced its own car classifications for racing, based on that used by the SCCA and these Conference classifications dictated that Production rules would be strictly enforced. The new classification was based on performance as bought, and this put the Morgan Plus Four into D Production, along with the Austin Healey 100 Six. The Triumph TR3 was in Class E, whilst the TR2 was in a lowly Class F! The idea was to allow fewer modifications than acceptable in SCCA racing, hence giving cheaper racing for the participants.

Alan Sands bravely entered his Morgan Plus Four two-seater for the British Empire Motor Club's Canadian Winter Rally which started on

Alan Sands with his Morgan at scrutineering before the Canadian Winter Rally. Note the blanked-off louvres, the tow rope, and the extended upper edge of the sidescreen. (Alan Sands collection)

Friday February 8th and finished after covering 1,300 miles over the snow covered roads of Ontario and Quebec on the Sunday. As the temperature was well below zero (around minus 30 degrees Fahrenheit) Alan prepared the car by covering the underside of the bonnet louvres with tape to keep the snow out. He also pre-attached a tow rope to the front of the chassis for extracting the Morgan from ditches and he added upper extensions to the side screens to keep the snow from finding its way into the cockpit. Spotlights were also fitted, but he states they were useless in a snow storm. Driving in to one control they hit a frost heave, and as a consequence one of the two six volt batteries jumped out of its position beside the back axle, and disappeared, leaving just a cable with a terminal and some plates attached! Eventually Alan and his passenger Ray Liddle finished fifty-ninth out of 119 finishers.

We think it was on Saturday May 11th that the British Empire Motor Club ran its spring hill climb at Hockley Valley. Alan Sands driving his Plus Four made third fastest time of the day with 1 minute 11.9 seconds and took his class, but unfortunately spectators trampling on the timing wire succeeded in breaking it before all of the 91 entrants had run, so the event was declared 'no contest'. Hill climbs were very popular as the number of competitors indicates, because there was less chance of damaging the car than during circuit racing.

On Sunday May 26th the Sports Car Club of British Columbia ran the 'Empire Trophy Race Meeting' at Abbotsford. This venue was an airfield situated about sixty miles east of Vancouver and was under-utilised by the Royal Canadian Air Force,

Alan Sands corners hard at the Hockley hill climb, on his way to a class win. (Alan Sands collection)

Morgan Sports Cars — 1957

allowing the Sports Car Club of British Columbia (SCCBC) several race meetings per year since 1950. The usual course was a two mile triangular circuit utilising the main northwest runway and two taxi-ways. In Race 2 for Production Classes A, B, C, D and E the Morgan Plus Four of A James finished sixth overall, but second in Class D behind a Porsche.

The British Empire Motor Club ran its 'Canadian Carrera' race meeting at Harewood Acres airfield on Saturday June 8th, attracting the two Plus Fours of Alan Sands and Ed Russell. The weather was excellent and over 5,000 spectators came to watch the action. The third race saw production Austin Healeys, Triumphs, Porsches and Morgans do battle. A reporter for the British magazine *Autosport* was watching and wrote that one of the Plus Fours began to drag its exhaust and was promptly black flagged, allowing Alan Sands to take the Morgan class. Whilst that may well be the written *Autosport* report, we think this might actually be the event that Alan Sands remembers where he persuaded a spectating Morgan owner named Steve Broady to make up the numbers so that there would be the minimum number of competitors to run a separate Morgan class, namely three. The two Morgan racers helped Steve get his Morgan through scrutineering. At the start these two set off on their own race leaving Steve behind. After a 'neck and neck' battle Ed blew a tyre as he tried to take Alan on the inside of a right hand corner. He thumped into Alan's Morgan, giving him a nasty moment, but Alan was able to continue. One lap later Alan was black flagged for trailing his exhaust, leaving his protégé Steve Broady to take the Class Trophy!

The Sports Car Club of Saskatchewan held its first ever race on Sunday June 30th on Davidson airfield, an old abandoned Second World War BCATP airfield, using a 1.8 mile course, roughly triangular in shape but with the corners replaced by chicanes. There was one Morgan entered, a TR2 engined Plus Four, by a Mr Brooks. The Morgan showed signs of modification, having the exhaust system apparently re-routed under the car to run beneath the left side wings, rather than down the usual right side. His first race was the fourth six lap race for 2 litre sports cars, the field consisting of six TR3s an MGA and the Morgan. Despite making equal fastest lap at 61.5 mph Mr Brooks could only finish sixth, some way ahead of Ken Finnigan's MGA, and close behind four of the five TR3s ahead. Mr Brooks then contested the Davidson Handicap, the feature race of the day

Mr Brooks' Morgan at Davidson, ahead of Ken Finnigan's MGA. (Tom Johnston collection)

held over 30 minutes. He finished fifth overall behind the winning Austin Healey 100 Six, Ken Finnigan's MGA and two TR3s. On handicap he was demoted to seventh, but was third in Class E, behind the two TR3s.

There was another race meeting held at Harewood Acres on Saturday August 17th, attracting the two Plus Fours of Lincoln Kinsman and Stephen Broady. Sadly we have yet to locate results.

The western Canadian Morgan agent 'GB' Sterne had his own car dispatched from the Morgan factory on Monday March 18th 1957. It was a black, four-seater Plus Four, chassis number 3605, engine number TS13490, and trimmed with a black leather interior. The specification included a tuned engine, racing tyres and the shorter two-seater windscreen. During construction at Malvern it had received attention in the repair shop on Thursday November 15th 1956 when the following had been carried out: 'Take off cylinder head, match up and polish ports. Regrind in valves'. This was given a job code number 18, presumably signifying a pre-delivery modification.

The fourth of the SCCBC's 'Little Silverstone' meetings was held at Abbotsford on Sunday September 22nd to 'Conference' rules. Four Morgans appear to have been entered, there being a large field. GB Sterne had driven to the circuit accompanied by his wife Lydia in his black four-seater. There were three Morgan entries from the USA, namely the two Plus Fours of Clarence Middleton and Max Schulze and the 4/4 of Tom Rice. We think they lived around Kennewick in the southeast of Washington State, and they were all members of the same sports car club. Also entered was the Morgan of Peter Browning from Victoria. Sadly we have not located any results. George Sterne was now forty-five years old, and he was beginning what was to become a long and successful period of Morgan racing.

The British Empire Motor Club ran its fall hill climb on Saturday October 19th, probably at Hockley Valley once more. Four Morgan Plus Fours were entered. Alan Sands finished seventh fastest overall with a time of 1 minute 14.29 seconds, claiming third place in Class E. In nineteenth and twentieth places overall were Dave Elcomb and Stephen Broady, recording 1 minute 18.13 and 1 minute 18.30 respectively, giving them sixth and seventh in Class E. Lincoln Kinsman only recorded one run with his Plus Four, a time of 1 minute 20.78 seconds, and he finished in 29th place, eighth in Class E.

Dave Elcomb had bought his Plus Four earlier this year from Windsor Motorcycles. It was described by his wife, known as 'Scooter', as being painted in 'baby blue' which was regarded as a rather un-manly colour and Curly Ellis had had problems selling it. Dave wasn't bothered by the colour and purchased it around July! We think this car was probably chassis number 3538, a Ming Blue two-seater with beige leather interior which had been dispatched from Malvern on August 22nd in 1956.

The following day on the other side of Canada there were just two Morgan Plus Fours at Abbotsford. One was driven by A James, but the other was driven by GB Sterne. In Race 11 for Production cars of Classes A, B, C, D and E, 'GB' finished in fourth spot, just ahead of Mr James, and was second in class to a Triumph TR3.

Chapter 5
1958

The year began with the publication of a road test by John Bolster of the new works Plus Four TUY 875 in the Wednesday January 1st issue of *The Motor* magazine. Presumably it had been borrowed following the previous November's Goodwood test day. 'GB' plates had been fitted to the rear of the Morgan and John had taken it via Northern France and Belgium to the famous Jabbeke highway for performance testing. It was no slouch and John commented that the recorded 0 to 50 mph time of 6.8 seconds had only ever been beaten by two sports-racing cars that *The Motor* had tested, and they had had engines of 3.5 and 5.5 litres respectively! It was still the cheapest 100 mph car made in the United Kingdom. The handling was described as above average for its class and, in through-gears acceleration up to 80 mph (0 to 60 mph in 9.7 seconds), it was a match for competitors costing up to double the price. The improved cockpit dimensions were commented upon favourably as was the now adjustable rake of the seat backrest. John suggested that driving pleasure was unquestionably the Morgan's purpose, and he loved the handling with its safe breakaway characteristics. The hard suspension gave a ride on English roads that he described as 'lively' but on poor Continental roads the car pitched and bobbed, bottoming on the suspension stops on occasion. No doubt the Morgan directors were delighted by his report and particularly by the acceleration figures which were the best recorded for a Morgan to date by far.

The MCC held its 33rd Exeter Trial this January with ninety cars setting off from the three starting points of London, Launceston or Kenilworth on

Bob Grant on Stretes hill during the MCC Exeter Trial. (Norman Miller)

218

the evening of Friday January 3rd and finishing at Weymouth the following day after several observed sections in the Exeter vicinity. This year the cars were divided into classes, Class III being for specials on ordinary tyres and sports cars on 'knobblies' and Class V for cars of all types other than specials running on normal road tyres. The Morgan factory entered a team consisting of Jim Goodall in a Plus Four (presumably HUY 982), Peter Morgan in his 4/4 RNP 504 and Neville Jarrett in a Plus Four, all running on Dunlop Weathermaster 'grip' tyres. Also running was Ted Dennis in PUY 329, Monty Rogers in PLB 111, and Bob Grant in TKC 389. Damp, dismal conditions made the hills very difficult but Ted Dennis proved to be the best, taking Class V with a masterful display. Ted even managed to climb Simms, just getting over the summit without stopping, after some coordinated bouncing from his passenger in the rear (PUY 329 was a four-seater) and throttle blipping. Jim Goodall took a Second Class Award, whilst Jarrett and Rogers both took Thirds. The others failed to get awards.

One of the greatest and most versatile of Britain's motor sportsmen in the pre-war and post-war era had been the Midlander Ken Wharton. He was equally at home racing in Formula 1, rallying, doing trials or taking part in driving tests. His death in New Zealand in January 1957 whilst racing a Ferrari Monza had been hard to take and eventually it was decided by the Hagley and District Light Car Club that an annual inter-region driving test would be a suitable way to remember him. The first was held on Saturday January 25th, and this annual event still continues today. This first event was televised by the BBC, and featured teams of three cars representing Scotland, the North, the Midlands, the South West, Wales and the South. Each team consisted of one special, one saloon and one sports car. There were also individual awards for the three classes of cars with other entries for this competition. Winner of the team competition was the Midlands' team, whilst ex-Morgan driver Dave Warren won the sports cars individual award in his TR2. Les Yarranton finished third in his Plus Four PUY 306 behind another TR2. The car park of the Chateau Impney Hotel was the venue for the four tests.

By the end of January 4/4s were being dispatched from the Morgan factory fitted with radiators manufactured by the long established firm of E J Bowman in Birmingham, the first being chassis number A367. It was also now possible to request wire wheels for the 4/4, chassis number A370 being the first such built, but these were the cheaper 48-spoke wheels and were fitted with 5.20 by 15 inch tyres.

This year's Yorkshire Sports Car Club's Mille Miglia Rally avoided the usual snow, ice and fog, and competitors just had a steady drizzle to accompany them on their way from the start at Ilkley on Friday evening, February 14th. The weather gods of course had not gone away, for a deluge soon descended and stayed all night and all the following day! Mild fords through rivers became raging torrents, and Pauline Mayman had to retire when her poor Morgan TON 919 began to literally fall apart.

The North London ECC ran the Jacobean Trophy Trial over that weekend of Saturday February 15th and Sunday 16th. F A Freeman, navigated by R Randall, took home a First Class Award. That same Sunday the Morgan 4/4 Club ran its Banbury Rally for club members, attracting seven Morgans and a Borgward Isabella. Les Yarranton won the event in PUY 306 after beating Barrie Phipps in JNV 654 in the deciding driving test.

The Bolton-le-Moors Car Club ran a special rally of 300 miles of extremely tough Welsh motoring followed by four stiff driving tests, starting on Friday evening February 22nd from Stoke-on-Trent. This rally was only open to 'genuine clubmen', barring any previous winners of rallies of National or International status, and the amazing first prize was a brand new Austin A35! This was no ordinary Austin A35 but one with modifications by Speedwell Performance Components which were identical to those that had been used on John Sprinzel's successful racing

A35 during 1957! Three hundred and fifty entries were received, whittled down to 120 accepted, of which two were non-starters. The weather was foul with snow and a bitter wind but the TR2 of Ron Goldbourn, navigated by Stuart Turner, proved victorious, Ron collecting the A35 as his trophy (Ron was a car dealer anyway). R J Randall took the award for best performance in the driving tests in his Morgan.

A very special Morgan built for racing was dispatched from the Morgan factory on Thursday February 27th to the Midlands agency Hunts (Birmingham) Ltd. It was chassis number 3875, and was an off-white two-seater Plus Four fitted with a tuned and balanced TR3 engine, number TS 23684, which carried a large capacity finned aluminium sump. The bodywork was in aluminium and wire wheels were fitted. Two sets of tyres were supplied, four being Road Speed tyres and four Dunlop racing tyres. There was a spare back axle of 4.1 to 1, a Brooklands steering wheel and two aero screens. A full length tonneau and driving mirrors were also included, and the upholstery was in stone with black piping. The new owner was to be Alan Belcher and it was rumoured that his new Morgan was the most expensive ever built so far.

Alan Belcher was a larger than life character rapidly approaching his fiftieth birthday. During 1957 he had accompanied his motor racing-mad brother-in-law to Silverstone, but Alan had been rather bored by the poor performances of certain drivers and had commented that if he couldn't drive any better than they were doing he would pack it up. His brother-in-law suggested he should have a go, promising he would find him a good mechanic. Alan was always open to a challenge. Earlier in the 1950s he had decided to learn to fly, buying himself a light aircraft (a Miles Messenger) for the purpose. He was a craftsman and an inventor, making his money from spice blending for the meat industry. 'What car should I buy?' he asked his brother-in-law. 'Oh, a Morgan of course', was the reply, so on his return Alan had visited Peter Morgan to decide on the specification, and money did not appear to be a major problem. The new Morgan was given the personalised registration number VON 777 as Yvonne was the name of his second wife. It was to be maintained by Ron Timmins, a meticulous engineer who lived not too far from Alan's home in Dudley. Ron did not think the position of the original Morgan fuel tank was ideal for racing so he got Alan to specify two seven gallon fuel tanks which were situated on both sides of the prop shaft and located on the floor boards that usually carried the batteries. There were separate fillers for each through the modified rear panel; the plan was to use the right hand side tank for predominantly right turn circuits and the left hand side for left turn circuits. As a result of this modification the spare wheel could now be recessed into the rear panel.

The RAC Rally of Great Britain had never really appealed to Continental drivers as they regarded it as just an upgraded British car club rally, relying heavily on night navigation and driving tests rather than on driving skills as in Europe. The event did count towards the European Touring Championship however, so the organisers decided to abandon the night navigation and add a starting point of Le Touquet in France, hoping thereby to attract the Continental stars. It didn't work, for only one foreign entry was received and therefore the Le Touquet start was cancelled. Two hundred and six entries were received, starting from either Hastings or Blackpool, seven being Morgans. Starters from Hastings included the Morgan factory team consisting of Peter Morgan in TUY 875, Les Yarranton in PUY 306 navigated by J P Taylor, and Jim Goodall in HUY 982, navigated by J Thomas. Also with Hastings starts were Pauline Mayman navigated by Val Domleo in TON 919, Romek Michalkiewicz in TKT100, and Neville Jarrett in a Ford engined 4/4. Just one Morgan was due to start from Blackpool, the Plus Four of Bob Grant, but Bob had received a good offer for his car just prior to the event, and sold it to Roger Dobson, replacing it with a Triumph TR3 which he was now driving in this event.

Les Yarranton's Morgan had been back to the Morgan factory for work in early March, having a

TR3 cylinder head fitted as well as adjustments to fix clutch slip and a leaking exhaust. The car had also had steering adjustments. It now had a blister in the offside bonnet to cover the foremost SU carburettor, as did TUY 875.

The starters left Hastings and Blackpool on Tuesday morning, March 11th, the two routes converging at Prescott for the first test, a timed climb of the hill climb course, before making for the second test at Chateau Impney, this being a manoeuvring test on a loose surfaced track. Jane Morgan met the entourage here, congratulating Bob Grant on his excellent performance so far with the Morgan. She was not too impressed when Bob corrected her, pointing out that the programme was incorrect and that he was actually driving his new TR3.

After a meal break the competitors made for Wales and a sprint at Eppynt in which Peter Morgan was fastest in his class. Now the weather really began to deteriorate with ice on the approach to Lydstep hill climb, but this didn't prevent Peter Morgan again setting class fastest time. The conditions were now very severe with snow and ice causing chaos during the all night drive on minor roads through Wales. Peter Morgan was one who slid off course, badly damaging the front of the Morgan, and we think this may be the occasion when he detoured into a railway goods yard to find something solid to chain the bent front crosshead to whilst he reversed to pull it straight again. Hardly any cars survived unscathed or unpenalised, and Neville Jarrett abandoned his 4/4 by the side of the road and retired. Following further tests in the North West, Wednesday night was spent navigating through more snow in the Lake District, with Romek Michalkiewicz fastest in class in the Ulpha test. After visiting Charterhall early on Thursday for a sprint on the circuit, the battered competitors returned to Otterburn where Romek again was fastest in one of the tests. The day's tests finished with a classic pylon type driving test at the Ferodo factory at Chapel-en-le-Frith and the competitors then left by main roads for an early night drive to Snetterton where a sprint was held on the circuit during the early hours of Friday morning. From here the three circuits of Mallory Park, Silverstone and Brands Hatch were also visited for sprint tests on Friday before the entries made their way to the final destination of Hastings.

At last the competitors were now able to get a well deserved rest in bed, before tackling the final tests on the Hastings seafront. The final

The Morgans of Peter Morgan, Les Yarranton and Pauline Mayman set off on the Silverstone sprint during the RAC Rally. Jim Goodall waits on the second row for his turn. (LAT Photographic)

Peter Morgan completes the final test at Hastings in a very battered TUY 875. (Morgan Motor Co collection)

indignity was an inspection for damage, and 34 of the 128 finishers from the 196 starters lost a further 100 points here. The winner of the event was Rootes Group works driver Peter Harper in a new (and undamaged) Sunbeam Rapier. Despite the conditions the Morgans did well, for Les Yarranton won the 1,300cc to 2,000cc section of the class for Special Touring cars, and Standard and Modified Grand Touring cars. Jim Goodall came second, with Bob Grant third. As some reporters hadn't noticed Bob was in the TR3 it looked as though Morgans took the first three places!

On Friday March 21st Pauline Mayman collected a new Morgan. It was specially built for her at the Morgan factory, and she remembered seeing the incomplete car carrying a luggage tag with her name on it as it moved through the factory during the car's creation. It was chassis number 3886, a two-seater with wire wheels and TR3 engine number TS 26013. A strengthened chassis frame was part of the specification and Pauline remembered the car was supplied beautifully hand painted in grey, with black upholstery. It was given the personalised number EPM 324, EPM being Pauline's initials. Her previous Morgan, poor TON 919, came to a sad end when it was somersaulted by Pauline at her favourite venue, Prescott, but we are not sure of the date.

The SUNBAC club ran the Colmore Trial on Saturday March 22nd, with a special class this year on an experimental basis for production cars, attracting seventeen of them, several being Morgans. A slightly less severe course was used from that tackled by the trials specials in the main competition. The prize for the production cars was the Langley Trophy, and it was won by the Series II 4/4 of John Parry. He had managed to persuade fellow Hagley and District Light Car Club member Peter Anton to sell him his 4/4, RUY 255. John Parry also won the class for open cars with permitted trials tyres, whilst another Morgan, that of Frank Livingston, came second. The class for open or closed cars with normal road tyres also went to a Morgan, the early Plus Four two-seater of H B Geddes. He had also done well with his Morgan in the Shenstone and District Car Club's V T Fellows Memorial Trial held on Sunday March 2nd.

Also doing well in trials was Monty Rogers, for on Sunday March 23rd he took part in the West Hants and Dorset MC's Hartwell Cup Trial with his hard worked four-seater Plus Four PLB 111. The entry of 52 was split into the three classes: saloons, tourers and specials. It was dry, making the hills easy, but driving tests sorted out the field and Monty was the overall winner of the Hartwell Cup for an excellent performance. Tom Bryant, Joe Huxham's business partner, was also in a Morgan but he had trouble with sections at Liscombe Farm, near Dorchester.

Black ice was a major hazard encountered during the Wolverhampton and South Staffordshire Club's Express and Star Rally, run in March. Amongst the 91 starters was Ted Cleghorn in RVF 142, and he finished with a First Class Award.

The Mallory Park track had been considerably widened at Shaws corner since the end of the 1957 season. In addition, the previously very narrow hairpin and the large tree sited at a dangerous point at the hairpin exit, had also been dealt with. The opening meeting at the revised circuit was organised by the BARC on Saturday March 29th. During the seven lap scratch race for Marque sports cars to the BARC's own formula John Looker set fastest lap, but it was Donald Pacey in a 1954 two-seater Plus Four that finished in third place behind a TR3 and an MGA. Don Pacey was an undergraduate at the University College of North Staffordshire (which became the University of Keele in 1962), and he had purchased this Morgan from George Hulbert, Technical Director of Speedwell Performance Conversions Ltd, in January. This company had been set up by four enthusiasts in 1957 to supply tuning products for BMC cars, especially the Austin A35. These four were racer and future World Champion Graham Hill as Chairman and 'fitter', racer John Sprinzel as the administrator and publicist, Len Adams as salesman and George Hulbert as the development engineer. It was George Hulbert who had developed the Morgan, which was chassis number 3197, a green two-seater with black trim and engine number TS 2991. It had been dispatched originally on Monday November 15th 1954 and was registered 818 DMD. (Some vehicle registration authorities were now reversing the numbers and letters of their registrations to increase the capacity of the registration system).

In March the old Lucas type L488 rear lights and separate Remax reflectors of all Morgan models were replaced by the combined unit type L549, as fitted to other sports cars such as the MGA and TR3, but also fitted in their thousands to Morris Minors. The 4/4 was also fitted with the same grille as fitted to the revised Plus Four at this time, the first probably being chassis A 390, dispatched on March 23rd. Several Plus Fours were now being supplied with enlarged capacity finned aluminium sumps, particularly to the American market. Whilst the TR engine had reasonable oil capacity of eleven pints, hard use could cause the oil temperature to rise, giving a worrying drop in oil pressure and eventually causing damage to the bearings. These large sumps had twice the oil capacity of the original steel type, and the finned aluminium aided cooling. Some serious TR racers were experimenting with oil coolers as being a better option.

March 31st was the last day for competitors to register for the 1958 Autosport Series-Production Sports Car Championship, which was to be run on similar lines to those of 1957. The championship was to be open to all holders of an FIA International Competitions Licence, but this year the cars had to comply with the spirit of the regulations contained in Appendix J of the FIA Sporting Code, applicable to Grand Touring and Improved Series Grand Touring models. The Morgan Plus Four and 4/4 were both included. Lionel Mayman confirmed that he would be entering the competition.

The Easter weekend brought a huge choice of motor sport events, this being the first full Easter programme since pre-Suez in 1956.

The MCC's 50th Land's End Trial began from Colnbrook, Launceston or Kenilworth on Good Friday April 4th and used the same classes as used in the previous Exeter. This year for the first time the event finished at Newquay, rather than Land's End, to allow more time for socialising after the event. The breakfast stop was in Taunton and then the trial proper began. As always several Morgans took part. The Morgan team consisted of Neville Jarrett in a Plus Four, Peter Morgan in the 4/4

RNP 504, and Jim Goodall in a Plus Four (presumably HUY 982). Ted Dennis was in his Plus Four, PUY 329, and C R 'Bob' Parsons, a vet, was also in a Plus Four. It was cold, with a biting wind and snow flurries over the barren landscape of Exmoor and there were many delays, particularly at Hustyn which many failed to climb. The best Morgan performance was by Bob Parsons who won Class 5, with Ted Dennis also taking a First Class Award. The Morgan team did not do well, Jarrett getting a Second Class Award, Peter Morgan a Third and Jim Goodall retiring.

On Easter Sunday the Nottingham Sports Car Club ran a race meeting at Mallory Park. It was a cold but bright day and attracted some 25,000 spectators but there were numerous non-starters for the second race, a ten lap race for sports cars of 1,300cc and over, just seven lining up on the grid. One was Ray Meredith in NAB 217. Ray had a lonely race in third place behind the winning Aston Martin saloon and a Lotus MG.

The following day, Easter Monday, there was a good crowd at the Trengwainton hill climb in Cornwall where fine weather led to excellent motor sport. Despite the large number of TRs and the Morgans in the sports cars up to 2,000cc class, it was the Bristol engined Frazer Nash of R E Wright that was fastest with a time of 27.81 seconds. Second place, just 0.07 seconds slower, was taken by Jim Banbury in JJY 221, whilst John Looker was third in his Plus Four OWP 38 after lifting a wheel at the fast left hand bend. John had recently left the laundry business in Pershore and had moved to Rock in Cornwall where he had converted an old coal wharf into a boat building business. In fourth place was Robin Brown in UOL 490, whilst Ted Dennis had also entered but didn't compete.

Pauline Mayman had wasted no time in entering her new Morgan EPM 324 in a major rally when she entered Class 4, for sports cars of any capacity, in the Ulster AC's Circuit of Ireland. The event began with a choice of Dublin or Belfast as the starting venue on Good Friday April 4th and finished on the following Easter Tuesday, April 8th at Bangor. Val Domleo was to be her passenger. John Howe had also entered his venerable Vanguard engined Plus Four, and he was navigated by H Curry.

The first stage included the Wicklow Mountains where snowbound roads caused many to gain penalties before the welcome rest at Killarney on the Saturday evening. Pauline Mayman was running in second position in the ladies' class at this point, just behind the Riley of Pat Moss and Anne Wisdom. The second stage began in pouring rain on the Sunday morning with a drive to the famous Tim Healy Pass. For a change this year the formidable climb was to be tackled downwards, as a timed descent, and this struck fear into the competitors, especially those with suspect brakes! This was followed by a regularity test near Bantry before the cars returned to Killarney for a further rest. The final stage of the rally was a 27 hour drive from Killarney to Bangor, including a night navigation section, a hill climb at Corkscrew Hill in County Clare, a speed test at the Kirkistown circuit and two final driving tests at Bangor on the Easter Tuesday. Pat Moss and Anne Wisdom kept their lead to win the Ladies' Trophy in a works Riley 1.5. The event was won by Paddy Hopkirk driving a works Triumph TR3.

Pauline and Val hardly had time to recover from their Irish excursion before they were facing the start of the Midland Motor Enthusiasts Club's 6th annual Cambrian Rally. This started at midnight on Friday April 11th from the Fleur-de-Lys at Lowsonford in Warwickshire with a 200 mile overnight drive into Wales followed by a fifty mile section in the Midlands. They were still well able to rally however, producing one of five clean sheets, with the overall winner being the best performer in the driving tests (an Austin A35). The Mayman-Domleo crew took EPM 324 to a class win.

A bitter wind didn't encourage spectators for the South Western Centre of the BARC's 17th hill climb at Brunton on Sunday April 13th. The class for sports cars from 1,901 to 2,750cc was well supported with J R Rudd from London in a Frazer Nash victorious with a time of 25.36

The Mayman and Domleo Morgan EPM 324 waiting at the top of the Tim Healy Pass for the timed descent, in the Circuit of Ireland. (Val Morley)

seconds. Jim Banbury in JJY 221, and John Looker in OWP 38 both recorded 27.86 seconds to finish in equal third place behind another Frazer Nash, whilst A M Greig recorded 28.28 seconds to finish fifth. Writing up this event in the Morgan 4/4 Club's magazine *Miscellany* the editor, Robin Brown, commented, 'Somebody must grab J Banbury for the Club – he is the most polished hill climb driver and does astonishing things with an old and very hard used Plus Four.'

Mr Greig's October 1955 registered Plus Four was for sale for £600, and had been rebuilt 2,000 miles earlier. It was a red two-seater, chassis number 3299, originally dispatched to Rossleigh Ltd in Edinburgh on Thursday July 28th 1955.

A perfect spring day was provided for the Thames Estuary AC's 'Day of Dicing', a day of National driving tests held at Orsett Barracks, near Grays in Essex on Sunday April 20th. The eight rally-type driving tests attracted 118 entries. Having an excellent day was Sandy Blair in Nixie, even drawing applause from the critical spectators.

He took the class for standard open cars, 1,601 to 2,500cc, and was only beaten overall by a couple of specials.

Pauline Mayman returned her Plus Four EPM 324 to the Morgan factory during this week for some well deserved attention. The cylinder head was removed for new valves to be fitted, the front suspension was checked over as was the electrical equipment, a new horn being required. Attention was required to the right hand door lock and the offside rear wing was repaired and repainted. Pauline also had a hand throttle fitted, as used on works Morgans, to enable a fast tick-over to be selected for driving tests to prevent stalling. The speedometer, which indicated a mileage of 3,537, was replaced and badges were fitted to the bonnet.

The next rally for Pauline was the MAC's National Birmingham Post Rally which began from the civic centre car park in Birmingham city centre on Friday evening April 25th. She was to be navigated by Val Domleo as usual. Also entered was Romek Michalkiewicz in TKT 100 to be navigated by his usual passenger E Clarke and there was a Morgan factory team too. This team comprised Jim Goodall navigated by P Taylor, presumably in HUY 982, Les Yarranton in PUY 306 navigated by H Rumsey, and Peter Morgan in the 4/4 RNP 504, navigated by Les Yarranton's usual navigator Tommy Thompson. Peter had lent his Plus Four TUY 875 to Lyndon Sims for the Tulip Rally. There was mixed fortune for the Morgan entries during the 400 mile rally. Romek Michalkievicz failed to start, Peter Morgan retired and Jim Goodall failed to arrive at the breakfast control in Llandrindod Wells. Les Yarranton too was having problems, collecting several road penalties before breakfast, but he did put up the best overall performance in the driving tests. Best of the Morgan entries however was Pauline Mayman, and she beat Les to finish in an excellent second place behind a Triumph in the over 1,600cc sports cars class, Les being one place behind. Pauline and Val Domleo easily took the Regent Challenge Trophy for the best performance by an all ladies crew, an excellent day's work for Pauline and Val.

The weather was atrocious for the BARC Members' Meeting on Saturday April 26th held at Goodwood, the club's home circuit, which had undergone considerable improvements to the facilities over the previous winter. The heavens well and truly opened and gumboots were the order of the day, with the paddock area resembling a trials section! The third event was a Marque sports cars scratch race, which started in a downpour with the Plus Fours of John Looker, OWP 38, and Don Pacey, 818 DMD, on the grid. John's blue and black car now sported the new shorter type of Plus Four radiator grille. John took an immediate lead but it was short lived, for his helmet visor became obscured each time he went along the Levant Straight, forcing him to slow. Mud obscured the outside, and rain water was obscuring the inside! Syd Hurrell went by in his TR3 to lead at the end of the first lap, and on lap four Paul Fletcher's AC Ace took second place from John, soon also passing Hurrell's TR3 for the

win. John finished third, with Don Pacey just behind in his Plus Four.

The following day, Sunday April 27th the West Hants and Dorset CC ran another of its popular autocrosses, this time in the grounds of Lytchett Manor, near Poole. Sprints over three laps were used, with the cars running in pairs. Winning a class award in his four-seater Plus Four PLB 111 was Monty Rogers.

There was a change in the organisation within the Birmingham Morgan agency, Hunts of B'ham, on Thursday May 1st. The company closed down its Hagley Road service department and transferred servicing to the Maymans' Kay Garages in Shadwell Street. This was a consequence of a rationalisation following Lionel and Pauline Mayman joining Hunts as directors.

There was a major driving test meeting held by the Taunton Motor Club at the Army's Middleway Camp barrack square in Taunton on Sunday May 4th. Eighty varied vehicles were attracted to the afternoon's five driving tests, and the best of all with a brilliant display of precision manoeuvring was Peter Morgan driving the 4/4 prototype RNP 504. This was an amazing performance, and one of which Peter remained justifiably proud for the rest of his life, for he had beaten much more suitable short wheelbase cars. Peter was not alone amongst the Morgan entries in being victorious, for Mrs Peggy Livingston won the Ladies' Award in an ex-Neville Jarrett red Plus Four.

Peter's works Morgan was now running with a Willment overhead inlet valve head conversion, although this was never intended for production 4/4s, being quite expensive. Famed Ford driver and enthusiast John Willment had financed the production of this special cylinder head, originally developed in bronze by Bob Yeats, a prolific Ford special builder. It was probably the best of the various overhead inlet valve head conversions produced for the Ford 100E engine and capable of giving 61 bhp at 6,000 rpm. Unlike the Elva head the Willment used Jaguar valves and valve springs and didn't suffer from valve spring surge.

A special Lodge spark plug was used of unusual 10mm size, type HELS10, and Peter had one disappear during his trip from Taunton, driving on three cylinders to a garage where he was very lucky to find a replacement for this rarely used plug size. The Willment head was sold by Willment Powermaster Conversions, in Twickenham, Middlesex.

Also that Sunday the Bugatti Owners' Club ran a hill climb at Prescott in glorious weather. The class for sports cars up to 3,000cc was heavily oversubscribed, but the BOC did accept the two Morgan entries of Ray Meredith in NAB 217 and Robin Brown in UOL 490 within the nineteen accepted. Robin Brown was now running with ram pipes from Wilen Engineering poking out of the side of the bonnet to feed cold air to the carburettors and he was pleased with this addition, recording 51.56 seconds, whilst Ray recorded 51.68 seconds. They finished seventh and eighth in class, vanquishing a lot of expensive and potent machinery. The class was won by a Lotus Bristol in 48.84 seconds.

On Sunday May 11th fifty competitors were attracted to the sprint meeting held at Harleyford Manor, near Marlow in Buckinghamshire on a beautiful sunny day. On top form was Sandy Blair in Nixie, easily winning his class. *Autosport*'s reporter was most impressed, writing, 'Tremendous verve and consummate skill got him to the top in a best time of 25.32 seconds, easily the winner of his class and the fastest sports car of the day. In fact, racing cars apart he was almost the only competitor who managed to get inside 26 seconds, and a great many of the single-seater brigade failed to achieve this. Blair was well over a second ahead of the class runner-up A Baker (TR2) who recorded 26.81 seconds.' It was praise indeed.

That same Sunday the Morgan 4/4 Club co-promoted a Standard Car Trial with the Midlands Motoring Enthusiasts' Club, the victor being T D Smith in his 4/4. Finishing in fifth place was Cyril Charlesworth in his second Morgan, a four-seater Plus Four coupé registered UKP 61. Cyril was the second owner of this February 1955 red coupé, chassis number 3234, the first having been F R E Sharp, one of the 'Sharp's Creamy Toffees' family.

Robin Brown lines up for his run at Prescott, with Ray Meredith's Morgan behind. Note the carburettor ram pipes. (Charles Dunn)

His first Morgan had been burnt out during a journey in 1954. Cyril was to become a life long Morgan enthusiast, and his company in Curdworth, Sutton Coldfield, was a pioneer in plastic moulding, later supplying the Morgan factory with components.

The Aston Martin Owners' Club ran the David Brown Trophy race meeting at Silverstone on Saturday May 17th. Included in the programme was the famous relay race for the David Brown Trophy, which this year had been made longer, covering 140 laps or 225 miles. Each team was allowed three cars, with up to two reserves which could only be used in case of mechanical derangement to the specified three team cars. Team 10 was the entry from the Morgan 4/4 Club, there being twenty other teams starting. The 'A' car was Robin Brown in UOL 490. The 'B' car was Ray Meredith in NAB 217. The 'C' car was John Looker in OWP 38, and the reserve was Alan Belcher in VON 777.

Alan Belcher had been competing in minor club races with his new Morgan racer but was finding that motor racing was not as easy as he had first believed. Alan was not one to be beaten easily so he had enrolled with the Jim Russell Racing Drivers' School at the Snetterton circuit where he was tutored in a Cooper Climax, and also at Brands Hatch where a Cooper Monaco was the available tuition racer. He was now much closer to achieving his 'Best Driver in the World' ambition! Meanwhile Ron Timmins was busy preparing the Morgan by concentrating initially on the engine which soon had internals polished so brightly that you could see your face in them. The engine was balanced at Technical and Balancing Service in Birmingham and Ron began to gas flow the head and to raise the compression in stages.

One of the Morgan relay team had problems on the way to Silverstone, the oil pressure dropping alarmingly. Luckily this was found to be a simple problem in the oil filter head and it was rectified, although the car only reached the scrutineers with five minutes to spare when practice had already finished. Luckily practice was not essential for 'experts'. With the handicap decided by credit laps the Morgan team found it had 122 laps to complete, one less than a potent TR team.

The start was of Le Mans type and Robin Brown managed to get away safely. Each first team car had to make a compulsory pit stop to change a spark plug. The Morgan team, under the control of Jim Bishop, managed this much better than many teams and even without burnt fingers! After Robin had covered his allotted 42 laps the sash was handed to Ray Meredith in NAB 217, and he reeled off his forty laps uneventfully. The final stint of forty laps was down to the hard charging John Looker, who was driving with headlamps blazing. The handicaps were all now coming together, allowing the leaders to be identified more easily than in the earlier stages of the race, and after two and a half hours of racing the Morgan team was running in fifth place. John piled on the pressure and gained a further three places in the last thirty minutes, one being taken on the run into Woodcote Corner on the final lap. The winning team consisted of two MGAs and an MG TF and finished just half a lap ahead, but they had had to cover four less laps than the Morgan team. It was an excellent performance by the Plus Fours, and John Looker had so impressed one of the spectators that he was keen to buy his racer there and then! John was finding weekend racing difficult now that he was in the boat building business, for weekends were his busiest time. Reluctantly he decided OWP 38 had to go.

Another racing Morgan for sale at this time was John McKecknie's Plus Four MVJ 101, for John was now racing an AC Ace before undertaking his compulsory National Service. His Morgan was offered as having a highly tuned TR2 engine with special inlet manifold, SU H6 carburettors, and a four branch exhaust. The whole car had recently been rebuilt.

The Westmorland Motor Club held a hill climb at Barbon that same Saturday. Two apprentices from the nearby Leyland Motors took part. One, Pat Kennett, was in his modified side valve Morris Minor convertible, whist the other, John Edwards, was competing in the ex-Jimmy Ray Plus Four, MLV

Brian Harper undertaking the final driving tests at Morecambe during the Morecambe Rally. (Charles Dunn)

58. When he had bought this historic Morgan it was coloured blue and fitted with a Vanguard engine and 4.1 to 1 back axle, but John soon uprated it to a TR engine, and changed the back axle for a 3.73 version collected from Bowman and Acock in Malvern Link. The Morgan received a bulge to the offside bonnet to clear the foremost SU carburettor and the whole car was repainted red.

Also being held that weekend was the Lancashire Automobile Club's Morecambe Rally, attracting 125 starters. On the Sunday morning, after the overnight run through Lancashire, Yorkshire and Westmorland had been completed, the competitors returned to Morecambe for the final driving tests. Only one driver, Ken Walker in a TR3, had a clean sheet with no penalties whatsoever after the road section, but his times on the promenade tests in the wet Sunday morning conditions were beaten by the experienced Ron Goldbourn, who deliberately waited all morning for the test area to dry out before doing his tests in his TR3. The Ladies' Award was taken by Pauline Mayman and Val Domleo in EPM 324, whilst Brian Harper won a First Class Award for his performance in his Plus Four.

Brian Harper was from Cannock in Staffordshire where the family motor coaches business was known as Harper Brothers. He had been rallying a Triumph TR2, followed by a Renault Dauphine, with considerable success as a member of the Shenstone and District Car Club, but had experienced various problems with the Renault including finding the gear lever up his trouser leg when he got in quickly during one rally! As a consequence he had decided to upgrade to another sports car and had recently visited Hunts' showroom in Broad Street, Birmingham. They had sold him a white two-seater Plus Four that he had been told had been on a 1957 Motor Show stand. It was registered WOF 559. In actual fact this Morgan was chassis number 3473, and had originally been dispatched to Bolton of Leeds in April 1956, presumably not selling there and hence being taken on later by Hunts. Earlier in the month of May, with just over 1,000 miles on the clock, the poor Morgan had been in an accident and required new casing boards to a door and attention to the rear of the body. Brian had served an engineering apprenticeship at Leyland Motors and was well able to look after the mechanical side of the vehicles with which he was involved.

Morgan Sports Cars — 1958

Way back in 1956 Leonard Lord, the boss of the British Motor Corporation, had realised that there was a gap in the sports car market for a small engined sports car, after the introduction of the 1,500cc MGA had moved MG up market. He realised that there was only the Morgan 4/4 at the lower end, HFS Morgan of course having previously also spotted and targeted this gap. Leonard Lord chatted to Donald Healey at 'The Austin' and asked him to design a cheap, small engined sports car using as much as possible from the Austin A35 parts bin, an idea that Donald Healey had already been exploring. Donald's son Geoffrey actually did the design using mainly Austin A35 parts, but he did use new brakes, and also preferred the Morris Minor rack and pinion steering. The body was designed by the Donald Healey Motor Company designer Gerry Coker, and it was fitted with side-screens with sliding windows. The platform chassis was also designed in-house, by Barrie Bilbie. The A35's A-Series engine was fitted with twin SU carburettors boosting the power to 43 bhp. The new sports car, called the Austin Healey Sprite, reviving an old Riley name, was introduced to the press in Monaco during the Grand Prix festivities, this race being held on Sunday May 18th. The odd position of the headlights led to the new Sprite being affectionately nicknamed the 'Frogeye' Sprite in Britain, and 'Bugeye' in the USA.

The new Sprite was very competitively priced, and HFS Morgan drew the attention of the Morgan board to this at the meeting held on Thursday May 29th where he expressed concern that the price of the newcomer was £79 less than the price of the Morgan 4/4 and could well lead to a fall off in sales of the 4/4. At that same meeting George Goodall asked if he might be permitted to retire from the services of the Company in September, by which time he would have completed 33 years service.

Girling Limited, the supplier of brakes to Morgan, was now busy addressing the problems of fitting front disc brakes to the Morgan Plus Four model, for both the bolt-on and wire wheels. Girling supplied drawings for this conversion in May. Peter Morgan told us that the work was done very quickly and with little fuss, the Girling concern apparently making the Morgan conversion an example to the motor trade of how easily and quickly it could change the current specification drum brakes for discs. The disc brakes that were fitted used the Girling type 14 C caliper assembly and an 11inch diameter disc. No doubt the conversion for the wire wheels set up was fairly easy for the Girling engineers to do, as wire wheels of this type were common to many cars. However, problems did occur with the bolt-on wheeled fitting, and alterations to the hub castings were required. During the summer months TUY 875 reappeared fitted with bolt-on wheels in place of its original wire wheel set up, and we believe this change was for a trial of the Girling disc brake conversions.

It must have appeared very odd to many customers that the Plus Four and 4/4 could both be purchased with either 16 inch bolt-on wheels or 15 inch wire wheels as original fitments. The 16 inch Dunlop bolt-on wheel was now 'old hat', with the smaller 15 inch wheels being much preferred by the motor industry. The Dunlop Rim and Wheel Company supplied drawings of a 15 inch replacement of 4J section to the Morgan factory in June. Supplies were immediately ordered as a future replacement for the 16 inch version.

On Friday May 30th the last Plus Four fitted with a Vanguard engine, chassis number 3922, a two-seater, was dispatched from the Morgan factory bound for Sweden. All Plus Fours were now being supplied with TR engines.

There were interesting developments too at the Standard Motor Company. The Company Competition Manager, Ken Richardson, was facing problems in some international rallies, where the class limit was not set at 2,000cc, in getting the TR3As to stay with the larger engined Austin Healeys allowed in the same class. As a result he had fitted a TR engine with Vanguard liners which had the maximum permissible over-bore, this being approximately 86mm and giving 2,138cc. As Vanguard pistons were not too strong he arranged for Specialloid to manufacture some special 86mm pistons to suit. This new engine didn't give much more power than the original TR3 engine, but gained a useful increase in mid-range torque. Ken believed he first used this engine in the works TR3 rally cars in the 1958 Alpine Rally which was held in July. The success of this engine allowed the Standard Motor Company to offer this piston and liner set as an option for 1959.

The Royal Scottish Automobile Club's International Scottish Rally began on Whit Monday May 26th and finished five days later on Friday May 30th. This year there was just one Morgan entry, that of Romek Michalkiewicz in TKT 100, but he started badly when he spun at the hairpin on the first test, the timed climb of the Rest-and-be-Thankful hill climb. On the Wednesday on the second of the tests held on Crimond circuit Romek scored maximum penalties and he repeated this at Castle Grant on the Thursday on the widely sweeping forward and reverse test. He finished ninth of the fifteen starters in Class 10, for Grand Touring cars up to 2,600cc. The rally was won by ex-Morgan driver Frank Dundas in his Triumph TR3.

There were entrants from fourteen invited clubs for the Eastbourne and District Motor Club's Restricted event the 'Rally of the Downs' which started on Friday June 6th and finished the following day after 320 miles divided into three sections. It was brilliantly won overall by Horace Appleby in his 4/4, KDY 183, navigated by his friend, a Brighton doctor named Bob McGhie. Naturally they won their class too.

On Sunday June 8th the active Darlington and District Motor Club held a hill climb at Catterick barracks. Class H was for cars from 1,500 to 2,000cc, and attracted five Morgans to battle with three TRs and two Porsches. The class was won by Peter Bradley in his Plus Four, with a time of 42.2 seconds, pipping the fastest Porsche by 0.4 seconds. In fourth place behind the fastest TR was W A R Crowther in his Plus Four, whilst Jim Banbury in JJY 221 had a bad day for him with just fifth place, but ahead of John Edwards in MLV 58. The other Morgan, of F Winter, finished seventh but still beat the other two TRs and the other Porsche.

Peter Bradley was from the picturesque village of Dent, high in the Yorkshire Dales, and his Morgan

The Morgan 4/4 used by Horace Appleby to win the Eastbourne Rally. (Charles Dunn)

had been registered 9267 U on Wednesday March 19th. It was chassis number 3880 and had been dispatched to the Leeds agent Bolton of Leeds the following day. It was a black two-seater with beige upholstery.

The new Austin Healey Sprite was soon put under the influence of Speedwell Performance Conversions Ltd by George Hulbert, and the Sales Director Len Adams gave this Speedwell version its competition debut at the 750 Motor Club South Midland Centre's driving tests held on Sunday June 15th at Shening Aerodrome near Banbury. It came away with first place, but was pushed all the way by H B Geddes, now driving a Morgan 4/4 Series II, and also a diminutive 328cc Excelsior engined Berkeley which actually beat the 4/4 to take second place.

Monty Rogers' hard worked Plus Four four-seater PLB 111 was back in the Morgan factory repair shop during the week for a new frame front, new centrepins, front springs and rebushed stub axles, a new exhaust system and new floorboards carrying the seats. It had now covered over 46,000 miles. Replacement floorboards were needed because of damage from rocks during trials, which Monty found was made worse by the bouncing of enthusiastic passengers.

The Midlands Motoring Enthusiasts' Club ran a race meeting at Silverstone on a cold and wet Saturday June 21st. Three Morgan Plus Fours were entered, EPM 324 to be shared by Pauline and Lionel Mayman, VON 777 by Alan Belcher, and MLV 58 by John Edwards, but none featured in the prizes.

The MAC held a hill climb at Shelsley Walsh on Sunday afternoon, June 22nd with the regulations framed to encourage production sports cars and saloons rather than specialised racers. It remained dry for the first runs but then the rain swept down for the second set. Fastest time of the day was made by Les Yarranton in PUY 306 with a time of 47.7 seconds, whilst second fastest was Frank Livingston in his Plus Four just 0.3 seconds slower. Ray Meredith was third fastest in 48.5 seconds. Mrs Peggy Livingston, Frank's wife, recorded 51.1 seconds, presumably in her husband's Plus Four, beating several of the TRs. As Les, Frank and Ray also competed as the Hagley and District Light Car Club's 'B' team they naturally won the team competition too.

Waiting in the Silverstone paddock for a five lap sports car handicap during the MMEC meeting. Some last minute fettling is undertaken by John Edwards. Pat Kennett is with the Morris Minor behind. (Pat Kennett collection)

The 1958 Plymouth National Rally began on Friday evening June 27th from starting places at Plymouth, Birmingham, Bristol, Southampton and London and was oversubscribed with 116 competitors actually starting. After 150 miles the routes converged at Haldon Roadhouse where the first secret route card was issued covering 120 miles of tortuous Devonshire roads to be covered at an average of 30 mph. At Okehampton, as dawn broke, the second secret route card was issued, heading the crews towards Bude and a breakfast break. Road books were now issued for the final stage to return to Plymouth at 20 mph average, but interspersed with various driving tests en route. At the first test, held on the old Davidstowe racing circuit, Peter Morgan set the fastest time in his Plus Four, with Jim Goodall second fastest in his. The second test was a loose surface hill climb at Horsebridge, near Callington, and here the fastest time was performed by Pauline Mayman in EPM 324. The next test was a sprint at Brentor and once again Peter Morgan set the fastest time. After arriving at Plymouth on the Saturday the morning's rallying was concluded by a manoeuvrability test on the Hoe, where again Peter Morgan was outstanding, setting the fastest time. After lunch the drivers returned to their cars for the final two tests, Jim Goodall being second fastest in the first. It was the road sections that produced the rally winners however, with the first three places going to the only three crews with clean sheets. Sadly the Morgans were not amongst them.

On Saturday June 28th the BARC held an eight race programme Members' Meeting at Mallory Park. Alan Belcher did well with VON 777 in the second sports car handicap event, leading from start to finish at a race speed of 69.99 mph. He was tailed initially by a Triumph TR2, but this was demoted to third place on the last lap by a fast finishing Lotus Climax. In the later Marque scratch race Don Pacey started on the front row of the grid in his Plus Four 818 DMD but soon dropped down the field to finish out of the awards.

During the first half of 1958 Jeff Parker-Eaton had traded in his red two-seater Morgan Plus Four TOK 258 to a garage in Shirley in the West Midlands. He had now replaced the Morgan with a Triumph TR sports car. TOK 258 appears to have then passed through the motor trade to Performance Cars Ltd in West London where it was purchased in June by twenty-five year old Chris Lawrence with financial assistance and encouragement from his future wife Jenny, and his uncle Tony Sanderson. The aim was to further his career in motor sport with a really competitive car. Chris was unaware that TOK 258 had previously been raced.

Chris Lawrence's father had raced motorcycles as an amateur at Brooklands and had also been a founder member of the Vintage Motor Cycle Club. As a fifteen year old Chris had been allowed to take part in motorcycle grass track racing, then in 1952 he started hill climbing and circuit racing in a Morgan Super Sports three-wheeler. Chris joined the Royal Navy after leaving school and, after officer training at the Britannia Royal Naval College and at sea, he trained as an engineering officer and gained a B.Sc degree. However, he soon realised that his heart was really set on motor racing. He left the Navy to work first with Thornycroft and then as a development engineer working on aircraft gas turbine (jet) engine starting equipment at Rotax. This company was the aircraft component division of Lucas, located in Willesden, North London, which later became Lucas Aerospace. Chris's section leader, Geoffrey Price, became his mentor at Rotax and Chris told us what an important influence he had on him when developing his analytical engineering skills for the future. He also had the opportunity early on at Rotax to attend night school and learn advanced welding techniques that would prove useful to him.

After the three-wheeler, Chris had raced a Type 38 Bugatti, then 'Porthos', one of the pre-war supercharged MG NE Magnette 'Three Musketeers' trials cars, which we have previously mentioned. At first it was raced supercharged but because of the severe handicapping Chris changed to six Amal carburettors. Then, to save weight, the MG body was replaced with a streamlined off-the-shelf Mistral fibreglass body made by Microplas Ltd. After a crash in 1956 which damaged the chassis, Chris designed and built a tubular space frame with all independent suspension. The much-modified car became known as the 'Rotacks-MG' in honour of Chris's work place, Rotax, and its return to the track gave him some success. However in 1957 he was given the opportunity to race a rare car with more potential. His uncle Tony Sanderson bought an AFM from Major Arthur Mallock that the Major had brought back to the UK from Germany. The intention was for Chris to develop the car for racing whilst Tony used it for sprints and hill climbs

The AFM was one of the best of the racing cars and competition specials built in immediate post-war Germany using pre-war BMW 328 parts. An advanced design, with a tubular frame, De Dion rear axle and cast magnesium wheels with integral brake drums, Chris's car had been built as a single-seater but had been converted to a two-seater for sports car events. It had a BMW 328 engine, which had been 'destroked' from 2 to 1.5 litres by using a special crankshaft, which also allowed it to rev above its original design limit. This modification had been used in Germany, to enable cars to compete in different classes, but it was found that the engine was unreliable at sustained high rpm in races, although ideally suited to hill climbs and sprints. Chris found that the car oversteered, so he improved the handling by modifying the location of the De Dion axle, but the increased cornering forces caused engine oil surge. This didn't help the modified engine's inherent weakness so after a series of bearing changes, and in fairness to Tony Sanderson, the AFM was then used mainly for hill climbing. In retrospect, Chris told us what a fine car it was and how much he learned from the experience of tuning and competing with it. With more time and money he believes that he could have made it a force to be reckoned with.

Chris had a group of racing enthusiast friends at Rotax who supported him at events and spent evenings and weekends working with him on the cars in a lock-up garage close by in Ealing. The group included Les Fagg, ex-Merchant Navy and a development engineer, and John Harvey. John was an experienced toolmaker and experimental turbine fitter who worked in the assembly shop and had access to equipment that was useful to Chris. He was a precision engineer, and group member Roland 'Nobby' Smith told us, 'John could build a soul into an engine.' Roland was an apprentice who joined up with Chris when he had been allowed to machine racing parts for him at the engineering school. Around the time of TOK's purchase the group had been joined by Rotax technical author Len Bridge. After completing his engineering studies Len had trained as a pilot in the Fleet Air Arm during National Service, flying Supermarine Seafires and Hawker Sea Furies. At Rotax Len wrote the operating manuals for the company's turbine starting equipment, including units used on the RAF's 'V' bombers. The work carried out by Chris and the group during the day involved using skills that were ideally suited to their part-time racing projects where fine tolerances and attention to detail were also important. Spending so much time together no doubt gave them the opportunity to bounce ideas off each other and discuss at length what was to replace the AFM.

Whilst racing at BARC events Chris had had a close-up view of the Marque racing which he also followed closely in the motoring press. In 1958 for the first time the series of scratch races was to culminate in the award of the Fred W Dixon Challenge Trophy for the most successful driver. The trophy, donated by Freddie's widow Margaret, via the Middlesbrough and District Motor Club, was one of the flying Mercury statuettes won by this famous pre-war motorcycle racer, racing driver and engineer. A race programme for a BARC Members' Meeting explained the Marque series thus: 'The cars eligible for these races are five types readily available to buyers anywhere in the country – AC Ace (excluding Bristol-engined cars), Austin Healey 100 and 100 Six (except the 100S), MGA, Morgan Plus Four, Triumph TR2 and TR3. No restriction is placed on modifications. Drivers are awarded four points for winning a race, three for second, two for third and one for fourth place.' Marque eligibility would be reviewed and revised each season as necessary, the idea being for the cars to be clearly defined and evenly matched to enable close racing, although the provision for modifications and tuning was encouraged in the spirit of Freddie Dixon's racing Riley developments pre-war. However, at first *Autosport* somewhat haughtily considered it to be a poor man's version of its own Autosport Championship! Chris Lawrence and his friends knew that there was a lot of potential for tuning in the TR engine and considered the Morgan chassis to be more suited to racing than the Triumph TR version. Hence the purchase of TOK 258, the 1956 TR2 engined Morgan Plus Four that was a year younger than the TR2 also on offer at Performance Cars Ltd for exactly the same price.

The next BARC Members' Meeting was held at Goodwood on Saturday July 12th with cloudy but rain free conditions. Ray Meredith was entered in NAB 217 for the ten lap Marque scratch race, but the Morgan took a while to get going from the Le Mans start, and didn't finish in the places. The race was won by David Shale's Austin Healey 100 Six from Roy North's Triumph TR2.

At Silverstone the Aston Martin Owners' Club ran the St John Horsfall meeting that same day. Just one Morgan was entered, this being Alan Belcher's VON 777, in the second half-hour regularity speed trial. Competing in high speed trials was giving Alan excellent racing experience, and he won a First Class Award for covering the required nineteen laps.

We think this was the occasion on which Alan found his normally mild mannered mechanic Ron Timmins shaking with anger when he returned with the Morgan to the paddock after this event. 'What have I done Ron?' asked Alan. Ron exploded, 'Your wife should be shot, she's a menace, look at your lap times', and he thrust the lap times under Alan's nose. To Alan's astonishment they were several seconds faster than those Yvonne had been chalking on the pit board after each lap during the race for Alan to see. Alan had been driving faster than he had ever done before in response to Yvonne's times. Yvonne commented, 'I cooked them, knowing you would not get your finger out unless you had some sort of stimulation. I know how your mind works. Still what are you bothered about, you won didn't you?' We doubt she did this again!

A sprint was held at Catterick barracks by the Darlington and District Motor Club on Sunday July 13th using half of the usual hill climb course together with a detour around a hangar to give a distance of nearly three quarters of a mile. Class H, for sports cars of 1,501 to 2,000cc, attracted a large entry with many TRs and ACs, but 9267 U, the Plus Four of Peter Bradley, and the Porsche of L S Stross beat them all, dead heating for first place.

In July four-seater Plus Fours from chassis number 3967 began to be dispatched from the Morgan factory fitted with wider bodies. Four inches of extra width had been obtained by the body shop and this allowed front seats that were two inches wider to be fitted, which were adjustable forwards and backwards.

The Morgan Motor Company board meeting was held on Thursday July 17th. It was agreed that George Goodall would retire as works manager at the end of September, but that he would continue as a Morgan Motor Company director. The board also supported giving Arthur Cridland £100 towards a television set as a mark of appreciation of his long loyal service, latterly as foreman of the body shop. Following this retirement Arthur Frith took over the position. He had joined the Morgan factory following service in the Royal Flying Corps during the First World War and was a skilled carpenter as well as being the Company's pattern maker.

With the disc brake trials proving satisfactory the board agreed they should be fitted to the cars exhibited at the November Motor Show, and the Girling Company was to be pressed for a quotation and a delivery date for 100 sets.

The Mid-Cheshire MC held a race meeting at Oulton Park on Saturday July 26th. Practice was held on a wet morning, but the track had dried by the afternoon's races. The first event on the programme was a half hour high speed trial, and Alan Belcher in VON 777 and a K R James in his Morgan both won Plaques for covering the required number of laps.

Chris Lawrence's first outing with TOK 258 was at Aintree on Saturday July 26th in the first of the two seven lap Marque races on the BARC Members' Meeting programme. Don Pacey was also entered in his ex-Speedwell Plus Four 818 DMD. *Autosport* magazine reported this as the most exciting race of the day. It was dominated by the scrap between the TRs of Syd Hurrell and Roy North and the Austin Healey 100 of Julian Sutton fighting each other for second place, Julian Sutton finally getting the verdict from Syd. Meanwhile the very rapid Austin Healey 100 Six of David Shale, fitted with the optional disc brake set up, comfortably won the race by three seconds. Don Pacey overtook Geoff Bewley's TR on the fourth lap for sixth place, but Geoff retook this position before the flag, leaving Don in a creditable seventh place. A disappointed Chris Lawrence came last, but this was no disgrace as the whole field was on the finishing straight when the winner crossed the line. Also competing during this meeting was the Southport Morgan agent, Gerry Hoyle, in a red 4/4 Series II, but he doesn't appear to have achieved success in the seven lap sports car handicap race that he entered.

The seventh annual 'Inter-Club Invitation Speed Hill Climb' was held at Prescott on Sunday July 27th. Twenty-six clubs had accepted the invitation to bring a team of three cars and a reserve. The morning was devoted to individual competition in five classes, allowing the handicappers time to decide how to handicap the teams in the afternoon contest. Peter Morgan managed third place in the 1,501 to 2,000cc class with a time of 51.44 seconds. For the afternoon team event the second car in each team had to come to the start line whilst the first car was still on the hill and start the moment the first car completed its climb, being signalled to go by a green light. The same routine followed for the third team member. Two runs were possible for each team. It rained for the afternoon runs, affecting the times of the fastest

Gerry Hoyle circulating at Aintree in a 4/4 Series II. (John Holroyd)

runners, but the Morgan team was outstanding in the conditions and won the Team Challenge Trophy by 0.02 seconds from the West Hants and Dorset Club. It was an excellent performance from the Morgan 4/4 Club's team of Peter Morgan, probably driving TUY 875, Robin Brown in UOL 490, and Ray Meredith in NAB 217. Cyril Charlesworth was the reserve with his four-seater coupé UKP 61.

The Nottingham Sports Car Club meeting at Mallory Park on August Bank Holiday Monday, August 4th hosted a round of the Autosport Series-Production Sports Car Championship. The over 1,600cc entrants were joined by the 1,101cc to 1,300cc class entrants in the first twenty lap race and the Austin Healey 100S driven by D Protheroe virtually 'walked it', finishing some 28 seconds ahead of the second-placed Lotus Elite of John Lawry. Lionel Mayman, no doubt driving his wife's Morgan EPM 324, finished fifth. Pauline was back in her own Morgan for the twenty lap race for sports cars over 1,501cc. A crash between Protheroe in the Austin Healey and the spinning Lotus Climax of J Higham took out both cars, promoting Pauline to sixth place at the finish having completed eighteen laps, the winner being a Jaguar D-type.

That same day the Taunton Motor Club ran an autocross at Walford Cross. The cars came to the line in fours and the first pair set off with a thirty second interval before the second pair did so. The most successful of the eleven invited clubs was the West Hants and Dorset CC which took the Team Award with members winning five classes including Tom Bryant who made the fastest time of the day in his Plus Four. Also competing, in his Morgan PLB 111, was Monty Rogers.

Robin Brown took his Plus Four UOL 490 to Trengwainton for the hill climb held that same Bank Holiday Monday, August 4th. He climbed in 27.24 seconds, sufficient to give him second place in the class for sports cars up to 2,000cc, nearly a second slower than the winning AC Bristol of Tom Cunane. In fourth place behind a Dellow was Ted Dennis in a Morgan Plus Four with a time of 27.66 seconds.

The *Autosport* magazine of Friday August 8th carried another road test of TUY 875 by John Bolster. It was still fitted with wire wheels for this test, and looked in similar condition to when it took part in the April Tulip Rally; presumably it was tested shortly after this event. It still had drum brakes, and the prototype sliding window side-screens. John Bolster was a great Morgan fan and he concluded his report thus: 'Many a dreary duty journey will be rendered thoroughly enjoyable and routine maintenance will be found to be particularly easy. Above all the Morgan is a worthy partner for the art of driving fast safely.' He recorded a 0 to 60 mph time of 10.6 seconds, and he rated the hood as one of the best he had ever used.

The eighth annual National Six Hour Relay Race held at Silverstone by the 750 Motor Club was on Saturday August 16th, starting at 1pm and using the usual 'Holland Birkett' 2.5 mile circuit. The Morgan 4/4 Club had entered a team as usual, carrying race number '21'. The 'A' car was TUY 875, driven by Peter Morgan. It was running with bolt-on wheels and also experimental Girling front disc brakes. The 'B' car was NAB 217, driven by Ray Meredith. The 'C' car was EPM 324, to be shared by Lionel and Pauline Mayman, and the 'D' car was VON 777, driven by Alan Belcher. The team manager was Lionel Mayman, and fifteen credit laps were given to the team.

Peter Morgan did the Le Mans start and soon began lapping consistently fast such that the Morgan team was in sixth place after just over an hour's racing. By 4pm, after three hours, the Morgan team was in second place with 92.5 laps, half a lap behind the leading Speedwell Stable team of three brightly painted modified Austin A35s, all driven by that company's directors. Half an hour later the Morgan and Speedwell teams were level, and half an hour later at 5pm the Morgan team was ahead after some consistent lapping by Alan Belcher. All eyes were on this battle between these two teams. The Speedwell drivers threw caution to the wind and increased their speed, retaking the lead at 6pm with just one more hour to go.

Just before 6pm Ray Meredith had brought NAB 217 in to the Morgan pits and handed the sash over to Peter Morgan, but TUY 875's exhaust down-pipe then broke at the flange and at 6.18 pm Peter came back in and handed over to Lionel Mayman. He didn't stay out long before handing over at 6.35 pm to Ray Meredith once more, but then more disaster struck as Ray had to make two pit stops to try and secure a flapping bonnet. Finally Lionel Mayman went out again, but by now the Speedwell team had got away and went on to win by one lap, the Morgan team covering 186 laps (fifteen being the credit ones; the Speedwell team had thirty-two). It was still a most impressive result for the Morgan 4/4 Club, and also for Peter Morgan's disc braked car which had impressed all by lapping at least three seconds faster than any of the other team members' Morgans.

Alan Belcher's car VON 777 was now going really well under the supervision of Ron Timmins. Ron had soon realised that the standard Morgan brakes were not adequate for racing, so he had visited the Girling and Lockheed agencies seeking improvements. He eventually decided on a Lockheed set up of 10 inch diameter good quality cast iron drum brakes with 2.25 inch wide linings all round, as fitted to one of the Humber models. This conversion was a great success and Ron remembered that it wasn't even necessary to use special competition linings with these. Alan Belcher liked to begin a race with the tyres at low pressure, finding the tyre squeal useful in judging cornering speeds; as the tyres warmed during races the pressure rose to a more suitable level.

On Saturday 23rd August the BARC held its 31st Members' Meeting at Goodwood. The third

Peter Morgan does the Le Mans start in the 750 MC's Relay Race in TUY 875. Note the bolt-on wheels now fitted to this car. Behind to the left is Alan Belcher's Plus Four. In front (22B) is Lord Portman's Porsche, whilst the white Porsche setting off (22D) is being driven by the fastest of the Porsche team's drivers, a certain Jim Clark. (Val Morley)

Pauline Mayman's car EPM 324 by the pit wall. To the right, with pipe, is Ray Meredith. Near him and leaning over the pit wall is the larger figure of Lionel Mayman. (Val Morley)

race, a ten-lap Marque scratch race with Le Mans type start, was another runaway success for David Shale in his Austin Healey 100 Six who also put in the fastest lap at 77.14 mph. Syd Hurrell came second in his TR3 ahead of a group of cars racing closely for third and fourth places, which went to J C Quick's TR2 and Chris Lawrence's Morgan respectively. In the final race of the meeting, a five lap handicap race, Chris Lawrence rounded off a successful day by coming second to G H Breakwell's TR3. Mr Quick, on scratch, lived up to his name and drove a very rapid race but was unable to overcome his handicap and finished in fifth place.

On Saturday August 23rd the MG Car Club held a race meeting at Silverstone. Entered in a Plus Four was Bob Duggan. Bob was on leave from National Service in the RAF. In July his parents had written to him advising they had bought him a green TR2 engined 1954 Plus Four two-seater, registration OYO 874. This was chassis number 3136 fitted with engine number TS1688ME and it had a 3.73 rear axle as well as flashing indicators from new. It had originally been dispatched on Thursday July 15th 1954 to Messrs Gordon Cars Ltd in London. Bob's parents had taken the Morgan back to the factory on Wednesday August 13th for a new front bumper and over-riders, new hinges for the nearside door and to have play in the steering taken up. When he had flown back to the UK for his mother's birthday on August 21st Bob was advised he was entered in his as yet unseen present for the MGCC meeting! Needless to say his race result was not too impressive, considering he had hardly driven the car before!

It was a glorious summer day on Saturday August 30th for the Shelsley Walsh hill climb, and

Morgan Sports Cars — 1958

the spectators were treated to the excitement of witnessing Tony Marsh taking the outright hill record from Ken Wharton's ERA by recording a time of 35.60 seconds in his V-twin JAP powered Cooper. Class 3b, for sports cars from 1,501 to 2,500cc, had attracted the largest entry and three different Bristol engined cars took the first three places: Cottrell's Lotus in first place with 41.90 seconds, Wilson's AC in second and Rudd's Frazer Nash in third. Three Morgan Plus Fours competed, Lionel Mayman recording 48.71 seconds, Pauline Mayman 48.37 seconds, with Peter Bradley best of the three with 46.78 seconds. We presume the Maymans were sharing EPM 324.

The Lancashire Automobile Club attracted over seventy starters to its 'Lancashire Cup' Rally, which began on Saturday evening August 30th and finished the following day after 200 miles overnight in Wales. One unfriendly and infuriated native took it upon himself to bar a road through a hamlet with his motorcycle. Brian Harper collected a First Class Award with his Plus Four WOF 559.

On Saturday September 6th SUNBAC held its Silverstone race meeting, attracting several Morgan Plus Fours to the entry list. Alan Belcher was entered in VON 777, Chris Lawrence in TOK 258, Don Pacey in 818 DMD, Robin Brown in UOL 490, and Ray Meredith in NAB 217. There were three six lap handicap events, but the only Morgan to beat the handicappers was VON 777 driven by Alan Belcher, which finished second in the third race, just 0.8 seconds behind the winning Riley special.

The longest race of the day was a fifty kilometres event for 'popular sports cars' as defined by the SUNBAC club. This included Austin Healeys, Triumph TRs, Morgans, Jaguars and MGs. Roy North in his TR2 took an immediate lead but he lost this on lap six to David Shale's Austin Healey. One lap later however Roy was back in front and he was never to lose it again. After David Shale retired Syd Hurrell chased Roy hard in his TR3 but he eventually had to settle for second place. Finishing third was Alan Belcher in VON 777, but well behind the two leading Triumphs.

Whilst it is unclear whether Chris Lawrence was actually present at this SUNBAC meeting on the Saturday he was certainly present at Brunton on the Sunday for the nineteenth running of the BARC's hill climb at this venue. In fact he and his uncle Tony Sanderson were sharing both the Morgan TOK 258 and the AFM racer. Tony beat Chris in the AFM to record 30.68 seconds, but Chris was much faster than his uncle in TOK 258, recording 29.07 seconds. Unfortunately for Chris, Jim Banbury was there too with JJY 221 and he recorded 27.91 seconds to finish in third place in Class 11, behind Rudd's Frazer Nash and Tom Cunane's AC Bristol. Whilst both the Morgan and the AFM were road registered the latter tended to be a bit unreliable and it was usually transported on a rather brief trailer, pulled by Chris's tow vehicle. Earlier in the year this had been a rather sedate 1926 Rolls-Royce 20hp saloon, with bodywork by Mann Egerton, but this had since been sold to Len Bridge for £112.10.0 (all the cash that Len could spare at the time!) to part finance the Morgan purchase.

That same weekend the Liverpool Motor Club ran the 'Jeans' Gold Cup Rally. Much of the overnight section was held in the Lake District, some of the roads proving too rough for low slung exhausts. Unfriendly natives tried to block one road with a railway sleeper. The driving tests were an important part of the 'Jeans' and the winner was to receive a special silver model of an Aston Martin DB2, commemorating the sad deaths in 1955 of the rally's originators, Peter Reece and Barry Davies. It was won by Peter Baldam driving a Turner, but in second place was the Morgan of Roger Dobson, this being TKC 389, the ex-Bob Grant Plus Four. In the main rally results Pauline Mayman took the Sir Leslie Scott bowl for the best all-lady crew, driving EPM 324.

In early September Pauline Mayman's hard worked Plus Four EPM 324 was returned to the Morgan factory repair shop and fitted with a new engine, TS 35197. During the same visit the car was generally checked over, particular attention being given to the clutch release bearing, the front

The AFM on its trailer following tests early in 1958 at Goodwood, with the rear of the Rolls-Royce 20hp just visible. Note the double silencers on the AFM. Looking frozen standing behind the AFM is Chris Lawrence (behind the windscreen) with Roland Smith and Les Fagg to his left, close to the Rolls-Royce. (Roland Smith collection)

and rear suspension and the gearbox and transmission.

At the Morgan Motor Company board meeting held on Thursday September 11th it was reported that Girling Limited had not yet replied to the request for a quotation for the supply of disc brake sets, so the board decided it was best not to show Morgan cars fitted with disc brakes at the forthcoming Motor Show.

HFS Morgan had by now asked his son Peter to take over the position of Managing Director from George Goodall when he retired. Peter Morgan was delighted that his father had such faith in his abilities and was proud he had been given this position now rather than having to wait to inherit it from his father some time in the future.

Peter Morgan's decision to inset the spare wheel into the rear deck of the 4/4 had greatly improved the styling of the Morgan two-seater and so Peter had arranged for the two-seater Plus Four to follow suit. This new styling was introduced in September from chassis number 4023, with the petrol tank now repositioned lower, on the chassis itself. It was a milestone design for the big Morgan and one that was to continue throughout the time of Peter Morgan and beyond. At the same time longer steering arms were introduced to improve the steering.

The London Motor Club's ever popular London Rally, with over 250 starters, began on Friday afternoon September 19th, from starts at Ascot, Leeds and Taunton, the routes converging at Llandrindod Wells. After three driving tests the competitors were then handed 'The Map', a sheet of Ordnance Survey 140, with 27 controls marked upon it. The 200 miles had to be covered overnight at 30 mph average speed. After returning to Llandrindod Wells for breakfast the final stages were tackled, using Tulip Rally-type diagrams and no other instructions. These stages were followed by the long afternoon run back to the finish at Ascot. The event was won by two Shenstone and District Car Club members, Mick Webb and Ron Crellin in a Sunbeam Rapier. Pauline Mayman and Val Domleo took the Ladies' Award in EPM 324, despite having a puncture during the map reading section which took thirteen minutes to fix. Les Yarranton won the award for the best driving test performance.

The Coventry and Warwickshire MC held a hill climb on Sunday September 21st, and John

Edwards had his Plus Four MLV 58 working well, for he won the class for sports cars between 1,500 and 2,000cc with a time of 43.57 seconds.

On Saturday September 27th the BARC held its last race meeting of the 1958 season, at Goodwood. It was bright and sunny but with a biting wind. The Plus Fours of Chris Lawrence and John Looker were both entered in the ten lap Marque scratch race, which would decide the winner of the Freddie Dixon Trophy. Besides the two Morgans, the large field consisted mainly of TRs, MGAs, and Austin Healeys, with just two ACs. Syd Hurrell was first away from the Le Mans start in his TR3 but was soon overtaken by David Shale in his Austin Healey 100 Six and Roy North in his TR2, pushing Syd down to third place. Chris Lawrence stayed with the leading trio in fourth place in TOK 258 until the end, only briefly taking third from Syd Hurrell at Levant Corner, as he tried to squeeze between the two white TRs that drove close together in echelon for the rest of the race (they were both entered by Syd Hurrell's tuning company SAH Accessories, based in Leighton Buzzard). Chris Lawrence reckoned he was faster in the corners but the TRs were faster on the straights by virtue of their more streamlined shape. Despite being frustrated by the TRs, Chris was so confident of the Morgan's ability that towards the end of the race he held back from them, and then put his foot down to record the fastest lap, at 78.12 mph. John Looker also had an exciting race despite making a bad start when the starter solenoid initially refused to function. He eventually finished in sixth place in OWP 38. David Shale won the race as usual, at 76.7 mph, and took the Freddie Dixon Trophy for the season.

Chris Lawrence and his team of friends ended the season on a high note and felt vindicated in the choice of the Morgan to go racing with but could see where improvements could be made. In 1958 TOK 258 had been raced in virtually production specification, with attention paid mainly to careful preparation before each race.

The following day the Hagley and District Light Car Club held its second sprint meeting at Chateau Impney near Droitwich, attracting around seventy entries. Despite bad weather several thousand spectators were there for the action at this delightful venue. Several Morgans were there too, and Frank Livingston in his Plus Four recorded 29.28 seconds to win the class for sports cars from 1,501 to 2,500cc. In second place was an

Robin Brown in UOL 490 at Chateau Impney. (Robin Brown collection)

AC, whilst Ray Meredith came third in NAB 217 with a time of 30.06 seconds.

That same Sunday the Morgan 4/4 Club ran driving tests for club members, victory going to Peter Morgan, presumably in RNP 504, whilst Jim Goodall was second and Tom Smith from America in his 1958 coupé was third.

Racer Don Pacey had decided to sell his ex-Speedwell car, 818 DMD, as final year studies now took priority. In the copy of *Autosport* for Friday October 3rd this 1955 Plus Four was described as having a fully modified engine and suspension, and also as being fitted with an oil cooler, an undertray and an aluminium bonnet. It had wheels shod with Michelin X radial tyres, and racing brake linings. There was a new hood, an aero screen, spot lamps, tonneau cover and even continental air horns. It had been resprayed red and black and was offered with many spares, for £565.

The MCC ran the Derbyshire Trial on Saturday October 4th, after a start the previous night. Ted Cleghorn did very well to win his class with his Dellow, whilst Bob Parsons won a Third Class Award with his Plus Four.

On Saturday October 4th the Pembrokeshire Motor Club ran its Lydstep hill climb. Four Plus Fours took part, competing in the class for sports cars 1,501 to 2,000cc and also in the 2,001 to 3,000cc class. The victor in both classes was the Lotus Bristol of P Cottrell, followed by the Turner 1500 of J Rhodes. Jim Banbury was third in both classes with JJY 221, but Robin Brown in UOL 490, Ray Meredith in NAB 217 and E A Phillips in his Plus Four were all off the pace.

The following day five clubs co-promoted a sprint meeting at Harleyford. Sandy Blair with his TR3 engined Plus Four, Nixie, took the award for the fastest in the open cars class up to 2,500cc.

Over 140 drivers entered the Lancashire and Cheshire Car Club's end of season meeting at Oulton Park on Saturday October 11th including two Morgan Plus Fours, these being VON 777 for Alan Belcher, and the ex-Bob Grant car TKC 389 for Roger Dobson, but entered by a friend, Charlie Pashley, possibly because Roger's job, as a company sales representative, kept him away from home quite a lot and he had asked Charlie to enter him. The programme had a nice photograph of Ray Meredith in NAB 217 during the August 750 MC Relay Race on the cover.

The meeting started with a half-hour high speed trial, and both the Morgans were successful

Alan Belcher during the seven lap scratch race at Oulton Park, cornering ahead of Foden's Alfa Romeo and Bracegirdle's TR2. (Charles Dunn)

in becoming qualifiers. Event 6 was a seven lap scratch race for sports cars up to 2,000cc, but excluding cars with Bristol, Connaught, Coventry Climax, Ferrari, Maserati, Porsche and Stanguellini engines. Neither of the Morgans finished in the awards.

The Pauline Mayman and Val Domleo combination had yet another success with the Worcestershire MC's Autumn Rally, which began on Saturday October 11th and finished the following day. They actually won the open cars class, beating all the men, and Val won a Navigators' Award too.

At the board meeting of the Morgan Motor Company held on Thursday October 16th Peter Morgan reported that an order had now been placed with Girling Limited for fifty sets of front disc brakes and that delivery was expected in December. He hoped to offer these brakes as an optional fitment for wire wheel cars by Easter 1959.

The Shenstone and District Car Club ran its eighth Buxton Rally on Saturday October 18th. After starting at either Shenstone or Buxton the 45 starters joined a common route with a tough navigational section, before driving tests at Oulton Park. After lunch another navigational section led to further driving tests at Chapel-en-le-Frith, and then after a last stage during darkness there were final driving tests in the dark at the finish at Buxton. Only 28 competitors finished, only six of these having visited all the controls. Brian Harper in his Plus Four WOF 559 won the open car class, and also made the best performance by a British Trial and Rally Drivers' Association member. Another Plus Four, that of M Eaves, had done well in driving tests.

The 750 MC Southern Centre held a speed hill climb at Blandford Camp on Sunday October 19th. Just Jim Banbury took part in a Morgan, JJY 221, recording 34.50 seconds to finish third in the class for sports cars from 1,401 to 2,000cc. He was beaten, as usual, by Tom Cunane's fast AC Bristol which took first place and just behind Wilshin's TR in a class with an entry of thirteen cars.

The Motor Show began at Earls Court on Wednesday October 22nd, finishing on Saturday November 1st. Two 4/4s were shown, a red one with black trim and a USA specification version in Ming Blue with stone trim which also had wire wheels and a laminated glass windscreen. These were chassis numbers A445 and A446 respectively. Three Plus Fours were on show too. The four-seater had the newly introduced improved front seats and wider body, and was chassis number 4016, having a grey body with green trim. The coupé (chassis number 4018) and the two-seater (4024) were both to USA specification and had wire wheels, the two-seater also having a laminated glass windscreen and showing the new rear end with the spare wheel let into the rear deck. The coupé was coloured green with stone trim and hood, whilst the two-seater was white with red leather upholstery. Also on display was a Plus Four rolling chassis with a TR3 engine. The basic TR3 engined Plus Four two-seater cost £968.17.0 including Purchase Tax, whilst the 4/4 cost £748.7.0. In comparison the Triumph TR3 cost £1,049.17.0 and the MGA £993.17.0. Also of interest is that the Morgan Motor Company was still advertising the Vanguard engine as being the basic engine for the Plus Four, the TR3 being £80.0.0 extra, despite the fact that no Vanguard engined cars had been built for some time!

On the middle Sunday of the Show (October 26th) the Guild of Motoring Writers had its Press Day at Goodwood to try out the various examples of cars on show. The Morgan factory had a two-seater Plus Four available and Stuart Seager, the *Autosport* reporter, was able to drive it, commenting, 'I felt at home in this model from the moment I first sat in it, and once again revelled in the high-geared precise steering, the fine balance, the excellent visibility and the well-fitting cockpit layout – all of which go to give confidence.' He continued, 'An ideal club competition machine, it was in its element at Goodwood, but it might be thought a little stark for everyday transport unless one is a complete "addict".' Bill Boddy, the editor of *Motor Sport*, drove it too reporting, 'This year's

Pauline Mayman completes the final test of the Bournemouth Rally in front of a large crowd. (Val Morley)

specimen seemed longer in the bonnet than previously, had bags of poke, and hurried sufficiently to keep a Jaguar at bay.' We are not sure which car the Morgan Company had made available for the test.

On the preceding day, Saturday October 25th, 84 starters were flagged off from the pier approach at Bournemouth by the Mayor, setting off in the West Hants and Dorset CC's Bournemouth Rally. The overnight road section was tough and only 38 crews were classified as finishers, one of course being the crew of EPM 324, namely Pauline Mayman and Val Domleo who took the Ladies' Award.

The following weekend the Liverpool Motor Club ran a rather unusual rally, the winner being sponsored by Victor Horsmann Ltd to run a Morris Minor in the following January's Monte Carlo Rally! Several Morgan drivers took part, including Pauline Mayman and Gerry Hoyle, but the prize was won by Eric Mather navigated by Ian Hall in an Austin A35, with Monarch modifications.

By November some Plus Fours were being dispatched from the Morgan factory fitted with 15 inch bolt-on wheels instead of the previous 16 inch version. In addition Girling Ltd supplied an improved version of the standard drum brake system fitted to Plus Fours, as from chassis number 4096.

Following the BARC season, Chris Lawrence and his team of friends set about improving TOK 258 over the winter for a serious assault on the following year's Freddie Dixon Trophy. Chris decided that little needed doing to the basic Morgan chassis set up. The rear lever-arm shock absorbers were retained but their action was stiffened up by replacing the fluid with EP90 grade oil. The standard steel bodywork remained unaltered except for the addition of an aluminium undertray. There was a small Perspex aero screen fitted

Detailed attention was paid to lubrication of the front suspension but the standard positive camber angle was retained at this stage. The main effort really concentrated on engine tuning for this winter, particularly on gas flowing the cylinder head to enhance the TR unit's torque characteristics that combined so well with the Morgan's superior handling on the typical UK circuits. A primitive flow rig was built, enabling the flow through the cylinder head to be investigated. At this time TOK 258's TR2 engine was fitted with the original low port head, which had smaller diameter inlet ports set lower than the later high port TR3 head. Chris Lawrence told us that he liked the low port head, for he discovered that the low port set up could easily be worked upon to enable the induction flow to attack the valve at a better angle and pass the valve into the open part of the chamber with more velocity. However, it was found that it was also too easy to damage the TR2 heads, when over enthusiastic machining broke into the waterways. Consequently a scrap head was sectioned to provide a good look inside. Chris told us that when they obtained a TR3 head there was more material to safely work with but he had been disappointed when the flow rig showed only a small increase in flow over that of the earlier head.

The camshaft design was to be a key item, thought up during the winter and developed at Rotax whilst on the night shift. (Chris had been studying books on camshaft design and cylinder head design, including the work by Ricardo.) It was a simple, harmonic design that was to work successfully first time out and, remarkably, wasn't altered at all during the time he would spend racing Plus 4s. The valve timing was 43-76, 76-43. The American Iskenderian cam was normally the favourite to have in a racing TR engine at this time but Chris claims he couldn't afford to buy and try one, and believed anyway that it would be too 'wild' for his needs!

The standard twin SU H4 carburettor set up was retained but a lot of work was done to gain optimum performance. W H M Burgess was the SU agent nearby in London and their staff gave invaluable help with trying different needles, springs and piston weights, eventually settling on 'RH' needles.

A surplus ex-wartime aero-engine oil cooler was obtained and fitted to TOK's engine. Unfortunately it was damaged during one of the Morgan's test runs down the long straight road that ran alongside nearby Northolt Aerodrome. Chris related how Les Fagg drove straight across the roundabout at the end of the run and hit a sign when he became distracted in the early morning mist by an unusual engine noise. It transpired that TOK's flywheel had become loose after too hasty an engine assembly by Chris in his eagerness to try out the latest tuning! Temporary repairs were made to the oil cooler but for racing it was replaced with a new unit bought from the NW London heat-exchange engineers Delaney Gallay Ltd who supplied parts to the car and aircraft industries. Several of the TR drivers had been racing for some time with oil coolers fitted to their engines and certainly Vic Derrington's car used a Delaney Gallay product.

A substantial four branch free-flow exhaust manifold was obtained from Servais Silencers Ltd. Chris liked the arrangement of the pipes on the Servais system but when he went to buy one he discovered that it was too expensive for him. He must have looked dejected because the manager offered him a redundant experimental manifold for nothing! However, it wasn't a conventional tubular manifold but one that had been fabricated by welding steel strips together and was consequently square in section, matching the shape of the exhaust ports. Chris thought this ideal, its construction making modifications possible without special equipment. The pipes from cylinders number one and four joined together into one, as did those from two and three. With this split arrangement Chris could easily develop the whole exhaust system, using the two pipes to feed a pair of Servais straight-though silencers side by side, or join into one with a 'Y' piece ahead of a single silencer.

Peter Morgan organised a Restricted rally for the Morgan 4/4 Club over the weekend of November 29th and 30th. The 350 mile rally began at Birmingham, Shipston-on-Stour or Eardiston, the routes converging near Worcester. There then followed two navigation sections demanding good map reading and one section using a route card, with the event finishing at a hostelry near Malvern for breakfast on the Sunday. Barrie Phipps in a Riley won the Morgan Cup for best performance, whilst Pauline Mayman collected the Committee Cup for second place, presumably driving EPM 324. Les

Yarranton won the sports car class in PUY 306. The organiser was congratulated on an excellent event.

1958 had seen the number of private cars registered in Great Britain and Northern Ireland top four and a half million. Congested cities were becoming commonplace. On Thursday July 10th the first parking meters to be installed in Great Britain came into use in the Mayfair district of London. A new type of high speed road system, designed to allow through traffic to continue at undiminished speed by bypassing cities, had received parliamentary approval in the late 1940s, but construction of these new roads, to be named 'motorways', had not begun until 1956. The very first to open was a short eight mile stretch of the Preston bypass, later to become part of the M6, which was opened by the Prime Minister, Harold Macmillan, on Friday December 5th. Meanwhile other motorways were now either under construction or well on in the planning stage.

The Falkirk and District Motor Club held a pleasant Yuletide Rally on Sunday December 7th. It required no maps, simple route directions being given to each of the 22 competitors for the 60 mile route. Despite this no crew failed to pick up penalties, a short regularity section catching out many, but Ian Bennie finished in the winning team with his Morgan coupé.

In the classified advertisements of *Autosport* for December 12th was Ray Meredith's Morgan NAB 217 advertised for sale for £575. Ray had decided he would like a new Plus Four for the 1959 season, and had been to see Peter Morgan to agree a specification. NAB 217 was advertised as having a TR3 engine, and a green all aluminium body. It was fitted with a heater, tonneau, windscreen washers, a radiator blind and spotlamps. There were seven spare wheels and recent work had included new brake drums and linings, and new centrepins, tyres and batteries etc.

Another Plus Four requiring yet more work to the front suspension at the Morgan factory this week was Monty Rogers' car PLB 111 which had new centrepins, bushes and shock absorbers fitted just six months after the previous front suspension overhaul. He obviously drove it hard! New rear brake drums and shoes were also required. This Plus Four had now completed nearly 53,000 hard miles.

As usual the annual competitions of the British Trials and Rally Drivers' Association had been held over the year and the prizes were awarded at the end. The best performance in the Silver Star rally competition was by Brian Harper with forty points in joint ninth position, but Pauline Mayman easily won the Ladies' Silver Garter competition with twice as many points (31) as second placed Anne Hall. Not only that but she was also third in the 'men's' Gold Star rally competition with fourteen points (!), the runaway winner being TR3 driver Ron Gouldbourn, the second time in a row he had won this competition.

Continental Europe

For the 1958 year the FIA had produced an updated version of 'Appendix J', the regulations deciding which production cars could compete in international events. There were two classifications, one being 'Touring' cars, requiring 1,000 examples to have been produced in the previous twelve months, and the other being 'Grand Tourisme' which required just 100. After 100 cars with similar bodywork and mechanical parts had been built for the GT class, the type could be homologated and there was then freedom in the shape of the body, providing it weighed the same as the manufacturer's production versions. There were various requirements including windscreen height (minimum 20cms, and full width only), and luggage capacity (150 litres over 1,000cc engine size). This latter regulation did not specify one boot, but allowed all sorts of areas to be boxed up as 'luggage space', thereby allowing in the Morgan two-seaters, for 150 litres could be accommodated in the area behind the seats, if the seat back was adjusted to the furthest forward position. The cars were also divided into 'Normal', 'Improved' and 'Special', according to the degree of modifications permitted.

Morgan Sports Cars — 1958

There were 76 British entries for the 10th International Tulip Rally, starting on Saturday April 26th. As we have mentioned, Bob Grant and Ted Cleghorn had tried to interest Peter Morgan in a team of three Morgans for this event at the 1957 Motor Show, but he had declined. He did allow Lyndon Sims to borrow the works car TUY 875 however, whilst Ted Cleghorn was probably driving his own Plus Four, RVF 142. Bob Grant of course had since sold his Morgan.

Lyndon Sims was to be navigated by Ralph Stokes and chose to start from London, whilst Ted Cleghorn was to be navigated by the experienced Barrie Hercock and start from Noordwijk in Holland.

Lyndon was a formidable rally driver. He had competed with a 2.5 litre Riley from 1953 until 1955, but for 1956 he had bought an Aston Martin DB2, with which he had won that year's RAC Rally outright. During his rallying he had got to know Peter Morgan, and Peter had been happy to lend him TUY 875 for the Tulip Rally, although all running expenses were to be paid by Lyndon. His passenger, Ralph Stokes, recalled that Lyndon collected the works car one week before the event began, but then found a piston was cracked, so he rang Ralph, who lived in Malvern, to collect a replacement set of pistons from the Morgan factory. These Lyndon fitted, but the car was obviously still 'running-in' for the rally start. This works Morgan was fitted with special sliding window side-screens which Peter Morgan had on trial, and there was also a blister on the offside bonnet over the foremost carburettor to improve air intake to this item.

It was not good weather for this the tenth Tulip Rally, with fog and heavy rain for the initial run to the Nurburgring in Germany, and it didn't help when the competitors found the road blocked by extensive road works entailing diversions to get to the circuit on time. The circuit itself was very slippery, but Lyndon managed to do a very fast time, despite an overhead thunderstorm. The Ted Cleghorn car soon began to lag behind and by the third of the special stages, from Tournus to Lamastre, they were one of 39 crews from the 196 starters that were late.

Meanwhile the Sims-Stokes combination continued apace in TUY 875. Ralph remembered that Lyndon seemed to spend every rest moment working on the Morgan, and as a result they forgot all about meals. Realising it was 24 hours since either had eaten they rummaged about in the back of the Morgan finding a stale bread roll, which they shared between them. Thick fog made the Abreschwiller stage of 100 kilometres, which had to be tackled in less than 90 minutes, the 'Pièce de Résistance' of the entire rally, and TUY 875 lost five minutes here.

The final event of the Tulip Rally on Wednesday

Lyndon Sims in the works Morgan stays ahead of the TR3A of Annie Soisbault at Zandvoort during the Tulip Rally. (The Motor)

248

April 30th was a series of races held at Zandvoort in reverse direction of the motor racing circuit, but held in fine weather. Before this Lyndon realised that he had no hope of beating the un-penalised TR3A of Ron Gouldbourn, navigated by Stuart Turner, which was then running in ninth place overall but that it was possible to claim second place in the class for GT cars from 1,601 to 2,000cc if he could stay ahead of the other TR3A driven by Annie Soisbault and navigated by Pat Ozanne. Lyndon duly managed to stay ahead, to split the Triumphs and claim the second place for Morgan. He finished in 37th place overall, just ahead of the Soisbault TR3A. Ralph Stokes was so impressed by Lyndon that he described him as the best rally driver ever!

Claude Savoye tasted success with his Plus Four at Montlhéry at the AGACI's Coupe de Paris meeting held on Sunday June 15th, finishing second in his class.

South Africa

Once again the van Riebeeck Trophy race was held at Eerste River aerodrome near Capetown this year and it was held on Saturday 29th March. Two Plus Fours took part, with Dave Coleman finishing tenth overall and fifth on handicap whilst Reggie Biggs was twelfth overall but improved to fourth on handicap.

This year the Sports Car Club of South Africa's Transvaal trial had been enlarged to a 400 mile rally through the Western Transvaal with driving tests held at various sites en route. It began at the Milner Park Showground in Johannesburg with a gymkhana type test involving changing a front wheel, driving round the ash track and negotiating a 'wiggle-woggle'. The cars were then routed to Grand Central Aerodrome Halfway House circuit for sprints held in the wrong direction to normal races, and with a chicane on the straight. Gene Bosman did well in this test in his Plus Four. The route now disappeared along bush tracks to Thabazimbi, thence to Nylstroom and back to the Grand Central track once more. Gene Bosman found himself baulked by a Chevrolet Fleetline at the chicane, and he wasn't in the winners.

There was a good crowd at Krugersdorp for the hill climb held on Saturday September 13th. There was one Plus Four in the class for sports cars exceeding 1800cc, in addition to ten TRs, seven Austin Healey 100 Sixes, one Mercedes Benz 190SL and a Ferrari 250GT. Only the TRs managed to get under 60 seconds for the climb, and the Morgan was well beaten.

Robb Motors' importing of Morgan cars seems to have come to a halt towards the end of this year.

Australia

The reduced performance of the detuned R4 was becoming apparent at the sprints and time trials run at Caversham by the WASCC on Australia Day on Monday January 27th. Standing quarter mile times were now slower by more than three seconds; Bill Richards, the owner, averaging 16.59 sec, Don Hall 16.54 and David Van Dal the best with 16.25 sec. Similarly, Bill and Don were both only able to record 104 mph over a flying quarter mile and David 105 mph. Don Hall recalls that his third run only managed 96 mph.

Despite the failing motor of the R4 sufficient repair and maintenance must have ensued because on Saturday February 15th David Van Dal was back at Caversham to record three second places in three six lap Southport-style events, in each case behind the TS Special, driven on this occasion by Norm Rossiter. Don Hall gave the timing crew something else to worry about by driving the R4 over the timing signal lamp at the start. This closed to club meeting also saw the appearance of John Haynes, who had a favourable handicap and captured first place in a twelve lap handicap race for sports cars in his blue TR2 engined Plus Four.

Racing returned to the town of Albany over the April Easter weekend, organised by the

WASCC and the Southern Districts Car Club. The last event there had been the Albany TT in 1940 over a 2.5 mile circuit around the central business district, when Arthur 'Digger' Wright had started in the repaired Jack McIntosh Coventry Climax engined 4/4. A new circuit of 1.9 miles was to be used this year, situated near the Showground, and three Morgans had entered, these being the two specials and the Plus Four of John Haynes. All could be well satisfied with their 300 miles trip south from Perth to compete.

The Albany meeting began on Easter Sunday April 6th with the West Australian Hill Climb Championship which was staged over the 0.59 mile ascent of Mount Clarence and saw David Van Dal fourth fastest in the R4 with John Haynes well down behind a field of Austin Healeys, TR2s and Bill Downey's supercharged MG TF in the section for sports cars. On Easter Monday, in a seven lap handicap race for racing cars, Barry Ranford Junior finished second behind Doug Green's MK V Cooper after the R4 had retired on lap 4. In a five lap race, again for racing cars and on handicap, the tables were reversed, for David Van Dal came in second behind Syd Negus's Cooper Bristol and in front of Barry Ranford who held third place. Meanwhile John Haynes held the Morgan flag high by winning the five lap event for sports cars, this time in front of Bill Downey's supercharged MG TF followed by John Cummins' HRG and the TR2 of Gerry Hilton. The main event, the Albany TT race was held over twenty laps of the new circuit. Syd Negus was fastest in his Cooper Bristol, lapping in 1 minute 38 seconds with Barry Ranford close behind. Peter Bond was third with the Bondley Special, and John Haynes finished fourth. When the handicaps were taken into account Barry Ranford (3 minutes 20 seconds) demoted Syd Negus (scratch) into second place, becoming the victor, with Peter Bond (4 minutes) third, Noel Aldous fourth with his MG and John Haynes in the Plus Four fifth. It was estimated some ten thousand spectators had lined the course in gloriously sunny weather. The R4 went really well and mixed it with the Cooper Bristol and Vin Smith's Alpha but, despite some very quick times, was forced to retire after twelve laps along with six others.

David remembered that the R4 was usually equipped with cheap 'Olympic' brand four-ply tyres for practice at race events. These tyres were then changed towards the end of practice for 'race tyres' to scuff the new tread and get used to the different handling. Originally Dunlop racing tyres

David Van Dal at Albany.
(David Van Dal collection)

were used, but later testing showed Pirelli HS Radials gave better adhesion.

1958 was the last year that the old Second World War airstrip at Mount Druitt near Ropes Creek in New South Wales was used for racing, having been the home circuit of the Australian Racing Drivers Club since 1950. On Sunday April 27th the Manly-Waringah Sports Car Club held a day of sprints, and J Williams, competing in the over 1,500cc sports car division recorded a standing quarter mile in the slow time of 20.90 seconds, with the flying 1/8 mile being completed in 6.15 seconds in his stock standard Plus Four.

The Kelmscott (Turner Road) hill climb was run on Sunday May 4th by the Western Australia Car Club in ideal weather conditions. Fifty entrants were attracted, including some members of the WASCC, and after trial runs before lunch they assaulted the climb in two classes, under and over 1,500cc. Barry Ranford Jnr recorded second fastest time of the day and the results sheet shows Jack Emery as second in the under 1,500cc section. There are no details available and it is not known whether Jack still had the Coventry Climax engined 4/4 he used so successfully in the late 1940s.

John Haynes appeared again in three of the minor races of the next WASCC meeting at Caversham on Monday June 2nd along with the R4 and the Ranford Special. The driving of the R4 was again split between Don Hall and David Van Dal. John Haynes also competed in the Le Mans start six hour race, that was now known as the 'Sunday Times Six Hour Race for Production Cars', with GA Bowra as co-driver. Somehow the Ranford Special qualified to start in this race for 'production' cars and Barry Senior was accompanied by his son, Barry Junior.

In Victoria W M Wright entered his 1,172cc Morgan special in a number of meetings, the first being the Rob Roy hill climb held on Sunday July 27th. On this occasion S L Fisher drove it into a second place for cars of 1,101-1,500cc.

For the WASCC State Racing Car Championships at Caversham on Saturday September 20th Bill Downey had the pleasure of driving the Bill Richards-entered R4 in the first two heats. Although his lap times were competitive he was unable to get into the places. John Cummins took over the R4 in Heat 3 but he fared little better and ended up in fourth place behind Syd Negus's Cooper Bristol, the TS Special (driven by Norm Rossiter) and Doug Green's Cooper. John Haynes in his Plus Four had replaced Vin Smith's Alpha, but could only finish seventh. The Sports Car Championship race over ten laps saw John Haynes battling in third place at the end of lap 7, but completing lap 8 in last place! Although his lap times recovered he couldn't regain any positions.

In Victoria, on the airstrip at Fisherman's Bend, W M Wright drove into his Morgan Plus Four into first place in an invitation race organised by the VSCC. The Morgan was again first, this time with S Fisher back at the wheel, in a hill climb organised by the AMSC at Hepburn Springs on Sunday November 16th.

The Christmas Cup meeting was run at Caversham on Saturday November 22nd. In 1955 this race had been the scene of triumph for David Van Dal and the Bill Richards R4 Morgan, for together they smashed the lap record and became the quickest in Western Australia. The 1958 event saw this combination on the start line for the last time. In the five lap race for racing cars, starting on scratch, sadly the R4 sat on the line refusing to move for several seconds whilst the field disappeared at the end of the main straight.

John Cummins then drove the R4 in the fifteen lap Christmas Cup Handicap, but his lap times were now 1 minute 52 seconds or thereabouts, possibly reflecting the fact that the brakes were failing, and after five laps he retired. John Haynes also failed to finish in his Plus Four in the Christmas Cup, after leading at the end of lap 9. He was just out of the places in three of the minor events also.

The R4 Morgan had had a number of 'pilots' in addition to David Van Dal during the four years (1955-58) it raced, including Bill Richards himself, Merv Dudley, John Cummins, Noel Aldous, Don Hall, Peter Nicol and Bill Downey. Of these Merv Dudley was the most frequent and he still regards the R4 as the best balanced car he ever drove. All the others also attest to the R4's superb handling except for John Cummins who has maintained almost to this day that in his hands it understeered and he was not adept at handling an understeering car. He apparently never knew that the brake system was biased to provide 70% of effort to the front and only 30% to the rear drums. Whilst visiting David Van Dal in Perth in 2001, for the fiftieth anniversary of the 1951 Australian Grand Prix in Narrogin, he became acquainted of this fact for the first time!

The records indicate that the R4 participated in at least forty-five major events, plus sprints and a few hill climbs. The results have been incompletely recorded but of those that have there were eight firsts, five seconds, five thirds and six fourth places. The car established a new lap record for Caversham in 1955-56 that was only bettered when the Ferraris, Maseratis, and Coopers came to town for the Australian Grand Prix in 1957.

David Van Dal had found it hard to recover his physical and mental fitness after his bout of polio in early 1956, and had not been able to develop the R4 as he would have wished. In addition his flourishing radiographic equipment business took him out of Western Australia for long periods. He had actually designed a cast iron skirt for the base of the engine block of the Vanguard engine carrying intermediate bearings for a five main bearing bottom end, together with a suitable steel crankshaft. He also designed a fabricated hemispherical alloy cross flow head, which had individual ports, for using Amal RN carburettors to the left of the head and for the exhausts to the right. The pushrods and rockers were arranged somewhat like the BSA Gold Star engine that David admired so much, and David had calculated a power output of 180 bhp at 6,500 rpm. None of these projects was brought to fruition, and the purpose built racers (Ferrari, Cooper Bristol and Alta) were now getting faster, and pushing the R4 down the finishers list.

Bill Richards and David talked through the future, and decided to approach Jack Ayres, a well known and successful Holden saloon racer, who came to see David to confirm that the R4 could be converted into a sports car, and then bought the car. He took it to Caversham in late 1958 to learn its foibles, but the engine destroyed itself comprehensively on the third lap. The next day Jack and car body builder Cliff Byfield visited David. As Jack knew how to tune Holden engines, David agreed to modify the R4 frame to accommodate a Holden engine (lengthening it by 2.5 inches), and also to accommodate doors, whilst Jack drew a body outline that Cliff could translate into an aluminium body shell. The remaining modified Vanguard engines and parts were sold to Peter Bond for the Bondley Special, whilst David gave the five bearing bottom end and the cross-flow cylinder head designs to his friend the great Merv Waggott, a Sydney based tuner particularly of Holden engines.

Cliff Byfield rebodied the modified R4 chassis in Perth in late 1958. Its smooth lines were similar to the most expensive of European sports racing cars of the time.

Whilst David Van Dal was no longer to drive his R4 creation, he did continue helping fellow enthusiasts with the design and procurement of 'go faster' bits. In November he and John Cummins had formed a company to supply 'parts and accessories for speed, power and roadability'. As a back-handed tribute to the American Offenhauser engine company they tried to register their new business as 'Krappenhauser Components', but the Registrar of Companies took a dim view of this, so they were forced to change one letter, becoming 'Klappenhauser Components'. David's great sense of fun also led him to produce a 'Team Cognisance' after the fashion of the time to name teams after the European greats. This was for John Cummins in Melbourne with his Bugatti Type 37, Jack Meyer with his Cooper Holden, Greg McEwin's HRG special etc in Adelaide and the R4 in Perth. It was entitled 'Scuderia Illa Gitima', and featured various rude bits on the shield, as well as crossed arms holding a steering wheel, and a broken piston and conrod!

Sadly David passed away in 2003. However two panels from the original car body, namely the bonnet and rear end, had been discovered in Jack Ayres' Perth workshop the previous year and were photographed with their designer.

David Van Dal standing with the rediscovered parts of the R4 in 2002. (Craig Atkins)

New Zealand

A large crowd was attracted to the two day New Year holiday beach racing at Tahunanui, organised by the Nelson Car Club. On the first day, Wednesday, January 1st, Roy Watson finished third in the Nelson Electroplaters Cup, a handicap race for cars over 2,000cc. Presumably Roy, another ex-Club President who was a car salesman for Keith Roper, was driving an early Vanguard engined Plus Four to run in the over 2,000cc class. His boss, Keith Roper, won the event in an Austin Healey.

In the heats for the Frosty Jack Rosebowl open handicap race, Halsey Logan took third place in Heat 2 in his blown Morgan 4/4, but didn't finish in the places in the final. He had really stripped

Halsey Logan racing his stripped supercharged 4/4 at Tahunanui. (Kevin York)

Morgan Sports Cars   1958

the Morgan to save weight for this event, even removing the wings, and was using a pair of special 13 inch rear wheels to give better acceleration. On the second day Halsey entered the Morgan in a handicap race for Ford 10 engined cars, finishing in first place ahead of the specials of Frank Pope and Gordon Fisher.

Dave Edmiston's success the previous year had attracted welcome sponsorship from the petrol company BP New Zealand for his entry at the New Zealand Grand Prix meeting at Ardmore on Saturday January 11th. Dave was actually working for this company now. He had worked long hours on the Morgan the week before he left Dunedin for Auckland. In the Ken Wharton Trophy Race for sports cars held over 25 laps the Morgan had the race well sewn up for his class but just two laps from the finish it ran out of petrol as Dave had miscalculated how much he would need. Apparently Dave had found the supplied BP petrol to be of poor quality so he had refilled the churns with decent fuel. He had realised during the race that he would need to refuel and signalled this to the pits each time he had passed. Unfortunately only Bernadette his wife was actually in the pits, the BP people having gone off to watch the racing from elsewhere!

The following weekend Russell Buckthought was entered with the black coupé at Levin, but we have no results for him. This tight kidney-shaped circuit with a lap of just over one mile was situated near the town of Levin in the North Island and had been opened in 1956. It was the first purpose built post-war motor racing track in New Zealand and owed its existence to racer Ron Frost, who lived in the town.

This year's Wigram airfield races were held on Saturday January 25th. Halsey Logan was entered in his 4/4 in the 12 lap open car handicap race, which was won by Lawton's Austin Healey. Halsey didn't finish in the first three.

The Dunedin road race was held on the Wharf circuit on Saturday February 1st, with several support races on the programme. Merv Neil brought his ex-Jack Brabham Cooper Climax through the field to win the 23 mile handicap open car race but Dave Edmiston failed to finish in his Plus Four. Dave had lost the car at McGregors Corner and it mounted a sand bank, leaving him stranded.

Dave Edmiston's Morgan is stranded on a sandbank at McGregors Corner at Dunedin, with the tower at the Railway Station visible in the background. (Dave Edmiston collection)

He was back in action for the following race, the 27 mile 'RedeX' sports car race, which featured a Le Mans start. Dave finished sixth, the winner being Frank Cantwell in a Tojeiro Jaguar.

Pat Fitzgerald had acquired Allen Freeman's old red Plus Four four-seater, P2290, and he did well with it at a hill climb held at Jugerford on Tuesday February 4th with fastest time of the day.

Dave Edmiston took his Plus Four to the first international car race meeting at Teretonga held on Saturday February 8th. Despite lapping in 1 minute 24 seconds, he failed to finish in the places this time.

At the end of February the Nelson Car Club held a closed to club series of nine races on the grass of the 36 acres of Nelson Airport land that the club leased from the city council. The club reasoned it seemed the only cheap way to control the grass! Halsey Logan did well, winning two of the races in his Morgan 4/4.

In May Dave Edmiston sold his Morgan to the local Bennett brothers (Ivan and Cliff) who were to continue its competition career. As bought the TR3 engine was fitted with the Triumph low compression kit comprising a compression plate to fit between head and cylinder block, longer push rods and new gaskets, making it more suitable to the everyday low octane petrol normally available in New Zealand. This kit dropped the compression ratio to 7.5 to 1. When Ivan began racing the Plus Four the compression plate was removed and standard push rods fitted, but he only did this for the major meetings as racing fuel was quite expensive.

The Nelson Car Club held a sprint meeting at Waimea West, with Roy Watson recording 20.1 seconds for the standing quarter mile, and finishing fourth in his Morgan (his boss Keith Roper won in a Cooper JAP 1,100cc).

In August the Nelson Car Club took part in a hill climb at Pig Valley where Keith Roper set a new record in his Cooper. Halsey Logan was third in his Morgan 4/4 with a time of 43.3 seconds. His Morgan had been re-engined however, and now sported a Ford Consul engine, probably the Mark 1 EOTA version of 1,508cc and still with a three speed gearbox. Introduced in 1951 this ohv engine produced 47 bhp at 4,400 rpm in standard tune. This conversion is particularly interesting as of course HFS Morgan himself had considered using the enlarged Mk 2 version of the same Ford Consul engine (1,703cc type 204E) for the Morgan range in 1955-6.

The Otago Sports Car Club ran a grass hill climb on Friday November 7th, with Ted Reid competing in his Plus Four and taking fastest time of the day.

USA

In California the tremendous drives by Lew Spencer in Baby Doll No 2 in the last few months of 1957 had caught the attention of the motoring press. In January Richard Knell of the *West Coast Sports Car Journal* published a road test of this car, reporting a 0 to 60 mph time of 9.0 seconds. What really impressed him, however, was the car's handling. 'This is undoubtedly one of the finest handling production cars available to the public today, bar none' he wrote; praise indeed. Claude Brun informed the journalist that the engine had been 'matched and balanced to perfection', and 6,000 rpm was allowed for the acceleration tests, although a normal limit of 5,800 rpm was used for racing. To keep the car race-worthy Claude checked the engine bearings after every event, and so far found they were lasting around two to three meetings.

Worldwide Imports had of course been highly delighted by the remarkable success of Baby Doll No 2 in racing, and no doubt sales interest in the Morgan marque was thereby increased. The team thought they could do even better with a lighter, right hand drive Plus Four, so Rene placed the order at Malvern. The new car was to become Baby Doll No 3, and this wire wheeled racer was supplied complete with racing tyres and strengthened frame front. It had a set of aluminium wings for lightness and was right hand drive because of better weight distribution on the clockwise tracks usually used for sports car racing (excluding Pomona). It was coloured green, with black upholstery and given chassis number 3853. After testing at the Morgan factory during the week of January 13th it was dispatched for California on Tuesday February 4th.

Meanwhile the next appearance of Baby Doll No 2 was at Pomona for the Cal Club's meeting held over the weekend of February 8th and 9th. Lew Spencer was joined in the Saturday's ten lap race for Production Classes D and E by Al Gebhard with his Plus Four. Lew was fourth overall behind two Porsches and an Austin Healey, whilst Al came home eighth. In the Sunday's thirteen lap race for Classes E and F Production Lew was again fourth, behind three Porsches, whilst Al was eleventh, and sixth in class.

Rene Pellandini had this year decided that Worldwide Imports would also contest the ladies' races, with Barbara Windhorst, the wife of Austin Healey 100S racer Bob Windhorst, driving. She drove a brilliant race, finishing just ten seconds behind the Porsche Spyders of Ruth Levy and Betty Shutes. The spectators were on their toes for the whole event and Barbara was justly rewarded with first in class and first in Production cars.

That same weekend Roger Slowi, an employee of the Western Electric Telephone Company, was beginning his own racing career at Hour Glass Field, San Diego, in an event organised by the Road Racing Training Association (RRTA). This organisation had been set up by top racers Ken Miles and Sam Hanks to put something back into the sport they loved by encouraging beginners. Roger was third overall and first in class, driving his new green Plus Four. Another Western Electric employee was his mechanic. He was Stu Haggart.

After he had moved from Chicago to California in 1956 Roger had been introduced to sports cars by a friend rallying an MG TD who needed a navigator. Roger took the job, was hooked, and his brother-in-law then convinced him that he really needed a Morgan.

For the weekend of March 1st and 2nd the Worldwide Imports' Baby Doll No 2 made the

Barbara Windhorst on the grid at Pomona, Rene Pellandini smiling behind the bonnet of Baby Doll No 2. (Lester Nehamkin)

256

long journey east to Phoenix, Arizona for the SCCA race meeting held on the airport circuit of nearby Bearsley in the 'Valley of the Sun', using a 2.5mile course. Bruce Wallace, the local Morgan dealer, was in support and three local Morgan drivers had entered their Plus Fours in the Saturday's novices' race, Roger Seargeant finishing first in class, Jim Crispelle third and Ed Harrington sixth. The course was rough and found to be very hard on tyres.

The 'novice' Morgan drivers were out again on the Sunday, joined by Lew Spencer, in a seven lap race for Production cars of 1,600cc and above. Lew finished third overall behind Hal Sharp's Corvette and Bob Winklemann's 'gull-wing' Mercedes, a very impressive performance. Lew won his class of course, supported ably by Roger Seargeant who was second in class, whilst Bill Doushkess, Ed Harrington and Jim Crispelle were fifth, sixth and seventh respectively.

Barbara Windhorst took over Baby Doll No 2 for the five lap ladies' race finishing second overall, losing by just one second to a Lotus, but taking first in class. This was despite losing time when she was forced off the track by a spinning Corvette on the first lap. Also competing in a Morgan in this race was Ruth Doushkess, driving the Plus Four she shared with her husband. She finished fifth overall and second in class.

Bill Doushkess and his wife Ruth had successfully raced an MG TF and an early MGA before Bill went to work for a Triumph dealer. Although he and his wife tried racing a TR3, the handling proved resistant to improvement, so they convinced their employer Bill Creighton that they should try the Morgan, which used the same engine. They visited an imported cars show in the autumn of 1957 at the Pan-Pacific Auditorium where they met Rene Pellandini. Rene was exhibiting a specially prepared powder blue two-seater Plus Four, with chrome wire wheels and much chrome added under the bonnet. After much to-ing and fro-ing Rene agreed to let them purchase this car at a special price. The SCCA Phoenix races were to be their first with this car.

The ten lap semi-main event for all Production cars turned into a Morgan benefit, for Lew Spencer was very impressive in Baby Doll No 2, finishing fifth overall behind two Corvettes, a Mercedes Benz 300SL and a Porsche Carrera, but was first in class. Roger Seargeant was second in class; Bill Doushkess came through the field to third in class, pleased at beating all the local Morgans. Ed Harrington was fifth after spinning but Jim Crespelle blew a tyre and failed to finish.

For this year's international Sebring 12 Hour Race, to be held on Saturday March 22nd, Tom Payne, the very experienced sports car driver from Ypsilanti, Michigan, was to drive the only Morgan entered amongst the sixty-five accepted starters. There is some evidence from the official Sebring records that Richard Kennedy (the 1957 Sebring Morgan driver) was this year's entrant, but he does not seem to have been much involved, and the co-driver was to be Charles 'Chuck' Sherman.

Curly Ellis, the Canadian Morgan dealer in Windsor Ontario, ordered from the Morgan factory two specially prepared Plus Fours, identical apart from having different rear axle ratios. These were chassis numbers 3871 (4.1 to 1 axle ratio) and 3872 (3.73 to 1). Both cars had tuned engines and also featured red upholstery. They were dispatched on Tuesday February 25th to Windsor Motorcycles.

On arrival both cars were prepared for Sebring, and painted in 'Ypsilanti colours', the special paint scheme used on their racing cars by Tom Payne and his supporters, featuring two horizontal yellow stripes across the red bonnet. Curly was to run the pits and he drove 3871 down to Sebring, whilst local Morgan enthusiast David Elcomb, drove 3872. At this time there were no interstate highways, but despite this the journey took them less than three days. Dave remembers the trip as, 'a great run'. Poor Curly had a bad ankle from his pre-war motorcycle injury and so he didn't use the gearbox as much as did Dave. Possibly as a result of this the gear change was not as easy on 3871 as on 3872.

On arrival they checked in to their rented downstairs rooms of a local rectory (the minister

The rolled Sebring Morgan on the course. Note the damaged right rear wing is being carried inside the car, behind the driver. (Bill Foster)

and his family moved upstairs) and the two cars were taken for scrutineering and practice, undertaken during unseasonable cold and windy weather.

The two drivers, Tom and Chuck, decided they preferred to drive 3871 for the race. Dave Elcomb suggested that they swap the gearboxes, but this wasn't done.

The Sebring course itself had received some improvements for this year. There was now a steep and narrow vehicle bridge sponsored by Martini-Rossi at the west of the pits giving access to the infield when the race was in progress. There was another bridge, sponsored by Amoco, for pedestrians at the east end of the pits. This was to become a favourite place for photographers to film the Le Mans start.

As in 1957 a 'GT' class was being used to give Production cars a chance of awards. The Morgan was in Sub Class 7, along with the TR3s, AC Bristols and Arnolt Bristols.

Practice was uneventful, but 'Wacky' Arnolt of the Arnolt Bristol team came over to the Morgan pit adjacent to his own to ask why their car was always going so fast, with equal times for the day and night time practice. Tom replied, 'because we're going flat out all the time!'

Dave Elcomb particularly remembers one practice evening when Curly and Dave were at a local restaurant where Irish stew was being served. Curly enjoyed it so much that he commented he wished he could get this for breakfast. The proprietor was happy to oblige!

Race day dawned to sunshine at last. After the preliminaries there was a near false start when several drivers were premature in running across the track to their cars, but eventually all was sorted out and they all set off together.

The Morgan ran without a hitch until over seventy laps had been completed when Chuck Sherman was impeded by a Porsche in the esses. The Morgan spun, hit a steel drum filled with water (a course marker) and rolled twice. Fortunately a substantial roll bar had been fitted to the Morgan and Chuck's injuries were minor. Chuck was able to right the badly bent Morgan and it was returned to the pits. Here frantic pit work soon had a door and wing removed from the other car and literally nailed into place on the damaged racer. The left front brake drum had also broken, so it was wired up. As these 'repairs' were all completed within the allotted two hours the team was keen to return to the race. The Chief Steward, Bill Smythe, had other ideas however so Tom Payne did just two more laps (to a standing ovation from the spectator stand near the accident site) before parking the Morgan on the back straight. As the chequered flag was shown at the end of the twelve hours Tom started the Morgan and drove it across the line, so that it was counted as a finisher, having completed 76 laps, being sixth in class and fortieth overall of the forty-one classified as finishers.

For the return trip back to Windsor Dave and Curly both shared the spare car (3872) with the wings and door reattached. This journey was not uneventful, for the State Troopers had closed roads in Georgia due to heavy snow, delaying the journey. When given the 'all clear' they were the second vehicle allowed through, following a bus - no doubt the Troopers reckoned that if the bus and the Morgan could get through then surely the rest could too!

Spectating at Sebring were two ex-college friends, both of whom had been racing MG T types. One, Tom Wright, was now living in Orlando, a rather sleepy Florida town in these pre-Disney days. Realising that the 1951 MG TD that he had raced whilst at Georgia Tec was no longer competitive in F Production since the introduction of the Alfa Romeo 1300, he had purchased in the autumn of 1957 a pale yellow (probably ivory) two-seater Plus Four, with red upholstery, from the brand new Orlando dealer. It was the first Morgan that the dealer had sold, and probably one of only two that he ever did sell, for the brick paved streets of Orlando were hardly ideal for Morgan suspensions!

The other friend was Arch McNeill, now living in New York, who had been racing an MG TC. Watching the racing at Sebring it occurred to Arch that he might do this, and after discussions with Tom they both resolved to try and be there in a Morgan in 1959. The Morgan seemed ideal as it was cheap, readily available, and didn't need much preparation to make it suitable for racing.

The same weekend as Sebring the San Francisco Region of the SCCA ran races at Stockton Airport. The weather was awful with rain throughout the meeting, making the 2.3 mile track pretty slippery. To add to their distress Rene's team found Baby Doll No 2 to have clutch problems, due to the gearbox mounts having broken, allowing the engine to move forwards when the clutch pedal was depressed. Claude Brun and Al Gebhard went to the town to buy some bolts and on return drilled the chassis gearbox cross-member to mount the gearbox rigidly to it. Rene had entered Al in Baby Doll No 2 in the novice race for Production cars over 1,600cc, held over twelve laps (31 miles). He was on the last row of the grid, with Corvettes and Mercedes 300SLs all around. The rain was so bad that when the flag dropped Al could see nothing but roosters of spray, which blinded his face visor. He ripped this off and pointed the little green Morgan between the rooster tails, weaving his way blindly through the pack. Al had tried his goggles (he started with them around his neck), but they were useless in the spray so he tried bare-eyed to squint around the windscreen as he couldn't see through it. He tried folding the aero screen flat but this brought instant pain as the rain hit his eyes. By now Al was coming up to lap slower cars and another Morgan spun in front of him, but Al did manage to stay on the track and finally came second in class and sixth overall, whilst Bill Hinshaw from Berkeley, a founder member of the Morgan Plus Four Club's Northern California Bay Area, was right behind Al. Returning to the pits Al was greeted by Rene and supporters who expressed some relief that he hadn't drowned!

In the twenty lap race for novices and senior drivers even Lew Spencer in Baby Doll No 2 couldn't avoid spinning on Turn 5 in the diabolical conditions, finally finishing fourth in class and fifth overall, whilst Cliff Wright finished eighth in class in his Plus Four. In the Saturday's ladies' race Barbara Windhorst took Baby Doll No 2 to victory.

Morgan Sports Cars — 1958

This was Bill Hinshaw's first race meeting after his obligatory drivers' school events in his red Morgan, which he had christened 'Little Red' (after Little Red Riding Hood). In Cal Club events a fair bit of engine modification, mainly related to lightening components, was permitted and Al Gebhard had told Bill what he was doing to his own car. Bill had felt some of these modifications would not be allowed by the more stringent rules applying in Northern California, so Bill had made several ten hour drives to Los Angeles to find out from Claude Brun what options worked best for reliability on Baby Doll and what didn't. He also learnt the easiest and quickest ways to remove the engine without removing the radiator etc. As a result Bill had the engine balanced and blueprinted and, after once burning an exhaust valve at drivers' school, it never gave any other problems. On his trips to Los Angeles Bill stayed at the bachelor pad of Rene Pellandini in the Hollywood Hills overlooking Sunset Strip. It had its own swimming pool and there were always abundant numbers of movie starlets around. His opulent lifestyle led Rene to be called 'The Penniless Millionaire'!

Meanwhile that same busy weekend the Cal Club ran a hill climb using part of the Willow Springs course from the pits up to the top of the hill, maybe seven to eight tenths of a mile. As Morgan enthusiast Curt Warshawsky was the event chairman he had managed to persuade twelve Morgan drivers to enter in ten different Morgans and was thus able to give them their own class. The top driver proved to be Bill Doushkess, some way faster than Roger Slowi, with Ruth Doushkess in third place. In fourth place was Kenny Deeter, an Irishman living in Southern California, working in the air-conditioning business. He had started racing in 1953 with an MG TD, but had not been impressed by the later MGA when he wanted something more modern. He was also not particularly impressed with the shape of the Morgan Plus Four, but when he drove one he had found that it handled superbly. As a result he had bought his green Plus Four from Ed Savin in 1956.

We think the Palm Springs races held on April 12th and 13th marked the debut of Lew Spencer

The retirement of Baby Doll No 2 with trophies. From left to right are Bob Windhorst, Barbara Windhorst, Nanette Spencer, Rene Pellandini, Lew Spencer and Claude Brun at Worldwide Imports. (Curt Warshawsky collection)

Lew Spencer at Palm Springs, in what we think is Baby Doll No 3, attempts to stay ahead of the very fast AC Bristol driven by Bill Love. The Arnolt Bristol is driven by Elmo Grimsgaard. Note the masking tape and the short cowl grille on the Morgan. (Lew Spencer collection)

in Baby Doll No 3, the right hand drive Plus Four with aluminium wings that Rene Pellandini had ordered from Morgan for racing. Certainly it was a right hand drive Plus Four that he brought home in thirteenth position (fifth in class) in Race 3, a five lapper, the winner being Richie Ginther in a beautiful Ferrari Tour De France coupé, followed by four Corvettes. For this race at Palm Springs the Pellandini Morgan had the front of the wings and the cowl covered by masking tape to try and minimise the abrasive effect of the desert sand on the paintwork.

In the ladies' race Barbara Windhorst took the same car to an excellent fifth overall and second in class.

On Saturday April 19th several Morgan owners took part in the Springtown hill climb in Pennsylvania, including Harry Reynolds taking part in his very first hill climb. Finishing fourth, fifth and sixth in the E Production class were the Plus Fours of Ike Williamson (69.8224 seconds!), Henry Baumann and Bill Worthington. In eleventh place was Jack Fetterolf in his Plus Four, with Harry sixteenth and Alan Maynard slowest of the Morgans in eighteenth place. That same weekend at Marlboro in Maryland the sky blue Plus Four recently used so successfully by Gaston Andrey was competing once more but sadly failed to finish. It was being driven by Charles 'Chuck' Kelsey, Gaston's mechanic, who had now taken over the Morgan. Gaston was now being offered far more exotic drives courtesy of sponsor Mike Garber and could see no further opportunities to campaign his old Morgan.

Chuck was out again at Cumberland on Sunday May 18th, along with Ike Williamson, but we have no results of the races.

Bill Hinshaw took 'Little Red' to the Tracy Sports Car Races held over a 2.7 mile circuit at Tracy Municipal Airport over the weekend of May 10th and 11th. He competed in Saturday's twelve lap over 1,600cc novice race, finishing sixth overall and winning Class E. Little Red was Bill's everyday car and proving very reliable, just needing a pre-emptive change of big-end bearings every third race meeting he did. All possible loose items were

Bill Dredge in the ex-Bob Oker racer finishes fifth in the Santa Barbara novices' race. (Dave Friedman)

safety wired. Bill used 5.90 x 15 Continental Racing tyre carcasses, but had them shaved and recapped at Bruce's Tires in Oakland for $13.75 each. These tyres, known as Bruce's Racing Recaps, far outgripped just about anything else available. The same tread was used by the California Highway Patrol Academy for training purposes on their skidpan!

Also competing at Tracy, on the Sunday in the ten lap race for marque sports cars, was Cliff Wright with his Plus Four, finishing thirteenth overall and fourth in the TR/Morgan class.

The Memorial Day holiday weekend of May 31st and June 1st marked the introduction of important new safety regulations by the Cal Club at its Santa Barbara races. These required fireproof clothing to be worn and car roll bars to be fitted.

Several Morgan drivers had entered the races. Lew Spencer and Barbara Windhorst were sharing Baby Doll No 3. Al Gebhard had ordered a new wire wheeled Plus Four from Rene Pellandini and had traded in his old car. As the new one hadn't arrived yet Rene had entered him in Baby Doll No 2 and he was trying out a new type of racing brake lining that worked best when hot. Bill Dredge, an editor and journalist at the Los Angeles Times, had purchased the ex-Ed Savin racer, previously driven to great success carrying competition number 59 by Bob Oker. This was the only Morgan with a TR2 engine entered, all the others being TR3 powered. It was now red. This was forty-five year old Bill's eleventh sports car and his second Morgan. His first sports car had been an Austin Nippy way back in 1937.

Roger Slowi was in his usual car and Bill and Ruth Doushkess were also sharing their usual Morgan. Bill recalls that the new roll bar regulations and a lack of time led to the installation of a hideous construction fabricated from cast iron water pipes by South Bay Imported Cars. When it was seen at the scrutineers Bill heard someone comment, 'My god, the flying bedstead!'

In the Saturday's novices' race Roger Slowi finished third, Bill Dredge was fifth but Al Gebhard failed to finish. Later that day Al finished ninth overall in Race 4, with Roger Slowi 16th, Bill Dredge 19th and Bill Doushkess 21st. Lew Spencer had problems with Baby Doll No 3, but these were put right for the ladies' race, where Barbara Windhorst had an exciting battle with Ruth Doushkess, beating her by less than a second.

The following day, in the fifteen lap Race 13

Al Gebhard in Baby Doll No 2 at Santa Barbara, sliding behind an Alfa Romeo. (Allen R Kuhn)

for under 2,000cc, Lew broke a tappet and Roger a push rod. Poor Al Gebhard was finding his new brake linings completely unpredictable, and spun off twice on the same corner. The marshals had seen enough and he was black flagged. So just two of the Morgans finished, with Bill Doushkess coming home sixth in class and Bill Dredge thirteenth.

Once again the ladies' race featured a tremendous scrap between Ruth and Barbara, with Ruth this time the victor by just one second.

The annual races at Put-in-Bay were held by the Cleveland Sports Car Club on Saturday June 7th, attracting the two Plus Fours of Richard Cook from Lakewood and Gordon Harrison from Pontiac to Race 5, a twelve lap race for Classes E Production and F Modified. The race was notable for the two Morgans leaving the course at the same corner. Richard Cook had bought his 'Baby Blue' Plus Four two-seater from MG Motors in

The Morgan of Richard Cook (number 12E) temporarily visits that of Gordon Harrison (number 34E) on the roadside at Put-in-Bay. (Joe Brown)

Lakewood as a replacement for an MG TD. It was the first wire wheeled Plus Four he had seen. He found the car understeered badly on the circuit, especially at Cemetery Corner where several times he left blue paint on the hill side, but not enough to prevent him finishing!

The RRTA ran a hill climb at the Arrowhead Springs Hotel in Southern California on Saturday June 14th. Three Morgan Plus Four Club members decided to have a go, these being Kenny Deeter, Roger Slowi and Bill Becker. Each competitor was scheduled for three timed climbs, but the 1.5 mile twisty course proved to be dangerous, with several cars rolling or crashing, and as the timing system was also temperamental the drivers were lucky to get two runs. Kenny was first in class, with Roger third and Bill fourth.

That same weekend Rene Pellandini's Morgan racing team returned to Laguna Seca with Baby Doll No 3 for Lew Spencer to drive. Also competing in Plus Fours were Roy Jackson-Moore, the distributor of AC cars in the western USA and also the former Jaguar XK140 driver Dr Cliffton Wright from Modesto, east of San Francisco. On the Saturday Lew Spencer started in twentieth position, but was up to second overall behind Dr Snively's Austin Healey when the race was stopped after only twelve of the scheduled fifteen laps. He would have been first, at the pace he was going, if the full distance had been run. Roy Jackson-Moore, we are pretty certain, was driving Baby Doll No 2. He knew Rene quite well and had been offered the spare seat in one of Rene's Morgans. This Morgan broke a push rod so Roy and Claude Brun spent the night replacing it ready for the Sunday's racing.

On the Sunday the Morgans ran in the twenty-five lap Class E and above Production race, with Lew making a brilliant start but then throwing it all away with a spin at Turn 9. Despite this he eventually finished fourteenth overall and seventh in class. Roy started last, having not finished on the Saturday, but worked his way to nineteenth place, with Cliff Wright twenty-sixth of the twenty-nine finishers. The twisty Laguna Seca circuit was fast becoming a marvellous circuit for Morgans, where much more powerful racers fell victim to the better handling of the little Morgan.

That same weekend, on the other side of the USA, the northeastern racers had congregated at Lime Rock for the SCCA's National races. Chuck Kelsey was proving a very effective racer in his ex-Andrey Morgan, claiming a fifth overall and fourth in class in the Production race for Classes D and E. He was still unable to make much impression on the all-conquering AC Bristols, which came first and second in front of an Austin Healey, and he was just pipped on the line by Harold Hurtley's Triumph after a race long duel.

The following weekend six Morgans entered the first of a series of annual races to be held at the county airport at San Luis Obispo in California by the El Camino Foreign Car Club. As this town was situated nearly mid distance between San Francisco and Los Angeles, the Morgan entrants were from both Northern and Southern California. From Berkeley in the north came Bill Hinshaw, whilst from the south came Al Gebhard, Bill Doushkess and Bill Dredge. From Santa Barbara came Jay David in a four-seater, and from Fresno came the local Morgan dealer, Don West.

The two mile circuit, with eight turns, suited the Morgan, for Bill Hinshaw finished fourth overall and second in class. Al was eighth overall and sixth in class whilst Jay David was seventh in class. Problems were encountered by Don West, who had brake troubles, finishing nineteenth, Bill Doushkess, who was twenty-fourth in class, and poor Bill Dredge, who broke a rod and failed to finish. Bill, Al and Jay beat all thirteen of the Triumph TRs entered, demonstrating the superiority of the Plus Four.

In the northeast the action was at Watkins Glen one week later for the SCCA Regional races. Two Plus Fours were entered, the drivers being W T Bosworth Jnr from Pittsburgh in

Pennsylvania and Jim Forno from Johnson City in New York. Jim had first been exposed to British sports cars during a tour of duty with the US Army 8th Air Force in England during the war. Whilst the USA had convertibles of course, Jim felt they had nothing to compare with the sports car. Jim was hooked and began his motor business 'Continental Motors' of Vestal, dealing in British cars. One of his dealerships was Morgan, cars being obtained from Fergus Imported Cars Inc. Jim was driving a red Plus Four with bolt-on wheels, purchased from Fergus. It was Bosworth who was the more successful of the two Morgan drivers with fourteenth overall and tenth in class, with Jim one class position behind but seventeenth.

Chuck Kelsey continued his losing battle against the AC Bristols at the SCCA's National meeting at Lime Rock, held on Saturday July 5th. The third race brought eight Class E Production racers to the line for twenty laps. As expected three AC Bristols went straight into the lead, the cars of Harry Carter, Jordan King and Evelyn Mull, but Kelsey stuck doggedly to the tail of the latter, hounding Eve all the way to the flag to finish fourth. Finishing last was the Plus Four of Dave Ruggles.

The weekend of July 5th and 6th saw sports car racing at a new purpose built circuit in Northern California. This was Vaca Valley Raceway, near Vacaville, some fifty miles from San Francisco and thirty from Sacramento. It was a mixed oval and road course with a lap distance of 2.1 miles and nine turns. Race 2 was for novice drivers in Production cars of over 1,600cc and three Morgans were entered, those of Bill Hinshaw, Bob Tara and Bob Kimball. Bob Kimball was the more successful, finishing sixth overall but second in Class E, just behind the TR3 of Frank Crane. Bill finished in fourteenth place overall and eighth in Class E whilst Bob Tara failed to finish in the coupé.

Bob Kimball had begun his love of sports cars with the purchase of an MG TF in 1954 after finishing his stint in the USAF. In 1958, after owning several sports cars, he joined Cambridge Motors, a Rootes Group dealership in Sacramento owned by Jim Reed, as a salesman. Cambridge Motors also held the Morgan dealership so Bob had bought a blue Plus Four, which he was now racing. He remembers the Morgan was always so much fun, being able to pass much larger cars in the turns, only to then lose out to some on the straights. 'You could see the frustration of the drivers when the little blue car could easily out handle them,' he said.

Bob Tara was a mechanic at Cambridge Motors and had previously been autocrossing a Jaguar XK120 and a 140, along with his wife Grace. As Grace had now reached the age of twenty-one they were now both eligible to race in SCCA races, so they purchased a black Morgan Plus Four coupé from Cambridge Motors and began racing. Grace was a naturally fast driver, such that she acquired the nickname of 'Racey Gracey'. She told us how she remembered the Morgan: 'It was the most perfect car, and the most beautiful black paint job, and boy was it fun to drive!'

Two weeks later, at Brynfan Tyddyn, the narrow course on the estate of Senator Woods near Wilkes-Barre in Pennsylvania, Ike Williamson finished second to Sam Moses's AC Bristol in the Classes D and E race, but he did beat all the Austin Healeys.

That very same weekend, down in Florida, a redundant ex-Second World War airfield was used for racing at Cocoa Beach by the SCCA. Tom Wright from Orlando was racing his 'pale yellow' Plus Four for the first time at this meeting. In his first race the line up included seven TR3s, a Jaguar XK120 and two Corvettes, amongst the thirty-five starters. Tom found the smooth runway surfaces really suited the Plus Four and had a race-long dice with the XK120, passing it in the twisty bits, but being overtaken on the long straight in front of the pits. Eventually brake fade slowed the Jaguar and Tom beat it to finish eighth overall, only beaten by the AC Bristols, a Mercedes 300SL, one of the Corvettes and a couple of Porsche GTs.

Tom Wright in the first race at Cocoa Beach. (Tom Wright collection)

In the second race Tom was doing equally well, when the bonnet came unhitched and began to rise at one side at speed. He was black flagged by nervous marshals to fix it, eventually rejoining at the back of the field. Despite this set back he still managed to catch and pass at least two TR3s in the few laps remaining. Tom wisely decided to fit a bonnet strap for the future.

Back in California Al Gebhard was at the RRTA's meeting at Hour Glass Field in San Diego on Sunday July 27th. Al had recently been to a drivers' school at this venue, where the Indianapolis 500 winner of 1957, Sam Hanks, was instructing. Sam stopped Al several times to tell him that his lines were good, but that he should go yet faster. Al complied and eventually spun off. Sam told him, 'That's what I've been trying to get you to do. You now know how fast you can't go!' Al had got the message, for he was first in class and second overall, behind D D Michelmore's Porsche Carrera!

The San Francisco Region of the SCCA held races at Minden-Gardnerville (Tahoe-Douglas) Airport over the weekend of August 2nd and 3rd, Minden being situated in the valley adjoining Lake Tahoe on the California-Nevada State line, at a height of over four thousand feet. Racing was held on a 3.4 mile circuit and in the forty-five minute race for Production Classes B to E inclusive Bob Kimball finished tenth overall and second in Class E in his Plus Four.

SCCA National races were held at Montgomery, New York, over the weekend of August 16th and 17th. Race Four, a twenty-lapper for Production Classes D and E saw the AC Bristols of Jordan King and Harry Carter finish first and second. Eighth overall and fourth in class behind three AC Bristols was W T Bosworth with his TR2 engined Morgan. Last of the finishers was poor Dave Ruggles once more.

For the weekend of August 31st and September 1st the Cal Club introduced a new car classification system for its ever popular Santa Barbara races, whereby the engine size classification used for production car racing was modified such that perpetual class winning models were reclassified into the next class up, thereby allowing other usually cheaper makes to have a chance. It was dreamt up by Elliot Forbes-Robinson, a racer himself, who believed a classification on performance, rather than just engine capacity, made for much closer racing.

Al Gebhard drove up to compete at Santa Barbara with his brand new wire wheeled Plus Four, coloured red with black upholstery, recently received from Worldwide Imports. As he removed the windscreen, taped the headlight glasses and fitted a straight pipe exhaust and new spark plugs Al realised that the new car would be a bit 'tight', and resolved to take it easy.

Also entered were eight other Morgans, although two cars subsequently had to pull out, those of JoAnn Stewart and Kenny Deeter. The other cars entered were those of Bill Doushkess, Roger Slowi, Lew Spencer and Barbara Windhorst with Baby Doll No 3, Bill Hinshaw and Bill Chapman (both from Northern California) and Chuck Lowry. Chuck Lowry, a film director from Hollywood, had recently bought Baby Doll No 2 from Rene Pellandini.

Bill Chapman had studied civil engineering at Cal Poly University in San Luis Obispo, and was now employed by the California Division of Highways. He had a British Racing Green wire wheeled Plus Four.

Baby Doll No 3 was now fitted with the earlier type of long radiator grille it retained for the rest of its racing career, perhaps to improve cooling, and this green Plus Four had two yellow stripes painted across the top of the bonnet, increasing in size as they went towards the rear of the car, and finishing on the rear panel. They were edged with black to make them stand out. The 'Baby Doll No 3' legend was painted across the upper front of both doors. On the left hand side bonnet were printed the legends 'Piloto Lew Spencer' and underneath 'Charme Barbara Windhorst' whilst the right side carried 'Owner Rene Pellandini' and beneath 'Mechanic Claude P Brun'.

On the Saturday there were twenty-six cars on the line for the six lap Class E race, comprising Morgans, TRs, Porsche Supers and early Carreras, and also included some Austin Healeys. The AC Bristols had now been reclassified from Class E to Class D by the newly introduced performance classification of the Cal Club. Also allowed in the Cal Clubs new Class E were ACs with non Bristol engines, Arnolt Bristols and MGA Twin-Cams.

Lew Spencer had worked his way to the front when engine trouble set in, finally finishing in fourth place. Al was fifth despite 'running in', with Bill Hinshaw seventh, Roger Slowi twelfth, Bill Chapman fourteenth, Chuck Lowry fifteenth and Bill Doushkess twentieth.

After the race Al was relaxing in the pits, having a drink with Rene and friends, when Ruth Doushkess came strolling by with helmet in hand.

Ruth Doushkess in Al Gebhard's Morgan at Santa Barbara. Behind the Morgan, left to right, are Rene Pellandini, Gerry Scott (Al's pit helper), and Bill Doushkess. (Lester Nehamkin)

She was looking for a drive in the ladies' race. Al offered her his car, for he knew she was a good driver. The offer was gratefully accepted and Ruth went out to her usual exciting battle with Barbara Windhorst, until the crankshaft broke on Baby Doll No 3, flooding the course with oil. Ruth continued, to finish first in class and fifth overall, before returning the Morgan to its owner. She mentioned to Al that she thought she heard a strange noise from the back axle, so Al and Claude Brun decided to check it over in the morning.

Saturday night was always party night for the racers. On the way to the motel Al too heard the noise and decided to stop to investigate. No sooner had he pulled off the road than the left rear wheel fell off! It turned out that the axle shaft nut had come undone, allowing the hub and wheel to come off and in the process chewing up the threads on the end of the halfshaft. After much searching Al found a suitable small file and appropriate deep socket and early on the Sunday morning Al woke Claude Brun to help him fix it.

Meanwhile the irreparable Baby Doll No 3 had donated various parts to other Morgans to make them race-worthy for the fifteen lap Sunday race for Class E Production. Six healthy Plus Fours started, with Al having been allocated a place on the front row of the grid because of his Saturday performance. He finished third, behind two Porsches. Bill Hinshaw came home fifth, Roger Slowi was seventh, Bill Chapman tenth, Chuck Lowry fourteenth and Bill Doushkess seventeenth.

The same weekend, the autumn meeting was being held at the Road America circuit in Wisconsin. Two Morgan Plus Fours were entered in the Saturday thirty lap race for Classes E Production and above. These were the TR2 engined, chrome radiator, two-seater of Curt Gifford from Williams Bay, Michigan and the cowled radiator two-seater of Viktor Schuppe, who was from Highland Park in Michigan. Viktor owned an ivory two-seater with red upholstery, which had been dispatched to Windsor Motorcycles on Thursday February 23rd 1956. He found himself in a photograph on the cover of the SCCA's magazine *Sports Car*, for the Canadian driver John Tidswell lost his TR on the first lap, near Station 12, and was swamped by the pack, including Viktor's Morgan. All but Frank O'Connor's Austin Healey missed the TR, with Viktor finally finishing sixth in class behind five AC Bristols. Curt Gifford failed to finish this thirty lap race.

Back on the Pennsylvania hills on Saturday September 6th Harry Reynolds was this time the

Viktor Schuppe manages to squeeze by John Tidswell's obstructing TR at Road America. (Pierre Perrin)

fastest of the Plus Fours at Springtown with a time of 70.0442 seconds, beating Alan Maynard by nearly three seconds and Dick Smith (grey Plus Four) by over four. Harry was enjoying hill climbing and determined to develop his Morgan for these events.

On September 14th and 15th the California Morgan racers returned to Cobb Mountain for another hill climb using a dirt and gravel surfaced, one lane, access road, a different course from the previous year's flood damaged one. The start was about half way up the mountain and the finish at Hoberg's Resort at the top. Baby Doll No 3 was still not repaired from the engine disaster at Santa Barbara, so Lew Spencer was to share Al Gebhard's car. From Northern California came the black drophead coupé of Bob and Grace Tara, along with Bill Hinshaw and Bill Chapman, who were running together as a team.

On the Saturday Lew was unbeatable, beating even the Modified classes. On the Sunday Lew managed third overall and first in class. Watching him was lifelong Morgan enthusiast Gerry Willburn, who spectated from the top of a small bank on a right hand curve. He marvelled that Lew could consistently take this curve in Al's left hand drive Plus Four with the right front tyre on the very edge of the course and the wing just an inch or so from the bank itself.

The last corner was of diminishing radius and Al on his final run hit the marker hay bales with the right rear wing, hooking one with the hub spinner and dragging it over the line. He finished second in class and Bob Tara was third. Al now had a somewhat flat wing that he later removed to find a goodly quantity of straw had been driven between it and the body of the car. Grace Tara took over the windscreen-less coupé for the ladies' event and posted the fastest time.

Returning down the mountain after their climbs Bill Hinshaw and Bill Chapman overtook a 1949 Ford amongst the leaving spectator traffic, which gamely tried to keep up. At Middletown at the bottom of the mountain, the Ford did not appear, so the two Morgan drivers retraced their steps, eventually finding skid marks on a bend and spotting the Ford lying on its boot in the gully below. They went down finding the female passenger in advanced stages of labour. Luckily a passing doctor kept her calm whilst an ambulance arrived, thankfully just in time!

One week later dismal weather greeted the major eleventh annual Grand Prix meeting held at Watkins Glen. Entered for the Dix Cup Race for Classes D and E Production and H and I Modified, over twenty-two laps, were four Plus Fours, although Chuck Kelsey's ex-Andrey car did not start. The starters

Jim Forno, with his mechanic Arnold Romaldini, on the grid at Watkins Glen. Behind is the Morgan of Howard 'Ike' Williamson. (Jim Forno collection)

were the TR2 engined Morgan of Ike Williamson, Jim Forno's Plus Four and the Plus Four of E Hewitt Clapham. Hewitt hailed from Columbus, Ohio and was always known as 'Brick' because of his red hair.

Once again it was the AC Bristols that stole the show, taking five of the first six places. Jim Forno was best of the Morgans, finishing thirteenth overall and tenth in class, with Williamson seventeenth overall and Clapham nineteenth.

By the weekend of September 27th and 28th Baby Doll No 3 had been fully repaired by Claude Brun, and was entered to be driven by both Lew Spencer and Barbara Windhorst at the SCCA races at Hour Glass Field at San Diego. On the Saturday Lew finished sixth overall, but he did even better on the Sunday with an overall fourth, behind Bill Love's fast AC Bristol (driven by Bob Harris), the GT Porsche of DD Michelmore and the Porsche Carrera of Dick Bellows. Barbara came third overall (first production car) in the ladies' race, beaten only by Josie McLaughlin in a Ferrari and Betty Shutes in a Porsche Spyder.

In the September issue of *Sports Cars Illustrated* Griff Borgeson described a road test of Lew Spencer's wire wheeled Plus Four coupé, a car to which Lew and Claude Brun had undertaken some under bonnet brightening. The radiator stay rods and some other items were chrome plated, an aluminium rocker cover was fitted and also an aluminium sump, as on Baby Doll No 3. The exhaust manifold had been coated in black porcelain by Pacific Porcelain Products of Los Angeles, a coating that lasted well and looked good according to Lew. Griff finished off his report with the comment that if a Morgan owner was to be asked, 'How come you bought a Morgan?' the response should be, 'For less than $3000 how can you possibly beat it?'

The article contained some interesting references to the racer Baby Doll No 3, which only had 65 miles on the clock then, suggesting the road test was actually performed in the spring. It was described as a 'Sebring model', because of the aluminium wings and beefed up frame and suspension. Whilst the Sebring entries were always given the latest specification for racing by the Morgan factory Dave Elcomb, who was involved with the 1958 Sebring Morgan entry, is sure both cars had normal steel wings. Perhaps the earlier dispatched Baby Doll No 3 had been produced to the intended Sebring specification, without Rene Pellandini being aware of the subsequent change. Lew Spencer believes Rene was always keen to have the aluminium bodywork option listed as a new Morgan model.

Griff reported that Italian 'Fren-do' competition brake linings were preferred by Rene's team for racing as they ably stood up to severe punishment. Lew was using 6,000 rpm as a maximum for the balanced TR3 engine, although 6,500 was safe, but with no power advantage. Claude Brun, whom Rene Pellandini described as 'a mechanic in a million', found the TR engines hard on bearings when raced, so he removed the sump after each racing outing and replaced the big-end bearings as a precaution. After every third race he stripped the engine, replacing in addition the main bearings, and also regrinding the valves.

After three weeks of wet weather it was sunshine for the weekend of October 4th and 5th for the first National meeting held at Virginia International Raceway. The very first novice race at the track held on the Saturday saw David Williams from Winston-Salem competing in the old green chrome radiator Plus Four, with a TR2 engine, driven so successfully at the Chimney Rock hill climb by Howard Kern. He worked his way up to second place, just failing to catch Henry Grime's Jaguar XK140. This was despite a shattered second gear. In the Sunday's twenty lap race for E Production and above David sadly failed to finish.

The first SCCA National race meeting to be held at Vaca Valley took place over the weekend of October 4th and 5th. In the second race, held over thirty laps for Classes E and F Production, Robert Kimball collected 800 points for an excellent second in class behind an AC Bristol, finishing eleventh overall. He had done well, beating several AC Bristols. One Morgan failed to finish, that of Jack West. As a result Bob was invited to compete in the over 1,500cc Modified race, where he finished back in the pack, but was able to marvel at the skills of the top drivers in their Italian racers.

For the Riverside races held over the weekend of October 11th and 12th, the first running took place of a soon to be famous annual race, the Los Angeles Times Grand Prix. It was being held jointly by the Cal Club and the United States Auto Club (USAC), which was a professional racing organisation more involved with oval racing, including the legendary Indianapolis 500. The event was heavily promoted by the Times-Mirror Corporation in its newspapers. It was stiflingly hot with a huge crowd watching the racing. In the 52.4 mile Production race for Classes E and above, Lew Spencer was battling with Corvettes and other heavy metal, finally finishing fifteenth out of forty starters. More importantly he was second in Class E behind the 1,600cc Porsche Speedster of Ronnie Bucknum. Failing to finish was the TR3 of R W 'Kas' Kastner. Lew was to enjoy many battles in the future with these two and Kas Kastner was to become the expert bar none on tuning TR engines.

The press caught the true significance of the event with its coverage of the mixing of amateur drivers with true professionals. *Road and Track* commented, 'Sports car racing, at long last, comes of age in the West.' The amateur based SCCA was not amused however and had severely warned its drivers from competing in professional events run by the Cal Club as from October 11th onwards. Those who ignored this faced a ban of one year.

One week later Chuck Kelsey contested the SCCA New York Region Championship meeting at Lime Rock, but was let down whilst leading in the ex-Andrey car when the throttle cable broke.

The Northern California racers made another trip inland to Minden in Nevada over the weekend of October 25th and 26th, this time for races held by the Cal Club. Regular Morgan racers Bill Hinshaw, Bob Tara and Bill Chapman were joined by two new Morgan drivers, Dan Scarbrough and Ed Leslie. The Tara coupé was also entered by Grace in the ladies' event.

Ed Leslie came from the delightful village of Carmel on the Monterey Peninsula. He had begun driving hot Model A Fords pre-Second World War before becoming a pilot. Having now returned from the Korean War, where he flew B29 bombers, he had discovered that sports cars were all the rage. He began by racing a new MGA before purchasing a new wire wheeled Morgan from a temporary dealer in Monterey who had three in his showroom. Ed had begun trading in Carmel as Leslie Motors, dealing in second hand British sports cars. 'I made enough to be able to buy new sports cars for racing,' he told us. The pale blue Morgan was soon driven all over Northern California and Ed was glad he could partially deflate the Moseley seat cushion, being quite tall. The only problem he recalled was that the central spotlight kept falling off. He raced with an aero screen, a racing mirror in the centre of the scuttle and had 'LESLIE' written on the scuttle side. Ed found the Morgan handled very well because the wheelbase was longer than a TR3, and it could be thrown sideways into a corner with complete safety.

The Saturday saw a real battle between Ed and the experienced Bill Hinshaw in Little Red, with the latter just having the edge and coming home first in class, whilst Bob Tara and Dan Scarbrough failed to finish. Sadly the duel was not continued on the Sunday, for Ed didn't race and Bill lost a certain victory when the throttle cable broke, leaving the Morgans of Bill Chapman, Dan Scarbrough and Bob Tara to finish

Morgan Sports Cars — 1958

Four Morgans battling at Minden. In the centre is Bill Hinshaw in front of Ed Leslie, whilst Dan Scarbrough, and Bob Tara in the coupé, are alongside them. (Dave Friedman)

seventh, eighth and ninth respectively. Grace Tara, 'Racey Gracey', was third out of five entries in the ladies' race.

For some time there had been much friction between the SCCA in California and its great rival the Cal Club. It was made worse when the Cal Club was given the sanction for the November Laguna Seca meeting, which had previously been awarded to the SCCA. Despite the politics there was a fine turn out of Morgans from both Northern and Southern California. From the north came Bill Hinshaw, Ed Leslie, Bob Kimball, Walt Chase and another ex-MGA racer Rick Hilgers from Carmel. Rick had been running his own sports car repair shop since 1954. From the south came Baby Doll No 3 for Lew Spencer and Barbara Windhorst, Baby Doll No 2 for Chuck Lowry, Al Gebhard, Ruth Doushkess and Bob and Grace Tara.

On the Saturday in the Class E race Lew Spencer was fourth behind the three Porsches of Dan Herman, Emil Pardee and Ronnie Bucknum. Morgan drivers Bill Hinshaw, Ed Leslie and Rick Hilgers were ninth, tenth and eleventh respectively. Al Gebhard was sixteenth, Chuck Lowry was twenty-eighth with Bob Tara, Walt Chase and Bob Kimball all non-finishers. Bob Kimball had the misfortune for someone to run into the back of his Morgan, puncturing the left rear tyre, but he found Laguna Seca to be, 'great fun driving on that course, with high speeds allowed and the thrill of the Carousel'.

The ladies' race featured the three Morgans of Barbara, Ruth and Grace. Despite having to pit to secure a coil lead, Barbara Windhorst finished fourth overall and first in a production car, just half a lap down on the winning Ferrari of Josie McLoughlin, the Porsche Spyder 550 of Betty Shutes and a Lotus XI. Ruth was eighth overall and fourth in Production, Grace was twelfth overall and sixth in Production.

The Class E race on the Sunday was a classic, with Lew Spencer having a tremendous battle with Ronnie Bucknum's Porsche Speedster 1600 and Dan Herman's Porsche Carrera. There were no less than thirty-seven starters and after one lap it was Bucknum in the lead, hard pressed by Dan and Lew. Lew took second on lap 2, but Dan came through to take the lead on lap 5. On lap 6 Ronnie was in front, but the following lap saw Lew ahead. Dan then pitted and fell back but Ronnie and Lew continued their scrap, both setting equal fastest laps (1 min 32 seconds). A trip off the track at Turn

3 cost Lew three places, but he regained the lost ground to lead into the final lap. A spin at Turn 6 meant Lew had to settle for second, four seconds behind Ronnie's Porsche. Behind Lew came Bill Hinshaw, Rick Hilgers and Ed Leslie in third, fourth and fifth places respectively. Further back came Bob Kimball in thirteenth place, Walt Chase fourteenth and Bob Tara seventeenth. Chuck Lowry had a disaster in Baby Doll No 2, for he got into the dirt on the outside of Turn 2, a fast right hander, and, as he attempted to regain the track, he hit the bank and turned the Morgan over. Chuck was thrown out of the car and taken to hospital with a chipped vertebra and damaged ribs.

Al Gebhard too had problems, for he ran off the course, unable to steer properly, damaging the front suspension. After the race the front suspension was dismantled to discover a hub ball-bearing race had completely disintegrated.

The badly damaged Baby Doll No 2 was lifted on to Rene Pellandini's trailer by an army tank wrecker and returned to the store at Worldwide Imports where the sad remains lingered for several months. When Chuck was finally out of his body-cast Baby Doll No 2 was broken up, and, comments Al Gebhard, 'given a decent burial'. A large dent was noted in the gearbox cover, consistent with Chuck's chest injuries.

On Sunday November 16th the Washington Region of the SCCA held races at Marlboro track in Maryland. Of interest is the decision to use the Cal Club classification of Production cars by performance. Despite this the sole Morgan of Harold Baumann could do no better than eleventh, behind a victorious Porsche, eight TR3s and an Austin Healey (the Austin Healey was down to Class E from D in the Washington Region's unofficial adaptation of the Cal Club's new system).

That same weekend a group of sports car enthusiasts in the Harrisburg area of Pennsylvania ran the first Hershey Hill Climb, using a 0.7 mile 'tight' tarmac course between groups of summer cabins used by employees of the local chocolate factory. It attracted 76 cars, and, to limit speed at the end of the straight before an acute bend, the organisers used a 'stop and reverse' line where drivers had to perform correctly before proceeding on their runs. Ike Williamson was the victor in Class E, and Ruth Meiss from Williamsport, won the ladies' event in a Morgan.

A six hour race was held at Pomona during the weekend of November 22nd and 23rd. Only one Morgan was entered, Baby Doll No 3, to be driven by Lew Spencer and Bob Windhorst. All was going well, with a likely fifth overall and second in class to be collected, when, after five hours of trouble free racing, an outer front wheel bearing failed. Claude Brun worked frantically to try and get the car back in the race, but to no avail.

On the Sunday, with the wheel bearing sorted, Lew Spencer finally managed to beat Ronnie Bucknum in his Porsche 1600 Speedster, after a

The remains of Baby Doll No 2 at Turn 2. (Curt Warshawsky collection)

twenty lap battle and by just half a second. Lew was eighth overall but won the class in this Production race for Class E and above. Roger Slowi was also competing in his Morgan, finishing a fine fourth in class and fourteenth overall.

Barbara Windhorst took over Baby Doll No 3 for the ladies' race, worrying Betty Shutes' Porsche Spyder all the way, and finishing second overall and first in Production, just six seconds behind Betty.

Baby Doll No 3 had been racing for some six and a half hours, without missing a beat. The use of ball-race bearings for wheel bearings was once again the cause of the only problems. Rene Pellandini was to write to the Morgan Motor Company requesting an urgent change in wheel bearing specification to the more modern taper roller type, these being better able to take the racing loads.

Races were held by The Sports Car Owners Limited at Lincoln Airport, near Sacramento that same weekend. This was a club of disenchanted SCCA members who tried to run non-sanctioned events, but they were to find it too difficult to carry on for long. Bill Hinshaw was competing in Class 2 in Little Red, and won, beating the Porsches.

Lew Spencer at Laguna Seca battles with his great adversary Ronnie Bucknum (31E) with Dan Herman of Eureka (177) alongside. The latter was known as 'Herman the German', and as his Porsche was red, he was listed in the results as 'Baron von Herman'! (Lew Spencer collection)

Also competing in the race for Classes 6 and 7 was Leslie Rose from Richmond. As he came third to two MG TDs we suspect he was driving a 4/4.

The Arizona Region of the SCCA held the 'Fiesta de Carreras' at Phoenix on Sunday November 30th. The fifteen lap race for all Production classes saw Lew Spencer finish sixth overall and third in Class E Production in Baby Doll No 3. Roger Seargeant was eleventh, and fourth in class, and L Hickerson was eighteenth and fifth. In the five lap ladies' race Barbara Windhorst took Baby Doll No 3 to fifth place.

Over in Hawaii that same Sunday the Armed Forces Foreign Car Club ran a 'Wee Alpine' Rally, attracting 38 starters to the Kaiser Lagoon parking lot on Oahu. After four hours rally driving Bill and Mickey Richardson came home in second place in their Morgan, behind Alan Dowd's winning Austin Healey.

The first weekend in December was the traditional date for the second of the two annual hill climbs held at Chimney Rock in North Carolina and the event was held in beautiful winter sunshine. The Class E record of Howard Kern in the old green Morgan was to remain unchallenged, even by Kern himself who was this time driving an Austin Healey.

The 1958 racing year was now over and the SCCA's Class E Champion was Harry Carter with an AC Bristol; indeed, of the thirty-two who scored points in the SCCA National races which counted towards the championship, no less than twenty-six were in AC Bristols. Harold Hurtley was best of the other makes with fourth place with his TR, whilst the only Morgan drivers to score were Chuck Kelsey, who was twelfth and Robert Kimball seventeenth. Most races were held in the northeast with the flourishing California racing not well represented in this championship.

To counteract this northeastern bias the two California Regions of the SCCA had this year run their own Pacific Coast Championship, for selected meetings. The Pacific Coast Champion in Class E was Lew Spencer, excellent reward for the hard working Rene Pellandini team. He had 3,400 points, whereas second placed Bill Love, with his very rapid AC Bristol, had 3,000.

The Cal Club also gave annual awards, and Lew won the Morgan class, ahead of Bill Hinshaw and Al Gebhard. Lew was the man to beat in California! Bill Hinshaw's Morgan Little Red was very tired after the year's racing so he decided to trade it for a Jaguar XK140MC that Frank Henry had in at his Morgan dealership, which Frank now ran from a used car lot in Berkeley.

It is interesting to note that just thirty-six new Morgans had been registered in California in the first nine months of the year, whereas some 3,270 MGs, 1,154 Austin Healeys, and 646 Porsches were registered in the same period. A larger percentage of the Morgans were raced however.

Canada

The very last races at Abbotsford were held on Sunday March 30th, for this airfield was to be reactivated by Transport Canada as a civil airport. Just about every British Columbia driver attended this 'Swan Song' meeting, with an entry list of 92 cars being obtained. The racing was run under Conference rules. There were two Morgan Plus Fours entered, by A James and GB Sterne. Thirty-two cars started Race 2, for the larger engined production sports cars, and Mr James finished in fifteenth place, but fifth in Class IV, the Conference using Roman numerals for the Production classes on this occasion. G B Sterne was three places behind him. The fifth race was for all comers and featured a Le Mans start. Again the two Morgans were part of the 26-strong field, this time finishing with James in seventh place overall and fourth in Class E, whilst GB Sterne was again three places behind him. The race was won by Jim Rattenbury in his Jaguar D-type. The SCCBC was now busy planning the construction of a replacement permanent circuit, to be built at Westwood, a mere twenty miles from downtown Vancouver.

The British Empire Motor Club held another

Morgan *Sports Cars* — 1958

Windsor Motorcycles in 1958. To the right is a UK built Nash Metropolitan and a range of Ramblers. (Morgan Motor Co collection)

hill climb on Saturday May 17th, probably at Hockey Valley. Just two Plus Fours took part, those of Alan Sands and Dave Elcomb. Alan's proved to be the fastest on this occasion by finishing fifth overall and fourth in Class E (behind the winning AC Bristol and two TR3s) with a time of 1 minute 13.85 seconds. Dave recorded 1 minute 16.77 seconds to finish thirteenth overall and eighth in Class E.

Ed Kowalski entered his chrome radiator Plus Four for the races at Harewood Acres on Saturday July 19th, but we have no results.

On Saturday October 25th P McCowan finished third in his Plus Four in the race for sports cars from 1,600cc to 3,000cc at Harewood Acres.

Another importer took delivery of its first Morgan during 1958, this being Birmingham Motors of Winnepeg. They continued importing during 1959 but then faded away.

Chapter 6
1959

The ever enthusiastic Hagley and District Light Car Club ran a production car trial on Sunday January 4th at Stourton, using a pub car park for the eliminator test and an adjacent large wooded field with lanes for the trial hills proper. The Morgan of G C Fidler won a First Class Award in the open production cars class for cars using RAC approved tyres.

The following weekend the MCC held the 34th Exeter Trial, with starts on the Friday evening, January 9th from London, Launceston and Kenilworth, and finishing the following afternoon at Weymouth. It was a cold night with some ice, but the ground was frozen, making the more usually muddy climbs easier. As usual the Morgan factory had entered a team, all Plus Fours this time, which consisted of Jim Goodall driving HUY 982, Peter Morgan in TUY 875, and Bournemouth Morgan agent Joe Huxham driving RXN 194, a 1955 two-seater. Jim Goodall's car was fitted with the special 'petrol' tank fitted at the rear on to a modified Morgan towing bracket, but filled with water for ballast, rather than the expected petrol! Also entered was Monty Rogers in PLB 111.

The climb at Tillerton stopped Joe Huxham, his rear number plate bottoming during his attempt. Jim Goodall and Peter Morgan were both stopped by Simms, despite Peter trying high speed as a way of beating this hill. The last hill, Knowle Lane, also stopped Monty, for his Morgan hit one bump with an almighty crash, which burst open the bonnet on one side. After the early-running Morgan team had smoothed the centre of the hill it became easier for the later runners.

Having failed just Simms, Jim Goodall and Peter Morgan both received Second Class Awards. Joe received a Third, whilst Monty Rogers missed out this year, failing on four hills.

In January H O Serck Ltd from Manchester, who manufactured various radiators for the

Jim Goodall in HUY 982, with the special trials 'fuel' tank during the Exeter Trial. (LAT Photographic)

automotive industry, supplied drawings of a four-row oil cooler specifically for the Plus Four. The Morgan Motor Company was currently supplying large capacity aluminium sumps as an option for those worried about rising oil temperatures, but perhaps the Morgan Motor Company was looking at this oil cooler as an alternative to supply to the racing fraternity.

One of the top trials drivers of this period was Horace Roberts who ran the Dunhampton Garage at Ombersley in Worcestershire. He had previously trialled a Coventry Climax engined 4/4 in the post-war years before switching to Allards, but he had continued his association with Morgans by 'passengering' for Terry Hall in the works coupé during the mid 1950s on many occasions. He had now decided to trial a Morgan again and had ordered a new Plus Four for the purpose. Having a young son he chose a four-seater, which was painted ivory and fitted with red leather upholstery. It was ordered with rear quarter-lights in the hood, for better visibility, and also wire wheels. A large fuel tank was fitted, together with a wooden 'skid board' beneath it to protect it from damage from boulders on rocky trials. There was an extra leaf in the rear springs too. Horace collected the Morgan from the factory on Monday January 19th. It was registered WAB 779, and carried chassis number 4105.

The Thames Estuary Automobile Club ran its Cats' Eyes Rally on Saturday February 7th and Sunday February 8th, using a similar format to previous years. The weather was kind and the rally was actually won by a 'bubble car', a four wheeled Messerschmitt TG500. The tandem-seated crew of Messrs Piper and Cooper was one of sixteen clear on the road section, and they managed to beat far more potent cars in the deciding driving tests to win the event outright! The Production GT cars 1,601 to 2,600cc class was won by Romek Michalkiewicz accompanied by his usual navigator E Clarke, but they were now using a Triumph TR3. In second place was Brian Harper in his Morgan WOF 559.

Brian's navigator, also from the Shenstone and District Car Club, was Ron Crellin, who had previously been navigating for several other prominent Shenstone Club members. Ron had learnt the business of navigating whilst passengering for his rally driving father, who was a member of the Lancashire and Cheshire CC. Ron always believed the best way to win any rally was to get local knowledge, so spare weekends were spent checking out 'white roads' (minor roads) on Ordnance Survey maps to see if they were worth using, or best avoided, when finding one's way from control to control.

WOF 559 had now been painted red. Brian had had a head-on collision with a farmer on a tractor whilst he was 'recceing' a rally in Wales. Following repairs Brian had decided to repaint the Morgan red, but hadn't known the type of original paint being used by Morgans, and the new cellulose paint didn't cover it too well, leading to some odd pink bits! The headlights also now had anti-glare 'peaks' fitted, and the two spotlamps were arranged to illuminate the far left and far right of the road.

That same Sunday the Morgan 4/4 Club ran its Banbury Rally, organised by Alan Smith, the club secretary, for the benefit of club members. There were only six starters and the event was won by Barrie Phipps in his Riley 1.5. In second place was Tony Perks in his early 4/4 whilst close behind was Richard Cashmore in his Plus Four. This was a blue Morgan with black upholstery and had been collected by Richard from the Morgan factory on March 1st 1957. It was chassis number 3640 and was given the personalised registration RC 30. Finishing fourth was NAB 217, in the hands of its new owner, a Canadian student named Fred Lockwood.

The Royal Military College of Science Motor Club started its first 'Rallye Militaire' on Saturday evening February 21st. It was only open to 'experts' who had won awards in Restricted, National and International rallies during 1958. There were four starting points from near London, Birmingham, Bristol and Southampton with the

Brian Harper and Ron Crellin with their many trophies after winning the Rallye Militaire. (James Wright)

routes converging at the RMCS at Shrivenham. The following common route contained six overnight sections requiring different types of navigation and timekeeping of which the fourth proved particularly difficult. It was a thirty mile loop to the south of Haldon around Dawlish and Teignmouth with some time controls only two minutes apart, requiring precision navigation and top quality driving on the muddy, slippery, meandering and undulating lanes. After the final driving tests had been held at Shrivenham it was announced that the overall winner was Brian Harper in WOF 559, with Ron Crellin being given the Navigator's Award.

After just 1,300 miles of use Horace Roberts took his new Plus Four WAB 779 back to the Morgan factory repair shop in February for a faulty seat to be replaced, and in early March he was back once more with engine vibrations to be looked at. As a consequence the original engine (TS 38855) was replaced by TS 45605, and a new gearbox was also deemed necessary!

Autosport magazine published details of its Series-Production Sports Car Championship in its issue of February 27th. The championship was open to sports cars complying with Appendix J, and permitted modifications included non-standard camshafts, and the removal of bumpers. Windscreens of vehicles above 1,000cc had to be at least 20cms in height and 100cms in width. The Morgan 4/4 Series II was eligible for Class B, 1,101 to 1,300cc, whilst the Plus Four was eligible for Class D, 1,601 to 2,000cc. The latter class also included the Bristol engined AC and Frazer Nash cars, as well as other exotica, to compete with the more mundane TRs etc. Alan Belcher had decided to enter this competition as had Chris Lawrence, but the latter was more interested in the BARC championship for Marque cars being held to that club's own definition for the Fred W Dixon Trophy which excluded the Bristol engines. Chris and his friends had been busily preparing his Plus Four TOK 258 during the winter specifically for this competition. The new season was eagerly awaited.

The BARC was also running its annual North London Enthusiasts' Car Club's Jacobean Trophy Rally which began from Paul Street Garage in the City of London with 58 crews setting off between 10 pm and 11pm on Saturday night February 28th.

Chris Lawrence powers his way to victory, 'taking the tricky Madgwick Corner at real speed' during the March BARC Members' Meeting. The oil cooler is visible beneath the Morgan's radiator as is the undertray, and the ram pipes to the SU carburettors project through the bonnet side. This wonderful photograph graced the front cover of Autosport for March 20th. (Autosport)

After 240 miles that took them through the North and South Downs, there were just 44 who returned the following morning. F Freeman won the class for over 1,600cc cars in his Plus Four.

Autosport produced an editorial on the problems facing rallying in the issue of Friday March 13th. The general public was becoming increasingly hostile to the increasing and apparent never ending use of minor roads in certain parts of the country that were popular for navigation rallies, and indeed the issue had been raised with Members of Parliament. It was suggested that the number of competitive events held on public roads must be reduced and more use made of closed circuits.

The club racing season started in fine style at Goodwood on a sunny but cold Saturday March 14th with the BARC Members' Meeting. It was TOK 258's first outing since its winter preparation and Chris Lawrence and his team were rewarded with two wins. Its first event was the ten lap Marque scratch race with points counting towards the Freddie Dixon Trophy competition. As usual there was a Le Mans start, where the drivers sprinted across the track to jump into their cars and start up before pulling out onto the circuit. Chris Lawrence took an immediate lead, which he kept by a steadily increasing margin, eventually finishing ten seconds ahead of second placed Bill de Selincourt who was followed in third place by Syd Hurrell, both driving TR3s. Although Chris Lawrence had won by a convincing amount, he was helped in his rapid start by a 'gadget' that had been developed by his team of jet-engine-starter engineers. In order to facilitate a swift getaway from the Le Mans start they had devised a series of switches and relays that activated the starter as soon as the Morgan's door was opened, and then deactivated it as soon as the dynamo gave an output after the engine fired. They were 'found out' by the officials but they argued that there was nothing in the regulations that prohibited such a thing! Although the club placed 'no restrictions on modifications' the response must have been that this was taking things a bit too far. The Lawrence team sportingly agreed to remove the system for future races but a regulation was quickly written by the club to make sure!

Chris's second race that day was a five lap handicap, which he won convincingly, ahead of Paul Fletcher's MGA Twin-Cam and setting the fastest lap at 79.7 mph. TOK 258 made such an impression that a dramatic close-up shot of it at speed was used on the front cover of the following week's *Autosport*.

Also taking part in the ten lap Marque scratch race at Goodwood had been Bob Duggan in his Plus Four OYO 874. Bob had finished his National Service stint with the RAF and was now a bank clerk in Llandrindod Wells. His fitness from his military service meant he had been able to make an excellent Le Mans start, and he had really enjoyed the first part of the race. Inexperience however had led to him overheating the engine and running the big-end bearings. Syd Hurrell diagnosed the problem in the paddock and gave Bob a set of new bearings which he proceeded to fit that night in a Chichester hotel garage. The following morning he set off for Wales but only got a few miles, as far as Midhurst, before the oil pressure vanished again and he left the Morgan at a garage for an engine overhaul including a new TR3 crank. Bob returned to collect it a few weeks later, finding there was no operative clutch! He decided to drive back to mid-Wales without one, luckily arriving safely.

On Sunday March 15th the Falcon MC ran its March Hare Trial with various start line handicaps allowing anything from a trials special to a family saloon to compete with an equal chance of success. Jeff Bradford in his Plus Four did very well on several of the hills to lead the sports car class but then suffered severe penalties when the Morgan jumped out of gear on one hill, and also when he messed up a time control. This left victory to P G Gough's Morgan, despite him using standard tyres.

Ray Meredith's new Morgan was dispatched from the Morgan factory on Monday March 16th registered XOV 555. This red two-seater with black trim was fitted with wire wheels and front disc brakes, these brakes now being available as an option on new wire wheel Plus Fours only. Aluminium wings and bonnet were part of the specification, with the bonnet having a bulge to clear the front carburettor. Front shock absorbers with stronger setting were also part of the package and, as Ray was to use the Morgan for daily transport as well as race it, windscreen washers were fitted too, despite not being a legal requirement at this time. For some time Ray had been using a mechanic from the Regal Garage, a local Bromsgrove Ford agency, to work on his previous Morgan NAB 217. Fortunately this expert, 'Tommy' Thomas, was keen to help prepare the new Morgan for Ray's racing events, and at no charge.

On Sunday March 22nd TOK 258 was the only Morgan entered at Snetterton for the meeting organised by the Snetterton Motor Racing Club. Heavy rain was the order for much of the day, making the track extremely treacherous, and there were several incidents and accidents during practice and racing. Chris Lawrence had entered for the eight lap scratch race for Series Production and Grand Touring cars to Appendix J specification. Despite the dreadful weather Chris was reported in *Autosport* as driving 'indecently quickly' and came second in the 1,201 to 2,000cc class although the Morgan developed 'engine problems' on the last lap. The Morgan 'sadly went home on the end of a tow-bar'.

Also driving in this class was Richard Shepherd-Barron in an Alfa Romeo Giulietta Sprint Veloce

Horace and Hilda Roberts in their four-seater Plus Four climb Hustyn during the Land's End Trial. (Norman Miller)

and Bill Blydenstein in a Borgward Isabella TS. Eventually both drivers would be associated with Chris and his enterprises.

At this time Chris's Morgan was taken to events on a tow-bar behind a Commer van, which had originally belonged to the 'Wembley Collar Service', a shirt collar starching company, and one of the team would sit in the Morgan to steer. The Morgan would be detached from the tow-bar when about five miles from the circuit and driven in, allowing the car to be nicely warmed up for practice. The Commer had replaced the original Rolls-Royce and trailer as team transport. With the latter it had been a matter of luck who slept in the tents or the car when an overnight stay was needed, but in the Commer the narrow shelves became makeshift bunks. It was a step up in the racing world so with tongue in cheek Roland Smith had sign-written the unofficial team name 'Scuderia Corlookat Imscarpa' on the sides of the van!

Also on March 22nd the Hants and Dorset Car Club ran the Hartwell Cup Trial over a course in South Dorset, attracting forty cars to a mixture of driving tests and trials sections. Heavy overnight rain had made many of the sections very tricky but Tom Bryant in a Morgan did well enough to win the 'Best in Opposite Class Award', the winner being David Williams in a Ford Popular.

As usual the MCC's 39th Land's End Trial began on Good Friday, March 27th with starts at Kenilworth, London and Launceston, the routes converging in the early hours of Saturday at Taunton. This year there were just three Morgan four-wheelers entered amongst the 140 or so cars, but there were five Morgan three-wheelers entered this year! The four-wheeler entries consisted of Peter Morgan in TUY 875, Horace Roberts in WAB 779, and Jim Goodall in Peter Morgan's old Plus Four KUY 387. The programme gives the engine size of Jim's entry as 2088cc, indicating a Vanguard engine, and we wonder whether Jim had originally intended taking the coupé JNP 239, but had then been offered KUY 387 which had a TR engine. We believe Jim's usual car, HUY 982, was being completely rebuilt and updated at the factory at this time with a new chassis and new bodywork. The three Plus Fours formed the Morgan team. It proved to be an easy Land's End Trial this year and all three won First Class Awards. Horace Roberts had clipped two bars of lead onto the back axle casing with 'jubilee' clips and maybe this helped him with the four-seater. The lead was 'on loan'. He also had a hand throttle in his car, as did the other works cars.

The Scottish Sporting Car Club held the Highland Rally over Easter, starting from Glasgow on Good Friday and finishing 1,000 miles later on Sunday. There were ninety crews entered, and Pauline Mayman took the ladies' prize back with her to Birmingham.

It was a fine day at Brands Hatch on Easter Monday, March 30th for the first event of the season. The meeting was organised by the BRSCC and attracted a large crowd of spectators. Event 5 was a ten lap race for GT cars. Overall winner and also first in the over 1,600cc class was Jack Sears in his Austin Healey 100 Six but Chris Lawrence drove TOK 258 into overall second place, ahead of R A Gibson's Jaguar XK 140, and also put in the fastest lap at 66.23 mph. It was an excellent performance considering the conditions. Richard Shepherd-Barron in his Alfa Romeo Giulietta Sprint Veloce was fourth overall and came first in the up to 1,600cc class.

Also held on Easter Monday was a hill climb at Trengwainton. Jim Banbury was entered, but not in his Plus Four JJY 221. In February Jim had part exchanged this car for an AC engined AC Ace at Wessex Motors in Salisbury, having previously been impressed with the performance of an apparently similar car driven by Alistair Park on the hills. Unfortunately the AC proved slower at Trengwainton than the Plus Four and he failed to feature in the awards.

The next BARC Members' Meeting was at Mallory Park on Saturday April 4th. David Shale with his Austin Healey 100 Six wasn't contesting the series this year. Consequently the fastest half dozen cars lining up on the grid for the seven lap Marque scratch race were the two SAH TR3s of Roy North and Syd Hurrell, Bill de Selincourt's TR3, the AC Ace of Bob Staples, Colin Hextall's ex-Roy North TR2 (he was driving for SAH too) and TOK 258. It was an incredibly close race that was just won by Roy North followed by the others in the above order. In fact there was only 0.6 seconds between Roy North and Syd Hurrell, with Bill de Selincourt 0.2 seconds behind. Colin Hextall put in the fastest lap in his TR2, at 76.41 mph, but everyone was surprised at Chris Lawrence's disappointing sixth place. *Autosport* reported that the morning before the race there had been frantic activity in the paddock around the Morgan, with welding equipment in evidence. However, the *BARC Gazette* subsequently reported that his poor performance in the race was actually due to a leaking head gasket, although Chris

The Mallory Park paddock at the April BARC meeting. Alan Belcher is on the far right in front of VON 777 (32), with his mechanic Ron Timmins on the floor checking the front end. To the side of the car is Alan's wife Yvonne. Chris Lawrence wearing a bow tie, and Roland Smith wearing a cap, are examining an SU carburettor from TOK 258, the rear of which can just be seen. Car 33 is Bob Staples' AC Ace. (Alan Belcher collection)

remembers having problems with the carburettor float chamber mountings. Also competing in this race was Alan Belcher in VON 777, but he apparently hit trouble too and didn't finish in the places if he finished at all.

There were starts on Saturday evening from Maidstone, Brands Hatch and Manchester for the Maidstone and Mid Kent MC's National Hopper Rally, which finished early on Sunday morning at London Airport after 180 miles of night driving. The Manchester starters, which included Brian Harper, were disadvantaged by a re-route which considerably lengthened their journeys, but Brian still managed to finish second overall in WOF 559, just one point behind the winning Volvo.

That same Sunday the 750 Motor Club ran the second hill climb held at Blandford Camp in Dorset, using a modified version of the course used the previous year. In the class for sports cars over 1,500cc Tom Cunane's AC Bristol took the class, but Tom Bryant took second place in his Plus Four after an 'earnest experiment in practice with Cuckoo Corner', according to the *Autosport* reporter.

Over in America at the New York International Motor Show, held at the Coliseum between April 4th and 12th, a new British sports car was unveiled. It was the Daimler Dart SP 250, powered by a 2,547cc V8 engine designed by Edward Turner, and producing 140 bhp at 5,800 rpm. In England enthusiasts waited to see how well it would perform on the track.

There was good news in Great Britain too, for the Chancellor of the Exchequer had announced that from April the Purchase Tax on new cars would drop from a punitive 60% to a more acceptable 50%. There was even better news for commercial vehicle purchasers, for the current rate of 30% (half that on new cars) was now abolished completely.

The Birmingham Post National Rally, organised by the MAC, took its usual format of a start from the Civic Centre car park in Birmingham one Friday evening, taking the competitors on a 400 mile journey into Wales overnight and finishing at Bromsgrove the following afternoon. As usual the driver and navigator were handed the first route card, together with the relevant map references, just as they were started and had no time to plot a route before departure. There was as always a good showing of Morgans for this event, which began on Friday April 10th, with no less than five being entered in Class E, for Grand Touring cars over 1,600cc. There was also a Morgan team, comprising Les Yarranton (presumably in PUY 306), Peter Morgan and Jim Goodall, whilst in addition Brian Harper was entered in WOF 559 navigated by Ron Crellin, and Pauline Mayman was in EPM 324 navigated by Val Domleo. At the breakfast stop Peter Morgan, Jim Goodall and Pauline Mayman were all unpenalised, and Jim went on to make no mistakes whatsoever and win his class. Indeed he only missed an outright win by 0.8 seconds! Pauline Mayman also did well to finish third in this class, whilst Brian Harper was fourth. Pauline and Val also collected the Regent Trophy for the best performance by an all ladies crew whilst the Morgan team also won the team prize. It had been another good showing in this Rally by the Morgans.

On Tuesday April 21st Horace Roberts returned his Morgan Plus Four four-seater WAB 779 to the Morgan factory's repair shop once again, this time to have disc brakes fitted to the front wheels, to also have damaged floor boards replaced (the result of trials damage) and for a steering wobble to be corrected. Horace had now covered just over 3,400 miles in this car.

The BARC Members' Meeting on Saturday 25th April at Goodwood saw a return to winter weather, with cold temperatures, incessant rain and strong winds. Nevertheless, in the ten lap Marque scratch race Bill de Selincourt and Syd Hurrell in their TR3s and Chris Lawrence with TOK 258 made the best of the Le Mans start, Bill leading Chris who led Syd. They stayed in those places, only a few lengths apart from one another until virtually the end of the race when Syd was held up whilst lapping the rest of the field. Bill de Selincourt actually lapped the eighth placed man as he took the chequered flag for victory.

Brian Harper sets off on the Birmingham Post Rally. Note the extra lights and the electric demister on the inside of the Morgan's windscreen. (Birmingham Post and Mail)

Chris Lawrence's fine drive into second place had seen him record the fastest lap at 75.13mph. Also running, in OYO 874, was Bob Duggan. Bob had learnt the hazards of overheating engine oil and now had a large oil cooler fitted. Unfortunately he retired.

Another Morgan returning to the Morgan factory repair shop was XOV 555, Ray Meredith's Plus Four. On Wednesday April 29th a new radiator was fitted, together with a Derrington exhaust system. The Morgan had covered just under 2,000 miles.

Bob Duggan was to invest in an exchange Derrington gas flowed TR2 head around this time, fitting a pair of SU H6 carburettors too. The SU Company let Bob have a selection of needles with which to experiment. The fan blades were removed, as was the thermostat. Bob made a lightweight but not particularly attractive bonnet in aluminium to save weight and continued this theme with the fitting of an alloy driver's seat. The ash frame of the body was also liberally drilled with 0.75 inch holes, causing quite a stir amongst the mechanics at the Morgan factory with whom he had become friendly. He also got to know Peter Morgan and Jim Goodall well during these factory visits.

Robin Brown was keen to upgrade his Plus Four UOL 490 to disc brakes so he wrote to Peter Morgan on Thursday April 30th inquiring if this was possible on disc wheeled Plus Fours. Peter replied on the following Monday to explain that although the prototype disc brake layout had been assembled on a car with disc wheels there were problems because of reduced clearance with this type of hub and wheel. Only two sets of the new suitable hubs had been obtained from the Company's malleable casters. He offered to let Robin know when the conversion would be possible. Robin had discovered that the standard drum brakes faded badly after five laps of racing, so he decided meanwhile to restrict his entries to races of no more than five laps!

The British Racing Drivers' Club's prestigious International Trophy meeting held at Silverstone on Saturday 2nd May saw the debut of the short lived, front engined Formula 1 Aston Martins, but Jack Brabham showed the way forward by winning the main race in his rear engined Cooper Climax.

The meeting started, however, with a high profile twelve lap race for Grand Touring cars and both Chris Lawrence and Alan Belcher entered their Plus 4s TOK 258 and VON 777 in the 1,601 to 2,600cc class, running as required in closed trim. Stirling Moss, who was to drive a BRM in the main race, took an immediate lead in the Aston Martin DB4, closely followed by Roy Salvadori in John Coombs' 3.4 Jaguar. Colin Chapman's Lotus Elite, in third position, was soon overtaken by Jack Sears in his Healey 100 Six. Chris Lawrence started well and had a fine dice with Colin Chapman and three other Lotuses but had to let them all through, eventually finishing in a still creditable eighth place overall. Stirling Moss won the race, some fifteen seconds ahead of Roy Salvadori, and setting a class lap record of 1 minute 58.8 seconds in the process.

In the 1,601cc to 2,600cc class Chris Lawrence came first and made the fastest lap of 2 minutes 6 seconds (83.63 mph) whilst Alan Belcher had his own battle close behind a couple of MGs and a Porsche Carerra but came home third in class behind Roy North's TR3. Chris Lawrence's lap time was a new class record for Grand Touring cars on the Grand Prix circuit.

On Sunday May 3rd the Bugatti Owners' Club ran its seventeenth National hill climb at Prescott, unfortunately in drizzling rain for most of the day. Two Morgans took part in Class 1C, for sports cars from 1,601 to 3,000cc, Robin Brown in UOL 490 beating Ray Meredith in XOV 555 by just 0.02 seconds when he recorded 56.49 seconds.

There were over 110 starters on Friday May 8th for this year's Morecambe Rally. The routes from the starting points at Glasgow, Buxton, Morecambe, Luton and Pontefract converged at Copster Green in Lancashire for the common 200 mile overnight special section. This covered the counties of Yorkshire, West Cumberland and Lancashire. After arriving in Morecambe the following morning there were the traditional driving tests on the promenade to conclude the event. The event was won by John Sprinzel in a Speedwell modified Austin Healey Sprite, navigated by Stuart Turner. This year the Morgans were out of the awards, but Dr E J Townsend did make the fastest time in the famous 'Monte Morecambe' final test. Dr Townsend was from Newark in Nottinghamshire, and he had purchased his 4/4, chassis number A220, from the Nottingham agency Bennetts, on September 4th 1956.

The second round of the Autosport Championship was held at Silverstone on Saturday

Alan Belcher in VON 777 races with hood erect to comply with the 'closed' rules during the International meeting at Silverstone, and leads a Turner. (Charles Dunn)

Robin Brown at a damp Prescott in his Plus Four. (Robin Brown collection)

May 9th by the Maidstone and Mid-Kent Motor Club. There were two separate twenty lap races, the first being for Classes A, B and C, whilst the second was for the larger engined sports cars of Classes D and E, and Alan Belcher took part with VON 777. From the flag the 4.4 litre Chevrolet

The grid for the second round of the Autosport Championship, during the Maidstone and Mid-Kent MC meeting at Silverstone. The rear end of Alan Belcher's Morgan VON 777 is visible showing the twin fuel fillers, one to each of the two special fuel tanks, and the recessed and enclosed area for the spare wheel with the fibreglass cover made by Ron Timmins. On the front row, second from the left, is the Chevrolet Corvette of Sir Gawaine Baillie which won the race. (Alan Belcher collection)

Corvette driven by Sir Gawaine Baillie took a lead it never relinquished, whilst three Bristol engined cars, a Frazer Nash and two AC Bristols, took the first three places in Class D. Scoring his first points in the championship, with three points for fourth place in Class D, was Alan Belcher.

The British Racing and Sports Car Club's meeting at Brands Hatch on Sunday May 10th was blessed with perfect weather giving an excellent day's sport. Chris Lawrence had a runaway victory in TOK 258 in the 'marque' race for production sports cars. He was followed by Roy North in his TR3 who couldn't get close enough to seriously challenge him. Chris was beginning to dominate this type of racing.

The Whit Monday BARC meeting at Goodwood on May 18th, held in perfect weather, saw Chris Lawrence entered in two exciting races against his closest rivals. Front disc brakes had recently been fitted to TOK 258 but it still retained the original bolt-on wheels. Whether this was using newly developed Morgan factory hub castings, or whether Chris had adapted his own, we cannot be certain. In the fourth event, a ten lap Marque sports cars scratch race, Chris made his usual rapid start and raced into the lead, with Bill de Selincourt's TR3 and Alan Foster's MGA Twin-Cam chasing after him, followed by Syd Hurrell's TR3. Syd Hurrell fought his way past the MG and then Bill's TR3, and took the lead from Chris Lawrence on the inside at Fordwater and there then followed a tremendous dice between Chris and the two TR3s. On lap 7 Bill de Selincourt finally squeezed past Chris, but the battle was not over and Chris retook second place going into Woodcote Corner on lap 9. On the very last lap Syd Hurrell fell back and it was Chris Lawrence who took the flag just ahead of Bill de Selincourt. Syd Hurrell's fan belt had failed and he had switched off the engine as the water temperature rose. Nevertheless he coasted over the line to take third place just ahead of the MGA.

The last event of the day was the Second Whitsun Handicap, which saw Chris Lawrence, Bill de Selincourt and Syd Hurrell in his repaired TR3 move quickly through the field. They were unable to catch the winning MGA Twin-Cam of Paul Fletcher but Bill de Selincourt came in second with Chris Lawrence close behind, the Morgan and the TR sharing the fastest lap in the process.

That same day the third round of the Autosport Series-Production Sports Car Championship was being contested at the Nottingham Sports Car Club's meeting at Mallory Park. The twenty lap race for Classes D and E was won by Dick Potheroe's Jaguar XK120, but second in Class D behind a Frazer Nash was Alan Belcher in VON 777, beating an AC Bristol.

VON 777 was going really well now in this difficult championship, the Bristol engined cars usually having the edge. Ron Timmins had been gradually raising the compression of the TR engine, and spent much time 'fettling' SU carburettor needles. He claimed 6,800 rpm was possible with this engine, and he always ran the SUs without the carburettor dampers for better breathing. As VON 777 was purely used for racing it was trailered to meetings, and Ron was busy working on the Morgan most evenings and weekends. The special drum brakes had been a notable success, lasting a whole season on one set of linings. The crank was to be changed for each season, a major expense, but failure to do this had resulted in a broken crank on the first race of the new season.

On a warm sunny Saturday May 23rd the Aston Martin Owners' Club ran its annual National race meeting at Silverstone which included the 200 mile team relay race for the David Brown Challenge Cup. This year somewhat surprisingly there was no Morgan 4/4 Club entry for the relay race, the two Morgans entered at the race meeting having to be satisfied with just entering Race 3. This was a five lap scratch race, with an additional handicap, for ACs, Bentleys, Coopers, Austin Healey 100s and Sprites, Morgans, TRs and VWs. Alan Belcher was entered in VON 777, and Ray Meredith in XOV 555. From the start A Searle's AC Bristol built up an unassailable lead, with Bill de Selincourt's TR3 some distance behind in second spot. On lap 2 Alan Belcher took third position from Bob Staples' AC Ace, which had a rather special 'works' cylinder head, and Alan went on to finish third after an excellent drive, keeping ahead of all the other Bristol engined ACs. When the handicaps were taken into account it was an Austin Healey that took first place, with Alan again being third behind Bill de Selincourt's TR3. VON 777 had had another good meeting.

That same Saturday the Westmorland Motor Club ran its main event of the year, a hill climb at Barbon. The hot weather brought a lot of entries and spectators, and control of the latter gave rise to concern, with some small children crossing the track at will just after the finish. Peter Bradley won the sports cars up to 2,000cc class with a remarkable 34.31 seconds for the half mile course, beating all the cars in the next class up. Peter's Plus Four 9267 U was now going really well, being suited to his aggressive style of driving. The engine was fitted with a Barwell cylinder head, an American Iskenderian camshaft and a Derrington manifold for extra performance.

The Stafford and District Car Club ran its Stafford Rally over the weekend of Saturday May 23rd and Sunday May 24th attracting 37 local starters. Finishing in fifth place was Brian Harper in WOF 559.

At the next BARC Goodwood meeting, held on Saturday June 6th, Chris Lawrence led all the way in the ten lap Marque scratch race in TOK 258. The TR3s of Bill de Selincourt and Syd Hurrell came second and third respectively, nearly eight seconds behind the Morgan, which had lapped at 81.36 mph. This meant that Chris and Bill now shared the lead for the Freddie Dixon Trophy with fourteen points each, just one point ahead of Syd Hurrell. Bill de Selincourt and Chris Lawrence had become good friends but so close and keenly fought was the Freddie Dixon contest that Bill dare not miss a race in case Chris got ahead. Bill had agreed to drive an MGA at the Nurburgring this weekend so after he had practised in the MG he had flown back to England to race his TR3 and his new Lotus Eleven at Goodwood, then had flown back to Germany to race the MG on the Sunday!

For this meeting TOK 258 was running with two silencers (a similar system had been used on the AFM), as experiments with the exhaust system continued. Each modification to the engine induction was matched by a modification to the exhaust to maximise the mid range torque, which was the strong point of the TR engine. Different exhaust pipe lengths, diameters and both twin and single silencer set-ups were all tried, although it would be found later on that exhaust tuning was more critical with Webers than with the SUs.

Following the work during the winter Chris and his helpers continued to try new ideas throughout the season, including different spark plugs and different jets for the carburettors. They had changed from the 1.5 inch SU H4s to the 1.75 inch H6s when the ever helpful SU agents, WHM Burgess, supplied them with a special inlet manifold for the TR2 cylinder head. Work continued in the search for more performance as they then went on to develop the TR3 cylinder head for TOK. Len Bridge told us that maintaining the correct fuel mixture to get the most power provided a constant challenge. The neoprene grommets on each float chamber mounting on the H6s insulated the chambers from engine vibration that would otherwise cause the fuel to 'froth' and weaken the mixture. However, as the team had found to their cost at Mallory Park, the grommets could deteriorate and consequently needed changing regularly. To prevent fuel starvation under racing conditions a pressure control valve and Jaguar specification electric SU pumps were experimented with to boost the AC mechanical pump.

HFS Morgan always enjoyed seeing his considerable family. On Friday June 12th he drove over to the Morgan factory in his blue Plus Four four-seater coupé, MAB 696, from his home at Oakwood, Cannon Hill near Maidenhead and then went to spend the weekend with his son and daughter-in-law Peter and Jane at Braeside, Wyche Road in Malvern. Their children were coming home from school this weekend and he wanted to see them. On the Saturday morning however all was not well with HFS at breakfast, for he found he was unable to speak. Peter decided he ought to stay with his father so Jane went and collected her daughters alone. Sadly HFS was developing a stroke, and he passed away peacefully at Braeside on the Monday, June 15th. His passing at the age of 77 was a major loss not only for the Morgan family, but also for the Morgan factory workforce, many of whom had been with him from the early days, and for his many friends in the motor trade.

His long-standing friend and colleague Harry Jones sent out a short letter to all the Morgan agents and other business friends on Tuesday June 16th. It read:

Dear Sirs, It is with regret that we advise you of the death of Mr H F S Morgan on 15th June 1959. A Memorial Service will be held at Stoke Lacey Church, near Bromyard, Herefordshire, at 3pm on Friday 19th June 1959.
Flowers to Mr A P Russell, Funeral Director, Malvern Link.
Yours faithfully,
Morgan Motor Co Ltd.

The memorial service was to follow a private cremation.

In his will HFS left the 'avowson' of Stoke Lacey to his son Peter, and the residue of his estate was divided, with Peter having two parts to each daughter's one. HFS had written, 'I bequeath to my son, Peter, rather more than his sisters, as he has the trouble and worry of running my old business (now under the control of my family), which may have to be sold owing to the increasing difficulty of running a private business'. Several years earlier, after he had reached the age of 70, HFS had transferred ownership of the Morgan Motor Company to his children in a Deed of Trust which was implemented as from February 1952. The Trustees were Peter Morgan and Major Kendall. Peter Morgan told us that his relationship with his father had been more like that with an older brother rather than a father. Peter had always told him everything and held no secrets from him.

He was to miss him greatly. Whenever HFS had visited Peter in his office at the factory he had enjoyed a cigarette with him, and biscuits, which HFS kept for the purpose in the bottom drawer of a desk in Peter's office. HFS was a trained draughtsman, and had done many of the Morgan drawings at his home, reducing the frequency of his visits to the Malvern factory in the recent years. Peter Morgan remembered his son Charles asking him why he used a pair of compasses for works drawings, when his grandfather preferred to draw curves freehand!

Charles Morgan remembers that on the day his grandfather died he was taken outside and it was explained that his grandfather would not be coming back any more. Although HFS had a reputation for being shy this was not true for his family and especially the grandchildren. Visits to Oakwood had always been exciting for Charles because HFS was brilliant with children. Charles would run up the stairs to 'his' room on arrival because his grandfather always put some new Dinky toys in a drawer in the room for him. He also had an amazing collection of bigger toys available for the children, many of which he had made himself, such as a tandem pedal car. He drove his blue Morgan coupé at amazing speeds according to Charles, and would race anything. He had lived his life as a great adventure. One thing Charles didn't like was HFS' breakfast, just bread and milk!

HFS Morgan had been a great engineer, whose philosophy had always been to produce simple yet effective cars that appealed to the sporting motorist. Above all they were cheaper than their competitors and gave better performance because they always had a high power to weight ratio. HFS had only ever really used two chassis types, both of which were originally used for three-wheelers. Although four-wheeled versions of the earlier V-twin chassis were built they were not proceeded with, but the four cylinder Ford engined F-Type three-wheeler chassis did evolve into the successful 4/4 and Plus Four four-wheeler version. HFS's simple designs were amenable to his factory's traditional production methods, and each chassis style was constructed so that it could easily be fitted with different body styles and seating arrangements to capture an adequate public market. HFS always liked to try different bodies on the same chassis to achieve the greatest customer appeal.

A newspaper from the Maidenhead area (sadly not identifiable) in its obituary on HFS summed him up thus: 'His trips into town in recent years were made in his little blue Morgan four-wheeler. He was of a shy and retiring nature, his absorbing interests being his family and his business.'

On Sunday June 14th, whilst the sad events were unfolding at Braeside, the competitors at Shelsley Walsh were blissfully unaware of these goings on and concentrated instead on getting up the hill as quickly as possible. Three Plus Fours were entered, those of Peter Bradley, Ray Meredith and a Mr R Soans. Peter Bradley was the best by far in 9267 U, with a second run of 44.53 seconds, Soans being 3.5 seconds slower. Ray Meredith had a dreadful day in XOV 555, only managing one run in a time of 60.32 seconds. As usual the Bristol engined sports cars took the class trophies. Ray had a 'moment' at the esses when the Morgan climbed the outside bank, but luckily returned to earth on its four wheels. The following day XOV 555 was taken to the Morgan factory repair shop, where a new frame front was required!

By June, after completing three hill climbs at slower speeds in his AC Ace than previously achieved with the Plus Four, Jim Banbury had realised he had made a mistake in part-exchanging his Morgan in February. Consequently he returned to Wessex Motors in Salisbury where the deal had been done, and managed to buy back his old Morgan, JJY 221, the unscrambling of the deal costing him £50.0.0. He had entered the inter-club team hill climb event to be held at Brunton on Sunday June 21st as part of the Morgan 4/4 Club team.

The BARC meeting held at Aintree on Saturday June 20th was conducted in a tropical heat wave. In the ten lap Marque scratch race Chris Lawrence again had a runaway victory in TOK 258, some nine seconds ahead of Bill de Selincourt, and he also recorded the fastest lap at 75.69 mph. Earlier in the meeting, Les Fagg, one of Chris Lawrence's team of helpers, achieved a fine third place with the Morgan in the second of three seven lap sports car handicap races.

Fred Lockwood, the Canadian owner of NAB 217, was now working for the Rootes Group in Coventry and had decided to further prepare the Plus Four for motor racing. He was sharing digs with Peter Marten, a new Rootes apprentice who worked in the Engine Test Department and who also owned a Morgan. Peter had recently left the Army where he had managed to damage the top of the chrome radiator on his early Vanguard engined four-seater NLY 723 after losing a bet that he could fold flat the windscreen and drive under the barrier at the barracks! He had improved his high speed driving skills in the Morgan when stationed in Cumbria by trying to beat his personal record each time he made the late-night return journey from leave in London via the A1 trunk road and the Yorkshire Dales. Peter came from a racing background, his father having raced an MG Midget at Brooklands, so the two Morgan enthusiasts worked many late evenings together on Fred's car. Unfortunately in June the engine broke a connecting rod during testing, so Peter took over the entry for the Midland Motor Enthusiasts' Meeting at Silverstone on Saturday June 20th in his own road-going Morgan. He had a good race but finished down the field. Meanwhile, Fred frantically finished-off the engine rebuild for Brunton on the Sunday.

As mentioned, it was on Sunday June 21st that the South Western Centre of the BARC ran the fourth of its inter-club team hill climbs at Brunton. The Morgan 4/4 Club's team consisted of the Plus Fours of Fred Lockwood

Sandy Blair in Nixie, with tuned TR3 engine, competing at the inter-club team hill climb at Brunton. (Charles Dunn)

(NAB 217), Jim Banbury back in JJY 221, and Sandy Blair in Nixie. Jim and Sandy were closely matched, just 0.13 seconds separating their best runs, with Fred two seconds slower, but then he had only just rebuilt the engine. The club finished in eleventh place.

The Plymouth MC's Plymouth Rally began on Friday June 26th from starts at Plymouth, Bristol, Birmingham, Southampton or London, the routes then converging at Haldon for a 'Northern Section' followed later by an 'Eastern Section'. The drivers then made for Plymouth for the final driving tests. Brian Harper and Ron Crellin took part in WOF 559, and finished in the winning Shenstone and District Car Club team.

Brian Harper and Ron Crellin during a driving test on Plymouth Hoe at the end of the Plymouth Rally. (S A Wightman)

The start of the MCC high speed trial. Horace Roberts in his white Morgan is following a Peerless GT, also Triumph powered, whilst Bob Duggan follows a Lotus. (James Brymer)

Brian had made several visits to see Peter Morgan at the Morgan factory during 1959 to personalise an order for a new Plus Four two-seater. Being somewhat tall and lanky Brian had asked Peter if the seat back could be made thinner to give more room for his long legs. Peter took him to meet Bert Gulliver, the foreman of the trim shop, who 'hummed and hawed' thinking it unlikely it could be done, but eventually it was. Bert Gulliver had been at the Morgan factory since 1916, having learnt his craft on horse drawn carriages. This wire wheeled Plus Four, chassis number 4265, was painted red, a colour Brian had now decided was lucky for him, and fitted with disc brakes, a heater and a Brooklands steering wheel. It was to be dispatched on Thursday July 16th to Hunts (Birmingham) Ltd and registered YOM 798.

On Saturday June 27th the BARC was back at Goodwood for its 38th Members' Meeting. There was another easy win for Chris Lawrence in TOK 258 in the ten lap Marque scratch race, the press remarking how the Morgan had been very fast and well driven. Syd Hurrell came second in the TR3 but had been challenged briefly by Bill de Selincourt who had been trying a bit too hard, spinning off in his TR3 and then retiring, allowing Alan Foster in one of Dick Jacobs' MGA Twin-Cams to take third place.

The Motor Cycling Club ran its tenth annual Silverstone race meeting the same day. As usual it catered for cars and motorcycles with the traditional high speed trials as well as some scratch and handicap races. There were three Plus Fours entered. Horace Roberts had entered his four-seater WAB 779 and we wonder whether the engine had now been fitted with the balanced Laystall crank it was to receive courtesy of Basil de Mattos, a manager for that company who was also a keen MCC trials enthusiast. Representing the Morgan factory was Jim Goodall in HUY 982, which had by now received a major updating including a body to current two-seater Plus Four specification. The third Plus Four was Bob Duggan in OYO 874. MCC events were all about having fun and we expect plenty was had by all. All three Morgans managed to complete nineteen laps in the high speed trial to win First Class Awards, but they didn't feature in the prizes for the races.

Also held that same Saturday was a Restricted speed hill climb at Castle Howard in Yorkshire using the estate roads and main drive of the

Peter Bradley impresses at Castle Howard. (John Holroyd)

eighteenth century stately home. The event was run jointly by the Yorkshire Sports Car Club, the Yorkshire Centre of the BARC and the East Yorkshire Car Club. Fastest in the class for sports cars up to 2,700cc was Peter Bradley with his very quick Plus Four 9267 U. Winning the class for Touring cars up to 1,300cc was a mop salesman named Brian Redman, then beginning his motor racing career with a supercharged Morris Minor.

On Sunday June 28th Jim Banbury was at Wiscombe Hill Climb near Honiton in Devon, with JJY 221. The meeting had a full programme and he was listed as a reserve, but he did get to run, coming home second in the class for sports cars under 2,000cc behind Searle's AC Bristol. Also entered in a Plus Four was Tom Bryant, but he was over two seconds slower than Jim. This hill climb was held along the drive to the house of Major Richard Chichester, and the very first event there had been held in August 1958. It was quickly to become a very popular venue.

The British Racing and Sports Car Club (BRSCC) ran an excellent race meeting at Mallory Park that same Sunday and included in the programme was the fifth round of the Autosport Series-Production Sports Car Championship. There were three twenty-lap races as part of this, the first for Class A, the second for Classes B and C, and the third for Classes D and E. Included in the latter race was Alan Belcher in VON 777. The track was very wet for the start but gradually dried as the event continued, and Alan finished in an excellent third place behind Dickie Stoop and John Tallis in Bristol engined Frazer Nash models. Alan managed to stay ahead of John Mitchell's AC Bristol after a fine scrap.

The Mid-Cheshire Motor Club ran its Oulton Park meeting on Saturday July 11th on a dull and rainy day. The event started with a half-hour high speed trial, and the poor conditions only allowed one competitor to qualify. He was Alan Belcher in VON 777, and he covered thirteen laps of the wet track at 71.59 mph.

That same Saturday at Goodwood, where the BARC was running its 37th Members' Meeting, the weather was better. Chris Lawrence made the headlines again by winning the ten lap Marque scratch race in TOK 258, his only challenge being by Bill de Selincourt who finished second in his lightweight and special bodied TR3. Syd Hurrell's TR3 had been stranded at the Le Mans start when it refused to fire, but after a delay he stormed through the field to take a well deserved fourth place, although unable to get close to the leaders, whilst Chris Lawrence set the fastest lap at 81.36 mph. Two races later Chris was back in action, but this time driving a Lotus Eleven (probably lent to him by Bill de Selincourt), in the five lap scratch race for sports cars up to 1,500cc. Unfortunately he left the track at Lavant on the first lap!

The Morgan board met on Tuesday July 21st. Just four directors were present: Peter Morgan, George Goodall, Harry Jones and Major Kendall. After a short tribute to HFS Morgan, it was unanimously agreed that Peter Morgan should succeed his father as the new Company Chairman.

Two-seater Plus Four models were now leaving the factory with new cranked windscreen brackets, the first, chassis number 4277, going through its pre-dispatch tests that same week.

The BARC North Western Centre held a sprint meeting at Aintree on Saturday July 25th attracting sixty or so competitors, one of which was Peter Bradley with 9267 U. He didn't disappoint and took the class for sports cars from 1,501 to 2,700cc, even beating a Cooper Bristol by 0.6 seconds, with a time of 32.0 seconds for the half mile course.

On Sunday July 26th the Bugatti Owners' Club ran its eighth Inter-Club Challenge Trophy hill climb at Prescott. As usual the morning was devoted to individual competition, with the afternoon being for the handicap team competition for club teams of three cars. There was only one team featuring Morgans this year, that of the Morgan 4/4 Club. In the morning session the fastest Plus Four was UOL 490, driven by Robin Brown with a time of 51.00 seconds. Barrie Phipps recorded 51.49 seconds

Chris Lawrence at Goodwood, winning as usual. Note the unusual silencers. (LAT Photographic)

in JNV 654; Ray Meredith recorded 52.54 seconds with XOV 555, whilst Richard Cashmore managed 54.40 seconds with RC 30. In the team competition during the afternoon the handicap defeated the three Morgans of Barrie, Ray and Robin.

The Snetterton Motor Racing Club's meeting at Snetterton on Sunday July 26th contained a round of the Autosport Championship. Alan Belcher took part with VON 777, and was going well until the last lap when he was forced to retire. His mechanic, Ron Timmins, didn't like the Snetterton circuit, finding the long straight difficult to gear for and likely to cause a rod to give way when racing hard. Perhaps that is what happened here.

The August Bank Holiday BRSCC meeting held on Monday August 3rd at Brands Hatch attracted a crowd estimated at 50,000 to watch an excellent day's racing which included two Autosport Championship races. Chris Lawrence had previously been concentrating on the BARC championship races so this was his first race in this series. TOK 258 had by now been converted to wire wheels, and ran with full windscreen and a new hardtop. The latter had been made by taking a production TR2 fibreglass hardtop and removing two inches or so from the centre of the roof. It was then rejoined with an aluminium strip that was laminated over. This was then fixed to a purpose-built rear section, fabricated from aluminium sheet and Perspex that wrapped around to the sides.

Classes D and E of the championship were combined into one race, with only five starters, just two being from Class D. These two were Chris Lawrence in TOK 258 and Bob Staples in his AC Ace. Chris found himself competing against Sir Gawaine Baillie's Chevrolet Corvette, Dick Protheroe's Jaguar XK120 and Jack Sears in an Austin Healey 3000 from Class E. Chris shot into a commanding lead, with the Corvette and Austin Healey behind but not able to make a serious challenge. Eventually Dick Protheroe's Jaguar XK120, which had made a hesitant start, took the Austin Healey and then finally passed the 'very wide' Corvette on the tenth lap at Druids. He set off after Chris and finally passed him for the lead on the sixteenth lap of the twenty lap race. *Autosport* reported TOK 258 as having, 'lost the edge off its brakes'. However a second place overall and a first in class was an excellent result. Afterwards, the petrol company ESSO carried a typical full page advertisement in the motoring press proudly announcing that all the successful cars had achieved their results on Golden ESSO pump fuel. Sponsorship from major companies was fairly low key in those days, being mainly in the form of occasional free spark plugs, free oil and fuel etc dispensed in the paddock, in return for publicity gained from winning cars in the high profile events. It was no wonder that most racing car transporters in those days were fitted with petrol engines rather than diesel, to make use of the free fuel on offer! When Chris became successful in the Morgan he also received a retainer from ESSO and some support from Dunlop. Richard Shepherd-Barron made the most of his Alfa Romeo successes by negotiating a fee from each of several companies to advertise their products on the sides of the tuned Austin A35 van that carried his racing spares and was also his everyday transport!

The Austin Healey 3000 model raced by Jack Sears was brand new, having just been announced in the press in July. It differed from the previous 100 Six in that the six cylinder engine had been redesigned and bored out to 2,912cc, giving 124 bhp and much improved torque. It was also fitted with Girling type 14 front disc brakes, the same as those fitted to the Plus Four.

The Taunton Motor Club ran an autocross on Bank Holiday Monday at Walford Cross. The master, as in the previous year, proved to be Tom Bryant in a Plus Four, for he made the second fastest time of the day overall and took the class for sports cars over 1,500cc by a clear second.

On Saturday August 8th the BARC visited Oulton Park for the first time and the ten lap Marque scratch race once again provided a close

Richard Shepherd-Barron stands between his Alfa Romeo Giulietta Sprint Veloce and his 'souped-up' Austin A35 van, at Spa in 1960. (Richard Shepherd-Barron collection)

one-two-three for Chris Lawrence, Bill de Selincourt and Syd Hurrell. So close was Bill's second-placed TR3 to TOK 258 that, not for the first time, they both shared the fastest lap time, Chris being just two seconds ahead at the flag.

The following day the West Essex Car Club ran a Restricted race meeting at Snetterton, but on the programme were two ten lap races for the Autosport Championship. The second of these was for Classes D and E, but the only Morgan entered was TOK 258, driven by Les Fagg, who was not eligible for championship points as he hadn't entered the competition. He didn't finish in the first three places.

On Saturday August 15th the 750 Motor Club ran its National Six Hour Relay Race at Silverstone. This year the club was forced to use the 1.6 mile Club circuit rather than the traditional 2.5 miles Holland Birkett circuit. After just failing to win this event in 1958 the Morgan 4/4 Club had made a special effort this year to try and win it, and the club was supported in its effort by the Morgan factory. Its strong team consisted of Alan Belcher in VON 777 as the 'A' car, Sandy Blair in Nixie as the 'B' car, Ray Meredith in XOV 555 as the 'C' car, Peter Morgan in TUY 875 as the 'D' car, Jim Goodall in HUY 982 as the 'E' car and finally Chris Lawrence in TOK 258 as the 'F' car. The team manager was Robin Brown, and the team, known as the 'Morgan Plus Four Team', was given twenty credit laps over the scratch team of Jaguars. There were twenty-two teams entered. Practice unfortunately resulted in Sandy's car running the big-end bearings, so the Morgan factory mechanics in attendance changed them and it was decided he would only run if disaster struck the others. He spent the race running in the new bearings on the inner roads of the Silverstone track. The fastest drivers in practice had been Chris Lawrence and Alan Belcher, and it was decided that they would therefore drive the major share of the race in a 'do or die' approach to winning it.

Chris Lawrence had a reputation for quick starts from Le Mans grids, so Robin gave him the honour of the first stint and at the 1pm start he was actually the first car away. At the end of the first lap Chris was running second and after 30 minutes of racing the Morgan team was in sixth position. Chris was really racing hard rather than sticking to consistent lapping. At 2 pm the team was up to fourth and Alan Belcher was now lapping very neatly. By 2.30 pm the team was in third place, and by 3pm the team was second behind a team of Fairthorpe Electrons. Strong performances by the Morgan team drivers brought the team into the lead by 4.30 pm, but they were now being challenged by the 'TR Team' (3 TR3s and 2 Peerless GTs). By 6.15 pm Syd Hurrell in his TR3 was challenging the Morgan of Chris Lawrence, who was doing the final session for his team. Syd began to close and the final few laps became very exciting, although the Morgan team believed that the commentator's lap scorers, who had the TR Team on the same lap as the Morgans, were wrong and that the Morgan team was actually a lap or two ahead. Chris Lawrence refused to be caught however and crossed the line ahead of Syd Hurrell to take a well deserved Morgan Plus Four Team victory.

The team cars were then lined up alongside each other and the journalists took many photographs of the victorious team, the drivers adorned with laurel victory wreaths. Sandy Blair was included, but always felt he shouldn't really have been in the line as he hadn't driven in the race. The event had provided a rare opportunity for Chris Lawrence to see Peter Morgan race, and recently Chris told us how impressed he was with Peter's driving on the track. Chris noted that through skilful driving Peter was able to turn in consistently fast lap times in a Morgan that wasn't nearly as highly tuned as TOK!

Alan Belcher had made a major contribution to the success, his excellent consistent driving impressing the reporters. Alan had a weak right hand as a result of a motorcycle injury sustained many years previously. It began to be very painful and difficult to use following the strain of the many hours of racing and he eventually resorted to putting his right elbow through the spokes of the steering wheel to hold it steady whilst he changed gear. He thought back to the great driver Archie Scott-Brown, who had a mal-developed right hand but had still driven amazingly well, and Alan decided if Archie was able to do it then he too would carry on regardless.

After the event Alan mentioned to Peter Morgan how important his car's preparation had been to the Morgan team's success, suggesting his mechanic Ron Timmins deserved special praise. Ron himself had been amazed but delighted that the Morgan had lasted so long at racing speeds.

Jim Goodall returns to the pits, having just handed over the team sash to Robin Brown (also holding his hat!) who is on his way to transfer it to Alan Belcher waiting in the white Morgan, VON 777. Note too the updated bodywork on Jim's car, HUY 982. '7A' is the Jaguar XK120 of C Clairmonte. (Robin Brown collection)

Chris Lawrence in front at Crystal Palace, leading Bill de Selincourt's much modified TR3. (LAT Photographic)

When the 750 Motor Club finally checked the lap charts it was discovered that the Morgan Plus Four Team had actually beaten the TR Team by three clear laps, vindicating the Morgan team's own lap scoring of the event.

Immediately after the race Peter Morgan drove his Morgan to Cornwall to rejoin the family in their holiday home 'Pentewan' at Polzeath. His young son Charles was most impressed with the laurel garland, which he still remembers Peter bringing with him. It was Jane Morgan who had bought this cottage, possibly in 1958, and she was to take her family there annually for the whole of August, Peter joining as and when business permitted. Charles believes it was an excellent break from the stress of running the business for his father. Previous holidays had been usually spent caravanning.

That same Saturday the Bolton-le-Moors Car Club National Rally began from evening starts at Bolton, Stoke-on-Trent and London, finishing the following day. There were over 100 finishers, none with a clean sheet, but in sixth position was Pauline Mayman in EPM 324, naturally winning the award for the best ladies crew.

The BARC held a National race meeting at Crystal Palace in glorious sunshine on Saturday August 22nd. Chris Lawrence put in the fastest lap during the Marque scratch race in TOK 258, breaking the class record. Chris naturally won the race in his 'staggeringly fast Morgan' after what was also reported by *Autosport* as a 'demonstration of immaculate driving', leaving Bill de Selincourt in second and Syd Hurrell in third place. Chris had now built up a commanding lead in the Freddie Dixon Trophy series. He had a total of 34 points; Bill de Selincourt had 26 and Syd Hurrell 21.

On Wednesday August 26th the British Motor Corporation launched what became known as the Mini. It had been designed by Alec Issigonis after Leonard Lord had asked him in March 1957 to produce something a bit better than the 'bubble cars' which had become popular during the Suez crisis. Although designed to appeal to the family man having limited funds, the new technology of transverse engine and front wheel drive put off many within that group of purchasers and the Mini tended to appeal to a more up-market clientele. It was initially sold at £500.0.0 as either the Austin Seven (written as Se7en) or the Morris Mini-Minor and fitted with an 850cc version of the BMC 'A' Series engine, but the amazing road holding and manoeuvrability soon had the sporting motorist interested. The sports car market had a new and unexpected challenger for the future.

The suspension on the new Mini was by a rubber system devised by Dr Alex Moulton. His very first attempt at using rubber for a car's suspension had been on his own Morgan 4/4 in 1948. The coil spring of the front suspension had been replaced by a slightly longer stack of square section rubber rings, interposed with aluminium stabilising plates. The Morgan steering damper was necessary to prevent torsional wind up it but it was quite successful overall so Alex invited HFS and Peter Morgan for lunch at Manvers House, the Spencer Moulton offices, to show them the system. The main problem with the modified suspension proved to be the inherent friction of the slider on the centre pin and Alex suggested at the time using a tapped supply of engine oil to lubricate the front suspension. The suspension was not further developed although of course HFS did introduce the 'one-shot' lubrication system to the front suspension on the Plus Four which was then under development.

The BARC ran a Members' Meeting at Aintree using the Club circuit on Saturday August 29th. Competing in the seven lap handicap Race 'D' for Marque sports cars was Pat Kennett in a Morgan Plus Four, but he spun off the circuit. It is possible that this was Pat's 1955 coupé LKY 699, blue with black wings, which had replaced his previous Morris Minor. Bob Duggan also took part in this meeting and achieved fastest practice lap and pole position with OYO 874, but to no avail. Front runners in the Freddie Dixon Trophy, Chris Lawrence, Bill de Selincourt and Syd Hurrell discovered that it was not really convenient for each of them to make the long journey up to Aintree that weekend because they had other pressing commitments, so they agreed that they would all miss out the round and maintain the status quo on points.

Shelsley Walsh ran a National hill climb on Sunday August 30th in fine weather. Only one Morgan was entered, namely the Plus Four of R Soans which recorded 45.95 seconds in the class for sports cars from 1,501 to 2,000cc. The class was won by Cottrell's Lotus Bristol with 41.79 seconds.

The other Morgans were probably at the Morgan 4/4 Club's driving tests, held that same day in the factory grounds of L G Harris and Co Ltd, paint brush manufacturers near Bromsgrove. Eleven had entered but with the 'driving test master' entered, namely Peter Morgan in his Willment overhead inlet valve 100E 4/4 RNP 504, the winner was obviously a foregone conclusion.

On the same Saturday, September 5th, that the RAC was running its International Tourist Trophy race meeting at Goodwood, the SUNBAC ran a club event at Silverstone using the Club circuit. Alan Belcher had entered VON 777, and collected a First Class Award for the half hour speed trial. He had also entered one of the six lap handicap races, and had a marvellous battle with E C Booth's Frazer Nash and a Jaguar powered Healey Silverstone, eventually finishing in third place at 71.75 mph. Also entered at this meeting was Peter Marten, but he was driving a 4/4 Series II, YDV 386, which he had recently purchased second-hand. It had the Elva overhead inlet valve head fitted and also a vacuum operated Handa overdrive on all three gears. It didn't prove successful.

The following day at Snetterton Les Fagg had entered TOK 258 for the Snetterton Motor Racing Club's Scott-Brown Memorial Trophy race meeting. The last race of the day, for saloons and GT cars over 1,301cc provided plenty of entertainment with a battle between Russ Taylor's Jaguar XK 120 in the largest class, and Syd Hurrell (TR3) and Les Fagg in the 1,301 to 2,000cc class. Russ Taylor led for the first four laps but was then passed by both Syd Hurrell and Les Fagg who then proceeded to pass and repass each other in a contest for the lead. Then, on the final lap the Morgan and the TR3 touched at Coram Curve and both spun off the track. Russ Taylor was forced to spin too to avoid them but caught the Jaguar expertly and carried on to win. Les Fagg was able to continue into second place and first in class but Syd's TR3 mounted the bank and was too badly damaged to continue. This informal meeting also gave Roland Smith and Len Bridge a chance for a Morgan drive on the track when the opportunity arose during the day, as they weren't entered to race. We think it is likely that Peter Morgan lent his works Plus Four (TUY 875) to the group to try out, after work had been carried out on it by them. The photo on the front of our dust jacket, which was taken at this event, shows TUY 875 with an undertray and oil cooler that both look very similar to TOK's.

Jim Banbury in JJY 221 was the only Morgan entry for the BARC South Western Centre's 22nd hill climb held at Brunton that same Sunday. On this occasion his time of 28.64 seconds didn't put him in the prizes.

The Liverpool Motor Club ran its classic Jeans Gold Cup Rally that same weekend, but only attracting just over forty cars to this famous event. Once again Pauline Mayman in EPM 324 won the trophy for the best performance by an all-lady crew.

The last but one of the qualifying rounds for the Autosport Championship for Series-Production Sports Cars was held at the Nottingham Sports Car Club's Mallory Park meeting on Sunday September 13th. Alan Belcher had entered Class D, being one of five starters in this class, the race being combined with the three contestants in Class E and three non-Championship racers. Dick Protheroe went away from the field to win the twenty lap race and take Class E (for over 2,001cc) whilst Alan finished fifth in Class D, after a long fight with Peter Sutcliffe's Frazer Nash. Syd Hurrell finished third in his TR3, the highest placed of the non-Bristol engined cars.

Just two Plus Fours took part in the Bugatti Owners' Club National hill climb held at Prescott that same Sunday, September 13th. R Soans recorded identical times of 51.28 seconds on his two runs whilst Robin Brown in UOL 490 recorded 51.67 seconds on his second run.

A directors' meeting was held at the Morgan factory on Wednesday September 16th, with Peter Morgan in the Chair. It was agreed to send a chassis to Italy, following help and advice from Rene Pellandini, the Western US Morgan distributor. The aim was to get some ideas for a new more modern body design to try to improve overseas sales of the 4/4, as this car just wasn't popular outside the

This photo and the one on the front cover, both taken at Snetterton in 1959, required much detective work to identify the event, the conclusion being they were taken at the Scott-Brown meeting. Les Fagg is on the grid in TOK, next to Peter Morgan's works Plus Four (the driver appears to be Chris Lawrence), and in the foreground is Peter Sargent's Jaguar C-type. This could have been prior to the sports car race or a practice session. (Len Bridge)

home market. In actual fact it was a Plus Four chassis that was dispatched! Peter also announced plans to repaint the front of the works and modernise the waiting area, which would include the provision of a fitted carpet.

The 4/4 model was now being produced with a five inch wider body, the body frame having been modified in the same fashion as previously undertaken on the Plus Four model in 1958. The first to be produced was A517, which had been tested in the week of September 7th. In addition, the wider windscreen used on the Plus Four was now fitted to the 4/4 and flashing direction indicators were standard fittings to all models.

On the Friday evening of September 18th the London Motor Club's famous annual London Rally commenced with starts at Ascot, Leeds and Taunton, the routes converging at Craven Arms in Shropshire. There were now two driving tests before the complicated night-driving section took the competitors into South Wales. A compulsory one and a half hour breakfast halt was held in the early hours of Saturday at Llandrindod Wells. After further excursions into South Wales the rally finished at Ascot later that day after 700 miles of rallying. There were five clean sheets from the over 200 starters, and best of all of these was the Morgan Plus Four YOM 798 of Brian Harper and Ron Crellin, which won the event. That was not all, for Pauline Mayman and Val Domleo won the Coupe des Dames in Pauline's Morgan EPM 324. It had been an excellent rally for the Morgans.

Brian Harper had found the new front disc brakes fitted to YOM 798 were not as likely to lock the wheels on hard braking as the rear drum brakes, so he purchased a Remax Baldwin F B Brake Booster kit for £7.10.0 which was a small 6 inch by 2 inch cylinder, containing a shouldered piston in a compound cylinder system, which he fitted only to the front brakes. The brakes were then superb and he could even out-brake Peter Morgan. We are not sure exactly when Brian fitted this.

The BARC Members' Meeting held at Mallory Park on Saturday September 19th started off pleasantly with fine weather and a large entry but was marred at the beginning with a fatality in the Formula 3 race during an overtaking incident. Despite the shadow cast over the event there was some fine racing and Chris Lawrence produced the expected result in the seven lap Marque scratch race driving TOK 258, with the TR3s of Syd Hurrell and Bill de Selincourt in second and third places.

On the following day Jim Banbury took his Plus Four JJY 221 to Yeovilton for a sprint meeting run jointly by the Yeovil Car Club and the West Hants and Dorset CC using an 800 yards pear-shaped one lap course at the Naval Air Station. Jim recorded 40.35 seconds, eighth overall fastest of the day from 43 starters. He beat the four TRs competing in his class by a considerable margin.

The BARC Marque sports car championship's final race of 1959 was held on Saturday September 26th at its BARC Goodwood meeting. Chris Lawrence had already enough points to secure the Freddie Dixon Trophy, but he rounded off the season in style by scoring his usual runaway victory in the ten lap Marque sports car race. As normal Chris was first away after the Le Mans start in TOK 258 and was never passed. Bill de Selincourt and Syd Hurrell took second and third in their TR3s.

Bill de Selincourt had also been racing his sports racing Lotus Eleven during the season in addition to his TR3, and was three points ahead in the contest for the Brooklands Memorial Trophy for the driver collecting the most points overall in the year.

Bill had borrowed works driver Peter Ashdown's Mk I Lola for the day and took a popular win in the ten lap scratch race for 1,100cc cars and collected his trophy from Mrs Margaret Dixon, alongside Chris Lawrence who had won the Freddie Dixon Trophy in such a convincing manner. In twelve of the thirteen rounds for the trophy Chris had finished sixth in one race, come second in two and won no fewer than nine races at five different tracks, including Oulton Park on the occasion of BARC's first visit. He had won convincingly with forty-two points, his rivals Bill de Sellincourt and Syd Hurrell in their TR3s finishing with thirty-one and twenty-six points respectively.

Although Chris had concentrated on the BARC races he had competed at every other opportunity with outstanding results, including setting a new GT class record at Silverstone. The team's hard work had paid off and remarkably there had been no retirements. Len Bridge told us how well the group of friends had worked as a team, and that Chris was a charismatic team leader as well as being a skilled and smooth driver who was able get the best from any car. Reputedly there was interest shown in him by one or two works teams but Chris had other plans.

Whilst Chris was winning the championship at Goodwood Alan Belcher's Morgan VON 777 was at the prestigious International Gold Cup meeting at Oulton Park, but in the hands of a new owner, namely Lionel Mayman. He had entered the Morgan for the final qualifying race for the Autosport Championship for Series-Production Sports Cars. Ron Timmins was not part of the deal, but he came to the circuit anyway to see the action, arriving just after the finish of practice due to traffic delays en route to the circuit. He discovered the SU carburettor representative in attendance, checking the carburettor needles, which of course Ron had previously modified and were not standard SU. Lionel Mayman spotted Ron and told him that he wasn't getting the revs from the engine that Ron had told him he should be getting. Ron lifted the bonnet and removed the carburettor dampers, telling Lionel that was all that was needed.

The second race on the programme was a ten lap race for Classes D and E in the championship and at the start Dick Protheroe's Jaguar stalled on the line with a broken throttle linkage. Dick Stoop took the lead in his Frazer Nash, followed by John Mitchell's AC Bristol, Jack Sears Austin Healey and Tony Lanfranchi's Frazer Nash. Behind this leading group was Lionel in VON 777, ahead of Sir Gawaine Baillie's mighty 4.4 litre Chevrolet Corvette. Lionel held off the Corvette for four laps, an amazing sight for the spectators, before it eventually powered a way past. Lionel seems to have hit problems then and faded from the results, but Ron remembers how the crowds flocked to see the little Morgan in the paddock after the race, marvelling at how it had held off the big engined American car for so long. It had been a true David and Goliath performance. Ron felt very proud of his development of the Morgan that day.

On Sunday September 27th the Hagley and District Light Car Club held its second speed trial at Chateau Impney in perfect weather, attracting Robin Brown in UOL 490 and Ray Meredith in XOV 555. Vic Hassall in an AC Bristol proved fastest in the up to 2,000cc Grand Touring cars class with a time of 27.03 seconds, whilst Robin finished second with a time of 27.85 seconds on his first run. On his second run disaster struck when the brakes failed as he approached a ninety degree bend at 70 mph and he disappeared into a laurel hedge, bending back the front suspension and damaging the front wings. It turned out that the offside front brake pipe which connected the two wheel cylinders together on the back plate had been rubbing on the front main suspension spring, wearing through at the critical moment. Ray Meredith finished third.

The MCC ran the Derbyshire Trial on Friday October 2nd, finishing the following day. The Morgan factory had entered a team, consisting of Jim Goodall in HUY 982, Horace Roberts in WAB 779 and Peter Morgan in the 4/4 RNP 504. Also entered was George Edwards in his red Plus Four OCO 738. George was a West Country civil engineer. The event proved easy for the Morgans, all collecting First Class Awards, whilst Jim Goodall actually won Class 5, for sports cars.

Not content to literally rest on his laurels, Chris Lawrence entered the end of season BRSCC event at Brands Hatch, held on Sunday 4th October. Having a conventional start, the first event was a ten lap race for series-production sports cars. Chris was on pole position on the grid in TOK 258, alongside the Lotus Elite of Edward Lewis,

Driving in shirt sleeves with customary bow tie, Chris Lawrence leaves the field behind at Brands Hatch in TOK 258. (Len Bridge collection)

Alan Foster's MGA Twin-Cam and Peter Tomei's Elva Courier. Chris made his usual great start and led the field for the first five laps until Graham Warner passed him in his Lotus Elite and eventually went on to win, two seconds ahead of the Morgan in second place, which was closely followed by Alan Foster's MGA. Chris had a class win however, ahead of Tony Lafranchi's Frazer Nash and Gibson's Jaguar XK 140.

Also on the programme was a twelve lap race for the increasingly popular international Formula Junior, and this was the first really significant race in the UK. This formula had originated in Italy for single-seaters powered by either 1,000cc or 1,100cc tuned mass-produced engines (different car weight requirements for each engine size), and production gearboxes and other parts, allowing cheap yet effective racing for the aspiring world champions. At this race meeting a grid of eleven came to the start, the bulk being front engined Elvas, Elva being one of the first British companies to see the appeal of this new cheap formula. One of these cars was driven by Chris Lawrence and he managed to cross the finish line in third place, behind two sister cars.

The BARC South Eastern Centre ran another hill climb at Firle on Sunday October 4th. Jim Banbury took part with JJY 221, being the only Morgan entered, taking part in the class for Special Touring and Grand Touring cars from 1,601 to 2,000 cc. He finished in seventh position of the fourteen entries, being beaten by a Frazer Nash, three ACs and two TRs.

That same day the Allard Owners' Club ran speed trials at Harleyford in Buckinghamshire. Sandy Blair now had Nixie running well once more after the Relay Race disaster, and took his class. Not only that but he was part of the winning team together with a Cooper JAP and an MGA.

During October the Ford motor Company introduced a new small car, the Ford Anglia 105E. The '105' related to the Ford model number and the 'E' related to it being an English Ford factory production. It was a revolutionary design, including a four speed gearbox seen for the first time on a British Ford passenger vehicle, and it had a brand new engine too. According to Fred Hart, who was in charge of the engineering for this car, the gearbox had been designed by Alf Haig, and the engine by a team led by Alan Worters at Rainham and Dagenham. The principles of an over-square engine, previously introduced by Ford on its

Consul and Zephyr models, were taken further, and the stroke to bore ratio of the 996.6cc ohv engine was 0.6 to 1 (80.96mm by 48.41mm). The compression ratio was 8.9 to 1 and 39 bhp was claimed at 5,000 rpm. The new engine was to be the first of a series of small capacity Ford engines, all using the same engine block with the same bore and bore centres. Various engine capacities of up to 1,390cc were possible by using three bearing crankshafts of different strokes. The new car itself was to be shown at the forthcoming Motor Show, where comparisons would doubtless be drawn with the new Mini.

This new Ford engine was to have a major effect on British motor racing, for the over-square design meant high engine speeds could be achieved, thereby producing more power with better breathing. One of the first to tune this engine was Keith Duckworth who ran Cosworth Engineering Ltd from small premises in Friern Barnet Road, North London. Keith had founded this company in 1958 together with Mike Costin, whom he had met whilst working at Lotus. Mike still worked at Lotus so Cosworth was basically a one man outfit. Keith ran it using a Heenan and Froude type GR3 dynamometer. The company initially specialised in tuning Coventry Climax racing engines, but Keith was also interested in the increasingly popular international single-seater Formula Junior, which effectively replaced Formula 3. As mentioned before, the formula specified engine, gearbox and other parts to come from production cars of 1,000 or 1,100cc. Overhead camshaft designs were not allowed and initial work at Cosworth was with the Fiat 1,100cc 'Millicento' engine, but this was expensive to buy. Consequently when one of Keith's evening helpers, Howard Panton, who was working for Ford at this time on the Anglia project, told Keith of the forthcoming 105E engine, its likely suitability for tuning and its cheap price, he decided it would be more profitable to be one of the first to concentrate on this new engine.

Another very interested party was Chris Lawrence. Chris had decided to try and make a living in the competition preparation and racing car engineering business, and had persuaded his mother and step-father, Robert Neale, to finance the purchase of garage premises in Westerham, Kent. He formed a company named Westerham Motors Ltd and asked John Harvey and Les Fagg to leave Rotax and join him in September. Roland Smith and his friend Willy Edwards had not completed their apprenticeships but were invited to carry out the last year with the new firm, becoming 'Aeronautical and Automobile Development Engineers'! As well as preparing customers' sports cars, particularly those fitted with the Triumph TR engines, Chris had an ambition to race single-seaters and wanted to design and build a Formula Junior car powered by his own tuned Ford 105E engine.

Chris was to produce a range of tuning options for various production cars, which he grouped under the LawrenceTune title. With all this activity it looked as though Morgan racing might have to take a back seat in 1960. Unfortunately the garage deal fell through in Westerham so Chris rented premises at 69A Avenue Road in Acton, West London, which he learned about from Len Bridge's landlord. Despite the new location the name Westerham Motors Ltd was retained. (Later, LawrenceTune Engines Ltd was formed, the words being joined in such a way as to promote 'LT' as the company logo. Len Bridge told us that a local businessman, not knowing Chris's first name, had a habit of calling him 'Mr Tune'!) The property in Acton had previously belonged to an upholsterer, and punctures became a problem for the new tenants until a good clear up of discarded tacks was undertaken, aided by a magnet!

As Chris focussed in on the Formula Junior car he realised he needed extra help, so Len Bridge agreed to join Westerham Motors from Rotax in November. Len and Chris lived close to each other and they often travelled to Acton together in TOK 258, using the journey as an opportunity to fine tune the car and test ideas, something they continued to do in later years with other road legal cars on which they were working. The company was to buy its own dynamometer and experiment with tuning the Ford 105E engine with help from Keith Duckworth. One false alley they went down on Chris's insistence was to make a manifold for the 105E engine to take four Amal Monobloc carburettors, following Chris's motorcycle and MG tuning experience. Len remembers the engine was gutless below 5,000 rpm, and then it took off like a rocket and died! The idea was quickly abandoned. A set up using a pair of H4 SUs and a single H6 was more promising but complicated.

During the autumn the correspondence columns of *Autosport* contained a series of letters on club racing, the originator suggesting the fall off in entries for club events in the classes for sports cars up to 2,000cc might be explained by the fact that any Bristol engined cars always won against the clubman's more likely entry of his daily transport TR, MG or Morgan. It was suggested that the BARC Marque formula, which excluded the Bristol engined cars, was the solution. Another correspondent suggested the BARC formula was not the complete answer as cars for that series now arrived at racing circuits on trailers, being too modified for road use.

Chris Lawrence then took up his pen with a slightly tongue in cheek reply, which was published in the issue of Friday October 16th. He explained that his Morgan was bought second-hand, and was only worked on in the evenings by his team of friends and himself. He stated that the engine conformed to the maker's original specification in all respects. All modifications that had been carried out were on original pieces with no replacements being made whatsoever. The chassis and bodywork were completely standard in all respects, no modifications having been made to the suspension, brakes and steering. He did mention three additions to the car, namely an oil cooler, a flat aluminium undertray, and a special home made exhaust system. He suggested that to win races required mental effort and hard work, not money. He pointed out that it was true that some of the Triumph cars he competed against were rather special and had cost their owners a great deal of money, but explained that all that this showed was that the Morgan was much more suitable for racing than the Triumph when it came off the production line. Commenting on the ban on Bristol engined cars taking part in the BARC series he suggested frustrated potential AC Bristol racing drivers should heed the following advice: 'Sell it. Buy two second-hand Morgans, one to race and one to go to work in'!

There was continual rain at the Bodiam hill climb held over 670 yards in a Guinness hop farm on Saturday October 10th by the Hastings, St Leonards and East Sussex Car Club. Jim Banbury had entered his Plus Four JJY 221 the only Morgan within Class 9, the opposition being four TRs and a Dellow. Jim won the class and finished fifth overall of the 77 starters, just being beaten by *Motor Sport* magazine's Denis Jenkinson with his Porsche.

At the directors' meeting held at the Morgan factory on Wednesday October 14th Peter reported a reduction in demand for the 4/4 model although the Plus Four was selling satisfactorily. Peter hoped that the newly introduced Ford engine from the new Ford Anglia 105E would be made available to the factory, but noted that the four speed gearbox was wider than the currently used three speed gearbox from the Ford 100E.

Revised starter motors were now being fitted to new Plus Four models as from chassis number 4335, tested in the week of October 5th.

The London Motor Club's Norwester Rally was held in gale force winds in the West Country over the weekend of Saturday October 17th. Trees and assorted storm wreckage littered the roads and only ten of the eighty-two starters actually qualified as finishers. One of those failing to finish was AC Lorkin who's Morgan broke a stub axle on a fast corner, the freed wheel sailing into a field leaving the crew high, but far from dry as rain heralded the dawn. The best performance by a mixed crew was awarded to Morgan 4/4 Club members Barrie and Angela Phipps in their Riley.

The London Motor Show was opened by the Prime Minister, the Rt Hon Harold Macmillan MP, at Earls Court on Wednesday October 21st and ran until Saturday October 31st. The Morgan stand showed one of the new wider bodied 4/4s and four Plus Fours, two being left hand drive, and three being fitted with front disc brakes which the Morgan Motor Company was now introducing as an option on both wire wheel and disc wheel cars, at an extra cost of just £10.0.0. The usual three body styles were shown (two- and four-seater sports, and coupé), as was the specially prepared Plus Four chassis.

There were around 100 entries for the Bournemouth Rally, organised by the West Hants and Dorset Car Club, 400 miles of rallying taking the competitors from Bournemouth on Saturday October 24th to Bournemouth on Sunday October 25th! There were final driving tests after the finish of the road sections. Pauline Mayman once again won the award for the best lady crew in EPM 324.

Cambridge University Automobile Club ran a speed trial at Snetterton on Sunday November 1st. Jim Banbury was entered in the largest class, Class 3A for sports cars, and finished sixth of the fourteen taking part. Ahead of Jim in JJY 221 was the winning Frazer Nash, an AC Bristol, a supercharged Tornado, an Austin Healey and a TR2. Tom Smith, from Indianapolis in the USA, also took part in his black 1958 Plus Four coupé, finishing over three seconds slower than Jim and in eleventh position. Tom was in England as part of his tour of duty with the United States Navy.

At last the British motorist had something to celebrate. On Monday November 2nd, the new M1 motorway, stretching from Berrygrove to Crick and including the M10 and M45 spurs, was opened by the Minister of Transport, the Rt Hon Ernest Marples MP. It stretched for nearly sixty miles with three carriageways in each direction and had no speed limit, except for any vehicle pulling a trailer when a 40 mph limit applied. Many drivers took the opportunity to try it, and the motorist organisations, namely the AA and RAC, were kept busy as poorly maintained and commonly pre-war cars expired in clouds of steam! Furthermore, lane discipline was poor as drivers were often not sure just how to drive on the new road. One poor driver was later to be televised stopping to change a wheel in the middle lane! For the blossoming tuning industry it gave a marvellous unofficial venue for testing speed modifications!

During 1959 the busy non-motorway roads began to receive the newly introduced double white line system in an attempt to prevent overtaking in dangerous areas. Today there can be few roads without them. Speed limits on these roads were still set at 30 mph for most goods vehicles, including small vans, but lorries pulling trailers could still do no more than 20 mph.

The 1959 RAC Rally had a new organiser, Jack Kemsley, and he had shaken up the event in an attempt to make it worthy of entries from Europe, as it was actually a round of the European Touring Championship. The rally had been moved from the traditional March date to November, and the night navigation exercises had been scrapped and replaced by route cards, helping to make the event more European in nature. Furthermore it was expected that this rally would be won on the road and not in special driving tests as on previous occasions. The days of the RAC Rally being called the Rally of the Tests were on the wane!

Sixteen foreign competitors were attracted, making an entry list of 146. There were three Morgans entered, making up the Morgan factory team. Peter Morgan was navigated by Tommy Thompson in Jim Goodall's car HUY 982, Brian Harper was accompanied by Ron Crellin in YOM 798, and Pauline Mayman was navigated by Daphne Freeman in EPM 324. Pauline's usual passenger Val Domleo had been recruited to navigate for Annie Soisbault in a works Triumph TR3A.

The Event was to start from Blackpool on the Tuesday, with a driving test soon afterwards on the promenade and then the rally competitors were to make for the Yorkshire Moors. This was to be followed by a requirement to cover the Hardnott and Wrynose passes in the Lake District at an average of 30 mph, covered overnight, before making for Scotland on the Wednesday morning for tests at Charterhall and Rest-and-be-Thankful.

After visiting the Western Highlands the competitors were to travel alongside Loch Ness to Inverness before heading for the Cairngorms and Balmoral, and hence to Perth. On the Thursday, after driving tests at Aintree and Oulton Park, the entourage was to make for Wales. The rally had a stop planned at Cheltenham for breakfast on the Friday morning. It was then on to Prescott Hill Climb for special tests, and from there on to Harleyford and Brands Hatch for other tests before finishing at Crystal Palace. On the Saturday the final five lap races were held at the Crystal Palace circuit to decide any ties.

Of the 146 entries 131 actually started from Blackpool on Tuesday lunch time November 16th. By the control in Brough seventeen had already retired, and even Pauline Mayman arrived four minutes behind schedule. At the Charterhall test Peter Morgan made the fastest time in Class 8, with Pauline Mayman third behind Jimmy Ray's Sunbeam Alpine. Peter took the class again at the Rest-and-be-Thankful hill climb, again beating Jimmy Ray. Rumours soon began to circulate of heavy snow in the Cairngorms, with likely problems on the road leading from Great Britain's highest village at Tomintoul to Braemar. As a consequence many drivers began to fit winter tyres and chains. It was soon obvious the road was impassable, many cars getting stuck and then having difficulty in turning round to return back down, where they faced the rest of the competitors still trying to get up. Brian Harper and Ron Crellin got further than most, before having to admit defeat. Some were able to find an alternative route to the Braemar control, sixteen did so in fact, one of whom was Peter Morgan. All the others collected 300 penalty points. Many crews were also hopelessly behind schedule, and by Cheltenham only sixty cars remained in the rally. All the Morgans were still there. By the time the final stretch to Crystal Palace was finished there were just fifty-three left, again including the three Morgans. On the racing circuit on the Saturday both Peter Morgan and Pauline Mayman won their tie-braking five lap races.

Sadly protests marred the results, which had Gerry Burgess provisionally the victor in his Ford Zephyr with just 33 penalty points. Peter Morgan was in sixth place with 48, Brian Harper in 38th place with 378 and Pauline Mayman in 45th place with 693. Peter Morgan won Class 8, for Grand Touring cars from 1,301cc to 2,000cc, and the

Peter Morgan in Jim Goodall's Morgan during the final Crystal Palace races of the RAC Rally. (LAT Photographic)

> **WESTERHAM MOTORS LTD**
> SPECIALISTS IN PREPARATION FOR COMPETITION
> (Sole Concessionaires of LAWRENCE TUNE)
>
> We are now able to undertake the preparation of a limited number of cars for competition. Three stages of **LAWRENCE TUNE** are available for TR2 and TR3 engined cars, giving both **PERFORMANCE AND RELIABILITY**, as proved during the 1959 Season on C. J. Lawrence's Morgan Plus Four
>
> **RECORD OF 22 RACES: 16 WINS, 4 SECONDS, 2 THIRDS — TOTAL 22**
> INCLUDING: NO RETIREMENTS
> Freddie Dixon Trophy Winner — (42 points)
> International Win Silverstone (Lap Record G.T. 1600 — 2600 c.c.)
> 3 National Wins
> Winning Team Six-Hour Relay Race Silverstone
>
> Available from stock :— **LAWRENCE** modified camshafts for TR2 and TR3 engines on exchange basis. Four branch manifolds. Split exhaust system. Oil coolers for any car
>
> ENQUIRIES TO **WESTERHAM MOTORS LTD**
> 69a, AVENUE ROAD, ACTON, LONDON, W.3. ACOrn 0129

Westerham Motors advertisement from Autosport November 20th.

Morgan team had finished in fourth place. Pauline Mayman was fourth in the competition for the Ladies' Award. Perhaps the greatest achievement however was that all three Morgans that had started had finished. No other make, with more than one entry, had all the cars finishing.

The protest centred on whether the snow-blocked road over Tomintoul should have caused the Braemar and possibly the Blairgowrie controls to have been scrubbed. If the protest had been upheld then the new winner would be decided by special test results from all those without penalties on the rest of the road section. This would actually drop Peter Morgan to fifteenth as he had gained three penalties in Wales. The protests were not upheld, and the Morgan Motor Company was very proud of its achievement, taking out advertisements proclaiming, 'Three Morgans entered, three Morgans finished.'

At the Morgan directors' meeting held on Wednesday November 25th Peter Morgan reported that a Ford 105E engine was currently being fitted to the 4/4 chassis, and that he hoped to have the prototype running by Easter 1960. It was suggested it might be necessary to widen the chassis to allow the wider gearbox to be fitted and Peter hoped a conventional gearlever might be possible too.

When HFS Morgan had run the Morgan Motor Company he had relied heavily on George Goodall to deal with the day to day running of the factory as works manager. Peter knew that this had been a good system so he reported to the meeting that he had asked George Goodall's son Jim, currently foreman of the machine shop, to take over this role as from Sunday November 1st. Some time earlier George had inquired of Peter if he would continue to employee his son Jim in the future factory structure. He pointed out to Peter that sadly Jim did not seem to take after his father, but behaved more like his mother! As Peter didn't particularly like George Goodall's personality this was, unbeknown to George, actually a good thing! Jim's old position of foreman went to F Whickett. He also announced that he was exploring the possibility of appointing an experimental engineer for a trial period of six months.

Peter was finding the running of the Morgan Motor Company now took up much of his time. Whilst his father was alive there had never been a need to even think about an experimental engineer as HFS had always been looking at new developments for the Morgan models himself, but following his father's death it was a different story. Plus Four sales in Great Britain had virtually dried up, with over 90% of production going to the USA. Even the British and European agents, particularly Basil Roy in London, were selling their Plus Fours to the American market, often undercutting the American distributors in the process. Peter was naturally a little concerned the Plus Four was being regarded as too old fashioned for the UK market, losing out to the TR3 and MGA opposition.

On Sunday November 29th the Morgan 4/4 Club ran a 160 mile rally for club members, starting at Droitwich and finishing in Malvern. The organisers were Club Secretary Alan Smith, Jim Goodall and Terry Hall. Only ten crews took part and very heavy rain made some of the country lanes near the Welsh border impassable. Barrie Phipps was the winner in his Riley 1.5, with Peter Morgan making the best performance in an open car, and best performance in a Morgan. All the other competitors were outside the time limit!

Hazel Chapman, the wife of Colin Chapman of Lotus Cars, presented the trophies at the British Trial and Rally Drivers' Association end of season dinner and dance in Buxton on Saturday December 12th. Once again Pauline Mayman had won the Silver Garter competition for lady rally drivers. In the Gold Star Rally competition John Sprinzel just beat Brian Harper by one point for the winner's trophy.

Australia

It was now four years since any Morgans had been imported to Australia, and with the sale of Bill Richards' R4 the last involvement of an Australian dealership with the marque had finished in 1958.

The R4 itself was now transformed into a sports car with a Holden engine and known initially

Jack Ayres at first test of the new R4 Holden, note his rude facial gesture to the cameraman! (David Van Dal)

as the Byfield-Ayres-Holden. It was first tested by Jack Ayres in its new form towards the end of February at Caversham, with David Van Dal present to record the event with his camera.

The first real action for the modified R4 was at Caversham for the WASCC Closed Meeting held on Monday March 2nd. The 'Holden' was fastest over the standing quarter mile with a time of 16.88seconds, and reached 102.9mph. In the State Championships at Caversham on Saturday October 24th Jack Ayres and the BAH won the Over 1,500cc Sports Car Championship, and on Saturday November 28th Jack was back at Caversham , for the Valvoline Xmas Cup races, gaining a second and a fourth place in three races.

Barry Ranford too had sold the Morgan Special that he had built for the 1957 Australian Grand Prix to Colin Metcher, who continued to race the car for the next two years. His first appearance was at Caversham on Friday September 4th, where he won the five lap scratch race for novices, and also scored second place in a five lap handicap for sports cars. The following day, at the WASCC Closed Meeting at the same venue he recorded the relatively slow time of 18.05 seconds for the standing quarter mile, and reached just 90 mph for the flying quarter, suggesting that the Vanguard motor was tiring.

Although the R4 now showed little of its Morgan roots, we think a brief resume of its later history may be of interest. Lionel Beattie was Jack Ayres' co-driver in the Holden in 1960 when they won their class in the six hour endurance race at Caversham. Lionel then bought the car and fitted a Repco head and larger front brakes. The R4 continued in this form and known as the 'Repco-Holden-Special' was a very successful sports/racing car in Lionel's hands, winning the Western Australia Sports Car Championship in 1961 and 1962 among a host other of trophies. Rod Waller, a notable artist and cartoonist, then owned and raced the car for five years before selling it to Bob Webb, a local BP service station owner. After competing in a six hour race at the new Wanneroo track in Perth he and Bob Kingsbury took the car to the Gold Coast in Queensland in Aug-Sept 1968 for the Surfer's Paradise Speed Week. It is not clear what happened to it then but in 1974 Neil McCruddin purchased a wreck for $45 from a house that was being demolished; this turned out to be the Repco Holden Special/R4, and it has now been restored.

New Zealand

The annual beach races at Tahunanui were once again held over the New Year holiday by the Nelson Car Club, and attracted several Morgans. On the first day, Friday January 2nd , Halsey Logan finished third in his Consul engined 4/4 behind the two fast Ford 10 specials of Frank Pope and Les Fahey in the R W Martin Cup handicap race. On the second day Halsey finished in second place in Heat 2 of the Bishop Cup consolation handicap, and second again in the final, behind Keith Roper's Cooper JAP. Ivan Bennett took part with his ex Dave Edmiston Plus Four and had the bonnet come up on the driver's side. He stopped and refastened it, continuing to the race finish.

There was a record crowd of 10,000 to watch the racing at Teretonga Park on Saturday February 7th. The opening event was an eight lap race for sports and racing cars, but poor Ivan Bennett struck disaster in the S-bend section of the circuit when the throttle cable jammed in the Plus Four. This led to a spectacular accident, the Morgan spinning into sand and rolling several times, throwing Ivan out and causing him to suffer concussion. Luckily he recovered consciousness in hospital. The accident was caused by the throttle cable having become frayed, jamming the throttle open. It was possible to make temporary repairs to the car that allowed it to be driven the 100 miles or so back to Dunedin.

The Plus Four was stripped and the body taken to Anderson's Motor Bodies in Dunedin, where Cliff Bennett worked as an apprentice panel beater. Unfortunately the work area used by the employee who was to rebuild the body frame was then gutted by fire. Ivan therefore wrote to the Morgan factory in England advising the Company

Ivan Bennett's damaged Morgan at Teretonga. (Ivan Bennett collection)

of his plight, and requesting a set of body frame drawings. These were duly sent, but turned out to be for the early twin spare wheel Plus Four. Some parts made from the drawings were fine, other parts were specially made to fit undamaged panels, and yet others were made by calculated guesses. When Cliff came to fit the rebuilt body there were discrepancies of five eights of an inch or so in a couple of places, and this necessitated some adjustment.

Cliff and Ivan purchased a number of items from a written off 1957 4/4 belonging to racer R J Blackburn in Christchurch, including good wheels, replacing the Plus Four's damaged ones. Mr Blackburn had used several of the other 4/4 components to complete a Mistral car for his own racing. The Mistral was a New Zealand kit sports car supplied by Elmslie and Stockton Ltd using a locally built space frame chassis together with a British designed Mistral body (by Microplas Ltd) and Ford running gear. The Plus Four was complete again and ready to compete at the Nelson Beach race meeting at the end of the year. In view of the problems encountered with the bonnet lifting on the beach at the beginning of the year Ivan and Cliff fitted a bonnet strap to prevent a recurrence. The body patterns received from Malvern went to Camille Kuzmich, who owned a Vanguard engined chrome radiator Plus Four.

Racing resumed at the Ohakea airfield after a two year absence, on Saturday February 28th. Pat Fitzgerald took part in the ex Allen Freeman Plus Four four-seater P2290 in the Ohakea Sports Car Race and Ohakea Clubman's Handicap, but we have no results for him. During October Pat Fitzgerald took his Plus Four P2290 to the Moonshine hill climb and was rewarded with the second fastest time of the day.

Around the middle of this year Cliff Bennett had purchased a two year old 4/4 fitted with an unmodified Ford 100E engine and gearbox. This red Morgan with black interior carried chassis number A302, had engine number 290301 and was originally dispatched on Thursday May 30th 1957 to T R Taylor of Dunedin. With the car in otherwise unmodified form Cliff travelled together with Ivan in his Plus 4 to the Nelson meeting to be held at the beginning of 1960.

USA

The success of the fledgling Pacific Coast Championship, introduced in 1958 by the Californian Areas 9 and 10 of the SCCA, led to a revised championship being introduced for 1959, with eight Regional races being included from the west of the USA and, to make it truly Pacific, two from Hawaii. A new performance related classification was to be used (but not elsewhere in the SCCA), taken from that used by the pace setting Cal Club. The Plus Fours were placed in Class E, along with most other 1,600-

2,000cc cars, and Class E also included the standard Austin Healeys. Into Class D went the AC Bristols, the Austin Healey 100S, the Porsche Carrera and Carrera GT models.

For some time there had been a downturn in the racing of Triumph sports cars in California. As this was a very important market for these cars the local distributor, Cal Sales Inc, of Gardena, run by Dorothy Deen, decided to back a plan devised by their service manager to try to remedy this. The service manager was R W 'Kas' Kastner, and the plan was to help a band of local TR enthusiasts to form the 'TRT' or 'Triumph Racing Team'. 'Kas', originally from Salt Lake City, had been racing TRs since 1955, and was determined to be the best there was, buying tuning books from England and the best German tools he could afford. He was now in a position to share his experience on tuning and competition driving with the other TRT members, and even designed the team logo for the side of each car.

For some time the rules of the Cal Club had allowed limited tuning. Engine compression ratios could be taken to the maximum as listed by the manufacturer's workshop manuals. Kas had discovered that TR engines were usually manufactured with a slightly lower compression than this, allowing some scope for improvement. It was permitted to remove metal, but not add any, so reground camshafts etcetera became possible, as indeed did the porting of inlet and exhaust tracts. The SCCA, on the other hand, did not allow removal of any metal, and would only allow options brought in by the manufacturers themselves, which were often quite expensive, and often difficult to find. This included using alternative differential ratios.

Of the two clubs it was the Cal Club which was by far the most popular sports car racing organisation in Southern California. The SCCA's rules on 'no tuning' were very difficult to police, and the saying was, 'He can't be stock because I'm not stock and he beat me!'

The Cal Club got the Southern Californian racing season off to a fine start at Pomona over the weekend of January 31st and February 1st. Morgan entries in the Saturday Class E race were Ken Deeter, Roger Slowi, Al Gebhard and, of course, Lew Spencer in Baby Doll No 3. To his surprise Roger Slowi found himself on the front row next to Lew, but it was Al Gebhard who followed Lew into Turn 1. At the end of the first lap Al was back in third place, but then retired with a broken valve. Meanwhile the revitalised Triumph team 'TRT' was doing really well and, working as a team, two of them boxed in Roger, demoting him to fifth overall. Ken Deeter was ninth. Lew won, and treated his then wife Nanette to the victory lap.

Lew and Nanette Spencer celebrate victory on Saturday at Pomona. (Bob Tronolone)

Saturday night was party time of course, and Roger Slowi's supporters, 'Ecurie Fatigue'(!), spent a particularly notable night at Crestline. The Sunday was a different story, for a push rod collapsed after two laps in Baby Doll No 3, losing Lew two further laps before he could rejoin. He came in fifteenth overall. Roger Slowi, Al Gebhard and Ken Deeter came in fourth, fifth and sixth. In the ladies' race Barbara Windhorst was caught in traffic, with Baby Doll No 3 sustaining a bent wing.

Whilst Morgans bought for racing were supplied to California already fitted with Dunlop racing tyres from the Morgan factory, Englebert 'Competition P' racing tyres were actually preferred by Rene Pellandini's team. It was also possible to have the used Engleberts recapped, and not only did Baby Doll often run thus equipped but the Morgans of Roger Slowi and Al Gebhard also ran on old Baby Doll covers that had been recapped. Al Gebhard told us that he had located an excellent tyre man in Long Beach, who was also a Triumph owner. He was a perfectionist and would recap Al's tyres as many as three times. First the old tread was removed on a tyre lathe. A racing compound was then added and baked at high temperature and pressure. The tyres were then spun to 120 mph on the car. Usually there was no need for balance weights, he was so good, and there was no visual indication that they had been recapped. He used a Pirelli-type tread and the tyres were always completely reliable.

Two of the Northern California drivers had new Morgans for the new racing season. Bill Hinshaw had disliked the Jaguar he had bought at the end of the 1958 season. He found it wasn't as much fun on the track as a Morgan so Bill quickly disposed of it and bought the 1958 Plus Four (Wembley Blue with black leather upholstery) that had belonged to the Bay Area Morgan Plus Four Club Vice President Jack Kane and prepared it for racing. He had logically named the new Morgan 'Little Blue'.

Bill Chapman's new Morgan was none other than Bill Hinshaw's old car, 'Little Red', which he had bought from Frank Henry after selling his green Plus Four. Bill Hinshaw wished he had asked him about the car first before buying it, as he knew Little Red was very worn and tired.

During the winter RKO Pictures wanted publicity for the Arthur Swerdloff film 'Roadracers' then showing in San Francisco, which was about a father who disowned his sports car racing son, blaming him for the death of another driver. Any local racer whose sports car was licensed for road use was invited to take part in the '1st Grand Prix de San Francisco', meeting at Market Street on the evening of Wednesday February 18th at 8pm for a police controlled run through the Tenderloin district to finish near Union Square. Both Bill Hinshaw in Little Blue and Bill Chapman in Little Red went along, joining some twenty other sports cars, including Aston Martin, Maserati, Ferrari etc. Unfortunately the police escort failed to appear, so they roared off on the route without them, several abreast, but stopping as required at traffic lights. One little old lady half way across a crosswalk raised her hand bag above her head as the cars parted either side of her. Hearing approaching police sirens they dashed to park as quickly as they could near the RKO Golden Gate Theatre and ran inside, whilst the box office directed the police to a nearby soup kitchen. The San Francisco Grand Prix was never run again!

For the weekend of March 7th and 8th the USAC and Cal Club were once more promoting big time racing at Pomona, sponsored by the *Los Angeles Examiner*. Four Morgans were entered, these being Baby Doll No 3 for Lew Spencer, and those of Al Gebhard, Ken Deeter and Willie West. Willie was from San Diego where he had made his reputation driving an Alfa Romeo. He was working on the sales staff at British Motor Sales, which was a Morgan agency. As a result he decided to buy a red two-seater and had prepared it for racing, helped by Dale Shoupe. This was his first Morgan race.

Race 2 was a five lap race for Class E only. For the first two laps Lew was right behind the familiar Porsche 1600 Speedster of Ronnie Bucknum, but on the third the Porsche Carrera of Chuck Parsons got through into second place. Once again the new TRT team worked well together, for on the very last corner of the race the TR of Gary Pickens blocked Lew, thereby allowing the TR of Kas Kastner through with Lew finishing fifth. Willie West drove well into seventh place, with Ken Deeter twelfth. Al Gebhard was trying to pass a TR on the outside of a curve when he was nudged by the twitchy TR and sent backwards towards the snow fencing at around 80 mph. He looked in his rear view mirror to see the crowd parting but luckily he stopped just short of the fence, eventually rejoining the race in last place. Despite this he picked off a few cars to finish fourteenth.

Al's poor finish put him on the back of the grid for the Sunday, but he drove a tremendous race. By lap two he was up to tenth position and, six laps later, he was sixth and closing on the leading five. On the twelfth lap he passed Lew Spencer for fourth position and everyone watching believed he could have finished second if the race had been longer. Unlike Lew, Al was using a standard 3.73 rear axle ratio, making his performance even more impressive. Lew unfortunately had gearbox problems, finishing fifth with the box jammed in top.

Willie West finished seventh, but Kennie Deeter retired with high oil temperature rather than ruin the engine. The winner of this twenty lap race was Chuck Parsons in his Porsche Carrera, with the TRs of Kas Kastner and Gary Pickens second and third.

Meanwhile, the two enthusiasts, Arch McNeill and Tom Wright, who had decided whilst watching the 1958 Sebring 12 Hour Race that they should enter Sebring in 1959, were about to realise their dream. Arch had contacted Peter Morgan directly at the Morgan factory to see what options they could supply to equip a suitable racer. Gradually a specification was drawn up for the Sebring car, and construction began following the placement of the order with Fergus Imported Cars Inc in November 1958. An all aluminium body (except for the scuttle and radiator cowl which Morgan felt needed to be in steel for strength) was built on a Plus Four. The engine was balanced and ported, and the compression raised by shaving 0.030 inch from the cylinder head. A Derrington exhaust manifold specially designed for the Plus Four further increased power. The front

A magnificent drive by Al Gebhard (13) at the March Pomona. Here he leads the MGA Twin-Cam of Jim Parkinson & the Morgan of Willie West, alongside the TR of Jerry Ostland. Number 100 is the Austin Healey of Peter Bundy, ahead of the similar car of Robbie Mackenzie-Low. At the rear is a Citroen ID19 saloon! (Al Gebhard collection)

suspension was reinforced and a bracing strut joined the top of each centre pin to the chassis. Dunlop triple-laced wire wheels were fitted with Dunlop R3 racing tyres with two spare wheels and three spare tyres. It was to be right hand drive (because the Sebring track was run clockwise), a bonnet strap was fitted and also Lucas type 51337E driving lamps for the night racing. The most important part of the specification was the brakes, as for the first time on a production Morgan, they were Girling disc brakes, of type 14. Indeed the shipping of the car was delayed whilst the Morgan factory awaited delivery of these items from Girling. The Morgan was given chassis number 4127, had TR3 engine TS 39202 and was coloured green with black leather upholstery. It was dispatched by boat on Wednesday February 11th 1959.

During the negotiating period for the Morgan Tom Wright realised he must pull out of the project, although he and his wife Jane were to form a valuable part of the Sebring pit crew. Mike Rothschild heard there might be a drive available, so he contacted Arch and introduced himself, offering to help with the project. Arch was delighted to accept this offer from such an experienced Sebring Morgan driver.

The Morgan arrived at New York docks where it was unloaded and spent several days parked under an elevated road. Arch met Mike at Mike's New Jersey home, and they went in Mike's Jaguar Mk VII saloon to view the car and briefly check it over. They left it there and returned home. Mike arranged to take the Morgan to his mechanic, Ed Brown, who checked everything in detail and prepared the car. He also fitted an Iskenderian 'TR 555' camshaft having 24-64, 64-24 profile with 0.435 inch lift.

Ed Iskenderian had set up his Ed Iskenderian Racing Cams company just after the Second World War, when a boom in demand from hot-rodders overwhelmed the few racing cam manufacturers available. Ed built his own cam for his Ford V8 engined Model T hot rod, and orders followed. His company was now the largest racing cam manufacturer in the world, based in Gardena, California. Success with American car tuning had lead to a range being developed for foreign sports cars, although these could not be used in SCCA races.

Arch McNeill's Morgan was not a cheap car. The basic price of the Plus Four two-seater was $2,453.00, the tuned engine added $125.00, the aluminium body $97.50, the disc brakes and wire wheels added $152.50 and the racing tyres $97.50. The total less Federal Excise Tax was $2,968.00, but Fergus Motors discounted $600, leaving Arch to pay $2,605.00 (including tax).

The Morgan was dispatched to Sebring by fruit truck whilst Arch went with Gus Ehrman, in company with the Jaguar of Mike and Honey Rothschild. The Jaguar lost its power steering on the way, but Mike was very resourceful, and soon had it repaired at a gas station. Arch knew his parents were nervous of him racing, so he hadn't told them about Sebring. Unfortunately he was spotted in South Carolina whilst in a restaurant, a mere twenty-five miles from their home!

There were problems in practice, possibly due to the new camshaft, so Mike asked his friend Jean Behra, a top sports car and Grand Prix driver, to check the plugs. He took the Morgan onto the highway at top speed, before switching off. The plugs seemed fine. Unfortunately for Arch he took a right hand bend a little too fast during practice, embedding the Morgan on a sandbank. There was no damage, but whilst he was digging the car out the photographers appeared. The next day a photograph of Arch and the stranded Morgan was syndicated in newspapers throughout the USA. Arch's secret drive was now well and truly exposed to his parents!

Practice had been held in a downpour of rain, flooding part of the pit apron, but the drivers hoped for better on race day, Saturday March 21st. There was a heavy fog first thing, but it had lifted by the time of the Le Mans start at ten o'clock. Mike Rothschild took the first stint in view of his greater experience, and the race was fairly uneventful for the Morgan team, although a battle did develop with the Arnolt Bristol of Ralph Durbin and Max Goldman. After about five hours the rain returned, making driving difficult on the partially submerged track, but just before dusk it stopped and there was a magnificent Florida sunset for the spectators to enjoy.

During the rainy period the Morgan came in for its last pit stop, and the opportunity was taken to put up the hood, for the inside of the windscreen was becoming increasingly difficult to see through. This manoeuvre put the Morgan behind the Arnolt Bristol, but had a demoralising effect on that team, for they had no such simple answer to the conditions.

The Morgan came home in twenty-sixth place overall, but fifth in the GT Class 7, behind three AC Bristols and the Arnolt Bristol. As with the Arnolt Bristol, 155 laps were completed.

After the race Arch was called back to New York by his business, so he drove the Morgan to Atlanta, Georgia and flew back. A few weeks later he returned to Atlanta, adjusted the tappets and drove the Morgan back home, ready for some SCCA racing. He wrote to Peter Morgan advising him of the Sebring result, and of the success of the disc brakes, (Arch had happily told Tom Wright at Sebring that at last he had 'A Morgan that Stops!'). Peter replied

The Morgan being prepared for Sebring. Mike Rothschild is to the left and Tom Wright to the right. Note the covered speedometer and special lamp for the race number. (Richard Vogel)

Mike Rothschild leaps into the Morgan after the Le Mans start at Sebring. (Tom Wright)

congratulating Arch and Mike on their success, and noting that they were beaten in their class only by cars costing almost twice as much as the Morgan.

Saturday April 4th was the date of the spring hill climb at Springtown in Pennsylvania. Harry Reynolds knocked nearly three seconds off his previous best time to record 67.0239 seconds, Henry Baumann and Ike Williamson both being unable to beat 69 seconds.

Over the weekend of April 18th and 19th the Northern California racers descended en masse on Stockton for the usual airport races. Rene Pellandini's Baby Doll No 3 was there too. On the Saturday Bill Hinshaw had high hopes for his new Morgan, Little Blue, but engine trouble soon stopped him. Bill Chapman and Bob O'Brien, both in red Plus Fours, showed much promise in novice and senior races respectively and the former was leading his race in Little Red, until a carburettor float chamber disconnected. Bob O'Brien worked as the Lodge Spark Plugs area representative at British Auto Parts in San Francisco, the importer of motoring products from such British manufacturers as Lucas, Girling, Lockheed, Borg and Beck, Mintex etc. His Plus Four was right hand drive.

Ralph Bohn, who was a policeman in Alameda, and Herb Atkins were sharing a pale blue Plus Four, but the Morgan was savaged at both ends during practice, Herb returning the Morgan to the pits on a tow rope.

Robin Jackson was going well in his Plus Four, but he hit a hay bale marker! Robin's green Plus Four was actually his second. The first, purchased from dealer Frank Henry in Telegraph Avenue, Berkeley, hadn't lasted long, for one wet evening the crimson Morgan was totally destroyed after Robin spun off the Shoreline Highway near Sausalito, and the Morgan went end over end to destruction. It was replaced by another Plus Four from Frank Henry (green with black upholstery) and as Robin had the remains of his old one for spares he decided to race this one. He had joined the Morgan Plus Four Club and prepared the Morgan for racing, with the engine being balanced, the ports relieved and matched to the manifolds and the head gas flowed.

Luckily for Saturday's Morgan enthusiasts Lew Spencer in Baby Doll No 3 and Rick Hilgers in his well prepared red Morgan both went well. In the five lap over 1,600cc Production race Lew started near the rear, but was leading Class E after just three laps. With just two Corvettes ahead Lew

Rick Hilgers mounts a hay bale at Stockton Airport in Snoopy. (Rick Hilgers collection)

eased off to take the class win, after indicating over 6,500 rpm on the tachometer.

In the ladies' race Grace Tara had the misfortune for the drophead coupé to lose all its water.

On the Sunday however roles were changed, for Baby Doll was sick and Rick Hilgers mounted a hay bale in his Morgan. Rick had christened his Morgan 'Snoopy', the Morgan sporting a large Snoopy logo on the side of the car. Bill Hinshaw now had first place in Class E sown up, but the Morgan was blowing out oil so he wisely eased off to take second. He had just four pints left in the sump at the finish.

After the main event there was an impromptu fifteen lap marque race. Bill Hinshaw and Rick Hilgers just dominated the field of TRs and Austin Healeys to finish one-two. A protest was filed against Bill's car, but the engine was found to be within the rules on compression testing and wasn't dismantled further. The race results stood, to the delight of the Morgan supporters.

This year Bill had decided to try and do better in Cal Club events, which, as mentioned earlier, had more liberal rules for tuning. To help him he had found a tuner named Morgan Keaton who ran Keaton Machine Works, a machine shop in Berkeley. He had made his reputation preparing engines for Oval and Drag racing, being completely unknown amongst the sports car enthusiasts. Keaton developed an engine for Bill that appeared outwardly to be unmodified, but put out a considerable increase in torque in the useable 3,500 to 5,000 rpm range. The engine was barely finished for this Saturday and it wasn't until the early hours of Sunday morning that Bill managed to get the camshaft timed correctly, returning to the track somewhat tired and unsure how the engine would perform.

Bill had started from the back of the grid, having not finished on the Saturday, but had positioned himself so that he could see the starter's knees, and as soon as he saw one bend he was off, racing down the outside of the pack where he wasn't too obvious to the officials, getting a good position into the first turn. Acceleration with his new engine had proved to be excellent. It was the way he had overtaken a theoretically more powerful Jaguar right in front of the officials' start/finish platform that had led to the protest in the second race. This was not a good place to demonstrate the potential of the new engine!

The previous oil leak was from a poor seal at the fuel pump. Unfortunately the oil loss had led to some damage to the big-end bearing journal of number 4 rod, leading to problems for the future. Included in the engine specification was a Pontiac V8 drag racing cam grind by Hubbard Racing Cams of Oakland, and oversized straight eight Buick exhaust valves, whilst the SU carburettors used Jaguar specification WO-2 needles. The cylinder head had been shaved .090inch giving a compression ratio of over ten to one, but because of the considerable overlap in the Pontiac camshaft timing, it didn't appear to be above standard when the engine was turned over at cranking speed for compression reading via the spark plug hole! Luckily there had been no enthusiasm to check the engine further at the Stockton protest. One of the problems Bill now faced was of converting his car from one specification to another depending on which club ran the race meeting.

On the weekend of April 25th and 26th, the seventh Chimney Rock hill climb, 'The Vernal Veloce', was held in North Carolina. David Williams from Winston-Salem was the pilot on this occasion of the long time competing old green Plus Four, and in practice he was 5.5 seconds faster than the 2 litre class record held by the same car. On his first proper run the throttle linkage stuck, but worse was to come on the second, for the Morgan rolled down a thirty foot embankment, luckily with no injury to David. This was put down to a chassis brace bolt stripping its threads and allowing the crosshead to bend. After repair David set off again to finish fourth in class behind the two Austin Healeys demoted into Class E, and also a Porsche 1600S. He still beat all four of the TRs in the class.

The California racers were at a new track at San Diego on May 2nd and 3rd. This was Del Mar, a 1.5 mile course with ten tight turns and a 2,600 foot straight, laid out in the parking lot of the local horse track. The tight course suited the Morgan of Willie West however for he took Class E on the Saturday in an eight lapper, and again on the Sunday, in a twenty-five lap race. Making his debut in the novice race was a future Hollywood actor named Steve McQueen, driving his Porsche 1600 Super Speedster.

Over in the northeast at Lime Rock, Chuck Kelsey, in the ex-Gaston Andrey Plus Four, finished second to Harry Blanchard's Porsche Carrera on Saturday May 9th in a twenty lap race put on by the SCCA New England Region. Chuck had previously advertised this pale blue Morgan for sale from his home town of Cambridge at the end of March as he hoped to continue in motor racing in more powerful cars. The Lime Rock track had now banned Sunday racing, following a court injunction from certain local residents who disagreed with motor racing, particularly on Sundays.

Harry Reynolds drove his wire wheeled Plus Four to Fox Gap Hill Climb, in the Pocono area near Stroudsburg in Pennsylvania for the event held on Saturday May 9th, finishing second in the 'no TRs Class E Production'. He had decided to increase the engine torque for future events, so had ordered a set of 2,196cc pistons and liners, Derrington manifolds and an Iskenderian camshaft, to be fitted during the summer whilst he worked for Haddon and Williams, a local 'foreign car' shop.

Unfortunately he couldn't fathom out how to fit the new camshaft, so he abandoned that. However, he did take the crankshaft assembly and pistons to Dick Simonek's shop in 'Gasoline Alley', a famous group of garages associated with preparing Midget racers, in a rough area of Peterson, New Jersey. Here they were meticulously balanced, the bottom end on a Hudson Crank Balancer. The head was shaved, the ports polished and the distributor advance recalibrated. Harry then reassembled everything for the fall hill climb season.

In Maryland the seventh annual Cumberland races were held over the weekend of May 16th and 17th. Just two Plus Four drivers contested the Class E race at this SCCA National event, Ed Zurhorst and Harold Baumann, but they were overwhelmed by the AC Bristols, finishing eighth and thirteenth respectively.

Little had needed doing to Arch McNeill's Sebring car to prepare it for SCCA racing. Although the

Iskenderian '555' camshaft was strictly speaking forbidden by the rules of the SCCA it was left in, and Arch didn't think it gave any real advantage over standard as it sacrificed bottom end torque for more power at the top end. His first SCCA race with the Morgan was the National event at Bridgehampton over the weekend of May 30th and 31st (Memorial Day weekend). Arch contested the sixth race, for Classes B, C, D and E, over twenty laps of the dusty circuit. Arch could make no impression on the three AC Bristols ahead, finishing fourth in class and twelfth overall.

Also on Memorial Day weekend the Western New York Region ran its third annual Lake Erie Invitation Races at Dunkirk Municipal Airport over a 1.4 mile circuit. Upholding the Morgan name in the forty lap Grand Prix was Jim Forno in a Plus Four. He finished sixteenth overall, having covered thirty-six laps, the winner being Dr Wyllie in a Lotus Climax.

The Cal Club was also active over the Memorial Day weekend, running its very popular races at Santa Barbara, attracting another huge entry, such that the Class E entry was split into two races. On the Saturday the best Morgan driver was Willie West, who finished third behind the Porsche 1600 Speedster of winner Wayne Beitel, with the Porsche Carrera of Ron O'Dell second. Roger Slowi was fourth behind Willie, Ralph Bohn was fifteenth and Chuck Lowry seventeenth. Rick Hilgers retired with a bent pushrod in Snoopy. Poor Bill Chapman ended up in the ditch at Turn 3, consequently spending the rest of the day and all Sunday repairing Little Red, before he could drive it back to San Francisco. Al Gebhard had generously offered his Morgan to his friend Chuck Lowry for the Saturday race, to try and boost his confidence after his write-off of Baby Doll No 2 at Laguna Seca.

On the Sunday it was Rick Hilgers' turn to finish third to two Porsches, the Carrera of winner Chuck Parsons and the 1600 Super of Bob Herda. Al Gebhard was back in his own car for this race but managed to spin, finishing in eighth position, just behind the blue Plus Four of Alameda driver Ralph Bohn.

In the fifteen lap race for Production Classes D to I, Roger Slowi finished fifteenth, and sixth in Class E, whilst Willie West had problems, finishing three laps behind the winning Austin Healey in twenty-sixth place, seventh in class. Lew Spencer was driving, but we are not sure if it was the Morgan. Whatever it was it had gearbox problems and he had to retire.

Rick Hilgers loaned Snoopy to Barbara Windhorst for the Sunday ladies' race, and she finished fourth of the twenty-three starters, and second in Class E.

One week later the California racers were at Laguna Seca for the SCCA Pacific Coast Championship races. The Saturday contained a series of twenty-minute qualifiers for the Sunday races, and ex-Morgan racer Ed Leslie was the winner of the Class E Production race in his Austin Healey 100 Six, with Lew Spencer second in Baby Doll No 3, with Rick Hilgers third in Snoopy. Race 3 on the Sunday, over forty-five minutes, was for E Production, and turned into a Morgan parade, with Lew Spencer and Rick Hilgers ahead of the field, finishing first and second. At the start it had been Ed Leslie in the Austin Healey who took the lead, but his front offside wheel broke its spokes and the wheel collapsed. Lew and Rick then took over, closely followed by Stan Peterson of Oakland in Prudence Baxter's Plus Four, until his wheel bearing broke and he retired in the pits. Lew and Rick fought wheel to wheel for the entire race, getting further and further ahead of the rest of the pack, with Lew becoming the victor by just half a car's length and winning the enormous LeJon Trophy. 'I lost', Rick informed us, 'because Lew did not make any mistakes.' Jack Dalton finally came third in his MGA Twin-Cam.

Willie West ended up in the ditch with his red Plus Four, and Bill Hinshaw was also racing Little Blue. Stan Peterson had been offered drives in Prudence Baxter's Plus Four because he in return could offer Prudence drives in the ladies' races in his Lotus Eleven. Whereas Scott Baxter could never make the Morgan perform well, Stan, by just working on the carburettors, was able to transform the car.

The ladies' race saw second and third keenly contested by Barbara Windhorst in Baby Doll No 3 and Ruth Doushkess in Scott Baxter's Morgan. They finished in that order.

Lew Spencer at Laguna Seca Turn 9 nearly loses it but manages to hold off Rick Hilgers' challenge. (Bob Tronolone)

The year of 1959 was the last year for the unique Put-in-Bay races to be held on the island of South Bass in Lake Erie. Five Morgans were attracted to the twelve lap race for E Production and F Modified, watched by around 15,000 spectators. New to racing his Morgan on tarmac was Alton Rogers, of Niles in Ohio. He had begun racing with a VW in 1956 and 1957, but then switched to a 1955 green Plus Four. This he regularly raced on the quarter mile oval dirt track at Canfield Speedway, fitting an oversize tyre to the right front wheel to aid cornering. Racing on ovals was frowned upon by the SCCA, so, to express their rebelliousness, Alton and his pit crew devised an emblem patch for their overalls, an arrow pointing left. This stood for the 'Scuderia Left Turn Club', because speedway ovals were always tackled anticlockwise!

Other Speedway circuits also let sports car drivers have a go, including one near Cleveland, where the man to beat was Herb Swan with a Porsche RSK. He offered a prize to the first to beat him. Al Rogers claims he was the first to do so with his Morgan.

Curt Gifford, of Williams Bay, Michigan, was also entered in his chrome radiator Plus Four. He had particular reason to remember this race, for his TR2 engine completely lost its fuel line and associated hardware. Luckily he was approaching the town section of the course so he coasted to a stop in front of the general store from where he was able to purchase a piece of suitable tubing and wire it in place before rejoining the racing!

Richard Cook from Lakeland and Gordon Harrison from Pontiac drove two of the other Plus Fours.

Of the five Morgans entered the only two to finish were those of Al Rogers and Richard Cook, with Al sixth overall and second in class behind Quay Barber's TR3.

Al Rogers fell in love with Put-in-Bay as a result of this visit and regularly visited for holidays. He remembers the circuit as being narrow and quite dangerous, particularly where it passed a couple of wineries, where drinkers sat on the kerb side watching the racing! The circuit was getting dangerous but what finally

Actress Jill St John, later to become famous as a James Bond Girl in 'Diamonds are Forever', poses with Lew after his victory at Laguna Seca. (Curt Warshawsky collection)

killed it for the future was a new law in Ohio prohibiting racing on public roads. It was aimed at drag racers, but obviously the roads of South Bass Island were also within the jurisdiction.

The Cal Club put on races at Hour Glass Field, San Diego over the weekend of June 20th and 21st. On the Saturday, in the eight lap race Willie West took the lead, but produced excitement at the start/finish line on lap three when a tyre burst (he used Englebert Racing tyres, usually most reliable). Luckily he was able to use his skill to bring the car to a stop safely. Al Gebhard managed

Curt Gifford passing through the town section at Put-in-Bay. (Morgan Motor Co Collection)

to stay ahead of Steve McQueen's Porsche 1600 Super for the early part of the race, but then Steve got by. Al followed Steve closely, and noticed oil appearing on his windscreen - Steve's engine had broken a con rod. Al thought to himself that at least there would be one less Porsche to contend with on the Sunday, but he was proved wrong, for Steve McQueen went back to Hollywood and persuaded Earl Callicut to sell him his own Porsche GT Carrera and was back there on the Sunday!

On the Sunday it was Willie West who was victorious in Class E, finishing second to Jay Hill's Porsche Carrera. Willie had needed to send his mechanic to Worldwide Imports on the Saturday evening for some replacement bits. At least he beat Steve McQueen's new Carrera, which was third. Roger Slowi's Morgan suffered many knocks during the close racing, causing Nanette Spencer (Lew's wife) to question, 'How many cars can you borrow paint from in the same race?' when she wrote her report for the *Format* magazine of the Morgan Plus Four Club.

One week later Watkins Glen was running the annual Glen Classic meeting, attracting the wire wheeled Plus Four of Jim Forno as the only Morgan entry. The first race was for unrestricted capacity and Formula 3 cars, over eleven laps (25.3 miles). Jim was running second in class and challenging for the number one spot until the final turn when the fuel pump failed, allowing those behind to pass, and Jim finished twenty-second overall, but he was still fourth in class. The third race was for Classes E and F over eleven laps once more, with Jim coming home twelfth overall and sixth in class. Jim was carrying race number 777 as he believed that 7 was a lucky number and would give him good fortune, (7, 17 and 77 had already been taken at this meeting!).

On Saturday July 4th Arch McNeill took his ex-Sebring aluminium Morgan to Lime Rock for the SCCA's Northeastern Region National race meeting. Over twenty laps Al managed third in Class E behind the AC Bristols of Eve Mull and Harry Carter, and ahead of the other Morgan, that of George Valentine from Ithaca New York. One week later Arch returned to this track for the SCCA New York Regional race, finishing third in class behind Mull and Carter once more, although this time it was Harry Carter who was the victor of the fifteen lap race.

Jim Forno with his supporters at Watkins Glen. Left to right: Dr George Voigt, Mrs Dorothy Forno, pit crew Miss Virginia Johnson, son Robert Forno, mechanic Arnold Romaldini, SCCA Regional Executive Bob Stanton and Jim Forno. (E J Conklin)

The Sebring Morgan was racing again the following weekend, for Arch McNeill with Mike and 'Honey' Rothschild took the car to the Marlboro circuit in Maryland for the Washington Regional SCCA races. Arch didn't adapt to the circuit with his two races, finishing behind the usual ACs and a TR or two. Mike, on the other hand, made it look easy, winning the Morgan-Triumph-MG marque race in style.

That same weekend the SCCA ran a National race meeting in California at Riverside. The long straights did not really suit the Morgans and only one was entered, Baby Doll No 3, for Lew Spencer. Practice was held on the Friday and disaster struck when the right front wheel came off on the third lap, Baby Doll sustaining considerable damage to the front end as a result. Repair work took until three in the morning to fix, with Billie Bell wielding the welding tackle and Claude Brun the big hammer.

The race officials had not expected the Morgan to appear for Saturday's race, so Lew had to start last in the fifteen lap race for Production Classes E and above. The engine wasn't running right, pulling a poor 4,900 revs on the mile long back straight, but despite this Lew came in eighteenth of the twenty-five finishers, beating much bigger machinery. He was fifth in Class E, following home Kas Kastner's TR3 and the usual AC Bristols. The race itself was shortened by two laps when Tom Frank rolled his Corvette to destruction at Turn 3, luckily without injury, this being the second Corvette destroyed in the racing. The winner was the ex-Morgan racer Bob Bondurant in his Corvette. Barbara Windhorst took Baby Doll No 3 to seventh place overall in the ten lap ladies' race, but third in Class E behind two AC Bristols.

On Wednesday July 22nd Rene Pellandini was a welcome visitor to the Morgan factory in England. In discussions with Peter Morgan he expressed the view that the Plus Four would continue to sell well in the USA, but that the 4/4 needed to adopt more contemporary styling if it was to compete with the Austin Healey Sprite for sales at the lower end of the sports car market. Furthermore, the Sprite had better equipment, namely an overhead valve engine, four speed gearbox and twin carburettors. Rene offered to approach the great Italian automobile stylist Giovanni Michelotti, who was a personal friend, on behalf of the Morgan Motor Company to see if he would design a more modern body for the Morgan chassis.

The Northwest Region of the SCCA held its annual Seafair races over a 3.2 mile circuit at Shelton Airport, Washington over the weekend of August 1st and 2nd, with points counting towards the Pacific Coast Championship of the SCCA. In the fifteen lap race for Class E Production Jack Murray, who worked for Boeing in Seattle, took his Plus Four to eighth place. He had previously raced various other vehicles, including a Corvette and a Porsche special, and had earlier raced on American ovals. He tended to be a fearless driver as a result. The Morgan had been purchased from GB Sterne, and was a black two-seater with red upholstery, a heater and wire wheels. It carried chassis number 3885, and had been dispatched from Malvern on Thursday March 27th 1958.

Whilst this race was sanctioned by the SCCA the various car clubs of both Washington and Oregon State had formed an alliance with the British Columbia clubs in Canada, called the International Conference of Northwest Sports Car Clubs, to run races in this part of the world using a classification loosely based on that of the SCCA. The 'Conference' had begun sanctioning races in 1957.

Two Plus Fours were entered for the SCCA National races held at Montgomery in New York on the weekend of August 8th and 9th. Arch McNeill was driving his ex-Sebring car and the other was the red 1956 Morgan belonging to Gerald Rollo, from Endicott in New York State. Gerald was an engineer working at IBM in Poughkeepsie. He had been very impressed by the Morgan racing of Jim Forno, the Endicott Morgan dealer, so he had purchased Jim's old racing Morgan in 1958 to replace an Austin Healey he had been racing.

Morgan Sports Cars — 1959

In the twenty lap race for Classes E and F Production Arch was the better placed of the two, finishing fifteenth overall, but seventh in class behind six AC Bristols. Gerald finished twentieth of the twenty-four finishers.

That same weekend, over in California at San Luis Obispo, four Plus Fours were participating in the town's annual races at the county airport. They were driven by Robin Jackson, Bill Hinshaw, Doug Farrar and Bill Chapman. Robin Jackson was going really well, battling through the field from thirteenth to fifth place until, on the penultimate lap, engine problems intervened. Bill Chapman finished an excellent third whilst Doug Farrar had to retire with brake trouble. Doug's Plus Four was a right hand drive model. The problem with Robin's engine turned out to be a cracked cylinder head. However, he was able to drive home to Marin County by carrying a five gallon can of water in the passenger seat, and stopping to top up the radiator every few miles.

Rene Pellandini was always encouraging the Morgan factory to produce better and faster cars, so he had been delighted by the news of the all aluminium racer produced for Arch McNeill for the 1959 Sebring race. He asked the factory to produce replicas, and the first two were reported in the San Francisco based magazine *Sports Car Pictorial* of August 1959 as having been delivered, with one destined for Bret Morehouse and one being kept for Rene for racing. This latter car, a white car with blue upholstery, was also lent to *Road and Track* for a road test, and this was published in the September edition.

Road and Track noted this Morgan 'Semi-Competition' model had extras including an all aluminium body at $175, competition exhaust system (Derrington) at $125, front disc brakes at $158, triple laced wire wheels at $195, finned aluminium sump at $75, and electric fuel pump at $25. There were also a couple of items they could not understand being listed as extras namely the strengthened frame front and strengthened gearbox mounts at $40. They believed a production sports car should not need strengthening for racing. The car they tested was right hand drive and fitted with Dunlop racing tyres. It also had a wood rim steering wheel. In the test they achieved a 0 to 60 mph time of 9.9 seconds, and a top speed of 102 mph at 5,500 rpm. The report finished, 'There are cars and there are cars, but the Morgan is well on its way to becoming a legend as the very last of the "hang the comfort, let's have sport" automobiles.'

Although there is little doubt this white Morgan was originally planned to be Baby Doll No 4, Rene had been negotiating for some time to acquire the western United States distributorship for AC Cars and, following a recent visit to the AC factory at Thames Ditton in England, he had finally managed to convince the management that he was the right person for this role. He now needed to prepare an AC Bristol for Lew Spencer to drive instead of the Morgan and so he bought a suitable car at a good price from a US soldier returning from duty in Hawaii. Claude Brun completely stripped the car and prepared it for racing. It was named 'Beware 1', by Rene as he wanted to inform the other competitors that a 'fantastic, beautiful and powerful car will race them'. It was a red left hand drive car and was so well prepared by Claude assisted by his brother George, an aircraft mechanic, that many thought it was a special build AC factory car. Rene also persuaded Roger Slowi's mechanic, Stu Haggart, to join his organisation, with special responsibility to look after the AC cars.

Rene particularly remembered the close wheel to wheel racing Lew had had with Rick Hilgers at Laguna Seca, so the white Morgan was now offered to Rick, as Rene was keen that the new Morgan should be raced by a talented driver. Rick collected this car, with little more than the *Road and Track* road test mileage on the clock and prepared it for racing. We think it was chassis number 4141, originally dispatched from the Morgan factory on Monday March 9th. Because of its white colour it was perhaps more appropriate that this Morgan should carry Rick's nickname of Snoopy complete with the cartoon drawing of Charlie Brown's dog on the scuttle, than his previous red one. Its first race was at Tracy Municipal Airport for the SCCA San Francisco Region races on August 14th and 15th.

Also entered was Robin Jackson who, after working late hours all week repairing the engine damaged at San Luis Obispo, finally made it to the start, joining several other Morgan drivers at this event. On the Saturday there was a novice event for Class E and above, and the Plus Fours of Ralph Bohn, Bill Chapman, Robin Jackson, and Doug Farrar finish third, fourth, sixth and eighth in class respectively.

The ladies' event Production class was won by Laurayne Wood in an Austin Healey, but second to her was Marion Lowe in a Morgan (she had been more famous in previous years for successfully racing her Frazer Nash with the men).

There were twenty-four Class E cars taking part in a twenty-four miles race on Sunday named the 'British Bash'. Pru Baxter's Morgan was being driven by Lotus exponent Stan Peterson, and he nosed out Rick Hilgers to take third place, with Rick fourth in Snoopy, Bohn seventh, Chapman tenth and Jackson eleventh. Two races later was a fifty-six mile race for senior and junior drivers, and Class E was won by Dr George Snively in an Austin Healey, with Bob O'Brien second in his Morgan ahead of the MGA Twin-Cam of Lester Hartman. Bob Bondurant was an impressive overall victor, for he was racing a borrowed Corvette.

Several of the Northern California racers had become good friends, such that they liked to meet at 'The Red Garter', a 'banjo, beer and peanut joint' in North Beach. They became 'The Red Garter Sports Car Club'.

We have tended to ignore the many rallies taking place in America. They were often just local club affairs, and more importantly, the reports were unhelpful to the historian, often even omitting the makes of cars with which the participants competed. On Saturday August 15th the Californian Morgan Plus Four Club ran its Nameless Rally, starting from UCLA parking lot with a 'hare and hounds' format. It was important because amongst the competitors was Kenny Deeter, driving another of the aluminium 'Competition' Morgans.

Kenny had ordered this new racer via Worldwide Imports, but decided to collect it himself from the Morgan factory whilst visiting his family in Ireland. This green Morgan, chassis number 4203, was right hand drive for racing and fitted with Dunlop racing tyres. Besides the aluminium body, front disc brakes, Derrington exhaust, strengthened frame front and gearbox mounts, a wood-rim steering wheel and Simmonds locknuts completed the 'Competition' model specification. It was collected by Kenny on Friday May 15th, registered in the UK as WOF 305. Kenny drove it via Glasgow to Stranraer and then over to Ireland, before it was shipped to California. He was now to prepare it for racing in the forthcoming Cal Club Santa Barbara races to be held on September 5th and 6th. To show his Irish ancestry an orange stripe was painted along the bonnet, thereby giving the car the green and orange of the Irish tricolour.

The Cal Club classified Production cars by performance now, so when an ex-Morgan-owning official informed the club about the specification of the Competition Morgans it was decided to move them into Class D, where they were up against the AC Bristols of course, these also being aluminium bodied and having had front disc brakes fitted since 1957. The ACs had full four wheel independent suspension and the excellent Bristol six cylinder 100D engine, which was good for 125 bhp, twenty more than the Morgan.

Kenny was very upset at having to race in Class D and suggested to that great Morgan enthusiast Gerry Willburn that the aluminium car with him driving weighed no less than a steel car with Gerry driving, Gerry being somewhat slightly built. In fact the Competition Morgan weighed 250 lb less than the steel car according to *Sports Car Pictorial*.

With Kenny re-classed into D, there was only one Morgan in Race 4, for Production Class E, this being Roger Slowi's Plus Four. He was in fifth place on lap 5, but was then sidelined with a

Morgan Sports Cars — 1959

Kenny Deeter at Santa Barbara battling Harry Peck's Corvette and an AC Bristol in Race Four. Note the damaged rear wing. (Ken Deeter collection)

shattered clutch pressure plate. Roger and Stu Haggart borrowed Rene Pellandini's station wagon on the Sunday morning to tow the Morgan back to Los Angeles, and it was soon fixed.

Race 5 on the Saturday was for Production Classes D and above, and Kenny was the only Morgan driver, although Lew Spencer was in Rene's AC Bristol, Beware 1. Nothing went right for Kenny, for he accidentally switched off the ignition, but managed to rejoin the racing to finish twenty-first out of twenty-three finishers. The Morgan's near side rear wing suffered a crease after the Corvette of Harry Peck made contact.

Meanwhile Lew Spencer was finding the AC much to his liking, finishing fourth overall behind three Corvettes and beating several Jaguars and Mercedes 300SLs.

On the Sunday Kenny did better in Race 12, for Class D and E drivers not qualifying for Race 13, finishing fifth overall out of twenty-two starters, and third in Class D.

Lew was in the AC for the next race and battled with Chuck Parsons in the Porsche Carrera, swapping the lead between them until Lew took the chequered flag to win.

That same weekend, on the other side of the USA, the Sebring car of Arch McNeill was competing at Thompson in the Northeastern Region of the SCCA's National meeting. Whereas the Cal Club had reclassified the aluminium cars into Class D in California, the SCCA still classified just by engine capacity, so Arch was entered in Class E. On the Sunday Arch was third in class in a fifteen lap race, behind the AC Bristols of Harry Carter and Pierre Mion. In the thirty lap race on the Monday he was fourth, another AC Bristol, that of Pettit, joining the previous two ahead of him.

On the Saturday September 12th Arch was out again, this time at Lime Rock for the Long Island Sports Car Association races, and in the race for Classes E and F he came home first overall in the fifteen lap race. Arch was having his Morgan maintained and prepared by David Junceau, who ran 'Formula Two Inc' in Poughkeepsie, New York, this garage handling Triumph, BMW and AC Bristol cars.

For the New York inter-club races at Bridgehampton on Sunday September 20th Arch drove the Sebring Morgan the 125 miles from his home in Dobbs Ferry, New York, accompanied by Mike and Honey Rothschild. He had entered the 150 mile race for Production cars of Classes F and above, the field including an ex-Le Mans Ferrari California, Corvettes, Jaguars, AC Bristols, Austin Healeys, a Frazer Nash and Porsches. Derrington inlet and exhaust manifolds were fitted for this event, giving a noticeable increase in performance (6% according to Derrington).

Both Arch and Mike practised, but Arch wondered whether he might drive this race single-handed, so enough fuel was to be carried to hopefully last the distance. There was concern about tyres during practice, for Arch thought the left rear felt 'loose'. Closer inspection revealed the tread was beginning to strip from the tyre carcass. Arch used Dunlop racing tyres, which were retreaded at the World Wide Tire Co of Hicksville, for $13 each. Mike, on the other hand, used Pirelli racing tyres, also retreads, and he was able to find and buy a suitable Pirelli from another competitor to replace the damaged Dunlop. Come the race and all went according to plan so Arch signalled to Mike that he was staying out. He finished a fantastic third overall, behind just the Ferrari and a Corvette, but was obviously class winner. This was a brilliant performance in this long race, considering the opposition. Inspection of the Pirelli tyre showed it was now down to the canvas in places, Pirelli presumably using a much softer compound than did Dunlops in the tyres Arch usually used. The Morgan hadn't missed a beat and was now driven the 125 miles back home.

Whilst the aluminium cars were not an official model at the Morgan factory, the specification of the alloy body, Derrington exhaust, strengthened frame fronts and gearbox mounts, front disc brakes and Simmonds lock nuts, was being advertised by Rene Pellandini. He advertised it as the 'Competition Sebring' model and it was available to special order. When the eighth of these replicas of the Sebring car was completed at the Morgan factory (chassis 4305 which was dispatched on Wednesday September 16th) the factory sales records show a new description, namely 'Baby Doll specification'. As we have shown no Baby Doll so far raced had been one of these, but presumably the factory had thought that the car sold to Rick Hilgers would have become Baby Doll No 4.

That same weekend marked the third running of the Del Mar races by the Los Angeles Region of the SCCA, using the tight 1.2 mile course around the horse racing track parking lot. The first of the Sunday races was a ten lap race for the ladies, and Barbara Windhorst managed fourth place in Baby Doll No 3 behind Betty Shutes' Porsche and two Lotus XIs. Lew Spencer took over the Morgan for Race 4, an eighteen lap race for Production Classes D, E and F, finishing in fifth place behind four Porsches, but, like Barbara earlier, he was first in Class E.

Arch McNeill was the only Morgan entrant amongst the two hundred and fifty competitors at Watkins Glen for the Grand Prix meeting over the weekend of September 25th and 26th. He raced in the 22 lap 'Harold W Jacques Memorial Race' for Production cars of E and below, one of twenty-five starters. He finished sixth, just behind the first non-Bristol powered car, the TR3 of Al Ackerley, but the winning AC Bristol was subsequently disqualified, so he moved up to fifth.

Once again the *LA Times* sponsored the annual Grand Prix races held at Riverside on October 10th and 11th by the Cal Club. Roger Slowi was the only Morgan entrant for the Production race for Classes D and E on the 'amateur' day of Saturday. He started well back in the pack, but by the eighth lap he had fought his way up to third in class and fourth overall. He held this position to the end of this fifteen lap race, to receive a well deserved trophy. Lew Spencer was in Beware 1, the AC Bristol, for the next race for Classes D and above, and he finished second in class and third overall behind a Mercedes 300SL and an Austin Healey, despite a blown head gasket. The Corvettes wondered what had hit them!

Rene Pellandini had now added another foreign make to his distributorships: the French manufactured DB Sports coupé and Formula Junior cars.

The American rally enthusiasts were catered for by a new event in October, the first ever American International Rally. It was designed to rival the famous Monte Carlo Rally, covering 3,300 miles over four days. The rally had six different starts, with the routes linking at Santa Fe in New

Morgan Sports Cars 1959

The McKinney/ Bru Morgan in spectacular scenery during the American International Rally. (Morgan Motor Co collection)

Mexico for a split second regularity run into the finish at Las Vegas in Nevada. This last leg was nearly 900 miles in length, with 177 different speed changes and instructions to observe. It was riddled with hidden check points, with little or no time for refuelling or resting, and was a major test of the crews' stamina and endurance. There was a disappointing entry of just sixty-eight, but all except

Arch McNeill collects the chequered flag at Lime Rock for his victory lap. (Arch McNeill collection)

330

five were flagged in as finishers. There was one Morgan entry, a Plus Four starting from San Francisco. It was driven by G C McKinney and navigated by H R Bru, and it came home in fifty-second place. The winner drove a Nash Rambler Station Wagon, and a Ford Thunderbird was second.

On Saturday October 17th Arch McNeill took his Sebring car to Lime Rock for the New York Regional SCCA races, where, in a fifteen lap race for Production Classes F and above, he at last beat the AC Bristols and took Class E, a brilliant performance.

Back in Pennsylvania Harry Reynolds' Plus Four was proving a formidable car for the hill climbs with its 2.2 litre engine. The bottom end torque was just what was needed for hill climbing, so Harry decided to name his car 'The Torking Dog', the name being applied to the side of the car behind the driver. At the fall Springtown hill climb held on Saturday October 3rd Harry's was the only Morgan, and he shattered his previous best time, recording 65.9207 seconds. He was now running in Class D Modified because of the engine modifications.

Over the weekend of October 24th and 25th Harry took The Torking Dog to the Big Pocono Hill Climb near Stroudsburg in Pennsylvania where he dominated the F, D and H Modified class, recording 94.0038 seconds. Also competing, but in Class E for standard Plus Fours were Janet Possinger and Dick Smith, finishing fourth and fifth respectively, Dick's time being some ten seconds slower than Harry's. Ten seconds is a long time in hill climbing!

Laguna Seca was just down the road for Rick Hilgers, and Morgans always did well at this twisty circuit, where good handling was more important than brute power. Rick entered the new Snoopy for the weekend meeting of October 24th and 25th. Three Morgans were also entered from San Francisco, the green Plus Fours of Doug Farrar and George Pridmore, and the red one of Bill Chapman. George Pridmore was an Englishman from London, who worked as a salesman for British Auto Parts. He was driving chassis number 3831, which had been dispatched from the Morgan factory on Tuesday February 4th 1958 to Worldwide Imports, fitted with a tuned engine. George was the first owner, and the Morgan was always immaculate, complete with enamel Union Jacks on the bonnet sides. It was a right hand drive car. Stan Peterson was also to drive the Baxter's silver Morgan in this meeting.

Rick had high hopes for Snoopy, but the tight course saw him on the outside of Stan Peterson at Turn 2. They touched, with Snoopy's left front wheel

Behind the AC Bristol of Frank Crane, Stan Peterson and Kas Kastner (TR3) take tight lines, whereas Rick Hilgers appears somewhat ragged on the fast Turn 2 at Laguna Seca. (Dave Friedman)

hitting the right rear wheel of the Peterson car. This pitched Snoopy into the hay bales at about 90 mph, flipping the Morgan end over end. Luckily Rick climbed out of the wrecked Morgan with little more than a cut lip and chipped teeth. Meanwhile Lew Spencer stunned the local boys by lapping faster than the Corvettes in Beware 1, on his way to victory by fifteen seconds in this Production D and E race.

1959 saw the completion in Florida of a very important American speedway, the famous Daytona International Speedway. It was the brainchild of racing enthusiast Bill France and was built in swamp land behind the town of Daytona. The speedway track had three banked turns, two of 31 degrees and the other of 18, giving a 2.5 mile circuit. Inside the speedway track was a road section, allowing different courses to be used with various parts of the outer track, depending on the racing. It had cost $3,000,000 to construct and the impressive facilities included several stands, trade buildings and restaurants. There was a lake in the centre of the track, filling the area from which soil had been excavated to make the bankings. This was to be used for speedboat racing and fishing, so no area was wasted.

On Sunday November 15th the Central Florida Region of the SCCA ran National races at this impressive new venue, using part of the infield course to give a 3.1 mile circuit, part speedway banking and part road circuit. The second race of the day was a thirty lap event for Classes E and above, but sadly only eight entries faced the starter, two being ladies. One of these was a school teacher from Key Largo named Lalah Neuman, and she was driving a Morgan Plus Four with bolt-on wheels, carrying her racing number 13. Lalah had a real battle with the other lady, 'Smokey' Drolet in her TR3, the two ladies racing side by side with nothing between them until the TR3 finally dropped out. Lalah finished fourth, but had a chance of third, for George Robertson ran out of fuel 200 feet short of the line in his Corvette and had to push it home.

The fall Hershey hill climb was held that same weekend. Rain slowed Harry Reynolds to a time of 73.2410 seconds, but Ike Williamson had a great climb, in 64.2736 seconds to take Class E Production. The 'stop-reverse line' had now been abandoned, with consequently less damage to transmissions.

The conditions were not pleasant for the eighth running of the Chimney Rock hill climb in North Carolina, which was held near the end of the racing season. It took place over the weekend of November 28th and 29th causing the event to be named 'The Turkey Trot'. It was very cold, with 16 degrees F, well below freezing, recorded at the top. Ex-Morgan driver David Williams had forsaken his Morgan for a drive in George Trask's TR3 and came in second in class with the fastest ever ascent in a Triumph. The only Morgan entered didn't finish in the first four places.

No Morgans took part at Riverside in California on December 5th and 6th. Roger Slowi was entered, but clutch trouble at the last minute made him scratch from the event.

Only one Morgan driver featured in the SCCA National Championship end of season standings. This was Arch McNeill, who finished sixteenth equal in Class E Production; his Morgan was the highest placed non Bristol engined car. In the New York Region's own Championship it was a different story, for Arch won the over 1,600cc category, a most impressive performance. Arch wrote to Peter Morgan to tell him of the ex Sebring car's 1959 achievements, reporting that it had started fifteen races during the year and had completed all of them usually finishing within the first four places in class. The only major attention to the engine had been the routine fitting of a set of exhaust valves and one set of big-end bearings. He finished his letter thus: 'The above just goes to show that the Morgan is a very competitive machine selling at a reasonable price. It is nice to know that someone still has such a combination in mind!'

During 1960 Arch wrote to Peter Morgan inquiring how many Morgans had been built before January 1960 with aluminium bodies and wings, and received the reply that the number was 58. We have been unable so far to find anywhere near this number in the Morgan records and wonder at the accuracy of this figure. The number of 'Competition Sebring' or 'Baby Doll' specification cars listed is only 17.

However, 1959 had been a particularly important year for the Morgan Motor Company in America for sales back home were still poor, the Morgan being perceived as out of date. The USA sold over 90% of Plus Four production for the year, and over 40% of 4/4s.

Hawaii

The United States of America had administered the Hawaiian Islands since 1893, but on August 21st 1959 Hawaii became the fiftieth State of the USA. The Hawaii State flag is of particular interest because it rather surprisingly contains a Union Jack on a background of eight stripes, representing the eight main islands. The flag had been designed much earlier when the Union Jack was a sign of friendship towards visiting British seamen. Unlike other States which mainly had speed limits of 65 mph for cars (55 mph for trucks), the limit in Hawaii was just 45 mph.

The USA had important military bases in Hawaii, of which Pearl Harbor is perhaps the most well known. The University of Hawaii was also very popular with mainland American students. As a consequence there was a transient population of young mainland Americans, including some with an interest in sports cars, who wanted to race. It must be said though that drag racing was still the more popular motor sport here. To run sports car events the Hawaii Region of the SCCA and the MG Car Club of Hawaii had formed a company known as the Associated Sports Car Clubs of Hawaii Ltd. This company actively promoted races, gymkhanas and other sports car events on the Hawaiian Islands. The main venue for racing was the ex Army Air Field of Kahuku, which was situated on the northern point of Oahu, between the Pacific Ocean and the Koolau Mountains. Originally built in 1942 the airfield had enjoyed only a short active life, and had then been further damaged by the tsunami in 1946. It did have two parallel runways, one of 5,000 feet and the other of 3,800 feet and an acceptable circuit of approximately two miles was possible using imaginative cross links between the two runways. The owner of the land was the Castle Corporation and for each race meeting it insisted on seeing a certificate of insurance from Lloyds of London. It was also possible to run drag races here and the money from these helped subsidize the sports car racing.

Towards the end of 1959 a foreign-car and tyre dealer named KP Motors, Inc took on the Morgan agency, possibly obtaining cars through Rene Pellandini. KP Motors was run by Les Kangas and Charlie Potts (hence the KP) and was advertised as a 'Rally and Race Center'. It was situated at 933 Kapiolani Boulevard in Honolulu. Both Les and Charlie were very keen sports car enthusiasts, and Charlie had also been an American football star at Iolani High School. The 'Rally and Race Center' had its own racing uniform for the Morgan drivers, consisting of a light blue driving suit with white Bell helmet.

Charlie entered a Plus Four at the Kahuku races held on Sunday September 6th, and finished second in the five lap Class E Production race behind the Triumph importer Walter Vail in a Triumph TR3A.

On Sunday November 22nd both Les Kangas and Charlie Potts were entered for the 'Turkey Trot' races at Kahuku. In the twenty lap main event Les Kangas finished in fourth place, behind a Chevrolet engined Healey, a Corvette and a Buick engined Healey, specials being a particular feature of racing in Hawaii. In the programme for the Turkey Trot, KP Motors proudly advertised their appointment as Morgan agents.

KP MOTORS, INC.

We are proud to announce our appointment as Hawaii's exclusive dealer for the sale and service of the following fine sport cars:

AC — ACE / ACECA / BRISTOL / ACECA BRISTOL

MORGAN — Plus four roadster / Plus four Drop-head Coupe / Plus four 4-seater Roadster / 4/4 series II Roadster

Some models NOW ON DISPLAY at your "RACE AND RALLY CENTER"

933 Kapiolani   Ph. 57-406, 59-362

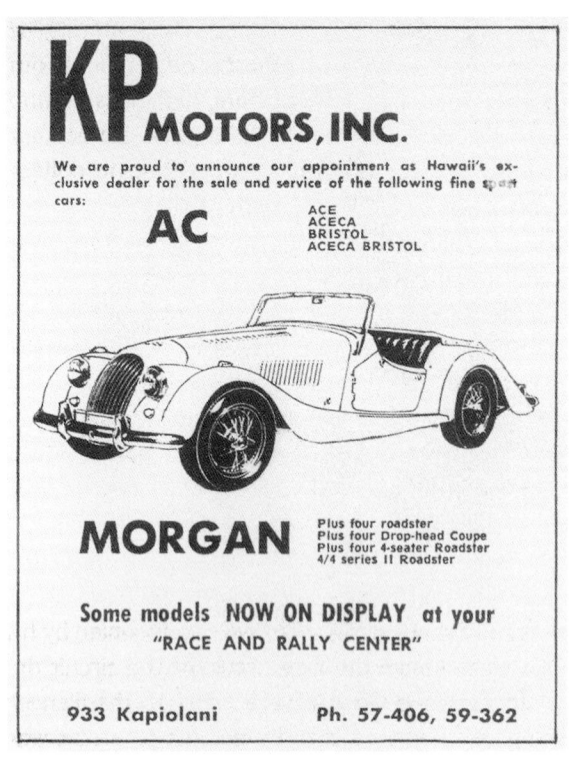

Canada

Morgan racing in Ontario continued with Gordon Harrison from Pontiac, Michigan contesting the races held at the old BCATP airfield at Green Acres near Goderich in Ontario on Saturday May 30th, and also Saturday July 4th where he was joined by the Plus Four of William Schwedler. Sadly we don't have results for either meeting.

On Sunday June 14th the Quebec Region ran races at St Eugene, in Ontario. Bud Mackley drove his Plus Four to second place in the over 1,500cc sports car race.

The SCCBC's new Westwood circuit opened on Sunday July 26th. A huge crowd estimated at between 10,000 to 18,000 spectators turned up on a glorious day to watch the action and assess the new circuit. The beautiful wooded venue surrounded a 1.8 mile course, featuring everything a European circuit should have, from uphill to downhill sections, to a hairpin and a carousel. It was a very challenging circuit, attracting just under one hundred drivers and it had excellent viewing points for the spectators.

Several Morgans were there for the inaugural meeting. GB Sterne was present in his four-seater Plus Four. Jack Murray, a Boeing assembly line worker, had crossed over the border from Seattle with his Plus Four. Also entered in Plus Fours were regular contestants Max Schulze, Clarence Middleton and Pete Browning. Dr Robert Brisco, a chiropractor from Trail in southeast British Columbia, had previously raced an MGA, but had now entered a green Morgan 4/4, to which Buckler close ratio gears had been fitted to suit the mountainous area in which he resided. Also running a 4/4 was Tom Rice. Tom, Clarence Middleton and Max Shultze had all made the long journey from Kennewick in Southeast Washington State over the border in America. There was a small Morgan dealership in this town, which presumably explained the existence of this small group of Morgan racers. Peter Browning was an enthusiastic member of the Victoria Motor Sports Club, and was to remain so for the rest of his life.

GB Sterne's Morgan was running equipped with wire wheels. It is possible the car was supplied with these having been fitted at the Morgan factory, being one of the first so equipped. However, there is no record of this and we suspect George had fitted them himself. The only Morgan to feature in the results was Jack Murray's, finishing second in Class D to an Austin Healey in the Class D and over Production race.

Another meeting was held at Westwood on Sunday August 9th but this time in front of only 2,000 spectators as it was an intra-club event for SCCBC members. Entered in Morgans were GB Sterne, Clarence Middleton, Peter Browning and Max Schulze in Plus Fours, with Tom Rice in his 4/4. Race 2 was for Production Classes E and above, and George Sterne tasted success by finishing in second place overall behind Al Doyan's AC Bristol, but he was first in Class D. The fifth race was open to all comers with a Le Mans start and George did well to finish in fourth place, the race being won by Jim Rattenbury's Jaguar D-type, ahead of Al Doyan's AC, with a modified TR2 third.

On Sunday August 16th another race meeting was held at Harewood Acres. Three Morgan Plus

The drivers' meeting at Westwood on July 26th before the Class D and over race. GB Sterne's car is visible. (Sterne collection)

Fours took part in the race for Production Classes D and E, Robert Rice finishing 19th, Gordon Harrison 22nd and Dr Warren Ross in 28th place.

Another Westwood meeting was held that same Sunday August 16th. The Plus Fours of GB Sterne, Clarence Middleton and Max Schulze were entered, as were two 4/4s. One belonged to Tom Rice and the other was entered by Lloyd Messersmith from Wenatchee in Central Washington State in the USA. Lloyd had bought his red 4/4 from the Morgan dealer in Kennewick, who gave him a good price as he was having difficulty in selling it. Lloyd fitted a luggage rack on the rear deck and for races he would pack a tent and Primus stove and drive accompanied by his wife to and from the race circuit. At the circuit the windscreen and silencer were removed, the silencer being replaced by a straight exhaust pipe that was wired under the car on the journey to the track. Having a 4/4 Lloyd tried to get the race number 414 allocated to him, but it was already taken by another 4/4 owner named Jack Thompson, so he had to take 434. We have no results for this event. Meetings continued to be held at Westwood until the end of the season on November 1st. Sadly results have proved to be elusive for this period.

On Tuesday September 15th the Winnipeg Sports

Dust is thrown into the air as GB Sterne runs off the track at Westwood Hairpin during the opening meeting in July. (Vancouver newspaper clipping)

A 4/4 at one of the Westwood meetings in the line up for the Class 1 Production race. (SCCBC archives)

Car Club ran races on the abandoned BCATP Paulson Airport at Dauphin in Manitoba using a 2.2 mile circuit. Bill Sullivan finished first in the under 2,700cc Race. Bill lived in Winnipeg where a new agent, Birmingham Motors, had become a low key Morgan agent, importing the first of their Plus Fours in 1958. This became Bill's car. It was a green two-seater, with black leather upholstery, wire wheels and a heater. It carried chassis number 3964, and had been dispatched on Thursday September 18th 1958. Bill bought it in April 1959 and at the time of writing Bill still has this car!

Birmingham Motors imported three more Morgans, all during 1959. One was a 4/4 chassis number A506, a Competition model finished in red, with wire wheels. It had been dispatched on Thursday July 30th, and became the property of Art 'Ginger' Millar, who raced it too.

On Monday October 19th B Neeve competed with his Plus Four at Harewood Acres, finishing ninth in Race 5, for Production cars over 1,500cc. In Race 7, for Production cars over 1,600cc he finished seventh.

Lydia and George Sterne with trophies won with his Morgan. Note too the radio aerial and wire wheels. (Sterne collection)

Chapter 7
1960

Early in January all new Morgans began leaving the Morgan factory fitted with Bowman radiators, and on Friday January 8th a black four-seater Plus Four, chassis number 4368, was dispatched with ordinary bolt-on wheels and the optional front disc brakes, being probably one of the first of the bolt-on wheeled cars to be so equipped.

The Ford 100E engines changed numbers from a six number series to perhaps a continuation of the same series but prefixed with 'S'. Car A544 was dispatched on January 25th fitted with the first prefixed number, S153693.

HFS Morgan was famous for using the cheapest possible materials in his production Morgans consistent with good performance, and all four-wheelers had been using front hubs with ordinary ball-bearing races. This was old motoring technology and the superior design of taper roller bearings was now far better, particularly in coping with the cornering stresses of racing. Some new Morgans fitted with disc brakes began leaving the factory in early 1960 with Timken taper roller bearings fitted to the front hubs and by April all disc braked cars were so fitted.

There was a new Morgan agency, 'The Cedar Motor House', situated in Cheltenham. It had been acquired by John McKechnie who was intrigued by the possibility of running a team of specially prepared Morgan 4/4s in the Autosport Championship, once the Ford 105E engine was made available. He believed a Ford 105E engine to Formula Junior specification would make these Morgans unbeatable.

For 1960 the FIA had altered the regulations for the Grand Touring (GT) racing category. Five years had passed since the 1955 Le Mans disaster, following which the engine capacity for the then newly introduced GT category was fixed at below 3 litres. The public outcry against powerful sports racing cars had now subsided, so the engine capacity limit was removed for 1960, allowing in such cars as the Chevrolet Corvette. The windscreen dimension regulations were toughened, however, ruling out the 1959 Sports Car Champions Aston Martin from competing in the GT class in 1960 with the same cars. As a concession to the possibility of bad weather conditions an oblong could be cut out of the windscreen in front of the driver for better visibility. For recognition as GT cars there had to be a minimum number of 100 identical units manufactured in twelve consecutive months. However two different carburettor specifications of number or size were permitted within each 100 built.

There was a new event for the motor sports enthusiast to visit in January (from Saturday 2nd to Saturday 9th). The Racing Car Show was organised by the British Racing and Sports Car Club (BRSCC) at the Royal Horticultural Old Hall in London. Included was a display of racing cars old and new as well as there being twenty-two stands where speed equipment manufacturers could show their products. The event proved to be a great success and it was decided to hold the show annually. Of interest to the Morgan owner in particular was the large stand of VW Derrington, as a conversion for the TR3 engine to use twin Weber carburettors was prominently on show.

Weber carburettors had usually been associated with exotic Italian sports and racing cars. They had also been used by Jaguar, Aston Martin and several Formula 1 teams, including the 1959 World Champions Cooper. Many of these teams were now investigating fuel injection, but the Italian Weber carburettors had gained a growing reputation as the best of the carburettors for racing. Although expensive they were becoming more affordable as die-casting enabled them to be produced in volume for the likes of the 'Veloce' Alfa Romeos. The most popular version was the series 'E' derivative of the 'Doppio Corpo Orizontale' or DCO, translating as the double bodied horizontal version of the twin choke Weber. Derrington claimed an extra 8 bhp using Webers on its tuned 2.2 litre TR3 engine.

There was a huge Morgan entry of thirteen Plus Fours for the MCC's Exeter Trial, held over the Friday night of January 8th, and finishing the following day at Weymouth. All had TR engines except one. There were two Morgan teams. The Morgan factory team consisted of Peter Morgan in TUY 875, Jim Goodall in HUY 982 fitted with the external bogus fuel tank containing water for ballast, and Horace Roberts in WAB 779. The other team, 'The Union Jacks', consisted of George Edwards in OCO 738, vet Allin Penhale in PYK 24 (Vanguard engined, but cowled radiator) and Ted Dennis in YDV 286. The team name came from the colours of these three cars, being red white and blue respectively. P Scott drove YNP 838, Tom Bryant WUO 529, Malcolm Kemp RXN 194, John Charnaud 744 FCV and B B Jones had the personal number plate BJ 4 on his blue 1959 car. There was also D Bowles, who was driving the old Monty Rogers four-seater Plus Four PLB 111 which carried three passengers.

Tom Bryant was the business partner of Joe Huxham, the Bournemouth Morgan agent. WUO 529 was one of the cars at the 1957 Motor Show, and was a green two-seater with dark green trim, chassis number 3559. Malcolm Kemp, also from Bournemouth, was driving a car previously campaigned by Joe Huxham himself. It was another green two-seater, but with black upholstery. It carried chassis number 3292 and had originally been dispatched to Henry Garner, the Birmingham agent, on Wednesday May 25th 1955. Garners could not sell the car and it was returned to the Morgan factory before being taken by Basil Roy Ltd in London on Thursday July 22nd that same year.

John Charnaud's father ran a garage outside Truro called Playing Place Motors, and John had ordered his green Plus Four through them in 1959. He collected it personally from the Morgan factory late that year, on Friday November 4th, after travelling there by train. Naturally his father's garage was to sponsor his motor sport, which consisted of some local rallies as well as the classic trials. This Plus Four, chassis number 4347, a green two-seater with black leather upholstery, had been delivered having several unusual features, such as door pockets, a clock instead of the glove box, bucket type seats and Dunlop Duraband radial tyres.

There were three starting places for the 108 starters on the trial: Kenilworth, London and Launceston.

The overnight conditions were dry, as proved to be most of the hills, making an easy trial for many, with 56 claiming First Class Awards! The members of both Morgan teams collected First Class Awards, with 'The Union Jacks' claiming the MCC's Team Award and Ted Dennis collecting the individual Class V Award. Firsts were also collected by P Scott, and Malcolm Kemp, with B Jones and D Bowles collecting Seconds. Tom Bryant and John Charnaud took Thirds.

Ted Dennis remembered seeing 'fuel' spilling from the extra tank on the rear of Jim's Plus Four at the finish. He dashed into the hotel to tell him his precious fuel was leaking away, only to be told by Jim it was just water ballast! Ted too used ballast, but he used lead wool. He found the TR engine had enough power to allow him to deflate the rear tyres to around 5 lbs per square inch pressure for the observed sections. To prevent the tyres moving on the rims at this low pressure and pulling out the tube valves he used to paint decorators' sticky gold size on the rims before inflating the tyres to 40 lbs per square inch overnight. This stuck the tyres to the rims and they were fine after that. His preferred make of tyres was the Firestone Town and Country, using over-size ones on the rear. The rear exhaust pipe was re-routed out of harm's way, and the rear number plate fitted upwards for the same reason. It was on this event that Peter Morgan, impressed with Ted's ability,

George Edwards on his way to the Team Award tackles Stretes during the MCC Exeter Trial. (Norman Miller)

suggested he might like to join the Morgan factory team in future. His teammate George Edwards from then on replied to anything Ted said with, 'Yes, Mister Morgan', to Ted's irritation!

This year the South Wales Automobile Club's Welsh Rally received sponsorship from the TV magazine *Television Weekly*. It was oversubscribed, only 120 entrants being allowed to start from the three starting places of Gloucester, Shrewsbury and Cardiff on Friday January 8th. From there the crews made for Cross Gates, near Llandrindod Wells, an easy drive. This National rally now began to bite, with a night navigation section over the mountainous roads of mid-Wales. After completing this there was a 30 minute break before the final navigation section sent the crews to the border counties. The final route card section included a to-the-second regularity test, before bringing the competitors back to Cardiff for the final driving test. Brian Harper and Ron Crellin were outstanding in YOM 798, having accrued just 67 penalties during the 400 rally miles. Furthermore, they were only seven seconds outside an exact schedule during the Regularity Test. They won the rally, collecting £50 and the Wellsteed Trophy for best driver, the George Heaps Trophy for the best navigator and the Shrewsbury Start Award. Brian commented at the time that it had been, 'a rally that puts relentless pressure on vehicles and is tough on the crew with never a let-up'. The navigators were really important on this event, and no doubt the local knowledge acquired by checking out the Welsh roads against maps over preceding months had paid due dividends for Brian and Ron. Pauline Mayman also did well in her Morgan EPM 324, collecting a Second Class Award.

At the first Morgan board meeting of the year, held on Thursday January 21st, Peter Morgan reported that the new 105E engined 4/4 was nearly ready for testing on the road. He commented that a slightly different gearlever system (designed by him) would be fitted rather than that used on the earlier 100E model, but that it should be satisfactory. He was wondering whether the body frame should be wider. Peter also announced the appointment of an experimental engineer, namely Neville Carlton-Oatley for a trial period of six months.

This appointment was necessary because Peter was finding the running the Company gave him little time now for any developmental work. Peter

Morgan Sports Cars — 1960

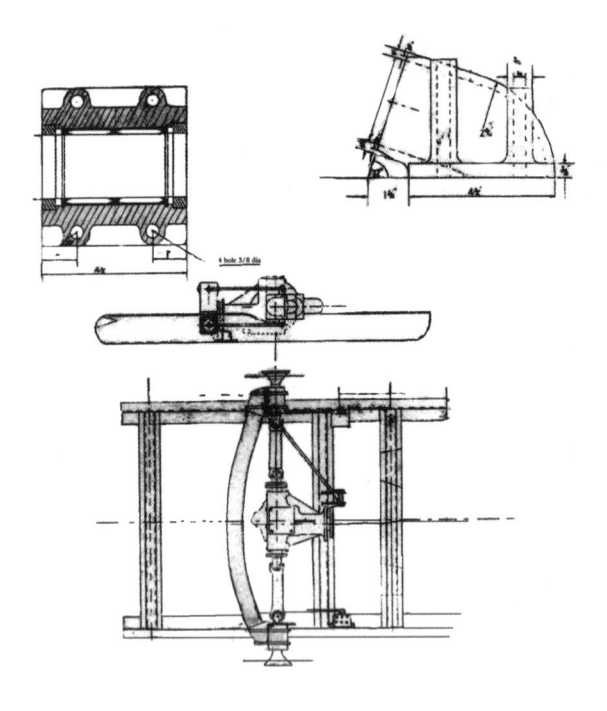

The Morgan factory drawing of the De Dion rear suspension. (Morgan Motor Co with assistance from Lorne Goldman and Chris Acklam)

wanted Neville to look particularly at a softer suspension for the Morgan, to take account of criticism Morgans received on the hard ride. Neville used to wear carpet slippers whilst working at the factory, soon leading to his nickname of 'Shuffle-shoes' from Peter Morgan!

Peter also announced at this board meeting that plans were now in hand to celebrate the fiftieth anniversary of the foundation of the Morgan Company as a vehicle manufacturer. These included the production of an illustrated brochure giving details of the history of the Company (to be written by George Goodall with Peter) and a luncheon at the Abbey Hotel to allow directors to entertain the press and friends of the Company. There was also to be a staff party and full page advertisements in *The Motor* and *The Autocar*.

On February 1st a De Dion rear suspension was drawn for the Morgan chassis, perhaps by Neville Carlton-Oatley, but it is not known if it was ever built. Peter Morgan was of the opinion that the De Dion didn't suit the front suspension characteristics, but this view may have followed much later experiments. When HFS Morgan was alive he had spent a lot of time with Peter trying different springs and also attempting to give the front suspension longer travel.

Whenever HFS Morgan had introduced a new chassis he had always tried different body styles. Thus, although the 4/4 Series II was only catalogued as a two-seater tourer, a four-seater had been built (dispatched in 1957) and so too

Stella Skinner's unique 4/4 coupé. (Morgan Motor Co collection)

was a coupé. The latter car, given chassis number A553, and painted Larkspur Blue, with stone leather upholstery, was purchased by Peter Morgan's sister Stella Skinner. Her son Tony went with her on Monday February 1st to collect the car from the factory and he recalled it had hardly enough petrol in the tank to drive out through the factory gates! Peter Morgan was asked to top up the tank for the journey back to Maidenhead, and Tony recalled his mother was not impressed that she was charged for it!

Brian Harper continued his winning ways in YOM 798 during the Thames Estuary AC's Cats' Eyes Rally, held on Saturday and Sunday February 6th and 7th. He took first place in the open cars class with just thirty penalties, beating David Seigle-Morris in a Triumph TR3A by five points.

The Morgan 4/4 Club's Spring Rally, a day rally, was held we think on Sunday February 14th, a cold but sunny day that attracted 24 starters. It was organised by Lionel and Pauline Mayman, with Peter Morgan stewarding. The victor was John McKechnie, but whether or not he was in his Morgan we are not sure. Fellow competitor Alan Smith commented that he thought the days of 'day rallying' were nearly over because there was now so much other traffic on the road.

At the Morgan Motor Company directors' meeting held on Thursday February 18th Peter Morgan reported that the fiftieth anniversary plans had progressed, with 1,500 copies of the Morgan history brochure to be printed, including 200 special presentation versions. The Commemorative Luncheon was to be held at the Abbey Hotel on Thursday April 7th, and full page advertisements were to be placed in the various motoring magazines in March. It was also reported that the Montagu Motor Museum would host a special Morgan rally on Sunday July 31st.

The Second Rallye Militaire held by the Royal Military College of Science MC took place on Friday night February 20th, finishing the following day, and Brian once again competed in YOM 798, hoping to win as he had the previous year. The new Triumph Herald proved to be the car to use, for the 'London taxi' turning circle of the little Triumph made it a master of the driving tests, and these cars won both the individual and team prizes.

One of the most famous makes of racing and sports racing cars made after the war had been those produced by the steel maker Cyril Kieft, first in South Wales at Bridgend and then later in Wolverhampton. In 1954 Kieft Cars Ltd was sold to Berwyn Baxter, who moved the firm to Birmingham in 1956. In the spring of 1960 the little company was bought by Hunts (B'ham) Ltd which moved it to Bordesley Road. Lionel Mayman and his fellow Hunts directors were keen to produce a Formula Junior car, and also to offer tune-up kits for production cars under the Kieft Power name. The company was to be run by Pauline's sister Wendy and her husband John Turvey, both of whom had previously joined the Hunts business. Lionel managed to persuade Ron Timmins to join the Kieft Sports Car Company venture as their development engineer, and of course Ron was also now able to continue his preparation of the ex-Alan Belcher Morgan VON 777. During the winter Ron had visited Hunts and had noticed his special drum front brakes had been removed on the instructions of Lionel Mayman and replaced by Girling discs, as on offer for production Morgans. Ron was displeased, believing his ex-Humber drum set up was still better than the new system.

Chris Lawrence too was busy designing and constructing a Formula Junior with the team at Westerham Motors. He was a frequent visitor to Goodwood, perfecting this new car during the off-season. It was bigger than most Formula Junior cars, and had a unique chassis design based on a tetrahedron using 1.5 inch 16 gauge tubing. This unusual car was to act as a design test bed for future Lawrence designs, just two being built initially as 'works' cars for the new racing season. The engine was a Ford 105E, modified by Chris, with advice from Keith Duckworth, and fitted with a camshaft by Ted Martin of Alexander Engineering Co Ltd, who was also tuning 105Es and supplying special components to other engine tuners. Chris Lawrence's future new cars, including the Formula Junior, were to be known as 'Deep Sanderson'. This unusual name came from a joining together of 'Deep Henderson', the title of a favourite song performed by his father's jazz band, and 'Sanderson', being the maiden name of his mother and surname of his supportive uncle. The first Formula Junior design was to be known as the Deep Sanderson (DS) 101.

Chris had finally decided to run his racing Ford 105E engine on Weber carburettors, and he also converted his Plus Four TOK 258 to run on them during the early months of 1960. Chris had bought cheaply a pair of old sand cast 45 DCO3s, which were racing carburettors with a very skimpy idling system, previously used on a D-type Jaguar. An inlet manifold design was fabricated for TOK's high port TR3 cylinder head to enable the set up to be developed before castings were made. Chris found that Webers suited his camshaft design, and exploited the engine's mid range torque much better than SUs. Previously Chris had known little about Webers, but was keen to learn more, so he visited Keith Duckworth of Cosworth Engineering who was making them work well. Keith spent some time with Chris, outside the workshop in the rain, explaining how they worked, and Keith's tuition meant that from then on Chris never had trouble setting up Webers. Keith told him what jets were required, which Chris obtained from Alan Southern in Hartney Whitney at his shop behind the Phoenix pub. The Plus Four required a hole in the offside bonnet to accommodate these carburettors, covered at first by an unpainted cowl.

Initially the Webers were directly bolted to the manifolds, but experience soon showed that rigid mounting caused fuel frothing, so Chris took a lead from Keith Duckworth, and used 'O' rings and Grover spring washers. A Bendix electric fuel pump was now used to boost the original AC mechanical pump.

Chris Lawrence's step-father, Major Robert Neale, had suggested Westerham Motors should eventually have a decent tow vehicle to supplement the 1940s Fordson 7V lorry that had replaced the Commer after the latter's engine had expired. Consequently he had organised the purchase of a Jaguar Mk VII, together with a specially made caravan which would accommodate the Morgan. It had a special chassis and a drop down rear like a horse box that also served as the loading ramp. Robert was very supportive of Chris at this time, even using his influence with the Standard Motor Company to buy engines cheaply.

Ray Meredith sent the TR3 engine from XOV 555 to Laystall Engineering for balancing and other work in February. To keep his Morgan mobile it was temporarily replaced by the old Vanguard engine previously owned by John Looker.

The Wolverhampton and South Staffs CC ran a National rally over the weekend of Saturday March 5th and Sunday 6th. This rally, named the 'Express and Star Rally' following local newspaper sponsorship, was an excellent and well run affair. There were starts at Wolverhampton, Liverpool, Hereford, Oxford, and Nottingham and these routes all joined at Knighton in Radnor, where the rally proper began with several overnight Welsh sections before the finish at Bridgnorth. The event was won by Tom Gold in an Austin Healey Sprite, navigated by Stuart Turner, but in second place after a brilliant performance was Pauline Mayman in EPM 324, navigated by Val Domleo. Winning the over 1,300cc open class was Brian Harper with Ron Crellin in YOM 798. It had been an excellent rally for the Morgan marque.

The 'Inter One-Make Team Driving Tests' had become the most important driving test event in the RAC calendar, and this year attracted fifteen teams to Honeybourne Aerodrome near Evesham on Sunday March 6th. This year the Mini took the event by storm, as the MG Car Club (Midlands) team of three Morris Mini Minors won by a huge margin. This was despite being on scratch, whilst the 'real' sports cars (Morgans, Triumphs etc) had a 7.5% advantage on handicap. It was so easy. The Morgan team did however salvage fourth place and Dr Townsend was second overall in the individual competition in his 4/4 Series II.

Dr Townsend was shortly to replace this Morgan with an Austin Healey Sprite and he advertised his 4/4 in *Motor Sport* for May. It was a rather special car as the advertisement makes clear: '1957 model, Willment ohiv conversion giving approx. 90 mph and up to 35 mpg. Handa overdrive all gears, strengthened gearbox, heater, radiator shutters, screen washers, special shockers and tyres giving superb road holding, special brake linings, full tonneau, revolution counter, vacuum gauge, and thermometer. A wonderful car in superb condition throughout with reconditioned engine nine months ago. £525.' The Morgan had actually been delivered in 1956!

There was already considerable press interest in the future Morgan fiftieth anniversary celebrations, and *The Autocar* carried a review of the fifty years of Morgans entitled, 'From Edwardian tricycles to Elizabethan Plus Fours' in its Friday March 11th issue. One of the photographs used showed Jim Goodall and Peter Morgan in the factory dispatch bay.

On Sunday March 13th the Falcon MC ran its third annual restricted 'March Hare' Trial, a road trial for saloon cars, sports cars and specials held in the Tring and Berkhamsted areas. Heavy rain led to the course being changed a week beforehand, but B B Jones still managed to clean every hill until the last. He won the class for sports cars in his Plus Four BJ 4.

That great pre-First World War Morgan three-wheeler competitor and motoring journalist W G McMinnies wrote his memories of HFS Morgan and the very early days of the Morgan enterprise in an article entitled 'The Quiet Man' which was published in the Wednesday March 16th issue of *The Motor*. He described HFS Morgan as 'a quiet and gentle man', and 'a genius in being able to

Jim Goodall and Peter Morgan in the Morgan dispatch bay. Note the shortage of windscreens on the cars behind! (The Autocar)

Joe Huxham, Jim Goodall and Peter Morgan with the prototype 105E engined 4/4 at the Morgan factory. (Morgan Motor Co collection)

make a thing cheaply and simply and also ensure that it did the job efficiently at the same time'. This article was ably supported by a letter to The Motor printed two weeks later from Len Coney, who had been a member of the Morgan Motor Company trials team in 1938. He commented that the title of 'The Quiet Man' was absolutely right and reminisced describing an incident that had occurred during the 1938 MCC Edinburgh Trial. Apparently the offside front wheel of Len's 4/4 CON 502 had hit a submerged rock hard whilst fording the swollen water splash at Costerton, the front crosshead being bent back as a result. After the evening dinner Len had decided to seek out HFS at his hotel to ask his advice as he now wanted to follow the forthcoming Scottish Rally in the Highlands. Len realised HFS would be very tired having just driven for twenty-two hours over 450 miles. HFS insisted there and then on walking the half mile or so to the garage to inspect the damaged Morgan himself. After examining the front end carefully HFS told him, 'Fortunately we use very good tubing. You will be quite alright to carry on but don't forget to bring a long piece of string with you tomorrow morning.' Len was wondering what he needed to tie up, but HFS then continued with a glint in his eye, 'You will need it to retrack the front wheels.' Needless to say there were no further problems, and Len held HFS in great respect for being so ready to offer help and advice in such an adverse situation.

At the Morgan directors' meeting held on Thursday March 17th Peter Morgan reported that the new 4/4 with the Ford 105E engine had been out on test, with the Ford Motor Company representative being 'extremely pleased with its performance'. Although a reported 85 mph had been achieved Peter was disappointed with the lack of torque developed by the new engine.

The weather was wet and a bitter wind blew on the occasion of the BARC's Member's Meeting held at Goodwood on Saturday March 19th. Chris Lawrence was there with the two 'works' DS 101 Formula Juniors, but both returned to the paddock behind the same breakdown truck after the ten lap Formula Junior race. It was not a great start for the Deep Sanderson enterprise. The Formula Junior event was followed by a ten lap Marque scratch race, which began with a Le Mans start. Bob Duggan had entered OYO 874 and managed to finish fourth, the winner being Paul Fletcher in an AC Bristol ahead of Roy North in a TR3. Bob had now fitted his Morgan with an Iskenderian camshaft and alloy push rods.

Grand Prix driver Tony Brooks sitting in a Plus Four as part of Girling disc brake publicity. (Morgan Motor Co collection)

The various companies supplying parts to Morgan were also warming to the Morgan fiftieth celebrations. Girling sent the Vanwall Grand Prix driver Tony Brooks for some publicity shots with a Plus Four, to be used in a Girling disc brakes advertisement for publication in April.

The very active West Hants and Dorset Car Club ran its annual Hartwell Cup Trial for production cars on a fine March day. The winner of the Harwell Cup was Edgar Wadsworth with his unusual rear engined Denzel, but there were excellent performances from the Morgan participants with class awards going to B B Jones, in BJ 4, Tom Bryant, presumably driving WUO 529, and Monty Rogers in PLB 111.

Jim Banbury had decided he ought to update to a more modern Plus Four for this year's sprints and hill climbs. As a consequence earlier in the year he had bought a beige Plus Four two-seater that a dentist in Hove had had rebuilt after an accident. It was virtually new (registered PNJ 350 in June 1959). On Saturday April 2nd he took it to the Pembrokeshire Motor Club's Lydstep hill climb, contesting two classes: Class 5, for sports cars 1,501 to 2,000cc, and Class 6, for sports cars 2,001 to 3,000cc. He was second in both classes behind Cottrell's Lotus Bristol.

Graham Morewood of Sheffield had been an enthusiastic motorcycle trials competitor in the mid 1950s before moving to two Morgan three-wheelers, one Matchless powered and the other Ford powered. After a brief excursion with an HRG he had now bought a green 1958 Plus Four two-seater, registered 774 ACV. He took his Plus Four to the Wirral 100 MC's Rhydymwyn Sprint, also held on Saturday April 2nd, and finished fourth in the marque sports cars class behind a Lotus 7A, an Elva with overhead inlet valve Ford conversion and another Plus Four driven by D G Allen. The two Morgans were well ahead of the TRs.

That same Saturday there was a huge crowd of 30,000 at Oulton Park for the BARC's Spring Meeting, which included a major Formula 2 race and attracted most of the top drivers. The last race of the day was a 10 lap Marque scratch race, contested by Chris Lawrence in TOK 258 and Lionel Mayman in VON 777. Ray Meredith was also entered in XOV 555. During practice Ron Timmins timed VON 777 and found it slower than when Alan Belcher had driven it. He blamed the change to disc brakes initially, but then he realised that Lionel's driving style was more flamboyant than the smoother style of Alan. Ron instructed Lionel in how Alan took various parts of the circuit and some improvement in times was achieved, eventually recording 2 minutes 14.8 seconds. Chris Lawrence recorded 2 minutes 9 seconds dead, and Ray 2 minutes 18.4 seconds.

Peter Bolton took an immediate lead from the start in Ron Atkinson's AC Bristol, followed by TOK 258 and VON 777. Paul Fletcher and Bob Staples had problems at Knicker Brook in their AC Bristols, the former overturning and the latter finishing up in the lake, for the second time that day! Alan Foster managed to take third place from Lionel with his MGA Twin-Cam, but Peter Bolton was unmatchable and won by five seconds from Chris Lawrence. Ray Meredith finished eighth.

It was an amazing site at the Abbey Hotel in Malvern on Thursday April 7th when just under ninety sat down for the Morgan Motor Company's '50 Years' celebratory lunch. It was an all male event, with representatives from the Morgan agencies, suppliers, clubs, and the press all enjoying an excellent meal, the main course being roast saddle of Welsh lamb. All the guests were from the UK, and many were personal friends of George Goodall. The top table comprised Ted Grinham, (ex-Standard engine designer), Chris Jennings (*The Motor*), George Goodall, Evan Price (Dunlop), Arthur Bourne (*The Autocar*), Peter Morgan, Basil Roy (London agent), Sydney Duckitt (Moss Gears), W G McMinnies (pre-WW1 Morgan driver and journalist) and Godfrey Russell (HFS's lawyer).

The toast to 'The Company' was given by Arthur Bourne of *The Autocar*, recalling numerous nostalgic moments, and suggesting the firm owed its success to the firmness with which HFS resisted the temptation to over complicate the design.

Peter Morgan gave the reply, having typed his speech. He started by saying how disappointing it was that his father had missed this event by such a short time. After a three-wheeler story about his father he continued by pointing out that his father had always been tremendously enthusiastic about motor sport, realising how useful it was in developing the car. He had taken it very seriously since as a manufacturer he appreciated there was a lot to be lost as well as gained and during his whole life, right up to the end, he never missed checking up on any results of events in which the cars had competed.

Peter also mentioned his mother Ruth, who passengered for his father in the three-wheeler whenever pregnancy allowed. She had told Peter that it was more by luck than cunning that he was not born during a certain six days trial, (presumably

Chris Lawrence chases Peter Bolton through Lodge Corner during the Oulton Park Spring Meeting. (John Holroyd)

referring to the ACU 6 Days Trial held in September 1919). Peter continued by paying tribute to his grandfather Prebendary H G Morgan, to George Goodall, to Harry Jones, to Major Kendall, to the loyal factory workers, to the suppliers, to the press and finally the distributors and agents.

George Goodall proposed the toast to 'The Guests', giving a witty speech that caused the audience to roar with laughter. Bill Boddy, writing up the event for *Motor Sport*, regretted the stories were often not suitable for printing but did mention that George had said he wasn't sure whether the Company had suffered most in the hands of the technical, or non-technical press! The reply was given by Evan Price of the Dunlop Rubber Company.

Jack Sylvester, the original Nottingham Morgan agent (Bennetts of Nottingham) gave an impromptu address from the floor. He was devoted to the Morgan family and business and had decided to donate to Peter his most treasured possession, namely a solid silver reduced size 'Spirit of Ecstasy' Rolls-Royce mascot. These had been awarded very rarely by the Rolls-Royce Company itself for really outstanding achievement (Bennetts were Rolls-Royce agents too). Jack had decided that Peter Morgan and the Morgan family deserved it for the same reason of outstanding achievement. It remained a treasured possession of Peter's for the rest of his life.

The lunch had been a marvellous occasion and many letters of appreciation were received from the guests. Peter's brother-in-law, John Hardwicke, wrote a congratulatory letter to Peter, but suggested it might have been a blessing that HFS did not live to partake in the event, believing it might have been too much for him. He wrote, 'Certainly he would have been in a state of jitters, especially at having to make a speech, whilst the fact that he would not have had Mrs Morgan (Ruth) by his side to share in the tributes would I think, for him, have turned what should have been a joyous occasion into a very sad one!'

Many others, not invited or unable to attend the lunch had been sent complementary copies of the commemorative booklet produced by the factory. Again many appreciative letters were

One half of the Top Table at the 50th celebratory dinner at the Abbey Hotel. Seated from left to right are Ted Grinham, Chris Jennings, George Goodall, Evan Price, Arthur Bourne and Peter Morgan. (Morgan Motor Co collection)

Pauline Mayman and Val Domleo winning the Regent Challenge Trophy in the Birmingham Post Rally for the third year in succession. (Pauline Mayman collection)

received from the recipients. Peter also received one from HFS's elder sister Freida, living in Harrogate. In her thank you letter for the booklet she also wrote, 'Your father told me how good you were with the men, how proud he was of you.' How nice for Peter to learn this from his aunt.

The Midland Automobile Club's Birmingham Post National Rally began on Friday evening April 8th, finishing some 400 miles later at Bromsgrove. Heavy rain in the Welsh mountains made some tracks very slippery, but there were still twelve clean sheets at the finish out of the 124 starters. Final results were therefore decided by the combined times in two driving tests held at the finish. Two of the 'clears' were achieved by Pauline Mayman with Val Domleo in EPM 324 and Brian Harper and Ron Crellin in YOM 798, whilst Peter Morgan made spectacular times in the final tests despite having lost time elsewhere.

Naturally Pauline and Val took the Regent Challenge Trophy for best performance by an all ladies crew, for the third year in a row. The Class Award for cars over 1,000 cc was taken by Brian and Ron, with Pauline and Val runners up. It had been another excellent event for Morgans.

On Sunday April 10th Jim Banbury was at Brunton for the BARC South Western Centre's 23rd hill climb at that venue. There was a large turnout of competitors including, incidentally, two DS 101 Formula Junior cars, driven by Len Bridge and Roland Smith. Jim's was the sole Morgan entry and he finished in fourth place in Class 6, behind three Bristol engined cars (two ACs and a Frazer Nash). His best time of 30.32 seconds compares well with Roland's Deep Sanderson time of 30.99 seconds, which was good enough to give him the Formula Junior Award, beating his teammate, a Yimkin and two Coopers.

Both Graham Morewood and Peter Bradley contested the 'hill climb' held at Castle Howard held on the same day. Graham wasn't impressed with the short 600 yards course, which had only two corners and a final level stretch of 400 yards, allowing sheer horsepower to have the advantage. The two Morgans finished just off the pace in third and fifth places. Peter Bradley's Morgan 9267 U was looking very stark this year as the front wings had been removed and replaced by aluminium cycle wings. Peter had also fitted disc brakes, joining the Barwell head, Iskenderian camshaft and Derrington manifolds.

Horace Roberts' four-seater Plus Four WAB 779 had spent most of February in the Morgan factory repair shop. Horace had had the cylinder head gas flowed and the ports matched, and a new radiator and replacement floor boards were fitted prior to Horace taking part in the MCC's Lands End Trial, where he was part of the Morgan team once more.

The MCC Lands End Trial took place as usual on the traditional dates of Good Friday and Easter Saturday, April 15th and 16th. Amongst the 134 cars there were no less than eleven Morgans, all Plus Fours except one, and including two teams. These two teams were as in the Exeter, 'The Union Jacks' and the Morgan factory team. 'The Union Jacks' once again comprised George Edwards in the red OCO 738, Allin Penhale in his Vanguard engined two-seater cowled car, PYK 24, and Ted Dennis in his blue four-seater YDV 286. The Morgan team comprised Jim Goodall in HUY 982, Horace Roberts in his four-seater WAB 779 and Peter Morgan accompanied by his wife Jane in his father's Vanguard engined four-seater coupé MAB 696. This was an unusual choice for a trials car and makes us wonder why he used it. It is probable that his old trials Plus Four KUY 387 was undergoing a major rebuild and update to current specification at this time. Also entered was B B Jones in BJ 4, Tom Bryant in WUO 529, Malcolm Kemp in RXN 194, John Charnaud in 774 FCV, and D Burke in a 1,098cc Morgan 4/4.

This year there was a new hill which turned out to be a real stopper. It had been suggested by Allin Penhale and was called Crossleigh, situated just four miles out of Bude in Cornwall. The approach was down a steep narrow lane, the hill rising very steeply in an elongated 'S' up the other side of the valley. The big catch was that the floor of the valley was covered by a sea of liquid slime, and the track itself by deep gelatinous mud. Whilst the first few competitors, including B B Jones, managed to climb clean, the hill then took its toll and few made it thereafter. There was doubt if the hill would count in the results, but then the later Morgans arrived and showed it could be done. George Edwards and Allin Penhale used the long approach to build up speed and roared up. Ted Dennis was also doing well, but then had the misfortune of the car jumping out of first gear. Jim Goodall climbed it too, but Peter Morgan in the coupé found it too tough. Just fourteen cars managed to 'clean' this hill.

The results saw George Edwards win a First Class Award and also win Class V, whilst Jim Goodall took a first too. Seconds were claimed by B Jones, Allin Penhale and Horace Roberts.

Peter and Jane Morgan in Peter's father's coupé MAB 696 on Hustyn hill in the MCC Land's End Trial. (Norman Miller)

Thirds were claimed by Peter Morgan, Malcolm Kemp and John Charnaud. Tom Bryant didn't take an award and D Burke retired. The Union Jacks once again took the Team Award.

Graham Morewood and Peter Bradley both contested the sprint meeting held at Catterick on Easter Sunday in their Plus Fours. Peter's modified Plus Four 9267 U showed the others how to do it, winning the class, whilst Graham was third in 774 ACV, behind a Frazer Nash Le Mans Replica, and just beating a Lotus XI Climax. Just 0.6 seconds covered the first four. It had been an impressive performance from the two Morgans, there being no fewer than twenty-six entries in their class. Graham's car was running with a modified cylinder head, and now had ram pipes to the H4 SU carburettors passing through holes in the offside bonnet.

There was a record turn out for the Easter Monday sprint meeting on April 18th held at Trengwainton, including several staying over from the Lands End Trial to enter this event. The course itself had been improved with a new paddock and spectator amenities. The class for sports cars up to 2,000cc had seventeen entries, of which four were Morgans. John Charnaud from Falmouth was in 774 FCV, Jim Banbury in PNJ 350, Tom Bryant presumably in WUO 529, and Ted Dennis in YDV 286, but Ted failed to start. The class was led by two AC Bristols, a Frazer Nash taking third place and a Dellow fourth. In fifth place was Jim Banbury with a time of 26.11 seconds. Tom Bryant recorded 26.54 seconds, and John Charnaud 28.27 seconds. There was also an Open Championship run for cars, Jim improving his time to 26.09 seconds (his was the only Morgan). The class was won by the 1,100cc Cooper of M Hatton who recorded 23.66 seconds.

The first event in this year's Autosport Championship for Series-Production Sports Cars was the Nottingham Sports Car Club's Easter Monday meeting at Mallory Park. There were two Morgan entries for this year's championship, Bob Duggan in OYO 874 and Lionel Mayman in VON 777, contesting Class C, for engines over 1,600cc.

Both were entered for the twenty lap race, which also included the field for Class A championship cars up to 1,000cc. The race as a whole was easily won by Peter Bolton in his AC Bristol but he wasn't entered for the championship so the second placed finisher, Lionel Mayman in VON 777 took the eight points. Behind Lionel, Bob Duggan was engaged in a furious battle with the Austin Healeys of Julian Sutton and Chris Ashmore, but the Morgan burst a tyre at the esses hitting the grass banking with spectacular results and failed to finish. It turned out a patched inner tube had finally had enough. Bob's Morgan was now running with a large port TR3 head, worked over and gas flowed by SAH Accessories, and a free-flow exhaust manifold.

Lionel Mayman also took part in the later twenty lap race for sports cars of unlimited capacity, and he was in fourth place after lap one behind two Coopers and the Tojeiro Bristol. He held this position to the finish in what was regarded as a rather processional race. It was a brilliant drive for Lionel, however, to stay with such company.

The Scottish Sporting Car Club's Highland Rally occupied the whole Easter weekend, starting on Good Friday evening and finishing on Easter Monday after three and a half days. A good navigator was essential, and indeed there were complaints from English entrants that the navigation was too tough for a National event. Pauline Mayman and Val Domleo had entered in EPM 324, but illness in Val's family forced withdrawal. The class for Normal GT cars and Improved Touring cars over 1,601cc was won by Scottish driver Ken Sturrock in his Plus Four.

SUNBAC held a hill climb at Ragley Hall on Saturday April 23rd. Lionel Mayman had entered in VON 777, and after a tremendous getaway unfortunately the engine 'fluffed' half way up, depriving him of success.

The fourth hill climb held at Wiscombe was held on Sunday April 24th. The course had been resurfaced and there was fine weather for the competitors and spectators. There were just six

Don Parker spins his Jaguar XK150S at Tatt's Corner during the Aintree closed car race, whilst Chris Lawrence in TOK 258 is engaged in a race long battle with Sir Gawaine Baillie's Jaguar 3.8. (The Autocar)

competitors in Class 7, for sports cars between 1,501 and 2,000cc, but two were Morgans. Jim Banbury was driving PNJ 350 and Tom Bryant was presumably driving WUO 529. Jim managed third place behind a Bristol engined Frazer Nash and an AC Bristol with a time of 41.75 seconds. Tom was fourth with 43.03 seconds.

On that same day the Morgan 4/4 Club's magazine editor, Robin Brown, was sampling a circuit new to him, namely Brands Hatch in Kent, which was being used by the Sevenoaks and District MC for a sprint meeting (two timed laps of the circuit). Robin would have liked more time to practise than the four laps allotted and finished fourth in class behind three MGA Twin-Cams.

The second round of the Autosport Series-Production Championship was held on Saturday April 30th during the Maidstone and Mid-Kent Motor Club's 12th Silverstone race meeting. There were only three cars entered in Class C so it should have been easy to pick up championship points during the twenty lap race for Classes B and C. However, Michael Bowling spun his Austin Healey at Becketts on lap 3, right in front of Lionel Mayman in VON 777, eliminating both of them, luckily without injury although both cars were damaged. The surviving Class C car, the Frazer Nash of Roy Bloxham, was able to tour round to the finish unmolested for four championship points.

That same Saturday the BARC ran an International meeting at Aintree, including a prestigious 200 mile race for Formula 2 cars, won by Stirling Moss in a Porsche. The day's racing had begun though with a ten lap race for closed cars, and Chris Lawrence had entered TOK 258, which complied with the 'closed cars' requirement by fitting the hard top to the Plus Four. The Morgan was entered in the class for 1,000 to 2,000cc. *Autosport* described Chris's Morgan as being 'indecently fast' for he even managed to get ahead of Sir Gawaine Baillie's Jaguar 3.8, and the latter couldn't pass him! Chris's excellent drive gave him fifth place overall, whilst he was third in class behind two Lotus Elites. There was also a seventeen lap Formula Junior race, in which Chris drove a Deep Sanderson. Although he was on the pace of a couple of Elvas, he couldn't make any impression on the Lotus and Cooper versions.

On Sunday May 1st the Bugatti Owners' Club ran the very last Prescott hill climb to use the original 880 yard course, as an extension at Orchard was nearing completion. It proved a good event for Morgans, particularly Ray Meredith in XOV 555, who recorded the first and only sub-fifty seconds Morgan time for this course, to take third place in the class for sports cars 1,601 to 3,000cc. His time was 49.39 seconds, whist Jim Banbury in PNJ 350 recorded 51.17 seconds. Class

Ray Meredith breaks 50 seconds on Prescott in XOV 555 on his way to third in class. (The Autocar)

winners were P Cottrell and M Morris in Bristol engined Lotus and Frazer Nash respectively, who tied with 48.78 seconds. Ray also won what the regular Prescott commentator Austen May described as a, 'little pot of gold over at Malvern'. This was an award by the Morgan Motor Company for the first sub-fifty seconds ascent of Prescott by a Morgan. We do not know how much gold was in the pot!

In Yorkshire the local BARC Centre had been having problems in locating suitable sites for sprint meetings. To the rescue had come club member Arnold Burton, who was from the famous high street tailoring firm of Burtons the Tailors. He made available the roads around the Montague Burton factory in Hudson Road, Leeds for a series of sprint meetings. One was held on Sunday May 1st and Peter Bradley achieved a time of 44.35 seconds to finish third in class with 9267 U.

At the Morgan directors' meeting held at the Morgan factory on Wednesday May 4th Peter

Peter Bradley displays his flamboyant driving style at the BARC sprint held at Montague Burton Ltd in Leeds. (John Holroyd)

Morgan highlighted the many letters of appreciation received following the anniversary luncheon at the Abbey Hotel. He also confirmed that a 'Works Party' was to be held on Saturday June 25th, consisting of a trip to London, 'leaving three hours for sightseeing and dancing'!

He also reported further trials of the new 4/4 with the Ford 105E engine, and of being disappointed with the lack of torque at the lower end of the rev range. He was trying the car with twin carburettors to see if they eliminated the 'flat spot'. Despite his reservations about this engine, which was also more expensive than the current 100E, Peter announced that it would be introduced at the October Motor Show, along with a new modified coupé body, which was being designed to reduce some of the current 'squareness' in body shape.

New Morgans were now starting to leave the factory with improved steering columns and drop arms, leading to lighter steering. Cam Gears Ltd had redesigned the steering worm to give better steering at the expense of 2.5 turns lock to lock instead of the previous two turns.

There also seems to have been a problem with TR3 engines, for many were reported by the test department as being 'rough', some cars being referred to Peter Morgan for final approval before dispatch, whilst other engines were removed and returned to the Standard Motor Company for retesting and attention.

On Saturday May 7th the BARC had glorious weather for the club's 40th Members' Meeting held at Goodwood. The first event of the day was a ten lap scratch race for sports cars up to 1,100cc and Chris Lawrence took to the line in Bill de Selincourt's Coventry Climax engined Lola Mk 1. He managed to finish third despite the fitment of Weber carburettors the night before having left the engine down on power.

The third race on the programme was a ten lap scratch race for Marque sports cars. Chris Lawrence was first away from the Le Mans start in TOK 258, and won by 48.8 seconds with an average speed of 79.54 mph, lapping almost the entire field. It had been a brilliant demonstration of Chris's ability in his reliable Morgan, and enthusiasts were beginning to ask Peter Morgan why the Morgan Company didn't offer Morgans fitted with Chris Lawrence built engines.

The next race was a ten lap race for Formula Junior cars. The sole Lotus failed to start so three Elvas took up the running, but maladies affected two such that Len Bridge in a Deep Sanderson finished second.

Bill and Chris were entered in Bill's Lola Mk 1 for the 1,000 kilometres race at the Nurburgring in Germany on Sunday May 22nd. Chris knew that it would be difficult to learn the 14.17 mile-long circuit which had over 170 corners, so he sought advice from the future World Champion Graham Hill. His advice was to practise ten laps a day for a month! When Chris told him he couldn't do that because he was entered in the Daily Express Silverstone meeting to be held on Saturday May 14th, just one week before the Nurburgring meeting, Graham's advice was, 'When you do your slowing down lap, come past Woodcote Corner and turn left. Leave the circuit and drive straight to Dover, get on a boat, drive straight to the Nurburgring and do ten laps.' Chris thanked him and decided that was what he would do, taking the Plus Four TOK 258 with which to learn the circuit.

The third round of the Autosport Championship was held at the BRSCC Mallory Park meeting held on Sunday May 8th. On this occasion there were sufficient entries in Class C for them to have their own twelve lap race. *Autosport* reported that the highlight of the event was the progress of Lionel Mayman in VON 777 who had got off line at Gerrard's Bend on the opening lap and had spun off, rejoining the race in last position. He pushed on extremely hard and was within a car's length of Handel's Jaguar XK120, which was running fourth, when the chequered flag was shown. It had been a wonderful display which drew a spontaneous cheer from the paddock's occupants when he came in after the race.

The Westmoreland Motor Club ran another successful hill climb at Barbon, near Kirkby Lonsdale, on Saturday May 21st. Peter Bradley had a great day with 9267 U, climbing the half mile course of 1 in 12 average gradient in 34.04 seconds, even beating Nutter's Bristol engined Frazer Nash.

The prestigious Daily Express International Trophy meeting was held at Silverstone on Saturday May 14th. The main Trophy race itself was won by Innes Ireland in a Formula 1 version of the Lotus 18 (fitted with a Coventry Climax engine), and this race was followed by a twenty-five lap Formula Junior event. Practice showed Chris Lawrence was some ten seconds behind the pace-setting Lotus 18 Ford Cosworth cars, and unfortunately in the race itself he had to retire with a failed water pump. He packed up and prepared to set off with TOK for the Nurburgring.

A sprint meeting was held at Catterick on Whit Sunday June 5th. Graham Morewood was using the new Dunlop Duraband radial tyres on his Plus Four. In addition he had now fitted the larger H6 SU carburettors on a Derrington inlet manifold. Sadly the modifications produced slower times than previously, although the finish line was crossed at a faster speed, so Graham blamed the Duraband radial tyres, and set about a trial of different tyre pressures. A Bristol engined special won the class, with Peter Bradley second in 9367 U. Graham finished fifth.

There was another round of the Autosport Series-Production Championship held at Mallory Park on Whit Monday June 6th during the Nottingham Sports Car Club's meeting. Unfortunately there were only seven starters for the combined Class A and C championship race, held over eighteen laps. Lionel Mayman led from start to finish for an easy victory. Bob Duggan, in OYO 874, battled with a non-championship contender, Baker's Aston Martin, eventually seeing it off and finishing second. Lionel and Bob shared the fastest lap with 75 mph, but the lack of numbers in the class meant that neither driver could claim any championship points. Bob's Morgan was now running with a homemade aluminium undertray fitted.

On the same day the BARC ran a National meeting at Goodwood. Bob Staples was entered in Event 5, the Marque scratch race, but he was not in his AC, driving instead TOK 258, which had now returned from its lap learning role at the Nurburgring. Bob's notes reveal that TOK was

Barry and Bob Staples with TOK 258 alongside Colin Hextall's TR3 at Goodwood. Note the bonnet cowl, now painted, covering the Weber carburettors. (Bob Staples collection)

running on Dunlop R5 racing tyres, size 5.50 by 15, running at 35 lbs/square inch all round. During practice one of the fuel lines detached from a Weber carburettor, and the throttle jammed fully open at Woodcote corner, both events luckily without mishap! In the race itself Bob found himself behind Colin Hextall's TR3, which was following the leading Austin Healey 3000 of John Turner, but the Morgan had dirty spark plugs, restricting speed. On lap 5 John spun, letting through the TR3 and the Morgan, but unfortunately the Morgan bonnet came loose on the very next lap and Bob was black flagged, having to stop to fix it, losing two places before continuing in fourth. With the spark plugs having cleared, Bob began a tremendous drive and managed to catch the third place car. He was being pushed very hard by Julian Sutton's very fast Austin Healey which had recovered after a slow first lap, and Bob lost his fourth spot on the very last lap when a melee at the chicane allowed Julian through on the inside. Also entered for this race was American Tom Smith in his black Plus Four coupé, but he was lapping some ten seconds slower than TOK 258 and only completed eight laps.

Another of the friendly hill climbs was held at Wiscombe on Whit Monday. Only seven starters contested the class for modified saloons and sports cars over 1,600cc, and the two Plus Fours did well. Jim Banbury recorded 42.34 seconds in PNJ 350 to take the class, whilst Tom Bryant, presumably driving WUO 529, came third.

On Saturday June 11th the North Midland Motor Club ran a sprint at Oulton Park, using one lap of the Club circuit. As the exhaust silencer mounting had broken, Graham Morewood ran 774 ACV without the silencer, just using the flexible down pipe. The noise was terrific and there was a flat spot in the power at the critical 3,000 to 3,500 rev range, although at just under 4,000 rpm the Plus Four really began to fly. The first runs were held on a damp track and Graham led the class after these. The second runs were held on a drying track and Graham tried a bit too hard at Druids, clouting the grass bank with the rear wing, and finishing in a slower time than earlier. Vic Hassel's AC Bristol went through to take the class, with Cresswell's Daimler SP250 second. Graham tied with another Plus Four, that of G W John of Chester, for third.

Ray Meredith was the only Morgan driver at Shelsley Walsh hill climb on Sunday June 12th. Although Peter Bradley was listed as an entrant no times were recorded for him. Ray and his mechanic Tommy Thomas had really got XOV 555 sorted, for Ray shot up to record 44.55 seconds.

The Eastern Counties MC's '100' meeting held at Snetterton on Sunday June 19th contained within the programme two ten-lap races counting towards the Autosport Series-Production Sports Car Championship. The final of the two was for Classes B and C and produced an enormous field and some drama when a Jaguar blew its engine just before a corner, causing others to slide off on the spilt oil. Bob Duggan finished in fifth place in Class C, but would have been pleased that he had beaten Roy North's potent TR3.

On Sunday June 19th the BARC South Western Centre held a hill climb at Brunton. There was a huge entry of 117, with eighty others turned down. The weather was glorious and there was a large crowd to watch the action. There were two Plus Fours within the eleven starters in Class 6, for sports cars over 1,600cc, and below 2,000cc. Jim Banbury was in PNJ 350 and was joined by Cardiff driver Brian Parsons in NAB 217. This famous old aluminium bodied Plus Four had been bought by Brian from Fred Lockwood. Fred had worked for Rootes in Coventry, and as Rootes used Servais silencers a prototype four branch exhaust manifold and exhaust system of this make had been fitted to the car. The engine had been balanced, and a high lift camshaft had also been fitted.

Jim Banbury was unstoppable, however, recording 29.43 seconds to win the class, whilst Brian recorded a more sedate 31.12 seconds to finish seventh.

Bob Duggan was the only Morgan entry, with OYO 784, for the BARC's 41st Members' Meeting at Goodwood held on Saturday June 25th. In Event

4, the scratch race for Marque sports cars, and counting towards the BARC championship, spins were the order of the day. There were at least six, with Fred Munns having the worst of it when he was thrown out of his AC Bristol at Madgwick on the second lap. Luckily he was not badly hurt although the AC was written off. Bob had a disaster at the approach to St Mary's on the third lap when the Morgan became a three-wheeler, and hit the hurdle. It turned out one of the original 16 inch rear wheels had broken in the centre allowing it to pull over the wheel nuts. As all four wheel nuts were still attached to the brake drum it was easy for Bob to fit a spare wheel for the journey home to Wales. When Peter Morgan found out about this he insisted Bob exchange his 16 inch wheels for the newer and stronger 15 inch equivalent, blaming the disaster on the onset of metal fatigue in the older wheels.

There were four Plus Fours entered for the Shelsley Walsh meeting held on Sunday June 26th. Graham Morewood was in 774 ACV, whilst Phil Veale was in a newly purchased car, a red 1959 wire wheeled Plus Four two-seater, recently bought from John McKechnie's garage, 'The Cedar Motor House'. J Bradshaw also had a new Morgan, but his was a four-seater. The final Morgan entry was the 1951 Plus Four of Brian Bannister. Graham was very impressed with Shelsley on this his first visit, describing it as the 'best hill I had ever been up'. Vic Hassal easily won the class for production sports cars up to 2,000cc in his AC Bristol with 43.63 seconds, whilst Graham's 47.13 seconds brought him second place. Brian Bannister was best of the other Morgans with 48.25, whilst Phil recorded 48.46 and Mr Bradshaw 48.55 seconds. We believe Brian's early Plus Four was running with a tuned and balanced TR2 engine.

Yet another hill climb was held at Wiscombe that same Sunday. Four Morgan Plus Fours were entered for the class for 1,600 to 2,000cc cars, although George Edwards' car non-started. Buncombe's AC Bristol took the class with a time of 41.55 seconds, with Jim Banbury second with 42.06 seconds in PNJ 350, whilst Tom Bryant was third with 43.92 seconds, presumably in WUO 529. The fourth Morgan was NAB 217 driven by Brian Parsons who recorded 46.75 seconds to finish last of the seven starters.

At the Morgan Motor Company directors' meeting held on Thursday June 30th Peter reported that the recent works party had been very successful.

He also reported that the Ford Motor Company had confirmed that the 105E engine would be available from April 1961, so he proposed to make the forthcoming 105E engined 4/4 (Series III) available to customers' orders only. Dr Steel had borrowed the prototype, and was very pleased with the engine, having averaged some 43 mpg. Peter reported he did not think there was any worthwhile gain in fitting twin carburettors.

Autosport magazine of Friday July 1st carried a road test by John Bolster of a new Plus Four. This particular car was fitted with disc brakes and wire wheels, with the latter being shod with radial tyres. These were the new Dunlop Durabands, introduced by Dunlop as opposition to the increasingly popular Michelin X, the pioneer radial tyre. Like the Michelin tyre the Duraband was also reinforced with steel wire. This Morgan was also fitted with the revised Cam Gears Ltd steering box and drop arm, which John found gave much lighter steering.

John always liked the Plus Four and found the radial tyres contributed both to improved cornering and traction, writing, 'The understeering tendency of earlier Morgans was not present in this instance and one could fairly fling the car through corners in a most refreshing manner.' Improved traction may have helped the Plus Four record a 0 to 60 mph time of 9.6 seconds, with a maximum speed of 104.6 mph, the fastest to date for a Morgan tested by *Autosport*. John really appreciated the disc brakes, commenting, 'In the past I have found that drum braked Morgans tended to pull to one side or grab when the brakes were applied repeatedly at high speeds. With discs one can rely on as many straight line stops as one wants, and there is never a sign of distress.' John concluded, 'If the object of the exercise is really high average speeds in absolute safety, there is nothing to compare with the Morgan at less than twice its price.' It was praise indeed. The car John had tested had only covered 500 miles when he borrowed it, but he added another 1,000. We suspect it was the newly rebuilt works car, KUY 387, complete with new body and chassis, being virtually a new car. It was built without external door handles, something John did not particularly appreciate.

The Duraband tyres had been available as an optional extra on new Morgans for a few months now, costing an additional £4.15.0. Older Plus Fours with 16 inch wheels could fit 6.5 by 16 Durabands, this size being the equivalent size to a 5.25 by 16 cross-ply. At this time there was no convention on how to mark the tyre sizes of radials, but eventually a metric width nomenclature was standardised. Dunlop recommended 18 lbs/sq inch pressure for the front tyres and 20 lbs/sq. inch for the rear for normal road use of the new radial.

On Saturday July 2nd the MCC held its annual Silverstone race meeting for cars and motorcycles, including the traditional high speed trials. The first proper race was a five lap scratch race, which was dominated from the start by Sturgess's Jaguar C-type, with Bob Duggan some way back at the head of the rest of the field. On lap 4 Mrs Bluebell Gibbs in her Lotus Eleven found a way past the Morgan for second place with Bob finishing third. In a later ten lap scratch race Tom Smith took part in his black Plus Four coupé, but he didn't finish in the places.

The BARC held its tenth Members' Meeting at Aintree on Saturday July 9th and the event was blessed by lovely hot weather. In the second of the two seven lap sports car handicaps D Martin, driving a new red Plus Four with wire wheels, OCK 606, managed to take first place ahead of MacKay's Lotus Climax and Pitt's Cooper Monaco, the latter having been driven brilliantly from scratch.

The last event of the day was a Marque scratch race. Mr Martin wasn't as fortunate this time,
having to be satisfied with a great dice with Wilby's MGA, and finishing down the field.

The Bugatti Owners' Club ran its ninth Inter-Club Invitation Team Hill Climb on Saturday July 24th at Prescott and announced it would also be its last such event. The Morgan 4/4 Club team consisted of Peter Morgan in the new KUY 387, Lionel Mayman in VON 777, Ray Meredith in XOV 555 and Jim Banbury in PNJ 350. Also competing in a Plus Four was M T Hughes, as part of the Liverpool Motor Club's team. The three fastest team members counted as the team, which meant leaving out Jim Banbury, and when the handicaps were taken into account the Morgan team finished in second place, with a time of 5 minutes 48.63 seconds, just 0.36 seconds behind the Sporting Owners' Club team of Austin Healey Sprites.

Lord Montagu of Beaulieu had kindly agreed to host a Morgan rally as part of Morgan's fiftieth anniversary celebrations, which was organised on Sunday July 31st. Unfortunately it coincided with a jazz festival at the same site, leading to disquiet on the Saturday night within the camping Morgan contingent at the carryings-on of the jazz enthusiasts! On a glorious sunny day some sixty three-wheelers turned up and twenty four-wheelers, the Morgan Three Wheeler Club being the larger of the two Morgan clubs at this time of course. Sadly the organisation by the Montagu Motor Museum was not highly regarded, and having to pay for admission was certainly not appreciated by the Morgan contingent. There was a concours competition, with the prizes presented by Mrs Jane Morgan.

The Nottingham Sports Car Club held a pleasant race meeting at Mallory Park on Sunday July 31st. Lionel Mayman had entered the twenty lap race for sports cars over 1,600 cc in VON 777, but he couldn't stop Brian Naylor's Cooper Maserati from romping off to an easy win, lapping the entire field in the process. Lionel finished second, holding off the Austin Healey of Chris Ashmore, and the AC Bristol of Vic Hassell.

On Sunday August 7th there was a hill climb at Wiscombe at which Jim Banbury competed in PNJ

Peter Morgan at Prescott in the newly rebuilt KUY 387 as part of the Morgan team. (Morgan Motor Co collection)

350 and Brian Parsons in NAB 217. Jim recorded 42.46 seconds to finish in third place in the class for modified saloons and sports cars over 1,600cc. Brian recorded 43.45 seconds to finish fifth.

Not long after returning from the Nurburgring Chris Lawrence discussed his intention with Peter Morgan to enter the prestigious RAC Tourist Trophy (TT) race, due to be held over three hours at Goodwood on Saturday August 20th. It was now run for GT cars. Peter could see that Chris's well prepared Plus Four TOK 258 could do well, with ensuing excellent publicity for the Morgan marque, so he agreed to enter Chris as a Morgan Motor Company entry. As the body on TOK 258 was rather the worse for wear Peter arranged for the Morgan factory to update the body to the current shape, panelling it in aluminium and fitting new aluminium wings. The original cowl with the long grille was retained. (We believe that part of the old body was subsequently used on a car that was constructed from parts in the nineteen-seventies). This all resulted in a weight loss of nearly 1cwt (112 lbs). The whole car was repainted in its original red at the Morgan factory too.

Chris told us that the chassis frame was also renewed at the factory as he had repaired it so many times, especially as a result of the pounding it received at the Nurburgring! Typical of the support that Peter gave to Chris in the early days, we believe that the work was done at minimal cost to Chris. Many chassis components were also renewed by Chris and his team, and new disc brakes were fitted. A 'new' engine was built up with much attention to detail, to ensure reliability for the forthcoming three hour TT race. John Harvey was to lap-in the knock-off wheel spinners to the threads of the hubs, allowing quick wheel changes if necessary without sticking spinner problems.

Also in mid 1960 a somewhat pedantic engineer bought a Lawrence Tune camshaft to fit into a TR3 engine, possibly not in a Morgan. He tried it in his car, then had it removed and replaced by an American Iskenderian version. He discovered the maximum power was similar for the two camshafts, but the Lawrence Tune camshaft gave better mid-range torque, as well as being kinder to the valve operating system. It was a better camshaft for road use and more reliable.

A record crowd visited Brands Hatch to see the Silver City Trophy race meeting on Bank Holiday Monday, August 1st. For this meeting the new 2.65 mile extended Grand Prix circuit was in use, construction of which had begun during the previous winter. There was a record crowd for this major meeting, which featured the fifty lap Formula 1 race for the Silver City Trophy.

The first event on the programme was the Wrotham Trophy race, held over ten laps for GT cars. Chris Lawrence was entered in the newly prepared TOK 258, running in the class for 1,601 to 2,000cc GT cars, TOK running with full windscreen and the hardtop. Unfortunately Chris was unable to get the better of Bill McCowen's potent AC Bristol, but did finish in second place some seven seconds behind. Chris reported problems with the near side front brake locking the wheel. Examination showed the disc to be faulty with heavy scoring evident, so the disc was renewed.

On Saturday August 13th the 750 Motor Club held its annual Six Hour Relay Race, attracting twenty-four teams to Silverstone to race on the Club circuit. Chris Lawrence wasn't in the Morgan team this year, probably saving TOK for the all-important TT the following weekend, but Westerham Motors was at Mallory Park for Len Bridge and Roland Smith to race the Formula Juniors. Consequently the Morgan team consisted of Lionel Mayman in VON 777 as the 'A' car, Ray Meredith in XOV 555 as the 'B', Bob Duggan in OYO 974 as the 'C', and American Tom Smith in his black coupé as the 'D'. Having won the event in 1959 the Morgan team was heavily handicapped this year, having to give eight laps to a Triumph team for example. The team manager was Lionel Mayman and he also supplied the pit crew from his garage, all wearing 'Kieft' emblazoned overalls. The night before the race Bob Duggan spent time with Tom Smith at Hendon, the pair motoring together to Silverstone early the following morning. Lt. Tom Smith was over in England stationed with the US Navy and had bought his black coupé, chassis number 3973, through the Navy Base Exchange scheme. His black coupé, with black leather interior was right hand drive, had wire wheels, a tuned engine and a heater. It had been delivered on Tuesday September 2nd, 1958.

XOV 555 was running with an oil cooler and oil temperature gauge as well as an undertray. Bob Duggan's car had been fairly recently fitted with front disc brakes as well as 15 inch wheels. Tom Smith's coupé had the engine set up by Derringtons, claiming a top speed of 120 mph. He was using Michelin 'X' tyres.

Ray Meredith took the Le Mans start at 1pm and ran second for a while to the Jaguar D-type of Peter Sargent before he broke a valve rocker shaft and had to pit to hand over the sash to Lionel Mayman. Ray's car was soon repaired by borrowing a rocker shaft from the Plus Four UOL 490 of a spectating Robin Brown and he set off again with the team sash. Unfortunately it was not noticed that the oil temperature gauge was not working correctly and after a while he returned with a very sick sounding engine. Lionel Mayman set off again for a long fast stint before handing over to Bob Duggan. His elderly Plus Four was also fast, but he was soon back in with rear brake trouble, caused it was believed by the balance between the newly fitted front discs and the rear drums not being right yet. Bob's rear brake shoes were the original 1.25 inch width, and they rapidly wore out. Robin Brown offered to donate his own rear brakes, but they were not correct for the Duggan car, so it joined Ray's in the casualty bay and Tom Smith set off with the coupé.

There were three teams of Austin and Morris Minis entered for this event, and all had shed road wheels at alarming rates. The organisers told them they must all retire, which they did. It was just as well because Tom Smith came through Woodcote corner backwards, sliding into the pit area and scattering marker drums and officials in all directions! He would have collected the Minis too if it had happened a few laps earlier! Luckily he had the presence of mind to hand over the team sash during his backwards entry! The coupé was driveable but not really race-worthy after its altercations.

Lionel Mayman waits in a rather battered looking VON 777 to receive the team sash from the incoming car of Ray Meredith during the 750 MC Relay Race. (National Motor Museum)

Lionel Mayman went out again in VON 777, but had the misfortune to seize the gearbox, so he returned to the pits. The only car left still driveable was the Duggan one, so it went out for the finish. In his article on the event written for the Morgan 4/4 Club *Miscellany* magazine Robin Brown wrote,'He finished the event going quicker and quicker as time went on, which is only natural I suppose if you haven't any brakes to slow you down.' Bob himself told us the race had been great fun, especially without brakes! The event was won by the Tornado team.

After the event Bob enlisted the help of a friend in a Ford Anglia to lead the way back home to Wales whilst he drove the brakeless Morgan behind it. He made it, using the back of the Anglia as a buffer from time to time!

The Bolton-le-Moors CC's Bolton Rally began from Spurstow in Cheshire that same Saturday at 11.30 pm, this National rally finishing the following morning at Capesthorne Hall near Macclesfield after 150 miles of tough navigation through Wales. Brian Harper and Ron Crellin won their Class Award in Brian's Plus Four YOM 798 whilst Val Domleo, now navigating for Anne Hall, finished third overall and won the Ladies' Award in Anne's Ford.

A hill climb was held at Shelsley Walsh on Saturday August 20th. Two Plus Fours took part, Lionel Mayman in VON 777 and Peter Bradley with 9267 U. It was Peter who made the fastest Morgan time yet recorded at Shelsley with 43.93 seconds on his sole run, sufficient for third in class. Lionel's best was 44.37 seconds.

The RAC Tourist Trophy race was run by the BARC at Goodwood on Saturday August 20th. This year it was no longer a qualifying round for the World Championship of Sports Car Manufacturers, for it was now open only to Grand Touring cars built to Appendix J and counted towards the International Grand Touring Cups awarded by the FIA. The BARC had further stipulated that the cars must run in closed form, encouraging fixed head coupés, and permitting hard tops and even requiring hoods to be erected on normally open cars. It was a move back to the roots of the TT when competing cars were not purpose built racers but were actually purchasable from manufacturers and were manufactured in some volume. On the same programme was the BARC Formula Junior Championship, and Westerham Motors had entered three Deep Sanderson Formula Junior cars for this, including the new DS 104, although the car to be driven by Richard Shepherd-Barron non-started. This was a big disappointment as Richard had interrupted his Formula Junior racing in Italy and had flown back specifically for this meeting. The Formula Junior event was run first with two seven lap heats, the fastest twelve from each then contesting a twenty-one lap final. Of the Deep Sanderson drivers, Bob Staples finished fourteenth in his heat, failing to qualify for the final, but Les Fagg finished eleventh in his heat and did qualify. He retired during the final from a lowly position.

Practice for the Tourist Trophy had occupied Thursday and Friday and grid positions for the Le Mans start were allocated by practice times. There were thirty-four starters, divided into three classes: over 2,000cc, 1,301 to 2,000cc, and 1,000 to 1,300cc. TOK 258 was running with the TR hardtop in place and side-screens fitted. Chris Lawrence managed a lap time of 1 minute 46.4 seconds, which was quick enough for third-equal fastest time in the 1,301 to 2,000cc class, Graham Hill managing 1 min 41.0 seconds and Joakim Bonnier 1 min 43.6 seconds in factory entered Porsche Carreras. In addition to the Porsche works entries there were three other Porsche Carreras, privately entered. Gerhard Koch's private entry and Graham Hill's works car had the specially commissioned lightweight Abarth bodies, introduced by Porsche earlier in 1960 for a competition version of the Carrera. The Porsche Carrera had been originally introduced by Porsche in 1955 as a sporting variant of the 356, but fitted with a special flat-four engine of 1,498 cc fitted with four overhead camshafts, two to each bank of two air cooled cylinders. By 1960 this engine had expanded to 1,588 cc and produced 128 bhp at 6,700 rpm. In addition there were two MGA Twin-Cams prepared by Dick Jacobs and driven by Alan Foster and Tommy Bridger, the fast AC Bristol of Bill McCowen and a team of three MG engined Elva Couriers in the same class.

The race got under way at 3 pm, Chris Lawrence being in twelfth position on the first lap. Chris settled down to consistent lapping in the 1 minute 46.5 to 47.0 range and soon began to draw ahead of the others in his class behind him, and began to catch the second-in-class Porsche of Jo Bonnier. On lap 29 Chris overtook this works Porsche at Lavant and began to draw away.

At the end of lap 47 the Morgan's planned pit stop was undertaken, all four wheels being changed and ten gallons of petrol being added in 1 minute 20 seconds. The refuelling took slightly longer than hoped for because the compulsory fuel funnel supplied for the purpose was too tight a fit in the tank filler neck, preventing air from escaping the filling tank.

With everything replenished Chris tried the starter, and disaster! It was clear from the noise it made that something serious was amiss. It had to be replaced, but this task was made especially difficult because of the adjacent hot exhaust pipes and the 'heat sink' of the engine block making the starter too hot to touch for long. Despite liberal dosing with water it took seventeen minutes to replace the starter.

Chris now lapped as consistently as before, between 1 minute 45.5 seconds and 1 min 47.0, but there was no hope of catching the leaders and the team had to settle for twenty-fourth place overall and seventh in class. The race was won by Stirling Moss in a Ferrari 250GT, whilst Graham Hill won the 1,301 to 2,000cc class with the Porsche-Abarth Carrera.

The faulty starter motor was immediately examined by the Lucas representative and it was found that the armature shaft bush had split, the pieces vibrating into the starter where half of the bush had jammed the armature immovably.

Although the starter failure had been a disaster, the performance of the Morgan on the

Chris Lawrence during the RAC TT at Woodcote corner in TOK 258. Note the flapping side-screen. (Louis Klementaski)

track had raised many eyebrows at the fact that such a cheap car could mix it with the works Porsches. Up until the pit stop TOK 258 was leading all but one of the Porsches, and the special Abarth bodied Carreras were truly rather special motors, having won their class at Le Mans in June, and having achieved 150 mph down the Mulsanne Straight in the process. To find themselves being humbled by the Morgan was not something they expected. Once again Peter Morgan received inquiries from potential customers who wanted such a Morgan with a Chris Lawrence built engine.

One such customer was the Morgan and general motor racing enthusiast John Sach, always known as 'Baggy' for obvious reasons. Baggy had been one of the invited guests present at the Morgan fiftieth anniversary lunch at the Abbey Hotel in April, working for the Anglo-Dutch oil company Shell Mex in public relations. He had been a noted fighter pilot during the Second World War. He fancied a Morgan with a Lawrence engine. Peter Morgan was to take these inquiries on board and had discussions with Chris Lawrence and his backer, his uncle, Tony Sanderson.

One week later Chris Lawrence was entered for the BARC's second Members' Meeting at Oulton Park. The first race was a seven lap sports car handicap, which had been preceded by a torrential rainstorm causing some flooding on the circuit. Several cars were in trouble, aquaplaning off the circuit, including the Plus Four of G W John, who found a ditch well infield. He did manage to extricate his Morgan, but obviously with no hope of a place.

Event 4 was a seven lap Marque scratch race, and Chris Lawrence disappeared into the distance in TOK 258, winning by fourteen seconds.

Event 7 was a seven lap scratch race for Formula Juniors, and for this Chris Lawrence was in the latest Deep Sanderson, the 104. The track was still very wet, but it had now stopped raining. Again Chris won, beating to his great satisfaction a couple of Lotus 18 Ford Cosworths and Major Arthur Mallock in his home built U2-Ford.

Chris Lawrence's Deep Sandersons hadn't had much success until this point. Chris had used as the required production car suspension, that from a VW. Under hard cornering the trailing arm front suspension had produced alarming camber angles, destroying cornering ability. Chris had mentioned this to Keith Duckworth of Cosworth one day whilst they were both waiting to collect Ford 105E engines from a Ford dealership. Keith suggested that he should modify the suspension as others did to introduce camber recovery. For the Oulton Park race meeting Chris raced the new DS 104, which had been built with the two trailing arm pivots modified by angling them down and towards the centre. As the results had now demonstrated, the system really worked well, and Chris christened it the Lawrence Link suspension system.

Roland Smith had persuaded Chris to let him use Chris's every day car, a Triumph Herald, for saloon car racing and he entered the scratch race with it at Oulton. Naturally the Herald had the Lawrence Tune treatment to the engine (camshaft and Fish carburetor). Roland was able to adapt to the car's handling and gave a good account of himself but was no match for Bill Blydenstein in his incredible Borgward.

The Morgan 4/4 Club held its autumn driving tests for club members on Sunday August 28th at the factory of Messrs L G Harris, the paintbrush manufacturers in Bromsgrove. The tests were organised by Philip Veale, and showers of rain made some of them a bit tricky with Robin Brown understeering his Plus Four into a low wall and bending back the offside front crosshead. The winner was a most consistent Dixon Smith in CAB 652, whilst Tony Thomas finished second. The 4/4 Series I was a very manoeuvrable car and ideal for driving tests.

On Saturday September 10th the BARC ran its 43rd Members' Meeting at Goodwood in glorious weather, attracting a goodly number of spectators. The most exciting race of the day was the ten lap Marque scratch race, which used a Le Mans start at which Chris Lawrence was still a master, with or without the starter relay gadget! He

A busy scene in the Westerham Motors corner of the paddock at the BARC Oulton Park meeting on August 27th. Chris Lawrence attends to TOK between the DS Formula Juniors and the Triumph Herald. Les Fagg is working on the wheel of a DS 101 whilst Roland Smith stands behind the Herald with his back to the camera, talking to Willy Edwards. In the corner Robert Neale and John Harvey have the bonnet raised on Robert's Standard Vanguard Estate. At the rear can be seen the Fordson, the caravan, the Jaguar MkVII, Bob Staples' AC Ace and the Standard van. (Len Bridge)

was first away, pulling out a good lead on the first lap. Bill McCowen in the 'Scuderia Light Blue' AC Bristol was second and started to pull back Chris's lead but having to lap back markers delayed him and he was five seconds adrift of the flying Morgan at the finish. The event had been televised on BBC TV and the commentator, Macdonald Hobley, was impressed by the way Chris, Bill and Colin Hextall had been drifting their cars through Woodcote corner. Colin Hextall had done enough by finishing fourth after a dreadful start in his TR3 to become the winner of the Freddie Dixon Trophy this year with twenty-three points. Chris, who had hardly entered any races, but had usually won when he did, came second with fifteen points.

The old RAF wartime airfield at Rufforth, 3.5 miles west of York was the venue that same day for a race meeting held by the Northern Centre of the BRSCC. Two Morgans took part in the ten lap race for sports and GT cars of any capacity, namely the Plus Fours of Peter Bradley and G W Graham. Peter finished in mid-field in twelfth place, with Mr Graham eighteenth. Peter Bolton won the race in his potent AC Bristol. Rufforth had opened for motor racing in March 1959 using a 2.1 mile circuit, but this had been shortened for 1960 to 1.7 miles, reducing the length of the straight.

The Bugatti Owners' Club ran a National hill climb at Prescott on Sunday September 11th, using the new loop for the third time. There were two Morgans entered, Ray Meredith in XOV 555 and Jim Banbury in PNJ 350. Ray's Morgan had not yet had the engine repaired from the Relay Race damage, so Robin Brown took over Ray's entry with UOL 490. Robin had spent a week fitting a new front crosshead to his Plus Four following the damage incurred during the club driving tests. Jim Banbury was fastest of the two, recording 62.24 seconds, with Robin recording 62.60 seconds. They finished sixth and seventh in class, behind the winning Cooper Monaco and various Bristol engined devices.

For some time there had been concern about the poor state of maintenance of some of the older vehicles used on British roads, many of which were originally built pre-war. As a result the Government decided all old vehicles should be tested annually. This Ministry of Transport (MOT) Test for roadworthiness came into effect on Monday September 12th for all vehicles over

The paddock at Rufforth. Behind John Busfield's MGA Twin-Cam can be seen Peter Bradley's much modified Plus Four with Cec Booth's Frazer Nash behind that. (Don Griffiths)

ten years old. These cars now had to be tested annually, and a fee was charged both for this and the issue of the required MOT Certificate by licenced garages. The MOT Certificate was required before the owner could tax the vehicle and use it on the road. Brakes, lights and steering were the main items originally tested, but the test was gradually modified to encompass other features of roadworthiness.

Autosport magazine for Friday September 16th contained a short paragraph in the 'Pit and Paddock' section announcing as follows: 'The Morgan Motor Company intend to market a competition Plus Four in limited quantities. It will be a standard disc-braked model with a Lawrence-tuned TR3 engine producing approximately 115 bhp, which will give the car a top speed of 116 mph with full weather equipment. The cost? Probably something in the region of £100 extra.' No doubt enthusiasts would be keen to visit the Morgan stand at the forthcoming Motor Show to find out more.

Robin Brown wrote in the September/October edition of *Miscellany*, 'Stop Press!!!. A "Super Sports" Plus Four will soon be on the market.' He had decided the specification must include Weber carburettors. This is the first reference we have found to the name 'Super Sports' being selected for this new car.

Lionel Mayman chose this time to publicise the Kieft Sports Car Co Ltd's range of Kieft Power conversions for the Morgan Plus Four and also the Triumph Herald. Pauline Mayman was now rallying one of the latter. The Kieft concern booked the Silverstone Club circuit one day in mid-September, and took along VON 777 and a standard Plus Four for comparison, as well as three Triumph Heralds. One was standard, one was running on twin SU carburettors and the third was Pauline Mayman's own heavily modified coupé, which carried her ex-Morgan personal number plate EPM 324. The motoring press was invited along to try them. One who did was David Phipps who wrote up his impressions in the *Modified Motoring* autumn issue. After driving the standard Plus Four (registration 534 BOK) he took the wheel of VON 777, describing it as a 'revelation'. The engine he found so much more responsive, with vastly improved acceleration and personal lap times some thirteen seconds faster than the standard car. 5,000 rpm (95 mph) was reached half way along the Club Straight. David concluded, 'Occasionally in the course of road testing I come across a car I am very loathe to return and of which I harbour fond memories. Such a one was Lionel Mayman's Morgan.' David recorded a 0 to 60 mph time of just over 9 seconds, the standard Plus Four recording circa 12 seconds.

Also testing the car was *Autosport* magazine, and VON 777 was so impressive that Lionel Mayman's approval was sought for a longer road test after the racing season. *Motor Sport* did likewise. Kieft described the engine conversions on VON 777 as having a 'Stage 2' modified cylinder block with high compression pistons and a 'Stage 1' gas flowed cylinder head with special valves and springs, costing £74.0.0 and £29.5.0 respectively.

Robin Brown sought more information for *Miscellany*, and received details from Les Newey who worked for Maymans. Les wrote, 'The Kieft Power Morgan has lowered suspension, twin braking system and a modified steering box incorporating an idler box to cut out front wheel hop on fast corners. The face of the cylinder head has been machined to raise the compression ratio and give a perfect joint with the block. Combustion chambers and valve ports have been machined to improve the gas flow and have been minutely balanced and polished. The special valves are precision seated and extra strong valve springs fitted to avoid valve bounce. Modified pistons, a four branch exhaust and a modified block complete the treatment and the result is an engine developing well in excess of 120 bhp. In spite of all these modifications it has been the aim of the Technical Director Ron Timmins to keep the Kieft Power

Morgan tractable for normal road use. This aspect has been a great success and all the gentlemen of the Motoring Press who have tested the car have found it a delight to drive on the road and the only difficulty has been persuading them to give the car back!'

According to Ron Timmins the lowered suspension was achieved at the rear by resetting the rear springs which had an extra top leaf and at the front by using his own specification of springs, but later photographs suggest the lower crosshead tube was cranked in three-wheeler fashion too. The final compression ratio Ron achieved was 12.4 to 1, the block being shortened to allow the pistons into the head. The camshaft and carburettors were never changed, Ron being ready to do this for 1961, but Lionel Mayman was keen to get the Kieft Formula Junior cars developed, using a Triumph engine, possibly then developing this for Formula 1 as Lotus had with its Formula Junior Type 18. The Morgan sadly was to be sold the following year.

The finale of the Autosport Series-Production Championship was to be the three hour race held at Snetterton on Saturday September 17th. The championship was to be decided by the best five results obtained during the series of races. Prior to the finale this put Lionel Mayman into third place in Class C with eleven points, sufficient for fifteenth position overall. The three hour race began at 5.30 pm with a Le Mans start, and within the first hour Julian Sutton, the runaway Class C leader, was in the pits with a boiling engine. Initial hope for the rest of the class was dealt a blow when the car reappeared five minutes later after replacing the broken fan belt and Julian went on to finish sixth to take the Class C Championship with ease and third place in the overall championship ratings. This third place overall moved Julian out of the class ratings and moved Lionel up to second place in Class C, for which he received a trophy. Lionel wasn't actually present at this event and his previous eleven scored points gave him overall eighteenth place in the championship. The race itself was actually won by Dickie Stoop in his Porsche Carrera, but he wasn't registered for the championship.

Lionel Mayman had taken VON 777 to the SUNBAC's Ragley Park hill climb that same day, recording 28.5 seconds, the Morgan rather unusually being beaten by a TR by just 0.2 seconds, but VON had been put up a class because of all the modifications and no doubt the TR was modified too. In the under 2,000cc class were the Plus Fours of Graham Morewood and J A White. The latter ran a four-seater and worked for the Rover car manufacturers. Graham was in his usual two-seater 774 ACV and he finished in fourth place in class, behind three AC Bristols.

The following day Lionel was at Mallory Park for the Nottingham Sports Car Club's meeting, taking part in the twenty lap race for sports cars over 1,500cc. The two Jaguar XKs of R A Gibson and D Hobbs took the lead from the start, but Peter Bolton managed to get his AC Bristol through into the lead and stayed there. Lionel Mayman managed to get past Hobbs for third place, and had a mighty battle with Hobbs to stay there, before the Jaguar finally retired, leaving Lionel unmolested in third place to the finish. D Hobbs' Jaguar XK 140 was fitted with his own design of automatic transmission, named the Hobbs Mecha-Matic, which ran on the epicyclic gears principle.

Jim Banbury was the only Morgan driver at Wiscombe on Sunday September 18th for another hill climb in PNJ 350, but he tasted victory in the class for sports cars over 1,600cc, recording 42.25 seconds and beating Michael Burn's Bristol engined Frazer Nash. The following Sunday he was again the only Morgan entered, but this time at Harleyford. He recorded 25.86 seconds to finish second in class to an AC Bristol. A pretty Jaguar left the course and was badly damaged on hitting a tree stump. As a result the RAC wanted improved safety measures instituted before allowing any more sprints at this venue.

Peter Bradley battles with his stark looking Plus Four during the BARC sprint held at the Burton factory in Leeds. (John Holroyd)

Once again the BARC Yorkshire Centre borrowed the factory grounds of Montague Burton in Leeds for a sprint meeting, held on Sunday September 25th. Peter Bradley did well in his stripped and tuned Plus Four 9267 U recording third fastest time in his class.

The Hagley and District Light Car Club held another of its sprint meetings at Chateau Impney, Droitwich on Sunday September 25th. The entire course had been resurfaced. Several Morgans entered, including Ray Meredith in XOV 555 and Robin Brown in UOL 490. Robin had the misfortune to misjudge his second run, ending up in the rhododendron bushes!

The Motor magazine in its issue of Wednesday September 28th carried a pre-Motor Show report introducing the new Morgan 4/4 Series III with the Ford 105E engine. The standard 105E engine was being used, giving 39 bhp at 5,000 rpm, and a Competition version was not planned, although in fact a handful of cars were built later for the Canadian and American market with twin carburettors. The Ford four speed gearbox was used too and this had necessitated some alterations to the profile of the chassis frame in order to accommodate the extra width of the gearbox and also provide increased foot room. Using the same 4.44 to 1 ratio 6HA back axle as on the 100E engined predecessor, overall gear ratios of 18.3, 10.65, 6.27 and 4.44 to 1 were achieved, with a reverse of 24.01. The gear lever was found to emerge from the gearbox inside the cockpit on the 105E engine, rather than in the engine bay as in the 100E. It was too far forward to use conventionally however so Peter Morgan modified his design of the 100E gear change to suit the new car. The body from the 100E Morgan was transferred with minimal alterations. Morgan had priced the new car at £520.0.0, some £22 higher than the previous model. With Purchase Tax the total price was £737.15.10.

John McKechnie had been thinking about using the forthcoming 105E engined 4/4 for racing in 1961, and *The Motor* report decided him to take action. On Thursday September 29th he wrote to Ray Meredith with the suggestion that a team of four 4/4s be used, with three racing as a team, to team orders in the Autosport Championship, the fourth car being used for practice and as a source

Morgan workshop manual drawings show the new 105E gearlever on the left and the earlier 100E on the right, both designed by Peter Morgan.

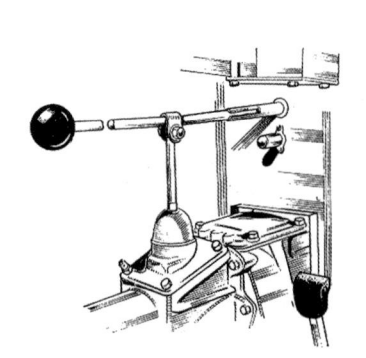

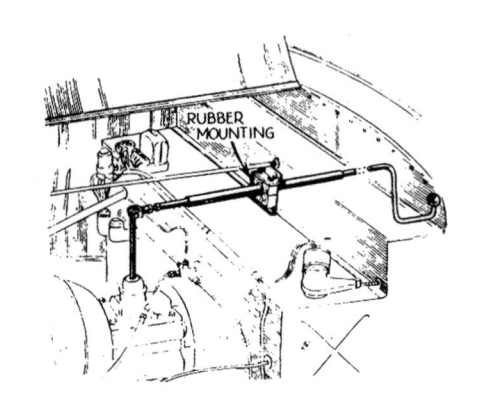

of spares. John had spoken to Ted Martin, the tuning wizard behind the Alexander Engineering Company of Haddenham in Buckinghamshire, and he was prepared to develop three very hot engines for the team. John suggested that with Ray's mechanic, Tommy Thomas, preparing his car and Harold Pugh preparing John's they should go very well indeed. The following day Ray replied, stating that he would like to meet up to discuss the idea further. He mentioned that Peter Morgan had said the factory wasn't very pleased with the 105E engine, and that a new Ford engine was expected pretty soon. Ray was eventually to decide that he would rather continue with XOV 555. This car was performing well with a Derrington high lift camshaft, and a Derrington inlet manifold, but Ray had also been to see Chris Lawrence and had arranged to collect from the Westerham Motors stand, at the forthcoming end of year Racing Car Show, a pair of 45mm Weber carburettors with Lawrence Tune manifolds and a Chris Lawrence camshaft.

The other person with whom John discussed this idea was Robin Brown, who had been thinking of selling his Plus Four anyway. He was to be more receptive than Ray, but was presently wondering whether to replace his Plus Four with an Elva Courier.

The Burnham-On-Sea Motor Club ran speed trials along the Marine Promenade at Weston-Super-Mare on Saturday October 1st. Three Plus Fours took part in Class 5A, Robin Brown in UOL 490, B B Jones in BJ 4, and P Scott. Fastest of the three was B B Jones with 28.1 seconds, sufficient to give him third in class behind two AC Bristols. Robin was fourth equal with 29.1 seconds. Mr Scott recorded 30.2 seconds.

A meeting of the directors of the Morgan Motor Company was held on Thursday October 6th. Peter Morgan advised that the new 4/4 with the Ford 105E engine would be on exhibition at the Motor Show later in the month. He mentioned the lighter steering of the 4/4 as a result of the revised Cam Gears Ltd steering box, and a revised facia with new toggle switches, and commented that all Plus Fours would now have front disc brakes. Flashing indicator lights were now standard too. Trials were underway to try and achieve softer springing for the Morgan range, this being led by Neville Carlton-Oatley.

The tenth London Rally, organised by the London MC attracted the maximum allowed number of entrants for a National rally, namely 250, to the four alternative starts of London, Birmingham, Leeds and Taunton. The event began at midday on Friday October 7th

Brian Harper and Ron Crellin get underway in the London Rally. (Brian Harper collection)

and the routes converged at Llandrindod Wells, from where the tricky night navigation section began at 5 pm onwards. After around 400 miles of twisting 'white' roads the weary competitors made for the finish at Llandrindod Wells, but only 64 of the 240 actual starters managed to do so! The class for Production Grand Touring cars 1,301 to 2,000cc was won by Brian Harper and Ron Crellin in YOM 798; a brilliant performance for the Plus Four crew. Pauline Mayman was now rallying her Triumph Herald, and she finished third in her class.

The sixth MCC Derbyshire Trial began on Friday evening October 7th, finishing the following day. The Morgan motor Company team consisted of P Scott in his Plus Four, Jim Goodall, presumably in HUY 982, and Horace Roberts in WAB 779. Also entered was Brian Parsons in NAB 217, but we have been unable to find any results.

The BARC held a sprint meeting at Aintree on Saturday October 8th, where heavy rain gave Graham Morewood an advantage over the very fast TR3 of J Kennerley. Graham took the class win for Triumph engined cars on the aggregate times of both runs, although there was later a protest that the TR which had been faster on one run should take the prize.

On Sunday October 9th Robin Brown in UOL 490 was the sole Morgan entry for the West Essex CC National hill climb at Stapleford Aerodrome. His best time was 58.35 seconds, giving him sixth place in the class for Grand Touring cars from 1,301 to 2,000cc.

There was unfortunately a fatal accident which marred the Hastings and St Leonards and East Sussex Car Club's sprint meeting held at Bodiam on Saturday October 15th. As a result the event was cancelled after the morning practice runs and only the third and last run of the morning was counted towards the result. Jim Banbury in PNJ 350 recorded 35.6 seconds on this run to finish third in the class for unlimited sports cars, but he had been over two seconds faster on an earlier practice run.

On Saturday October 15th Graham Morewood took his Plus Four 774 ACV to the Wirral 100 MC's sprint meeting held at Rhydymwyn, near Mold in Flintshire. The weather was very cold. Joining him in the class for specials and sports cars up to 2,000cc was D G Allen in his Plus Four

The start of the Brands Hatch GT race sees Gibson's Jaguar take the lead, with Chris Lawrence in TOK 258 about to be taken by Warner's Elite on his right. Colin Hextall's white TR3 is behind the Jaguar and Jim Clark in the Austin Healey is on the right of the photograph. (Autosport)

and Gerry Hoyle in a new front disc braked two-seater. This was THY 88, chassis number 4557, a light grey car with black upholstery, which had been dispatched to Lifes Motors in Southport on Wednesday June 29th. Gerry had now retired from running this business, although he was still competing in the agency's demonstrators, as on this occasion. The business was now being run by George Randall. The three Plus Fours were closely matched, heading the production cars section of the class with times within 0.4 seconds of each other.

The Club circuit at Brands Hatch had been resurfaced prior to the BRSCC's Lewis-Evans Trophy meeting held on Sunday October 16th. One of the best races was the ten lap Grand Touring car race, which was split into three classes, Chris Lawrence having entered TOK 258 in the 1,001 to 2,000cc class. From the flag Gibson's very fast 3.8 litre Jaguar XK 120 took an immediate lead, followed by Graham Warner's Lotus Elite, Chris in TOK and Jimmy Clark driving the Ecurie Chiltern Austin Healey 3000. When Gibson spun off Chris was up to second, behind the Lotus, but he began to be pressed hard by Jim Clark. Chris responded with faster laps and held him off to finish second overall and second in class to Graham Warner's Elite.

The Motor Show at Earls Court was held from Wednesday October 19th to Saturday October 29th. The Morgan stand featured the new Series III 4/4 with the Ford 105E engine and gearbox. The car on show was the first production car, chassis number A590, coloured blue with black interior. There was also a stripped chassis on display. There were four Plus Fours on display: a grey four-seater, chassis number 4646, two two-seaters, a red one, chassis number 4647, and a light blue one, chassis number 4649. The latter was the only Plus Four shown without front disc brakes. There was also a coupé in Westminster Green with stone upholstery and wire wheels, chassis number 4650. The item of greatest interest to the sporting motorist however was the display of a Lawrence Tune TR3 engine fitted with Weber carburettors, which, it was announced, Chris Lawrence was producing especially for the Morgan factory. *Autosport* commented: 'Very exciting indeed is the Super Sports Morgan Plus Four. The car is based on Chris Lawrence's successful machine and a separate engine is shown on the stand. Two twin-choke Weber carburettors are featured, and a special camshaft plus careful balancing form part of the modifications. The final result is 116 bhp which is enough to propel the Plus Four at 115 mph. What about a road test Peter Morgan?' Robin

The Lawrence Tune Super Sports engine displayed on the Morgan stand at the Motor Show. (The Autocar)

Brown in *Miscellany* noted that the production Super Sports was apparently to use a Derrington exhaust system. Although TOK still used the one-off 'square' manifold, a tubular version was available for Lawrence Tune customers, manufactured for Chris by RJV Engineering. Baggy Sach no doubt visited the Morgan stand, for he ordered an exact copy of the green coupé on show, but fitted with a Lawrence Tune engine!

On Sunday October 23rd the Guild of Motoring Writers held a test day at Goodwood of the manufacturers' new cars. The Morgan factory had two for the journalists to try, the Westminster Green prototype 4/4, now given chassis number A589 and registered 809 CAB on Friday October 14th, and Chris Lawrence's racer, TOK 258. Bill Boddy of *Motor Sport* loved TOK, but only described the small Morgan as 'nice', commenting, 'We never felt at home with the funny gearchange.' *Autosport* loved TOK too, describing it as, 'the greatest possible fun to drive', but again was not impressed with the 4/4, regarding the engine as 'lacking punch'.

Autosport magazine was able to borrow the Kieft Morgan VON 777 for a week in October. Apart from the engine modifications the journalist, Martyn Watkins, noted the lowered suspension, down by two inches, with Woodhead-Monroe shock absorbers all round. There was a Panhard rod at the rear, and a three-piece track rod at the front incorporating the idler box. The special exhaust system terminated at the driver's door. Lionel Mayman had lapped the Silverstone circuit at under 1 minute 17 seconds with the car in this trim on Dunlop R5 racing tyres.

The noisy exhaust was a particular problem, attracting unwanted attention from the police on two occasions! A week of rain prevented performance testing being done but a 0 to 60 mph time of around seven seconds was estimated (perhaps optimistically). The 'constant surge of power throughout the engine speed range' was favourably commented on as was the faultless handling. The only real down side (apart from the noisy exhaust) was the fuel consumption, which averaged a mere 16 mpg.

Motor Sport borrowed the Kieft Morgan too, some time in October after the Guild of Motoring Writers' test day. Once again rain precluded acceleration figures being taken. The journalist

The prototype 4/4 Series III, 809 CAB, circulates with a Jaguar 3.8 Mk II at the Guild of Motoring Writers' test day at Goodwood. (The Autocar)

noticed the polished ram tubes on the SU carburettors. The inlet pipes were lagged with asbestos and there was a heat shield between the carburettors and the exhaust manifold. A light alloy undertray was fitted. The TR engine modifications received favourable comment, making it 'really howl like a 1100 Climax'. The car was summed up, 'With the expenditure of something over £1,000.0.0 the Morgan buyer will receive from Kieft a very accelerative sports car of distinctive lines which will be capable of winning its class in races sprints and hill climbs without the expenditure of a great deal more money – what more can the enthusiast ask?'

The Knowldale Car Club ran its 'Mini Miglia' Rally over the weekend of October 29th and 30th, attracting 58 crews to a navigation test through the Llandrindod Wells area of some 200 miles. Brian Harper and Ron Crellin did well in YOM 798, finishing second overall.

The following weekend Brian and Ron repeated their success in the Stockport Motor Club's Regent Rally, by coming second in the class for 'Semi-Experts'. Somewhat unusually the rally included a class for military quarter-ton vehicles, attracting 22 entries from the Army, mainly in Austin Champs!

There was a meeting of the directors of the Morgan Motor Company on Thursday November 17th. Peter Morgan announced twenty orders had been received for the new 4/4 Series III at the Motor Show. The new coupé was progressing well and he estimated it would be in production in December. A supply problem had arisen with the 6HA axle for the Series II 4/4, holding up production. Salisbury was to switch to their new 7HA axle for both the Plus Four and 4/4 models and the company had originally produced drawings in 1959 of this axle for the Morgan Motor Company with a 3.73 to 1 ratio for the bolt-on and wire wheeled Plus Fours, and a 4.56 ratio for the 4/4. The Morgan Company was about to switch

Jim Goodall and Denis Moore in HUY 982 during the milder part of the RAC Rally. (LAT Photographic)

completely to this axle, which it did during the next year. We suspect there were teething problems with supply at this time.

Peter also advised the board that negotiations were in hand regarding the restructuring of the Company, particularly in the sale of unwanted assets.

Jack Kemsley was once again responsible for the organisation of the RAC's ninth International Rally this year, and he continued to try and attract Continental drivers by reducing the impact of the special tests to the role of tie-breakers, designing the rally to be won or lost on the road sections. This year he had introduced three forest stages and also a Tulip-type route book. There were three Morgans entered this year, forming the Morgan factory team entered in Class 7, for Grand Touring cars from 1,301 to 2,000cc. Peter Morgan we believe drove KUY 387, navigated by Tommy Thompson. Jim Goodall was in HUY 982, navigated by Denis Moore, and Brian Harper was in YOM 798, navigated by Peter Astbury. Peter ran a caravan company in Cannock, and was an experienced rally driver and navigator. Pauline Mayman was navigating for Rosemary Seers in a Sunbeam Alpine, whilst Val Domleo was paired with Anne Hall in a Ford Anglia 105E. A total of 180 crews were accepted for the event of which fifteen were from abroad, including Citroen and Mercedes-Benz works teams. This year the 2,064 mile route did not venture into Wales at all, but had the majority of its course in Scotland. The event started on Monday November 21st at Blackpool, the first day's runs eventually finishing at Peebles for breakfast the following morning. Fog and floods proved sufficient to reduce the number of clean sheets to just seven during that night. One of those forced to retire was Peter Morgan who hit a bridge near Keld, damaging the Morgan too badly to continue. Mike Duncan, who worked at the Morgan factory in 1961, told us that Peter later got a hefty bill from the bridge owner for its repair!

The special stage due to be held at Charterhall circuit was cancelled because of foot-and-mouth disease, although there was actually no restriction on motor vehicles using roads in this area.

After a two hour halt at Peebles the competitors left for the route to Inverness, facing a tie-breaking test on Rest-and-be-Thankful and then came the decisive road stage on forest land at Monument Hill near Dalmally. This was a rough winding two mile stretch of road leading to a steep final stretch and this all had to be completed in

Brian Harper tackles the Wolvey skid pan test during the RAC Rally. (Brian Harper collection)

three minutes from a standing start. It caused carnage and chaos, the only crew managing to complete the stage on time being SAAB works tester Erik Carlsson navigated by Stuart Turner in the little 841cc three cylinder two-stroke SAAB 96. Several cars were badly damaged, with holed sumps, punctured tyres, twisted suspensions, damaged bodies and lost exhausts. The British rally drivers were just not used to forestry stages.

After a night's rest at Inverness there were ninety minutes of 'fettling' time allowed between collecting the car from 'parc ferme' and the actual start of the Wednesday route, which consisted of two loops from and to Inverness. The following day the crews made south for England. There were special tests at Bo'ness and Elvington before the crews made for Lambcroft Airfield near Kelstern for another tie-breaker test, this replacing Cadwell Park again because of foot-and-mouth disease. On the Friday morning there was another tie-breaker test at Mallory Park, followed by driving tests at the Anti-Skid School at Wolvey, where the well soaped and watered skid pan required precision driving. After this Brands Hatch was the venue for overnight 'parc ferme', before further tie-breaker tests in the form of five lap races on the Saturday.

The rally was won by the amazing Erik Carlsson/Stuart Turner SAAB 96 which finished with the only penalty-free clean sheet. It turned out they had 'reccied' the unknown Scottish sections using a hire car just before the event, returning said car in a slightly the worse for wear condition! The Ladies' Cup was won by Anne Hall and Val Domleo in the Ford Anglia. The Morgans did not do well, but Jim Goodall put up some amazing times in the tie-breaker tests being fastest in his class for five of the seven. This was little consolation because these tests were only for tie-breaking purposes for crews finishing with identical penalty scores. Brian Harper finished the rally with a very painful right hand, a result of engine kick-back whilst hand cranking the engine. YOM 798 finished with some front end damage following an excursion into a fence at some stage.

The Morgan 4/4 Club ran a rally over 150 miles on Saturday December 3rd. Unfortunately this weekend marked the culmination of one of the wettest periods the Hereford and Leominster areas had ever known, and the poor competitors were all at sea in more ways than one, with only two finishing within the permitted limit of lateness. Jim Goodall, navigated by Denis Moore was the winner. Robin Brown writing in *Miscellany* suggested the broken headlamp on Jim's Morgan (probably HUY 982) was caused by having been rammed by a boat in one of the deepest bits!

Ron Crellin and Brian Harper with hand in plaster, at the Rally of the Vales with YOM 798. (Brian Harper collection)

That same weekend the Swansea MC ran its Rally of the Vales as a National event for the first time, it being the deciding round of the hard fought RAC Rally Championship. Obviously the organisers wanted a tough rally to sort out the best teams, but they couldn't have expected the deluge to have its rally route as its focal point with so many floods to contend with. Seventy-six cars took part, from starts at Cardiff, Swansea and Gloucester, the routes converging at Bishops Meadow near Brecon for the first Saturday night 160 mile loop. Floods made the route atrocious and one particularly deep ford at the Devil's Staircase on the banks of the river Nan y Fedw only allowed two cars through before the roaring torrent washed away an MGA! Most crews cut their losses and made for the next control in Lampeter. Brian Harper was particularly unlucky to arrive there 31 minutes late, one minute over the time allowed to qualify on that section. Brian was driving with his right wrist in plaster after the argument with a starting handle during the RAC Rally. The second loop of 170 miles proved more restful, although a tree across the road at High Noon caused some diversion. The loop was followed by a regularity test, and then the survivors, just one third of the original starters, congregated at Langrove Country Club near Swansea, the finish, for a hearty breakfast. We are not sure of the results, but do know Brian Harper collected sufficient points here to finish second overall to Bill Bengry in the RAC Rally Championship.

When the results of the British Trials and Rally Drivers' Association Competition for the year were announced during December the Morgan drivers had performed very well. Brian Harper and Ron Crellin were comfortable winners of the Gold Star rally competition, scoring 34 points to second placed Tiny Lewis's 27. Pauline Mayman finished fourth with 21 points after mixed drives of her Plus Four and Triumph Herald. In the Silver Star rally competition Brian Harper was third with 117 points. In the Ladies' Silver Garter rally competition Mrs Anne Hall finished in first place with 18 points whilst Pauline Mayman was second with 10. The Co-drivers' Award went to Val Domleo, who had navigated on occasion for both of them! It was the third year in a row that Val had won this award. In the Production Car Trial competition B B Jones was sixth after only competing in four of the contributing events.

On Thursday December 15th a board meeting was held at the Morgan Motor Company. Peter Morgan advised the directors that the new improved coupé was now well advanced, with some four or five cars awaiting the new windscreen. Peter commented he was also thinking of fitting lowering side windows to this model. The problem with the supply of back axles for the 4/4 model had now been resolved with Salisbury. The Company's experimental engineer, Neville Carlton-Oatley, was also now reported to have left for an appointment elsewhere by mutual consent.

In the issue of *Autosport* for Friday November 25th it was reported that Richard Shepherd-Barron had driven Chris Lawrence's TOK 258 at Silverstone using the latest version of the Lawrence Tune engine. He had lapped the Grand Prix circuit in 2 minutes 1 second, no less than 5.5 seconds faster than the 2 litre GT record, which Chris himself already held!

Richard had started his competition career in 1958 with a Fiat Abarth 750, after Army National Service in Germany had given him the opportunity for a close look at Continental performance cars. Coming from a sporting background, with a mother who had been a Wimbledon tennis doubles champion, Olympic medal winner and yacht racer, Richard had a natural racing talent. He quickly moved up to a 1,290cc Alfa Romeo Guilietta Sprint Veloce, achieving consistent success in 1959 and coming third in the 1,001-1,300cc class in the Autosport Championship. This was a notable achievement in a class dominated by the fast but fragile Lotus Elites.

Richard had chosen the Alfa, rather than a Lotus, for its combination of performance and ruggedness, the latter being important if you drove the car to and from circuits. However, Richard could stay ahead of all but the quickest Lotuses. It was just unfortunate for him that first in class was a certain Jim Clark! Jim had come to prominence racing in the Border Reivers team and Richard met him whilst racing in Scotland in 1958. Richard subsequently introduced him to his friend, John Whitmore, who would also campaign one of the first production Elites in 1959. Richard and John Whitmore were invited to race with the Border Reivers, and when Jim Clark and John shared the tenth placed Elite at Le Mans in 1959 Richard joined them as the reserve driver.

Richard's exploits in the Alfa had also drawn attention to him from Italy, especially when he achieved a sixth place at Monza, and he was invited to drive Taraschi and RAM Formula Juniors there. The friendship with Chris Lawrence during the year revealed to Chris that Richard's experience and ability could be useful. This resulted in Chris asking if he would like to join him for 1961 in a season of 'proper GT racing with the Morgan'. Richard agreed, receiving a retainer of around £400 as number one team driver, and being expected to help with preparation of the

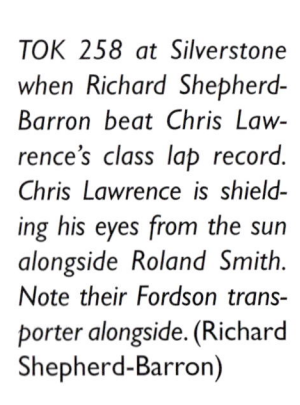

TOK 258 at Silverstone when Richard Shepherd-Barron beat Chris Lawrence's class lap record. Chris Lawrence is shielding his eyes from the sun alongside Roland Smith. Note their Fordson transporter alongside. (Richard Shepherd-Barron)

cars and the administration when not racing. It was to prove an ideal racing partnership as the styles of the two drivers were so similar. Richard told us that despite his 'record' run at Silverstone, their times racing the same car on most circuits were, to all intents and purposes, identical. Having thrown in his lot with Westerham Motors as a professional driver, Richard sold the Alfa to Tony Sanderson for hill climbs – no doubt a better bet for him than the AFM that he used to share with Chris!

A few weeks after Richard's drive at Silverstone the December 30th issue of *Autosport* carried a bit of a scoop, a test of TOK 258 by John Bolster. John of course was an ex-racing driver, and he loved Morgans, knowing how to get the best out of them. He mentioned that the Lawrence car was really the prototype of the recently announced Super Sports model, the only 'extra' on TOK 258 being an undertray and bucket seats, although it seemed likely Peter Morgan would make the latter optional on the new model. Len Bridge remembered that the bucket seats fitted to TOK 258 were off-the-shelf items purchased from racing driver Les Leston, who also ran a car accessories company.

At the time of the road test the engine fitted to TOK 258 was reported as being the TR2, with a compression ratio of 10 to 1. It was running on die cast 45mm DCOE Weber carburettors fitted to the high port TR3 head, and Chris told us that it is likely that TOK still had the set-up used for the long distance TT event at Goodwood in the August. However, he had discovered, at the recommendation of Alan Southern, that the 42mm DCOE6 Webers were even better suited to the mid-range torque of TOK's two litre TR engine than were the 45s. Chris found that the 42s more closely matched the inlet ports and gave better pick-up and acceleration, which was especially useful for shorter races on the tighter circuits. After using them on TOK Chris was to specify these carburettors for the 'production' Super Sports TR3 engine, which was intended for use on the track and the road. Chris explained that TOK's ultimate state of tune with SUs had been virtually 'full-race' and that the engine was rough at low rpm, as it was with the early Webers, but with the more sophisticated die cast Webers, especially the 42s, the Lawrence Tune engine would idle, 'and people went shopping with them'.

John Bolster took some performance figures for TOK 258 during the test, getting a top speed of 121.6 mph, and an amazing 0 to 60 mph time of 7.6 seconds. He pointed out that complete new TR3 engines to Super Sports specification, including balancing, Weber carburettors and manifolds would cost £220, and that there was also an exchange plan. The new Super Sports was priced at £1,250.0.0 including taxes. John commented, 'This must represent the greatest performance for the least money which is at present available.'

Peter Marten, whom we have mentioned racing Morgans during 1959, had been successfully racing a Ford 100E powered Lotus Seven during 1960. He had given up racing the Series II Morgan as it was not quick enough, and with the Handa system 'top gear' was really too high for racing. It so happened that Peter knew Richard Shepherd-Barron through his friendship with Peter's sister, Shelley, and during the year Richard asked Peter how he could help him with his racing for 1961. (Shelley took up club racing successfully in 1961 with a Turner 950). Peter was losing interest in the 750 MC 1172 Formula with the Lotus as the cars were so evenly matched, so Richard suggested he should buy a Plus Four and have Chris Lawrence work on it. Peter knew Chris vaguely and had been impressed by his Morgan drives, but Chris appeared rather reserved and Peter had been reluctant to approach him. Richard was persuasive so Peter bought an ivory 1954 Plus Four that he spotted for sale on a garage forecourt. It was registered PGP 123, and was chassis number T3129, originally dispatched on June 26th 1954 to Basil Roy Ltd in London. When Chris Lawrence saw it he said, 'I like the car. Bring it to Acton and we will breathe on it for you.' It was close to the end of the season so Peter decided to try it out on the track before finally committing himself and entered the GT race at Snetterton on 10th October. Although the car was in standard trim he had great fun with it in the race and was sufficiently impressed, so without further ado he

Peter Marten with his 4/4 Series II in the Snetterton paddock at a club meeting in 1959. (Peter Marten collection.)

took the car to Acton. Peter was on his way to racing his Morgan in 1961 as the first Lawrence Tune racing customer.

The issue of *Autosport* for December 30th that carried the TOK road test also included details of the following year's Autosport Championship. There were to be four classes, three (Classes A, B and C) being respectively for Appendix J Group 3 cars of up to 1,000cc, 1,1001cc to 1,300cc and 1,301 to 2,000cc. The fourth class was for over 2,000cc and Appendix J Group 4 (unlimited capacity). John McKechnie was still very keen to enter a Ford 105E engined 4/4 in Class A and put his order in with Peter Morgan for a 4/4 with all alloy bodywork and disc brakes, seeking help from Peter on homologation. John believed it should be possible to tune a 4/4 to produce close to 200 bhp per ton weight, his 'Holy Grail'. Peter did not share his enthusiasm for the new 4/4. The engine just had no bottom end torque and was useless for trials where trickling off the line with torque a-plenty was important. Peter was about to try a Shorrocks supercharger on the 105E in desperation, but he had learnt an important lesson with the Ford 105E engine that he was never to forget: Morgan cars needed an engine of at least one litre capacity. Discussions with the ever helpful Ford Motor Company advised that a 1,340cc engine using the same block casting was shortly to be introduced in the forthcoming Ford Classic model. Peter asked for this engine to be made available to the Morgan Motor Company as soon as feasible.

The BRSCC ran its now traditional Boxing Day meeting at Brands Hatch on Monday December 26th. The first race of the day was for GT and production sports cars over 1,000cc. Chris Lawrence led from the start in TOK 258, but on the third lap had to concede to Graham Warner's Lotus Elite. These two began to pull away from the field, and despite closing by the rest they were untouchable, finishing in that order, Chris winning the over 1,600cc class at 64.58 mph. It was a good result with which to end the year.

Not long after this event Richard Shepherd-Barron drove TOK 258 to the Koni shock absorber agent, Crowland Engineering in Spalding, Lincolnshire, for its conversion to telescopic Konis all round, the rears fitting onto a sub-frame attached over the chassis. Richard had long been an enthusiast of Konis and his racing Alfa Romeo had been partly sponsored by the Dutch company. This was a particularly unpleasant journey for Richard as it was very cold and the hardtop had been removed for easier access to the rear axle area!

On Saturday December 31st the British Racing and Sports Car Club's Racing Car Show opened at the Royal Horticultural Old Halls in London, closing the following Saturday. Chris Lawrence was there with his Westerham Motors Ltd stand. One visitor was Ray Meredith, collecting his Weber 45DCOE carburettors, inlet manifolds and Chris Lawrence camshaft.

On display was the revised Deep Sanderson Formula Junior car, complete with competition prepared Ford 105E engine and the Lawrence Link suspension system. Also on the stand were three Lawrence Tune engines. There was a Ford 105E in Stage 3 Lawrence Tune, fully balanced, with special camshaft, modified head, new exhaust manifold and cast inlet manifold with two double choke Weber carburettors, and there was a Triumph Herald engine in Stage 1 Lawrence Tune, with special exhaust manifold and silencers and a special inlet manifold with Fish carburettor. Lastly on display was a TR3 engine as supplied to the Morgan Motor Company for the Super Sports Plus Four. Of interest were the twin silencers fitted to the latter, but not used by Morgan.

The Lawrence Tune treatment of the Super Sports engines entailed stripping the new engines received from the Morgan factory, with the crank, flywheel, front pulley, rods and pistons being fully balanced at Jack Brabham's company, Jack Brabham (Motors) Ltd at Chessington in Surrey. Brabham

The Westerham Motors stand at the BRSCC's Racing Car Show. The Super Sports Morgan engine is in the left foreground. Note the silencers fitted. To the right is the Deep Sanderson Formula Junior car without bodywork, with a Ford 105E engine behind. The Triumph Herald engine is in the left background. (Len Bridge collection)

had a Repco balancing machine, and it was operated by a New Zealander called Steele Therkleson. Chris was so appreciative of the fine job that he did on the engines that when Steele said he wondered how well they went Chris told us that he lent him TOK to try one for himself! Meanwhile, the heads were gas flowed, and a Lawrence camshaft was fitted giving timing of 43-76, 76-43. The valves were polished and properly seated. The compression ratio was raised to 9 to 1. Much of the work was done by John Harvey, Westerham Motors' excellent engine man, who worked upstairs at Acton. He lowered the completed engines to ground level using a winch that had been used to manoeuvre furniture in and out of the workshop by the previous tenants, the upholsterers! Westerham Motors supplied the inlet manifolds for the Webers, which were matched to the ports. Morgan supplied the 42mm DCOE6 Webers but the carburettor linkage and the fuel lines were supplied from Acton. The completed engines were then returned to the Morgan factory, either in Chris's Jaguar Mk VII (the passenger seats were removed) or later in the firm's Standard 10 van.

Despite the appearance of the Formula Junior on the Show stand, Len Bridge remembered, 'The pace of development in Formula Junior was phenomenal and unless you had a new "tweak" each week you couldn't keep up with the other makes.' The formula was being dominated by Colin Chapman's first rear engined design, the Lotus 18 which, as mentioned before, was built in Formula 1, 2 and Junior versions. With limited resources available it was decided that future Deep Sanderson developments would concentrate on GT cars, which had a bigger potential market.

When Chris Lawrence was interviewed for this book, he summed up the Morgan thus: 'They were, and are, very competitive sports cars. Old man Morgan (referring to HFS Morgan) knew all about flexible chassis and how they worked. He was no man's fool. He set up a car with a really stiff front end, a flexible chassis and a great big axle at the rear. We never had to change that. We didn't have to do anything to the chassis by changing the geometry. The front suspension takes one look at a corner and locks solid. Look at Formula 1 cars today - you can see that the suspension doesn't move when you jack them up! We put decent tyres and shock absorbers on them, with wheels that didn't fall to bits and that's about it. All we did was to get reliable engines that gave loads of torque.'

1960 had been an interesting Morgan year, culminating in the racing achievements of Chris Lawrence who planned to race Morgans on the Continent. The rally drivers had done well too, but the use of forest stages was about to threaten the Morgan success, requiring much stronger suspension with more travel. Only the new 4/4 was casting a shadow, but Peter Morgan had plans in hand to use the larger Ford engine. 1961 promised to be very interesting.

Continental Europe

During 1959 Lyndon Sims had approached Peter Morgan asking if he could take a works Morgan through the 1960 Monte Carlo Rally. Peter had agreed to provide a special car for this event, and it was collected from the Morgan factory early in January, being registered YUY 224 on Wednesday January 6th. It was a red coupé, with black interior but had several works modifications to suit the rally, of which the most important was a non-detachable hard top. This had been manufactured at the Morgan factory out of four pieces of 18 gauge aluminium sheet, beaten into shape and wheeled smooth by Percy Sambrook, the sheet metal shop foreman. They were fitted around a wooden former made by Arthur Frith, the body shop foreman. The aluminium panels were then welded together by Percy to produce a unique hard top. Whilst the main reason for the hard top was to comply with the regulations for the Monte Carlo Rally, Percy believes that Peter Morgan was also considering whether it should be made available as an optional extra for the coupé, hence the construction of the re-useable wooden former.

The chassis number was 4394, and the engine number TS 45597. The coupé was fitted with a 3.73 rear axle, disc wheels and disc brakes, a heater, a large petrol tank (around 12 gallons) and two spare wheels.

Lyndon took it home to Brynmawr in Gwent where he ran his TV and electrical business. As he had little available time to run in the engine he set it running at 1,500 rpm parked behind his shop, checking every so often that it wasn't overheating. There were frequent oil changes too and this running in went on all week. The arrangement for the rally was that Lyndon would enter the Morgan personally, and pay his own expenses, fitting his own lights etc. The rally had starting points in Athens, Frankfurt, Oslo, Glasgow, Warsaw, Paris, The Hague, Rome and Lisbon, but Lyndon chose to start from Glasgow, his navigator being Roger Jones.

After the start on Monday evening January 18th, the Glasgow contingent made its way south to Dover for the ferry to cross the English Channel and enter France at Boulogne. The crossing was rough but 71 cars set off on the other side for Blois. In the mountains after Bourges true winter weather conditions prevailed and there were several crews who received penalties on the treacherous roads. By Figeac no fewer than 27 of these 71 had penalties. On arrival at Chambéry the Morgan had accrued just forty penalties. All the start point routes now converged for the difficult 570 kilometres to Monaco. Between Chambéry and Grenoble the road had been cleared by snow ploughs, leaving high walls of snow on each side, which Lyndon used as banks to help him corner the Morgan. Unfortunately on one corner the plough had cleared the snow over a road side ditch to match the true road level and the Morgan dropped into the ditch, with two wheels off the ground. There was frantic digging before the Morgan could regain the road. Lyndon 'pressed on' and got to Grenoble within the permitted time, and hence on to Monaco. Unfortunately a secret check point had revealed that they were very late at the first part and too fast from there to Grenoble. As a result the Morgan was excluded from the final ninety cars contesting the Mountain Regularity Test, which was really the main feature of the rally. Lyndon was very upset by this decision, which he thought was

A rear view of the Monte Carlo Rally coupé showing the unique hardtop, the twin spare wheels and the snow shovels fastened to the rear panel. (LAT Photographic)

Lyndon Sims on his way south through the UK towards Monte Carlo. (LAT Photographic)

totally unfair. Only nine of the 78 Glasgow entries actually qualified for this final test. Because of this the Morgan was only classified in 125th place with 9,180 penalties, but Lyndon did have the small consolation of coming third in the Manoeuvrability Test held at the end of the rally, behind two Porsches. Mercedes-Benz dominated the rally, taking the first three positions with 220 SE models and the Manufacturers' Team Award, having had a much easier journey from the Warsaw start in what had been a most controversial Monte Carlo Rally.

After the rally the works car was returned to Peter Morgan at the factory and Lyndon was pleased to be offered this Morgan again for the Tulip Rally in May. Lyndon had entered the Morgan in Class D, for under 2,000cc GT cars, for the 12th International Tulip Rally, which started from Noordwijk on Sunday May 1st. Lyndon's navigator this time was Barrie Hercock. The first stages of the rally were very easy, making for Liège, then Bouillon and Vichy. Then the rally began to tighten as the competitors hit the twisty mountain roads of the Massif Central. The tricky night sections ended with a detour to Mont Ventoux for a timed hill climb of the famous course. Lyndon Sims was easily quickest in the 2 litre GT category with a time of 7 minutes 22 seconds. The competitors made for the Alpes Maritimes where the cars were

given a set time of 11 minutes 59 seconds in which to do the twelve kilometres from Bollene to the Col de Turini. Many got penalties here, including Lyndon who was fractions of a second late, but he was the only one in his class to have just one penalty point. On arrival in Monte Carlo there were just ten competitors still with no penalties, but Lyndon did still lead his class.

On Tuesday May 3rd the competitors set off again for the Alps, where a timed climb was held on the Col des Leques. The road was slippery due to rain and Lyndon spun the Morgan, stopped and then restarted, just being beaten by Koiff's Alfa Romeo by fractions of a second in the GT class. After further Alpine sections the survivors made for the Nurburgring in Germany taking in a climb of the Trois Epis near Orbey first, where Lyndon led his class during the five kilometre climb. After the Nurburgring the crews made for Eindhoven, and then set off back to Noordwijk. Lyndon and Barry had a heart stopping moment just after leaving Eindhoven when the Morgan was trapped between the gates of a wide level crossing. They frantically edged the Morgan as far off the tracks as they could and the express train missed the rear of the car by a couple of feet!

At the finish it was confirmed that the Morgan crew had finished fourteenth overall, as well as

Barrie Hercock clocks in at the Chamrousse time control during a Friday night stage of the Tulip Rally. (The Motor)

winning the class. No doubt Peter Morgan was impressed with their performance when they returned to Malvern.

After the Daily Express Silverstone meeting on Saturday May 14th Chris Lawrence set off for Germany to try and learn the Nurburgring circuit,

Richard Shepherd-Barron competing at the Limonest Mont-Verdun hill climb meeting near Lyons on the weekend of September 17-18th 1960. He was on the way back to the UK after a summer racing Formula Juniors on the Continent following the Nurburgring and Spa meetings. (Richard Shepherd-Barron collection)

44 miles south of Bonn. Upon arrival he did as Graham Hill had suggested, that is he completed ten laps of the over 14 mile circuit in TOK 258. Unfortunately the chassis broke at the site where the jack fitted but Chris had taken welding tackle with him and the chassis was soon repaired. Another ten laps followed, and yet more batches of ten as he tried to learn the circuit. In the 1,000 Kilometres race Chris and Bill de Selincourt finished second of the three class leading Lolas, a car Chris described to us as 'The best car I have ever driven.'

Also competing in this event had been Chris's old racing adversary Bob Staples in an AC Bristol. His co-driver was Richard Shepherd-Barron. The drivers all got to know each other and became good friends.

The following week Chris Lawrence moved to Spa Francorchamps to continue racing Bill's Lola at the meeting held on Tuesday May 24th. The British all stayed at the same hotel and Chris and Richard in particular began to develop the particularly strong racing friendship that lead to Richard joining Westerham Motors later in the year.

Chris Lawrence finished eighth at Spa in Bill's Lola in the 128 mile race for Appendix C sports cars up to 1,600cc, whilst Richard Shepherd-Barron was second in the 81 mile race for up to 1,300cc GT cars in his Alfa Romeo Giulietta Sprint Veloce.

Bob Staples didn't have such a good time in Spa because the AC dropped a valve in practice. Work through the night had the car ready for the start, but it only completed four laps. Bob too had developed his friendship with Chris who offered to develop his AC for him.

Australia

With the demise of the Bill Richards Morgan Agency in Perth and the conversion of the Morgan R4 to the Repco Holden Special, there was now very little Morgan activity in Western Australia, or indeed anywhere else in Australia.

In the first couple of months Colin Metcher entered a number of events at Caversham but had no real success. However, he took the ex-Ranford Plus Four Special to Albany in mid April over Easter for both the hill climb and the Albany TT. Jack Ayres won the sports car section in Lionel Beattie's Repco Holden Special. The sliding pillar front suspension, Moss gearbox and differential were what were left of the Morgan components of the R4, so at least some Morgan bits won the hill climb! Colin Metcher did not feature in the hill climb but on the holiday

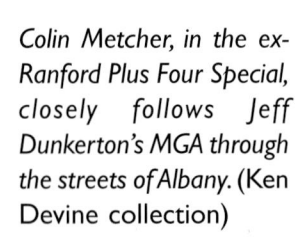

Colin Metcher, in the ex-Ranford Plus Four Special, closely follows Jeff Dunkerton's MGA through the streets of Albany. (Ken Devine collection)

Monday, April 18th came home fifth in the TT behind Sid Taylor in the TS Special, Ray Barfield's Aston Martin, Jeff Dunkerton's MGA and Syd Negus in his Plymouth Special; quite a creditable performance.

The ex-Ranford car was severely 'bent' by Colin at Caversham later in the year and passed to Max Fletcher who had Peter Lyons rebody the original Morgan chassis. The front suspension was essentially unaltered and the original drive train retained. However, Max modified the rear suspension to coil springs with telescopic shock absorbers and fitted a 2.2 litre GMH 'Grey' Holden motor with triple SU carburettors. Renamed the VMS (Valkyrie Manifold Special) Fletcher raced the car in 1965-66 when it was bought by Jim Krajanicich who stored it for some years before selling it to a local Jaguar enthusiast, Alan Shepherd. Finally, the by now quite neglected VMS was taken over by Dave Sullivan who, with his son David, has since restored it.

In Victoria J Thompson continued to campaign his Plus Four at hill climbs, gaining a second fastest in the under 2 litre class at Rob Roy on Sunday April 10th.

It was in Sydney that the most important event occurred in what was to amount to a new era for Morgans in Australia. A draughtsman and engineer named Ken Ward had been instrumental in founding, with a few others, the Morgan Owners Club of Australia (MOCA) in 1958. In 1955 he had purchased for £395 a tired 1949 4/4 drophead coupé, which he enjoyed so much that he became enthused with the Morgan marque. The MOCA started with an emphasis on competition, and club events were frequent in its early years. Ken helped keep Morgan owners on the road, and one day in early 1960 he and his photographer brother Barrie were asked why no new Morgans were coming into the country. Not having a suitable answer Ken decided to write to Peter Morgan. On Friday July 8th Peter replied positively, with a proposed annual quota of twelve cars. His letter indicated that the Plus Four was proving so popular in the USA that a larger quota at that time was not possible. Subsequently Ken and his brother Barrie, based in Ryde, were appointed Morgan agents for New South Wales, to take effect from Sunday January 1st 1961. The first two imports, both TR3 engined Plus Fours, one red and the other green, predated the appointment and arrived at Sydney's docks in October, having been dispatched from the Morgan factory on Wednesday August 31st. The red one, chassis number 4590, fitted with wire wheels, had been ordered by a local Rockdale watchmaker and jeweller called Ron Coulston.

Ron Coulston had become well known as a top navigator in Australia, particularly for the Round Australia events. He had recently asked the equally well known racing driver and journalist David McKay what sort of car he could buy suitable for both road work and competition. David had been watching the amazing successes of Chris Lawrence and his Plus Four in England with interest, and suggested Ron might try the Morgan. Ron then located the Ward brothers and put in his order. Morgan extras specified were Dunlop Duraband radial tyres on wire wheels, disc brakes, Derrington manifolds and a woodrim steering wheel.

A new motor racing circuit was being constructed at Warwick Farm horse racing course, inspired by the Grand Prix motor racing circuit at the English horse racing course at Aintree. The opening meeting was to be on Sunday December 18th, and it was decided the Coulston Morgan would be driven there by David McKay. David first suggested some modifications to the Morgan, which were put in progress. Firstly the back axle ratio (3.73 to 1) was completely unsuited to the short straights, so it was replaced by one of 4.27 to 1. Jerry Lister from Turramurra, who had a fast Vanguard engined hill climb special, worked on the engine. The head was ported and polished, and a racing camshaft from Hedley McGee & Co, of Kings Cross, Sydney was fitted. He replaced the cylinder liners with those used in Ferguson tractors, boring these to give a capacity of 2380cc. This raised the compression ratio to 10 to 1. Jerry replaced the distributor with a magneto and the oil pump pick-up in the sump was baffled, following advice from John Cummins regarding the problems David Van Dal had encountered. Eighteen hundred miles of running in were undertaken by Ron in the week before the race.

Morgan Sports Cars — 1960

On race day the weather was very wet as David drove the Morgan to the start of the very first event, a race over ten laps for production sports cars. Bob Cutler's Austin Healey 3000 took the lead, with the Morgan close behind, these two pulling away from the field, the Healey pulling away on acceleration and the Morgan closing up on braking and cornering. That was how it went for five laps, but on the sixth the Healey ran wide off the northern horse track crossing, under pressure from the Morgan. The Morgan was through into the lead, pulling away by three seconds a lap to win comfortably and set fastest lap, which obviously became the lap record in the process. David put the win down to the greater stability and adhesion of the Morgan in the wet. One particular problem David disliked about the Morgan was the 'austere seating', such that he had a tendency to finish up on the transmission tunnel when bouncing over the horse track crossings, something he found very uncomfortable. He wished individual bucket seats were fitted.

Several weeks after the event David took the Morgan (untouched since the race) over the *Sunday Telegraph* test route that he used in his role as a motoring journalist. Carrying a fourteen stone passenger, David equalled his outright record and also clipped a second from the hill climb record. He was able to report very favourably on the Morgan in his motoring column of the *Sunday Telegraph* of February 5th 1961, delighting the new importers.

Seconds after the start at Warwick Farm, with David McKay following leader Bob Cutler's Austin Healey. The horse racing track is clearly visible, separated from the motor racing circuit by a substantial earth bank. The variety of European vehicles in the Paddock car park is notable too. (John Hurst collection)

New Zealand

Once again the Nelson Car Club ran beach races at Tahunanui to start the year. Races were held on Saturday January 2nd and Monday 4th. The Bennett brothers both competed, and won the team prize.

During the meeting Cliff Bennett bought from Halsey Logan the special 13 inch rear wheels he had previously used on his own 4/4. We think these were Ford 100E wheels, re-drilled to fit the Morgan wheel stud fitting.

The seventh International New Zealand Grand Prix was held at Ardmore on Saturday January 9th. Competing in the supporting Ardmore Sports Car Trophy race held over twelve laps and with a Le Mans start was P Elford in a TR engined Plus Four, but we have no results for him. He also entered the 'Ultimate-EKCO Race Car Feature', a twelve lap handicap.

At Wigram on Saturday January 23rd Camille Kuzmich from Christchurch took part in the twenty lap sports car race in her Vanguard engined Plus Four. Also entered was Ivan Bennett in his ex Dave Edmiston car. There was a Le Mans start. Ivan had a good race, but cannot remember the placing.

For the races held at Dunedin on Saturday January 30th, a new round the houses circuit was in use. There had been no Dunedin races in 1959 when the previously used Wharf circuit was not available. For 1960 a new 'Oval' circuit of 1.68 miles was cordoned off, combining two hairpin bends, a steep climb and descent over Glen Hill. Ivan Bennett entered his Plus Four in the 'Festival Motor Car Race' (saloons and sports cars, with classes for both), but broke the crankshaft. Two ladies entered, Ivy Stephenson in a

On the beach at Tahunanui. Ivan Bennett is in his rebuilt Plus Four, complete with bonnet strap, behind Noel Orton's Austin Healey in a handicap event. (R Stewart)

Ivan Bennett in his Plus Four at Hooper's Inlet hill climb. (Ivan Bennett collection)

Buckler and Camille Kuzmich in her Morgan and they were reported as being 'rather lost in the crowd'.

The town of Waimate had run its own 'round the houses' race to replace the absent Dunedin event in 1959. The Town circuit south of Canterbury was in use again on Saturday February 13th. There were two Plus Fours entered in the 15 lap (19.5 miles) sports car race, the Vanguard engined Plus Four of Camille Kuzmich and the TR engined Plus Four of Ivan Bennett. Ivan did not compete as the TR engine had not been repaired, and we wonder whether or not Camille competed.

Allen Freeman's old four-seater Plus Four P2290 was in the hands of Eric Olvercrona for the races held at Ohakea on Saturday March 5th, but we do not have the results of his performance in the Ohakea Sports Car Race.

Ivan Bennett drove his repaired Plus Four at the Hooper's Inlet hill climb held in August. Ivan made third fastest time of the day in 37.09 seconds, with his brother Cliff recording 39.84 seconds in the 4/4.

Later during this year Cliff Bennett fitted a Willment overhead inlet valve conversion to the 100E engine in his 4/4, having purchased this

Cliff Bennett at the October Mosgiel grass track meeting. Note the special 13 inch rear wheels. (Cliff Bennett collection)

conversion from R S Rutherford who had been using it in his Mistral. Unfortunately he found the original three speed gearbox spoiled this modification as the car suffered from torque loss between 50 and 70 mph. He raced it at the Mosgiel grass track meeting held in October, the area about to be divided for building houses.

The first day of the New Year beach racing at Tahunanui was held on New Year's Eve, Saturday December 31st and the races attracted Ivan Bennett with his Plus Four and his brother Cliff with the 4/4. In Heat 1 of the 'Handicapping Purposes' race for scratch cars up to 1,200cc Cliff finished in third place behind Les Fahey's Ford 10 Special and Jim Lovell's Lloyd Special. In the similar race for scratch cars from 1,200cc to 2,000cc Ivan Bennett also finished in third place behind Mill's Humber 80 and Bob Stewart's MG TF. In the 'Frosty Jack Rosebowl' sports car handicap race Cliff finished in a fine second place, behind the MG TF of Bob Stewart. No doubt the New Year was celebrated in style by all the sand racers at Nelson that night!

USA

For the 1960 racing season the SCCA board of governors had decided to support the proposal made by its 1959 Contest Board that Production cars should be classified according to performance rather than by the previously used engine capacity system, thereby following the lead of the Cal Club. The SCCA's new list moved the Morgan Plus Four into Class D, where the opposition was to be the Jaguar XK, the new Austin Healey 3000, the BMW 507, the Porsche 1600 Super 90, and the Bristol engined cars of AC, Arnolt, and Frazer Nash. The TRs were still in Class E, along with the slower Austin Healey 100s (BN1, 2, 4 and 6), the MGA Twin-Cam, slower Porsches, Alfa Romeos, the Daimler SP250 and a few others. Morgan enthusiasts were dumbfounded, for they could see no way that the Plus Four deserved to be grouped with such expensive and more powerful sports cars. The Morgan drivers of the Washington DC Region decided to write to the Competition Director, John Bishop, requesting a return of the Plus Four to Class E. They pointed out that the TR and Morgan had much in common, including the same engine and a similar cost price. They suggested that the new classification was confusing the ability of the normal steel bodied, drum braked car with the rare aluminium bodied and disc braked 'Competition Sebring' models. In reply John Bishop quoted lap times of Morgans against those of AC Bristols at Elkhart Lake (3 mins 21 secs against 3 mins 20.4 secs) and lap speeds at Lime Rock (AC Bristol: 68.48 mph, Morgan 68.18 mph, TR 67.13 mph), and at Thompson (AC 61.18 mph, Morgan 60.68 mph, TR 59.86 mph), and said the Contest Board would keep the classification under review, but that it stood for this season at least. One is left thinking that the Washington group were probably right, for we expect it was the performances of Arch McNeill with the Sebring car that were actually some of the timings being used. The competition minded Washington DC Morgan owners had founded the Morgan Car Club in March 1959, and regularly entered events at the local Marlboro track as 'Team Rebel'.

The less popular Morgan 4/4 Series II with Ford 100E engine was initially left out of the new list, but the omission was later rectified, and it was placed in Class H, the class originally used for cars of between 500 and 750cc, but now including all the smaller cars, being the last class in the new system, and containing the popular Austin Healey Sprite and the pushrod Fiat Abarth 750.

There were still very strict rules as to what modifications were allowed to a sports car for SCCA Production Class racing and lists were produced for each accepted model detailing the specification to which entrants must adhere. Thus, for the Plus Four Morgan, the minimum weight dry was given as 1,900lb, with full details given of the engine, including camshaft profile, compression ratio (8.5 to 1), and even valve spring strength (166lb open). A list of acceptable options allowed 15 inch wire wheels, 9.2 to 1 compression ratio, 11 inch front disc brakes, a four branch exhaust and special inlet manifold. For the 4/4, which had a dry weight of 1,456lb, permitted

Morgan *Sports Cars* 1960

options were an aluminium cylinder head giving an 8 to 1 compression ratio, dual SU carburettors (1.25 inch) and 15 inch wire wheels.

The Washington DC Region of the SCCA began its Regional racing with a meeting at its home track of Marlboro over the January 2nd and 3rd weekend. It was cold, and this annual fun fixture was not known as the 'Refrigerator Bowl' meeting without reason! We have no results but do know that Hugh O'Brien was the local Morgan star, battling against the TRs for the places.

In marked contrast there was glorious weather with temperatures in the 70s Fahrenheit for the SCCA Palm Springs races over the weekend of January 23rd and 24th, with 213 entries attracted. On the Saturday Roger Slowi did well to finish first in Class E in the oversubscribed novices' race, but on the Sunday he had the water pump fail whilst again leading the class. It was left to Dr Ken Hayes and Dan MacManus, who was from Torrance in California, to uphold the Morgan marque by finishing tenth and eleventh overall and third and fourth in class. Lew Spencer in Beware 1 was the true star, with victories on both days. For some reason the Los Angeles Region of the SCCA had not yet decided to follow National SCCA leadership so the steel bodied Plus Four had yet to be reclassified from Class E into D Production.

Lew Spencer's driving skills had attracted the attention of sponsors, such that Lew now decided it was time to leave Rene Pellandini and try and seek his fortune as a professional driver. One of his last races for Rene was in the AC Beware 1, at Willow Springs over the weekend of February 13th and 14th. His amazing performance in finishing third overall behind two Corvettes should have left no doubt in the mind of his future sponsors that he was the right man to hire. Lew had already lined up a drive at Sebring. In the consolation race for Classes D, E and F Production Dan MacManus finished fifth overall and second in class behind the TR3 of Kas Kastner.

The Central Florida Region of the SCCA ran a weekend of races at the magnificent Daytona Speedway, we think over the weekend of March 5th and 6th. Once again the Key Largo lady driver Lalah Neuman was entered in her Morgan and this time Tom Wright had also driven his 'pale yellow' Plus Four from Orlando to compete. Race

Tom Wright in the pale yellow Morgan and Lalah Neuman are lapped by the leaders, Ed Harcum in a Porsche special and Ed Rahal in the D-type Jaguar at Daytona. Note the banking in the background. (Tom Wright collection)

preparation consisted of taping the headlights, replacing the windscreen with an aero screen, removing the bumpers and fitting a straight through exhaust pipe. The race number was made from 'sticky back plastic' shelf liner. The course used by the SCCA used part of the banking leading on to a twisty infield section, and Tom found that the banked part was really equivalent to a two mile straight, for which it was important to set up the car to stand a chance of doing well.

Sketchy details of the main race for the Morgans suggest it was held for all cars above 1,600cc. Lalah's Morgan had the edge on Tom's on the banking, for she would gradually come motoring by, giving Tom a quick wave as she did so. Tom would now have to work hard to pass her on the twisty infield segment, before the whole sequence was repeated once more.

The faster cars could get up to impressive speeds on the banking, so careful watching in the rear view mirror became imperative at Daytona. Come the final lap and Tom just managed to squeeze past Lalah before the flag, but out of the places.

On March 6th and 7th, the SCCA held its first race at Pomona, a familiar track though for the Cal Club. In the novices' race on the Saturday thirty-two cars started and Roger Slowi had an impressive race finishing an excellent third behind the winning Porsche 550 and a Corvette. On the Sunday Roger failed to finish with a probable broken piston, leaving Kas Kastner in his well prepared TR3 to win Class E, followed by the Morgans of Burton, Ken Hayes and Harris. Seventh in Class E behind two Austin Healeys was John Hodges in his Plus Four. Dan MacManus failed to finish in his black Morgan, failure of a rocker arm being given as the reason.

The Northwest Region of the SCCA held a Regional meeting at Shelton Airport on a cold, wet and windy Sunday March 13th. There was only one Morgan racing, the Plus Four of Jack Murray, the notable Seattle driver. Surprisingly he took part in the five lap novices' race for over 1,600cc Production and Modified cars, finishing eleventh overall, but fourth in Class D, behind an Austin Healey 3000 and two Jaguars. Later he took part in Race 5, a ten lap race for Production Classes D and E, finishing fourth overall behind two AC Bristols and a well driven TR.

For this years Sebring 12 Hour Race on March 26th Fergus Imported Cars had imported one of

Jim Forno's Sebring Morgan preparing to leave his Endicott garage. (Jim Forno collection)

the aluminium bodied and front disc braked 'Competition Sebring' cars for Jim Forno to enter on behalf of the Morgan Motor Company. This entry was painted in the USA racing colours of white with a blue stripe along the bonnet and tail, and was otherwise to Baby Doll specification. It was chassis number 4445, one of the last of these 'Competition Sebring' cars to be built. It was dispatched from the factory on Thursday February 25th. Jim's co-driver was to be Ike Williamson, the well known Morgan driver whom Jim had got to know whilst racing at Watkins Glen and who already had the necessary FIA licence. The Morgan was collected from New York City and taken to Jim's Continental Motors garage at Endicott, where it was checked over and made compliant with the race rules by fitting a roll bar etc. A Borgward station wagon was to be used to tow the Morgan on a trailer, which was also loaded with four spare wheels, on the long journey to Sebring. There was snow on the ground when they left Jim's garage in New York State, but bright weather welcomed them to Florida.

On arrival at Sebring the race numbers were applied. For easy communication with the pit crew Jim had devised a system using three different coloured lights which were fitted to the right hand front wing. The driver switched on the green to indicate no problems, red to indicate 'I have a problem and am coming in', and white to ask the pit crew to give instructions.

Jim knew that they were not going to win the race, but he promised his son that he would be the first away in the Le Mans start. Although now 41 years old Jim had been good at the 100 yards race at school, so he reckoned that if he left the car in first gear, with the key on and the ignition set slightly retarded he could hit the starter push

Jim Forno leaps into the Sebring Morgan for a brilliant start. Note the three signalling lights on the front wing. (Jim Forno collection)

The Sebring start photographed from the Amoco Bridge. Jim Forno's Morgan is well up with cars starting much further down the track. (Dave Friedman)

button as he vaulted over the door for an immediate getaway.

Once again the big sports car teams were entered, but there was a problem in that both Ferrari and Porsche refused to use Amoco fuel as these factories had contracts for fuel elsewhere. In the end they 'sold' their cars temporarily to others so that the cars still competed, but without being officially entered by their factories. The FIA was pushing hard its GT category, which required minimum sizes of windscreen and luggage compartments to comply with 'Appendix J'. Several of these GT entries looked extremely odd as a result.

Lew Spencer, the ex-Morgan racer but now a professional racing driver, had accepted an offer by the British Motor Corporation to drive an Austin Healey 3000, shared with Gil Geitner, whilst Mike Rothschild was driving an AC Bristol for the AC Cars team.

This year the weather was glorious for the morning of the race as the sixty-five drivers prepared for the Le Mans start at ten o'clock. True to his word Jim Forno out-sprinted the other drivers to their cars, leaped over the door of the Morgan and hit the starter button. The Morgan fired instantly in gear and he was away; probably the first to move and the crowd cheered the impudence of this underdog in out-starting the high and mighty. It was now a case of settling into a comfortable and non-breaking lap routine using a maximum of 5,800 engine rpm.

As the race progressed the Florida heat became intense with temperatures soaring well into the 80s Fahrenheit and by midday some drivers and pit crews wore painful sunburns. Several drivers were also troubled by the masses of insects splattering on the windscreens, and found it very difficult to see clearly.

The Morgan drive had been going to plan, with both drivers optimistic of a good class position until, after sixty laps and at around two-thirty in the afternoon disaster struck. Jim was driving the fast back part of the course on a long right hand turn when the left front wheel came off, complete with brakes. Jim held on to the steering wheel of the uncontrollable and brakeless three-wheeler as it careered off the course at high speed, and made for a parked B29 aircraft. It slid under the plane's wing, but luckily ground to a halt just before it came to the fuselage.

Jim climbed out and inspected the damage. It was obvious that the malleable steel hub casting had fractured. Some TR enthusiasts nearby offered to donate a front hub from their own car but although the wheels were the same the hubs were of course completely different. Jim decided it was best to just sit out the rest of the racing under the B29's wing, thereby getting much needed shelter from the sun.

Porsches took the first two places, but Lew Spencer did very well to finish fifteenth overall and second in class, completing 167 laps with Mike Rothschild completing one lap less in the AC for twenty-first overall and third in class.

Some time after the event the failed front hub casting was taken to Fergus Imported Cars and hence returned to Peter Morgan for examination. Peter was concerned about the failure, for HFS Morgan had used malleable iron extensively pre-war for castings without problem. Recent castings did not seem to be as uniform in consistency as before, seeming sometimes to have too much coke, which could have led to the failure. Peter eventually decided to seek an assurance from the hub casting suppliers that this could not happen again but to his surprise this was not forthcoming. Safety was obviously vitally important so Peter decide that forged hubs would have to replace the previous malleable castings. All this took time and the new steel hubs were finally introduced during 1963.

Whilst Sebring overshadowed all other racing held over the weekend of March 26th and 27th, at Stockton Airport in California Rick Hilgers was back in his rebuilt aluminium Morgan, Snoopy. The Morgan had required a total rebuild following the end over end flip at Laguna Seca in 1959, and Rick took the opportunity to make some small modifications, such as fitting a roll bar under the dashboard cowling and closing the exhaust hole in the right hand side of the chassis. His father Rudy was a retired mechanical engineer, but woodwork was his hobby, so he remade the whole rear section surrounding the right wheel well. It was indistinguishable from the Morgan factory's production. He also made a new dashboard out of Philippine mahogany, which looked better than the original. All the effort was well worthwhile for Rick took a first place in the races.

One week later, at Riverside International Motor Raceway, the second annual International Sports Car Road Races were run by the Cal Club, sponsored by

From this to this! After the rebuild Rick Hilgers takes a victory lap in 'Snoopy' at Stockton. (Rick Hilgers collection)

the *Los Angeles Times*. The amateur championships held on the Saturday attracted two Morgan drivers, Roger Slowi and Dr Ken Hayes with their blue Morgans. Roger's Morgan was in fact his original green one, now repainted Cadillac Blue. Nearly all of the press coverage featured the 200 mile International Grand Prix, held for professional drivers on the Sunday, (and won by Carroll Shelby in a Maserati T61), but Roger Slowi was reported as reaching 102.27 mph on the long straight. The class winner was Kas Kastner in his well sorted TR3, which clocked 109.

It was again wet for the spring hill climb at Hershey over the weekend of April 2nd and 3rd. Best of the four Plus Fours was that driven by Arthur Simmers, recording 69.8941 seconds, Harry Reynolds (in Class DM) being 0.8 seconds slower. Ike Williamson took over 72 seconds and Ralph Poe needed nearly 76.

The Northwest Region of the SCCA organised another race meeting at Shelton Airport on Sunday April 10th. The second race was a ten lap novices' race for over 1,600cc cars and Bob Austin from Aberdeen finished in fifteenth overall position, but fifth in Class D. The sixth race on the programme was a fifteen lap race for Production classes of over 1,600cc. Jack Murray took part in this race with his Plus Four, finishing eighth out of nine finishers from a field of fourteen. He was third in Class D however.

During Rene Pellandini's visit to the Morgan factory in July 1959 he had offered to approach his friend Giovanni Michelotti, the great Italian car designer, to see whether he could design a more modern looking Morgan, based on the current chassis. In September 1959 the Morgan board had approved Peter Morgan's suggestion that Rene's offer should be followed up by sending a complete chassis to Italy for Giovanni to measure and assess for a design.

Based in Turin Giovanni was a prolific designer, responsible to the Triumph company for many body designs, including the imaginative Triumph Herald, the Triumph Spitfire, and the soon to appear TR4.

Giovanni had agreed he would design for his friend Rene, free of charge, a closed coupé on the Plus Four chassis. As with many of his projects the Turin firm of Nardi Automobili Sport, run by Enrico Nardi, was involved and a complete Plus Four rolling chassis (number 4403) was dispatched to Nardi on January 1st 1960. The drawings were completed on Saturday April 16th, and a set was sent to Peter Morgan. It is possible a prototype body was actually built, as this commonly happened when Nardi was involved with a Michelotti project, but we have not been able to confirm this. Peter Morgan didn't think the car was ever built, or if it was he never saw it. Recently Edgardo Michelotti, the son of Giovanni, managed to find some of these drawings. What an interesting Morgan car it would have made.

Rene was delighted with this fabulous modern design for a closed coupé and believes that Peter Morgan too was intrigued. However, after thinking long and hard about the prospects of the new design, the calculated costs for production appeared too great and the project was dropped. Peter decided for the moment to stick with the current bodywork developed by his father. He did realise, however, that he might well need to change in the future.

As was predicted by many the standard drum braked, steel bodied Plus Four Morgan was not really competitive in Class D Production. At the SCCA National Presidents Cup meeting held at Marlboro over the Easter weekend, April 15th to 17th, Lindsey McKellips driving his Plus Four four-seater could finish no better than last in class, behind five AC Bristols and a Bristol engined Fraser Nash.

During the previous winter Arch McNeill had overhauled his Sebring Morgan, at last refitting the standard camshaft in the process. At Lime Rock at the Northeast Regional races on Saturday April 23rd he finished an excellent first in D Production, showing

The Giovanni Michelotti Morgan coupé design, commissioned by Rene Pellandini. (Edgardo Micholetti archives)

the great advantage of disc brakes. He finished seventh overall in the Production race for Classes B, C and D. George Burgess was thirteenth overall and fourth in class in his Plus Four. On Saturday July 4th 1959 Morgan agent Basil Roy Ltd in London England had taken delivery of a green 'Competition Sebring' Morgan destined for G.W Burgess of Stonington in Connecticut. It was fitted with a 4.09 rear axle, but a spare 3.73 was with the car. Basil Roy specialised in exporting Morgans to special order. This was chassis number 4230.

The same weekend the ninth Chimney Rock Hill climb was being held in North Carolina, but for this event and all subsequent ones a shortened course of 1.9 miles was being used, the start being moved up the hill from the bridge. This meant there was no longer any need for the 'stop box' halfway up and allowed better entrance and exit from the park. Tom Wright and his wife Jane took their Morgan up from Orlando and had a good weekend, for Tom won Class D with his Morgan finishing thirteenth overall. His time was 2 minutes 43.5 seconds beating two other Morgans, an Austin Healey 3000, and a Porsche Super 90. Dr Sam Miller was second in class in his white Plus Four, whilst Jane Wright took over from Tom in the family car to finish first in the ladies' class.

David Williams failed to record a time in his Plus Four.

At Springtown that same weekend Harry Reynolds was the only Morgan driver present, and he recorded 66.9798 seconds.

Dr Sam Miller was a family doctor from Abingdon in Virginia. In the early 1950s he was a keen follower of British sports cars, and when he decided to arrange a trip with his wife to Europe for the spring of 1959 he wrote to Peter Morgan to order a car. They collected this Morgan from the Morgan factory and then used it for touring in France. On their return to Malvern they left the car at the factory for it to be shipped home via the port of Norfolk Virginia. It was dispatched on Friday May 1st. This Plus Four two-seater was ivory with stone leather upholstery, chassis number 4188. Sam brought back an aero screen from the Morgan factory for use back in the USA in motor sport.

Also held that weekend were races at Cotati, an abandoned Second World War US Navy airfield, near Santa Rosa in California. The circuit was a 'T' shaped course of 1.9 miles made by using three limbs of the old crossing runways. This year the San Francisco Region of the SCCA had decided to use a different car classification

Approaching Turn 4 at Cotati, Pru Baxter leads Dave Christofferson (152) with George Pridmore (42) ahead of an Arnolt Bristol. (Dave Christofferson collection)

system to any other SCCA Region, dividing sports cars into 'Stock' (S) where showroom specification was required, including standard exhaust systems, full width windscreens and even bumpers, and 'Prepared' (P) for all modified or sports racing cars. Rick Hilgers in the aluminium bodied Snoopy was in Class P5, whereas Bill Chapman in Little Red, George Pridmore in his green car and Pru Baxter in her silver one were in S5. Also taking part was Dave Christofferson, who managed an industrial and truck parts store in Napa, and had been racing an MG TD. He had borrowed Bob Monk's red right hand drive Morgan for this event, a car we think was the ex-Bob O'Brien car. On the Saturday Rick finished third in Snoopy with Dave seventh, Pru ninth and George twelfth whilst Bill Chapman was disqualified. On the Sunday, in the over 1,601cc 45 minute race Rick was ninth and Dave tenth, whilst George failed to finish.

With Lew Spencer having now turned professional, Rene Pellandini needed a new driver for his AC Bristol. He chose Ronnie Bucknum, a surveyor, who was making a great name for himself driving his Porsche 1600 Speedster. He came to join Worldwide Imports as a salesman and driver. His first race in the AC was at Vaca Valley for the Cal Club meeting on April 30th and May 1st. Entered in Morgans for this meeting were Rick Hilgers in Snoopy in D Production, and Roger Slowi, Bob Monk, Bob O'Brien, Dave Christofferson and Bill Chapman in their steel bodied cars in E Production. In Race 8, Sunday's consolation Production car race over twelve laps, Rick Hilgers was outstanding, finishing fourth overall behind the three Corvettes, but just ahead of an AC Bristol, and well ahead of the Porsche Carrera and a Lotus Elite. Roger Slowi was lying second in Class E until one lap from the flag, when he had to retire his blue Plus Four. Ronnie Bucknum then took Beware 1 to victory, beating Ernest Maidenhall and Bill Hinshaw in Porsches, with Dave Christofferson and Bill Chapman third and fifth in Class E respectively. Dave Christofferson was soon to buy what we think was Bob O'Brien's right hand drive red Plus Four from Bob Monk, a Napa resident. Presumably the previous owner Bob O'Brien, Bob Monk and Dave were all sharing the car at this event.

In Washington State the Puget Sound Sports Car Club ran an event at Arlington airfield on Sunday May 1st using a 2.4 mile course. The event was run under the Northwest's Conference rules and attracted GB Sterne from over the border in Canada with his black Plus Four four-seater. No doubt he was well up in his class as usual.

The San Diego Region of the SCCA ran a meeting at Del Mar for the weekend of May 14th and 15th. Roger Slowi had a marvellous run in the E Production race, finishing first, followed home by Dr Ken Hayes.

Ike Williamson tried his luck in Class D in the SCCA National races at Cumberland on Sunday May 15th, but again found the ACs too much, finishing last, with six AC Bristols, a Frazer Nash and a Jaguar XK150 ahead of him in the class.

The Northwest Region of the SCCA ran its prestigious 'Forest Festival' races at Shelton on Sunday May 15th. It had been hoped to run a two day event, but insufficient marshals led to everything occurring on the Sunday. There were two Plus Fours entered, by Russ Austin from Aberdeen and Curt Chisholm from Olympia, both being newcomers to racing. Curt Chisholm had bought his red 1958 four-seater Plus Four from Tom Carstens the Morgan dealer in Tacoma in Washington. Tom had been a great influence in supporting sports car racing on the West Coast of America and traded as 'Carstens AutoHaus'. The Plus Four was Curt's daily family car (he was married with two children), but it was an easy thirty miles or so drive to Shelton where the windscreen and exhaust silencer were removed and he would go racing. Both of the Morgans took part in the thirty minute over 1,600cc novices' race and Russ beat Curt by

397

Curt Chisholm with his four-seater Plus Four. (Olympia newspaper)

one place, finishing fourteenth overall and fourth in Class D. Russ also took part in Race 5, a thirty minute race for over 1,600cc Production classes, but failed to finish. Perhaps Russ was another name for Bob Austin, who had contested the novices' race at Shelton in April.

Curt also took his Plus Four to drag races held at Shelton and Puyallup in Washington. Whilst true sports car enthusiasts would frown at such activity Curt did well, winning eight trophies in a row by beating other foreign cars. Curt was a specialist in fast up-shifts through the gearbox, which gave him an edge over the competition.

One way to get competitive racing was to enter the events of the smaller clubs which didn't use the current SCCA classification, such as the Oakland County Sportsman's Road Racing Club, which ran its 'Spring Sprints' at Waterford Hills in Michigan, some thirty miles north of Detroit, over the weekend of May 21st and 22nd. The twisty 1.5 mile circuit always suited Morgans and in the over 1,600cc ten lap novices' race T Barth's Morgan finished first overall and first in E Production, beating even Corvettes. In Race 4, for 1,600 to 2,700cc cars over twelve laps Gordon Harrison started sixth on the grid, but managed to finish third, behind an Arnolt Bristol and a Frazer Nash, just ahead of Stacey Crute's Morgan. Two races later Gordon was out again, in an all comers race held over twenty-five laps. He finished sixth, and second in class behind Tom Payne's Porsche.

Gordon had bought another of the 'Competition Sebring' Morgans, this being chassis number 4471, which had been dispatched from the Morgan factory on Tuesday March 29th, bound for Windsor Motorcycles. It was white, with blue leather interior, right hand drive, and had the usual 'Competition' specification of aluminium body, disc brakes, wire wheels, Derrington exhaust, aluminium sump and reinforced front suspension. Curly Ellis had managed to fit a 4.6 to 1 rear axle, making the Morgan particularly suitable for 'tight' circuits such as Waterford Hills.

In the State of Utah Morgan driver Steve Harris showed promise at the SCCA Utah Region's road races, held at Salt Lake on Sunday May 22nd, where he had a fierce battle with the AC Bristol of Bill Kalmar in the Production race, whilst duelling for fifth place. Steve's Morgan had clutch problems during this meeting, and Steve and his helpers were forced to strip the car down and replace the clutch between races.

That same weekend at Thompson, George Burgess came home eleventh overall and fourth in Class D in the Production race for Classes B, C and D. Bill Brandt was fourteenth overall in his Plus Four.

In California the exploits of Rene Pellandini's AC Bristol, Beware 1, had resulted in several interviews by the motoring press. In the Cal Club's *CSCC Notes* for May Rene's mechanic, Stu Haggart, revealed that they used 9.5 to 1 compression pistons for racing, adding that these were Cal Club approved. Sadly this approval was not true and, at the Santa Barbara meeting on May 28th and 29th where Ronnie Bucknum took Beware 1 to a sixth overall and a class win behind five Corvettes, the engine was checked and the 'illegal' pistons found. Although it was clear that there had been no attempt to deceive, and letters were sent from AC Cars in England in support, the punishment handed out was severe. Ronnie Bucknum was banned from Cal Club races for six months (later reduced to three months), whilst Rene was prohibited from entering Cal Club races for one year.

At this same meeting Roger Slowi was sixth in Race 4, with Bob Monk twelfth in their Plus Fours. In Race 10, for B, C and D Production, Rick Hilgers in his aluminium Morgan, Snoopy, came in seventh in class. On the Sunday, in Race 12, Dan MacManus, Bob Monk and Art White came in eighth, ninth and fifteenth in Class E. Race 13, the Production main event held over fifteen laps, was won by Ronnie Bucknum in Beware 1, with Rick Hilgers seventh overall behind two Porsche Carreras, Bob Windhorst's Austin Healey, a Porsche Speedster and an Elva Courier, making Rick fifth in class. There were thirty-three finishers, but Roger Slowi failed to do so.

There was the usual big entry at Laguna Seca for the June 4th and 5th meeting. It was organised by the San Francisco Region of the SCCA which was still using its own class system. This resulted in the aluminium Plus Four of Rick Hilgers being in Class P5, whereas the normal steel Morgans of Bill Chapman, George Pridmore and Doug Farrar were in Class S5. On the Saturday in the eighteen lap race for larger Production cars Rick Hilgers mixed it with the Corvettes, beating several to finish eighth overall out of twenty-six starters, and third in class behind two AC Bristols, one of which was the 'outlawed' Beware 1, driven by a fired up Ronnie Bucknum. He actually won the race! First of the steel bodied Morgans was the red Plus Four of Bill Chapman in seventeenth position, but winning the class (TRs and Morgans), with Doug Farrar twentieth and George Pridmore last of the twenty-four finishers. The following day there was a similar field for the twenty-nine lap Race 3. Once again Ronnie Bucknum beat everything in what was probably the last race for Beware 1 before suspension. The Morgans didn't do very well, for Rick Hilgers and Doug Farrar failed to finish. Bill Chapman again took the class win with sixteenth overall, and George Pridmore was the last to finish, some four laps behind the winner.

One of the most notable hill climbs in Pennsylvania was the famous Duryea Drive hill climb, near Reading, perhaps the most interesting and the longest of the Pennsylvania hill climbs at 2.6 miles. Half way up was a Japanese style Pagoda, built in 1908. That same weekend Ike Williamson took his Plus Four to this hill climb recording a time of 175.46 seconds, fast enough to give him second place in Class EP1 behind the hot TR3 of Bill Gurnee.

Arch McNeill certainly knew his way around Lime Rock, for at the Long Island Sports Car Association's meeting on Saturday June 11th he finished first overall in a fifteen lap race. One week later he was competing at Roosevelt Raceway, Westbury, on Long Island, New York. The New York Region of the SCCA had organised a meeting using a roughly triangular course formed from the parking lot and service roads of this horse-harness racing venue. There were eleven corners and a straight of just under eight hundred yards long.

Ike Williamson uses the entire available road as he climbs the hill at Duryea. (Jake Alderson collection)

Arch had entered the fifteen laps Production race for Classes B, C and D.

He started near the back of the grid, but had a great run on this enjoyable circuit, being detained briefly behind an AC Bristol before finishing second in D Production behind Walt Diver's Austin Healey 100 Six.

Arch's excellent results with the Sebring Morgan led the SCCA to query the eligibility of the aluminium body for Class D Production, suggesting too few had been built to homologate the car as 'Production'. Despite correspondence from Peter Morgan, stating that fifty-eight Plus Fours had been built by the factory prior to January 1960 with aluminium body and wings, and that a further twenty-one had been built up to the end of June 1960, Arch was told he would have to compete in 'E Modified' in future. We remain surprised at the claim that so many aluminium bodied Morgans had been built by the factory.

The Northwest Region of the SCCA held another of its popular Regional races at Shelton Airport on Sunday June 19th. Curt Chisholm was there with his red four-seater, along with newcomer Paul Montgomery from Seattle in his Plus Four. The weather was awful with heavy rain all day, and even hail at times. In the novices' race for over 1,600cc Production classes Curt finished in fourth place overall and second in Class D behind Harry Kersting's Jaguar. Paul was sixth overall, and third in Class D.

Watkins Glen held the fourth annual Glen Classic meeting over the weekend of June 25th and 26th. Just one Morgan was entered, the 1959 Plus Four four-seater of A Talbot Hodge ('Tab') from Rochester, New York. This was his first ever race, although he had won his class at drivers' school, also at Watkins Glen. 'Tab' had obviously learned the circuit well, for in Race 5, a twenty lap race for Production Classes D and above, he finished seventh overall and first in Class D, beating an AC Bristol, and several Jaguars and Austin Healeys. Tab's Morgan was chassis number 4220, a red four-seater with black trim, which had left the Morgan factory fitted with a raised compression engine and matched and polished ports on Friday June 12th 1959. It also had wire wheels.

The LA Region of the SCCA ran races on the newly resurfaced Pomona fairground circuit during the same weekend, using its own Production classification, such that the Plus Four Morgans were still in Class E. Kas Kastner was the man to beat, with Class E wins on both days in his TR3. On the Saturday Burton was third in his Plus Four behind Danny Stephen's Austin Healey, having taken his class in the earlier novices' race. On the Sunday Roger Slowi tried desperately to pass Boughton's TR for second place at Turn 3 on the last lap, spinning in the process and collecting the TR. The Morgan was badly damaged and Roger never raced it again. His spin gave Dr Ken Hayes the second position with his Plus Four, in front of Danny Stephens Austin Healey 100. Once again Burton took Class E in the novices' race.

The July issue of *Road and Track* contained a report of a visit to Peter Morgan at the Morgan factory where a journalist was collecting his new Plus Four after a three month wait. The journalists spotted the late HFS Morgan's four-seater drophead coupé looking rather sad in the dispatch bay. They seemed particularly interested in the 'Competition Sebring' model, asking Peter about the specially strengthened front suspension, which Peter informed them was more required for rallies than racing, but was now standard anyway. Derek Day, the sales manager, managed to find them a Competition model to look at in the dispatch bay.

In another area were half a dozen grimy Morgans, which Derek Day told them belonged to Americans who had taken delivery of them new from the factory for British vacations, and had then brought them back for shipping home to America. Nine cars a week were now being built at the factory, with 80% bound for the USA.

Arch McNeill was back at Lime Rock on Saturday July 2nd for the SCCA National races, but had to run in Class E Modified for the reasons mentioned above. In the main event of the meeting, a thirty lap race for Modified Classes B, C, D, E, F and G, Arch finished sixteenth of twenty-six starters, being sixth in class.

Competing in D Production in his Plus Four was George Burgess, but we think he too might have been driving his aluminium bodied 'Competition Sebring' Morgan. Presumably he kept quiet about it, if this is so! George finished sixteenth overall out of the twenty-six finishers in Race 4 for the larger Production classes, but, more importantly, he was fourth in class behind an AC Bristol, and two Jaguars, thereby gaining four points in the SCCA's National Championship for D Production, making George the first Morgan driver to score this year.

Roger Slowi collects J D Boughton's TR3 at Turn 3 at Pomona, sidelining both cars. (J W LaTourette)

The San Francisco Region of the SCCA held races at Vaca Valley over the weekend of July 9th and 10th. In the main Production race on the Sunday over twenty-seven laps for Classes 'S5, S6, S7, P6 and P7', the Morgan of Chuck Tanland was first in Class S5. (This Region was still using its own non standard classification of Production racers.)

The Colorado Region of the SCCA ran its allocated National meeting over the weekend of July 16th and 17th at the new track in Castle Rock, Colorado, some thirty miles south of Denver, called the Continental Divide Raceway. Steve Harris made the trip from Utah to what was probably the closest big race to his abode, and found another Morgan Plus Four entered, that of Robert Grueter. In the Production race for the larger classes Steve was outstanding, finishing fourth overall, behind two Corvettes and Gene Kurland's AC Bristol. His second in Class D gave him eight National points. Finishing fourteenth and fifth in class came Robert Grueter. There were thirty finishers, and the new track was thought to be quite tricky.

The very last of the Seafair race meetings to be held at Shelton Airport took place over the weekend of Saturday and Sunday July 30th and 31st. A new track would take over in 1961, the Pacific Raceways International Circuit nearing completion in an old gravel pit near Kent in Washington. A good crowd of around 8,000 turned out in fine weather to watch the action. There was only one Morgan entered, the Plus Four of Paul Montgomery, who finished sixth overall and second in Class D in the thirty minute novices' race for Production cars over 1,600cc.

A new regulation was mandated by the SCCA for all racing sports cars as from Monday August 1st, namely the compulsory fitting of metal-to-metal quick release safety belts. Military aircraft versions were highly recommended.

The New York Region of the SCCA ran it's annual National races at Montgomery Airport over the weekend of August 6th and 7th, but attracted just one Plus Four, that of Dick Brandt, for the twenty lap race for Production Classes B, C and D. He finished twenty-second of the twenty-five finishers.

That same weekend, over in California the third annual San Luis Obispo races were held on the 1.5 mile airport course. Just two Morgans took part, the usual white Plus Four of Dr Ken Hayes, and the new green Plus Four, with tan leather upholstery, of Bob Sheridan. Bob had moved to San Francisco in 1957 to undertake a course in hotel and restaurant management at the City College. He had soon fallen under the spell of sports car racing, being particularly impressed by the performances of Rene Pellandini's racing team and especially Lew Spencer. As a result the family Simca Aronde was traded in to the local Morgan agent Frank Henry in Berkeley for this new Morgan in 1958. After the usual rallies and autocrosses (gymkhanas), Bob undertook driver training at Riverside. San Luis Obispo was to be his first event, competing in the novice class.

One week later Cotati was the desolate venue for SCCA races co-promoted by the San Francisco Region and the Racing Drivers Club, the latter being an organisation of local drivers that ran a driving school once a month. Two Plus Fours were entered, one shared by Bill and Myrna Carter, and the other entered by Frank Crane. Frank Crane had been racing a TR3 for Rusty Hyde of Hyde Motors on Van Hess Avenue in San Francisco before he took over the business, adding the Morgan and AC franchises (via Rene Pellandini) and renaming the business Frank Crane Triumph.

Bill and his wife Myrna had been racing a TR3, but they had recently bought Ralph Bohn's old Morgan, which was in a bit of a mess following a collision with hay bales whilst Ralph was racing. When it had been rebuilt Bill brought it home for his wife to try, but she found she couldn't reach the pedals, and she was so upset that she felt like crying. To make the Morgan suitable for her short stature metal extensions were fabricated for the pedals and a special seat was made for Myrna using tapered cushions fastened to boards. This became known as her 'high chair' and was removed when Bill was driving. The Morgan was initially red, but later painted a navy blue.

In the ladies' race Myrna brought the Morgan home in fourth place (second was Prudence Baxter, this time in a Daimler V8). In the 45 minute Production race for above 1,600cc Frank and Bill finished eighteenth and nineteenth, but first and second in Class S5.

The 'Kentucky Derby Road Races' were held at Louisville by the Kentucky Region of the SCCA over the weekend of August 20th and 21st. These National races used a course shaped like a table tennis bat, around the outside of the Coliseum at the Fairground. Just one Morgan was entered, that of Lester Detterbeck who had towed it from Chicago for the races. He failed to finish in the fifteen lap B, C and D Production race due to engine problems. Lester had bought his Morgan second-hand a couple of years before, having been told that this white Morgan had competed in Sebring. To race back home in Chicago he had had to weld steel plates to the bolt-on wheel centres to prevent the wheel-stud nuts pulling through the wheel centres (as earlier required by the California Sports Car Club in 1957). Which Morgan this was we have been unable to determine, but possibilities are the 1956 Sebring car of John Weitz, later used by Joe Ferguson, or the 1957 entry for Weitz again, which did not actually take part.

The annual three day Labor Day weekend of September 3rd, 4th and 5th was the date for the Cal Club's ever popular Santa Barbara meeting, with twenty-one races on the card, four even being for motorcycles! Race 4 was for Production Class E only and held over eight laps but the first three places were all taken by Porsches. In fourth place was the Morgan of Frank Crane, whilst racing newcomers Art White and Bob Sheridan were eighth and eighteenth respectively with their Plus Fours. Poor Bob Sheridan had thought flagman Stu Haggart (a mechanic at Worldwide Imports) was black flagging him, so he had pitted, only to find Stu was misusing the flag to advise him other cars were close behind. As a result he missed the cut off for Sunday's final, the main Production race.

Race 12 was a consolation race for those unable to race in the main event, and was held over twelve laps for Classes D, E and F. It was won by the AC Bristol of A Horney, with Dr Ken Hayes tenth overall and sixth in Class E, with Bob Sheridan fourteenth overall and eighth in class. Bob Sheridan had several times chatted to Ken Hayes about how he made his Morgan fly, learning that Ken preferred Pirelli Stelvio six-ply tyres and used a 4.56 to 1 rear axle ratio on his white Plus Four.

The main event for Production classes was Race 14, held over fifteen laps. Jay Hills was the victor in his Porsche Carrera, whist Frank Crane finished thirteenth overall but was third in class behind two Class E Porsches. Art White finished nineteenth, and fifth in class. In the ladies' race Jan Gilmore borrowed Frank Crane's Morgan, finishing tenth overall of the twelve starters, but second in Class E.

Canadian chiropractor Dr Robert Brisco took his 4/4 Series II across the border from his home in Trail in British Columbia, Canada into Washington State for the Labor Day weekend of races held at Deer Park. This was a little town just north of Spokane in the east of the State in Washington. This course was first used in 1956, using the runways of an abandoned Second World War B29 bomber base, and had a lap distance just under three miles. It was very wet for the Sunday's races. In his first event Robert only got as far as the first corner before the gearlever became disconnected so he had to complete the ten laps entirely in the second of his Buckler gearbox's three gears. He claimed he could still hit 75 mph on the back straight and he still finished first in Class I (presumably Conference rules applied). It turned out that the bolt holding the Morgan gear lever to the original Ford one had sheared. After a repair Robert took to the track again for the main event and took the lead in his class once more, even holding off a couple of Austin Healey Sprites from the class above. On the third to last lap the bolt sheared again at the same corner, but this time leaving him coasting to retirement. Robert commented, 'This mishap was followed by a brief discussion with the pit crew!'

The following Saturday Arch McNeill once again demonstrated his mastery of the Lime Rock track at the Long Island Sports Car Association meeting. He won his class in a fifteen lap race, and came in fourth overall, only beaten by two Corvettes and a Lotus Eleven.

Frank Crane demonstrated that he too had great potential driving a Morgan. That same weekend at Cotati, in the forty-five minute race for Class E and above, he came home fifth, behind the victorious Corvette of Paul Reinhart, a 300SL Mercedes, and two AC Bristols. The organisers of the meeting, the San Francisco Region of the SCCA and the Northern California Corvette Association, also staged a rather unusual handicap race over ten laps, with fifteen entries, each of a different class (the San Francisco Region using its own profuse classifications). The handicaps were based on the Saturday qualifying times. George Pridmore brought his green Plus Four home third, behind the winning Porsche Speedster and a TR3.

The Road America '500' held at Elkhart Lake in Wisconsin was America's longest amateur road race and this five hundred mile annual event always attracted a large number of entrants and spectators to this enjoyable track every September. This year, for the race held on Sunday September 11th, there was a Morgan entered, and it was to achieve a most remarkable result. The Morgan was owned by Tommy Gallagher and was one of the 'Competition Sebring' aluminium bodied Plus Fours. Because of the aluminium body the race organisers felt it must be entered in the D Modified class, as insufficient numbers had been built to allow it to run in the Production class. Acting as co-driver with Tommy was Harry Heuer, a noted driver of the Scarab sports-racing cars. Sadly engine problems had sidelined the Scarab, so he was happy to be invited to join the little Morgan team.

Some 32,000 spectators were present for the start, the forty-four cars being set off in class order. Five hundred miles is a long way and the attrition rate was high. Towards the end of the race it began to rain and Harry, who was then driving, found the Morgan handled remarkably well in the wet, whereas the higher powered cars had all sorts of problems staying on the course. With all cars now on a virtual equal footing because of the weather Harry found himself actually gaining on the V12, 3 litre Ferrari of Augie Pabst, although it was many laps ahead. 'GET AUG' was the instruction held out by Harry's pit crew! Twenty-four cars splashed their way to finish, with the Morgan coming in seventeenth. What was amazing was that there were just two 'D Modified' cars ahead, namely the winning Maserati 61 and the Pabst Ferrari, making the Morgan an amazing third in class, and gaining six points for the SCCA National Championship!

At the Springtown hill climb in Pennsylvania over the weekend of September 17th Harry Reynolds did his fastest time yet, recording 65.1009 seconds to finish second in the Modified class for over 1,500cc capacity. Mike Krisiloff recorded 72.7695 seconds in his Plus Four.

The parking lot of the Del Mar horse racing course was used by the SCCA over the weekend of Sept 24th and 25th. This tight course always suited the smaller cars, but there was often much barging to disturb the shapes of the cars. The two red Plus Fours of Steve Dredge and Art White were both badly affected, but Steve did get through to win the class. Steve

Steve Dredge in his much battered Plus Four at Del Mar, where he took the class win. (Dave Friedman)

was driving the ex Bob Oker Morgan, recently raced by his brother Bill Dredge.

That same weekend three Morgans were competing at Watkins Glen in the twenty-two lap Schuyler Carrera Race for Class D, these being the Plus Fours of Gerald Rollo, Howard Williamson and Tab Hodge. Tab failed to finish, whilst Gerald and Howard came in fifteenth and sixteenth respectively, the last to finish, and well beaten by the AC Bristols and Jaguars.

In September the Morgan Motor Company Accountant, Major Kendall, visited Fergus Imported Cars Inc, in New York, meeting with Mr Doubey, Managing Director, and Mr Stanfill, Manager of the Repairs Department. He duly reported back to the Morgan board at its October meeting, relaying several requests. These included defrosting equipment, softer springing, a full spare parts list written in 'American English', and the need for help in improving the classification of the Morgan for competition in the USA. Mr Doubey had also expressed the hope that Peter Morgan would visit them shortly, something he was already considering doing.

Once again the *Los Angeles Times* sponsored the joint amateur and professional races held at Riverside on October 15th and 16th, but just Ken Hayes and Bob Sheridan were upholding the Morgan marque. Ken failed to finish the Class E race.

That same weekend the monthly sports car magazine *Northwest Sports Car News* sponsored the 'Northwest Grand Prix' race meeting held at the new Pacific Raceways course at Kent in Washington State. This course had been opened earlier in the year, having been built on a huge gravel pit surrounded by trees just seven miles east of Kent, and featuring a drag strip as well as 2.4 mile road course. The programme had ten lap qualifying races for the various classes, prior to a 150 mile Grand Prix. GB Sterne was there with his four-seater Plus Four, winning his class.

One week later, at Laguna Seca, Rick Hilgers was driving Snoopy, and in the forty-five minute main race he was truly outstanding, eventually finishing fourth and even beating Red Ferris's Corvette. He was only headed by the winning Corvette of Bill Sherwood, the AC Bristol of Ronnie Bucknum (now back in Cal Club racing), and the Mercedes 300SL of Peter Culkin.

A hill climb was also held at Yorklyn in Delaware that weekend on the Saturday attracting four Plus Four drivers. The fastest was Harry Reynolds in The Torking Dog with a time of 41.61 seconds, to finish second in Class III. Finishing fourth was the Morgan of John Jacobson, fifth was Garry

Greenstein both recording just over 44 seconds. Alan Hedgecock recorded 46 seconds.

John 'Jake' Jacobson has been a life long Morgan enthusiast. He had purchased the dark green, twin spare wheels 1955 Morgan previously used by Bill Worthington, and was enjoying using it in local events. For Yorklyn he had replaced the front wings with lightweight cycle type. Recently he described the Morgan as, 'a lovely, wonderful, joyful car, so much fun'.

The following day Harry Reynolds took The Torking Dog to the Pocono hill climb where he was the sole Morgan entry amidst four AC Bristols in Class D Production. Harry finished third in 42.0664 seconds. This hill climb in the Pocono Mountain area was situated just off Route 209, midway between Stroudsburg and Port Jervis, New York. The one mile climb with just one corner led to a resort known as 'Honeymoon Haven', a pink palace with ceiling mirrors etc.

It was raining for the Pomona meeting on Sunday November 6th. Three Plus Fours were entered, those of Ken Hayes, Bob Sheridan and the shared car of John Hodges and R Smith. The rain played havoc with the racing, and Bob Sheridan recalls passing an MG, with the rooster tail of spray going down his neck and under his driving suit. Despite the conditions Ken Hayes had few problems with the five lap race, finishing fifth overall behind four Class F cars. He won Class E however.

At the November hill climb at Chimney Rock Dr Sam Miller and David Williams were both driving their Morgans. Sam came twenty-second overall but was first in Class D Production with a time of 2 minutes 45 seconds whilst David finished second in this class.

Right at the end of the racing season, over the weekend of December 10th and 11th, the SCCA ran a race at Las Vegas, on McCarran Field Airport. Four Morgans were entered, two drivers from Utah and two making the long trail from California. The former two were Dee Burton and Bill Smith from Salt Lake City, and the latter two were Bob Sheridan and Steve Dredge. Despite the long haul, none of the Californian Morgans was successful.

It had been a rather odd year for Morgan racing. Whilst the SCCA had perhaps over-rated the performance of a standard Plus Four when it placed it in Class D, the action of the 'rebel'

Dr Sam Miller leaves the start line at Chimney Rock. (Dr Sam Miller collection)

California Regions by using their own classifications led to much confusion. The best Morgan performances nationally in Class D were those of Steve Harris (sixteenth equal) and George Burgess (twenty-second equal), but the best SCCA Morgan achievements of the season were those of Tom Gallagher and Harry Heuer at Road America, giving them thirteenth equal at the end of the year with the aluminium Morgan in Class D Modified, behind far more exotic Maseratis, Ferraris and an Aston Martin! In addition, in California the magazine *MotoRacing* published a West Coast Championship, which covered Cal Club events and possibly others. In this Dr Ken Hayes came fourth in Class E, George Follmer being the class winner with his Porsche.

Harry Reynolds had come to realise that Morgan drum brakes were not too good for frantic braking on the Pennsylvania hills he loved to hill climb. The drums had hard spots that machining failed to correct. As a result he corresponded with the Morgan factory in England, eventually purchasing the 'kit' needed to convert his Morgan, The Torking Dog, to Girling disc brakes, and the parts arrived packed in an impressive wooden case towards the end of the year. Harry remembered, 'freezing my backside installing them in an unheated garage at my parents' home near Philadelphia'.

1960 had also seen the penetration of imported cars into the American market start to slip, with a drop from a peak of 614,131 cars in 1959 to 498,575 in 1960. One of the reasons for this was the awakening of the domestic manufacturers to the foreign challenge, and the introduction of their own 'Compacts'. Thus, during 1960 Ford had introduced the Falcon, Mercury the Comet, Plymouth the Valiant, and finally Chevrolet the Corvair. The biggest importer by far was Volkswagen, and the success of this rear engined German car had inspired General Motors to equip the Corvair with a rear engine. 'If you can't beat them, join them,' was the General Motors motto.

Sports cars were not immune from the sales drop, probably suffering more from a downturn in the US economy. Some manufacturers failed to respond to the downturn in sales and had a very difficult time in 1960 and 61. The Italian manufacturer Moretti, for example had lines of imported sports cars stored at the Jersey docks, with not a buyer at any price.

In November Fergus Imported Cars had requested the Morgan factory to cancel further deliveries, one reason being a large stock of unsold Borgwards, for which Fergus was the Eastern USA distributor. The Borgward business was very important to Fergus, shipping some 1,200 to 1,500 per month. The downturn in American sales was a major contributor to the bankruptcy of Borgward in the summer of 1961. Deliveries of Morgans to Fergus were resumed the following month.

Hawaii

During the early months of 1960 a blue Morgan Plus Four, one of the right hand drive 'Competition Sebring' models, arrived in Hawaii, where it was to be raced by Charlie Potts. The huge Ala Moana shopping mall in Honolulu staged an Auto Show over the weekend of March 5th and 6th and KP Motors were represented. Several cars due to be raced at the forthcoming Open meeting to be held at Kahuku on Sunday March 20th were on display.

The first race on this Kahulu programme was a six lap novices' race of the circa 2 mile airfield course. There were several Morgans entered. A 'Chuck Sparks' was entered as driving Les Kangas' maroon car and George Keys and Peter Revson were also driving Plus Fours. Twenty-one years old Peter Revson was a son of one of the three brothers that had founded the American Revlon cosmetics empire. Although originally from the northeast of the USA he had just relocated to Hawaii with his mother and was attending the University. His Morgan was grey with black wings. The race was easily won by Danny Ongals in a Corvette, but Chuck Sparks and George Keys were second and third. Peter Revson finished eighth.

The third race was another six lapper, this time for 1,600cc to 2,000cc cars. George Reeves won in his 'Competition Products Special'. Second was an AC Ace, whilst Les Kangas came home third ahead of Walter Vail's TR3. In fifth place was Charlie Potts, just ahead of Hal Melleney, both in Plus Fours.

In Hawaii the car classification was more liberally interpreted than in the SCCA events held on the mainland.

The sixth race was another six lap race, this time for Production cars under 2,000cc. In this event a Porsche Carrera beat the AC to win, with Les in third place yet again. Hal Melleney was fifth; George Keys ninth and poor Peter Revson was last of the thirteen finishers.

A consolation race over eight laps was held for those who hadn't qualified for the final main event. Hal Melleney did well to finish third, thereby getting an entry for the main race. George Keys was fourth and Peter Revson seventh of the ten finishers. The main event was to be held over thirty laps and was won by a Corvette, followed by a Corvette engined Austin Healey. Hal Melleney did very well to finish sixth, whilst Charlie Potts came home ninth.

The Kahuku track had been spruced up and partly remodelled for the Hawaii Grand Prix meeting held over the weekend of Saturday May 30th and Sunday May 31st. Several five lap heats were held on the Saturday to determine starting positions for the Sunday races. In the first heat, for novice drivers, Greg Huehl finished second in his Plus Four.

In the heat for Production cars in Classes C, D, and E there was a great result for the Morgans, with Charlie Potts first, Peter Revson second, Hal Melleney fourth, Les Kangas fifth and Greg Huehl seventh.

On the Sunday Greg Huehl finished in second place once again in the five lap novices' race. In the five lap Classes C, D and E Production race Peter Revson improved to finish in first place, ahead of Walter Vail's TR3, whilst Hal Melleney, Charlie Potts, and Greg Huehl finished third, fourth and fifth respectively. Les Kangas finished seventh.

A six lap handicap race had Hal Melleney finishing third, with Les Kangas and Charlie Potts in fifth and sixth places. Peter Revson finished eighth and Greg Huehl was eleventh. The main race was held over twenty laps for Modified and Production sports cars. It was won by Jimmy Pflueger in his Fury Special, whilst the two Morgans of Charlie Potts and Les Kangas finished sixth and seventh, just beating the TR3 of Walter Vail.

We wonder if this might have been the race meeting in which Peter Revson was hauled before the stewards for being 'too aggressive' in his driving. In Peter's later autobiography he comments that he had been told he was, 'talking like a loose lunchbag' at the stewards' inquiry! Peter was to soon return to the northeastern USA.

Further races were held at Kahuku on Sunday September 4th. In the race for over 1,600cc Production cars Charlie Potts finished first, ahead of Les Kangas. Charlie was now beginning to dominate Production car racing.

He was back at Kahuku on Sunday December 4th. Whilst he had to settle for second place behind Walter Vail's TR3 in the race for Production cars over 1,600cc, he then beat Walter to take victory in the thirty lap main event in his Morgan 'Competition Sebring'. Earlier, in the race for all Production classes Charlie had finished second to Lee's TR3, with Les Kangas in third position.

Canada

The Activities Chairman of the Winnipeg Sports Car Club, Ron Routliffe, was keen to encourage racing during the tough Manitoba winters, and after organising a snow race at Pembina North Dakota Airport he organised an ice race in April. It was held on the Red River at the St Adolphe ferry crossing some twenty miles south of Winnipeg. A commandeered grader cleared the snow from a tight course of around a mile to the lap. Twenty cars took part on a cold (25 degrees Fahrenheit) but sunny day. The second race produced a battle for top spot between Kieth

Ralf's new Corsair and Art 'Ginger' Millar's Morgan 4/4, eventually settled in the Corsair's favour. Ginger was the only sports car driver who was brave enough to leave the hood down!

The sixth and final race was held over twenty laps and was a real bumper to bumper affair. It was won by the very experienced Dr Phil Smyth in his DKW, followed by Slim Routliffe's Volvo with Ginger Millar in third place with his Morgan.

The first race of the year at Westwood was scheduled for Sunday March 27th but heavy rains had left the course awash with mud so the meeting was postponed until Easter Sunday April 17th. GB Sterne had a new Morgan Plus Four for this year's races, having written the previous one off in a road accident. We think the new one carried chassis number 4416, which was another black four-seater. The specification included wire wheels, disc brakes and a Brooklands steering wheel. The TR3 engine, TS 61199, had raised compression, polished ports and a Derrington exhaust manifold. The front frame was braced for strength and the gearbox mounting was of the 'improved type', later fitted by Morgan as standard. Simmonds lock nuts were used. An electric fuel pump was fitted with duel fuel pipes, the ignition coil was moved to the inner wing valance and there were corner lights in the hood. The axle ratio was given as 4.09 to 1, and racing tyres were fitted. The windscreen had laminated glass. It was dispatched from the Morgan factory on Wednesday February 3rd.

GB fitted a roll bar as this was now required. The SCCA had insisted on this fitment for races in its Northwestern Region following an accident the previous April. Sports car racing elsewhere in Canada was often to a sanction from the Canadian Automobile Sports Clubs (CASC), an organisation founded in 1951 as a governing body for sports car racing in Canada. This organisation did not make a roll bar compulsory until 1962.

There was a good Morgan entry for the Westwood race meeting held on Sunday May 8th. Plus Fours were entered by GB Sterne, Peter Browning and Max Schulze, whilst 4/4s were entered by Tom Rice and Jack Thompson. Unfortunately we have no results.

The first race meeting of the year counting for Conference points at Westwood was held on Sunday May 29th. The second race was for Classes A, B, C, and D and GB Sterne finished in eighth place overall, but third in Class D.

Dr Robert Brisco's first race of the year in his 4/4 was held at Claresholm in Alberta. The venue was the RCAF airfield, an old BCATP base during the Second World War, which had finally closed in 1958 after use for NATO flight training. The event was run on Saturday and Sunday July 2nd and 3rd by the Calgary Sports Car Club. Robert entered two races, finishing third in Class 1 in the Production race, and second in class in the thirty minute Le Mans all-comers race. In both races he was soundly beaten by the Winnipeg vet, Dr Phil Smyth, in his much campaigned and very fast DKW.

At Westwood on Saturday July 23rd the 'International 200' a three hour endurance race attracted just two Morgans, the 4/4s of Lloyd Messersmith from Wenatchee and Tom Rice from Kennewick. Unfortunately we have no results. The following day the Triumph Tourist Trophy race was held, with GB Sterne entered in Class D Production in his Plus Four and Lloyd Messersmith in Class 1 Production in his 4/4.

GB Sterne continued his successes at Westwood on Sunday August 21st when he finished third overall in the race for Classes A, B, C, D and E Production and won Class D in the process.

There was fine summer weather for the race meeting at Westwood held on Sunday September 11th, attracting some 7,000 spectators. The ten lap race for Production Classes A, B, C, D and E was easily won by Bob Constabaris in his AC Bristol, but in third place behind Milt Davis' Porsche was GB Sterne in the black Morgan. He also won Class D, but he was the only finisher in this class.

GB also contested Race 7, the Senior Le Mans race, finishing in a very respectable seventh place considering the opposition. The race was won by Pat Piggot's 2 litre Lotus 15.

On Sunday September 18th a race meeting was held at St Eugene, near Montreal, attracting two Plus Fours, driven by Paul Villeneuve and Jacques Couture. In the novices' race Paul drove well to finish in second place. In Race 3 both Morgans were competing, Jacques finishing in third place, just ahead of Paul. Paul completed a good day's racing for him when he also took part in Race 9 finishing in thirteenth place.

Jacques Couture's Morgan was a green chrome radiator Plus Four. It had been owned by John Tannin, a British racer living in Canada, who had found it in the USA after it had lost a 16 inch wheel when it pulled over the wheel nuts. The Morgan had suffered quite a bit of damage as a consequence. Jacques bought the Morgan and rebuilt it. He was troubled by cracked road wheels, so he had bought two new ones. He would then practice and qualify on the old cracked wheels, but would substitute the new ones for the races!

As a grand finale to the season's racing at Westwood the BCSCC put on a two day meeting on Saturday and Sunday October 29th and 30th. The first day's race was the 'Twilight Grand Prix', a five hour endurance race. The following day club races were held in heavy rain. We think Dr Robert Brisco was competing in his 4/4 at this event. Westwood hairpin posed its own problems for the 4/4 as first gear had to be selected to enable reasonable acceleration up the short steep straight immediately following it. This often produced horrible noises from the Ford gearbox! Robert managed first in class and held off two Austin Healey Sprites in the process.

It had been an enjoyable year for the Morgan racers in Canada, none enjoying it more than GB Sterne, who had become a regular class winner at Westwood. The 1961 season was eagerly awaited.

Acknowledgements

We wish to acknowledge the considerable help given to our research by the following people. The list is not complete, and anyone not mentioned we sincerely thank for their help. A complete list would fill a book on its own. We have acknowledged photographers directly under the photographs used.

The book was the idea of the late Peter Morgan. He was involved extensively with the research and made the Morgan Motor Company archives available to us. His son Charles has been equally helpful.

Others include,

UK: Graeme Anton, Peter Anton, John Baker-Courtney, Jim Banbury, Tony Bancroft, Alan & Yvonne Belcher, Mrs Doreen Bennetts, Douglas Bertram, Alex Blair, Len Bridge, Robin Brown, David Burgess-Wise, John Charnaud, Roy Clarkson, Richard Colton, Ron Crellin, Derek Day, Basil de Mattos, Mrs Mibs Delf, Ted Dennis, T Dixon Smith, Val Domleo, Keith Duckworth, Bob Duggan, Mike Duncan, John Edwards, Peter Garnier, Graham Gauld, Lorne Goldman, Jim Goodall, Bob Grant, Terry Hall, Ian Hall, Brian & Val Harper, Fred Hart, David Hiam, Ken Hobbs, Derek Howard, Jim Hughan, Joe Huxham, Ken James, Ian Jervis, Martin Kemp, Pat Kennett, Chris Lawrence, 'Tiny' Lewis, Ross Lomax, John Looker, Geoff & Mary Margetts, Peter Marten, Pauline & Lionel Mayman, Sonny McCann, W G McMinnies, Ray Meredith, Edgardo Michelotti, Nancy Mitchell, John Moore, Sir Alex Moulton, Alec Newsham, Brian Odoni, Jeff Parker-Eaton, Bill Parkes, Brian Parsons, Allin Penhale, Herman Pol, Andy Polack, Jimmy Ray, Brian Redman, Ken Richardson, Horace & Hilda Roberts, 'Monty' Rogers, Dennis Rushton, Jack Sears, Richard Shepherd-Barron, Lyndon Sims, Tony Skinner, Mrs Nina Smith, Roland Smith, Dr John & Mrs Mary Spare, Jeff Sparrowe, Dr William Steel, Ralph Stokes, Jack Sylvester, Doug Taylerson, Dave Thomas, Tom Threlfall, Ron Timmins, Dave Warren, Harry Webster, Mrs Whiteley, Gerry Willburn, Hugh Willmore and Les Yarranton,

Australia: Craig Atkins, Russell Boughton, John Cummins, Terry Doyle, Merv Dudley, Don Hall, Ian McDonald, Terry McGrath, Barry Ranford, Gavin Sandford-Morgan, David Van Dal, Rod Waller, Ken Ward, Geoff Way and Terry Wright.

Canada: Frank Boulton, Robert Brisco, Marv Coulthard, Jacques Couture, Dave and 'Scooter' Elcomb, Michael Gee, Tom Johnston, Lincoln Kinsman, Roy McLaughlin, Lloyd Messersmith, Alan Sands, Lydia Sterne and Bill Sullivan.

France: Pierre-Henry Mahul and Claude Savoye,

Luxembourg: Paul Conrardy,

Macau: Dick Warrall

New Zealand: Ivan and Cliff Bennett, Dr Graham Cowie, Dave Edmiston, Allen Freeman, John Lancaster, John Moorhead, Ted Reid, Tony Shelly, Mike Stephens and Graham Vercoe.

Scandinavia: David Christie, Knut Hallan, Viv Hanstad-Pilcher and Harold Hellum,

South Africa: James Henderson and Peter Lawley

Spain: Pablo Gimeno

USA: Larry Albedi, Gaston Andre, Mrs Janet Aycock, Bob & Dick Bowie, Pierre Brun, Bill and Myrna Carter, Leo Caton, Bill Chapman, Curt Chisholm, Bill Claren, Harry Constant, Richard Cook, Kenny Deeter, Lester Detterbeck, Bill Doushkess, Ray Errickson, Joe Ferguson, Jim Forno, Al Gebhard, Mrs Grace German, Carl Goodwin, Ben Hall, Jim Haynes, Harry Heuer, Rick Hilgers, Bill Hinshaw, Robin Jackson, Roy Jackson-Moore, John Jacobson, 'Kas' Kastner, Bob Kimball, Charlie Kolb, Ed Leslie, Gordon and John MacKenzie, Arch McNeill, Dr Sam Miller, Jim Nichol, Augie Pabst, Tom Payne, Rene Pellandini, Stan Peterson, Harry Reynolds, Alton Rogers, Gerald Rollo, Mike Rothschild, Martin Rudow, Mike Savin, Bob Sheridan, Jim Sitz, Roger Slowi, Robert Smith, Lew

Spencer, Chris Towner, Dave Troffer, Richard Vogel, Kent Warshauer, John Weitz, Willie West and Tom Wright.

We would also like to thank Guy Loveridge and Richard Netherwood of Plus Four Books, for encouraging us and overseeing this book into production.

Last but not least we would like to thank Christine Chapman and Richard Shepherd-Barron for their assistance with the manuscript.

Index of Names

Acheson, Albert 22, 28-29
Adams, Ronnie 147
Agnew, L 154
Ahern, John 13-14, 21, 71
Alcaraz, Francis 150-151
Aldous, Noel 55, 103, 251
Allard, Sydney 142
Allen, Dennis "Conrod" 80-81, 85
Allen, DG 345, 369
Anderson, Don 101, 105, 151
Anderson, Syd 58-59, 103, 153-154, 194
Andre(y), Gaston "Gus" 7, 110-111, 113-118, 160, 163, 165, 168, 170-171, 203-204, 206-207, 214, 261
Anton, Graeme 42
Anton, Peter 42-43, 87, 131-132, 145, 222
Appleby, Horace 180, 184, 188-189, 231
Arnolt, "Wacky" 171, 202, 258
Arundell, Peter 179-180,
Ashley, Captain Mike 114-116, 118
Ashton, W 197
Ashworth, J 189
Astbury, Peter 373
Atkins, Herb 318
Austin, Bob 395
Austin, Russ 397-398
Avedon, Robert 63-64
Axon, JR 184
Ayres, Jack 252, 310-311, 384

Bailey, Major 20
Baille, Sir Gawaine 287-288, 296, 303, 351
Baker, Caroll 210
Baker-Courtenay, John 140
Balchowsky, Max 210
Banbury, Jim 76-79, 82, 86-87, 126, 177-178, 180-181, 184-185, 224-225, 231, 240, 243-244, 283, 291-292, 294, 301-302, 304, 306-307, 345, 348, 350-351, 355-358, 364, 366, 369
Bannister, Brian 356
Baptista, Frank 157, 166
Barker, Ted "Limpy" 54-55, 57
Barnes, Stu 211
Barrett, Gerry 166
Barth, T 398

Baxter, Berwyn 331
Baxter, Prudence "Pru" 321, 327, 331, 396-397, 403
Baxter, Raymond 38
Baxter, Scott 321
Beasley, JR 179-180
Beattie, David 101, 105, 151
Beattie, Lionel 311, 384
Beaulieu, Lord Montagu 357
Beaumann, Henry 261, 318
Beaumont, Tony 16
Becker, Bill 264
Behra, Jean 201, 316
Bekaert, Johnny 179
Belcher, Alan 220, 228, 232-233, 235-238, 240, 243, 279, 283-289, 294, 296-298, 300-301, 303, 341, 346
Belcher, Yvonne 283
Bell, Billie 325
Bell, Gordon "Dinger" 51-52
Bellairs, L 155
Bender, Bob 161
Ben-Dror, Michael 207
Bennett, Cliff 255, 311-312, 387-389
Bennett, Ivan 255, 311-312, 387-389
Bennie, Ian 247
Benson, (USA) 199
Benson, RS 126, 131
Bertram, David 131
Bertram, James 131
Bertram, W Douglas 82-83, 131
Bigger, Frank 147
Biggs, Reggie 249
Binney, Bill 115, 162
Birkett, Holland 182
Bishop, Jim 35, 43
Black, Duncan 114,
Black, Sir John 10, 12
Blackburn, Bob 195
Blackburn, RJ 312
Blackburn, Vic 155
Blair, Alex "Sandy" 21, 27-28, 34, 40, 78-79, 81, 93-94, 124, 126-127, 132, 134, 146, 182, 185, 225, 227, 243, 292, 297-298, 304
Blydenstein, Bill 282, 363
Boddy, Bill 77, 129, 244, 347, 371
Bodin, John 16
Bohn, Ralph 318, 321, 327, 402
Bolster, John 33, 88, 176, 218, 237, 356, 377

Bond, Peter 151, 194, 250, 252
Bondurant, Bob 7, 158, 161-163, 165-167, 169-171, 325, 327
Bondurant, Jackie 158, 161, 163
Bone, HJ 188
Boney, RD 77
Bonnier, Jo 361
Booth, Cec 364
Bos, Manuel 158
Bosman, Eugene "Gene" 190-191, 249
Bosworth, WT (Junior) 207-208, 264-266
Boughton, Jim 52
Bould, AR 34
Boulton, Frank 69, 118-119
Bourne, Arthur 346-347
Bowles, D 338
Bowra, GA 251
Boyer, Don 204, 206
Brabham, Jack 105, 193, 195-196, 379
Bradford, Jeff 281
Bradley, Peter 231, 235, 240, 289, 291, 294-295, 348, 350, 352, 354-355, 360, 364, 367
Bradley, W 174
Bradshaw, J 356
Bradshaw, PB 84
Brandt, Bill 399
Brandt, Dick 402
Brayshaw, Peter 127
Bridge, Len 234, 240, 289, 301, 303-306, 348, 353, 359, 377, 380
Bridson, Raymond 101
Brisco, Dr Robert 334, 403-404, 409-410
Broadbent, Don 118-119, 174
Broadley, Eric 179
Broady, Steve 216-217
Brook, Leslie 26
Brooks, (Canada) 216-217
Brooks, Tony 345
Brough, George 26
Brown, Alan 129
Brown, Ed 316
Brown, JF "Robin" 127, 132-133, 135-136, 138, 140, 147, 180-181, 183-185, 225, 227-228, 237, 240, 242-243, 285-286, 295-298, 301, 303, 351, 359-360, 363-365, 367-371, 374

413

Browning, Peter 217, 334, 409
Bru, HR 330-331
Brucher, AW 34
Brun, Claude 198, 208, 210-214, 255, 259-260, 264, 267-268, 270, 273, 325-326
Brunt, DIC 28
Bryant, Tom 13, 87, 223, 237, 282, 284, 294, 296, 338, 345, 349-351, 355-356
Bubman, AS 90
Buchanan, RC 171
Bucknum, Ronnie vi, 271-273, 314, 397, 399, 405
Buckthought, Russell 196, 254
Bullard, James 166, 168
Burgess, George 396, 399, 401, 407
Burke, D 349-350
Burkholder, Les 69
Burton 391, 401
Burton, Arnold 352
Burton, Dee 406
Butler, Hal 112
Butterell, Robin 16, 37, 93
Byfield, Cliff 101, 252

Cadrobbi, Alf 214
Caesar, Dick 129
Carefoot, J 78, 94
Carlsson, Erik 374
Carlton-Oatley, Neville 339-340, 368, 376
Carnegie, Robin 142
Carruthers, Dick 66
Carsten, Tom v, 397
Carter, Bill 402-403
Carter, Harry 206-207, 265-266, 275, 324, 328
Carter, Myrna 402-403
Cashmore, Richard 278
Caton, Leo 67-68
Chamberlain, Bob 53, 100
Chapman, Bill "Willy" 267-269, 271, 314, 318, 321, 326-327, 331, 397, 399
Chapman, Colin 286, 310, 380
Chapman, MT 154
Charlesworth, Cyril 227-228, 237
Charnaud, John 349-350
Chase, Walt 272-273
Chisholm, Curt 397-398, 400
Christofferson, Dave 396-397
Cizek, Les 168, 171
Clapham, Arthur 19, 29
Clapham, Hewitt "Brick" 270

Claren, Bill 65
Clark, Jim 80, 186, 238, 370, 376
Clarke, Bernard 14-15, 28, 30, 73, 122
Clarke, E 88, 127, 136, 176, 226, 278
Clarkson, Roy 15, 22, 26-27, 32, 40, 45-46, 79-80, 90, 97, 148
Cleave, Ashley 87, 143
Cleghorn, Mrs "Mibs" 78, 88, 136, 149
Cleghorn, Ted 40, 43, 78, 80-81, 85, 88, 91-92, 95, 122, 129-130, 136, 145, 149, 178, 180, 187, 223, 243, 248
Cleye, Rudy 117, 158
Cochrane, Tony 95, 125
Cole, Bob 212
Coleman, Dave 249
Colley, H 57
Collins, Peter 61
Colman, Dave 191
Colton, Richard 16, 22-24, 31-32, 34, 36, 43, 76, 81, 86, 95,
Coney, Len 344
Conrardy, Paul 48-49
Constant, Harry 169-170
Constantine, PWE 127,
Cook, Richard 263, 322
Copeman, Harmer 176
Corbett, Gerry 34, 82, 84, 90
Cortazar, brothers 151
Cosby, Wilson 211
Costin, Mike 305
Coulston, Ron 385
Couture, Jaques 410
Cowie, Dr Graham 61-62
Craddock, LE 194
Crane, Frank 402- 404
Creed, Lionel 74
Crellin, Ron 7, 278-279, 284, 292, 302, 307-308, 339, 342, 348, 360, 369, 372, 375
Cridland, Arthur 90, 235
Crise, Red 66
Crispelle, Jim 257
Crossan, Bob 174
Crossley, Miss J 74
Crowder, Gordon 203
Crowther, WAR 123, 231
Crute, Stacey 398
Cubley, Edgar 37, 95, 121
Cummings, Charlie 9
Cummins, John "Cummo" 53, 58-60, 99, 101, 194, 251-252, 385
Cunningham, Briggs 112, 115, 163

Curry, H 224
Curtis, Charlie 12, 73, 186

Dane, Benjamin 111, 114
Daniels, Joseph 207, 211
Darwent, Lorimer 126, 139, 149
David, Jay 264
Davidson, Dr J G 66, 163
Davies, Barry 35, 78, 88, 95
Davies, RA 60, 154
Davis, Mary 112
Davis, Sammy 133
Davison, Lex 105, 193-194
Davison, Ted 213
Dawtrey, Lew 53
Day, Derek 401
Day, Felix 9
Day, G 71, 74
De Blaby, John 34-35, 78, 127
De Bonde, Fred 102, 153
De Mattos, Basil 19-20, 76, 90, 293
De Selincourt, Bill 280, 283-284, 288-289, 291, 293-295, 297, 299-300, 302-303, 353, 384
Dean, Charlie 53
Dear, Geoff 44, 77
Deeter, Ken "Kenny" 260, 264, 267, 313-315, 327-328
Dennis, Ted 181, 188, 219, 224, 237, 338-339, 349-350
Denton, Hugh 14, 16, 20-22, 24, 26-28, 30-32, 34-38, 74, 76, 80, 82-84, 86, 95
Derrington, Vic 87-88, 246
Detterbeck, Lester 403
Dick, Alick 12
Dillow, R 78
Dingley, Peter 72
Dixon Smith T 132, 363
Dixon, FW "Freddie" 234
Dixon, Jeff 34, 43, 89, 142
Dobson, Roger 220, 240, 243
Dodd, John 17
Dolton, J 34
Domleo, Val 7, 179, 184, 188, 220, 224-226, 229, 241, 244-245, 284, 302, 342, 348, 350, 360, 373-375
Done, Denis 23
Donovan, D 88
Donovan, DJH 81
Doolittle, General Jimmy 157
Doushkess, Bill 257, 260, 262-264, 267-268
Doushkess, Ruth 257, 260, 262-263, 267-268, 272, 321

Index of Names

Dowd, John 116
Dowle, R 77
Downey, Bill 250-251
Drake, Bob 166
Dredge, Bill 262-264, 405
Dredge, Steve 404-406
Dreyfus, Rene 109, 201
Duckitt, Sydney 346
Duckworth, Keith 305-306, 341-342, 362
Dudley, Merv 151-153, 155, 191-194, 251
Duggan, Bob 239, 281, 285, 293 300, 344, 350, 354-355, 356-357, 359-360
Dukes, David 157, 163, 170
Dundas, Frank 37, 40-41, 74, 76-80, 88, 231
Dymock, Eric 79

Eaves, M 244
Edmiston, Dave 62, 156, 195-198, 254-255, 311, 387
Edwards, George 303, 338-339, 356
Edwards, John 232
Edwards, Sterling 66
Edwards, Willy 305, 363
Ehrman, Gus 316
Eisenhower, President Dwight D 65, 171
Elcomb, Dave 69, 217, 257-259, 270, 276
Elford, P 387
Elkington, I 13, 21, 30
Elliott, George 207
Ellis, Douglas "Curly" 69, 115, 118, 166, 217, 257-259, 398
Ellis, Harold 110
Elmer, Maxine 112
Emery, Jack 251
Errickson, Ray 66-67, 158
Everard, Tony 129, 132
Evidon, James 203

Fagg, Les 234, 241, 246, 291, 297, 300-301, 305, 361, 363
Falcon, Lou 64
Fangio, Juan 201
Farnell, Jack 65
Farrar, Doug 326-327, 331, 399
Ferguson, Joe (Junior) 62, 65-66, 107-109, 159, 200, 403
Ferguson, Joseph "JB" 62-63
Fetterolf, Jack 261
Fidler, GC 277

Finch, Victor 69
Finnigan, Ken 216-217
Fisher, SL 251
Fitch, John 203
Fitzgerald, Pat 255, 312
Fitzwilliam, R 142
Fletcher, Max 385
Fletcher, Paul 178
Flook, J 88
Ford, Gilbert 100
Forde, Dr Welles 208
Forno, Jim 265, 269-270, 321, 324-325, 391-393
Foster, Alan 179, 193, 288, 293, 304, 346, 361
Foster, FJ 127
Fowler, Dan 161
Fox, Tom 196
Franks, DL 20
Fredman, Leon 78, 126-127
Freedman, Bill 158
Freeman, Allen 61, 156, 197, 255, 312, 388
Freeman, Daphne 307
Freeman, FA 188, 219, 280
Freeman, Mary 36, 125
French, RA 21
Frith, Arthur 235, 380

Gallagher, Tommy 404, 407
Garber, Mike 207, 214
Gardiner, Sir Charles 58
Garner, Henry 338
Garnier, Peter 13-14
Gebhard, Al 169, 208- 211, 213, 256, 259-260, 262-264, 266-269, 272-273, 275, 313-315, 321, 323
Geddes, HB 222, 232
Geneve, Mick 103
Gifford, Curt 268, 322-323
Gilmore, Jan 403
Ginther, Richie 110, 261
Goldich, Bob 202
Goodall, George 10, 39, 43, 53, 87, 93, 96-97, 139, 209, 235, 241, 243, 295, 309, 340, 346-347
Goodall, WA "Jim" 7, 13-14, 16, 21, 28, 30-31, 34-36, 41, 71, 74, 76-78, 82-83, 88, 91, 93-94, 120-121, 123, 125, 127, 133, 135, 141, 144, 146, 177-178, 219-221, 224, 226, 233, 277, 282, 284-285, 293, 297-298, 303, 307-310,338, 343-344, 369, 373-374
Gough, PG 281

The Heritage Years

Gould, Horace 26, 43, 71
Gouldbourn, Ron 189, 249
Graham, GW 364
Grant, Bob 125-126, 129-131, 139, 144, 149, 178, 180, 183, 186-187, 189, 218- 222, 240, 243, 248
Gray, Cloyd 212
Gray, JT 123
Greenstein, Garry 405-406
Gregory, Masten v
Grieg, AM 188, 225
Grier, Bob 109, 201
Griffiths, Les 13, 16-17, 21, 27-28, 44
Grinham, Ted 346-347
Grueter, Robert 402
Guinness, Sir Algernon 27
Gulliver, Bert 293

Haas, Bob 206
Haggart, Stu 256, 326, 328, 399
Hales, Alfie 190
Halford, George 11
Hall, Anne 178, 247, 360, 371, 373-375
Hall, Ben 112, 115-116
Hall, Cecil 76, 82, 126
Hall, Don 57-58, 184, 249, 251
Hall, Ian 23
Hall, Terry 16, 21, 34-35, 41, 71-72, 74, 76-77, 91, 120-121, 125, 144, 146, 278, 310
Hammill, Des 129
Hancock, Ed 116-117
Hardwicke, John 347
Harper, Brian 7, 189, 229, 240, 244, 247, 278-279, 284-285, 289, 292, 302, 307-308, 310, 339, 341-342, 348, 360, 369, 372, 374-375
Harper, Peter 147, 222
Harrington, Ed 257
Harris 391
Harris, AG 88
Harris, Steve 398-399, 407
Harrison, George 263, 334
Harrison, Gordon 322, 335, 398
Harrop, Harry 39
Hart, Fred 304
Harvey, John 234, 305, 358, 363, 380
Hassan, Walter 129
Hassen, Chuck 161
Hastings, Daniel III 66
Hatch, Harry 10
Hauser, Eric 203
Hawes, Geoff 99
Hawke AG The Hon. 57

Morgan Sports Cars — Index of Names

Hawthorn, Mike 90, 108-109, 129
Hayes, Dr Ken 390-391, 394, 397, 401-403, 405-407
Hayes, Fred 172
Hayles, John 76, 97
Haynes, Jim 204, 206-207
Haynes, John 250-251
Healey, Donald 230
Healey, Graham 230
Hearne, J 57
Hebb, Edwin (Junior) 67, 111-112, 115-116, 163, 166
Hedgecock, Alan 406
Hellum, Erik 49-51, 98-99, 151
Henry, Frank 211, 275, 314, 318, 402
Herbert, B 125
Hercock, Barrie 248, 382-383
Herman, Dan 272, 274
Heuer, Harry 404, 407
Hextall, Colin 283, 354-355, 364, 370
Heyward, Dick 158
Hiam, David 80, 88-89
Hickerson, L 275
Hilgers, Rick 272-273, 318-319, 321-322, 326-327, 329, 331-332, 394, 397, 399, 405
Hill, Graham 224, 353, 361, 384
Hill, Phil 115, 199, 203
Hilliard, David 188
Hindsvaerk, Arne 99
Hines, Phil 154
Hinshaw, Bill 209-211, 259-261, 264-265, 267-269, 271-275, 314, 318-321, 326
Hitchin, Norm 112, 198
Hobbs, Alan 13-14, 121
Hobbs, Ken 121
Hobley, Macdonald 364
Hodge, A Talbot "Tab" 400, 405
Hodges, John 391, 406
Hoinville, Graham 101
Hollis, Hugo 196
Holmes, J 40, 93
Holmes, V 93
Homes, Peter 20
Hopkins, Tex 206
Horrocks, Brian 76
Houlihan, Ed 173, 174, 204-205
Howard, Derek 45- 47, 81
Howe, John 19, 22, 77, 79, 80, 224
Hoyle, Gerry 27-29, 31, 78, 236, 245, 370
Hubner, Peter 129, 137, 181, 183
Huehl, Greg 408
Hughan, Jim 76, 123, 130-131

Hughes, H 78
Hughes, MT 357
Hulbert, George 223, 232
Hunt, George 158-159
Hurrell, Syd 90, 132, 142, 226, 236, 240, 242, 280-281, 283-284, 288-289, 293-294, 297-303
Hurtley, Harold 264, 275
Huxham, EP "Joe" 13-14, 21, 71, 77, 223, 277, 344
Hyslop, Angus 196

Innocenzi, Tony 56, 58, 101-102
Ireland, Innes 179, 354
Irving, Phil 53, 103
Iskenderian, Ed 316
Issigonis, Alec 299

Jack, D 40
Jackson, Bill 204
Jackson, EG 72
Jackson, L 176
Jackson, Robin 318, 326-327
Jackson, Yvonne 74, 78, 82, 88-89, 123, 127, 130, 132-133, 142, 147
Jackson-Moore, Roy 264
Jacobs, Dick 179, 293, 361
Jacobson, John "Jake" 405-406
Jacoby, Harry 37, 40, 72, 74, 146
James, A 216-217, 275
James, Alex 173
James, Dick 77
James, Ernest 13-14, 21, 28, 71, 79, 91
James, Ken 23, 28, 72, 74, 121
James, KR 236
Jarrett, Neville 133, 175, 177, 219-221, 223, 226
Jenner, L 21, 71, 88, 121
Jennings, Bill 190
Jennings, Chris 346-347
Jensen, Ross 106, 196
Jervis, Aileen 25, 35-37, 93, 123-125, 127
John, GW 355, 362
Johnson, Bill 204
Johnston, Derek 147
Johnston, Sherwood 115
Jones, Alan 193
Jones, BB 343, 345, 349, 368
Jones, Harry 10, 42, 209, 290, 295, 347
Jones, Roger 381
Jones, Stan 60, 193, 194
Jordan, Bill 206

Kane, Jack 314
Kangas, Les 333, 407-408
Kastner, RW "Kas" vi, 271, 313, 315, 325, 331, 391, 394, 401
Kay, Stanley 15, 22
Keaton, Morgan 319
Keen, Stan, 93, 127
Kelly, Erskine "Rick" 203, 206-207
Kelsey, Charles "Chuck" 261, 264-265, 269, 271, 275, 320
Kemp, Malcolm 338, 349-350
Kemsley, Jack 307, 303
Kendall, Major William 10, 290, 295, 347, 405
Kennedy, Richard "Dick" 166, 169-170, 173, 201, 206, 257
Kennett, Pat 228, 232, 300
Kern, Howard 213, 270, 275
Keys, George 407
Kieft, Cyril 341
Kimball, Bob 265-266, 271-273, 275
King, Jordan 203-204, 207
Kingsbury, Bob 311
Kinns, Leonie 78, 88, 127, 142
Kinsman, Lincoln 173-174, 217
Kirkham, Bill 101
Koch, Gerhard 361
Kolb, Charlie 203-204, 206
Kowalski, Ed 276
Krisilof, Mike 404
Kuhn, Robert 204,
Kunz, Dr Hal 107, 109
Kuzmich, Camille 312, 387-388

Ladds, Hugh 20
Landau, Al 68
Langley, P 197
Lawley, Peter 190-191
Lawrence, Chris iv, 7, 179, 184, 233-234, 236, 239-242, 245-246, 279-281, 283-285, 288-289, 291, 293-300, 302-306, 341-342, 344-346, 351, 353-354, 358-359, 361-364, 368, 370-371, 376-380, 384-385
Lawrence, Edwin III 163
Le May, General Curtis v, 63, 68
Lee, Ken 34, 36-37, 40, 74
Lee, Leonard 129
Legat, Dr Peter 16
Leonard, Theodore "Ted" 114, 116
Leslie, Ed 271-273, 321
Levegh, Pierre 81
Levitt, Dan 158, 161-163, 164, 170, 203
Levy, Ruth 167

Index of Names

Lewis, Ian "Tiny" 43-44, 71, 74, 76-77, 82, 86, 88, 91, 95, 120-121, 123, 125
Lidden, HJC 44
Liddle, Ray 215
Lindsay, Keith 57-58, 60, 99
Lister, Jerry 385
Littlejohns, Arthur 55, 57-58, 99, 153
Livingston, Frank 188-189, 222, 232, 242
Livingston, Peggy 226, 232
Livingstone, Frank "Duffy" 64
Llopis de la Torre, Felipe 151
Lockwood, Fred 278, 291, 355
Logan, Halsey 197, 253, 254, 255 311, 387
Lomax, Ross 32, 84
Looker, John 83-84, 86, 89-90, 128-129, 132-137, 141, 143, 144, 175, 178-184, 186-189, 223, 225-226, 228, 242, 342
Lord, Leonard 230, 299
Lord, LK 93, 127
Lorkin, AC 306
Louth, Lord 190
Love, Bill 212, 214, 270, 275
Lovely, Pete 166
Lowe, Marion 327
Lowry, Chuck 209, 213, 267-268, 272-273
Lukey, Len 193-194
Lumsdaine, Sandy 134
Lyons, Peter 385

MacAfee, Dick 166
MacKenzie, Gordon 107-110, 115, 158-160
MacKenzie, John 114-115
Mackley, Bud 334
Macklin, Lance 81
MacManus, Dan 390-391, 399
Macmillan, Harold, Rt. Hon MP 306
MacNaughton, Ted 120
MacRae, L 20
Magenheimer, Bob 113
Mainwaring, 97
Mallam, Patrick 41
Mallock, Major Arthur 234, 362
Mann, Ed 63
Marples, Ernest, Rt.Hon MP 307
Marshall, 77
Marten, Peter 291, 300, 377-378
Marten, Shelley 377
Martin, D 357
Martin, Frank 209

Martin, Ted 341, 368
Maurice, "Morrie" 103
Mayman, Lionel 128, 136, 141, 178-185, 223, 226, 232, 237-241, 341, 345, 350-351, 353-354, 357, 359-360, 365-366, 371
Mayman, Pauline 7, 128, 132, 135-139, 141-142, 147, 177-180, 182-185, 188, 219-222, 224-226, 229-233, 237, 240, 244-245, 247, 283-284, 299-303, 307-310, 342, 348, 350, 365, 369, 375
Maynard, Alan 261, 269
McAfee, Ernie 160
McBratney, Jane Marie 67-68, 110
McCann, "Sonny" 13-14
McConville, Ken 99
McCowan, P 276
McCruddin, Neil 311
McDonagh, John 24-25, 36
McDonald, Ian 154-155, 194
McEachern, Bruce 173-174
McEwin, Greg 56, 194
McGhie, Dr Bob 231
McIntosh, Jack 250
McKaughn, Bob 213
McKay, David 385-386
McKechnie, John 82-84, 89, 126, 129, 132, 134-139, 142, 178-182, 184, 337, 341, 356, 367-368, 378
McKellips, Lindsey 395
McKenzie, Ian 14-15
McKinney, GC 330-331
McKinsey, Bob 65, 67
McLaren, Bruce 106, 196
McLaren, Les 106
McLaughlin, John 115
McMillan, Dr Ken 198
McMinnies, WG 343, 346
McNair, RD 130
McNamara, Dr Norm 207-208
McNeill, Arch 259, 315-318, 320, 324-326, 328- 333, 389, 395, 399-401, 404
McQueen, Steve 320, 324
Meiss, Ruth 273
Melleney, Hal 408
Melvin, Don 203, 206-207
Meredith, Mervyn 35, 74, 88-89, 93, 123, 127
Meredith, Ray 32, 37, 72, 83-84, 86, 90, 129, 132, 134-137, 139-140, 146, 177-178, 180, 182-186, 224, 227-228, 232, 235, 237, 238-240, 243, 247, 281, 285-286, 288, 291, 296, 297, 303, 342, 345-346, 351-352, 355, 357, 359-360, 364, 367-368, 379
Messersmith, Lloyd 335, 409
Metcalf, Johnnie 59, 60
Metcher, Colin 311, 384-385
Michaels, David 204
Michalkiewicz, Romek 78-80, 88, 122, 127, 136, 142, 176, 220-221, 225-226, 231, 278
Michelotti, Giovanni 325, 395
Middleton, Clarence 217, 334-335
Mildren, Alec 193-194
Millar, Art "Ginger" 336, 409
Miller, DA 180
Miller, Dr Sam 396, 406
Milliken, Bill 170
Miske, E Bernard 204
Mitchell, Nancy 34-35
Monk, Bob 397, 399
Montgomery, Paul 400, 402
Moore, Denis 373-374
Moore, John 13-14, 16, 18, 20, 25, 27, 28-31, 34-35, 37, 71-72, 74-75, 77-80, 82, 90, 127, 185
Moore, Robert 33
Moorhead, John 106, 155-156
Morehouse, Bret 326
Morewood, Graham 345, 348, 350, 354-356, 366, 369
Morgan, Charles iv, 290, 299
Morgan, Freida 348
Morgan, HFS 7-12, 14, 23, 26-27, 38, 73, 87, 93, 96-97, 106, 121, 124, 146, 180, 188, 230, 241, 255, 289-291, 295, 300, 309, 337, 340, 343-344, 347-348, 394, 401
Morgan, Jane iv, 35, 221, 299, 349, 357
Morgan, Peter 7, 9-14, 16, 21, 23, 25-26, 30-31, 34-36, 41- 46, 53, 73-78, 80-83, 85-88, 93-96, 121-123, 125-127, 130-132, 134-135, 144, 146-147, 175, 177-179, 182, 187-188, 200, 209, 219-224, 226, 230, 236-238, 241, 243, 247-248, 277, 282, 284-285, 290, 295, 297-303, 307-310, 317, 325, 332-333, 338-341, 343-344, 346-350, 352-353, 356-357, 358, 362, 367-368, 372-373, 375, 377-378, 380, 382-383, 385, 394-396, 400-401, 405
Morgan, Preb. HG 347
Morgan, Ruth 10, 38, 123-124, 346-347

Morris, William 36
Moss, Pat 123, 224
Moss, Stirling iv, 46, 90, 111, 286, 351, 361
Moulton, Alex 300
Mourning, Jim 166-170
Mull, Evelyn 165, 203-204, 207
Mundy, Harry 129
Murray, Jack 325, 334, 391, 395

Nardi, Enrico 395
Nasser, Gamal 144
Neale, C 13-14
Neale, CE 41
Neale, Robert 305, 342, 363
Negus, Syd 57, 153-154, 194, 250-251, 385
Neill, Andie 15-16, 22, 24, 27-30, 37, 40-41, 78-80, 93, 123, 130-131
Neill, Chrissie 15-17, 22, 29, 40, 79, 93, 123
Nelson, Rose 203
Neuman, Lalah 332, 390-391
Newby, F 132
Newey, Les 365
Newsham, Alec 16-18, 137-138, 142-144, 147, 177-180, 189
Newton, Al 118
Nichol, Frank 136
Nicol, Peter 194-195, 251
Nogueira, Felipe 151
Norgard, P 13, 20-21, 28, 30, 36, 71, 77, 81, 88, 91, 121, 168, 126, 145-146
North, Roy 181, 235-236, 242, 283, 286, 288, 344
Norwood, John 159

O'Brien, Bob 318, 326-327, 397
O'Brien, Hugh 390
O'Shea, Paul 114, 116, 165, 168
Oakley, D 35
Odoni, Brian 76
Oker, Bob 113-115, 117, 118, 156-157, 160-163, 165-169, 171, 199, 201, 203, 262, 405
Oker, Ila 162
Olver, LR 32
Olvercrona, Eric 388
Ord, Duncan 154
Orr, Maurice "Morrie" 61, 62
Ozanne, Patricia 145, 147

Pabst, Augie 169
Pacey, Donald "Don" 223, 226, 233, 236, 240, 243
Palfrey, Angela 34-35, 74, 83, 88, 90, 93-94, 124-128, 130, 137, 147, 177, 182,
Park, AM 184
Parker-Eaton, Jeff 139, 141, 233
Parkes, TA "Bill" 20, 82-83, 127, 182,
Parks, George 116-117, 165-166, 168, 170,
Parnell, Jock 66
Parnell, Reg 195
Parry, John 222
Parry, Marion "Pip" 15, 27, 72,
Parsons Chuck 314-315, 321, 328
Parsons, Brian 355-356, 358, 369
Parsons, CR "Bob" 224, 243
Parsons, Reg 110, 112, 115, 117
Pascoe, T 16
Pashley, Charlie 243
Patterson, Bill 193
Patton, Raymond 14-15
Paulsen, Tore 151
Payne, Tom 115, 166, 170-171, 257-259
Pearce, Dr Ian 85
Pellandini, Rene vi, 69, 147, 163, 171, 198, 200, 202, 206, 208-209, 211, 213-214, 255-256, 259-262, 264, 267, 270, 273-274, 301, 314, 318, 325-326, 328-329, 333, 390, 395, 397, 399, 402
Penhale, Allin 338
Perks, Tony 35, 278
Perriam, CP 185, 188
Peterson, Eric 66
Peterson, Ralph "Pete" 63, 101, 114,
Peterson, Stan 321, 327, 331-332
Phillips, EA 243
Phillips, Miss P 176
Phipps, Barrie 16, 18, 20, 23-24, 26, 28, 31, 32, 34-35, 37, 40, 74, 77, 79, 82-84, 86, 88, 90, 93-95, 123, 125-127, 130-132, 135-138, 145-146, 177, 180, 182, 219, 246, 278, 295-296, 306, 310
Pither, John 34, 83, 123
Poe, Ralph 395
Pol, Hermen 18
Polack, Andy 72, 78, 88, 120, 132, 136-137, 140-141, 145, 147,
Polinka, Jerry 172
Pollack, Bill v,
Portham, Colonel 149
Possinger, Janet 331
Postumus, Cyril 144

Potts, Charlie 333, 407-408
Potts, Billy 80
Price, Evan 346-347
Pridmore, George 331, 396-397, 399, 404
Pritchard, David 139
Pritchard, Dick 23, 43, 82, 94, 296, 301, 303
Pugh, Harold 368
Pugh, Peter 53, 101

Raby, Ian 181
Randall, B 125, 136
Randall, George 370
Randall, R 219
Randall, RJ 220
Ranford, Barry (Junior) 192-194, 250-251
Ranford, Barry (Senior) 192-195, 250-251, 311
Ray, Jimmy 7, 16, 18, 28-30, 33-40, 43, 46, 72, 74, 76, 89-90, 142, 147, 228
Ray, Kath 16, 18
Redman, Brian 294
Reece, Doreen 34-35
Reece, Jack 15, 32, 74
Reece, Peter 15-16, 23, 28, 30, 32, 35-37, 39, 72-74, 78, 81, 88, 90, 92, 95
Reeves, FET 74
Rehberg, Ralph 199, 202,
Reid, Ted 60-62, 106, 156, 195, 197, 255
Revson, Peter 7, 407-408
Reynolds, Harry 202, 261, 268-269, 318, 320, 331-332, 395, 396, 404-407
Reynolds, Richard 55-56
Rice, Robert 335
Rice, Tom 217, 334-335, 409
Richards, Bill 53-54, 60, 99, 101, 105, 151, 251-252, 310
Richardson, Bill 275
Richardson, Ken 45, 53, 76, 230-231
Richardson, Mickey 275
Riches, Fred 80
Rigg, Ken 172
Rigg, W 76
Roberts, Horace 71, 278-279, 282, 284, 293, 303, 338, 349, 369
Roberts, Hylda 282
Roberts, Jim 11, 73
Robertson, Charlie 18, 22, 25-26, 37, 40
Robinson, Jim 116-117

Index of Names

Rogers, Alton "Al" 322
Rogers, EM "Monty" 40, 41, 43, 71, 76-79, 82, 120, 134, 143, 177-178, 219, 222, 226, 232, 237, 247, 277, 345
Rollo, Gerald 325-326, 405
Romaldini, Arnold 269, 324
Roper, Keith 253
Rose, Harry 189
Rose, Leslie 275
Ross, Dr Warren 335
Ross, John 79
Rossiter, Norm 249, 251
Rothschild, Hanni "Honey" 67, 316, 325, 328
Rothschild, Mike 64, 67, 106-111, 113-118, 157-158, 200-201, 208, 316-318, 325, 328-329, 393-394
Roy, Basil 26, 28, 346-347, 396
Rubini, Gunnard 111, 113, 115-118
Rudd, Bill 162
Rudd, Ken 126, 132, 142, 177, 183
Ruggles, Dave 265-266
Rumsey, Harold 95, 226
Russell, Ed 172, 174, 217
Russell, Godfrey 346
Russell, JP 73
Rutherford, Ron 155

Sach, John "Baggy" 362, 371
Salmon, P 132
Sambrook, Percy 380
Samm, D 177
Samm, Robert 206
Sanderson, Tony 184, 233-234, 240, 362, 377
Sandford, Stuart 45, 148
Sandford-Morgan, Gavin 56-57
Sands, Alan "Al" 174, 214-217, 276
Sargent, Peter 301, 359
Savin, Ed 111-114, 158, 162, 166-168, 171, 199, 262
Savoye, Claude 148, 189, 249
Savoye, Guy 148
Savoye, Jacques 148
Scarbrough, Dan 271-272
Schade, Bill 203
Schroeder, LW 162, 166
Schulze, Max 217, 334-335, 409
Schuppe, Viktor 268
Schwedler, William 334
Scott Watson, Ian 186
Scott, David 34, 82, 90
Scott, Gerry 267
Scott, Miss 188

Scott, P 338, 368-369
Sear, Oliver 80-81, 85
Seargeant, Roger 214, 257, 275
Sears, Jack 80-81, 85-86, 283, 286, 296, 303
Seers, Rosemary 373
Seigle-Morris, David 341
Shale, David 235, 240, 242, 283
Shand, J 180
Sharp, FRE 227
Shaver, Robert J 163
Shead, Don 127
Shelby, Carroll 165-166, 199, 209, 394
Shelly, Jack 60
Shelly, Tony 60-62, 106, 155-156
Shepherd-Barron, Richard 281, 283, 296-297, 361, 376-379, 383-384
Sheridan, Bob 402-403, 405-406
Sherman, Charles "Chuck" 257-258
Shinn, Chas 111, 166
Shipman, PT 78
Shoupe, Dale 314
Shove, J 95
Simmers, Arthur 395
Simonek, Dick 320
Sims, Lyndon 123, 226, 248-249, 381-382
Sinclair, "Jock" 15
Sinclair, I 34
Skinner, Stella 340-341
Skinner, Tony 341
Slowi, Roger 256, 260, 262-264, 267-268, 274, 313-314, 321, 324, 326-327, 332, 390-391, 394, 397, 399, 401
Smith, Alan 135-136, 278, 310
Smith, Bill 406
Smith, Dick 269, 331
Smith, Dixon 132, 363
Smith, Jack 31
Smith, R (NZ) 197
Smith, R (USA) 406
Smith, Roland 234, 241, 282, 301, 305, 348, 359, 363, 376
Smith, S 187
Smith, TD 227
Smith, Tom 243, 355, 357, 359
Smith, Vin 154
Sneath, Ernest 22, 28, 33, 37-38, 42, 72, 81, 90, 95, 134, 146, 175
Sneath, Rodney 42
Snell, William 165
Soans, R 291, 300-301
Soderstrom, Bengt 165, 168, 171

Soisbault, Annie 249, 307
Sopinka, Michael 174
Southern, Alan 342, 377
Spare, Dr John 7, 16-17, 24, 26-28, 30-31, 34-37, 42-44, 71-75, 77-78, 82, 87-88, 93-95, 120, 121, 123-124, 126-128, 130, 133, 146-147
Spargo, Arthur 196-197
Sparks, Chuck 407
Sparrowe, Jeff 20, 25
Spencer, Lew iv -vi, 7, 63-64, 163-169, 198-199, 208- 214, 256-257, 259-264, 267, 269-275, 313-315, 318, 321-322, 325-326, 328, 332, 390, 394, 397, 402
Spencer, Nannette 260, 313, 324
Spiegler, Dave 206
Sprinzel, John 219, 223, 286, 310
Staker, Bill 102
Stallard, Graham 78, 93, 132
Standbridge, Bob 90
Staples, Bob 283, 289, 296, 346, 354-355, 361, 363, 384
Steel, Dr William 16-18, 356
Sterne, George "GB" 173, 217, 275, 325, 334-335, 397, 405, 409-410
Sterne, Lydia 217,
Stevens, Laurie 59-60,
Stewart, Gwenda 133,
Stewart, JoAnn 267
Stewart, Phil 161,
Stokes, Ralph 74, 78, 93-94, 123-124, 248-249
Stoop, "Dickie" 294, 303, 366
Stratter, Keith 207, 208
Stratton, Gordon 34, 82, 84, 90
Sturrock, Howard 15, 16, 22, 33, 39
Sturrock, Ken 123, 188, 350
Styles, Phil 213
Styles, Rod & Cliff 153
Sullivan, Bill 336
Sullivan, Dave 385
Sylvester, Jack 347

Tanland, Chuck 402
Tara, Bob 265, 271-273
Tara, Grace 265, 269, 271-272, 319
Tatham, Arthur 148
Taylor, A W 21, 88
Taylor, JP 220
Taylor, P 226
Taylor, Sid 55, 152-154, 194, 385
Taylor, TR 312
Temple, Bob 180
Therkleson, Steele 380

Morgan Sports Cars — Index of Names

Thomas, "Tommy" 281, 355, 368
Thomas, Alf 81
Thomas, Barry 82-83
Thomas, Dave 134, 140
Thomas, J 123, 127, 220
Thomas, Tony 363
Thompson, D "Tommy" 20, 34-35, 41, 78, 88, 93-94, 123, 125-127, 142, 146, 226, 307
Thompson, Dr Charles 110, 112, 171
Thompson, J 174, 385
Thompson, Jack 335, 409
Thompson, Mrs A 154
Thompson, Richard "Dick" 111, 165
Thompson, SJ 102
Thomson, MJ 56
Thorne, BJ 76-77, 91, 121
Threlfall, Tom 79, 120-121
Timmins, Ron 220, 228, 235, 238, 283, 287-288, 296, 298, 303, 341, 346, 365-366
Tomblin, K 88
Townsend, Dr EJ 123, 286, 342-343
Trelfall 21
Troffer, Dave 166
Trukke, Hayes 156-157, 161, 163-164
Trukke, Mickey 157
Tucker, R 82
Tucker-Peake, "Tucker" 188
Tufte, Clif 115
Tuning, William 171, 203, 208
Turner, Dr AG 178
Turner, Stuart 220, 249, 286, 374
Tweedel, Arthur 203

Ulmann, Alec 156, 159
Underwood, Lake 157
Uphill, Colin 105, 192

Valentine, George 324
Van Dal, David 7, 53-55, 58-60, 99-101, 103-105, 151, 154, 194, 249-252, 311, 385
Van Dal, Sydney 59, 105
Van Damm, Sheila 147
Vaughan, GWD 74
Veale, Phil 356, 363
Venn, John 184
Vernon, KT 182-184

Viall, Jim 203
Villeneuve, Paul 410
Vogel, Richard 159-161, 163, 169-170,
Von Neumann, John 203

Waddell, J 27
Waddington, John 74, 95-96, 128, 130, 133, 142, 147, 177
Waggott, Merv 252
Wakeland, George 105
Walker, Alan 81
Walker, DA 132
Walker, Ian 137
Wallace, Bruce 257
Waller, Rod 311
Wallwork, Johnnie 18, 39, 43, 90
Walter, Phil 109
Walton, LM 180
Ward, Barrie 385
Ward, Ken 385
Ward, Mrs 34, 82
Warner, Graham 304, 370, 378
Warner, Mike 18, 20
Warren, Dave 44, 78, 96-97, 126, 219
Warshawsky, Curt 167, 260
Watkins, John 118
Watson, Roy 253, 255
Way, Geoff 58, 102-104, 152-153
Weaver, George 207
Webb, Rob 311
Webster, Harry 11
Webster, WK 74
Weed, Al 69-70, 118-119
Weir, C 93
Weitz, John 107-111, 158-159, 200, 202, 403
Wells, Graham 156
Weslake, Harry 136
West, Don 264
West, Jack 271
West, Willie 314-315, 320-321, 323
Westwood, Bert 188,
Wharton, Ken 60, 219, 240, 254
Wherry, Joe 69
Whickett, F 309
White, Art 399, 403-404
White, Geoff 34, 82, 84
White, HE 84
White, JA 366
White, PWS 28-29, 31, 41-42, 74, 77-78, 88, 96,
Whiteley, Bill 15, 28-29, 123
Whitmore, Sir John 376
Whitwell, WR "Dick" 186
Willburn, Gerry 18, 269, 327
Williams, David 270, 320, 396, 406
Williams, J 251
Williams, Mr 88
Williamson, Howard B "Ike" 163, 166, 170, 203-205, 207, 209, 261, 265, 269-270, 273, 318, 332, 392, 395, 399-400, 405
Wilson, W 40
Winberg, Chas 165, 168-171, 198-200, 202
Winchell, Luther 174
Windhorst, Barbara 256, 257, 259-263, 267-268, 270, 272-275, 314, 321, 325, 329
Windhorst, Bob 256, 260, 273, 399
Winter, F 231
Wisdom, Anne 224
Woods, C 166
Woods, Pearce 117
Woods, Senator 165
Worters, Alan 304
Worthington, Bill 209, 261
Wright, Dr Cliffton "Cliff" 259, 262, 264
Wright, Arthur "Digger" 250
Wright, Don 58
Wright, Tom 259, 265-266, 315-317, 390-391, 396
Wright, WM 251

Yarranton, Les 14, 16, 20, 23, 27-28, 30, 34-36, 41-43, 74, 78-79, 82, 88-89, 92-95, 120, 123, 125-127, 130, 133, 142, 144, 146-147, 180, 188, 219-222, 226, 232, 241, 246-247, 284
Yedor, Cy 164
Yost, Charles 65,
Young, Laurence "Woody" 165, 168, 199, 203, 207

Zeigler, Ralph 66
Zoccola, Mark 191
Zuckert, Tony 207, 209
Zumich, Camille 387, 388
Zurhorst, Ed 320